ALSO BY SARAH SCHULMAN

Fiction

Maggie Terry

The Cosmopolitans

The Mere Future

The Child

Shimmer

Rat Bohemia

Empathy

People in Trouble

After Delores

Girls, Visions, and Everything

The Sophie Horowitz Story

Nonfiction

Conflict Is Not Abuse: Overstating Harm, Community Responsibility, and the Duty of Repair

Israel/Palestine and the Queer International

The Gentrification of the Mind: Witness to a Lost Imagination

Ties That Bind: Familial Homophobia and Its Consequences

Stagestruck: Theater, AIDS, and the Marketing of Gay America

My American History: Lesbian and Gay Life During the Reagan/Bush Years

Plays

The Lady Hamlet

Roe Versus Wade

Between Covers

Enemies, A Love Story (adapted from I. B. Singer)

Manic Flight Reaction

Carson McCullers

Mercy

LET THE RECORD SHOW

A POLITICAL HISTORY OF
ACT UP NEW YORK, 1987–1993

LET THE RECORD SHOW

SARAH SCHULMAN

Farrar, Straus and Giroux
New York

Farrar, Straus and Giroux
120 Broadway New York 10271

Printed in the United States of America
First edition, 2021

Photograph on title page and pages 1, 313, 409, and 531 by T.L. Litt. Poster on
pages 2, 314, 410, 532 courtesy of Gran Fury.

Library of Congress Cataloging-in-Publication Data
Names: Schulman, Sarah, 1958– author.
Title: Let the record show : a political history of ACT UP New York,
    1987–1993 / Sarah Schulman.
Description: First edition. | New York : Farrar, Straus and Giroux, 2021. |
    Includes index.
Identifiers: LCCN 2020056721 | ISBN 9780374185138 (hardcover)
Subjects: LCSH: AIDS (Disease)—United States—History—20th century. |
    AIDS (Disease)—Political aspects—United States—History. | ACT UP
    New York (Organization)—History—20th century.
Classification: LCC RA644.A25 S3633 2021 | DDC 362.19697/92—dc23
LC record available at https://lccn.loc.gov/2020056721

Our books may be purchased in bulk for promotional, educational, or business
use. Please contact your local bookseller or the Macmillan Corporate and
Premium Sales Department at 1-800-221-7945, extension 5442, or by email at
MacmillanSpecialMarkets@macmillan.com.

www.fsgbooks.com
www.twitter.com/fsgbooks • www.facebook.com/fsgbooks

10 9 8 7 6 5 4 3 2

Dedicated to us

"The AIDS Coalition To Unleash Power is a diverse, non-partisan group of individuals, united in anger and committed to direct action to end the AIDS crisis."

Contents

Note to Readers

Let the Record Show is a look at the individuals who created ACT UP New York. While ultimately there were 148 chapters of ACT UP around the world, each acted autonomously. New York was the "mother ship," and my study focuses exclusively on that community, covering the years 1987 to 1993.

AIDS is not over. Out of the 100,000 New Yorkers who have died of AIDS, 1,779 died in 2017. As of 2019, more than 700,000 people had died of AIDS in the United States, according to the Kaiser Family Foundation, including 16,350 in 2017, according to the U.S. Centers for Disease Control. As of 2019, according to UNAIDS, 32 million people worldwide had died of AIDS, with around 690,000 deaths in 2018.

ACT UP New York still exists. Learn more at https://actupny.com.

Preface

This is a book in which all people with acquired immune deficiency syndrome (AIDS) or with the human immunodeficiency virus (HIV) are equally important. Their experiences all matter. Therefore, their contributions to transforming the AIDS paradigm are represented as dynamic, interlocking parts of a bigger picture. In recent years the representations of the AIDS Coalition To Unleash Power (ACT UP) and AIDS activism in popular culture have narrowed, almost to the level of caricature. By decentralizing, yet still accurately representing, the remarkable contribution of those with the most access while juxtaposing those efforts with the phenomenal work of people with less access, a deeper, more complex world is revealed. People who must have change choose the playbook their social position demands. Historicizing ACT UP as an organizational nexus of a larger culture of resistance by people with AIDS (PWAs) invites all of us, in the present, to imagine ourselves as potentially effective activists and supporters no matter who we are. The story of ACT UP New York is much larger than its legendary Monday-night meetings. It is a political and emotional history of liaisons, associations, relationships, coalitions, and influences that cumulatively create a crucial reality of successfully transformative struggle under the most dire of circumstances.

I first started observing and writing about AIDS in the early 1980s, when I was a twenty-four-year-old city hall reporter for the *New York Native*, a gay male newspaper. I would go to press conferences given by Mayor Ed Koch to raise concerns about the inability of the New York City Council to pass a basic gay rights bill protecting New Yorkers from discrimination in housing, jobs, and public accommodations, like

restaurants. When AIDS became apparent to me, around 1982, I began
to ask questions about the looming crisis. In this way, by chance, I was
able to cover early stories like gay businesses being denied advertising
space because of AIDS hysteria, and the first case of AIDS diagnosed in
the Soviet Union. Soon, however, I was writing regularly about the early
stages of state oppression of PWAs, the closing of gay spaces, the
refusal of the government and pharmaceutical companies to respond
effectively or at all, and the nascent movement of resistance, including
early civil disobedience and organizing. Because I had been a reproductive rights activist and journalist, I contextualized this developing
story in the larger framework of the rise of the religious right as an elec-
toral force and the role of their president, Ronald Reagan, in obstructing progress on AIDS. In New York City, PWAs and their supporters
were also thwarted locally by the negligence of Mayor Koch, and so
we had both municipal and national battles to wage. I also, from the
beginning, focused my coverage on women, poor people, and children
and the impact of AIDS on their lives. These journalistic pieces can be
found in my book *My American History: Lesbian and Gay Life During
the Reagan/Bush Years*.

ACT UP was founded in March 1987 after a lecture at the Lesbian
and Gay Center by writer Larry Kramer. I had been writing about AIDS
for about four years before joining the newly formed ACT UP in July
1987. Although never in leadership, I was a rank-and-file member of
ACT UP until 1992, shortly after the organization split. I went on with
five other women to cofound The Lesbian Avengers, also a direct-action
group. While in ACT UP, I participated in countless actions, including
Seize Control of the FDA (Food and Drug Administration), Stop the
Church, and Storm the NIH (National Institutes of Health). I was arrested twice, at the Day of Desperation action at Grand Central Terminal
("Fight AIDS, Not Arabs") and at Trump Tower for the Trumpsgiving
action. I hovered on the outskirts of the Women's Caucus, attended the
first meeting of the Housing Works Committee, and participated in the
Shea Stadium action ("No Glove, No Love"). I organized one of ACT
UP's earliest fundraisers, held at Performance Space 122, across the
street from my apartment. But, like most of the rank and file, and unlike most of the people highlighted here, I was never an active member
of a committee, nor did I belong to an affinity group. I did bring AIDS

into my other community work, including coprogramming the MIX NYC Queer Experimental Film Festival, which I ran with cofounder Jim Hubbard from 1986 to 1993. I continued to write journalistic pieces about AIDS for the next thirty-five years, primarily in relation to gentrification and, most recently, HIV criminalization. This is my fifth nonfiction book with significant AIDS content, and I have also published four novels about some aspect of the lived experience of AIDS. My entire adult life has been surrounded by AIDS: the deaths of those around me and with whom I made my stand, advocating for and learning from people with HIV, and witnessing and sharing the survival of my closest friends. I have met, stood with, and advocated for people with HIV all over the world as an HIV-negative person, and consider myself to be part of the HIV/AIDS community.

THE ACT UP ORAL HISTORY PROJECT

In 2001, Jim Hubbard and I founded the ACT UP Oral History Project. Since the popular availability of protease inhibitors five years before, the AIDS activist movement had virtually disappeared from public view. Many were licking their wounds and trying to rebuild their lives. The emergence of internet culture left ACT UP behind, as most of its materials were not digitized or searchable. *AIDS Incorporated*, slang for the complex of AIDS-related government bureaucracies and pharmaceutical company alliances, had mostly replaced grassroots activism, and the community that had been built by activists was scattered. ACT UP, as a result, was undocumented and seemingly forgotten. There was no accurate data easily available to researchers. Distressingly, *The New York Times*—known in ACT UP as "The New York Crimes"—which had systematically under- and misreported the AIDS crisis, was being cited as a legitimate source in PhD dissertations and books. We had to make the history and experience of AIDS activism visible and accessible.

For the next seventeen years, from 2001 to 2018, Jim and I conducted long-form interviews with 188 surviving members of ACT UP New York. These transcripts form the heart of this book. We let people self-select with no exclusionary definition of what it meant to have been "in" ACT UP, gathering from all corners of the movement with one significant exception. By 2001, almost every HIV-positive woman in ACT UP New York, except one confirmed survivor, had died. And that woman did not want to be interviewed because her children's spouses did not know that she was HIV-positive. She has since died. Most of the dead, like Katrina Haslip, were straight women of color, but some, like Keri Duran, were white, working-class, and queer. A number were formerly incarcerated at the Bedford Hills women's prison and came to ACT UP after serving their terms. We tried to interview two white prison AIDS activists, Judy Clark and Kathy Boudin, who were still incarcerated, but we were refused permission by the warden. Upon release, Kathy declined to be interviewed. Judy is finally awaiting release as I write. Only secondhand, through Terry McGovern, Marion Banzhaf, Catherine Gund, Debra Levine, and other ACT UPers involved with prison work, do we have these activists' stories. A number of the men we interviewed have since died (RIP Jim Lyons, Michael Perelman, Herb Spiers, Andy Vélez, Larry Kramer, and Douglas Crimp); a number of men and women died before we could get to them (RIP Keith Cylar, Sally Cooper, Spencer Cox, Juan Mendez, and others). Some former ACT UPers later developed such chaotic drug habits that they repeatedly canceled interview appointments, sometimes until they died. One severely addicted man welcomed us into an apartment drenched in dog urine, where he babbled on for hours after not having slept for four days.

People of color in leadership in ACT UP who died, in some way, of AIDS include Ray Navarro, Katrina Haslip, Ortez Alderson, Robert Garcia, Keith Cylar, Juan Mendez, and Joey Franco. Women of color who worked on significant campaigns with us and have since died of AIDS-related conditions include Phyllis Sharpe, Iris De La Cruz, Carmen Royster, and Marina Alvarez. Although I knew them, and visited Iris in the hospital, I never had the opportunity to interview these people. In Jim's and my documentary *United in Anger: A History of ACT UP*, you can see footage of Iris, Phyllis, Robert, Ortez, and Ray speaking, and some cutaway shots of Katrina and Keith. Other people have more extensive footage of some of them. While I have asked surviving ACT UPers in our interviews to memorialize these activists of color, along with white people who also died, I do not have enough material from their points of view to adequately evoke them here. Because they died of systemic racism, and governmental and corporate indifference and neglect, their full impact on the movement cannot be accurately assessed. I have tried, throughout, to include other people's memories of their influences. And I have tried to assess the consequences for people of color that resulted from ACT UP's actions, failures, and victories.

The process of reconnecting with former ACT UPers as we interviewed them, the showing of interview clips in universities and community centers nationally and internationally, and our public discourse about the process resulted in a show at the Harvard Art Museum, curated by Helen Molesworth in 2010, almost a decade after we had begun. This exhibit was the first organized retrospective of ACT UP, the first display of objects, posters, and photographs from the group's inception. It also brought thirty former ACT UPers back together for the first time in official and public capacities. Later that year, through the work of filmmaker Ira Sachs, the show moved to White Columns gallery in New York, and the opening night served as the first ACT UP New York reunion. After that, an ACT UP NY Alumni page was formed on Facebook, and public consciousness about ACT UP was reignited. Some people returned to ACT UP, and some later created an anti-Trump activist organization called Rise and Resist.

When preparing the ACT UP Oral History Project, Jim and I looked at two Holocaust archives for guidance. The Shoah Foundation, organized by Steven Spielberg, had a structure that did not fit our needs. Designed to counter Holocaust revisionism, in which people who did not commit the Holocaust deny that it ever occurred, the project had hundreds of interviewers focused on a list of predetermined questions. We felt that the interviews were designed to emphasize the moments of trauma, of oppression and atrocity. As important as this was, we were more intrigued by a small archive financed by the Fortunoff department store family that investigated who each person was before the Holocaust, and then how they were impacted by the turn of events. This approach really appealed to us for a number of reasons. The primary purpose of the ACT UP Oral History Project, and of this book, is not to look back with nostalgia, but rather to help contemporary and future activists learn from the past so that they can do more effective organizing in the present. We wanted to show, clearly, what we had witnessed in ACT UP: that people from all walks of life, working together, can change the world.

In general, I am interested in individuals and the choices that they make. I am especially interested in why they make those choices. Unfortunately, most people do not participate in making change. My perception is that the fate of a society is determined by very small groups of people. Only tiny vanguards actually take the actions necessary, and even fewer do this with a commitment to being effective. The purpose of that combination is to open up new possibilities and set new paths for the larger community. I heard the second-wave feminist philosopher Ti-Grace Atkinson speak on this subject at the fortieth anniversary of the 1968 Columbia University student strikes, and she observed that women in society can only progress when men progress. If men do not move, women are suppressed. She suggested that these great leaps happen every forty years or so. Unfortunately, they cannot be forced; they depend on the zeitgeist. But in the interim periods, there are small groups of people practicing what the writer Gary Indiana called "the politics of repetition," trying to stop the rate of giveback and regression. Yet when the zeitgeist moment hits—and AIDS activism was one of those moments—there is a mass surge forward as a movement forces the creation of social space where persistent voices can finally be heard. That ACT UP was a combination of old-time activists with developed analyses and strategic experience, and newly politicized first-time activists with enormous energy for change and openhearted creativity, was central to its success, even if this dynamic was complex, difficult, and sometimes rancorous. Drive and commitment, invention and felicity, a focus on campaigns, and being effective are the components of movements that change the world.

What also influenced me to structure the interviews around the individual ACT UP members and their full lives was the novel *Enemies, A Love Story,* by Isaac Bashevis Singer, which I had the honor of adapting into a stage play that premiered at the Wilma Theater in Philadelphia in 2005. For example, Singer eschewed sentimental stories of pre-Holocaust Jews on the "happy natives" model, or victims who had to be innocent, clean-hearted, and pure to justify lament for their destruction. Also documenting a stigmatized and misunderstood group of people, he showed that individuals and communities who were complex and conflicted before the Holocaust were an extended version of themselves after the cataclysm. And that their fragile personhood, their contradictions, did not have to be scrubbed clean to give meaning to their lives, extermination, or survival. His novel focuses on a Jewish womanizing liar who breaks his family's heart before the Nazis come to power. Later, in exile in New York, he is traumatized and has been made crazy by his suffering, including the murder of his children, but he is still a womanizer. I found this model to be deeply humanizing. The woman he loves, Masha, suffered profoundly in the camps, and he attributes her psychic pain to those events, until he meets Masha's long-lost husband, who testifies that actually "she was crazy before." And so I was attracted to the question of who each person was *before* AIDS, hoping that by asking these questions, Jim and I could learn and come to understand what it was specifically that made this small group of individuals rise to the challenge of history. Why them and not others?

Let the Record Show relies on three sources: First, the literal interviews we conducted, containing what ACT UP members said about themselves and the movement, all of which are available online for purposes of comparison. Second, my own memories of participating in ACT UP from 1987 to 1992. And finally, my own awareness of and research into the histories of earlier movements, to trace their influences. The information that we most need in order to survive is something we have to unearth ourselves, analyze ourselves, and share with one another. The centerpiece of understanding ACT UP's history of success and failure is to look at the specific individuals who made up this movement, their backgrounds, and the relationships they formed. This is why I have written this book people-first and experience-first. More than just the leaders, regular members' voices and stories are essential in understanding an organization that was part of a larger coalition in which people were constantly dying and being replaced by people who also sometimes died, usually in front of one another.

I am not a trained historian, and this is not a cumulative, documented history beyond the testimonies of the people who created it. When interviewees disagree about events, I sometimes side with one version or another, or present multiple perspectives based on my own experience at the time, or what I came to learn, cumulatively, through the interview process over many years. It was impossible for me to use all 188 interviews in this book; it was also impossible for me to use the totality of the interviews I did include. However, readers can read all the full transcripts online for free and watch the complete tapes at the

New York and San Francisco Public Libraries, as well as the library of the University of Michigan, Ann Arbor, thanks to David Halperin. A full list of interviews appears at the end of this volume.

UNITED IN ANGER: A HISTORY OF ACT UP

AIDS has been grossly misrepresented and mis-historicized in lots of different ways, partially because for decades the corporate cultural apparatus favored works—both creative and journalistic—that made straight people into the heroes of the crisis, thereby deflecting the burden of guilt away from the powerful social and governmental institutions that abandoned people with AIDS. There are now two generations whose primary exposure to AIDS comes from a number of works that have become too big to fail, including the Oscar winner *Philadelphia* and the Pulitzer winner *Angels in America*, both of which show alone and abandoned gay men with AIDS, contrasted with a homophobic straight person who heroically overcomes their prejudices to support the poor gay man who has no community and no political movement to protect him. Of course, the opposite was true: gay men with AIDS were abandoned by most straight people, including their families, neighbors, and government. And they were defended by their community, who often shared their lack of rights and representation. Ironically, both of these corporate cultural products surfaced during ACT UP's most powerful years. *Angels in America* premiered in 1991 and opened on Broadway in 1993, and *Philadelphia* debuted in 1993. Yet they both ignored the political movements that transformed the crisis, just as they ignored the neglect of most straight people, to great reward. *Angels in America* ends with hope, symbolized by the drug azidothymidine (AZT), which by the year of the play's opening was considered lethal by many AIDS activists, who were themselves the real hope for the future. By contrast, Larry Kramer's *The Normal Heart*, the story of a group of white gay men heroically battling the government, differs because it did represent an accurate paradigm. Although produced downtown at The Public Theater in 1985, it languished on the sidelines for decades, only becoming mainstream with a 2011 Broadway revival and an HBO television version in 2014, when the world was finally ready for heroic gay men, if they were white. The problem with *The Normal Heart* was that it wasn't the only true story, yet it was the one that got heard, albeit eventually.

Angels in America, probably the most lauded American theatrical work of our time, is strangely disconnected from the reality of people with AIDS, relying on the conventional trope of a cowardly gay person who abandons his lover. Interestingly, in a 1992 interview in *The New Yorker* with theater critic John Lahr, Tony Kushner made no claims to *Angels in America* being an accurate depiction of the AIDS experience. He explained that the play was—in some ways—about his relationship with his best friend, a woman named Kimberly Flynn, who had had a serious brain injury. Kushner described how he had left her in her crisis. The guilt of this action of abandonment was the key personal experience at the heart of the play. This actually makes perfect sense, as the use of AIDS in *Angels in America* is a metaphor, not a central representation. And for that reason it is not reflective of the actual relational dynamics of the time. Coincidentally, this associative impulse produced a work that straight people loved and were comfortable with, and it as a result became iconic and incontestable. If it had been about straight people abandoning people with AIDS and gay people heroically overcoming heterosexual cruelty to save each other's lives, which would have been accurate, I don't know that it would have been so thoroughly praised and elevated. Decades later, in the 2018 book *The World Only Spins Forward*, by Dan Kois and Isaac Butler, Kushner changed his origin story, saying instead that he had been in love with a dancer who had died of AIDS. But that version resonates less accurately with the play itself, which is not really about love and loss, but instead about fear and abandonment by and of gay men, and recognition and transformation for straight people.

Institutional standards and dominant cultural insistence on tropes and themes for AIDS work pervade both independent and commercial filmic representations. When it came to making our feature-length documentary film, *United in Anger: A History of ACT UP*, Jim and I met with several prominent funders of documentaries. We were told over and over that a documentary film has to have four to six characters the viewer can follow on a "journey." Jim explained repeatedly that if we conformed to this, we would be distorting the history, because the successes and failures of ACT UP and AIDS activism were attributable not to individuals, but rather to the group. We were denied financial support every time.

"When you make a film that is a blueprint for challenging authority and the powers that be," Jim said, "you can't expect that the powers that be will reward you. To me, the story of ACT UP is the story of the group. It was always a story of fluidity of leadership, of ordinary people rising to the occasion. The structure of *heroism* in U.S. narrative works against that. Profiling individuals and enforcing this narrative onto them is not telling the real story." And in fact, most of the money that supported *United in Anger* came from social justice funds and from hundreds of individual community members making small contributions. We later sold our archive to Harvard Library to complete the work, but film money was not very forthcoming.

When it came to representing AIDS activism, among the many outcomes that we never predicted was that our open-source approach to making our interview footage and substantial archival footage accessible would get used to nefarious ends. A number of films emerged using our material to make claims that are not accurate. For example, David France's film *How to Survive a Plague* visually and formally argues for an understanding of AIDS activism on the heroic white male individual model, since he did subscribe to the four-to-six-characters prescription, while Jim's film, *United in Anger*, argues that the success of the movement was, by contrast, a consequence of the profound range of difference in the large group relationships that produced the AIDS coalition, reflecting our understanding that, in America, diverse grassroots movements for change must work together in order to be successful.

I also found the title of France's film to be misleading and disturbing. A trend of white male journalists proclaiming that "AIDS is over" began on November 10, 1996, with Andrew Sullivan's cover story for *The New York Times Magazine* titled "When Plagues End." Now here was France, more than ten years later, saying that we had "survived a plague." But journalist Linda Villarosa's shocking 2017 *New York Times* exposé showed that Black gay men in the U.S. South have rates of HIV infection larger than in any country in the world. Villarosa proved that AIDS was only over for white males who could access the standard of care, in a nation with no logical health system. Approximately thirteen thousand people still die of AIDS every year in the U.S., and most of them are poor. But even more broadly impactful than preventable death is the stigma itself, which not only is enhanced by lack of services, but keeps people from facing HIV by using pre-exposure prophylaxis (PrEP) or condoms, getting tested, and getting treated. Stigma feeds bizarre HIV criminalization laws throughout the country and around the world that mandate disclosure of one's HIV-positive status under threat of incarceration, often even if the person is virally suppressed and therefore biologically incapable of infecting anyone, or is using condoms. Yet when France's book with the same unfortunate title came up for review, *The New York Times* placed it on the front page of its *Book Review*, and the reviewer they chose was . . . Andrew Sullivan. It is not surprising to note that he was uncritical.

A public conversation between David France and Jim Hubbard, organized by Theodore Kerr at The New School in 2013—and viewable on YouTube—is very revealing about the competing strategies of how to tell AIDS activist history. When asked by an audience member, "Where are all the women and people of color in your film?" France replied that he focused on wealthy white men who "were able, perhaps more than other people . . . to work full time for years to fulfill their political work." But actually, if you read the ACT UP Oral History, over and over again women, people of color, and low-income ACT UP members report dedicating their entire waking lives to the movement. At another point France says, "I did not talk about housing issues, I did not talk about IV drug use, I didn't talk about women's issues, I did not talk about the complicated and knotty issues around race when that was something that ACT UP was addressing." The mainstream approval France received for his film, which relied heavily on footage others had archived, was depressing to us, not only because the impression it gives of how change is made and who makes it is false, but because the "heroic individuals" myth, aside from being inaccurate, could mislead contemporary activists away from the fact that—in America—political progress is won by coalitions.

We showed *United in Anger*, in person, all over the world, including in Palestine, Lebanon, and Abu Dhabi, where Arab viewers learned for the first time that ACT UP had interrupted television broadcasts during the first Gulf War with the slogan "Fight AIDS, Not Arabs." We brought the film to Brazil, India, and Taiwan—at the time of a bizarre HIV criminalization law prohibiting sex between people who are HIV-positive—as well as all over Europe, and even to Russia, just months after the anti-gay laws went into effect, when members of the dissident rock band and performance art group Pussy Riot had been disappeared into the prison system. People were afraid to come to public screenings, and venues were mandated to post signs saying 18+ ONLY because Russian anti-gay laws were based on fake charges of "corrupting" youth. There are people with HIV/AIDS everywhere in the world. Just recently Dan Glass and ACT UP London invited me to show the film for the tenth or so time in that city, and again we had a full house: people who had never seen images of AIDS activism, people watching the film for the first time, queer people and people with HIV from Bangladesh, Nigeria, and Macedonia, looking for inspiration, support, and tactics.

We made it available for free on Kanopy and YouTube, encouraging high schools and colleges with no budget for buying films to show this work to students for free. And queer studies professor Matt Brim wrote a study guide for teachers, which is available for free at www.unitedinanger .com/study-guide, so that instructors won't need a background in HIV or AIDS history to be able to share the film effectively with students.

WHAT IT WAS LIKE TO ASK THE QUESTIONS

Because I had been in ACT UP from July 1987 until June 1992, I already knew most of the people interviewed in some capacity. A number of the interviewees and I had had significant political differences in ACT UP, but that did not affect our ability to hold frank, open conversations. This was one of many signs of the everlasting bond between the people who had been in this movement together, sharing the epicenter of the mass death experience of AIDS and the knowledge that together we made a difference. Only one person expressed regret about his time in ACT UP. For everyone else, ACT UP was an experience that they were proud of and that had significantly impacted their lives. A tiny handful refused to be interviewed. Most of these were individuals who had become famous since their ACT UP days, ironically around subject matter related to AIDS. Of the two people who were interviewed by Jim Hubbard instead of by me, one was because my father died and I had to skip that appointment, and the other was because I didn't think I could handle the person's manipulations. Interestingly, out of all the interviews that I conducted, no one, in seventeen years, refused to answer a question. The only interview that ended abruptly was ended by me when a man who joined ACT UP after the 1992 split, and after the advent of effective medications, showed no respect for people who had come before. Ironically, the people he was insulting were the same folks with whom I'd had significant political differences. While I disagreed with those in question, I recognized their work and contributions and could not tolerate hearing them be ignorantly maligned. There is a difference between principled disagreement and character assassination. I always felt that one of the reasons people spoke so openly to me was because they wanted to make record of their achievements and were truly interested in discussing their ACT UP experiences, and since so many New Yorkers have been in therapy, they were used to telling their thoughts and feelings to a middle-aged Jewish woman.

There were patterns of response that broke down interviewees into a loose and generalized array of types. There were the people who, five, fifteen, or twenty years after the events, still held the same feelings and interpretations of their ACT UP experiences that they had held at the time. There was no introspection and no shift in discourse. On the opposite range, there were many people who, with hindsight, had rethought their own reactions and could now separate what they had felt and thought at the time from how they understood themselves and others after years had passed into new eras. A number of interviewees took the process of record making very seriously and reviewed files or thoughts in preparation for our appointment so that they could maximize the experience. Others were casual and did no preparation at all, ending up either unable to recall key information or surprised by the nature of the conversation. There were a significant number of men who did not mention women's contributions in detail unless prompted, while the women in question were comfortable crediting men with the work they did, while occasionally hedging about other women's contributions. There were those who looked closely at the website in preparation for our meeting, noting what previous testimony had produced, and taking in the nature of the questions. Others didn't even glance at the previously accrued materials. One man only read the testimonies of his friends; another only looked at what other men had recorded. And then there was the magazine editor who left us standing in the rain while he refused to buzz us into his building, and we never, ever learned why. There were a number of ACT UP alumni who—years after the trauma of mass death—became compromised by drug addiction, whose behavior vis-à-vis our interview reflected that conundrum.

And of course, like the blind men describing the elephant, most people had generalized ideas of ACT UP based on the small groups that they interacted with, the issues that attracted them, and the precise activities that they participated in. A number were surprised that I didn't know in advance of our conversation about events they had organized, which they experienced as central to the organization. Yet they often did not understand what others were doing at the very same moment. A small, very crucial group of individuals had spent their time in ACT UP observing and analyzing the full range of meaning and impact of ACT UP as a whole, and developed organizational overviews, which permitted broad analysis, recognition of large tropes, and a grasp of strategic reach. But most often, ACT UP did not theorize itself.

All of these methods, personalities, traits, and approaches make up the whole. It was a very human, complex, multifaceted society of activists who succeeded in winning significant victories, against great odds, that changed the world and literally saved lives. With flaws and significant limits, these human beings made the future possible.

HOW TO READ THIS BOOK

Because ACT UP's success was partially due to a strategy of difference facilitating simultaneity of response, a chronological history would be impossible and inaccurate. For that reason this book is organized by cohered themes and tropes, distilled from intense analysis of ACT UP's activities from its founding in 1987 to its distress and desperation in 1993, years that frame the epicenter of the AIDS cataclysm in New York.

Most of the activists engaged and evoked in this work, who survived past 2001, were interviewed in the ACT UP Oral History Project. If you are especially moved or intrigued by someone, you can read their full interviews by going back and forth between this volume and www.actuporalhistory.org, where you can watch five minutes of streaming video for each of the 188 people profiled, and you can download the full transcript of their interviews for free. The complete tapes can be viewed in person at the New York and San Francisco Public Libraries, and at the library of the University of Michigan at Ann Arbor. We also made available over a thousand hours of digitized archival footage at the New York Public Library. As of 2020, the website has had 14,165,294 views, and complete transcripts have been downloaded 645,855 times.

If you need a detailed time line of ACT UP's history and actions in chronological order, you can look at the one that appears at the end of this volume, and use this to help you situate the exact sequence of events. For example, there you will find that during the spring of 1990 ACT UP had a major action at the NIH, the Latino Caucus founded ACT UP Puerto Rico, the first Needle Exchange action took place on the Lower East Side, and the book *Women, AIDS & Activism* was written by the Women's Committee. Simply take the event you are reading about and look it up on the time line; in that way you will be able to understand how many different directions of activism were ongoing in the same moment, and you can fully comprehend the depth of difference in and related to ACT UP New York.

Throughout the book you will find small moments of remembrance. People died constantly throughout ACT UP. All of our experiences were shadowed by loss. Within each large action or significant political moment, I try to remember someone who was associated with that time. Sometimes I have extended testimony about that person's life, sometimes just a fragment. Sometimes their participation was central, sometimes peripheral. The richness and the sparseness parallel the experience of death in ACT UP. Sometimes the person who died was someone you knew well; other times it was someone you'd seen or spoken to once, or was a friend of a friend. But near and far, the landscape of disappearance and apparition is one I am trying to recapture here.

BOOK ONE

POLITICAL FOUNDA-TIONS

Do you resent people with AIDS?

Do you trust HIV-negatives?

Have you given up hope for a cure?

When was the last time you cried?

PART I

Change and Power

Part I includes an introduction that summarizes ACT UP's primary tactics and sources so that contemporary activists can have a stand-alone handbook of general principles and takeaway ideas. This is followed by a look at two influential Puerto Rican activists in ACT UP who worked in the context of four Latino-oriented committees, exploring how they negotiated and experienced power structures inside and outside the organization. Finally, an examination of the first wave of treatment activists analyzes how they started to unpack governmental and pharmaceutical obstructions to people with AIDS, and the ingenious methods they developed for direct action to combat them.

Introduction: How Change Is Made

This is the story of a despised group of people, with no rights, facing a terminal disease for which there were no treatments. Abandoned by their families, government, and society, they joined together and forced our country to change against its will, permanently impacting future movements of people with AIDS throughout the world and saving incalculable numbers of future lives. Some men and women with AIDS fought until the day they died. The dead and the living ultimately transformed the crisis.

This is an apocalyptic story of the first generation of AIDS activists, who experienced the virus in a way that no subsequent generation would ever have to experience it again. For some, their days, months, and years in ACT UP were the most important times of their lives. For others, it was a chapter in a series of contributions. Some people went on to find a place in the world; some lost their place forever. But because of commitment and brilliance, only these survivors carry the burden of the first years of the mass death experience that was AIDS. They made the world better, to some degree, for every subsequent HIV/AIDS generation, that is, the future.

This is a story that should have been impossible, which is why it is crucial for us now to understand how and why it happened. These were the people least likely to make substantive change, participating in the broadest possible coalition, most of whom, in some or all aspects of their lives, were excluded from basic rights. As Dudley Saunders points out, in a way, "the win obscured the process," one that we need to learn from right now. And our distorting cinematic concepts of what constitutes heroism have also made it impossible to look at the flaws clearly, as well as at their consequences. Understanding mistakes does not undo successes. Learning to hold both, at the same time, is necessary in order for new generations of people under attack to feel capable of moving forward.

On July 25, 1989, 150 members of ACT UP demonstrated in front of the *New York Times* publisher Punch Sulzberger's residence at 1010 Fifth Avenue and then marched to the West Forty-Third Street offices of the paper. After threatening a sit-in in Times Square, the protesters were finally allowed to picket on the sidewalk opposite the *Times*. Several demonstrators held a die-in in front of the building. The demo was preceded by a Sunday zap in which outlines of dead bodies were stenciled on the streets around Sulzberger's houses, and his neighborhood decorated with stickers emblazoned with ALL THE NEWS THAT KILLS. "AIDS Crisis Escalates While N.Y. Times Sleeps" was the headline on the leaflet ACT UP distributed, which asked: "Why, instead of actively investigating the work of federal health organizations, does the *Times* merely rewrite [their] press releases? . . . Such compliance makes the *Times* a mere public relations agent for an ineffective government . . . Why did the *Times*, in its June 29 editorial (Why Make AIDS Worse Than It Is?) dismiss a new federal study finding a 33% under-reportage of AIDS infections in the US? This callous editorial assured its general readership that AIDS will be over soon, once infected members of undesirable risk groups die off."

From left to right: Steven Helmke, Rob Kurilla, Jody Rhone, Conyers Thompson, Glenis Redmond, Rand Snyder, Donna Minkowitz, Lee Arsenault, Dan Keith Williams, Wayne Kawadler, Julie Clark, Marc Rubin, Tom Blewitt, David Falcone, Blaine Mosley. (Photograph by T.L. Litt)

FACING THE PAIN

Although the story of AIDS activism is one of heroism, it actually starts in suffering. AIDS without medication is a grotesque display of loss. Every faculty disintegrates: the brain, the lungs, the nerves in one's legs, the ability to control shit, the tongue covered in thrush, the broken skin. Even the normally unconsidered capacity to swallow and then to retain nutrition disappears. The body is no longer a mystery of synchronicity; it is a trap of literal pain and confusion, but also of social isolation. The diarrhea machine; the literal scarlet letter of cancerous Kaposi sarcoma eating away one's face, torso, legs, and arms; the rambling dementia; the shooting flames of neuropathy making walking impossible or a horrific ordeal—even the fungal toenails—don't usually allow someone to make new friends.

With the lack of treatment and services also came the abandonment by family—if they hadn't already thrown you out or driven you away for being queer. Life was surrounded by death. There was the systematic loss of the friends who were your support network and the witnesses to your life, the deaths of whom became the end of context and memory. There was the loss of jobs, the end of careers, the disappearance of income, the losing of your apartment, the stares on the street, the shunning by neighbors, acquaintances turning their backs or fading away, the silence of the government. Inevitably came a horrible death, possibly while you were lying on a gurney in a hallway of an overwhelmed hospital or on a sofa in a friend's cramped apartment, emaciated and swimming in endless diarrhea.

But, surprisingly, while many people joined ACT UP NY to end their own suffering, others came to confront someone else's pain. ACT UP was simultaneously a place of decline and a place of defiance of loss. Every Monday night those few hundred people entered the ground-floor meeting room at the crumbling old school that had become the Gay Center, then the Lesbian and Gay Center, and now the renovated, corporate Lesbian, Gay, Bisexual & Transgender (LGBT) Community Center on West Thirteenth Street, next to the disappeared St. Vincent's Hospital to the east, and across from the still-present Integral Yoga Institute to the north. They came to save lives with humor, commitment, profound innovation, genius, will, and focus, and sometimes wild acting out, ruthlessness, and chance. But that meant that they also came to die and to watch disintegration. Because, to make something better, we have to face it at its worst. And only a small group of people on this earth are willing to look pain in its real face, assess it accurately, listen, and then criticize themselves with rigor, find a productive way to cooperate, and rise to the occasion to solve a problem. People who are desperate are much more effective than people who have time to waste.

Most of the men and women in New York City with AIDS never came to ACT UP, even at the height of its impact from 1987 to 1992. Most of the people who loved someone with AIDS and wanted their lives to be saved, most of the people who felt empathy or identification with people with AIDS, never came to an ACT UP meeting or action. Most people, after all, do not act to create change, no matter what. Then there were specific obstacles: there were many thousands of people who died in the closet rather than come to ACT UP. There were literally thousands, if not millions, of people who wanted AIDS to end who never could imagine themselves in a state of overt, physical, and public opposition to the police, the mayor, the president, *The New York Times*, science, government, art museums, and pharmaceutical companies. The thought of being handcuffed and arrested on television—publicly associated with AIDS, drugs, and anal sex—disrupted their image of their futures, which were never going to happen, but, in fantasy, depended on being appropriate. Being oppositional instead meant "no business as usual," which for many was itself a loss of order and ambition. In order to change institutions, we have to confront institutions. And institutions, as well as the individuals who gain their power by being associated with them, become angry and punitive when they are questioned. In order to get out of hell, you have to be in hell, so pretending it's all fine and will all be fine won't get you out. Going to ACT UP meant attending every Monday night for the general meeting, and for some most every other night of the week, and mornings before work for demonstrations or zaps (creative but confrontational protests that inherently challenged frames of power). This decision toward action required constantly committing every literal day to face the disgusting, overwhelming, unbearable suffering of the fragile, devastated, deteriorating, enraged, sad, ingenious, committed, and very young people with whom we chose to be.

The AIDS Coalition To Unleash Power was founded in New York City in 1987; it split in 1992 when twelve people left to form Treatment Action Group (TAG). The year 1996 saw the popular availability of protease inhibitors, the compound medications, taken daily, that make it possible for people with HIV who have access to health care to live. In that short time:

- ACT UP designed a fast-track system in which sick people could access unapproved experimental drugs, and then, through direct action, forced the U.S. Food and Drug Administration to adapt it.
- ACT UP ran a four-year campaign to change the U.S. Centers for Disease Control's definition of AIDS so that women could get access to benefits and be included in experimental drug trials.
- ACT UP made needle exchange legal in New York City, and started Housing Works, a service for homeless people with HIV/AIDS.
- ACT UP also helped force pharmaceutical companies and the government to change priorities in medical research to stop the same failed drugs from being studied over and over again.
- ACT UP's "Countdown 18 Months" campaign influenced a refocus of research onto opportunistic infections, thereby reconceptualizing the image of effective treatment. Reality made us evolve from the fantasy of one pill that would "cure AIDS" to diversified, individualized treatment combinations that would address the impact of HIV on each body.
- ACT UP ended insurance exclusion for people with AIDS and confronted the Catholic Church's attack on public school condom distribution, abortion, and needle exchange.
- Images of ACT UP fighting back on the nightly news and through posters, community-distributed video, and still photography created a new face for the world of people with AIDS and their allies as a vibrant and powerful grassroots force. This new queer/PWA stood publicly with power and grace, and this defiant determination had long-range influence on how people with HIV and queer people saw themselves and were in turn understood by others.

While very few people joined ACT UP, larger numbers were involved in helping people with AIDS. Most volunteers preferred to participate in social services, from being a "buddy" through Gay Men's Health Crisis, walking dogs of people with AIDS through PAWS, serving meals through God's Love We Deliver, and working with many other crucial, life-enhancing organizations. Yet only a very small number were actively involved in what ACT UP called "direct action to end the AIDS crisis." At its height, ACT UP had about five to eight hundred people at a meeting. Our largest demonstration, Stop the Church, had only seven thousand people. A few committed activists, when focused on being effective, can accomplish a lot.

WHO MAKES CHANGE?

What kind of person decided to be in ACT UP, and why were they so effective? After all, AIDS activism was, perhaps, the most recent successful social movement in America. It was "successful" in that, over fifteen short years, the broad coalition of people working on AIDS was able to transform the disease, and—in part—the society that surrounded it. The AIDS coalition of activists, scientists, medical personnel, journalists, and social service workers was able to force industry and government to take the necessary actions to go from a state of disaster, with no treatments for people with no rights, to the creation of medications that render a seropositive person with health insurance so virally suppressed that they are biologically incapable of infecting anyone and can live a normal life-span. They created complex social services, tried to change public representation, and impacted how bureaucracies function so that a more truthful story could be told that supported and helped a wider range of people.

However, while advocates were able, in a sense, to beat HIV, they could not beat capitalism. And so, today, because of the greed of international pharmaceutical companies and various health industries, large numbers of people with HIV in the United States and around the world cannot receive medications that already exist. For this reason, around three-quarters of a million people throughout the world still die every year of a disease that is entirely manageable. In the United States, infected people without insurance, living in states with no targeted funding, do not have access to the current standard of care because we don't have a coherent health insurance system. Direct care workers have told me that in New York City today, many AIDS deaths are diagnosed in the emergency room, often because the person had no health care. According to *The New York Times*, reporting on the fiftieth anniversary of Stonewall, "of the 1,790 people who died of AIDS in New York City in 2016, 1,471 were black or Latinx, and more than half were living in extreme poverty. Across the country, according to the U.S. Centers for Disease Control (CDC), African-Americans accounted for 43 percent of H.I.V. diagnoses in 2017, though they represent just 13 percent of the population."

So now, in 2020, as we in the United States are in the middle of a national cataclysm of corruption, illness, and racism, it makes sense to look back at the structure and strategies of ACT UP that were successful and unsuccessful, and why they worked and didn't work. Some of these ideas are applicable and helpful to those of us today who are committed to transforming our contemporary crisis of scapegoating, deprivation, brutality, greed, and neglect. This is the time to learn from our activist past, a history that has not so far been told in Oscar-winning movies and Pulitzer Prize–winning plays and books, from HBO to the nightly news.

What kind of person takes on this responsibility? What kind of person actually rises to the occasion of a mass calamity? I think the answer is very surprising. ACT UP's motto, recited at the start of each Monday-night general meeting, was "The AIDS Coalition To Unleash Power is a diverse, non-partisan group of individuals, united in anger and committed to direct action to end the AIDS crisis." And as this book will show, this is an accurate description. The people interviewed in the ACT UP Oral History Project are from very different backgrounds and experiences, with different temperaments and abilities. In trying to understand what they all had in common that brought them together, I started out expecting some kind of shared foundational preparation. In the beginning of the interview process, Jim and I thought that perhaps they might have all grown up with some value of community. For the first few years I asked a lot of questions about early family sense of belonging. Did they go to church? Were their parents community-oriented? Part of the PTA? But this line of questioning led nowhere. Many reported no early orientation toward collective responsibility, while others came from generations of activists. There was no thread.

Once Jim and I discarded that idea, we thought that perhaps they had all had fundamentally transformative relationships to AIDS or the gay community, but over the years even this did not pan out. Of course, many ACT UPers had AIDS or were HIV-positive, feared becoming infected, or had lost lovers, close friends, or even, as in the case of Alexis Danzig, her father. There were others who had an impulse connection. Sharon Tramutola was sitting with her friend in Newark watching television when an ACT UP demonstration came on. The next day she took the New Jersey Transit into the city, went to Greenwich Village, entered the Gay Center, and joined ACT UP. Karen Timour, working as a bookkeeper, saw images of ACT UP and thought that it might be a great place to make some friends. At a meeting someone asked for a volunteer to work on insurance. She thought, *Sure, I can try that.* And Karen ended up masterminding an enormous campaign conducted by snail mail in fifty states that led to winning basic insurance eligibility for people with AIDS. Over six hundred thousand HIV-positive Americans became eligible for insurance because of her work. Some of ACT UP's most effective members had little or no relationship to AIDS when they first joined the organization. What did these people have in common with Peter Staley, a bond trader who came to ACT UP when he himself became infected? Or with Jim Eigo, an HIV-negative gay man who had been a playwright and theater critic?

At this point I focused on people whose demographic was unusual in the ACT UP collective, hoping that the exceptions would reveal the commonality. Karen Ramspacher was one of a handful of straight people who were entirely integrated into the heart of ACT UP's work. But when I asked her and other straight people why they had joined when most heterosexuals in America were shunning and blaming people with AIDS, they didn't seem to understand the question. In almost every case I had to make overt my goal: that I was trying to comprehend why they joined ACT UP when most straight people refused to help. Repeatedly, respondents would tell me that they didn't understand why the others weren't there! It seemed so obvious a step for each of them that they found other straight people's indifference to be perplexing.

I entirely gave up this thread of pursuit after I interviewed Patricia Navarro, the mother of Ray Navarro, a much-loved Chicano gay artist who died a brutal AIDS death that included blindness and dementia. Patricia had come from her Latino community in Los Angeles to be with Ray in New York, and subsequently became a well-known member of ACT UP. But when I asked her why she was the only parent of a person with AIDS who joined ACT UP, she was confused. She insisted that she wasn't alone. She did belong to a mother's group that overlapped slightly with ACT UP, but none of those women were activists in the ACT UP mode but her. Patricia Navarro had just never noticed that she was an exception because it seemed to her, as it did to Karen Ramspacher, that joining ACT UP was the only logical choice. But of course, if the families and straight friends of people with AIDS had followed the exceptional Karen and Patricia, the world would have been an entirely different place.

It was almost eight years into the process that I suddenly realized what the common denominator was. We were interviewing Rebecca Cole, by then a well-known TV personality associated with upscale urban gardening. But when Rebecca first came from the Midwest to New York in the 1980s to be an actress, she had a job working in a bar while going out on auditions. A coworker there told her that the newly formed AIDS Hotline needed volunteers to get off the ground; she signed up, even though she knew nothing about AIDS. But actually very few people at the hotline knew much more, because there were no treatments, there wasn't that much to know, and the calls reflected this lack. SPREE, whom we interviewed at the Radical Faeries homeland of Short Mountain, Tennessee, told us about her time at the AIDS Hotline, and the content of the average call.

"Here's a typical one. Someone from the city, the big city, visits the country. They give it to a cow . . . Can you get [AIDS] from eating a hamburger from this cow? . . . This woman was doing her laundry. She dropped some of her laundry onto the floor. She then rationalized that, what if someone threw a used condom onto the sidewalk. Someone steps in it. Then goes into the laundromat and walks where she had dropped her laundry. Is she in any danger of getting it?"

But one day Rebecca received a phone call from a woman in Connecticut who had AIDS and had been refused entry into a local experimental drug trial because they were not accepting women. Rebecca was outraged. On her own, she phoned the Centers for Disease Control, made an appointment, went there with another young woman, met with them, and in this way initiated the movement in solidarity with women with AIDS.

Hearing this remarkable story, I suddenly realized that what all these ACT UPers had in common was not experiential. That there was no common concrete factor in their lived lives. Rather, it was characterological. These were people who were unable to sit out a historic cataclysm. They were driven, by nature, by practice, or by some combination thereof, to defend people in trouble through standing with them. What ACT UPers had in common was that, regardless of demographic, they were a very specific type of person, necessary to historical paradigm shifts. In case of emergency, they were not bystanders.

THE DIVERSE INFLUENCES ON AIDS ACTIVIST POLITICS

Since I knew that our interviews told the previously ignored story of women and race and drugs and housing in regard to the AIDS crisis, and, most important, told a story about the power of groups over individuals, I decided to try to write a cohered synthesis of what is actually revealed by the ACT UP Oral History Project in order to unearth its real lessons for the future, which is now our present. In the process, I have come to understand that, for one thing, AIDS activist history has been mistakenly placed in the trajectory of gay male history. I can understand why this connection would be made: gay men were very significantly victimized—individually and collectively—by the criminal indifference of the U.S. government, by private pharmaceutical companies, and by familial homophobia that abandoned them to the virus. And gay men were at the forefront of both leadership and rank and file of the resistance to this greed and indifference. It was the gay male media that focused on AIDS, and activists met in gay-controlled and gay-funded spaces. But my research shows that the ideologies and values that served as the foundations of the applied practices of AIDS activism did not only come from the trajectory of gay male history.

Of course, there was a grassroots tradition in gay liberation politics of deliberately organized "zap actions" and acts of nonviolent civil disobedience conducted by early groups, such as the Gay Activists Alliance, the Gay Liberation Front, and the Lavender Hill Mob, aimed at forces like the American Psychiatric Association. And individuals from these movements—like the late Marty Robinson—were influential early members of ACT UP. However, while many people in ACT UP had not been previously active politically, my interviews reveal that some folks in ACT UP also came from, and were influenced by, other political histories. Members of ACT UP came from Black liberation movements, civil rights organizations like the Congress of Racial Equality (CORE), radical student movements in Central America, anti-Fascist movements in Latin America, U.S. labor movements, sectarian Left parties, the Communist Party and its counterculture, and other movements where they may or may not have been open about their sexualities. We also had key members who came from the Jewish Left, Zionism, Quakers, and the Catholic Left. A significant number of productive ACT UPers came from the Prairie Fire/May 19th Communist Organization, a spin-off of Students for a Democratic Society (SDS) and the Weathermen. Interestingly, one of the earlier movements with the most direct tactical and analytical influence on ACT UP was reproductive rights, most specifically the movement against sterilization abuse. How both access and consent were conceptualized, especially by women in ACT UP, is directly inherited from earlier movements that they participated in, opposing how Puerto Rican women (in New York and on the island) were tricked into sterilization by coercive governmental/medical programs. This history in fighting sterilization abuse provided a heightened sensitivity to how HIV-positive women of color, and their HIV-positive children, were treated by science, especially in issues demanding "consent," like drug testing and placebo use. The way reproductive rights activists understood the right to have children as the necessary balance to their demand for free abortion rights established a practice of multi-issue thinking.

One reason that ACT UP has been historicized in the gay male trajectory, instead of as part of the histories of these other traditions, is because we queer people were the weak link in the coalition at the time. The very reason why there was an autonomous gay movement in the first place was that historically no one else would have us, beyond tiny groups of the Trotskyist Left, like the Spartacist League. The broad exclusion of queer people from families and from political coalitions was not because of any kind of desire on our part to be separate. So the gathering of queer people into sexuality or identity-based movements was a result of exclusion from other places, and by other people, including other people with whom each of us identified: women, racially organized communities, and national, ethnic, disability, ideological, and geographically rooted resistance. Throughout the history of ACT UP there was a tension about working with non-gay-identified groups, not because we didn't want to, but because they didn't want us. Even as a reporter, I started covering AIDS in the early 1980s, but it wasn't until as late as 1991 that I was finally permitted to publish the first piece in support of people with AIDS to appear in *The Nation* magazine. But it was about homeless people with AIDS, which was more acceptable to them as a subject than gay people, because it fit into a traditional Left understanding of class. These imposed separations clouded the diverse histories of influence on ACT UP, making it look like a gay male movement that had emerged out of the air.

Another powerful reason ACT UP has been awkwardly shoved into the gay male historical trajectory is that it was misrepresented over and over by the national media as exclusively, instead of predominantly, white and male. This is a significant difference because women and people of color transform the movements that they choose to join. And this enormous influence was hidden by corporate control of representation. A review of major media coverage of ACT UP from the 1980s and '90s repeatedly shows white male newscasters interviewing white male ACT UPers, or using shots of white male protesters. And we must remember that at that time the media was almost entirely white and male, and most gay men with influence were closeted. If anyone out there cared at all, it was because AIDS was sold, initially, as "tragic," because the young, robust, white male body was reduced to rubble, allowing the straight viewer to feel sorry while simultaneously being comforted by the weakness and punishment of the queer. This issue was addressed at the time, repeatedly. ACT UP photographer Donna Binder described her extensive experience with newspapers and magazines seeking out images of very sick and dying people, and how she had to fight to make them understand that her pictures of people on the front lines of opposition were also images of people with AIDS. I know from my own experience that in a public conversation that I held with Larry Kramer at OutWrite in Boston in the early 1990s, I suggested, in front of an audience, that the next time Larry was called by the media, he could refer them to a person of color or woman in ACT UP. And Larry responded, "But Sarah, shouldn't we use our best people?"

THE INTERSECTION OF RACISM AND HOMOPHOBIA DISTORTED OUR UNDERSTANDING OF AIDS FROM THE BEGINNING

To see the role of racism in the public perception of AIDS, we have to go back to the era directly preceding the recognition of the virus. And just to be precise, although the famous gay cancer study appeared in *The New York Times* in 1981, we now know that AIDS existed for decades before medicine finally recognized patterned symptoms in gay men. In 2008, I interviewed Betty Williams, a straight Quaker who came to ACT UP because of her long affiliation with homeless people and the Haitian community. She reported that homeless people, a New York City population in which people of color have consistently been overrepresented, used the term *junkie pneumonia* to describe what we later came to understand to be pneumocystis pneumonia (PCP), and they also identified *the dwindles*, a street term for what later was identified as wasting syndrome. So homeless people knew about the AIDS crisis at such a level of common parlance that support workers were aware of this initial street-level vocabulary. But because poor people cannot get adequate health care in America, this epidemic, so well known as to inspire language, remained invisible to science.

In 1990, Princeton University Press published an overlooked book, *The History of AIDS*, in which the author, Mirko D. Grmek, described sixteen cases of the virus going back to the 1940s, involving patients who traveled, including doctors and sailors, and those who denied homosexual experience but died with symptoms of "anal trauma." They exhibited a range of AIDS symptoms, and in some cases, lung cell samples later indicated PCP. So we can trace AIDS in America back to the 1940s, and some theorists place its origins at the end of the nineteenth century. Even though we now understand that some homeless people knew about AIDS early, and that doctors and sailors in Grmek's study probably had it as well, it is still accurate to refer to those years, before 1981, as "before science recognized the crisis."

The men diagnosed with Kaposi sarcoma ("gay cancer") in 1981 were privileged enough to have health-care practitioners who paid enough attention to notice a pattern of disease. Yet they all died terrible deaths. The race and class privilege that allowed their illness to become noticed, theorized, and reported did not save their lives and could not protect them from intense suffering. It did not protect them from being stigmatized by the homophobia that thought of a certain cancer as "gay." That a concept of "gay cancer" could have ever existed is painfully illustrative. The idea that cancer could be gay reinforced biological concepts of homosexuality, and the persistent racial disparity in health care created twin illusions of white gay cancer and poor people of color nothing. The first name affixed to this illness, which would eventually be called acquired immune deficiency syndrome (AIDS), was gay-related immune deficiency (GRID). The idea of a "gay disease" reflected a number of pervasive anxieties. First, that homosexuality had some biological component, that homosexuality was itself a disease, and that the disease of GRID was related to the pathology of homosexuality. And simultaneously, this thinking evoked the contradictory idea that homosexuality was contagious and could be caught. The term *GRID* reflected the lack of recognition that homeless people could be gay, or be men having sex with men, just as in later years gay men with AIDS were assumed to have not shared needles. Grmek reports that 30 percent of infected Haitians (in his 1990 study) reported homosexual activity as sex workers for tourists, a fact overlooked by researchers assuming exclusively heterosexual practices among Haitians. At the time, despite low rates of reported HIV infection, even lesbians were prohibited from donating blood because we were perceived to have the biological disease of homosexuality, which was assumed to cause AIDS. The incredibly important transformation of breaking down the disease into *behaviors*, instead of *identities*, took many years and required the participation of people with AIDS from the spectrum of humanity. The multiple stigmas follow AIDS to this day. One journalist friend was recently told, off the record, by an AIDS scientist that, in his estimation, by July 3, 1981, when the *Times* headline announced "Rare Cancer Seen in 41 Homosexuals," there were already two hundred thousand people infected in the United States.

ACT UP AS A FEMINIST MOVEMENT

To understand the context for the ideological roots of the activist values that produced ACT UP's victories for women, people of color, and poor people, let us travel back in time to when I was born, many years ago, in 1958. In 1958, if a woman was raped in New York City, she could not get a conviction in court without a witness. Her own testimony was not acceptable. In the 1960s, the second-wave feminist movement emerged in the context of global radical liberation movements that were anti-colonial as well as offering visions of personal and societal liberation. In that context, the state was experienced as literally the enemy of women. In fact, very few women were even in the state as lawyers, law enforcement, elected officials, or judges. As a consequence, grassroots feminist movements opposed protectionism and were not oriented toward relationships with the state. In a sense, you could say that their strategies were rooted in what we now call "restorative justice," even though that language did not exist at the time. But projects like illegal abortion networks, self-defense classes, and rape crisis hotlines, where a woman who was raped could speak to another woman who had been raped, bypassed the state. Battered women's shelters, feminist health centers, consciousness-raising events—these types of projects and the visions behind them were focused more on empowering women and less on working with the state to punish men. A significant number of internally influential lesbian ACT UP members came directly from these feminist movements of the 1960s and '70s into ACT UP, where they were highly effective at conveying ideologies and values from feminism that were grassroots in theory and approach. This influence was in part the reason why ACT UP never applied for 501(c)(3) not-for-profit status, and never asked for government funding. I just want to mention two of many examples here of 1970s feminists who literally carried those values into ACT UP: Jamie Bauer and Marion Banzhaf.

Jamie Bauer transitioned decades after their work in ACT UP, and now is nonbinary, but they came from the women's peace movement and the lesbian activist community and functioned in ACT UP as an emissary of those legacies. Here I found that Nan Alamilla Boyd's pioneering 1999 article "Looking for Lesbian Bodies in Transgender History" is very helpful to those of us telling lesbian and transgender histories through the same individuals. Jamie had particular experience in the Women's Pentagon Action, in 1979, had great knowledge and commitment to nonviolence, and was learned and skilled in civil disobedience training from a feminist perspective. In fact, in our pretransition interview for the Oral History Project, Jamie details how they and others like John Kelley, BC Craig, Robert Vázquez-Pacheco, and Alexis Danzig (straight, bi, future trans, queer, gay, lesbian, white, Black, Brown, female, and male) educated ACT UP about nonviolent civil disobedience; organized and ran trainings for protesters, marshals, and legal observers; and basically supervised and organized ACT UP's unwavering use of nonviolent civil disobedience. This work was so natural to ACT UP that while a motion to officially refuse violence never actually came to the floor, ACT UP never committed an act of violence. This was true even when its own members—many of whom were very ill and knew they would die—suffered at the hands of the police, the state, and pharmaceutical executives. Clearly from all footage of ACT UP demonstrations, and from repeated testimonies in many interviews, being trained in nonviolent civil disobedience was part of the personal enrichment experience of being in ACT UP and was a key factor in ACT UP's ability to win campaigns and influence policy.

My second example, Marion Banzhaf, came from a number of political legacies, including the feminist Women's Health Movement of the 1970s and Reaganite '80s. In fact, she was on the staff of the Tallahassee Feminist Women's Health Center, where she had direct experience fighting for abortion rights, against sterilization abuse, and for the integration of lesbian rights into a reproductive rights agenda, while taking on the rising religious right and the right-wing omnibus bill, the Family Protection Act. In this way she was part of the development of the feminist concept of "patient-centered politics," which was antiracist and incorporated class and access into its approach to treatment and demand for services. ACT UP formed in 1987, and Marion joined that same year. The issue of mandatory testing came up, with William F. Buckley Jr. and other right-wing figures seriously proposing tattooing people with AIDS and putting them in isolation or internment. Marion proposed that, should this come to be, ACT UP could consider building "underground testing" on the model of feminist illegal abortion networks. She then learned that the men in ACT UP had no idea of what that was. So she participated in a teach-in on the feminist concept of "patient-centered" politics. And of course, like nonviolent civil disobedience, patient-centered politics was a fundamental of ACT UP's vision and organizing principle. Throughout the interviews, people would often say, "People with AIDS are the experts," a viewpoint that was learned inside ACT UP from feminism, that drove our agenda, and that we shared with the world.

GAY MEN, HOMOPHOBIA, AND SEXISM

The sexism of white gay men in this period reflected complex combinations of supremacy and oppression. The closet, whether a punitive, isolating, and diminishing personal experience or a reality of private networks of gay men in power, enabled some gay men to access the full privileges of straight men, and sometimes more. At the same time, openly gay men often faced job discrimination and exclusion, legal discrimination, street violence, and familial homophobia. Still, in a country where white women earned seventy-five cents to every dollar a white man made, households or communities funded by white men's incomes had discretionary buying power beyond any other configuration. Whoever partners with a white man, in America, partners with the nation's highest earning capacity. Yet this did not shield white gay men from AIDS. On the contrary, AIDS was a sudden, shocking reality check that the powers that be in the U.S. government, and in industry, and in family, did not care what happened to gay male lives, even if some of those institutions included gay individuals in power positions.

AIDS literally made gay men visible as they sickened and died in public, but even then many industries, including traditionally gay-friendly ones like arts, design, and entertainment, refused to represent the AIDS experiences accurately or at all. Fields with decimating numbers of dead, like ballet and opera, did not represent their own experiences onstage. Professional groups did develop to help, like Design Industries Foundation Fighting AIDS (DIFFA, 1984) or Broadway Cares/ Equity Fights AIDS (1988) and Visual AIDS (1988). But fields that suffered high levels of AIDS deaths often hesitated to change course and disrupt the long-held traditions of cooperation with power.

These hypocrisies drove some individual gay men into AIDS activism. While some had previous political organizing experience, the vast majority had actually never been in an activist movement before. Even the ones with expertise in business organization, public relations, advertising, graphic design, and health care often had never thought deeply about how to organize a popular meeting, or how to build an action outside of established institutional frameworks. This combination of shock at how little their lives meant to powerful institutions, and the need to quickly create a functional grassroots movement, meant that lesbians with tested organizing experience from the lesbian and feminist movements were—for once—noticed, needed, and very welcome.

Gay men, in that era, had experienced emotional and cultural consequences of their exclusion from exercising the full range of power available to heterosexual or closeted men. There was often a kind of fawning for straight male approval, both toward a signification of power as well as a kind of repair of familial homophobia. Generational disdain of women was born not only in sexism but also in the humiliating and constant imposition of women candidates for intimate relationships by parents, bosses, and general society, in whom gay men growing up, or living in the closet, were supposed to painfully feign interest. The liberatory moment of AIDS activism meant not only a releasing of the gay and AIDS closets but also the opportunity for queer men and women to bond, to build, to integrate, and to rise together in a way that had never been possible for some before. In a sense, gay male separatism, rooted in the desire to access straight male power, had to give way to working and living with women, often lesbian or bisexual, of all ages, as equals. And this was widely embraced in ACT UP. For men in ACT UP were not only free to be themselves, with AIDS, but also finally free to love women, to learn from women, and to listen to women, especially gay women, in a way never desirable before. And some gay men, gay women, straight men, and straight women came out into bisexual identities in ACT UP. For some lesbians, who had worked with impoverished constituencies, excluded from power institutions, this was our first opportunity to apply political knowledge and experience to a context that was able to amass serious funding. For some of us, this was our first experience of a kind of heterosexual privilege: access to white male resources. What Alexandra Juhasz called "privilege and principle" met together, for many, for the first time in that movement.

While writing this book, I got an email from someone asking me to introduce them to women who worked as "caretakers" for gay men who died of AIDS. I said that I could introduce them to women who were influential leaders, but that my data in the ACT UP Oral History Project showed that there was no difference in numbers between women who cared for dying friends and men who cared for dying friends, that this work, in ACT UP, was not gendered. And she wrote me back, "Thank you, can you refer me to someone who might know some women who cared for gay men during AIDS?" So these sexist and racist clichés exist: that it was some heroic white male individuals who, alone, transformed the AIDS crisis, that women were important because they were the caretakers of men, and that people of color simply didn't exist at all. But the reality is that women—and trans men who at the time identified as women—especially feminists and lesbians from the 1970s movements, were actually some of the principal theoreticians of ACT UP.

This is not to say that every white man in ACT UP became a feminist or every white woman an antiracist. Rather, ACT UP was able to make progress for people of color and women without every white person and man in ACT UP coming to consciousness. It is true that AIDS only got addressed at all because white men with access had it. They got it just at a moment when it seemed that some social progress was being made and that there might soon be some recourse from the crushing practice of anti-gay bigotry, the lack of legal protection, and one of the greatest unrecognized forces of history, familial homophobia. They had it at a time when that very same oppression and discrimination inadvertently produced a current of invention and elevated aesthetics, born of separation from the dreariness of historical whiteness. Perhaps because gay people were often forced out of their families and small towns, there were creative and cultural advances that surpassed the banality of white American culture. And AIDS activism's most radical and socially revolutionary vision evolved when those white men were in the same boat as everybody else who had AIDS: desperate. Because when they were desperate, they acted differently. They listened. Anyone with no way out looks for a way out. And it is only in that moment that their prejudices, conventions, and egos are up for grabs. As a result, without a small group of those white men finally listening, and then using every ounce of energy, currency, connection, assertion, insistence, and culturally recognizable imagination in coalition with those with less power, AIDS would never have been transformed.

KEY STRATEGIES THAT ARE USEFUL TO ACTIVISTS TODAY

Direct Action

In his landmark expression of American Radicalism "Letter from Birmingham Jail" (1963), Dr. Martin Luther King Jr. laid out the tactical structure of civil rights protest: "In any nonviolent campaign there are four basic steps: collection of the facts to determine whether injustices exist; negotiation; self purification; and direct action."

Even though it was never expressly stated, and even though we did not realize it, repeated examination of ACT UP's approach revealed that we used a version of this analysis. While most ACT UPers were too old to have studied Dr. King in school, most of us grew up watching the civil rights movement unfold on black-and-white television, and some had family and community who participated in or identified with the movement. We saw images in *Life* or *Jet* magazine of Black people being attacked by police dogs, sprayed with water cannons, arrested, and murdered. We saw repeated footage of Black people doing nonviolent civil disobedience, sitting in, and being arrested. I can speculate that for queer children of all races born in the 1940s, '50s, and '60s with no public recognition of our realities, and growing up in hostile communities and families, these images of Black resistance had an even more searing power. The way that Dr. King's description of activist process manifested in ACT UP was roughly thus:

1. Experience-Based Agenda: Identify your issues based on the lived experiences of people with AIDS.
2. Education: Become the expert on your subject.
3. Design the Solution: Instead of acting in an infantilized relationship to those in power, begging them to solve problems, ACT UP used their acquired and innate expertise to design reasonable, doable, and winnable solutions.
4. Present This Solution to the Powers That Be: And when they refuse to listen . . .
5. ACT UP's process of "self-purification" was a combination of nonviolent civil disobedience training, emotional and political bonding through the creation of affinity groups, and the putting in place of highly organized support systems of marshals and volunteer lawyers to ensure that no one would get lost in the system. Teach-ins created a highly informed rank and file, all of whom were encouraged to be spokespeople because "people with AIDS are the experts." Sophisticated media workers combined grassroots video activism and high-level media contacts to present ACT UP's demands.
6. Then ACT UP would perform nonviolent direct action to, as facilitator Ann Northrop would say, "Speak through the media, not to the media."
7. Thereby, ACT UP created public pressure on the powers that be to move toward ACT UP's reasonable, doable, already designed solution.

It was the Black civil rights movement's interpretation of "direct action" that best represents ACT UP's, although this, too, was not made explicit at the time. Probably the best historical example would be the events of February 1, 1960, when Black students from A&T State University sat in at the segregated lunch counter of a Woolworth in downtown Greensboro, North Carolina. While they did have a supporting picket outside on the street, they did not *only* have a picket. Instead of *asking* through chants and posters for the segregated lunch counter to lose its whites-only restriction, they also did direct action. They literally sat at the counter, thereby actually integrating the counter. For one moment, before being beaten, being threatened with death, facing real violence, and enduring the humiliation of food spilled onto their heads and clothes while being called racial epithets, before being punched and then arrested, these young people created an image that has survived the decades and become emblematic of protest: they created the world that they wanted to see. While ACT UP never studied "Letter from Birmingham Jail," it is certain that many of us saw these images of Black resistance, with which we identified and internalized, and from which we learned.

In this tradition, through the trajectory of gay and lesbian liberation and feminism, most of ACT UP's public protests were creative actions. Instead of marching around with signs and listening passively to speakers as the sole end-all of an organizing experience, ACT UP created elaborate images of the obstacles they were fighting and the world they wanted to live in. So, for example, in the famous Stop the Church action in December 1989, ACT UP went beyond using signs to protest the Catholic Church's interference with condom distribution in public schools. While seven thousand protesters did do a conventional demonstration outside, a small group of activists literally went inside the church and nonviolently disrupted mass. This direct action showed that because the church's actions jeopardized people's lives, ACT UP would not abide by traditional standards of secular movements, targeted by the church, who usually stayed out of religious rites. As Dudley Saunders observed, it was "invisibility made visible at the center." If we truly knew that our lives mattered, then we showed this by literally stepping into the church's space, just as they were doing by interfering in the public sphere of city schools. The form of a direct action was part of its message. This created more opportunity for our ideas to reach the public. It also kept ACT UP's creative and imaginative membership ever interested and engaged in fulfilling the artistic vision conjured in our minds and hearts to accompany and highlight each issue and event on the organization's political agenda.

Direct action was a concept by which theoretical discussion was not separate from action. Of course, individual ACT UPers were influenced by theory. A number of young video activists had studied in the Whitney Museum Studio Program. Many older activists came from highly theorized earlier radical movements, and some members, like Douglas

Crimp, wrote theory. But on the floor of the Monday-night meeting, theory was never debated unless it was tied to creating actions, or to setting active campaigns. As Maxine Wolfe, one of ACT UP's most influential leaders, would say, when planning and carrying out an action, "theory emerges" as a concrete result of actual decisions that are being made for real-life application. Instead of the Gramscian concept of "praxis," which is the application of theory into practice, ACT UP first chose a practice—an action—and then evolved a theory necessary to make it work toward our larger goal of "direct action to end the AIDS crisis." In this way campaigns were structured as a series of interconnected actions, designed to produce a larger outcome. ACT UP would never just do a demonstration, zap, or action to stand on its own. These public expressions were designed to build to the next step. That's why every event had a sign-up sheet, or leaflets announcing further actions, and participants were informed of the next step in the series on any specific issue. Every action included a component of giving participants and observers something else to do. In this way, energy was not wasted, and events had purpose, as part of a larger schema. Not wasting energy, effort, or goodwill was essential to being effective in a movement of people who literally did not have time.

There is an intimacy to direct action that no other tactic creates. In other approaches, the people who are being harmed are usually kept out of sight and thereby made invisible through a series of shunning techniques. They are repressed by illegality, lack of representation, hatred. Stigma keeps people from speaking out. The media distorts the experiences of people who need change by presenting reductive or wrong renditions of their experiences or by ignoring them altogether. The media also appoints mainstream people to explain points of view that they actually do not understand. By the time a "feminist" or gay person or person of color or trans person—and all the overlaps therein—finally makes it into mainstream media, that chosen person's perspective is often years behind the movements they claim to speak for. The history and range of ideas that produced these movements is never acknowledged or referenced. Direct action disrupts this systemic falsification. It forces a *direct* confrontation between the people with power and the people whose lives are demeaned or damaged by the ignorance and indifference of the person with power. But in this moment of collision, the message must be impossible to avoid. It can be funny, but it has to be attention getting; it needs to be insightful. It has to be visually arresting; it cannot be a cliché. In that brief moment of stepping into the sight line of the powerful, shunned people use direct action to be understood. And they are making two things clear: (1) the specific content of their demand for change, and (2) that they will never stop fighting for their survival.

Simultaneity of Action, Not Consensus
Although it wasn't made explicit at the time, ACT UP's process of dealing with such dramatic difference and diversity of experience and approach among the members was to practice a kind of radical democracy. In this way, individuals and cliques had to give up any thought of successful control over the entirety of the organization. A thorough investigation of the roots and expressions that led to ACT UP's tragic split in 1992 reveal that subverting this range of difference and trying to channel it through open and hidden moves was ultimately its downfall.

But during its height of influence, ACT UP never demanded full agreement for an action or campaign to be taken up. For example, if I wanted to participate in an illegal needle exchange on the Lower East Side in order to get arrested and wage a test case trial, and you didn't want to, you wouldn't stop me from doing it; you just wouldn't do it. If instead you wanted to organize a demonstration against the Catholic Church, and I didn't want to, I simply wouldn't do it. In this way, many different expressions of direct action were carried on simultaneously, none of them requiring full consensus, total participation, or universal agreement. Although it was never overtly stated or theorized at the time, this method allowed each ACT UPer to respond in a way that made sense to them and reflected where they were at individually. The only requirement was that it was direct action, with a goal related to ending the AIDS crisis, and not provision of social services. The differentiation between direct action and social services was rooted in the understanding that activists created change that required policy, and social service providers, and later AIDS Incorporated professionals, institutionalized and carried out policy.

All of this was handled through a loose structure: General Monday-night meetings were run with a relaxed version of Robert's Rules of

Order. Facilitators like Maria Maggenti, David Robinson, Ann Northrop, Alexis Danzig, Robert Garcia, Kathy Otter (later known as Kathy Ottersten), and Karl Soehnlein were profoundly influential in attracting people to ACT UP, engaging them, and instructing them in process and moving meetings of large numbers forward. People were asked to voluntarily refrain from voting unless they had been to three meetings. But soon after the implementation of this requirement, no records were kept and no one was challenged. Focusing on something so bureaucratic as membership records would have been considered unimportant and not focused on direct action to end the AIDS crisis. The Monday-night agendas were set by the Coordinating Committee and adjusted by the two elected facilitators, who would include and prioritize reports or motions for action from the main committees. People had to be called on to speak, and the facilitators looked for new voices before calling on the same person repeatedly, although this also was not rigid. It was not stated or theorized, but simply collectively understood through shared values, that the facilitators had the humane discretion to determine that a person was so implicated that they deserved to be heard more than once before others had spoken.

The facilitators' primary job was to move the discussion toward action, and to make sure that repetitive, circular conversation did not eat up valuable time. Committees changed over the years, but some examples are the Actions Committee, which coordinated large organization-wide actions; Fundraising; Treatment and Data (T&D); Majority Action, which was a gathering of ACT UPers of color; and Media. Each committee sent a representative to the weekly meetings of the Coordinating Committee, where responsibilities were assigned, money dispersed, and efforts synchronized. At the same time, people self-divided into small affinity groups that were not accountable to the larger body and that did not have to clear their activities with the floor. People would collect their legal paperwork from within the affinity group, and bring it to the legal team, in case they did get arrested and had to be supported through the system. So, for example, when the Monday-night general meeting decided to do an action at the Food and Drug Administration, it was organized through the Actions Committee, sitting at the Coordinating Committee. But at the demonstration, individual affinity groups appeared with their own artistic and creative expression that no one had approved.

When it came to enacting nonviolent civil disobedience, often affinity groups would take trainings together, participate together, and get arrested together. When people got sick and died, affinity group members would transition into being care teams. Affinity groups like the Marys, Wave 3, or the Costas would involve ten to twenty people, who met on their own time in their own apartments, and would keep their presentation or actions a secret, so that the presumed police infiltrators would not be tipped off. Every general meeting started with the announcement, "If there are any uniformed or plain-clothed members of the New York Police Department, or any law enforcement agency including the FBI here, you are required by law to identify yourselves now." Even though no one ever did identify themselves, ACT UP always assumed that, because they were having an impact, they were being watched. Police files on ACT UP obtained through the Freedom of Information Act (FOIA) were highly redacted, indicating informants. See more details of FBI and police involvement at the end of this book in Appendix 1.

This freedom of expression within the movement was born not of theory but of necessity. Many people in ACT UP did not have long to live. They were working against the clock to try to save their own lives. This lack of time made people more efficient, creative, and flexible, and it turns out that that flexibility was exercised in a way that created more efficiency. For example, if it came up at a Monday-night meeting that a letter needed to be written to a commissioner, someone would volunteer to write it. Often that person would simply be trusted to write the letter and send it. There was sometimes no process whereby a large committee would vet the letter, changing words here and there, arguing over punctuation or vocabulary. We just didn't have time for that level of control. In this way, people were allowed and encouraged to take responsibility for their task and to complete it without being micromanaged. Because the stakes were so high, overall this was a successful approach. It kept the organization moving actively forward and allowed each individual a kind of freedom of expression to respond to AIDS in the way that made sense to them. And ultimately, this very wide range of simultaneous responses, in multiple social milieus, with different concrete aims, and involving different targets and participants, strengthened ACT UP because it created a large, resonant, cumulative impact that singular activity never could have produced.

HOW A PREDOMINANTLY WHITE MALE ORGANIZATION WON THE MOVEMENT'S SINGLE GREATEST VICTORY FOR WOMEN, PEOPLE OF COLOR, AND POOR PEOPLE

It is very unusual for movements or groups that are dominated by men and white people to achieve transformational victories that improve the lives of women, people of color, and poor people. And certainly, the fact that ACT UP did this stands in great contrast to the history of white gay rights politics, which has led to race- and class-based reconciliation with the state.

The impact of racism on people of color in ACT UP is documented over and over again by my interviews. In one example, ACT UP New Yorker Moisés Agosto-Rosario, one of the founders of ACT UP Puerto Rico, testified that he had to take on the extra burden to enter the all-white Treatment and Data Committee so that he could get the latest treatment information and stay alive. And he succeeded. And there are many stories like his. But, interestingly—and this is where it gets really unpredictable—despite profound racism and sexism, ACT UP managed to win what I and many others consider to be the most significant victory for women, people of color, and poor people in the history of American HIV, which was when ACT UP's four-year, multifaceted campaign succeeded in changing the Centers for Disease Control's official definition of what symptoms constituted AIDS.

How this happened is worthy information for women and people of color working in coalition today. Because of ACT UP's patient-centered politics, learned from feminism, people with AIDS were the experts. And the experiences of women with HIV and people of color, of poor people and health-care providers in ACT UP, and in coalition with ACT UP, were the basis for campaigns and analysis. The enormous amount of time that people spent together had a significant influence on determining strategy. For many, ACT UP dominated their lives and particularly their social lives, not just with meeting time and demonstration time but also with shared jail time, eating together in between meetings, moving into one another's homes, traveling long distances together, hospital visits, parties, dancing, teach-ins on new treatments, and all kinds of combinations of sexual and romantic relationships, as well as caretaking together and organizing memorial services and funerals. ACT UPers often felt emotionally alienated from their former friends and communities who now remained passive in the face of the AIDS crisis, and sometimes felt that they could only relate to others who were actively working for positive change. This enormous amount of shared time, in person, made possible deep and authentic discussions of the lived experiences of AIDS. Since the common lens was one of direct action, once problems were acknowledged, activist solutions were imagined, together, as a natural form of relationship.

But even more important, once issues relevant to women and/or people of color (POC) with AIDS were articulated, women and/or POC ACT UP members did *not* waste their time trying to teach their white male comrades to be less sexist and racist. Discussions on the floor of the Monday-night meeting often raised issues of gender and race, sexism and racism, in the way actions were being approached and constructed. But women and people of color did not employ consciousness-raising groups about racism or sexism that were separate from information about campaigns and actions. In fact, there were very few official gatherings—other than parties—that were not geared to an active event or campaign of some kind. Women and/or POC members did not stop the drive toward action to correct or control language or to call out bias. Instead, people of color and women in ACT UP stewarded ACT UP's considerable resources—literal money, group energy and passion, and more elusive connections—for projects that primarily aided women, poor people, and people of color. And in some key cases, they won the complete commitment of the larger organization, and in some cases they did not. The larger group's involvement or indifference was sometimes crucial, and in other cases, it was not. But during ACT UP's most effective period, the larger group's approval did not get fetishized. The story of the founding of ACT UP Puerto Rico, for example, was a case in which the ample financial resources of ACT UP NY were used to allow a cadre of Latinx (or, in the parlance of the day, "Latino and Latina") members to go to Puerto Rico repeatedly with allies, and to jump-start AIDS activist organizing there. In other words, the language and behavior of racist and sexist ACT UPers was not the focus, but their energy, money, and connections, diverted to larger communities and broader goals, were.

Changing the CDC definition of AIDS was the greatest example of this kind of action-oriented intervention. At the time, the U.S. government defined AIDS by symptoms that infected women did not often manifest, like the parasitic skin cancer Kaposi sarcoma, while simultaneously excluding female-specific symptoms like uncontrollable yeast infections or severe pelvic inflammatory disease. As a result, women with HIV, who were overwhelmingly poor, could not qualify for benefits and could not participate in experimental drug trials, and thus treatments were not developed on a female model. Even today, the most effective standard-of-care compound drugs work more slowly in viral suppression in women than they do in men, possibly because not enough women comprised the original test models. As ACT UP used to say, "Women don't get AIDS; they just die from it." In the campaign to change the definition, women, people of color, and their supporters were able to help guide AIDS activism, often an extension of feminism, to become a movement that would win the most significant victories for women, people of color, and poor people with HIV in American history.

1

Mechanisms of Power: Puerto Ricans in ACT UP

When there were no treatments, everyone was going to die. Before any functioning AIDS medications had been developed, people with homes died in bed while the homeless died on the street. People with homophobic families died on someone's couch. People with good food and health care might live longer, but not necessarily. For everyone from Hollywood movie stars to the hungry, AIDS was a terrible death.

And this was uniting.

The desperation of inevitability—in some key cases—overwhelmed traditional supremacy behaviors of not listening. People who took on the responsibility to end this apocalypse had to be open to ideas and experiences they had never considered before, from people they had never known or taken seriously. And when everyone was committed to transformation, we all moved forward. This emergency allowed those who had never previously crossed paths to be in the same room, even if it was the hallway of an overcrowded hospital.

Yet as soon as one tiny step of progress was made, the relative equality of being doomed together subsided and was replaced by the great American arbiter of supremacy and subordination: access.

Any crumb that was seized went first to the privileged, even if that privilege was relative. Even if they had no civil rights and no family support but had a big bank account. Even if their boyfriend had already died, but they had the lease. Even if their diarrhea was so bad they couldn't go outside, but they still knew someone who knew someone who could get them into a drug trial. Even if they were poverty-stricken but not incarcerated. Even if they had families who loved them, but they were born HIV-positive into a world with no treatments. Once a resource was forced into existence by activists, its distribution depended upon sometimes infinitesimal degrees of difference of relative privilege, given that all people with AIDS—before functional medications—suffered from neglect, indifference, stigma, and, most important, the horrifying ravages of AIDS itself.

ACT UP was predominantly white and male. But its history has been whitened in ways that obstruct the complexity. Because AIDS has been wrongly historicized exclusively from a white perspective, I want to start here with the stories of two central ACT UP members who are HIV-positive and who have ties to Puerto Rico: Robert Vázquez-Pacheco and Moisés Agosto-Rosario, one a Black Nuyorican, one a Latino born on the island. Their interviews reveal some of the very complex and unpredictable dimensions of positionality—in AIDS itself and then in AIDS activism—most of which ultimately convene on the question of power and how it is constructed.

The story of access in ACT UP is the story of a collective that intended to do good, and actually did in fact truly make the world a better place. Inside those accomplishments are realities of a human dimension: people who do great things also do bad things, sometimes out of bias and supremacy, and sometimes out of vulnerability, fear of demise, the desire to live, or all of the above. And when white people, and men, do things out of bias and vulnerability, people with less access pay a price. Sometimes that price is stress, or being forced to strategize, or being blindsided as a way of life. Sometimes that price is exclusion from treatments, from participation in decision-making, or from the machine of power. Sometimes that means death, and sometimes that means long-term and systemic deprivation for the collective as well as the individual. When we evaluate how we have spent our lives, we have to look at our cumulative impact, not at the moments of failure or bad faith. Assessing this history is not a game of call-out. Instead, it is an effort to really understand and make clear how the AIDS rebellion succeeded, and to face where it failed, in order to be more conscious and deliberate, and therefore effective, today.

ROBERT VÁZQUEZ-PACHECO

When he was twenty-four, Robert Vázquez-Pacheco was at the beach with his lover, Jeffrey, a "nice Jewish Boy from Queens whose parents didn't like him having a Puerto Rican boyfriend." Jones Beach was packed with throngs celebrating the 1981 July Fourth weekend. Lying on the sand, six months into their loving, romantic relationship, the two young men noticed an article in *The New York Times* describing forty-one cases of cancer found in gay men in California, eight of whom had died. Robert remembered thinking, *Those sluts in San Francisco are getting some disease.*

Three months later, Robert was planning a surprise party for Jeffrey's thirtieth birthday, when Jeff called and asked him to come to New York Hospital. The stately building, with gothic archways and elaborate brickwork, Robert said, "has this gorgeous Art Deco lobby, like a hotel or a train station." Waiting in entrance halls, Robert looked up to find Jeffrey coming down the stairs, crying. Small marks that had appeared on his skin had just been diagnosed as Kaposi sarcoma lesions. Robert took Jeffrey in his arms, and then went to the pay phone to cancel the birthday party. For the next six years, Jeff was treated with chemo for the cancer, but he got sicker and sicker. The only thing that actually helped him was smoking pot to counteract the side effects of chemotherapy. The young couple didn't personally know any other people who were dealing with AIDS. There were no support groups yet. They were both already volunteering at the Gay Switchboard, which was a vital and popular anonymous hotline that anyone could call for information, or just to talk. Jeffrey and Robert integrated whatever AIDS information they could find into the hotline's foundation, but there were no other places, that they knew of, to put their knowledge and experience of living with AIDS.

Robert's family included Jeffrey in their gatherings and treated them with kindness. When Robert's sister had a newborn baby, she handed it to Jeffrey to hold. But Jeff's family was rejecting. When his own sister had a baby, she wouldn't let her brother touch it. Six years after his first lesion, Jeffrey died. Robert remembered having swollen lymph nodes himself, as far back as 1980, but decided not to start on any of the new medications. A Nuyorican, Black Puerto Rican, born in New York City, he'd heard that the one available treatment, AZT, caused anemia in Black people. Well aware of the sinister history of medical experimentation on Black people, he resolved not to take AZT unless it was tested on Black people and proven to be safe. Due to the particular strain of virus that he had been infected by, his subsequent fairly good health, and his suspicion of drugs, he didn't actually start medication until 1995.

After Jeffrey died, Robert was very, very angry. He wanted to do something, something active, and not just rely on social services. He went with his best friend, David Kirschenbaum, to ACT UP's first anniversary party and talent show in 1988 at the bar Siberia. It was filled with "in-jokes," like "a familial setting." He saw Vito Russo there, the well-loved popularizer of gay images in Hollywood cinema, known for community screenings and for his 1981 book, *The Celluloid Closet*. Robert saw someone singing Broadway show tunes, clad in leather gear, cracking a whip. But he wasn't inspired to join the group. Eventually, though, he and David did stop by an ACT UP meeting when the two of them happened to be at the Gay Center on a Monday night. It was packed. The first thing Robert noticed was, "There are a helluva lot of cute boys here."

"Where should we stand?" David asked.

"Stand where the power is," Robert said. And after watching the group dynamics for a while, they situated themselves near Avram Finkelstein, Maria Maggenti, and Maxine Wolfe. "The big cheeses." The Gay Switchboard had had women in leadership; it was not unusual for Robert to see women being listened to.

Robert's first step forward in ACT UP was at a meeting when he noticed that the person writing notes on the chalkboard had terrible handwriting. Robert jumped up, took the chalk, and wrote out notes in architectural lettering. The crowd applauded because they could finally read what was going on. He had found a way in.

There were only a handful of people of color in the first years of ACT UP. Ortez Alderson, who had come from a Black Power/antiwar background in Chicago, would hold the floor and talk passionately about issues affecting poor people. Robert Garcia, a young, bright, slightly yuppie Latino party boy, had never been political before. Dan Williams, a Black former sailor, was there. "We stood out like a fly in a glass of milk." Robert joined with these men and a few others to form the Majority Action Committee, which was a committee made up of people of color within ACT UP. Their first meeting had ten or fifteen people of color out of three hundred or so ACT UPers. Even though Robert had a full-time job, he represented Majority Action at the Coordinating Committee, which was ACT UP's principal planning committee (the floor rejected the term *steering committee*, because they didn't want to be steered). He then created and took on the expanded task of general welcoming. He would orient all new members by pulling them off the floor at Monday-night general meetings and spending twenty minutes with each new group, bringing them up to snuff on current issues in ACT UP so they could jump right in. He told them, "We need people who will be working as opposed to posing." Often Robert was the first person someone joining ACT UP would meet.

Perhaps because he had come to ACT UP out of anger at how his lover had suffered and died, Robert put most of his efforts into peace-keeping. He became a marshal for the organization's first major action, Seize Control of the FDA, which took place on October 11, 1988, in Rockville, Maryland, just outside Washington, D.C. He was not one of those, like attorney David Barr, negotiating with the government for a more flexible approval and distribution system of new drugs to people too sick to wait for the elaborate bureaucratic process. He was "an action person," more interested in the nuts and bolts of creating actions on the street and opening doors inside ACT UP. Robert focused on the crucial issue of safety at the planned demo. "Safety" for sick and dying people was literal. But, like most ACT UPers, he was always informed about the issues at stake in the fight, which in this case was with the Food and Drug Administration. In fact, he was part of a teach-in for the membership on the specifics of the clinical trial system, and specifically the issue of "compassionate use," where ACT UP campaigned for access to unapproved drugs that had shown some benefit in trials.

The philosophy of marshaling appealed to Robert. ACT UP calculated that for every four hundred people at a demonstration, seventy-five marshals would be needed. Their stated job was to make sure our people did not get physically hurt, and simultaneously that our side remained nonviolent. The marshals—identified by colored armbands—did crowd control, functioning as a physical barrier between cops and demonstrators. Our people listened to and trusted the marshals, and most ACT UPers had experienced civil disobedience trainings that were held for free before large actions. Marshals also helped with chants or kept people going if there was a legal, moving picket, which would fall into illegality if the crowd stood still. Marshals had to be good-natured and remain calm. If people got arrested, marshals had to note their names, so that no one would get lost in the system. For this reason, marshals normally would avoid arrest. But at Seize Control of the FDA, a group of people tried to open a locked set of glass doors, and suddenly the glass broke (footage of this is included in the film *United in Anger*). At that moment, the police overreacted and swept up everyone in their path, and Robert got arrested, with his walkie-talkie in hand, as cell phones were not yet in general use. The FDA arrests were so numerous that people were taken to a big gym, where they hung out and got to know one another and "some lesbians played tampon basketball." But Robert was careful to never get arrested in New York. "Because Puerto Ricans disappear there."

While so much of AIDS activism was about getting access to treatments, Robert did not experience a lot of open conversation in ACT UP circles about which drugs each person was trying, even though there were constant teach-ins about new approaches, and even though treatment activists were always sharing information about different medical strategies. "We didn't have these kinds of conversations about *What are you taking, what are you on?*" The business of saving lives and literally changing the world was an intimate experience, but while "there was a presumed intimacy . . . there were tons of people I saw on a regular basis and I didn't know what they did for a living."

There were other topics that were rarely raised. "One of the subjects we didn't discuss in ACT UP [was] socioeconomic issues . . . I was surprised by how many people in ACT UP went to college." Robert had dropped out after one year of college, sold drugs, took up painting, and worked a variety of jobs. He was working for a lighting designer when he first came to ACT UP. He remembered working-class Jews like Maxine Wolfe, Avram Finkelstein, and Gregg Bordowitz talking about class issues. "The spectrum played itself out in the different committees people joined. The folks who joined Treatment and Data, those boys were all college educated and fairly middle-class . . . Middle-class people look at a situation and say *I can do that!*"

Being of the generation that got infected before AIDS was even identified was a very specific experience for Robert. "I've never been *negative*, I don't know what that means." Yet he passed no judgment on people who got infected after modes of transmission were identified. "I don't know if I could have stayed negative realistically . . . Desire is not a rational process." Included in all its demographic diversities, ACT UP also had a wide range of people with a variety of HIV experiences and stances from the beginning. "There were folks in ACT UP who were very publicly HIV-positive . . . and folks who were not out about their status in ACT UP." In a sense, this, too, was a coalition of difference. No one position was enforced. One could say there was a gentleness about how each person handled their own virus.

Robert had a number of relationships and affairs in and around ACT UP, including with Gregg Bordowitz, who was the Romeo of the group. Women and men in ACT UP mention him in their interviews as a love partner or love object more often than any other individual. "Relationships in ACT UP were very public. You knew who was dating who." The open sexuality and the vulnerability to love and attraction in ACT UP were partially an extension of pre-AIDS gay male sexual culture, but also formed a foundation of group bonding. "Gay men jump into bed to meet each other."

Like a number of other significant early members of ACT UP, Robert envisioned the future of AIDS activism as a movement for universal health care for all Americans. "What I saw was the opportunity in ACT UP for social change . . . using AIDS as a nexus of all the problems in society we could address . . . a lever for us to be able to talk about the health-care system. I actually did think that AIDS was going to change health care, access mostly."

In 1989, Robert got a paid job managing the PWA Health Group, a buyers club where members could pool resources to obtain hard-to-get treatments. Now he had an AIDS day job where he saw firsthand the racial disparity in access. The PWA Health Group imported or otherwise got a hold of drugs that were not readily available, and therefore people had to pay out of pocket because none of it was covered by insurance. Two of the drugs that they went to great lengths to get were dextran sulfate, imported from Japan, and a lipids compound called AL-721, which was made by natural foods people in California for folks to spread on their toast in the morning to build immunity. Unfortunately, none of these drugs actually worked. But the movement put a lot of effort into getting access to them because there was nothing else.

Even though many of those efforts may seem futile in retrospect, they strengthened the collective understanding that access to new treatments was a right, and that government obstructions were not to be obeyed. In this way, action cohered principles. This reach for patient control of decision-making around experimental treatments permeated the culture of AIDS resistance.

From this job, Robert went on to become an outreach worker for the Minority Task Force on AIDS, finally working directly for people of color with AIDS and bringing all his skills back to the POC community. Unlike ACT UP, "I saw that they were prevention oriented," mostly emphasizing condom distribution and not discussing treatment. The POC organizations provided services, like helping people with AIDS get housing, and emphasized prevention. Throughout the history of AIDS activism, there has been a dichotomy between prevention and treatment. Prevention is an effort focused on HIV-negative people, while treatment is the agenda of HIV-positive people. Robert experienced this lack of focus on treatment within the Minority Task Force on AIDS as particularly a POC political empowerment issue. "I was seeing that in communities of color, people were intimidated by science and there wasn't much treatment education." Robert remembered Moisés Agosto-Rosario as another Puerto Rican from ACT UP who was also now employed at the Minority Task Force on AIDS. Moisés, he noted, "was one of the first people to do treatment education" for people of color. "ACT UP was about treatment. 'Drugs into bodies.' I don't remember a lot about prevention."

Clearly the issue of expanding clinical trials to include people of color and women continued to be of utmost importance to obtaining cutting-edge treatment for marginalized people, as well as to having studies for future medications modeled on POC and female bodies. And these principles were brought by Robert and Moisés from ACT UP to the Minority Task Force on AIDS. Looking historically, Moisés and Robert moving from ACT UP to the Minority Task Force on AIDS is one of the first times that openly gay people of color moved into leadership of general POC organizations, bringing overtly queer activist politics with them to the table. Of course, gay people like Bayard Rustin had been at the forefront of the Black civil rights movement of the 1960s, but not with overtly queer activist political orientation. And while Rustin was not closeted, he wasn't out, in a modern sense, to the membership of his movement. It wasn't yet possible. In fact, Rustin's sexuality ultimately marginalized him politically from Black civil rights. Kevin Mumford's 2016 book, *Not Straight, Not White: Black Gay Men from the March on Washington to the AIDS Crisis* (UNC Press), discusses a number of Black gay religious leaders whose significant work inside their churches to advance Black queer people was cut short by AIDS. But this specific shift of openly gay men bringing openly queer politics to the leadership of POC organizations was made possible by the emergency of the AIDS crisis. Moisés and Robert contributed a trajectory seen in later broad coalition movements, like Black Lives Matter, which were formed with openly queer and trans Black people at the helm. Using overtly radical queer POC frameworks to articulate a freedom vision eventually became a frame for movements for many Black and oppressed people.

In addition to their time together at ACT UP and at the Minority Task Force on AIDS, Moisés invited Robert to be part of a new invention, the Community Constituency Group (CCG). The CCG was a collection of people who were not scientists, but who had AIDS or who represented grassroots organizations of people with AIDS, together dialoguing directly with government and big pharma.

"We were there as community members to share our wisdom . . . how trials were designed and run." The CCG was actually part of the government. It fed into the AIDS Clinical Trials Group (ACTG), which consisted of meetings of researchers doing trials on AIDS drugs. This was the chance for people with AIDS and community leaders to be able to sit down with scientists and explain to them what people actually needed. It was run by the National Institute of Allergy and Infectious Diseases (NIAID), which in turn was part of the National Institutes of Health. It was an instance of direct access to the governmental bodies that were making decisions about what would happen to people with AIDS, medically. It was headed by Anthony Fauci. And it was all paid for by U.S. government money.

For Robert, the CCG was there to deal with "the antiseptic world of research." He felt it was as if the scientists "were not used to interacting with other human beings." The CCG had to explain to researchers that if they were recruiting people to trials from low-income communities, they needed to have people from those communities involved in explaining the purpose and options of the organizations and its policies. The CCG told researchers that they needed Spanish-speaking people working in all services for Latinos. The community needed to be a part of the whole research process.

"I like to organize and get stuff running for people around me," Robert noted. So, true to form, he started organizing trainings for people from the community newly part of the CCG.

Being a person of color in ACT UP was a highly pressured experience, even for individuals fully integrated into the organization's political and social life. There was the constant demand for people of color with AIDS to be seen and to have their experiences placed at the forefront of ACT UP's agenda, yet there was simultaneous need for individuals to protect themselves from the exhaustion of tokenism, unless it served a large purpose. Robert experienced this intense push and pull within both the artistic and the treatment arms of ACT UP, all within the hyperdramatic and surreal environment of mass death of the young.

For example, while Robert was working at the Minority Task Force on AIDS, his friend Debra Levine from ACT UP was working at the public arts organization Creative Time and was involved with commissioning an AIDS information piece that Robert became involved with at El Museo del Barrio. In this way, he had officially entered the world of AIDS art creators, working in organized, and sometimes funded, capacities. Later, at a conference on art and AIDS in Ohio, Robert was listening to speakers from the ACT UP art collective, Gran Fury. Robert raised his hand and said to ACT UPer and filmmaker Tom Kalin, "Of course you have no people of color in Gran Fury." Then came the phone call. So he joined Gran Fury and worked with them for three to four years. Robert was a model in one of Gran Fury's best-known art projects, a poster designed for the sides of public buses commissioned by the Public Art Fund. Three couples—Julie Tolentino and Lola Flash, Mark Simpson and Jose Fidelino, and Heidi Dorow and Robert—are all pictured kissing, under the slogan KISSING DOESN'T KILL: GREED AND INDIFFERENCE DO.

Kissing Doesn't Kill
(Courtesy of Gran Fury)

The posters did not end up in Manhattan, but they were placed on buses in the Bronx, where one of Robert's cousins saw him. "Robert, was that you, kissing a girl?" She thought it was an ad for the clothing label Benetton.

In an interesting parallel, a few months after ACT UP split in 1992, Robert was at a conference in Amsterdam listening to David Barr, formerly of ACT UP, then of TAG, speak. Robert raised his hand and said, "There are no people of color in TAG." A few days later, he got a phone call from Mark Harrington, one of ACT UP's most influential leaders, as well as a leader of the split, asking him to join TAG, which was invitation-only at that time. Robert went to his first meeting at someone's Fifth Avenue apartment. "It was unfriendly. No one felt comfortable there." Robert found it off-putting socially, and the room was filled with "people with a level of knowledge that I don't have." So Robert left. "I was not getting anything out of it." In and outside of ACT UP, unless he was working for an explicitly POC organization, racial exclusion and inclusion had to be constantly negotiated.

Of course, being an individual with such a high level of contact to information and resources, Robert also found it hard to assimilate all the scientific information, and he never became a "heavy-duty treatment activist" who had "access to every drug." Even after he had been taking daily HIV treatment medications for years, Robert felt confident that he could rely on his ACT UP connections for information. "If I have a question about treatment stuff, I can call Moisés. He still sits on all those committees. I know Mark [Harrington]. I know Peter Staley. I know treatment people. I can get on the phone and talk to them." These relationships, fostered in ACT UP, are still the lifeline to health.

"The activism that we did, the stuff that we did at the FDA, definitely resulted in the fact that now there are all of these drugs that are out there that people can access. Unfortunately, we didn't do anything about cost."

MOISÉS AGOSTO-ROSARIO

Compared with Robert Vázquez-Pacheco, Moisés Agosto-Rosario had a very different experience of being Puerto Rican in ACT UP, starting with the fact that he grew up on the island. When Moisés was in college in Puerto Rico, he had a boyfriend, but he wasn't afraid of AIDS, which he thought of as "the gringo thing." He simply resolved to never have sex with Americans. Then he started dating a new guy, also local, but Moisés wondered why his boyfriend had the most complete set of vitamins he had ever seen. Eventually, even though he had only ever had sex with two people, he decided to get tested for HIV, "to get it out of the way." This was 1986, at the only testing site in Puerto Rico. To his shock, he tested positive, and the clinic workers advised him to take a lot of vitamins.

AIDS was a "non-conversation" among gay men in Puerto Rico and certainly undiscussable with his family. "I remember thinking, *I can't tell anyone. What am I going to do?*" Since he came from a working-class family with no health insurance, he decided to read everything he could find and learn whatever he could on his own. He found a book in Old San Juan called *Living With AIDS: Reaching Out* by Tom O'Connor, published in 1987. "It became my bible." The book recommended reducing toxins, so Moisés changed his diet and gave up red meat. But after a year with no medical care, he started to plummet into depression. A gay professor (who later died of AIDS) took him in as a therapy patient for free, and the two of them started the first AIDS support group in Puerto Rico.

"I started to hear about this radical group in New York," and soon he came to the city to go to graduate school in literature at Stony Brook. Moisés quickly found his niche in New York City. He got his health care at the Community Health Project (CHP), which was situated inside the Gay Center on West Thirteenth Street. He had eight hundred T cells—lymphocytes used in the creation of immunity—which are the main measure of how well or poorly a person with AIDS is doing. Eight hundred was low, but by premedication AIDS standards, it was pretty good, considered stable. He got a job as a literacy teacher in the Bronx, in Soundview, helping Latinas on welfare learn how to read and write in Spanish so that they could qualify for English as a Second Language courses. Thus began his exposure to Puerto Rican life in New York City. As a light-skinned, blue-eyed Puerto Rican, Moisés grew up thinking more about class than skin color. "I came to this country, already with an identity formed . . . Our issues had mostly to do with class . . . You could be a Black person with money and we would call you 'blanquito,' 'little white person.' I had to learn race politics."

One day in 1989, he ran into a friend who said he should check out ACT UP because "they needed someone to translate." Since he was already familiar with the Gay Center for his health care, that was not an obstacle.

"When I walked into the room at the Center it was like a religious experience. Coming from not having people to talk to, to a bunch of fired-up people really wanting to make a difference, fighting for their lives literally. I could relate to them."

His first task was to translate leaflets and signs for the Stop the Church demonstration at St. Patrick's Cathedral. So, from his beginning in 1989, Moisés entered ACT UP in an intentional way, to serve Latinos and to raise their issues. When he got to Stony Brook, his first letter from the administration had opened with "Dear *Minority* Student," but when he arrived at ACT UP, there already was a *Majority* Action Committee. Moisés worked in the Spanish Translation Committee with ACT UPers César Carrasco, Cándido Negrón, Brad Taylor, and Juan Mendez. And he worked with the Majority Action Committee. But he felt a need for something more political and Latino than just translation, so people came together to form the Latino Caucus. There also was the Immigration Working Group, which included Carrasco, Negrón, and Allan Clear. ACT UP ultimately had four committees expressly involving and serving Latinos.

Moisés's foundational experience in ACT UP was with other Latinos. In a sense he helped build a complex and active Latino subculture in ACT UP that made it possible for Latino AIDS activists to work in majority Latino communities. And so the differences between the Latino members' backgrounds, which may have been invisible to whites, Blacks, and Asians in ACT UP, were enormously significant to Moisés. "Within ACT UP there were no Puerto Ricans from PR. Some people were Latin Americans, Latinos from the states. For Puerto Ricans, we are always between. We're not Latin Americans, but we're not from the states." The range of Latino activists in ACT UP was broad. There was Gonzalo Aburto, a Mexican student activist; Andy Vélez, a Bronx-born Nuyorican; César Carrasco, an interior designer from Argentina; Patricia Navarro, the Chicano mother of PWA Ray Navarro; Marina Alvarez; and a number of women who had come from Bedford Hills prison, among others. The range of Latinos in ACT UP crossed the lines of class, national origin, race, gender, and HIV status. When I asked Moisés to name the members of the Latino Caucus, he only mentioned men. But when I prompted him by raising the question of women, he was enthusiastically forthcoming. He felt that "the dialogue between gay men and the straight women was very good. Their issues of course were related to having kids and feeling that they had been left aside."

The Latino Caucus at Storm the NIH on May 21, 1990
(Photograph by Dona Ann McAdams)

ACT UP PUERTO RICO

As Latinos in ACT UP spent more time together, and talked more about Puerto Rico, AIDS started to become more widespread on the island. The activists learned that Louis Sullivan, President George H. W. Bush's secretary of Health and Human Services, was planning to visit. The National Commission on AIDS, founded in 1989 by an act of

Congress, was getting ready to go as well. By 1990, the Latino Caucus decided that they, too, should go to Puerto Rico and start an ACT UP chapter to confront government inaction. The proposal was endorsed by the floor at the general Monday-night meeting, and ACT UP paid to send its members to run the campaign.

This action is a good example of ACT UP's flexible leadership style. The Latino Caucus knew that there were "touchy issues" involved in their mission to Puerto Rico. Having experienced American imposition all of their lives, whether living in PR, Latin America, or New York City, the members of the Latino Caucus were now themselves potentially imposing on people doing grassroots work on the island. They decided, in advance, that while they were formally attempting to create ACT UP Puerto Rico, they actually wanted to get some kind of direct action going, and they were not wedded to leading or controlling whatever formation was produced by their efforts. It wasn't about spreading the ACT UP brand; it was about supporting people anywhere in the world with AIDS to do direct action. So Moisés—along with ACT UPers José Santini, Carlos Cordero, Gilberto Martínez, Cándido Negrón, Juan Mendez, César Carrasco, Carmen Hernández, and others—set off.

Upon arrival, their first action was a typical ACT UP media-savvy move. They met with the director of the Associated Press on the island and told him their intentions: their aim was to meet with the government to tell them their plan for addressing AIDS. In this way, the Spanish Translation Committee and the Latino Caucus communicated "through" the media to the government. And, as in all ACT UP actions, they took on the responsibility to propose the solution, rather than asking an ignorant but powerful body to paternalistically solve the problems. Through a friend, they rented a condominium cheaply, and everyone from ACT UP crowded into it. They did outreach by going to the gay bar armed with Spanish-language SILENCIO=MUERTE stickers.

Moisés and Carlos would "go to the bar in our ACT UP outfits, little short jeans and boots, go to people with a smile, put a sticker on their chests. 'What's this?' 'Ohhh, you want to know? Come to a meeting!'

"Of course, at that point people were getting sick and dying." So the bar owner opened the place for political gatherings. "I remember in two weeks we had a meeting of like two hundred people," which was large for Puerto Rico. "And it was a really rough conversation to negotiate if they really needed an ACT UP chapter, or [if] they just needed to start the fire and take it from there, and we leave. Because we were not going to stay, which was my main concern. You don't go there and say, *You need to have an ACT UP.* Because we were not there." They had a series of demonstrations, including a public protest in front of the hotel where Louis Sullivan was having a meeting with the Department of Health. "We had like ten, twenty people, but we got media coverage. Then we had another demonstration at the commission meeting."

Most of the cases in Puerto Rico at the time had to do with intravenous drug use. Within the gay community, there was still a wall of stigma around needles. Richard Elovich, one of ACT UP's main advocates for AIDS activism related to intravenous drug use, came down to help. He went to an area called La Perla to run a needle exchange, where users could turn in dirty needles and get free clean ones in return. Richard described the scene to Moisés as "devastating." While most gay men in ACT UP were focused specifically on the sexual transmission of AIDS, current and former drug users were speaking up as well. The HIV-positive Latinas in the group kept the drug issue on the table with the gay men. "We began to get more people and more people."

By the summer of 1990, activists finally realized their goal of an AIDS activist march in Old San Juan, chanting, "*El gobierno tiene sangre en sus manos* (the government has blood on its hands) . . . So it was pretty powerful, because it was the first time there was a very activist-like direct action taken there." People with AIDS and their supporters in San Juan ended up starting an ACT UP chapter. Moisés knew for sure that it was not going to continue forever as ACT UP. In fact, they met for a couple of years, but then other groups started "with their flavor, with their needs." Even a chapter of Parents and Friends of Lesbians and Gays (PFLAG) started. But Moisés was satisfied. "For me, it was not about having a successful ACT UP chapter. It was just to set the fire up."

WHO IS ACT UP?

When the Latino Caucus returned in triumph to New York at the end of 1990, Moisés felt that they'd become "pretty recognized on the floor." Their next arena of ACT UP action became focused on making Latino leaders in New York City accountable to people with AIDS. In what Moisés described as a difference in "mentalities and ideologies," conflicts arose over the question of targeting the Hispanic AIDS Forum in February of 1991. This was the first community-based organization that provided AIDS services and prevention education to the "Hispanic" community in New York City. Funded by a combination of city and private funds, the Forum was directed by Miguelena Maldonada De Leon. Some activists felt that the Hispanic AIDS Forum was not addressing the needs of IV drug users, not getting involved in needle exchange, and not doing enough prevention work generally. Moisés disagreed with this focus.

"I knew that, when you had to look at the bigger picture, it was pretty dangerous in the movement to [target] a community-based grassroots group that was trying to put services together to service the community . . . In my mind it was like, *No, I cannot make them a target when they have to struggle to fight for their own funding.*"

This raised a larger question for the organization—whether ACT UP should target another community-based AIDS group or focus instead on the big power: government and pharmaceutical companies. This debate is a typical example of how theory emerged out of action in ACT UP. A concrete proposal for action would be on the table, and then the larger philosophical and strategic questions it revealed would be addressed. The events around this question were very upsetting to Moisés. In our interview, as he started talking about his frustrations with "ACT UP," I thought he was going to tell me about white racism in ACT UP, and in fact, this was information that I was looking for and wanted to hear in order to document the range of experiences of people of color in the organization. But in this case, he was actually talking about his frustrations with other Latinos, whom he was centering when he used the term *ACT UP*. Like most ACT UPers, Moisés functioned in a small but effective subset of the larger organization. And, importantly, this was a consequence of the larger unstated but de facto structure that made ACT UP effective, which can serve as an example for our organizing today. Members did their parallel but resonant activist work in whatever realms and ways that made most sense to them, with the people with whom they shared the most "affinity" or agreement.

Like Moisés, most ACT UPers saw the organization principally defined by the people with whom they worked most intimately and the actions that they focused on together. The conflicts they had, the successes and failures they experienced, were often attached to the concept of ACT UP as a collective simultaneity of very different actions, all cohered by two elements: (1) direct action (as opposed to social service provision) and (2) "to end the AIDS crisis."

Most of the Latino Caucus wanted to take on the more mainstream Hispanic AIDS Forum, and some people did an action confronting them, including ACT UPers Alfredo González, José Santini, and Marina Alvarez. Only Moisés and Luis Santiago were uncomfortable. At that point, the Monday-night meetings had moved from the Gay Center to Cooper Union on Astor Place, because they had gotten too large. The Latino Caucus brought a motion to the floor to officially target the Hispanic AIDS Forum. "Most of the caucus members went to the floor at the front" of the room to show support for the motion. But Moisés "decided to stay in the audience," with Luis. When the proposal was presented for discussion, Moisés spoke out against it from his seat. He argued that if ACT UP wanted to work with other communities, it would not be productive to oppose them organizationally, and as a consequence of his argument, the proposal for a demonstration against the Hispanic AIDS Forum was killed.

"It cost me a lot of friends . . . But it also gave me an understanding of making a differentiation between what was ACT UP, what was activism and what was a movement." So, even though the greater ACT UP sided with him and defeated the proposal, he thought of his opponents in the Latino Caucus as ACT UP.

However, when our conversation moved on to treatment activism, an entirely different group of people took on the emblematic meaning of "ACT UP" for Moisés. Once he was alienated from the Latino Caucus, "ACT UP" became the Treatment and Data Committee. "If [not] for ACT UP, we wouldn't have people from the community, and patients, participating in the science protocols," he said.

By the end of the 1980s Moisés's T-cell count dropped to five hundred, and he started taking AZT, which had just become available. AZT, a failed cancer drug made by Burroughs Wellcome Pharmaceuticals and recycled as a therapy for AIDS, was being widely advertised as the only significant treatment focused on the general condition of being HIV-positive, being diagnosed with AIDS-related complex (ARC—a concept that has disappeared from the lexicon, but indicated an "almost AIDS" condition). At that point all other approved medications were targeted to particular opportunistic infections. Because of his own failing health and the fact that he was starting medication, Moisés's interests expanded from a Latino-specific focus to the broader question of treatments. But most treatment activists in ACT UP were white. Forced by personal necessity, Moisés stepped out of his comfort zone and for the first time walked into a white committee. "I was curious about the Treatment and Data Committee. I would always go and sit in the back. My English, it was a process of adjusting to a whole new language as well."

As the movement progressed and he got more treatment-oriented, Moisés was increasingly invited into the nascent formulations of the AIDS bureaucracy, governmental committees, and social service agencies. He was invited by the National Latino Lesbian and Gay Organization to get involved in clinical trials, because it was the first time the National Institute of Allergy and Infectious Diseases funded Black and Latino groups at a national level to look for leaders in local communities who could be trained to participate in clinical trial design. Moisés was brought to Washington and trained. He met important government actors like Anthony Fauci, NIAID's director. Then he was put on a committee of people with AIDS inside the ACTG. His first assignment was to look at the question of pharmacology. So this literature student did what he had done when he first tested positive: as part of the foundational tradition of ACT UP's autodidacticism, he started studying. Moisés bought a book, *Pharmacology Made Easy*.

In ACT UP, though treatment activists often did educationals, they could be very technical and hard to understand. While the use of advanced language may have given them authority, at the same time, no one was ever dissuaded from the course of treatment that they personally chose. After all, nothing really worked, so people had to make the hard decisions for themselves. "The whole spirit of nonjudgmental, open-minded mentality, I think, gave me kind of a strong sense of respect for people's choices, and not to judge what they were doing . . . You would see someone doing just alternatives and die, and someone doing just clinical trials, and die . . . For me, information saved my life. So that is why I thought my duty was to make sure others would get it."

After a number of false starts, Moisés finally felt able to fully participate in Treatment and Data. As he got more involved, week after week he was able to observe that T&D members were overwhelmingly healthy in comparison to other groups of people with AIDS in ACT UP. At that time, most people with AIDS were taking AZT, but as he spent more time with T&D, Moisés came to realize that some people in T&D were not taking AZT. Instead, they "were in clinical trials for ddI, 3TC when it just started. There were some studies on d4T. It was all the beginning of a non-nucleocide." And Moisés realized that the reason was because "they had access to the information . . . They had access to Fauci. They had access to all these people. And I started to [think], *I want that.*" He wanted everyone else to have that access, too, of course. But he had to get closer to the people in T&D with access to the cutting-edge elite treatments of the future if he wanted to stay alive.

"Being here in New York, and having coworkers . . . and having my dear friends in ACT UP getting sick and dying, it really affected me in the way I looked at the future. I remember that it got even to a point of non-comprehension—I had kind of a breakdown in 1991, when my best, best friend died in Puerto Rico. It was a period of time in which every week, every week, there was a coworker that died, there was a friend that died, there was a volunteer that died, there was another friend that was in the hospital, there was another friend that needed this, there was another friend that needed that. There was this sense of, like, we had no future. I couldn't look that further to the future, because everything was just falling apart around me. But at the same time—I just kept going, kept going, kept going, kept going, kept going, kept going. And I saw it in other friends. I saw it in myself. Just keep working, working, working, working, working, work, work, work, work to a point where you get sick and then you go."

It was this constant awareness that his life depended on his positioning that enabled Moisés to continue to seek and find access. At one point his pharmacology committee was frustrated because the protease inhibitors, which would eventually become the standard of care, were just beginning to be studied, and there was not enough data to determine safety. Moisés was charged with writing a letter to Fauci expressing these concerns.

"I would go and ask the guys from T&D once in a while, but I would try to learn, myself, as much as I could. That was a time where I realized I knew more than I thought. I always was with this kind of insecurity that I didn't know enough. It's like that feeling, I always say, when you're a person of color here. It's like you have to prove yourself twice and three times. In the treatment and research area, you have to prove yourself like five times." To the scientists or to T&D? "Both . . . First, you come with a thick accent. People think that if you have an accent, you're stupid. I got that a lot of times."

Whereas initially Moisés situated himself with Latinos out of comfort and familiarity, the more sophisticated he became to the role of access in America, the more he moved back toward working with grassroots POC communities. "That was where I wanted to go—communities where this was an item added to the list, communities that already were disenfranchised . . . Access to care was not that much of an issue for the majority of the members who had access to Fauci, who had access to trials. They could go into the trial because they had a good doctor, while all these people that I felt more identified with didn't."

Now, for Moisés Agosto-Rosario, the white men with access whose work had helped other community leaders open up government committees to people of color had become his new definition of *ACT UP*. What about most of the other hundreds of people in ACT UP—did he think they had the same access?

"I don't know about everybody in ACT UP. I can't say that they did. What I knew was that the people that I knew that were working on care, and treatment, and research had that access . . . I was disappointed with some of the answers I would get from people, like *We can't fix everybody's life* . . . A majority of the people that I looked up to because I thought the work they did was critical were not really that much into doing work related to access to care and treatment in disenfranchised communities . . . I felt that I was hitting my head against the wall."

Perhaps I was just doing my job as an AIDS historian, perhaps I somehow wanted Moisés to feel better, perhaps I was again advocating for him to see and recognize the women in ACT UP. So, at this point in the conversation, I brought up all the enormous work that the Women's Caucus, and women with HIV, did in ACT UP. I reminded him that they ran a successful four-year campaign to allow women and poor people access to benefits and experimental drugs and studies, the very thing he was saying ACT UP didn't do. And he did acknowledge that. I wanted him to recognize *my* identification arena as just as authentically ACT UP as any other.

"It was a significant campaign," he acknowledged, "and it was driven by women in ACT UP. You see, if it weren't for the women that got involved and then pushed their issues through—because you remember, you had to push your issue through. It was not *You come and everybody understands.* There were a lot of heated discussions about women issues, about people of color issues. But again, it had to be driven by those people affected. If it were left to the hands of those that had the power within the organization . . . Do you understand what I mean?"

As someone coming from the feminist and lesbian movements, I totally understood. Democracy requires participation, even if the people who are already demeaned or excluded have to do most of the work to get the conversation elevated. The burden is on those of us who are not heard, and that is on top of the *consequences* of not being heard. It sucks, and you have to be hard-core to fight it, but if women and people of color and other disenfranchised people don't fight for it, it will not happen. Women have to fight and insist and strategize and organize for our issues. It has always been that way, and in America, it has always been that way for people of color, too. This is what politics is, and this is what coalition politics in American social movements has always been: marginalized people have to be smart and organized and tough. Yet Moisés's analysis was rooted partly in the fact that, because he had come from Puerto Rico, he had not spent his life justifying being Puerto Rican to white people. This reaction was imposed on him as an adult when he moved to New York. He wasn't used to it, and he resented the hell out of it. He also had his own theories.

"The fact that I was born and raised in Puerto Rico gave me the sense of entitlement, and a sense of *What do you mean I cannot ask for something?* When, for what I have experienced with my family in New York, or disenfranchised communities, this internal programming that haunts you forever, in which this is your destiny. You are growing up with being a minority, with a kind of fatalistic kind of attitude."

So he was appropriately outraged and empowered in his perspective at the way women and people of color had to agitate internally. And yet that is what was required to move forward. The Latino Caucus had done this successfully inside ACT UP in order to support people with AIDS in Puerto Rico, and women and our supporters did this successfully within ACT UP as well. And yes, there is a cost, as Moisés explained so clearly—an extra burden, or a series of extra burdens, that the white men with good doctors who did great work simply did not face, even though they were fighting against the clock to save their own lives. And who we were as a group, in this complex, intense relationship, was a manifestation of feeling, but even more, of power.

"The same way I found myself struggling, I saw others—like women's groups—struggling for their issues. That doesn't mean wonderful things didn't get accomplished—which they did—but it was because of the force of those internal groups in the organization. Which, if you think about it, it was beautiful to see. It is what democracy should probably be—it was beautiful to see that people would bring their issues [to the table]. Some people would not understand them. And it was there, it was there, it was there until it would somehow click, and we got something accomplished. But it wasn't a flow of total openness to all the issues that needed to be addressed."

When Moisés left ACT UP, he brought all of his insights and skills with him to organizations that more directly served Latinos in the fifty states and Puerto Rico. He worked with the Latino Commission on AIDS, the Latino Treatment Issues Group, and the National Latino Lesbian and Gay Association. Then he took a job in Washington with the National Minority AIDS Council (NMAC).

"What ACT UP gave me is invaluable. I learned, and I learned, and I learned not to be afraid. I learned to speak out. I learned to work in teams, to work with other people, to connect with that human thing. AIDS made us be more human . . . It just connected me to the human side, and to see and understand how AIDS first was a personal issue. First it was about me, then it wasn't just about me. It was other guys, too, and other issues with other problems. Then it was about other people in other communities. It's kind of like you go [forward], and it's still about you, but the picture keeps getting bigger, and bigger, and bigger.

"The beautiful thing about ACT UP, that I miss so much now, was the sense of camaraderie, not just on the political side, but also in a community/personal side. We knew how to have fun with what we did, because our hearts were there three hundred percent. But also, there was no judgment to be[ing] a naughty boy, or to hav[ing] fun and go[ing] out dancing . . . So in terms of social life, it gave me a very strong social structure in New York. If it wouldn't be for ACT UP, it would have taken me a long time to find a family of friends in New York. ACT UP gave me that, not in a shallow way. It was a very here, in your face, real-life, and these are your friends, and these are your friends that are dying, these are your friends that are getting sick with you. And fun. It was fun. We would go out and do a demonstration, and then we would go out and party. Any kind of thing you could think of would happen. There was no judgment."

2

The First Treatment Activists

The Treatment and Data group that surprised Moisés Agosto-Rosario in 1990–91 with their advanced reconceptualizations of research, growing dialogue with pharmaceutical companies, and special access to cutting-edge drugs was actually that committee's second iteration. When ACT UP first began in 1987, Treatment and Data was inaugurated with a different orientation. The first T&D Committee had to start from scratch, figuring out the government bureaucracy, setting emergency priorities, and inserting ACT UP into the equation for federal agencies. Many of the people in the first T&D Committee were HIV-negative. There were no treatments, after all, so in the chaos, lack of information, and panic of the first years, there was less focus by nonscientists on the systematic development of new medications.

ACT UPers had an intense work ethic, and their activism, across the organization, was intellectually, emotionally, and physically labor-intensive. These men and women had to do the work of rethinking solutions and kick-starting a direct-action course while also forcing the government and pharmaceutical companies into new approaches and policies. Often the greatest obstacle to change is that people do not conceptualize beyond their understanding of their task. Being brave enough to learn enough to be able to create new paradigms was the first step toward real change in treatment development and availability for people with AIDS.

T&D's vision:

1. Get existing experimental drugs released quickly.
2. Make them available through fairly enrolled drug trials.

3. Let people with AIDS know where the trials were and how to get in them.
4. Insist that new drugs had to be developed.

Gay liberation veterans Marty Robinson, Herb Spiers, and Vito Russo; straight cancer scientist Iris Long; gay playwright Jim Eigo; and two dedicated young activists, David Kirschenbaum and Margaret McCarthy, were among the initial fundamental players in T&D. Later, a second wave of treatment activists—many of whom were HIV-positive—would evolve this preliminary group's work to focus on new drug development and to change the way research was conceptualized. But first, ACT UP had to simultaneously learn the basics of the American health-care bureaucracy and figure out how to work from the ground up to make the government understand that from this moment on, it would have to listen to people with AIDS.

INVENTING TREATMENT ACTIVISM

IRIS LONG

Iris Doerr Long was born in New York City in 1934. She took a chemistry course at Washington Irving High School, and was later inspired to get a master's in chemistry at Hunter College in the Bronx when she was thirty. It was the first year that the previously all-female school admitted men, so it was still a supportive environment. Her first job was at Columbia-Presbyterian Hospital. Then, as an organic chemist at Sloan Kettering, she worked on a class of cancer drugs called nucleosides. "It all had to do—in 1953—with the discovery of DNA and the role of DNA—the helix, and everything else . . . Not quite 10 years later, they were making these drugs for cancer—nucleosides—[which were] the building blocks of the DNA.

"We were fooling around with . . . all types of derivatives. As a chemist, you try everything. And then they were tested, some of them . . . And . . . our group had association with Burroughs Wellcome," the pharmaceutical giant. Some of these nucleosides were somewhat successful with cancer. A midwestern researcher, working in the same paradigm, came up with a new cancer drug called AZT, but it did not have enough success to make it to the stage of being tested in humans. When AIDS hit, twenty years later, pharma and science first went to old drugs that had already been developed to see if any of them could be recycled to work for AIDS. The National Cancer Institute (NCI), under the direction of Dr. Samuel Broder, became interested in AZT. An argument erupted with Burroughs Wellcome. As a failed cancer drug, AZT wasn't important to the company, but when it started to be considered for HIV, Burroughs Wellcome asserted that AZT was not in the public domain, and as a result, they were able to get a patent. This deliberate privatization was an act that would have immense negative consequences for people with AIDS and would consume activists' energy for a decade.

Iris, in the meantime, had gone on to earn a PhD, furthering her work in nucleosides. After a few more jobs, she was home with her husband in Astoria, Queens, and looking for something else to do. She had kept up with scientific journals, and when she saw that AZT was being considered for HIV, she became interested. "Of course, that attracted me, because I was a nucleoside chemist." First she looked into the AIDS Medical Foundation, later known as the American Foundation for AIDS Research (amfAR), founded by Dr. Mathilde Krim, also a cancer doctor who had worked at Sloan Kettering. Earlier in her career as a researcher, she had specialized in interferon, a cancer drug that also was applied to HIV.

Iris knew it wasn't just an antiviral that was needed—they needed to treat the many opportunistic infections. *AIDS* is, in a sense, a catchall term, like *cancer*. It manifests differently in each person, and there are multiple strains. Once someone's immune system was compromised, they would get different infections, ranging from brain diseases to pneumonia, skin cancer, blindness, wasting, and more. It was the infections that debilitated and killed the person, not AIDS. Until the virus itself could be controlled, the second strategy was to try to control the infections as they appeared.

Iris volunteered with Community Research Initiative (CRI), operated by Dr. Joseph Sonnabend, who had worked with Mathilde Krim on interferon at amfAR. PWA activist Michael Callen, ACT UPer Susan Brown, and a number of others made up the core at CRI. Frustrated with the lack of action by the government and private pharmaceutical companies, CRI was conducting its own community-based, independent research on potential drugs. At the time Iris joined them, they were working on AL-721, the egg lipid compound that men were spreading on their toast in hopes it would improve immunity. CRI seemed "more in front," and Iris knew that hospitals did not take scientists as volunteers, while the AIDS community needed and welcomed them. She had never been involved in a grassroots community effort before; she had never been politically active. She knew no people with AIDS. She had no gay friends.

JIM EIGO

Jim was born in Paterson, New Jersey, and grew up in the Bronx and, later, the Philadelphia suburbs. His father was a postal worker, and his mother was a secretary and worked in a drugstore. In his all-boys Catholic prep school, Jim was both a football player and a theater kid, an unusual combination. He got a partial playwriting scholarship to California Institute of the Arts.

Jim came out in his late twenties and early thirties in the late 1970s—"Not only just came out, but that was the first time I had sex with another guy, too. Although I'd known for years." He'd heard rumors about a gay cancer, rumors about clusters of people who were ill in New York and Los Angeles and San Francisco.

For Jim, as for anyone who lived through that time, the information about AIDS came in fits and starts; it was contradictory, and it was frightening, "particularly for those of us who lived in the East Village . . . At that time we were an art center, but we were also a drug center. And the combination of lots of gay men and lots of people who used injection drugs in the same neighborhood meant that . . . all throughout the eighties, lots of people on your block and among your friends were getting sick and dying."

Jim was never part of the disco and drug scene. He had nothing against drugs, and supports decriminalization, but it was not a scene he traveled in. A lot of the places Jim went to be gay instead were more anonymous sexual spaces, like the series of gay porn movie houses on Third Avenue. It was a different feeling, he thought, from gay discos, where there was a crowd of people who knew one another, saw one another every weekend or maybe every night, "and suddenly knew people among them who were getting sick and dying."

In the early eighties, Jim started to volunteer for the Gay Men's Health Crisis (GMHC) and worked in their financial advocacy unit, which at the time—because the caseload was a lot lower—could actually assign one-on-one financial advocates to patients. The goal was to get people onto disability, or Social Security, or—for those few people who qualified—Medicaid and Medicare. "It was just very difficult, at the time. The city was trying to avoid AIDS like a plague. And of course we were, unfortunately, saddled with the Reagan administration that didn't even want to breathe the word *AIDS*. So there was very little to try and get the clients." After about a year or a year and a half of volunteer work, it wasn't that Jim was dissatisfied with what GMHC was doing— and certainly not what client services, the area he was working in, was doing—but it became incredibly clear that there was a political dimension to the problem. "It sounds naïve, in retrospect, but those first few years, people were so busy digesting what was happening to them that politics only came up after five or six years of being knee-deep in a crisis." The first emergency response now was to try to take care of the people who were sick, and then to try to "make sense of it for oneself, and change one's own behavior to the degree you thought you had to." So the first several years of the emergency were very confused. ACT UP really was the first political organization to emerge in the AIDS crisis, and that was only in 1987, so at least six years after GRID and four or five after we'd first had the word *AIDS*. "But, I guess I wasn't alone in only coming to the realization that there was a huge, political dimension to this problem, because it was only then that ACT UP came into being." Most of the people who went to the Monday-night meeting had come to a point where grief was not enough. They were angry, and in that anger they were quite prepared to shut down the whole city, if need be.

"It just really started with a handful of people who sat down at Wall Street. But ACT UP snowballed awfully quickly, and word got around that on Monday [nights], ACT UP gave a home to people who were sick, people who were not yet sick, and to their friends and people who cared for them. It was not long before a hundred to two hundred people were meeting in that room every Monday night. Pretty soon, it would be four hundred and even more . . . and people become courageous awfully quickly. I certainly am not alone in saying—everyone who was active in ACT UP wound up drawing on resources they had inside them, that they never dreamed they had . . . But, it only could have come out of them because they were locking arms with a hundred other people, at that point. And, I've always believed in community and ACT UP, during those two or three years of its height, is the most splendid enactment of the idea of community I've ever been a part of."

Jim got to ACT UP by chance. In November of 1987, when the group was nine months old, Jim went to the Center to attend a Lambda Legal forum on the Supreme Court's 1986 *Bowers v. Hardwick* decision, which reinforced the criminalization of gay sex. The event was scheduled for the second floor, but Jim thought it was the first floor. The choice to meet in the Gay Center was crucial to building ACT UP. People already were used to going there and had positive associations with the place. It is a good lesson for those organizing today to choose meeting spaces that already have positive roles in the lives of the community. Jim's first meeting proved to be essential.

"I was very lucky that first week, in that Iris Long took the microphone."

IRIS LONG

It was with a group of people from CRI that Iris first got to the Gay Center on Thirteenth Street for one of ACT UP's Monday-night meetings. "Well, there was a lot of people there. It was standing room only, at that point. I liked what was going on, and what was happening. People were looking for the drugs, and it was very interesting." At the meeting Iris brought up basic information that activists did not already have, about how clinical trials were done and the role of the National Institute of Allergy and Infectious Diseases, and she shared the crucial, transformative information that 80 percent of the current trials were of one drug, AZT, whose patent was held by Burroughs Wellcome.

Her takeaway was that ACT UP's main demand must be that other drugs should be tested, and that this should be the group's main focus. "There were these other potential drugs out there. Everyone could name these drugs. It didn't seem right to me or anyone else, so I said, *Well, okay, this is where we have to go. This is the government, this is what the government is doing. We have to put pressure on them, to expand their program to other drugs.*"

Iris saw AZT as a "potential" drug. It had gone through all the steps to get to the testing-in-humans stage, but it was no miracle drug. It wasn't a cure. That was certain. But people wanted it. Obviously, there were side effects—these were very toxic drugs. "Cancer patients go through the same thing. The drugs are very cytotoxic. So, it was obvious that a lot more work had to be done, or we had to find better drugs to prevent these toxic effects from occurring. Plus, the drug wasn't getting rid of this virus."

Since Iris was a chemist, she hadn't really been trained to think about what the patient wanted. But she knew patients had to fight because of her own experience with her mother and another close friend who had strokes. She knew that people had to be advocates—whether it was for themselves or others. "You had to stand up and fight . . . actually fight! . . . Larry Kramer was there, at that time. And, he immediately jumped on it." This was 1987. ACT UP accepted her contributions and put them on the meetings' weekly agenda. She started writing papers, with data, and putting them out on a long table at the back of the meeting room, where people would pick up new information every week.

JIM EIGO

"Iris, at the time, was a *Queens housewife*, as she frequently called herself. But, not just any Queens housewife. She had advanced degrees in chemistry and on and off throughout the years had worked for drug companies including Wellcome, who was the forerunner of Burroughs Wellcome, the company that at the time owned AZT . . . Iris was brilliant, but Iris was not very articulate or very organized. [One Monday], she took the microphone and talked about a group she wanted to get together of people who would look into the drug approval process, and what drugs were in the pipeline right now, to try and eliminate those barriers toward approving potential agents for people with HIV and for the opportunistic infections associated with HIV."

Vito Russo took the floor immediately after Iris, grabbed the

microphone, and said he thought the floor had been insufficiently interested in what she was saying—that, for his money, what Iris was talking
about was the area that ACT UP should be most involved in because it
was the one that had the potential for doing the most people the most
amount of good, in a quick amount of time. Jim Eigo was a writer and
was pretty good at research and organization. "I was a quick study and all
of that, and I thought, maybe this is the area I could get involved in,
and make a very quick dent in. This was just the very first week."

Iris announced she would meet anyone who was interested the next
Monday before the meeting. Jim was there and Vito and Marty Robinson, another long-term gay and AIDS activist. Both Marty and Vito
have since died of AIDS. "Marty and Vito had this incredible love/
hate relationship with each other." At that very first meeting, they
were shouting at each other. Jim found it hard to know what to make
of it. But he saw immediately that Iris had an incredible amount of
knowledge—not just about chemistry and about drugs, but also about
the greed of the drug companies, how perverse the whole process was.
"Iris was deeply motivated by a sense of justice, and she knew what was
wrong, and she could almost put her finger on it, and she thought she
could help us, because here is—like I said, she had no reason to be in
the midst of—at that time, a bunch of mostly white gay guys, and she
was interested in helping us."

Within a few weeks, Jim was "Iris's guy Friday," and together they
were drafting and shooting off paper after paper to the floor of ACT UP.
Iris's study group was associated with the Issues Committee of ACT
UP. Issues was one of the two biggest committees, alongside Actions.
Issues thought of itself as the think tank, and Actions organized all of
the street actions for the group at large. Within a month, Jim was sitting on the Coordinating Committee of ACT UP, representing Issues.

ACT UP consolidated its base in New York City and soon became
a national organization with lots of international chapters. "But at that
very beginning, there were a handful of about five of us that were working with Iris Long. And by February of 1988, we had put out papers
that formed the basis of all the treatment work that we would do [as a
national organization] within the next three years." Over the next few
years, ACT UP secured the approval of several drugs and undeniably
changed the drug approval process. "Although there were some things

about the rapacity of capitalism that we could not change. And we always were working within a very limited framework."

But, looking back on it, Jim found the degree and speed with which ACT UP was able to change things amazing. "It was only because we were embedded within a community like ACT UP. And when ACT UP later dissipated, it was because, in some ways, the brain and the body split again." Jim felt that it was only when we were quite literally working hand in hand, when Issues and Action Committees worked very close together and targeted the local AIDS treatment units—like the teaching hospitals in New York where experimental drugs were being tested on patients—that all of the membership, the several hundred active members of ACT UP, could get behind and put their bodies on the line. "It worked for about two to three years, splendidly. I know ACT UP has done good work since then. I don't mean to trivialize what has been done since then. But there was a time when we had four hundred people a week in the room, and we were able to effect change on several different fronts."

Jim spent the first few weeks around Christmas 1987 learning all he could about the drug approval process. He recalled the government setting up twenty to fifty teaching hospitals for drug trials, five in New York City, so "there were lots of targets for us to sit-in at those first few years." By February, Iris's research group called themselves the Treatment and Data Committee. "David Kirschenbaum—who's really an underrated treatment hero of those first year or two of ACT UP—had a one-man data gathering operation going since July of '87 . . . I mean literally, volumes of information under the Freedom of Information Act. So we would weekly just [dive into] boxes and boxes of stuff."

DAVID Z. KIRSCHENBAUM

David Z. Kirschenbaum is a second-generation Ohioan who grew up in a Reform Jewish community, where his mother was president of Hadassah, but not religious. He came out two days before his twentieth birthday at Case Western Reserve, in a class called The Anthropology of Sexual Deviance, and transferred to Pratt in New York, where he switched from biomedical engineering to architecture.

David first learned about AIDS through the gay newspaper *New*

York Native in about 1983. He had a boyfriend whose earlier lover had died of AIDS. Then he heard that a close friend moved to Texas and got into the IMREG trial. IMREG was, David said, "one of the bogus drugs that came out along the way that didn't do anything. And [my friend] was abused, horribly, in the trial. He was under the impression that he was going to be medically taken care of—because he didn't have any insurance and things—and they didn't take care of him, and they just let him progress, even when other things came along. I thought that was pretty bad . . . Then he got into another trial on co-enzyme [Compound] Q, to get some care, and that also didn't do anything. And then, he would go to emergency rooms at other hospitals, and in Texas, they just turned you away. I went to visit and I actually went to the hospital one time with him, to go for the trial. And then, basically, shortly thereafter, I came back to New York." David found out about ACT UP at a gay dance at Columbia University, a very popular gathering place at the time for gay men from across the city. ACT UP had an information table there, and David joined the Issues Committee, which was being chaired by Herb Spiers.

JIM EIGO

"Eventually, we had lots of people within the system that liked us—or, at the very least, were sympathetic with us—some who were closeted gays," Jim said. T&D wound up befriending the head biostatistician at the National Cancer Institute, David Byers, who was gay and dying of AIDS. He was not out, but he passed on information to activists. "There were people that were both hero and villain, at different times. It was a very complicated thing." AIDS was increasingly revealing its complexity, highlighting and reflecting most of America's social problems. Jim and his colleagues realized that they always had to be very concrete in their demands. They couldn't be too theoretical; they had to distill everything to a few points. "It had to do with the rapacity of capitalism, and the inability of this country to ever recognize how all of our services are being eaten away." And, of course, the fact that we had a Reagan administration that simply would not begin to deal with AIDS.

DAVID Z. KIRSCHENBAUM

David and Iris Long met at Herb Spiers's loft. Margaret McCarthy, Bill Bahlman, Steven Spinella, and Garry Kleinman were some of the regulars, and there were usually about ten to twelve people. They started going to meetings at the National Institutes of Health, talking with Anthony Fauci, and with Ellen Cooper at the Food and Drug Administration. The demands were "more compassionate protocols, more drugs into the system." One of the chief concerns was getting drugs that already helped with opportunistic infections, like Bactrim and aerosol pentamidine for pneumonia, into trials as prevention or prophylaxis, which the doctors weren't allowing. Activists felt that people with AIDS should not lose their lives to treatable infections in order to get access to new drugs. That was a decision being made by cold science, not from the point of view of the patient who wanted to live.

ACT UP literally asked Fauci, the director of the National Institute of Allergy and Infectious Diseases within the NIH, which trials were going on and who was being enrolled, and he refused to answer.

"The government up to that point took the position that, *We don't need to tell anybody anything. We're not accountable.* And so, we held them accountable . . . There was a conflict going on. It was not a kissing match."

David and his roommate Margaret McCarthy started sending Freedom of Information Act (FOIA) requests through attorney William B. Rubenstein at the American Civil Liberties Union (ACLU). They went through literally cartons of documents trying to find out what drugs were being tested to treat AIDS, who was being enrolled, and the distribution of those people—"whether they were white, gay men or whether they were Black or Latino or women with children they were enrolling, were they looking at any children? . . . I would be calling all these people all the time." David would literally call Tony Fauci directly. In this way, ACT UP got meetings with the government. It was the interactive, actual conversation that allowed these early activists to start to put the pieces together.

MARGARET McCARTHY

Margaret McCarthy came from an Irish Catholic family in East Flatbush, Brooklyn. When she started college at Columbia in 1983 she jumped into the anti-apartheid movement, which was employing civil disobedience to win concessions from the administration. During her sophomore year, a student died of AIDS. McCarthy joined Laura Pinsky and Paul Douglas's Gay Health Advocacy Project on campus. For a summer job after her first year of law school, she worked at the New York City Commission on Human Rights in the AIDS Discrimination Unit under Mitchell Karp, one of the cofounders of Black and White Men Together.

Margaret worked on a range of AIDS discrimination cases, and was outraged at what she was seeing. "We had a whole bunch of cases where patients had filed against dentists who refused them treatment. Then we also had handled the case for a dentist who was gay. The dental practice wanted to kick him out because he was going to have patients with AIDS." Her office at the Human Rights Commission was downtown, right by city hall on Duane Street, and when ACT UP had a demonstration in July of 1987 at Federal Plaza, she participated and then went to the next Monday meeting. Soon she joined the Issues Committee and the Lavender Hill Mob.

The activists would go to Washington, super prepared, and meet with Fauci and Margaret Hamburg, who later became the health commissioner of New York City. This was the beginning of ACT UP's collaboration with the government. There was Jack Killen, who was Fauci's assistant, and a couple more officials. ACT UP would set the agenda for what they wanted to talk about, and the discussion would last sixty to ninety minutes. Margaret McCarthy and David's apartment was stuffed with boxes of government documents. "We didn't even have a living room." It was filled with an actual photocopy machine, which in the 1980s was the size of a stove. David had developed a relationship with Hamburg, so they would talk on the phone, and she "would tell him what to ask for in his Freedom of Information [Act] requests." The phone again! Real conversations.

Margaret's focus was on all people who were being excluded from access to drugs, either officially or because of social inequality. "People whose kids had AIDS are the most disenfranchised people." Were those parents represented in ACT UP? No. But people took it on as an issue because they really understood that nobody was advocating for those kids. The doctors and nurses who treated HIV-positive children really wanted their patients to get treated decently, "and so they were kind of aligned with the people in ACT UP who were working on those issues."

IRIS LONG

Iris started a study group inside the Issues Committee that met separately every week. She found herself working on it all day long, calling drug companies, finding out, *Here's a drug, let's find out where it is, how can we get it!* One drug they focused on was DHPG (ganciclovir), which was used for AIDS-related blindness, called cytomegalovirus (CMV) retinitis. The activists wanted DHPG to be available to PWAs, so they had to learn about the Food and Drug Administration and the approval process. Of course, this was before the internet. Members, some of whom had no science background, were doing heavy-duty research through medical journals and conversations with scientists. The more they learned, the more they began to understand about the specificities of the government bureaucracy. They had to face and deal with learning how all of the byzantine agencies worked. They then understood how and why the FDA was not functioning in a timely way. As a consequence, PWAs were going blind.

DHPG could help people, but the FDA was caught up in the bureaucracy of the review. They had tons of paper they had to go through, committees that would review the data, and then the drug would have to be put on a calendar. This was followed by more review, more presentations. The whole process was very slow. "The drug company [Hoffmann-La Roche] agreed, everything was slow, so they had an ally in us." The pharmaceutical companies also had an interest, from the beginning, in speeding up approval.

DAVID Z. KIRSCHENBAUM

ACT UP's relationship with government officials was dynamic. David recalled that "occasionally, they would leak information." For example, DHPG was on compassionate use protocol, and the FDA wanted a real clinical trial of it, which would have limited the access. "Tony mentioned this to us in a meeting so we would create a big huff about it. And it did happen. We made a big huff, and compassionate use protocol stayed . . . At some point he learned to use us, as well—not just work with us, but to use us for his goals, which were not necessarily in conflict with our goals."

David and Iris wanted their own forum for developing ideas and their own "airtime" at the Monday-night meeting. So they officially made Treatment and Data a committee in ACT UP's first year, 1987. "Well, she was *Treatment*, I was *Data*. I did lots of data gathering, and we didn't think we were getting enough time at the Issues Committee— what we needed to look at and talk about."

JIM EIGO

The first drug battle, over DHPG, was a question of access. Treatment and Data knew that they had to force the FDA to make it available, and that they had to focus on campaigns that were winnable.

"You can't deal with the ocean—you really can't. You might want to, but you really have to be very rigorous. And so, early on, for example, one of our first big successes was [with DHPG]." It was the standard of care, in the sense that it was an unapproved drug but every doctor gave it to his or her patient if they had AIDS and they came down with CMV. And yet at one point, the Food and Drug Administration refused to approve it, claiming they didn't have good data. "And they *didn't* have good data." But that meant anyone who couldn't afford paying for it out of pocket themselves was unable get it, because the drug was only legal for other purposes. So no insurance would pay for it, and certainly not anyone who was on Social Security, Medicare, or Medicaid would be assisted. "We had a very potent issue there. It was an issue that affected lots of people."

IRIS LONG

This first and early incarnation of Treatment and Data established a relationship with Ellen Cooper at the FDA. One of their face-to-face meetings with the FDA became, in a sense, ACT UP's first show of theatrical protest toward government officials. In 1988, as Ellen Cooper was speaking at a hearing in Washington, ACT UPers made paper and cardboard clocks, held up to show that time was passing and people were dying. The FDA officials were "somewhat stunned."

"They weren't looking to make the system work better. That wasn't their job . . . They would say, *That's someone else's job.*" ACT UP knew that they had to put pressure on and change the FDA, specifically how they did business, because the drug development system was just taking too long. There was too much bureaucracy. Eliminating it became our job.

JIM EIGO

As the activists interacted more and more with government officials, they had to find a way to understand them in order to work with them. Getting along with people with power, without being co-opted by them, is one of the tightropes of being effective. Jim found that: "None of them were homophobic. I really, honestly, have to say that. I think Tony Fauci has lots of faults. He is a vain man and he sees himself as a great man, and he wants to protect that legacy, and he saw AIDS as a way to further that legacy. I'm under no delusion that he was just doing it just to help us, or just to save the lives of people with AIDS. I do have to say, he was one of the straight men of his generation from whom I never detected a whiff of homophobia. I have to say that. Ellen Cooper, in fact—after she worked with the FDA, worked with amfAR. So we in some ways—I think she was deeply hurt by us, to begin with. And then, she listened to us. And then, she wanted to work at a community level, in order to develop AIDS drugs. Frank Young, her boss, left pretty quickly and he was something of a well-meaning blowhard . . . A lot of the community doctors, a lot of the people who worked in teaching hospitals, saw themselves as great champions of people who were ill. They were working to get them drugs. They were highly insulted if you suggested that what they were doing was not in the best interest of people with AIDS, or that it was too slow. And, in part, you could see that.

"Everyone works from mixed motives, and they work from their own vantage point. What I do have to say about it was there was—in all of the bureaucracy—the major goal of any individual is usually to protect his or her ass, to advance his or her position, to preserve his or her legacy for those few, like Fauci, who do see themselves on a much larger scale. And so they all have little fiefdoms. And most of them are working in all their adult lives in a very specialized field. They see very little. None of them had much day-to-day contact with people with AIDS, although some people who were researchers had AIDS patients. But, up until ACT UP started speaking, they were just, *Oh, those poor AIDS patients*, or guinea pigs, in the worst scenario. One great thing that ACT UP accomplished was to give a face to AIDS."

DAVID Z. KIRSCHENBAUM

A friend of David's who was close friends with Margaret Hamburg told him that one day Tony Fauci and Hamburg were sitting in a room and saying, *These people are yelling at us, trying to get us, blah, blah, blah.* And as they're having this conversation—*What should we do?*—it was decided at the meeting that *the best way to get them to work with us is to invite them in.* And that's what happened. They invited ACT UP into all the government's ACTG meetings. They put people in ACT UP on committees. And dramatic shifts started to take place with the government looking for ACT UP's support. "We started arguing for their funding— more so—to keep them going. And we became their vocal advocates . . . The fact that they invited us in, rather quickly at one point—obviously, they figured they could use us . . . Some of their goals were simply to keep the money stream going, which isn't necessarily doing good research. They're not the same." Despite these strategic points of alliance between government officials and ACT UP, David felt that often the political people did not understand the moral issues involved.

David was a major advocate for children in clinical trials— specifically in giving them Bactrim. At one meeting, he was sitting with "the NIH gang," and they mentioned they were going to now allow Bactrim prophylaxis for all their adult trials. And he said, *Adult trials? What about children?* And they were going on and on—*Well, there's just not enough data.* Getting children involved became a rallying cry for David. And eventually, through NIH meeting minutes, he got copies of the recommendations that they were talking about, and went ahead and published them before the NIH had announced them. David and Garance Franke-Ruta published these recommendations at the San Francisco AIDS conference in June of 1990, distributing them to every

member in one of the plenary sessions to show that the NIH was excluding children. Project Inform then published it in their newsletter.
"It took too long," but eventually, children were given prophylaxis as
well. "I always thought you worked for the weakest denominator in
any link to get the most for everybody. And if you could get children
certain things, as well as adults, then you could get everybody to get
everything."

These early meetings with the NIH could be very frustrating, indeed upsetting, for ACT UP. Most people getting the opportunity to
be face-to-face with the government had friends who were dying at that
very moment, many due to governmental delays. The officials were not
having this experience. David had a good friend, John Bowen, who was
in the original AZT trial. He was in the placebo group, and he had originally come down with pneumonia. So he was on Bactrim prophylaxis.
To get in the trial, he had to go off Bactrim prophylaxis. Consequently,
his disease progressed as part of the placebo group. He recovered again.
After the trial, he tried to get on AZT, as compassionate use, but the
doctors wouldn't give it to him because one of his blood values was off.
In June of 1989, John went to the Montreal AIDS conference, and at a
session where Ellen Cooper was talking, John stood up and said, *Here
I am, I'm developing pneumonia, and you wouldn't give me any drugs for
the pneumonia. You won't give me anything for pain. And you just let me
go on. And then, finally, you wouldn't give me any drugs after the trial,
once you reached your end point. Well, I have like twenty-five T cells, and I'm
walking around.* "It never occurred to any of these people that anyone
with such low T cells could even walk or still be alive. They hadn't even
looked at that stuff."

This story is so emblematic, not only as a concrete example of people
dying in the face of government bureaucrats, but also of how David,
after all of his fighting, has had to carry this story with him for the rest
of his life.

PLACEBOS AND CONSENT

Although the only drugs being tested were AZT and DHPG, treatment
activists were starting to realize the layers of complex issues involved in

clinical trials. One early controversy involved the use of "double-blind," or placebos, in the studies. Scientists wanted the best research, and this required having something to compare the treatment to. So when a patient entered a study, they never knew if they were getting the actual drug, or a benign, empty pill—a placebo—as part of being in the comparison test group. The standard was that the doctors and the patients both did not know who got the drug and who got the treatment, so that no one would be biased in their approach. The doctors would not know who would die, and who might live. Although the use of placebos was status quo in scientific studies, for a movement organized from the patient's perspective, it was far from acceptable. No one wanted to be the test person who was denied the treatment and, in practicality, condemned to die. And so activists developed a perspective that opposed testing new drugs against nothing. At first it was very difficult, because there were no treatments whatsoever. Later, when AZT was in place, new drugs could be tested against AZT or whatever was the standard of care.

Since I was part of ACT UP and shared the pro-patient perspective I had learned in the reproductive rights movement, in 1988 I wrote an article for *The Village Voice* investigating the use of placebos in trials for infants who were born HIV-positive. I opposed these trials, in part because my history in ACT UP made me view HIV-positive infants as "people with AIDS" deserving treatment. But I also had a second realm of influence that would become crucial later on in ACT UP's 1992 split—a reproductive rights definition of *consent*.

In 1979, when the Supreme Court upheld the Hyde Amendment depriving poor women of Medicaid funding for abortion, I joined a newly formed organization, the Committee for Abortion Rights and Against Sterilization Abuse (CARASA). At that time there were three different kinds of abortion rights movements. There were "single-issue" abortion rights groups, like the National Abortion Rights Action League (NARAL) and the National Organization for Women (NOW) abortion rights committee. These groups had one focus: keeping abortion safe and legal, and trying to fight anti-abortion strategies to limit access. Then there was International Planned Parenthood, which was very far from the front-line service organization known as Planned Parenthood today. International Planned Parenthood was involved in population control, programs funded by first-world countries to limit birth rates in the global south without empowering women to make their own informed decisions about whether or not to have children. So, just as many women were forced into motherhood by law and custom around the world and in the U.S., global population control kept women *from* motherhood through methods like sterilization—a widespread and diverse series of programs to sterilize mostly Black and Brown women from poor countries, often without informed consent. For radicals supporting abortion rights, forced sterilization was the flip side of the issue. This was the original source of the concept of reproductive rights, the third type of abortion rights movements and a political analysis that supported abortion rights for women who did not want to carry pregnancies to term, while opposing sterilization without consent for women who did want to have children. CARASA was part of the reproductive rights movement and emerged from groups like the Committee to End Sterilization Abuse (CESA), which had been organized by a Puerto Rican doctor, Helen Rodriguez-Trias, working in New York. CESA was instrumental in creating New York's 1978 sterilization regulations, which demanded informed consent for sterilization.

For those of us who came out of the multi-issue reproductive rights movement, before coming to ACT UP, "consent" was a crucial concept that we linked to antiracist politics. And a significant number of women in ACT UP had been previously trained in this perspective. The feminist concept of reproductive consent was particularly resonant with PWAs' concerns about placebos, and about being forced into trials under conditions to which they did not consent. When I wrote against the use of placebos for infants born with AIDS, I was very aware that in New York City, most of these children were Black and Brown because so many women with HIV were people of color. And my reproductive rights training reminded me that, since as infants they could not consent, being subjected to placebo testing was consistent with the racist history of nonconsensual medicine in America and internationally. Also, in these cases, the mothers were often dead or dying of AIDS, and couldn't protect their children. Or, if they were alive, many of these poor women of color felt guilty about having inadvertently infected their children by giving birth to them. This was especially true if their own HIV infections came from intravenous drug use. And through this guilt the women could be emotionally coerced into submitting their very sick newborns to placebo trials in which they might get sugar instead of medicine. So ACT UP and CARASA were my two influences in writing the article.

Unfortunately, my white male editor at the *Voice*, Richard Goldstein, who was also HIV-negative and gay but not in ACT UP, supported placebo use in pediatric AIDS trials. He came from the traditional perspective that favored scientific standards over the immediate needs of patients. This was a very difficult debate between two profoundly different perspectives inside white gay journalism. Obviously the more rigorous the study, the better in the long term. But if he were the person who needed the medication in order to stay alive, I felt that he would have had a different perspective. And being in ACT UP meant looking at everything from the point of view of the person with AIDS and their desire to live. AIDS activists argued that if patients were admitted to clinical trials and drugs were tested against the standard of care, instead of against placebos, it might take longer to get the ultimate information, but more lives would be saved in the immediate. This was a representative example of the kinds of historical, experiential, and emotional complexities surfacing early in the process of finding a way out of the disaster of AIDS. Despite my arguments, Goldstein killed my story at the *Voice* because of his own belief in placebo studies, and it was subsequently published in the *New York Native*.

MARGARET McCARTHY

Many researchers used death as "an endpoint."

"So a lot of the studies were set up so that they would be comparing people getting the drug and people in the placebo group, [and] say[ing], *We're going to see how many of them die*, and so death was considered the endpoint of the study . . . [The scientists] were looking at: in the *got the medication* column, this number of people died, and in the *we didn't give them anything* column, the same amount died, so we can't say it worked . . . They didn't have any other treatments, right, so there's nothing else to compare it to except for nothing. Later, I think it makes sense to do studies where you're comparing a proven treatment to a new treatment, right, so that you have arms of the study comparing Drug

A to Drug B to Drug C or some combination. But at the time that I joined ACT UP, like, there were no approved treatments. AZT was the first one."

JIM EIGO

A lot was learned from the DHPG campaign. In the winter of 1989, the Food and Drug Administration felt they had to reopen the case, drag in all the information they could and become proactive, in order to extract something useful from the data they collected—which Jim knew was "sloppy, terribly done, disparate, and lots of it was coming from local AIDS doctors." But ACT UP was able to have the FDA reverse themselves and approve the drug. Because the American government operates on so many different levels—federal, state, and local—and so much of the health-care industry is strangled by private industry, it is very difficult to push drugs forward. But Jim recalls that, at least within those few years, "if you could identify an obvious problem—if you could get the media on board about it, if you could get two hundred to three hundred ACT UP people sitting in at a very particular target and making it very, very uncomfortable for the powers that were, you could affect very, very quick change." And within only a year, ACT UP reversed the unapproval of DHPG, and got another AIDS drug—didanosine (ddI)—approved.

DAVID Z. KIRSCHENBAUM

But with the drug release came other problems. The doses for AZT were way too high. Originally, the approval for AZT was twelve hundred milligrams a day. ACT UP conveyed crucial information through talking to doctors and then communicating back to the NIH that they were concerned about AZT doses. *People are doing fine with three hundred milligrams a day, so why are you giving them all this drug?* Some of this thinking had to do with cancer therapy, where doctors hit the patient with everything they could, in order to get rid of the cancer. And as long as they don't die, there's some benefit. David knew of one trial that took place at Sloan Kettering that had to do with Kaposi sarcoma—AIDS-related skin cancer—where "they gave these patients full dose chemotherapy, and they all died. So, then they cut the dose in half and they didn't die so quickly, and some of them actually lived. So what did they do with those remaining patients—they upped their dose . . . to see if they could treat it better . . . and so then they died."

IRIS LONG

Iris was spending every day of her life making calls to find out about different drugs. People with AIDS would phone her at home asking for help getting medicine. She even helped a woman with tuberculosis get a drug from Canada. Now her life was surrounded by gay people and people with AIDS.

"I sort of just accepted it, that's it. I said, *This is what I'm doing. These are the people I'm involved with. I like the people. It's a whole different thing I'm doing here, and I think I'm doing the right thing, and I'm very interested in what I'm doing.*" She liked the interaction. Iris had always been a laboratory person, so interacting with people was something she had never done before. She was not "a joiner" before, at all. But she was "a fighter type person that would fight for somebody's rights."

When her friends started to die, she said, "it was very hard on everyone—myself, the group. There were funerals, meetings, memorial meetings for people, and it was very moving, to see all the people that came." The epidemic was escalating, in the world and inside ACT UP.

THE AIDS TREATMENT REGISTRY (ATR)

DAVID Z. KIRSCHENBAUM

As ACT UP started to understand how the trials were organized, and where they were, they realized that PWAs had no way of accessing this basic information. So, as part of the access component of their work, in February of 1988, Treatment and Data began to solve the problem themselves by compiling extensive lists of trial sites and distributing them by hand to PWAs. "It was decided that everyone in the room should be on the board of the AIDS Treatment Registry." They included John Wagenhauser, Peter Hochschild, Garry Kleinman, Margaret

McCarthy, Bob Huff, Michael Cowling, Richard Elovich, Ann Gorewitz, and Nancy Adams. A number of these Treatment and Data members, including Margaret McCarthy, also formed an affinity group called Wave 3. The name came from a tactic invented for the Wall Street action, where affinity groups would wait in "waves" to follow one another as, one by one, a group sat down, disrupted traffic, and got arrested. In this way, a small number of people could have a longer impact. So the people compiling the registry were often the same people being arrested together and planning actions.

MARGARET McCARTHY

The first thing Margaret and others did in creating the AIDS Treatment Registry (ATR) was to put together a publication that ultimately became *Deciding to Enter*, the first of its kind in the United States, initially as a book and then also as a pamphlet. It explained the whole process of getting into and going through a clinical trial. *Why would I want to get involved with it or not?*, *What would it entail of me?*, and *What are the risks and benefits?* They tried to use simple language, and it got translated into Spanish and Creole. It also included information about whether or not the trial included a placebo.

Because so many ACT UPers who had been arrested were sentenced to community service, the ATR got them to work off their debt to the court by collating the mailing of hundreds of copies of the registry. Tony Malliaris did a lot of transcribing because he had a secretarial job. But Margaret knew that making the trials accessible involved more than just telling people where they were located. The ATR folks were aware of the U.S. history of abuse of prisoners and people of color in clinical trials. These people sometimes were not told that they were even *part of* clinical trials, and sometimes were not given a choice. In the case of AIDS, often being on other medications was forbidden as a prerequisite to get into a trial. Women of childbearing age were excluded from almost every trial. The conductors of trials didn't want to have people who were considered noncompliant, and so they made a lot of race- and class-based assumptions about who would be noncompliant, which affected women with AIDS who were often poor and/or of color. There was a lot of exclusion. And since there were no available treatments, people were desperate. They wanted to be in the trials.

Access to trials also depended on where people lived. There were practical issues: Patients had to be able to get to the study site. The trials might not offer transportation assistance. For example, the Community Health Project, located in the Center, had a trial for aerosolized pentamidine, to prevent pneumonia. So people living outside of the city were never going to get that medication. Their doctors often didn't know about the trials. They were not written up in the medical journals. A person would have to go to an AIDS-specific conference to learn that information, and most people, if they had a doctor, had a family doctor. This is where the ATR came in. Outside of big cities with major research universities, "there weren't many practices that would have this information, like, *Oh, I read in the back of, like, the PWA Health Group magazine that they're having this treatment.* Well, how many doctors are reading that?"

DAVID Z. KIRSCHENBAUM

David and others were watchdogging the AIDS Clinical Trials Group at the National Institutes of Health, which was finally getting a national clinical trials program going. He looked at who they were enrolling, looked at their protocols. In his FOIA requests, he asked for the copies of all the protocols as they were being developed. ACT UP discovered that the NIH wasn't enrolling women. In most cities, they weren't enrolling Blacks and Latinos, either, except in Baltimore, at Johns Hopkins, where AIDS seemed to have been developing most among Black men, their patient pool. Some AIDS trial groups were sitting on their money for years, without enrolling a patient. "At Case Western Reserve, the guy who started the ACTG there was homophobic. He was coming from a hemophiliac background and just wasn't enrolling anybody."

The government was highly biased against enrolling women. Often women with AIDS had more complicated lives, could be drug users, or there just weren't enough women that doctors could identify, as most women were not being diagnosed properly. Also, the government researchers wanted a more homogenous group. "They wanted to keep it *as narrow a focus as possible,* in their patient pool, so they could see differences among their patient pool easier." This translated into racial and gender exclusion.

David felt that the reason that the male patients were mostly white was the same reason that there were so few women—a desire for homogeneity. And no one inside the government was objecting to it. "Inclusion was not that important to them." ACT UP started getting the statistics on who they were enrolling at each ACTG, and would point out, *This one had so many women, this had so many Blacks, this had so many this and that.* And David and his colleagues would also look at each trial and see which locations were enrolling who. "No one else was looking at those statistics."

At the Food and Drug Administration, it took four to seven years to approve drugs, and people with AIDS got some access through the 1983 Orphan Drug Act, which sped up the process. "We got commitments that they would approve AIDS drugs quicker than normal. Was that a good thing or a bad thing? I can't say, but they could get drugs out there, sooner." Often, drugs got used for populations that may have not needed them yet, like AZT for asymptomatic people with a high T-cell count—did that actually extend their lives? Sometimes it sped up their demise. It is hard to do that kind of work, to get the right answers, when people are dying and scared.

ACT UP dealt with this dilemma by emphasizing that each patient had to make their own decisions. No one really knew when to start certain medications. Basically, the patient was left making a decision based on their best information, which was rarely widely available. Jim Eigo got involved in that process with the FDA, early on. "Jim Eigo was brilliant, very articulate, and quite wonderful at voicing our concerns at that time . . . Jim sat with officials on a regular basis, working out these various programs."

IRIS LONG

Soon Iris was putting all her energy into the ATR. It was a xeroxed, hand-stapled pamphlet, sent out through the mail directly to patients, activists, and doctors, because the doctors alone could not be relied on to get information about clinical trials out to people. As it evolved, the ATR included more and more information. It started to list if a trial was financed by a drug company, if there were payments involved. The first edition of the ATR, in 1990, listed thirty to forty trials. The more PWAs pushed, the more trials were opened.

It was very hard to get information on drug company trials, because they were more secret than government trials. The ATR was contacting each of the hospitals that were holding these trials, and found the key person that would tell ACT UP what was going on in trials for AIDS. By the time Iris stopped coordinating in 1993, the ATR listed sixty to seventy ongoing trials. The updated editions went out through the mail, every four months at first, and then more frequently. The directory listed entry criteria, the required blood work, locations, and more. The work became so overwhelming that Iris had to leave the Treatment and Data Committee to run the ATR. Iris ultimately spent ten years in ACT UP, finally leaving in 1997, five years after the split with TAG, and right after protease inhibitors—the current standard of care—became widely available. When TAG split off in 1992, Iris stayed in ACT UP. She never went to a TAG meeting.

"There was some sort of animosity between certain ACT UP people and TAG. I wanted to go, but I never pushed myself to go . . . Meetings are a dynamic. And you can either feel wanted at a meeting or you don't. And I felt that some of the meetings, later on, were not very friendly. In fact, I saw one woman, who was a friend of mine—she was trashed. This had to do with [peptide T], and she was at the meeting and really made to feel not very welcome. So I wasn't comfortable with TAG. And there were other people, also, that were not comfortable with TAG . . . There were ACT UPs all over the country. Somehow, that should have been stabilized, rather than gone downhill. And with the internet and everything, it could have become a national, viable organization. But it's not so easy to form an organization . . . In the beginning, everyone was treated fairly. Everybody could be heard. Nobody was shouted down too much. And I feel that was lost . . . I think that anyone can make a difference. And that you really have to seek and listen to many voices . . . What are the different pieces to make something work? You have to reach out to all different types of people—whether they're doctors, different communities, churches, whatever. To get things done, you have to make a chart of where you have to go. So there has to be some sort of a plan, too. You have to plan . . . Doctors have to be receptive.

If they're not, you have to force people, you have to *act up*. That's what you have to do."

THE INVENTION OF PARALLEL TRACK

JIM EIGO

In 1988, Jim Eigo, David Kirschenbaum, Iris Long, and Garry Kleinman wrote a letter to Tony Fauci, at this point the de facto AIDS czar, with a proposal that they'd worked on. It stated that PWAs who had exhausted AZT and had no treatment options, and were too sick to get into any clinical trials, should have what the activists were calling *parallel trials*, so that PWAs could access what were, at the time, the only treatment options. They understood the reasons for keeping people with advanced issues out of the pristine trials to get a drug approved, so that these PWAs didn't have to stop taking other medications. But to give sick people the chance, ACT UP proposed the creation of parallel trials where a PWA could still get the drug. They argued for this access, even though the data produced from one of these "informal" trials might not be absolutely clean, because the person was too sick to obey certain parameters required under a more clinical trial. They argued that this *real-world data*, itself, would be invaluable, if the state actually kept it.

Fauci didn't answer.

The following spring, when Fauci came to New York to talk at the local branch of the Institute of Medicine, Jim was in the audience and peppered him with questions. Fauci later told *Gay Community News* that he had gotten the letter, that he had read it, that he thought it was very smart and thought there were a lot of things that the government should be doing, and that they should act upon a lot of the things that were in the letter.

"Now, I don't for a minute think it was only out of the goodness of his heart that he was doing it," Jim said.

"He also was coming up against the Food and Drug Administration. So we're dealing with internal politics within government agencies here, and sometimes one agency would play us off against another agency. But we tried to keep our eyes open about that, and tried to never allow ourselves to be co-opted too much by one agency against another. But Fauci would have been very happy to almost do away with the Food and Drug Administration, because they were standing in the way of his glory, of his approving virtually everything they wanted to get approved. The FDA always saw itself as the gatekeeper, and people who were doing the investigations, who were doing the experiments—the scientists [at the NIH] always thought of the FDA as almost this dowdy, old, fusty organization that was standing in the way of science. Whereas, of course, the Food and Drug Administration looked upon the experimenters as being quite willing to throw any drug out into the market that might help someone or might not—might harm someone or might not, just because they thought it would."

Within five months, Fauci was behind the idea. He renamed it "the parallel track," Jim said, "because he had to remake it in his own image, of course." But ACT UP had won. Jim found that ACT UP was establishing a pattern of success. They were able to find a great need, narrow the focus, and articulate it through the people who were working intensively in that area and then, always—"and I cannot say this enough"—back it up through direct action. ACT UP rank and file came down to Washington, to Bethesda, "to all the places where drug approval gets done, and put their bodies on the line. There is something incredibly powerful about seeing hundreds of people just sitting there or yelling—or—if it's a different sort of meeting—people with AIDS who are themselves sick and need a drug, getting up at a microphone and telling the powers that be, *You are not serving me*."

THE BIRTH OF THE INSIDE/OUTSIDE STRATEGY

What Jim is articulating here is the developing strategic dynamic that would drive ACT UP to success, and ultimately be a source of its demise: the strategy of having one arm of the movement in direct, personal relationship to government or corporate officials—working with them, cajoling them, proposing solutions, having intimate interactions, and creating identification. This dynamic later came to be known as Inside. At the same time, a different sector of the organization provided backup and pressure through street actions, civil disobedience, and direct action, playing the role of Outside. Sometimes they were outside the system, and sometimes they were literally outside, doing actions. In 1987, most people in power were white males from middle- and upper-class backgrounds, and this dramatically determined which AIDS activists had the potential to be Inside and which ones would be relegated to Outside. But in addition to demographics, character also played a part. And so did ideology, as different personalities were attracted to different forms of response.

At first the development of the Inside player was natural, a product of activists pursuing personal, face-to-face contact with government officials out of desperation and necessity. Once contact was established, these activists then had to show officials that they understood the issues, could talk as peers, and could offer solutions that would elevate the officials in their own pursuits: both for the common good and in relation to their professional goals. To some extent, the success of the Inside part of this strategic approach did depend on government officials, in certain ways, taking the people in front of them seriously. Relating to them, or identifying with them with some kind of begrudging respect, had to occur for the Inside strategy to be viable.

It cannot be overstated the extent to which, in the 1980s, the vast, overwhelming majority of people in government, corporate leadership, the legal and justice sectors, and the media were white males. It would be very hard for a young person today to understand the extent of the white male wall when it came to power. Although, today, white males still have more power than anyone else and continue to own most of private space while controlling much of public space, the 1980s were very, very different. When women, lesbians, people of color, and sometimes openly gay men looked for images of themselves in seats of power, they just weren't there, or they were hiding. Women, people of color, and openly gay people were almost *always* on the outside of all representation and decision-making. So it is important to at least think about why these government officials were able to find a place inside themselves that allowed them to connect to ACT UP's first rendition of Treatment and Data. It is impossible to know to what extent the demographic makeup of the individuals in question was a factor. Margaret Hamburg was a biracial Black Jewish woman, and therefore highly unusual as a government official. Anthony Fauci was Italian in a world of WASPs. They both had urban backgrounds. The ACT UP people they were dealing with were white; some were ethnic whites from working-class backgrounds. Some, like Iris, had impressive scientific knowledge, even though she was not charismatic, and had a working-class affect. Margaret and David were well educated, from Columbia and Pratt; Jim was white and had an impressive, elastic mind. Although all were upstanding individuals, at the time they came across as unusual, somewhat bohemian, and eclectic. Iris was a middle-aged woman, Jim and David were openly gay, David was young and wore his hair in bangs. Margaret was a young woman. While these nuances may not seem important today, at the time of supreme white male monopoly on power, they did signal these individuals as out of the mainstream, not from the ruling class, and against the profile of most of the people with real power in policy development. All of our folks were autodidacts and incredibly hard workers, like most ACT UP leaders. We will never know what would have happened if the people in ACT UP who self-selected to approach the government were less familiar to the officials, if they would have been as successful. If the Latino Caucus, or a group of out lesbians, had been the first hand that reached out to the government, would it have been grasped? I would guess that the answer would be no. Was there a reason that those highly activated sectors of ACT UP, made up mostly of lesbians and people of color, situated themselves, initially, away from direct negotiating contact with the government? This is one of the legacies and mysteries that we all have to grapple with.

While we can never fully know how these demographics worked at the time, one thing is certainly clear: when the first Treatment and Data activists formed direct relationships with government officials, they did not do so deliberately, consciously or unconsciously, as Insiders. They did not hold ideologies about their class, race, gender, or affects. How can we surmise this? Because the people Jim Eigo cites as the force behind the Inside—the hundreds of ACT UPers who acted as Outside, who got on buses to come to support the Inside at meetings, to demonstrate and to do direct action—were not overwhelmingly different from the Inside. At the beginning, being a researcher/

negotiator and being a street activist were not two separate endeavors in ACT UP, for two different and separate kinds of demographics. Obviously, people were attracted to different milieus and to different focuses through a number of lenses: character, medical desperation, sexual or platonic attraction, previous skills, aspirational reach, self-image, political analysis, recruitment, coincidence. And in this way people did self-select what role and sector most attracted each person inside the complex ecosystem that was ACT UP. But watching the Inside/Outside strategy cohere, consciously and unconsciously, over the course of ACT UP's growth and demise, creates an uncomfortable but important place for all of us committed to progressive change to pay attention.

EXPANSION OF DRUG AVAILABILITY AFTER PARALLEL TRACK

JIM EIGO

In June of 1989, ACT UP sent a few hundred people to the fifth annual International AIDS Conference in Montreal. Reagan-era bans on PWAs entering the United States meant that all international meetings had to be held outside of the country. "Those of us who were interested in treatment issues actually had a chance to go to all the papers and grill the scientists . . . There was no excuse for what they weren't doing. Because again—because of the media glare and because we were now able to bring hundreds and hundreds of people from all over the country to bear on this."

By the end of that summer of 1989, Jim was asked by the Food and Drug Administration to come to a meeting at which they were going to be deciding the application of the parallel track idea, with ddI as the pilot project. He addressed the commission at the conference, which was a daylong event in which many from around the U.S. spoke. Many ACT UP members came and were a quiet, but palpable, presence in the audience, and several ACT UP members spoke very movingly. And by the end of the day, to everyone's lasting shock, the FDA finally decided that they were going to embark on parallel track for experimental AIDS drugs. They used Jim's proposal as the rough draft of the plan, and they named him to the commission that was going to be organizing it. So it was "shocking, scary. But it was also terrific, too." As much as he looks back upon it as a victory, Jim is still very conscious of what we were not able to accomplish and how broken the health-care system within the United States continues to be. "So I don't want to overstate what we did, but within the world we were handed at the time—when five ACT UP members would die a month—we, at the time, felt it was a great victory."

The whole process, from the letter to parallel track access for ddI, took eighteen months. More than a thousand people got access to ddI right way. Like AZT, it was toxic, but because the toxicities were different, at least, in theory, the idea was that PWAs could lower the doses of both drugs—if they did them together—and lessen the side effects. This mixing and matching, in a sense, was the beginning of the concept of the "cocktail"—moving away from the idea of one pill that would "cure" AIDS, to the idea of "compound" medications, interacting in different doses, depending on the situation of the individual taking the drugs. This idea is what is currently the standard-of-care practice: compound medications, like the subsequent quad pill, which has four drugs compounded into one pill, or Atripla, which has three.

The parallel track made it easier for PWAs to get access to new drugs, but some of these medications that were so hard-won actually didn't work. Still, because the drug approval process was now easier, drug companies that before had not been willing to put money into developing drugs for exotic, opportunistic infections could now do so, because they were not looking at a ten-year approval process, but maybe a three-year one. So in some ways, the new system worked better to treat opportunistic infections. However, Jim is quick to point out that we still "don't have a cure. We don't have a vaccine."

UNIVERSAL HEALTH CARE WAS SUPPOSED TO BE THE NEXT STEP

JIM EIGO

"The biggest disappointment of my life was that at this point, we could not hold ACT UP together, to do it just a bit longer or somewhat longer. A lot of us who were working in drug approval wanted to push the fight to universal health care and to reforming things like Social Security, Medicare and Medicaid . . . There was a vice president of a drug company who told me in 1990 that he thought the health-care system in America was so broken, served the people of this country so badly, that definitely, before the turn of the century, we would have universal health care. I mention that because, if certainly—some guy bringing down a six-figure salary within a drug company felt this, of course those of us within ACT UP were thinking this. You have to remember, '92 was when Clinton was elected, and within that first year he and Hillary Clinton tried to push the whole idea of universal health care. Several of us in the few years before that were obviously thinking in the same way. And after we secured parallel track, a few of us wanted to move us into other areas.

"By then, Treatment and Data had moved from Iris's four-person study group to . . . literally sixty people a week, just to the sub-committee meeting. There were many people who came to Treatment and Data meetings and never came to an ACT UP meeting—that's how big it was. So because of that, there were some of us who wanted to work more in the health-care end of things, rather than the narrower area of drug approval. And some of them left Treatment and Data before I did. People like David Kirschenbaum and Garry Kleinman were much more working on state issues by that time and trying to get the state to pay for health care."

Jim spent the next few years serving on various governmental and independent commissions; when that time was up, he wanted to gradually extricate himself from the drug treatment end of things. He started a study group with Jay Lipner, who was the lawyer that masterminded the plaintiff settlement after the Love Canal disaster, to devise an approach toward universal health care. When they went to the FDA in 1988, Jim said, "one of the slogans I came up with was . . . 'Health care is a human right.' And it was pressing. And that was the first time, I think, that ACT UP officially articulated it, but it was very much [what] the majority of the floor felt, and I thought the more that we could press that as a moral cause, [it] was something that we could ally ourselves with many people outside of the gay world and the AIDS world." The movement could not secure benefits for the people we were fighting for if we didn't tackle some of these larger structural problems. And so, Jim and a few others started a study group, which included Peter Staley, a former bond trader who was one of ACT UP's principal fundraisers during its first two years.

As Jim saw it, the problem was that, by then, ACT UP was falling apart. It was a disagreement about "how important community was to what we've been doing." Jim was HIV-negative, and was sitting on a number of AIDS panels. "The only way I saw myself as having any legitimacy, and even opening my mouth on AIDS issues, was as long as I had a vital grassroots organization behind me." When ACT UP was at its most efficient, Jim felt it was because the group agreed on certain very basic core issues and, most important, on how to apply these beliefs.

As David, Garry, Margaret, Iris, and Jim started to branch out onto other access-related issues, and Richard Elovich moved into Needle Exchange, a new group of activists came to Treatment and Data and "almost exclusively came to work on drug approval, and how can we get drugs approved. It was much more technocratic, it was much more scientific." Jim's expertise was never in the science of the medications in question. Even when he became a quick study, what he became a quick study of was the maze of drug approval, and the byzantine U.S. government, and the factions between different branches and sub-branches of U.S. government. He never wanted to become a doctor. "A lot of people in Treatment and Data . . . in some ways were more interested in the drug than in a lot of other things. For me, I was always interested in the community of ACT UP, because that was the only basis on which I felt I had a leg to stand on."

But on the other hand, a lot of the core of (new) T&D were, themselves, HIV-infected people. And they felt they were being true to the whole principle of, *I have a right to self-determination; I have a right to be part of the process of drug approval, because it eventually affects my life directly.* Perhaps because he was HIV-negative, Jim didn't want to be an AIDS professional. He wanted to be a community activist. Certainly by 1991, and even midway through 1992, just when he started wanting to hit the Social Security Administration, "the floor of ACT UP was less and less inclined to want to even deal with the Feds at all. It was just hard. After a few months of trying to work at that, it was hard to see how you could even begin to get the full approval that I wanted for dealing with the federal government . . . I felt so very bad, because there were people within all the various factions of ACT UP that I was personally close to, and there were people who were doing work that I thought was so important and had to go on, and it would be so diminished if ACT UP flew apart. But in the end, I just couldn't see how to do it. And also, some of it was personal, in the sense that, by then, I can't tell you how tired I was—how draining [it was]. I hated the halls of power as much as—more than I thought I would, having always been skeptical of power."

This question, illuminated by the search for treatments, of who could get a seat at the table and who could not, and the consequences of these differences, would become central not only to the future of ACT UP but to the global future of the virus itself.

Remembrance: Marty Robinson

In the end it all boiled down to the personal experience of watching one another die. And even the most advanced and informed members of ACT UP were not yet able to access medications that actually worked. So when Marty Robinson died at forty-nine in 1992, even his friends didn't know which way to turn. He was a veteran of gay liberation, part of the first group of gay activists to emerge from the Stonewall riots. A former construction worker, Marty cofounded the Gay Activists Alliance. But it was in his role as cofounder of the Lavender Hill Mob, formed a few months before ACT UP, that Marty had a strategic influence. The "Mob" used the technique of zaps: for example, they showed up at a CDC conference in concentration camp uniforms, and at St. Patrick's Cathedral dressed as priests, shouting that government officials and gay leaders alike were not doing what was needed.

MARGARET McCARTHY

The first time he was hospitalized, Marty was in Beth Israel. "He was totally in denial. He said, *I have regular pneumonia, so it's not AIDS!*

David Z. Kirschenbaum, Marty Robinson, and
Bill Bahlman at the March on Washington,
October 11, 1987
(Photograph courtesy of Jon Nalley)

"He was on a regular ward. They had that Center of
Excellence, the special AIDS floor where they had extra staff-
ing and everything, and he wasn't on that. He was just on
a regular ward with the oxygen tube they give you if you're
having trouble breathing. My impression is that there were
different ways to go with your HIV treatment, and he picked
the one where you're taking interferon, which turned out in
the long run to be not the one to take, but, you know, who
knew, right? Other people took the road that was AZT, and
maybe they lived or they didn't, but the interferon way just
didn't work. He was working on all these issues, but when
push came to shove, it's really hard to acknowledge, like, *This
is what I have. This is why I'm sick.* Then I know it affected his
brain. He was never the most focused person, but he just was
completely demented. I ran into him on the subway once, because we lived in the same neighborhood, and he was clearly
demented at that moment. But people would come in and out
of the HIV-related dementia. I know David Kirschenbaum
was very involved with taking care of him . . . He was telling
me how he had died . . . at home with a morphine drip.

"Everything had someone pushing it, right? I think that
the problem was, if you just take that stuff, we don't know if
it works, and [we don't know] if there is actually something

you could take that could help you. I remember one of my friends in ACT UP had already taken AZT and couldn't take it anymore because of the side effects, and so we all chipped in money to buy him dextran sulfate, which wound up never being approved. It didn't work. But we thought it did, because it worked in a test tube. You had to order it from Japan, and so we each had contributed, like, a bunch of money. I know it was like hundreds of dollars to get it, but it didn't work."

PART II

The Dynamics of Effective Action

This detailed analysis of the anatomy of ACT UP's first major action, Seize Control of the FDA, reveals why, and how, it worked: the innovative choice of the right target, the infrastructure of internal lobbying within the movement, the national reach of organizing, the complex media strategy, and the use of the Inside/Outside approach, sometimes with and sometimes without the knowledge of the full body. All of these elements and agendas converged, effectively forcing the government to change. This analysis is contrasted with a look at Stop the Church, ACT UP's notorious action at St. Patrick's Cathedral. Given ACT UP's flexible organization, two actions could emerge that had dramatically different origins, that grew somewhat organically, and that landed with distinct consequences, creating very different kinds of long-lasting impact.

3

Choosing the Right Target: Seize Control of the FDA

ACT UP's action at the Food and Drug Administration headquarters on October 11, 1988, was the first major victory for the movement, and also its first national mobilization. It significantly improved the lives of thousands of people by getting them access to experimental medications. Although hundreds, if not thousands, of people created the action Seize Control of the FDA, here we can only look at four emblematic individual activists who, thanks to their cumulative insights and approaches, facilitated the overtaking of the federal drug approval process by a grassroots activist movement of sick and dying people and their friends. David Barr was among those who strategized this bold action to pressure for change. Gregg Bordowitz was one of the implementers, creating consensus on the ground. Michelangelo Signorile and Ann Northrop were media professionals who, with their colleagues, reinvented and reinvigorated the role of media/public relations activists. The initiating action of choosing the right target—one that was not predictable—in a sense allowed all kinds of innovations in preparation, execution, and communication of both the movement and its demands to follow. Understanding the inner workings of Seize Control of the FDA can serve as a primer for activists in all movements, specifically how innovation must be expressed at all levels in order to produce the dynamic synchronicity that creates substantial change.

GREGG BORDOWITZ

When Gregg Bordowitz was growing up on Long Island, he was threatened and got into fights in high school "for being kind of a faggy teen," because of the things he was interested in, like punk music. "I was one of these art geeks who used to get picked on all the time."

He moved to the East Village and lived in an open relationship with his girlfriend, while also having sex with men and with other women. "Gay identity was for clones that had their culture going on on the other side of town. We were *free of labels*. I didn't know anyone who was identified as *gay*." In the mid-1980s, Gregg became aware that he might have picked up HIV from having unprotected sex with men, and, like Moisés Agosto-Rosario, he found his way to the Gay Center to get health care from the Community Health Project. He felt welcomed there and supported.

Going to the Gay Center was a very profound experience for Gregg, and it changed his worldview. First, it was then and there that he decided he would become "a citizen of this gay community, whatever that meant." He felt very indebted to the gay community. Gregg remembered looking up at the Center's sign, pondering what the notion of community was, and realizing that a community is a group of people who need one another. The people at the Center and the Community Health Project didn't know him, but he could tell that they had dealt with a lot of people like him. As a result, it was the pivotal turning point in his life around that time, the moment when he started to get more politicized about issues of identity and became much more knowledgeable about AIDS.

As an art student in the Whitney Museum Independent Study Program (ISP), Gregg focused his first video project on AIDS. *Some Aspect of a Shared Lifestyle* took its title from the *Morbidity and Mortality Weekly Report*, which first published the news about gay men in New York and San Francisco who had cancer and pneumonia. With David Meieran, another video maker and graduate of ISP, Gregg started showing up to gay demonstrations with cameras. The first events they taped were protests in response to the Supreme Court's 1986 *Bowers v. Hardwick* decision. This 5–4 ruling upheld the Georgia sodomy laws maintaining that gay sex in a private home between consenting adults was illegal. Gregg started to identify for a time as gay.

Five years into the AIDS crisis, the Supreme Court's ruling was devastating for gay Americans. At a time when the governing powers should have been helping people with AIDS, forty thousand of whom had already died, the Court hurt and punished gay people even more. Justice Byron White wrote for the majority that sodomy is neither "deeply rooted in this Nation's history" nor "implicit in the concept of ordered liberty." Chief Justice Warren Burger agreed, adding that decriminalizing gay sex would "cast aside a millennia [*sic*] of moral teaching." This focus on "sodomy" unleashed even more public hysteria about anal sex as a mode of AIDS transmission, leaving the embattled gay and AIDS community more isolated and abandoned.

In March 1987, David and Gregg saw a poster in the Christopher Street subway station advertising a demonstration by a new organization, ACT UP, at Wall Street. "We said, *We're gonna go there with cameras. That's the next step. That's what the Hardwick protests are leading us to. This is the most important issue that's confronting the gay community* . . . So we had been making these links." They were aware of the growing homophobia around them, the threat of quarantine and mass mandatory testing, "which was a legitimate fear at the time." Earlier that year, conservative pundit William F. Buckley Jr. had written in *The New York Times* that "AIDS carriers" should be tattooed.

The ACT UP demonstration, later known as First Wall Street, was called for 7:00 a.m. in front of Trinity Church on March 24, 1987. There were seven demands:

1. Immediate release by the Federal Food & Drug Administration of drugs that might help save our lives. [These drugs included Ribavirin (ICM Pharmaceuticals), Ampligen (HMR Research Co.), Glucan (Tulane University School of Medicine), DTC (Merieux), DDC (Hoffmann-La Roche), MTP-PE (Ciba-Geigy), and AL-721 (Praxis Pharmaceuticals).]
2. Immediate abolishment of cruel double-blind studies wherein some get the new drugs and some don't.
3. Immediate release of these drugs to everyone with AIDS or ARC.
4. Immediate availability of these drugs at affordable prices. Curb your greed!
5. Immediate massive public education to stop the spread of AIDS.

6. Immediate policy to prohibit discrimination in AIDS treatment, insurance, employment, housing.
7. Immediate establishment of a coordinated, comprehensive and compassionate national policy on AIDS.

President Reagan, nobody is in charge!
AIDS IS THE BIGGEST KILLER IN NEW YORK CITY OF
YOUNG MEN AND WOMEN
You must be on time!

ACT UP had been founded only a few weeks earlier. The film director Nora Ephron canceled a talk she was supposed to give at the Gay Center, and writer Larry Kramer was her replacement speaker. Larry had already cofounded the Gay Men's Health Crisis in 1982, initially to stimulate research, but he quickly found himself at odds with the other leaders about tactics of confrontation, which he favored, and was excluded from the organization. These events are depicted in his 1985 play, *The Normal Heart.* Larry called a number of friends and activists and asked them to come to the Center. He made a passionate, desperate plea to the audience that night to take action. He famously informed the crowd, "In five years, half of you will be dead!" A few days later a larger group came together, chose the name AIDS Coalition To Unleash Power, and planned their first action. Listing the names of pharmaceutical companies in their first leaflet showed ACT UP's orientation from the start. It was a movement that addressed corporate power and greed as strongly as governmental indifference. Their demands also revealed that, from the start, the Food and Drug Administration was seen as a key obstacle to getting treatment.

The ACT UP action at Wall Street was a turning point for Gregg. There he met his future collaborator, the lesbian film and video artist Jean Carlomusto. He also confronted the anger of the movement for the first time. "I was upset that people were shouting, *You could get it, too.* I thought it was politically bad. I thought it would be politically alienating . . . It was a kind of anger, and vibrancy, and honesty that I hadn't encountered yet in other kinds of activism or protest. It seemed very personal." Approximately 250 demonstrators showed up for this first action, and 17 were arrested for civil disobedience.

David and Gregg showed up to the next Monday-night meeting with cameras, seeing themselves as traditional "documentarians." They didn't conceptualize themselves at first as being part of the action. So they were upset when people didn't want to let them film, and when Larry and others had no interest in being interviewed. Everyone who was present was expected to be active. Gregg's first real participation was on June 1, 1987, when he went to Washington, D.C., on an ACT UP bus to join other gay groups in a mass civil disobedience on the steps of the Supreme Court.

Gregg and David Meieran were accompanied by videographers Hilery Kipnis, Robyn Hutt, and Sandra Elgear. They formed the Testing the Limits Collective together, and in the process of filming every action as ACT UP grew, they also started to develop a conceptual role for documentary filmmaking that functioned as part of a movement instead of being separate and outside. This would come to be known as video activism.

Gregg got together with Charles Stimson and Ortez Alderson, an activist from Chicago who had moved to New York to become an actor and who was working in Black gay theater with Assotto Saint. They decided to get together to "do a kind of activism that was not necessarily authorized by the large group." They were annoyed by what they felt was a slow pace as ACT UP grappled to develop their perspective. They called themselves "MHA," which actually didn't stand for anything, but had flexible uses. For example, they used "Metropolitan Health Association" in order to get a meeting with Stephen Joseph, the health commissioner of New York City.

At that time, Joseph was talking about various kinds of punitive measures against prostitutes. He had engaged in some "very panic-causing kinds of rhetoric" about the threat that people with AIDS, for whom he was considering internment and other repressive measures, caused to the general public, particularly around tuberculosis. MHA showed up. "We said, 'We're the Metropolitan Health Association.' They said, 'Please come in.'" They were in a large conference room with Stephen Joseph. It quickly became apparent, though, that MHA was not any kind of interborough health consortium. They started asking Joseph about the slow pace in the city's response to AIDS. When Joseph realized that they were AIDS activists, Gregg and company were arrested and the story appeared in the press.

At the next ACT UP meeting, Gregg remembers rising and saying, "Look, you can just do this. You don't have to go to the large group to get authorization. In fact, it's better that the large group is not involved with these kinds of actions because they don't have to be held accountable. So you can just do stuff. ACT UP is just this place we all meet on a weekly basis to talk about strategy and prioritize issues." He remembered saying over and over again, *You can just do this. Just go out and do this.* And people were very enthusiastic. This happened at the same time that the concept of affinity groups, which were inherently autonomous from the larger body, was gaining more popularity in ACT UP.

Then, in 1988, Gregg tested positive for HIV.

"I did a crazy thing. I tested positive in the afternoon, on a Monday, and I went directly to the meeting and announced that I had tested positive. I have spent many years thinking about why I did that, particularly since I had sexual partners in the room. There was a number of people I was sleeping with at that time, who were in the room, whom I hadn't told before I announced it to the group. In the end, I think it had to do with fear—and economy. I didn't want to go through this alone, and I also didn't want to have face-to-face meetings with anybody. I was just like, *I'll announce it and it will go through the rumor mill. And I just won't have to tell anybody. Everyone will know who needs to know, and that's it.*"

But also, the decision coincided with something else. There was a period in ACT UP when Gregg felt it was taboo to identify as a person with HIV within the group. "It's hard to imagine, but you'd be sitting in this room and you would assume that most of the men in this room were positive or had lovers who were positive." But Gregg felt that almost no one spoke out—he remembered that only Michael Callen and Griffin Gold would announce that they were people with AIDS before they spoke. He doesn't recall anyone else doing that in ACT UP at any of the early meetings. Gregg decided that it was important that people in the group be honest about their status to one another, that we couldn't have a stigma, a secrecy within the group. "There was no need within the group to internalize the stigma attached to being a person with AIDS out in the world. It was nothing to be ashamed of."

Gregg remembered that announcing his HIV status at the meeting produced stunned gasps. "A few people rolled their eyes. Later, Mark Harrington told me he thought it was the cheapest, most manipulative way to get people to come to my action. It was in the context of some needle exchange I was organizing. But a lot of people came up afterward and asked if they could be of any help. You know, at that time I was crazed. I was told that I had like a year or two to live, statistically. I knew through ACT UP that there were people with AIDS who were living longer than that, but statistically at that time in history I had a year or so. I was twenty-four or twenty-three . . . I wasn't going to live with it alone."

There weren't many treatment decisions to make in those days. It was AZT or not AZT. And the existing drugs were harsh, so Gregg had to decide on the basis of how he was feeling whether or not it was worth it for him to continue with a medication. He went on AZT when it was being administered in a huge dose, and he had to get a pillbox with an alarm to be reminded to take it three times a day. After he started taking AZT, they cut the dose in half, but the side effects of the first dose lingered. "That was terrible, awful—jittery, diarrhea. There was this awful feeling of 'blech' throughout your entire body."

STRATEGIZING INTERNALLY FOR THE FDA ACTION

One day, in 1988, David Barr and Mickey Wheatley, two members of the newly named Treatment and Data Committee, invited Gregg out to lunch at the Cloister Cafe on Ninth Street, then one of the nicest places to eat in the East Village. By this time, Gregg had become very comfortable speaking at meetings, and he spoke often. "I remember having this kind of conscious realization that if you stood up and said exactly what you meant and didn't trail off into some kind of rambling incoherence, which is often the style of many people in meetings, that actually your opinion would be respected or at least heard."

David Barr and Mickey Wheatley had picked up on this. *Gregg*, he remembered them saying, *you're becoming a very visible leader within ACT UP. When you speak, people listen to you and your opinion carries a lot of weight within the group.* They said, *Look, we have this idea for a strategy that would be very different than things that have been tried before in activism . . . Many groups have gone to Washington and protested in front of the White House. Many groups have protested in front of Congress. For our movement, we need to go to the Food and Drug Administration. This is very specific. This is an institution that is very specific to the issues that we're facing.* They wanted to cut through the bureaucratic red tape of the FDA. "But more than that, [they wanted] people with AIDS [to] be involved in every level of decision-making concerning research for a treatment and a cure for our disease." It was the seventh year of the AIDS crisis, and the FDA had shown a sluggishness on approving drugs. There was also an unwillingness to test HIV drugs. There were about thirty drugs in the pipeline that ACT UP thought were promising and that the FDA had back-burnered and not pushed through to the testing process. So there was a history of slow response. It was on the basis of that history that they had the idea.

At first Gregg was kind of reluctant.

"It was very strange. It was like . . . some kind of Hollywood pitch. They literally took me out to lunch . . . and said, *You, you're the new leader. Don't you understand? People listen to you. When you stand up, people listen to you . . .* I didn't think I was a leader or anything like that at that point. They said, *No, you're really like one of the up-and-coming leaders and you have to take responsibility for that. We want to do this. We want to approach the group to do this.* So they convinced me. I think I made an announcement that a working group would form around this idea. Then, because I was going to at least one meeting, sometimes two meetings a night, the idea got filtered out pretty quickly among the various smaller groups . . . David was working in the Treatment and Data group to gain consensus about the FDA being the target. I was working through the various action committees to gain consensus for the idea."

Soon ACT UP embraced Gregg's proposal.

"So I became aware of this, and I'm sure other people were aware of this as well, that if you wanted to present an idea to the group, and you wanted to win consensus, then you had to do a certain amount of campaigning within the group. You couldn't just come up with a speech that would sway hearts and minds on the floor on Monday night. You had to develop that speech, you had to develop that rhetoric, and you had to do a lot of face-to-face politicking along the way in order to gain consensus. I don't think there's anything ominous about this. This is how grassroots democratic politics [works]. To a certain extent, this is how democratic politics is supposed to work in general. You convince people of the validity of your ideas. You have to go out there and convince people . . . Why would it be important for people of color to go to the FDA? Why would it be important for women? What would be the issues for people of color? What would be the issues for women? What would be the issues for gay men? What would be the issues for people with AIDS, in general?

"It was a constant process, this process of ideas having to meet the test of consensus. Even though it wasn't a consensus-driven group, we voted. But in order to get votes, you had to develop a certain amount of foundational consensus. And in order to get foundational consensus, the ideas had to meet a series of tests on what were the concerns of the group . . . and the concerns of the group were coalition politics, feminist politics, race politics, sexual politics, the causes of the members of the groups and their various interests and needs."

DAVID BARR

David is a third-generation New Yorker involved in social justice. His father, Sherman Barr, a social worker, was one of the founders of Mobilization for Youth, a foundational antipoverty program in the 1960s. At experimental public high school John Dewey, he became exposed to avant-garde theater and enrolled at New York University (NYU), but he dropped out in 1972 to be part of The Performance Group, an environmental theater company run by Richard Schechner and Joseph Chaikin.

In 1982, David started as part of the first class at the City University of New York (CUNY) Law School, which was dedicated to public interest. There he was mentored by a series of lesbian activist lawyers, including Rhonda Copelon, who had represented a client challenging the Hyde Amendment in front of the Supreme Court. She got him interested in gay rights litigation. He interned with Nan Hunter, a free speech activist, at the ACLU, and "was the only guy in the room" who witnessed her high-pulse debate with antipornography attorney Catharine MacKinnon at the Women and the Law Conference. Abby Rubenfeld was codirecting Lambda Legal—a civil rights organization focused on LGBT people and HIV-positive people—down the hall, and David interned there as Lambda tried to challenge the licensing of the newly invented HIV test, because there was no confidentiality mandate. They lost. This was followed by an "AIDS legal crisis" of discrimination cases with no precedent. Logging information as the intern answering the phone, he started *AIDS Update*, the first AIDS legal newsletter. "It was all moving very fast . . . and there was no sense of control over anything that was happening."

Because of the lack of confidentiality, activists took a position against being tested for HIV. The reality was that there were no treatments anyway, so testing positive created new problems and produced no solutions. Very little was known about the disease. "At the time it was all myth and rumors." AIDS was attributed to poppers, fisting, having a thousand partners—theories ran wild. In 1986, while clerking with a housing judge, David noticed white spots on his tongue but ignored them.

He was hired by Lambda to do AIDS policy law in 1987. Early focus was on discrimination, immigration, and confidentiality. He read about ACT UP's action at Wall Street and went to a general meeting that was held at NYU Law School to plan the concentration camp float for Gay Pride. "Everybody was fighting but it was passionate," and "the erotic energy was really compelling." He joined the Issues Committee, which soon merged into its subgroup Treatment and Data. They met at the loft of Herb Spiers on Nineteenth Street and Park Avenue. The first group included Iris Long, Jim Eigo, David Kirschenbaum, Margaret McCarthy, Bill Bahlman, Marty Robinson, and Carey Stiegel.

The focus of discussion when David joined was clinical trials. Where were they? How did people get into them? How could ACT UP get access to their results? How do they contact the NIH? T&D filed a FOIA request to get information from the government, which did not want it released. "They didn't know who we were." It was Iris Long who really "started it." David remembered her saying, *"You people need to learn about how drugs are developed, you need to understand the biology, you need to understand clinical research.* And she just started to teach everybody." He finally decided to undergo testing in 1989 and was confirmed to be HIV-positive.

David also told me a story different from Gregg's about the origins of the FDA action.

"The idea for the FDA demonstration came out of a lunch that Gregg Bordowitz and I had at Dojo, on St. Mark's Place. And we were talking, Gregg was talking about the need to do a national action . . . By this time ACT UP chapters had sprung up around the U.S., just by word of mouth. It wasn't like ACT UP in New York said, *Let's create ACT UP Kansas City*. Somebody would read an article in some paper and say, *Oh, let's do it here.* And then it was global, ACT UP chapters [sprang] up in other countries all over the world using our model . . . I don't know if they knew what we were actually doing, or what the model really was. But it meant it flashed for people, and they took it on . . .

"It seemed like it was time to bring everybody together and do something together. And Gregg wanted to organize a national action; the first national action. And I was heavily involved in fighting with the FDA over expanded access, and felt like *This, right now, that is our key issue, is access to experimental drugs, and dealing with the FDA on this.* And that should be the focal point for this demonstration. We need to go there en masse. And so Gregg and I sort of talked it through. We came up with the vision of what it ought to be; and we brought it to the floor. And [we] presented the idea, and said, *We want to do a major demonstration at the Food and Drug Administration. Do you want to do it?* The floor talked about it; voted and approved it, that night."

This is one of the key moments in AIDS activism on a number of levels. Most important, I assert, was the creative thinking of organizers—and I lean toward Gregg's version of events unfolding, so I will attribute the original thinking to David Barr—that the *target* was conceptually so important. The target couldn't be generic. It couldn't be a place demonstrators had been to over and over again. The target could not be a *symbol*; it had to be *actual*. It had to be the exact building where the problem was being housed. And so by choosing to break the mold of *location*, David and Mickey Wheatley opened the door for a whole new wave of creative thinking.

But also hidden in these two conflicting versions is, I think, that while David was doing something necessary and game-changing strategically, he chose to do it in a way that reinscribed whatever instincts or remnants of identification with white male power structures he was still invested in. He was playing puppet master in a way that created a new prince, one who had already captured people's hearts. He didn't go to a Black or Latino PWA, or to a woman. He kept the power network on the old model. This practice, this way of doing queer AIDS politics white man to white man, would not negate the lives saved; in fact, given how white and male the power structure was, this approach may have been more effective. But the impulse toward secrecy, toward a hidden game plan inside ACT UP, would be the shadow of future structural conflicts that contributed to the split and thereby the diminishment of the organization. People were dying, and perhaps they felt, in the sense of emotional *feeling*, that having another white man front the action would be more effective. And being effective was the larger objective. And, as uncomfortable as it is to consider, without ever being able to know for sure, perhaps they would have been right in the short term for people who only had a short term. Perhaps, however, at a very high cost to those who live in the long term.

By 1988, New York wasn't the only player. As David noted, ACT UP chapters had started to spring up around the country and around the world. Therefore, the next step was to try to get national consensus. A few weeks after the FDA plan began, ACT UP New York sent a handful of activists to a national gathering in San Francisco on July Fourth weekend. This was the very first meeting of representatives from different ACT UP chapters. Gregg says that the messengers were him and Robert Vázquez-Pacheco and Deb Levine. David says that he went with Gregg and Robert. Mary Patten and Ferd Eggan of ACT UP Chicago were there. ACT UP LA was represented, as were ACT UP San Francisco and a few other groups.

GREGG BORDOWITZ

In San Francisco, Gregg and ACT UP New York found opposition to their innovative concept. They went through a three-day process during which, Gregg said, "we just basically, through repetition and will, convinced everybody that the Food and Drug Administration was the place to be." There was a contingent of people that thought the action should go to Congress . . . *Why bother with this regulatory institution?* . . . Go to the White House, the president. Gregg had to battle and work through again with the national folks his and Robert and Deb and David's belief that to make the AIDS activist movement significant and singular, and directly address the issues that were specific to us, we needed a new kind of thinking, a savvier notion of what the target should be, a savvier way of dealing with the media. And they succeeded in convincing the national group. They came back to New York with a sense of victory, and Gregg remembered being ecstatic that they had convinced all the national groups to all go to the FDA. Gregg, Robert, Deb, and David went directly from the airport to the ACT UP meeting, thinking they would announce their success and the group would be excited and appreciative, but the ACT UP meeting couldn't find time on the agenda. "We had to wait until the next week."

DAVID BARR

In David's memory, the national groups were all fighting with one another about what the object of the demonstration should be: *We should go to the White House; we should go to the Capitol; and we should go to Health and Human Services.*

"I felt like Gregg and I were just kind of sitting back. Because, we were *New York*. We were three times more people than all those other chapters put together, and we just kind of let the conversation go on. And then eventually, we said, *The action's going to be at the Food and Drug Administration. New York's already made this decision. You can go anywhere you want, but New York is going to the FDA.* And—that shook everybody up real bad. And then there was some compromise, which was, there'll be a rally the day before at HHS."

The national coalition to build the FDA action was called ACT NOW, and Gregg was the official representative from New York. The coordination was conducted by telephone, on conference calls. Propelling such a complex and large demonstration both inside ACT UP New York and nationally took focus and influence.

GREGG BORDOWITZ

There were many different informal structures within ACT UP. The group was very intimate. "Like all groups, there were lines of communication, various loops—you know, popularity, credibility, all these things played a role . . . The group also had a very kind of anarchic quality to it." Gregg stood up every week in front of the group and talked up the action, built up support for the action, dramatized it. He came up with the idea that he would start counting the days until we took over the FDA, "because it didn't seem real. It didn't seem real to people."

It was the largest event ACT UP had tried to date. It was the first time we were going to be busing people to another city. The machine was still being built. Gregg started to realize that from the organizational standpoint, people weren't really jumping into action. There were housing issues that needed to be sorted, and poster making, and signing up people on the buses. "Were we really going to deliver a significant contingent? How were we going to interact with all the other ACT UPs? Could we do something coordinated? In the end, we adopted the kind of brilliant strategy of the decentralized model, the affinity group model." In this way, affinity groups could do anything they wanted, within parameters. There was a lot of difference within the groups and among the groups. Gregg had started using a kind of language—"I had a kind of fantasy about what kind of activist language it should be. So I had come up with this slogan, 'Seize Control of the FDA.' That was frightening to many people, this notion of seizing control. But I was very insistent . . . *People with AIDS are going to take over the agency and run it in our own interests.*"

ACT UP was not one monolithic institution. It was a group of people who met every Monday night. Many of them were parts of smaller groups, or cells, or affinity groups within the larger group. And those affinity groups to some extent had, if not a separate life, a life outside the group. So it was much more molecular in structure.

"The meetings were very interesting. Once I really got in the inside of ACT UP, there was a period where I never sat on the large meeting. I was always doing business on the side . . . It was roiling. The feeling of ACT UP in its heyday—this was like 1988—when the room was packed, and you could hardly get into the ground floor of the Gay Center. If the weather was nice, the meeting spills out into the courtyard. There is business happening all over the place. It's very difficult for the people who are actually running the meeting to get the attention of the group. There is all kinds of sexiness going on, as well. There is all kinds of cruising going on the sides, and eye catching, and chattiness. There was an energy in the group that was amazing, because it was filled with people who had ideas, filled with people who had energies, filled with a kind of erotic energy. And all that came together. It was in some ways like a bazaar of desires. So it was amazing that anything got done. An enormous amount got done."

Gregg watched as the FDA action planning shifted the group away from a defensive posture to an offensive posture. The FDA action put ACT UP on the offense and enabled us to come up with a vision for the way that health care should be implemented in this country, the way that drugs should be researched, and sold, and made available. Most important to Gregg was the idea that people with AIDS should be at the center of the public discussion. We weren't just making statements that responded to assaults from the right. We had our own agenda. "We were just going to seize control of the FDA and run the fucking thing ourselves. We knew that we weren't actually going to do that, but this was it. We were just going to seize control. This was why it was so important, even though many people found that frightening—I was told, *Gregg, back off of that rhetoric.* But I just thought it was incredibly important to stay on point."

The day before the action, there was the rally at the U.S. Department of Health and Human Services (HHS) in Washington, D.C. An important tactical insight was established by separating the rally from the action. ACT UP actions did not have speakers talking to passive audiences. ACT UP actions were participatory for everyone, as facilitated by the affinity group structure. But because of the needs of the national groups to have some kind of experience of coalescing, it was decided that we would all gather and hear a speech. And that was the rally where Vito Russo made his historic "Why We Fight" declaration.

WHY WE FIGHT

A friend of mine in New York City has a half-fare transit card, which means that you get on buses and subways for half price. And the other day, when he showed his card to the token attendant, the attendant asked what his disability was and he said, I have AIDS. And the attendant said, no you don't, if you had AIDS, you'd be home dying. And so, I wanted to speak out today as a person with AIDS who is not dying.

You know, for the last three years, since I was diagnosed, my family thinks two things about my situation. One, they think I'm going to die, and two, they think that my government is doing absolutely everything in their power to stop that. And they're wrong, on both counts.

So, if I'm dying from anything, I'm dying from homophobia. If I'm dying from anything, I'm dying from racism. If I'm dying from anything, it's from indifference and red tape, because these are the things that are preventing an end to this crisis. If I'm dying from anything, I'm dying from Jesse Helms. If I'm dying from anything, I'm dying from the President of the United States. And, especially, if I'm dying from anything, I'm dying from the sensationalism of newspapers and magazines and television shows, which are interested in me, as a human interest story—only as long as I'm willing to be a helpless victim, but not if I'm fighting for my life.

If I'm dying from anything, I'm dying from the fact that not enough rich, white, heterosexual men have gotten AIDS for anybody to give a shit. You know, living with AIDS in this country is like living in the twilight zone. Living with AIDS is like living through a war which is happening only for those people who happen to be in the trenches. Every time a shell explodes, you look around and you discover that you've lost more of your friends, but nobody else notices. It isn't happening to them. They're walking the streets as though we weren't living through some sort of nightmare. And only you can hear the screams of the people who are dying and their cries for help. No one else seems to be noticing.

And it's worse than a war, because during a war people are united in a shared experience. This war has not united us, it's divided us. It's separated those of us with AIDS and those of us who fight for people with AIDS from the rest of the population.

Two and a half years ago, I picked up *Life* [magazine], and I read an editorial which said, "It's time to pay attention, because this disease is now beginning to strike the rest of us." It was as if I wasn't the one holding the magazine in my hand.

And since then, nothing has changed to alter the perception that AIDS is not happening to the real people in this country.

It's not happening to us in the United States, it's happening to them—to the disposable populations of fags and junkies who deserve what they get. The media tells them that they don't have to care, because the people who really matter are not in danger. Twice, three times, four times—*The New York Times* has published editorials saying, don't panic yet, over AIDS—it still hasn't entered the general population, and until it does, we don't have to give a shit.

And the days, and the months, and the years pass by, and they don't spend those days and nights and months and years trying to figure out how to get hold of the latest experimental drug, and which dose to take it at, and in what combination with other drugs, and from what source? And how are you going to pay for it? And where are you going to get it? Because it isn't happening to them, so they don't give a shit.

And they don't sit in television studios, surrounded by technicians who are wearing rubber gloves, who won't put a microphone on you, because it isn't happening to them, so they don't give a shit. And they don't have their houses burned down by bigots and morons. They watch it on the news and they have dinner and they go to bed, because it isn't happening to them, and they don't give a shit.

And they don't spend their waking hours going from hospital room to hospital room, and watching the people that they love die slowly—of neglect and bigotry, because it isn't happening to them and they don't have to give a shit. They haven't been to two funerals a week for the last three or four or five years—so they don't give a shit, because it's not happening to them.

And we read on the front page of *The New York Times* last Saturday that Anthony Fauci now says that all sorts of promising drugs for treatment haven't even been tested in the last two years because he can't afford to hire the people to test them. We're supposed to be grateful that this story has appeared in the newspaper after two years. Nobody wonders why some reporter didn't dig up that story and print it 18 months ago, before Fauci got dragged before a congressional hearing.

How many people are dead in the last two years, who might be alive today, if those drugs had been tested more quickly? Reporters all over the country are busy printing government press releases. They don't give a shit, it isn't happening to them—meaning that it isn't happening to people like them—the real people, the world-famous general public we all keep hearing about.

[Legionnaires' disease] was happening to them because it hit people who looked like them, who sounded like them, who were the same color as them. And that fucking story about a couple of dozen people hit the front page of every newspaper and magazine in this country, and it stayed there until that mystery got solved.

All I read in the newspapers tells me that the mainstream, white heterosexual population is not at risk for this disease. All the newspapers I read tell me that IV drug users and homosexuals still account for the overwhelming majority of cases, and a majority of those people at risk.

And can somebody please tell me why every single penny allocated for education and prevention gets spent on ad campaigns that are directed almost exclusively to white, heterosexual teenagers—who they keep telling us are not at risk!

Can somebody tell me why the only television movie ever produced by a major network in this country, about the impact of this disease, is not about the impact of this disease on the man who has AIDS, but of the impact of AIDS on his white, straight, nuclear family? Why, for eight years, every newspaper and magazine in this country has done cover stories on AIDS only when the threat of heterosexual transmission is raised?

Why, for eight years, every single educational film designed for use in high schools has eliminated any gay positive material, before being approved by the Board of Education? Why, for eight years, every single public information pamphlet and videotape distributed by establishment sources has ignored specific homosexual content?

Why is every bus and subway ad I read and every advertisement and every billboard I see in this country specifically not directed at gay men? Don't believe the lie that the gay community has done its job and done it well and educated its people. The gay community and IV drug users are not all politicized people living in New York and San Francisco. Members of minority populations, including so called sophisticated gay men are abysmally ignorant about AIDS.

If it is true that gay men and IV drug users are the populations at risk for this disease, then we have a right to demand that education and prevention be targeted specifically to these people. And it is not happening. We are being allowed to die, while low risk populations are being panicked—not educated, panicked—into believing that we deserve to die.

Why are we here together today? We're here because it is happening to us, and we do give a shit. And if there were more of us, AIDS wouldn't be what it is at this moment in history. It's more than just a disease, which ignorant people have turned into an excuse to exercise the bigotry they have always felt.

It is more than a horror story, exploited by the tabloids. AIDS is really a test of us, as a people. When future generations ask what we did in this crisis, we're going to have to tell them that we were out here today. And we have to leave the legacy to those generations of people who will come after us.

Someday, the AIDS crisis will be over. Remember that. And when that day comes—when that day has come and gone, there'll be people alive on this earth—gay people and straight people, men and women, black and white, who will hear the story that once there was a terrible disease in this country and all over the world, and that a brave group of people stood up and fought and, in some cases, gave their lives, so that other people might live and be free.

So, I'm proud to be with my friends today and the people I love, because I think you're all heroes, and I'm glad to be part of this fight. But, to borrow a phrase from Michael Callen's song: all we have is love right now, what we don't have is time.

In a lot of ways, AIDS activists are like those doctors out there—they're so busy putting out fires and taking care of people on respirators, that they don't have the time to take care of all the sick people. We're so busy putting out fires right now, that we don't have the time to talk to each other and strategize and plan for the next wave, and the next day, and next month and the next week and the next year.

And, we're going to have to find the time to do that in the next few months. And, we have to commit ourselves to doing that. And then, after we kick the shit out of this disease, we're all going to be alive to kick the shit out of this system, so that this never happens again.

DAVID BARR

The FDA demonstration was pivotal. It solidified the affinity group structure, because so many affinity groups were created for that action. It was the first national action with participation from other chapters. It was the point where the joining together of the theater and the media machine became solidified. "They had done the press work so well that I remember Michelangelo [Signorile], being on the bullhorn, in that weird rubber jacket he used to wear—*Person with AIDS from Minnesota, here*, to bring the Minnesota-paper [reporter] guy over there."

According to David, there were only a thousand people at the FDA action, yet the action itself was the prototype for many to come. It was not a traditional "rally," with people standing passively listening to speakers or marching around with signs. It was a simultaneous happening. Affinity groups had been formed to do small, independent actions—one group appeared in white lab coats with bloody handprints on their chests, another did a die-in, holding cardboard gravestones over their heads. Peter Staley climbed on top of the awning structure with a warrior headband around his brow. Everywhere people were responding at the same time in different ways that made sense to them. It looked much, much larger on television than it actually was because it was so theatrical. And there had never been a demonstration at the FDA before, ever. The headquarters was a completely nondescript office building in the middle of suburban Maryland, and it was suddenly on the front page of every major newspaper in the country except *The New York Times*, where it was buried. It was the lead story on all the nightly newscasts. This was really the start of the national AIDS movement.

MEDIA FOR A MOVEMENT

The FDA action was the debut of ACT UP's media strategy, one that required seizing the message. Experienced journalists, publicists, and newcomers developed original strategies for getting the message out in an environment in which corporate media ignored or distorted the reality of AIDS and its consequences.

ANN NORTHROP

Ann Northrop's family were "all rock-ribbed Republicans. And the most political involvement they had was sitting around the dinner table, complaining that Richard Nixon got a raw deal."

At Vassar in the fall of 1966, she had a transformation and became a demonstrator against the Vietnam War. She graduated in 1970, a turbulent moment with the invasion of Cambodia and the killings by the National Guard, at both Kent State and Jackson State. Hers was one of several hundred colleges that were on strike that spring. Classes were canceled; exams were canceled. The students all wore peace signs on their mortarboards when they graduated. Ann was instrumental in getting Gloria Steinem to be the graduation speaker, and Steinem quoted Black Panther Party cofounder Huey Newton in her speech. "It was a tremendously fascinating time, and I was enormously compelled intellectually and emotionally by what was going on."

She began a career in television and media, but also had known for a long time that she was a lesbian. "People who think they have the most to lose are the most reluctant to come out, I think, and I think that was partially my story . . . People who don't come out now—men in corporate jobs, for instance—are people who are afraid of assuming minority status, and I think that was a lot of what I felt." So she decided that what she would do was have a big career and no social life. And, in fact, that did happen through most of her twenties. Ann didn't end up coming out until she was almost thirty.

Fascinated by war correspondents and by the media, she ended up finding a job in Washington, at the *National Journal*, which covers the federal government. She went to the Supreme Court for the hearings on the Pentagon Papers case, then got a job in New York, working on a local feminist talk show on Channel 2 called *Woman* in the fall of 1971. After the show was canceled, she worked in local operations at Channel 2, then freelanced for ABC Sports. She worked on the first is-sue of *Ms.* magazine, then as a writer at *Good Morning America* in 1981, and at *CBS Morning News* from 1982 to 1987, when she quit, decid-ing to pursue something more meaningful. She soon met her longtime collaborator, Andy Humm, then at the Harvey Milk High School for LGBT students who had been harassed out of regular public education. Many of them were sexually active early, and became infected. Harvey Milk High School was an AIDS-saturated environment. Both of the founders, Dr. Emery Hetrick, a psychiatrist, and Dr. Damien Martin, a professor at NYU, died of AIDS. Andy hired Ann to be an advocate for AIDS education at the school, even though she had not known anyone with AIDS. When she arrived, there was a funeral for a student who had just died.

"I immediately figured out that this was the Vietnam War all over again." For Ann, the AIDS crisis was about people in power not caring about the lives of people who didn't have power, and being willing to accept a system of attrition in which people would die, and while cer-tainly it was about gay men, it was also about race and sex and class. It became very clear to her that the AIDS crisis was the equivalent of the war, all these years later. And when she then found out about ACT UP, about six months into her new job, and learned that there were peo-ple going out in the streets and demonstrating, as she had done some of in antiwar and women's movements, Ann thought, *Wow, here's my home. This is what I can get involved in, because this is what feels good to me.* On March 1, 1988, she attended her first Monday-night meeting of ACT UP.

"It was truly love at first sight for me, in that room. And I immediately recognized it as a bunch of cranky individualists who clearly couldn't get along with any authority figure anywhere and were just all there, being themselves and arguing with each other, and getting stuff done, and having a great time. I never looked back . . . and got arrested for the first time, at the end of that month, in the first anniversary action at Wall Street on lower Broadway with a couple of hundred people . . . Why, in a country as rich as this, do we have so many people living in misery and in terrible conditions? And it's because people in power don't care. It's because all they care about is their own ambition . . . I think that gay white men thought they had privilege in this country and were shocked to find out they didn't, and that people in power were prepared to let them die. And when they figured that out, they got very angry about it—a lot of them."

Ann had a lot to do with helping activists understand and manipulate the media, in order to use it to our own ends. What she understood when she went to the Harvey Milk High School and got involved in ACT UP, and started to learn about the epidemic, was "how ignorant I was—as a journalist, in spite of having been aware of [AIDS] from the first reports of 1981. I really didn't get it, as a journalist. And that made me understand that journalists, in general, don't get it." She also discovered, in going to work for a social service agency, that journalists "do not understand life, in general, and that they sit in their little submarine offices with no windows and work very long hours and work very hard but have very little interaction with human beings and do not understand what's going on out in the world." That was shocking to her—to learn how ignorant she had been, and how ignorant journalists in general were.

Ann did a lot of thinking and started hosting media trainings for ACT UP, where she would begin by saying, "There are two words you need to know, in thinking about journalists: ignorant and arrogant. They know nothing, but they think they know everything. And therefore, they don't want to listen. If you're going to teach them, you have to do it in a manipulative way, because if you go to them and say, *You don't understand this*, they say, *Fuck you, go away. I know everything, I am a journalist* . . . You had to know that the main approach is to flatter the press."

THE PURPOSE OF A DEMONSTRATION

Ann had the insight that the whole point of demonstrations was about bringing issues to public attention, with the hope of putting public pressure on people in power to make change. It was the movement's analysis that the reason change didn't happen was that there was no pressure on people in power to make change. So the strategy was to bring things out into the open so that people would be horrified, and so that the people in power would be embarrassed and would make change out of that embarrassment—"a strategy which, I think, worked, to a great extent. But that was the equation."

The Media Committee's job was to make sure the press covered the action. How do you get the press to pay attention? Ann laid out the fundamental points of doing media for a radical political movement:

1. Well, first of all, you do plan an action that is interesting enough, that you think the press is going to care about it. But you have to woo the press. You have to find a way to get them there.

2. Some of that is about writing a press release that you send to the press that's interesting enough to make them look at it and say, *Oh, I better go cover that—that's going to be important or interesting or crazy, and will make good pictures and put wild people on television.* But we also know that the press doesn't generally read press releases, so don't expect to get the press there, just by sending them a press release, because they're going to throw it in the wastebasket, and you're just going to have to do it all over again.

3. So you have to *call* them. And you have to find the right person to speak to. So you have to know how to call a newspaper or television station and say—not ask to speak to a specific person, but say—*I'm calling about this, who should I speak to?* And let them tell you who to speak to.

4. Then you have to know how to talk to that person, and how to present [the issue]. And you do it first by asking them questions, and saying, *What do you know about this? What's your opinion of such and such?* Rather than just throwing something

at them. And then, lead them into being interested about this, and say, *Well, what you may not know is such and such.* Or, *We're doing this, that you might find interesting,* and sort of make them think it's their idea to come do this, rather than haranguing them or lecturing them about—*You should be there, and you should be covering this.* That will make them sit home, guaranteed.

Part of infiltrating the media's messaging was through simple education, in the hopes of getting our message, and not the state's, or the corporation's, across.

"The press was so stupid and so lazy, that they would come to every demonstration and ask one question: *Why are you here?* That was it. And they had no understanding of any issue, and no ability to ask questions about any issue. Ninety-five percent of any news story is what the reporter is saying. The sound bites are a very tiny part of any story. I would tell people, *Watch the evening news, and time how much of a story is the reporter's narration, and how much is the sound bite,* and you'll find that the sound bite is a very small portion of the story. So it's far less important for you to come up with the right sound bite than it is for you to talk to the reporter before they do the story and educate them, so they will reflect your point of view in their narration."

Even when we did everything we could, it was often hard to get the media to pay attention. ACT UP's actions were planned, for the most part, to be quite dramatic, with the understanding that that was how we got the media. Ann felt that activists have two audiences when we do an action—one is the audience of people immediately there, wherever we're targeting, and the other is the public in general. And one of her well-known insights is that *you're not talking to the media, you're talking* through *the media.* The news media are a vehicle to talk to the general public, or people in power who are watching. Activists are trying to reach the people immediately on-site, and both approaches can be valuable, and important. "But actions are always, always, always planned to be dramatic enough to capture [the] public's attention."

This principle is even more relevant today in the age of social media. The actual action is crucial in terms of its impact on the people on-site, and the responses of law enforcement. But the media around the action—both corporate media shown on television and online, and movement-created media posted online and through social media, that is, the *representation* of the action, can be more important for spreading the word than the event itself. The video can be the most important aspect of an experience of resistance. Yet its goal is to inspire more individuals, groups, and communities into public action. If the media does not inspire real people to act, then it is not effective; it is entertainment.

Ann felt that the fact that ACT UP members were arrested repeatedly was an indication of the powers that be trying to stop us. The fact that we were held longer and longer—held overnight, ultimately—instead of just a couple of hours, as at first, was an attempt "to shut us down." The fact that the judicial system—meaning the politicians who control the judicial system—were willing to impose higher and higher charges against people, and less and less willing to let ACT UP off with probation, was, in Ann's view, "an indication of a crackdown." The fact that ACT UP was barricaded farther and farther away from our targets was an indication of repression. "But, mostly, the fact that we were infiltrated by the FBI, which we found out sometime afterwards" proved to Ann that the state had become increasingly concerned about ACT UP, while at the same time they were unable to actually understand it (see Appendix 1).

MICHELANGELO "MIKE" SIGNORILE

Mike grew up on Staten Island. He later came to understand his younger self as "one of these people who was very apolitical, in the gay scene in New York," going to a lot of parties, going to nightclubs to cover them as a journalist. In the early to mid-1980s, he worked for a publicity firm that would plant items in gossip columns, and he would go to a lot of parties, collect a lot of gossip and dirt, and give that dirt to the columnists, and in exchange, they would write about his clients. He also wrote for *Nightlife, People,* and other kinds of popular lifestyle outlets.

"What was interesting about the world—even the world of celebrity and fashion and gossip and journalism—entertainment journalism in New York—is that even though we all thought we were out, we weren't really out. We were out to each other . . . We were certainly known to be gay to the other straight people around us—but nobody ever talked about it . . . If you figured it out, you figured it out. If you didn't, you were clueless. And that seemed to work for everybody. Homosexuality was something straight people were and are uncomfortable with, so they didn't want to talk about it. The gay people who wanted to move up didn't want to really talk about it. And you can convince yourself in that atmosphere, though, that you are accepted, because nobody was attacking you . . . You were keeping it quiet, and that was all fine."

AIDS, of course, changed everything about this fragile closet. Mike and his friend, the *Village Voice* columnist Michael Musto, started talking about the lack of response. There were very formalized benefits that socialites and others were organizing. And they had a bad taste about that, too, because those supposed benefits were just becoming other parties to go to, simply people taking pictures. AIDS was becoming glamorized, in a way, but there still was no anger about what was happening. Besides, by the mid-eighties, Michael and Mike weren't very political; their anger was less about the government and more about the media. They started asking each other crucial questions. *Why aren't we seeing more discussion of what's going on, or what's not going on? All we see are these benefits and whatnot, and aren't we just helping it all to keep going by writing about these benefits?*

One night they were at Boy Bar, in the East Village, and two guys came up and started talking to them, trying to get them to go to ACT UP. Mike's first recollection of ACT UP was that he had probably seen something on television or in a magazine and he immediately thought, *ACT UP are these crazy radicals. They get arrested.* But these guys in front of them—"they were nice guys and they were cute." And so they were talking them up for a while, and then they went away. And then Michael Musto said, *Well, what do you think? Is this what the answer is? Do you think we should go to this group, because we've been talking about wanting to do something? Maybe we should go there.* And Mike said, *Michael, this group—they protest in the street, they get arrested, they throw things, they have signs, they're crazy.* And Musto said, *Yeah, but these guys are really cute.*

In 1988, they went to ACT UP, where both went through a real eye-opening transformation. Suddenly, everything they'd been perceiving, but couldn't get the words out about, was articulated. On top of that, they were exposed to facts, figures, and data. Mike felt electrified. And Michael Musto went home and wrote the first piece for *The Village Voice* about ACT UP. At that time, in 1988, the *Voice* had still not done a piece.

THE INSIDE/OUTSIDE STRATEGY

Michelangelo immediately got involved with the Media Committee because he saw it as an area where he could make a difference with his contacts, and what he had learned, and what he was seeing. Bob Rafsky was a member. He had been a closeted, married advertising executive who now had AIDS. He had worked for Rubenstein Associates, which was handling Donald Trump and others, so he had good contacts at *The New York Times*. Vito Russo was chairing the committee at the time. David Corkery had come from ABC and also had many contacts. As with most of ACT UP, the Media Committee did not commit to one single strategy, but instead focused on several simultaneous approaches. In the spirit of a movement led by the visions and needs of people with AIDS, the Media Committee never told ACT UP what to do, and never stopped or altered an action because of messaging concerns. The actions led, and media was there to do support. Literally.

The Media Committee's strategy was to utilize whatever the group was doing, whether it was actions and protests that were going to get a lot of attention, or people in Treatment and Data or another committee who were uncovering information that needed to be put out there. Their approach was to work on several fronts: publicize the demonstrations, but also work on editors and reporters to get the information into circulation that wasn't being written about.

The Media Committee also emphasized building relationships with the press instead of acting in consort with ACT UP activists.

"The Media Committee of ACT UP was starting to [establish] a better relationship with *The New York Times* and with reporters there than the rest of the group. It sort of became a good cop/bad cop scenario. The rest of the group might protest the *Times*, but we would be on the phone with those reporters, sort of in a more neutral position. We would be there to get them the information, after ACT UP might have attacked them for not putting something there. Even though we knew a lot of these reporters were terrible, we knew [that] we had to ed-ucate them. We could not just yell at them and scream at them and say, *Okay, they're bad.* We had to be the ones to be nice to them—always be there, call them up, leave messages, let them believe that they actually came up with the story that we educated them on, do damage control when they got it screwed up—call them up, try to get it corrected. We tried to really work them, in the way that publicists do . . .

"So it was a very interesting dynamic, because we weren't just rep-resenting a group that needed publicity. We were representing a group that was attacking the media, often. And I think in that sense, it put us in a very interesting position. But we approached it, I think, in a very business-like manner. We had information that they needed, if they really wanted to get ahead on this epidemic. And we also had a very theatrical group here, that caused a lot of commotion, and [the media] wanted to be plugged into that. And as ACT UP became more success-ful at getting the message out, many more reporters wanted to have a contact in ACT UP, or with ACT UP. And so, we found ourselves having more and more connections with reporters."

One project was an AIDS buzzwords poster that listed all the terms reporters were using that were constantly wrong, like *AIDS victim.* Using these words telegraphed bias and did not acknowledge the point of view of PWAs. ACT UP preferred the term *people with AIDS* (PWAs). The media committee created this poster and mailed it to over two thousand journalists around the country, and it was on walls in news-rooms at television stations and at newspapers. This was *media activism*, on its own, irrespective of the floor. And like the rest of ACT UP, this type of project was never brought to the Monday-night meeting as a proposal, only as information. There was no micromanaging. There wasn't time.

In this relationship between the Media Committee and the rest of the group, there were different strategies supported simultaneously: one of confrontation with power in public, and one of cohesion with power in private. The Media Committee acted in accordance with the Inside/Outside strategy. In this approach, some people in the organization had contacts or relationships with people at important media outlets, or with scientists working in the government, while other people in ACT UP provided the street energy, organizing impressive, innovative, visible street rebellions designed to pressure the institutional power. Again, this method was ultimately effective, and yet—in a media realm—still reflected hierarchies of influence and access. While street activists came in all genders, races, class backgrounds, and ages, the Inside players, working with reporters and government officials, tended to be more like the journalistic contacts they were trying to win over: white and usually male, industry-based and trained. For a while this dichotomy of roles worked. The Inside activists were schmoozing the same *New York Times* that the Outside activists were calling "The New York Crimes" for never covering the epidemic while thousands died. That this strategy was not made explicit to the general membership may not matter. The difficult fact is that ACT UP would probably not have been as successful without providing a mirror internally for the people who controlled the media to see themselves.

ACT UP'S MEDIA STRATEGY AT SEIZE CONTROL OF THE FDA

MIKE SIGNORILE

Pre-Publicity

"Sometimes, you laugh at the technology we used . . . We had, [in] 1988, what was then considered a cell phone, these giant, battery-operated things, with giant antennas. And that was like, state of the art . . . We were really on the edge of the technology." ACT UP Media had a significant and incredible pool of people with a wide range of skills. We had Chip Duckett, who had been doing publicity for cookbooks, so he was familiar with pre-publicity. He knew how set up publicity in markets around the United States, "little mini-Oprahs in every city."

As a result, ACT UP NY did not have to send anybody on tour. We had people in every single city, in every market, thanks to the organizing skills of people like Chip. So, before the protest, he booked people on local TV shows and on local radio, nationwide. The Media Committee sent out hundreds of press kits, and would follow up with outlets and say, *Did you get our press kit? There's this huge action coming. It's going to be huge news—the largest thing since the storming of the Pentagon.* Mike kept saying that line even though he didn't realize how big the Pentagon action during the Vietnam War actually was. "We just kept saying that." The storming of the Pentagon in 1971 was thousands and thousands of people—but that was the Media Committee's pre-publicity mantra. And of course, the reporters would hear that and say, "Well, we have to book somebody locally on this." And so the coverage of the actions grew. It was a sophisticated hype machine: "You know, we're going to tell them it's going to be big, and they're going to then make it big. Then the day it happens, they have to cover it, because it's *the largest thing since the storming of the Pentagon.*"

The local people with AIDS, living across the country, were there to speak to "a middle-America audience." They talked about families devastated by AIDS. They talked about mothers and their sons and their daughters.

"We had people in those markets who were people with AIDS, as well as mothers and fathers. So we very much played to St. Louis, and Denver and Detroit and all these places . . . In addition to getting, of course, perhaps one of the few talk shows in those markets that probably ever dealt with AIDS—in addition to getting visibility for people with AIDS—doing this also forced all the newspapers and the TV in those markets to have to cover the demonstration when it happened, because there'd been all this pre-publicity. And what we were also doing, in the process, was empowering the local activists in all of those communities to do media, because we were doing it from New York, but we had people from Media Committees in every one of those cities . . . We'd do the booking, and then we'd say, *Okay, now you have the contact, put it in your book, and these people are going to become very valuable for you, for publicizing AIDS, from here on in—for all the protests that you're going to do.*"

The night before the Seize Control of the FDA action, the Media Committee was watching the local news on television in Washington, D.C. Yellow tape was all outside of the FDA, and they were pre-publicizing the whole demonstration for the next day. And the television reporters were saying, *The FDA is gearing up for what is going to be the largest demonstration since the storming of the Pentagon.* "And I was just like, *oh my God . . .* Numbers-wise, it wasn't, but in the larger, mythical sense it was, because the media said it was." Our estimates are between five hundred and fifteen hundred people.

Prepping Spokespeople

The idea of official spokespeople was problematic for members of ACT UP. Certainly, the idea of leaders was always in and of itself a problem for people with AIDS, who—at that time—were excluded from power and had little investment in the status quo. The Media Committee had enormous respect from the floor. "We were not a controversial committee. There was never any division. There were never any big fights. There was always good news coming from the Media Committee. And if there was an issue about spokespeople, I feel it was blunted by people really trusting the Media Committee to make the right decisions."

Localize the Experience

Another extraordinary piece of media that helped ACT UP to bring the demonstration local came courtesy of Urvashi Vaid, who was at that time the public communications person for the National Gay and Lesbian Task Force; she had helped to organize a demonstration at the Supreme Court steps, after the *Bowers v. Hardwick* sodomy decision. She devised a plan that then she brought to ACT UP, and she worked with the Media Committee in ACT UP New York to use it for the FDA demonstration. It was her plan to make sure that we got front-page placement for the demonstration the next day in papers around the country.

The Media Committee had reporters coming to the demonstration from every media market; Washington, D.C., was home to bureau chiefs from every paper in the country. And so ACT UP lined up protesters with signs from the cities that they came from and made an announcement to reporters: *You will now find people from your cities who are here.* And they found them—Cincinnati, Detroit, Denver, Portland, and more. "And those reporters all just ran [to cover it] . . . and the television people. And that made the difference between the protests getting page five in the Arizona paper, or *The Dallas Morning News*, and being on the front page, because there was a local person there . . . So we [ensured] that kind of detail, for the publicity. And I think that, to me, was the beginning of really using every tool you could."

GREGG BORDOWITZ

On the bus down to the FDA, Gregg Bordowitz, David Barr, and Peter Staley started planning the next step, which they believed should be back in New York, what would end up being the Target City Hall action. "I think it was me," Gregg said. "I said, *Look, we have to go to city hall. Make it local. That's the next action* . . . Michael Nesline was there. I remember because Michael Nesline was teasing us that we were some kind of cabal, or something like that. But I said, *That has to be the next action.*"

When he got back from the FDA, Gregg immediately started working on the Target City Hall action and started building consensus for it within the group, going to individual meetings and "saying that this is our next target, probably the best next target." After City Hall, and after an action in Albany where ACT UPer Mark Aurigemma debated Governor Mario Cuomo, Gregg started to feel frustrated. He felt that ACT UP was all over the place. Gregg felt that now, in the wake of the FDA action's success, was the time to dig in for a long campaign, because ACT UP had the opportunity "to get universal health care for the state." That brought him into tensions with "a whole bunch of people." Just like Jim Eigo, Gregg felt a conflict emerging between those who wanted ACT UP to become a broad health-care movement, and the emerging "drugs into bodies" mantra of new treatment activists. Jim, who is HIV-negative, coined the slogan "Health care is a human right," and was a long-term activist for access; Gregg was HIV-positive and also wanted an access focus. Was ACT UP's goal primarily to force the creation of necessary treatments, or was its goal to do so with an eye toward the larger vision of accessible health care for all people? Although treatment activists who focused on "drugs into bodies" of course wanted health care in America, the focus and goal of their work was developing new medications.

"By this time, I'm an out person with HIV within the group. And yet, that goes against the grain of the position of being an out person with HIV within the group, because to be out with HIV within the group, you are really a kind of drugs-into-bodies first and foremost as a politic. I guess it had to do with treatment decisions and stuff like that. I didn't really feel like there were a lot of treatment decisions in front of me. I don't know if I had faith or not faith that there would be a cure in my lifetime. I pretty much thought that I was going to die from this thing. And I felt that it was pretty clear that ACT UP and the AIDS movement was a catalyst for the growing health-care movement at that time. So I was very much interested in that, and that ACT UP could join unions, and the unions could come together. It was this coalition politics idea that sexual politics, and race politics, and feminist politics could come together in such a way with the unions . . . That increasingly brought me into alienation with the group, because the group was going in another direction. The group did not want to slow down for a long campaign." Of course ACT UP would soon embark on a four-year campaign to change the CDC definition of AIDS so that women would qualify for benefits and treatments. But those were not the same people arguing for "drugs into bodies."

Peter Staley protesting at the FDA headquarters in
Washington, D.C., in October 1988 (Photograph by Donna Binder)

DAVID BARR

For David Barr, the FDA action was a huge success. Before the action, David had a hard time getting the FDA to return his calls. After the action, "they returned the call the next day."

In his experience, the action opened the doors to an ongoing relationship and to communication. And the relationship with the FDA was really transformed; it changed tremendously from where it started, from *You're wasting my time* to *We need to work with you people.* And the expanded access definition also changed; the drug approval standards improved. The demonstration was a really important piece in forcing the agency to realize that they had to deal with ACT UP in a way that was different from how they were used to dealing with consumers.

"And so that was important . . . Because it was such national visibility; for the first time it presented a different vision of what a person with AIDS is. And I can't stress enough how important that was. We were victims; and we were vectors. We were bad guys and victims. And through the work of the people involved in Denver, creating the Denver Principles, through the work of ACT UP and others, we developed a different vision of the person with AIDS as hero. And that really was personified at the FDA. *Look at these people, they're fighting for their lives. And they may not look like we all look out there, in America. But, oh, they're dying, and they want medicine. Hm. I can wrap my mind around that.*"

The Denver Principles were created by a gathering of people with AIDS at a gay and lesbian health conference in 1983, four years before ACT UP's founding.

THE DENVER PRINCIPLES

The 1983 statement from the People with AIDS advisory committee:

> We condemn attempts to label us as "victims," a term which implies defeat, and we are only occasionally "patients," a term which implies passivity, helplessness, and dependence upon the care of others.
>
> We are "people with AIDS."

RECOMMENDATIONS FOR ALL PEOPLE

1. Support us in our struggle against those who would fire us from our jobs, evict us from our homes, refuse to touch us or separate us from our loved ones, our community or our peers, since available evidence does not support the view that AIDS can be spread by casual, social contact.

2. Not scapegoat people with AIDS, blame us for the epidemic or generalize about our lifestyles.

RECOMMENDATIONS FOR PEOPLE WITH AIDS

1. Form caucuses to choose their own representatives, to deal with the media, to choose their own agenda and to plan their own strategies.

2. Be involved at every level of decision-making and specifically serve on the boards of directors of provider organizations.

3. Be included in all AIDS forums with equal credibility as other participants, to share their own experiences and knowledge.

4. Substitute low-risk sexual behaviors for those which could endanger themselves or their partners; we feel people with AIDS have an ethical responsibility to inform their potential sexual partners of their health status.

RIGHTS OF PEOPLE WITH AIDS

1. To have as full and satisfying sexual and emotional lives as anyone else.

2. To quality medical treatment and quality social service provision without discrimination of any form including sexual orientation, gender, diagnosis, economic status or race.

3. To full explanations of all medical procedures and risks, to choose or refuse their treatment modalities, to refuse to participate in research without jeopardizing their treatment and to make informed decisions about their lives.

4. To privacy, to confidentiality of medical records, to human respect and to choose who their significant others are.

To die—and to LIVE—in dignity.

Signed by
Phil Lanzaratta, Richard Berkowitz, Tom Nasrallah,
Matthew Sarner, Bobby Reynolds, Artie Felson, Bill
Burke, Dan Turner, Michael Callen, Bobbi Campbell,
Bob Checci.

4

Collective Leadership: Stop the Church

Stop the Church took place at St. Patrick's Cathedral, on Fifth Avenue in the heart of midtown Manhattan, on December 10, 1989, cosponsored by ACT UP and Women's Health Action and Mobilization (WHAM!). It was ACT UP's most controversial action, internally and internationally, but in a sense, it was ACT UP's boldest act of broad leadership, as a collective. It started from a truly radical platform uniting AIDS and abortion rights. It confronted one of the most powerful institutions in the world, the Catholic Church, one that most progressive movements feared to address. Nothing could have been more counter to assimilationist or respectability politics than Stop the Church. Even the name of the action, in the tradition of Seize Control of the FDA, was the opposite of conciliatory, explanatory, or appeasing, even if what actually occurred in the church was not what ACT UP had originally agreed upon or planned. And it was organized in parts by different kinds of people, with different needs of expression, creating an unruly but impressive whole.

Stop the Church was, in some ways, ACT UP's most grassroots action. It was not masterminded as part of an organized campaign toward a policy win. And this was partially what made it controversial. ACT UP's actions were usually aimed at government and pharma, and came equipped with reasonable, winnable, and doable concrete demands for policy changes to help save the lives of people with AIDS. Stop the Church was different. ACT UP was not trying to change the Catholic Church, nor were we trying to negotiate. Stop the Church was a raw display of power, in the only way we could manifest it—through direct action, to demand that they "stop killing us." It grew from a fundamental emotional frustration and anger on the part of the rank and file,

From left to right: Ann Northrop, Charles King, and Sharon Tramutola
in front of St. Patrick's Cathedral at the Stop the Church action,
December 10, 1989 (Video still by Stuart Marshall)

who were overwhelmed by the dying of their friends, and the lack of
treatment progress. It was designed as a confrontation, a revolt, a rebellion, a resistance, and it was designed to take place on enemy territory.

Looking at the evolution and development of Stop the Church,
we see that ACT UP not only functioned with simultaneity of *action*,
meaning different kinds of actions taking place at the same time. It
also was powered by simultaneity of *approach*—in other words, different kinds of actions went through different kinds of processes. How
something happened was not systematized, and therefore not bureau-
cratized. AIDS was chaotic, and the kinds of people attracted to the
battle to transform AIDS were iconoclastic. Fortunately, the organization's functional capacity was flexible enough to allow different events
to occur in different ways. In this analysis of Stop the Church, we see
how much personal relationships—friends, siblings, roommates, eve-
nings of cocktails, feelings of exclusion, histories of acting out, a kind of
desocialization that came from being excluded both by the larger society and by ACT UP itself—all converged as catalysts for an outlandish
expression of rage, alongside humor, that propelled cultural transforma-
tions for both people with AIDS and the church itself.

Traditionally, the Catholic Church of New York conducted its own parallel educational system, through Catholic schools, which constructed rules and curricula as they wished in relation to Catholic dogma, which was historically anti-gay and anti-abortion. As the AIDS crisis grew, the church escalated its efforts to influence public education as well. It opposed sex-education classes in the public schools, it opposed condom distribution, and it opposed the "Rainbow Curriculum," a long-gestating plan to update New York Public School education to include queer people and people of color in classroom curricula. Finally, the church compounded its injurious impact on the people of the city of New York when Cardinal O'Connor opposed needle exchange, a centerpiece of ACT UP's politics.

Many Catholic members of the ACT UP community, and its growing numbers of supporters, came from generations when they had experienced bitter oppression from the church. Not only had gay people and women been repeatedly attacked and humiliated by church policy, but people with AIDS faced terribly degrading behavior from Catholic hospices. Even getting buried was difficult. Redden's Funeral Home on West Fourteenth Street was one of the first places to hold AIDS funerals, and people brought their dead to the oasis of Redden's regardless of their denomination. Similarly, the many Jewish members of ACT UP—mostly secular—did not consider the church with any sense of sanctity. A cursory examination of the membership, I think, reveals that most members of ACT UP were Catholic or Jewish. There were, of course, heartland white Protestants of the full spectrum, but since it was based in New York before the full impact of gentrification, ethnic whites (Jews, Italians, Irish) and Latinos created a cultural affect that was passionate, confrontational, and direct.

On December 10, 1989, for the first time in history, the world—and the world literally watched this event—saw homosexuals with AIDS and women wanting the right to abortion interrupt a Sunday mass in a world-famous cathedral to assert their power and insist on the sanctity of *our* lives. There had long been pickets and demonstrations outside St. Patrick's. And about a year before ACT UP's founding I participated in a small demonstration inside the cathedral when some gay activists stood quietly and calmly turned our backs on the cardinal in response to him expelling Dignity, the gay Catholic organization, from meeting on church property. But going inside with significance, instead of deference, was brand-new. And to dare do this as despised outcasts with AIDS was the paradigm shift. Ironically, Stop the Church made palatable the future assimilationist agenda of the gay rights movement, which uplifts pro-natalism, nuclear family, monogamy, and marriage. Because when the world saw women wanting abortion rights and homosexuals and people with AIDS refusing to adhere to the boundaries of Catholic Church property, the prospect of the much more controllable, integrationist concept of gay marriage suddenly seemed reasonable and, in fact, desirable.

It is fascinating to trace the origins of this action, how it unfolded, and what kinds of politics and character types drove it to international notoriety. Because, of all of ACT UP's actions, Stop the Church was driven the most by feeling. While literally hundreds of ACT UPers were involved in the planning, and thousands carried out the demonstrations and action, the compelling order of events can be told by focusing on a few individuals: Dolly Meieran, Karen Ramspacher, Robert Garcia, Vincent Gagliostro, Victor Mendolia, Emily Nahmanson, Neil Broome, Michael Petrelis, and Tom Keane, each of whom propelled a different key phase of the event.

WOMEN'S HEALTH ACTION AND MOBILIZATION (WHAM!)

DOLLY MEIERAN

Dolly Meieran was born in 1967 in Pittsburgh. Her father was a robotics engineer "who spent more time playing his viola," and her British mother was an educator of the blind. Her grandfather was a Holocaust survivor from Eastern Europe by way of Norway. "There was this kind of a tense relationship to history and the Holocaust, that because it was still so raw and so new, I mean, it's so strange to think, in the sixties and seventies, World War II was closer in history than ACT UP is to the present day, in a way, like there's this weird elasticity to time."

Her gay brother, the video activist David Meieran, had joined ACT UP. She organized a screening of his collective's film *Testing the Limits* at Oberlin, where she went to college, but "it was just so kind of difficult to make people aware at that time." During summers she would come to New York and do video work for ACT UP.

Dolly took her evolving video skills and started working with ReproVision, a collective with Dana Dickey, Julie Clark, and Dina Mermelstein that was shooting footage on women's health care. They were documenting Operation Rescue, a group of radical anti-abortion activists who had started standing in front of clinics with signs of aborted fetuses and other graphics, trying to upset and obstruct women who were on their way into abortion clinics. They created a situation that was so harassing and distressing that abortion rights supporters started doing "clinic defense," a process in which they would stand in front of the besieged clinics and try to accompany women trying to enter to get an abortion. Sometimes the clinic defenders would physically get between the woman and the Operation Rescue people, but they had to quickly convey to the overwhelmed women what was going on and differentiate themselves from the assaultive anti-abortion teams. It was often chaotic and very confrontational. Numbers of women were so overwhelmed by the presence and aggression of Operation Rescue that they were deterred from getting the abortions that they needed and wanted.

Being a bridge person between ACT UP and reproductive rights, Dolly saw clearly that, politically and religiously, it was the same enemy. It was New York's Cardinal O'Connor who was letting Operation Rescue sleep in the church. It was Cardinal O'Connor who was stopping the distribution of condoms and clean needles and lifesaving information. "It was the same political senators and representatives who were opposing abortion who were also opposing anything that would lead towards decriminalizing—I mean, there were still sodomy laws . . . Those were the same people who were banning abortions . . . Most people understood."

Then, in 1989, in *Webster v. Reproductive Health Services,* the Supreme Court upheld a Missouri law that imposed restrictions on the use of "state funds, facilities, and employees in performing, assisting with, or counseling on abortion." Nonprofits like the ACLU and the Center for Constitutional Rights were fighting anti-abortion laws, but "they were limited by their 501(c)(3)s . . . So we're like, *Oh, well, this is where we can come in,* because this is our lives, our issues and health." These young women decided to start their own direct-action group modeled on ACT UP that would take to the streets for abortion rights. The new group, Women's Health Action and Mobilization (WHAM!), included women who were also in ACT UP, like Karen Ramspacher and Catherine Gund. Their first action was to show up at the Supreme Court for *Webster*'s oral arguments wearing T-shirts that said US OUT OF MY UTERUS and KEEP YOUR LAWS OFF MY BODY, and they got arrested. By December 1989, "after a particularly heinous fall," Operation Rescue escalated harassment at clinics, and WHAM! and people from ACT UP did clinic defense every weekend, literally accompanying women who were trying to enter the buildings to get abortions, to shield them from the gauntlet set up by Operation Rescue. The artist and ACT UPer David Wojnarowicz came out a couple of times to help.

"Earlier in that fall [Cardinal] O'Connor was just really lambasting needle exchange, even though the data was already starting to pour in, *Needle exchange works, needle exchange saves lives.* And hospitals being so under the thumb of the Catholic Church, even St. Vincent's [a primary AIDS hospital in Greenwich Village] . . . actually wouldn't even perform abortions . . . Why is a church controlling a hospital? I mean, to me, that really just seems wrong. I mean, a hospital should be controlled by medical people, not religious people."

One night, after getting very, very angry, Dolly and some other activists were on their way back from an anti–Operation Rescue event in White Plains. Dolly was particularly mad at O'Connor and decided to go spray-paint on the sidewalk, O'CONNOR SPREADS DEATH. Well, unfortunately, "some very large cop from Midtown South saw us and chased us, and that was not a fun evening . . . And suddenly like eight police cars and four unmarked taxis just kind of converged. And it was just kind of, you know, without the three-thousand-strong force of ACT UP behind you and you're all alone at three o'clock in the morning, it's really not pleasant." One of the men, Scott Sensenig, was taken down on the ground and the police were "kicking and kicking and beating him and beating him."

KAREN RAMSPACHER

Karen Ramspacher was born in 1965 in Havertown, Pennsylvania. Her father worked for IBM, which in the 1970s stood for *I've Been Moved*, people joked, because of how frequently its employees were transferred. Karen's parents were Catholic Democrats. They used to pray to stop the war in Vietnam. This is the way she was taught Christianity. "You're supposed to look out for people who are in a bad circumstance . . . So, yes, I was the kid in the neighborhood who was standing up for the kid being picked on, because that was the sense I was getting from home and from church, that that's what we do and that's how we make the world a better place." She later was a "club kid" in New York City; her favorite night spot was the Peppermint Lounge. She went to Studio 54 in her prom dress with a gay friend, to CBGB to hear punk, and to Danceteria.

BRINGING REPRODUCTIVE RIGHTS FEMINISM TO ACT UP

The personal overlaps of people from WHAM! and ACT UP mirrored the overlaps in values and concerns "because the principles are the same. It's about respect of your body, control of your body, health of your body, rights of your body." One of the T-shirts that Karen loved at the time was YOUR LAWS STOP WHERE MY SKIN STARTS. "I mean, it's all about sex. It should be all good stuff, so if it isn't, we need to fix that." Karen worked with women who had been in the feminist health movement before joining ACT UP, including Risa Denenberg and Marion Banzhaf. They ended up doing a daylong teach-in on the parallels between the women's self-help movement and the AIDS movement. They started by laying out feminist principles, and then built to the issues of women and AIDS, leading to the AIDS movement with men. The point was to spell out specific strategies that women had used to build feminist activism, to articulate methods that the men could borrow and learn. They wanted the men in ACT UP to know that "*this wisdom already exists*, let's quickly teach it instead of reinventing the wheel." That teach-in led to the book *Women, AIDS & Activism*.

ACT UP's integral support for abortion rights extended to research within T&D. Karen joined the subcommittee Fetal Cell Group inside Treatment and Data, with Marty Robinson and David Lopez, investigating if fetal tissue could be used to improve the immune system. There was a governmental ban in place to stop those studies, motivated by the anti-abortion movement. The subcommittee wrote a 138-page report concluding that there were valid scientific reasons for pursuing fetal cell investigation, not just for HIV but also for Parkinson's and Alzheimer's, but that, despite all this potential, it was being stonewalled because of the abortion issue. "We tried to bring the science to the fore . . . and help push through the abortion block, which was essentially a religious right block . . . Somebody needed to do it. I don't think that the AIDS scientists would have touched it, because it would have been too political, but by having us do the research, hopefully we helped move that cause forward. That was the idea."

Karen was living in a loft with three queer roommates, including Robert Garcia, who became her best friend. As a result of his relationship with Karen, Robert got involved with clinic defense.

"I campaigned hard to be able to live in the loft where he lived with Catherine Gund and Jocelyn Taylor, and I was the fourth roommate." They had four bedrooms, and then there was an extra bedroom above the bathroom, and some other activists from North Carolina lived there for a while, too. And then at one point, all four had one other person living with them. Karen had her sister; Robert had his brother. It was a very busy loft, and there were a lot of meetings at 60 Warren Street, between Church and West Broadway. It was a fifth-floor walkup, which was really nine flights, because they were the double flights. It was grueling for sick people to come to meetings there, because there was no elevator. It was a huge loft and zoned for commercial use only. There was a company name, *Look Mom Comics*, on the door. The fire department used to come and knock because they knew people were living there. "We'd be real quiet, so we wouldn't get kicked out. But it was a great space." Robert was part of the POC art collective House of Color, and Jocelyn was cofounding the Clit Club (a lesbian nightclub) with Julie Tolentino, while Catherine was making documentaries, and Karen was involved with WHAM!, working for reproductive rights, while all of them were working in ACT UP. "We were all doing everything together."

A whole new subculture emerged from the WHAM!/ACT UP relationship forged through clinic defense. A group of ACT UP men went to Buffalo in 1991, when Operation Rescue heavily targeted abortion clinics in that city. On the bus ride up, Brian Griffin and Donald Grove and a few others formed an affinity group, Church Ladies for Choice.

"They decided to do bad drag in order to be the USO of the pro-choice movement. So they sang songs." They took traditional songs like "God Save the Queen" or "This Land Is Your Land," and they rewrote them to be pro-choice, taking "hymns" and making them "hers." They would come to the WHAM! events to do clinic defense. "There [were] a lot of blockades back in the late eighties and early nineties by the anti-choice groups, and . . . it's nice to be able to always balance what you do with a sense of humor so that you can maintain your own level of interest and the public's level of interest in what you have to say."

WHAM! members in ACT UP were involved in planning Stop the Church, and WHAM! wanted to cosponsor. "WHAM! talked about it and said *ACT UP's doing this big action.* A bunch of us, Diane Curtis, Julie Clark, myself, Tracy Morgan, Elizabeth Meixell, were all talking about it. *ACT UP's going to do this action. Let's do it. Yeah, let's do it . . .* because the issues were the same."

PLANNING HOW TO STOP THE CHURCH

VICTOR MENDOLIA

Victor Mendolia was born in 1961 in Huntington, Long Island, which "just was a cultural wasteland; really nothing for kids to do." Victor's mother was in social work school at Stony Brook. So he often went to school with her, and either sat in classes or hung out in the student union, and he later joined a campus program called Interns in Community Service. There were different speakers on different subjects, and one that really clicked for him was a speaker from the United Farm Workers. In short order, Victor had set up a picket line in front of his local grocery store, to boycott lettuce and grapes in support of the United Farm Workers' efforts to unionize. He was fourteen.

Only a few years later, he moved to New York City and quickly became "an East Village boy." At first he didn't really know his way around, and would often do the West Village Christopher Street strip. But soon he got to the Pyramid Club on Avenue A, and immediately felt, *Oh wow, this is where I belong, this is home.* "It was gay-centric, but it was a completely mixed crowd. The straight people that were there were completely open to everything that was going on. Most of the shows tended to be either gay or gay-oriented. But it was a very accepting, open community . . . It was very exciting. There literally was art everywhere, and it was the start of the gallery boom there." His best girlfriend from Long Island was also living in the city, and they started producing club events under the moniker Anonymous Productions. He was Victor Anonymous, and she was Jeanette Anonymous. Their first club night took place in the East Village, at a venue called the Lucky Strike on Ninth Street. Madonna was the bartender. From there, they started doing events at Pyramid, and went on to bigger clubs, particularly Danceteria. For a while, they were doing two or three parties a week. And they loved it. They gave Karen Finley her first show in New York. Victor's experience was that, for most young people in the East Village in the early 1980s, AIDS was something that was happening to older guys who frequented sex clubs like the Mineshaft and the Anvil, on deserted side streets of the far West Side, rooted in seventies gay culture where the hypermasculine but stylized clone culture still prevailed.

"And while I went to those places occasionally, at the time, I was very shy about any kind of public sex, or hooking up, and things like that. I rarely hooked up in those kinds of situations. So I think for a while, most people there just didn't feel like it was our issue—it wasn't our problem, and it wasn't something that we readily wanted to address or deal with. But I remember specifically what it was that got me involved with ACT UP. I was at Uncle Charlie's, on Greenwich Avenue. And there was a poster that said—and I don't remember the number—but it was like, *1500 AIDS deaths: haven't you been silent long enough?* And I was like, *You know what? I'm going to go to that meeting. I'm going to go to that meeting this weekend.*"

Like many people who joined ACT UP, Victor was attracted by the vigor of a specific leader. "I was particularly drawn to [facilitator] Maria Maggenti. I thought that she was just so incredible. I thought that she always held the room together properly; she . . . was usually right on. She could always cut right to it. And I was always really impressed with her. In a way, I was inspired particularly by her."

Victor took over as a chair of the Outreach Committee, which oriented new members. Vincent Gagliostro started coming to the meetings, and he and Victor organically became cochairs. "We never even discussed it or voted on it; it just happened." They started building "propaganda" for ACT UP. Vincent was a highly skilled and talented art director, and each week, they would try to come up with some new, great visual tool to reach out and get more people to join the group. When they were pointing out Gina Kolata's misreporting in *The New York Times*, they made stickers that said BUY YOUR LIES HERE, and put them on newspaper vending machines. The information about Kolata's misreporting came out of the Treatment and Data Committee, and Victor always felt that everyone at T&D was so smart that all they had to do was say it and he'd believe it. With Richard Deagle, he made a poster targeting the mayor, Ed Koch. It said 14,000 AIDS DEATHS. HOW'M I DOIN'?—Koch's catchphrase. "We made those specifically so that they would fit in the overhead subway ads."

At that point, Cardinal O'Connor had been increasing efforts to get Catholic Church control of sex and AIDS education in the public schools. He was lobbying against two things: condom distribution in schools, and the Children of the Rainbow, a new public school curriculum that had POC and gay inclusion. Victor, Vincent Gagliostro, and Robert Garcia were hanging out one night, "and we had had more than a few cocktails. And I said, *If he's going to go meddling in the public schools, then we should just shut down his cash machine, and close the church down.* So that's how it came about."

They brought their proposal to the floor, and there was a lot of support. "A couple of people spoke against it, about people's right to worship, and things like that. But in general, I remember Bob Rafsky just going on and on saying that *we need to do this.*" The official plan was just to do a picket outside. But when it became clear that some people were going to do something on the inside anyway, ACT UP held in-depth discussions about how to make the action pointed and coherent. "What we tried to do is to steer it so that whatever happened on the inside would happen during the homily, which is the non-sacred part of the mass. It's where the priest or the bishop or the cardinal says his own opinion to the congregation. So it's not classified as part of the sacred liturgy."

Neil Broome and Michael Petrelis and others were very vocal about wanting to go inside. Eventually, ACT UP decided that the people who chose to go inside the church would do a silent die-in during the homily. Victor felt that the Catholic Church "has caused more death and destruction and more chaos and problems on the planet than anything else." So he didn't have a problem confronting the church. But his concern was "just that we wouldn't lose the message, because we didn't want it to be seen as just throwing a tantrum at the Church; we wanted it to be about specific issues, and to counter them." He remembers going to WHAM! directly, and "they immediately said, *Let's do it.*"

EMILY NAHMANSON

One of the youngest people in ACT UP, Emily Nahmanson arrived as a teenager, like Garance Franke-Ruta and a few others. Emily was seventeen, and an undergraduate at NYU. She had come out a week after starting college. "I was sitting in the fountain in Washington Square Park watching these three women—who looked like they had been house painting . . . eating these sandwiches, and they were kind of tough and sexy . . . and I was, like, *I think those women are dykes.* And then, I looked again and I thought—*Wow, I really like that.* And it was, like, boom. And that was it."

Stop the Church was a centerpiece of Emily's ACT UP experience. She also remembers the floor being clear that we would not disrupt the service. There were two slogans that were developed for the action: "Stop the Church" and "Stop this man." "*Stop the Church* was a phrase that was met with a lot of objections. I understood the objection because that wasn't what the demonstration was about." Emily felt that the action was really a demonstration against Cardinal O'Connor, much like a demonstration citing Koch as an enemy. She saw it as "an awareness campaign" designed to "demonize" Cardinal O'Connor. "It was left up to the people who wanted to do what they wanted to do to just do it." No official ACT UP support was organized for any action inside the church, yet it was agreed upon that anything that would happen inside would not disrupt the service.

VINCENT GAGLIOSTRO

Vincent Gagliostro was born in 1955 in Hackensack, New Jersey. He grew up in a "kind of a split personality Italian environment because my father's side of the family was very, very old world and refused to speak English." He had been political since he was thirteen, primarily in the antiwar movement. Vince had an aunt who, he feels, was responsible for all of his activism. She was his mother's partner in their beauty salon, but she always wanted to be a journalist.

Vince introduced his best friend, Don Yowell, to artist Avram Finkelstein and the two fell in love. Then Don died in 1984 without admitting to his friends that he had AIDS. In 1987, Vince went to ACT UP's second meeting, where he found an immediate sense of acceptance. "Because you were there, you were trusted." Working at an ad agency, Vince brought his gifts as a graphic artist directly to ACT UP. He felt that ACT UP, at first, didn't fully realize the extent to which AIDS could potentially be a political minefield. "There was curiosity, which is always great. There was a lot of fear, which is always great for a provocative activist group. Because propaganda feeds on fear." He found the group process to be very empowering; to have a floor talk about a graphic was inspiring to both the designers and the rank and file.

Vince and the other organizers set about to build a mass demonstration, the largest in ACT UP's history, for Stop the Church. They built a fierce campaign to recruit people: a poster campaign, ads in *The Village Voice*, making and distributing large quantities of stickers around the city. As the campaign developed, Vince found out how many people had a problem with Cardinal O'Connor, and he found out how much power the church had in our city. "We were threatened by them. I had phone calls from Cardinal O'Connor's office. I was followed by people that I know worked for Cardinal O'Connor . . . to find out where I lived. Where I lived was an old building, a little old brownstone, and the mailbox was a slot mailbox. Every day there would be heinous things on the floor, threatening me."

Phone calls told him, *You're going to rot in hell.* Some said, *We know you live at 21 West Sixteenth Street, and we are going to kill you.* Then one day he was walking home from an ACT UP meeting and realized a guy was following him. "You know when you are being followed. And I turned around and he was really, really cute." Vince turned to him and said, *Can I help you?* He said, *What? Well, you're following me,* Vince insisted. *No, I'm not,* the man insisted, yet when Vincent continued walking, the man still followed him. Finally, Vince blurted out,

I'll save you, 21 West Sixteenth. "I just don't think any of us were ready and equipped. Ready for what we were up against and equipped to deal with it at all . . . It was totally out of control."

At a time when ACT UP meetings were at around five to seven hundred people, seven thousand people came to the protest outside the church. Many did civil disobedience on Fifth Avenue in front of the cathedral, and 120–130 were arrested. Organizers had no idea that that many people were going to show up. It was the largest demonstration against the power of the church to that date.

VICTOR MENDOLIA

"The night before the action, as usual, Ann Northrop gave one of her speeches on sound bites. And her advice was that we're not trying to convince people to change religions, and we not trying to say that their religion is no good, and we're not trying to convince them of anything other than we're trying to get the public to understand that *we are the ones fighting for people's lives, and they are the murderers.*"

THE DEMONSTRATION OUTSIDE

EMILY NAHMANSON

Emily's life was organized around ACT UP.

She joined the affinity group the Costas, named after ACT UPer Costa Pappas, who had already died. Other Costas included Lee Schy, Rand Snyder, Walter Armstrong, Heidi Dorow, Marion Banzhaf, Maxine Wolfe, Phil Montana, Terry McGovern, Maria Maggenti, and Avram Finkelstein. They mostly met during the Monday-night meetings, off in a little corner, plotting their next action, or what role they were going to have in the next big group event. A lot of the decisions were organically made, "because everyone had the same idea about the message that we wanted to get across." Emily remembered that in some ways the Costas didn't really care about the consequences if they thought the action was just, because "after all, what's the worst that can happen? Well, the worst that can happen is you die. Well, guess what? People were going to die anyway. And then, the second worst thing that could happen is that you get arrested. Well, that was par for the course."

She recalled that Maxine Wolfe often had a lot of really good ideas and influence, and often "people just took her ideas and implemented them. I thought she was amazing. She had been doing this for a long time, and it was just incredible that here's this woman who . . . she was always an old lady, in my mind. I kind of felt like, *Well fuck, if Maxine is willing to do that, then yeah, I'll do it.*"

For Emily, the reason for Stop the Church was that the Catholic Church as an institution was "just horribly evil" and had all this power to use for good in the world but was not doing it. She cited the context of a lot of anger toward the Catholic Church in the gay community and among women, and in the AIDS activist community that the church was "overstepping their bounds, that's for sure." In preparation for the action outside the cathedral, Emily, Bill Monahan, Glenn Belverio, and David Lopez decided to get in the face of the Operation Rescue people, who were at the Stop the Church demonstration, "these crazy anti-abortion fanatics." They dressed up in clown makeup, and became Operation Ridiculous. They found themselves on Fifth Avenue among thousands of demonstrators on the block facing the cathedral. "It's the most fabulous, insane energy to happen, I think, in the AIDS activist movement. We had worked so hard to get there. It was just going off incredibly well." They needed to get across the street, but the police were protecting churchgoers and not allowing demonstrators to cross. So Operation Ridiculous went onto the side street and hailed a cab. In their clown costumes and full makeup, they had the taxi circle north and come down Fifth Avenue with the traffic and then stop on the east side of the Avenue, in front of the cathedral. Then the five clowns burst out of the cab and exploded onto the sidewalk in front of St. Patrick's, having outwitted the police barriers. Once the police saw them come out of that cab, Emily said, "We were gone. We were arrested so fast." And soon she was standing in the back of a paddy wagon with all these people wearing clown makeup. Emily ran into David Lopez some weeks after that, but she didn't remember him because they had met in clown-face. David died within months.

KAREN RAMSPACHER

Karen didn't go into the church. That was a choice. She thought about it, but "I was like, *Oh, I think I'll have flashbacks from Catholic school.*" So she decided to stay outside and was supposed to be part of Operation Ridiculous, but she missed the timing, so she ended up in the demonstration, lying down in the street. When she was arrested, she was put on a big school bus full of people charged with disturbing the peace. She went limp—*passive resistance.* "I weighed all of 105. I'm sure it was really annoying for them to have to carry me onto the bus."

THE ACTION INSIDE THE CATHEDRAL

I was there that day, and I went into the cathedral expecting to be part of a silent vigil. This is what we had decided at the pre-action meetings, and what I was anticipating. When I walked in, I saw a number of other ACT UPers wandering around, all of us acting incognito and not really acknowledging one another. When the homily started, a few affinity groups began their actions. Vincent Gagliostro, while organizing the protest to take place outside, had designed a mock program that some ACT UPers handed out to parishioners inside. "Welcome to St. Patrick's Cathedral." Some people started reading these out loud. The parishoners were shocked. They seemed totally repulsed. Another affinity group started lying down in the aisles, doing a silent die-in; I contemplated joining them, but the horrified reactions of the Catholics around me kept me in my seat.

The yelling clearly upset people who were praying, and while I opposed everything that they stood for, I didn't understand the impact, externally, that this was all going to have. Altar boys started dropping flyers—statements from the Catholic Church—on the folks lying in the pews, and the police entered the cathedral, swarming, stepping over and arresting protesters as O'Connor continued the service. Then Michael Petrelis stood on top of his pew and began screaming, and some other people joined him. I heard Ann Northrop yelling as she was carried away, "We're fighting for your lives too."

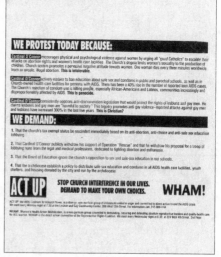

We do not challenge anyone's right to worship as they choose. However, recent actions by the Catholic church go beyond its constitutionally protected right to worship. The church, through its immense political power, restricts access to information that can save lives and access to health care, including abortion. The church should not interfere with the state's function to protect public health. These actions of the church ensure the spread of HIV (the virus thought to cause AIDS), deny women control of their bodies and endanger all of our lives. The intrusion of O'Connor and the church hierarchy into politics and public health guarantees that ALL people will suffer from the murderous policies of the church.

ACT UP flyer distributed to parishioners during the Stop the Church action, December 10, 1989 (Vincent Gagliostro)

NEIL BROOME

Another ACT UPer who had gone inside the church was Neil Broome. By the time Neil got involved with Stop the Church, he was seasoned. A Queens native who had been severely harassed in high school, and an HIV-positive club kid, he'd come to ACT UP because people on the nightlife scene were not talking about AIDS. By the time of Stop the Church, Neil had already organized a "Freedom Ride" through the U.S. South to support the Ray family of Arcadia, Florida, whose house was firebombed when three children contracted HIV through blood transfusion.

"It was a small town with a wooden courthouse and people came in their pickups. They were demented. I don't even know how to characterize it. They were angry, drunk, crazy, pickup trucks, rifles—it was frightening. I was [thinking], *Oh my God, what is this* . . . They had about two hundred people assembled, coming there in their trucks, surrounding us. And they were saying, *Wait until the cameras go off, we're going to kill you* . . . We had to leave the town in an entourage of fifteen cars and they made us lie down in the well. It was scary, frightening . . . All these people that came with tube tops and bad perms, pasty skin. All these images were swirling. This is like the worst of *Jerry Springer*."

It wasn't difficult, then, for Neil to decide to go into the church. To him, O'Connor was "another demented, delusional freak in New York—another power hungry, hateful person, who all these fools worship." Neil found O'Connor's role regarding HIV to be "abysmal." "People have this idea of New York as being liberal and progressive, but there's a lot of strong conservative elements in the city, and a lot of power players who are not progressive . . . Look how long it took for a gay rights bill to pass—seventeen years!"

Neil and his close friend Gerri Wells went inside the church. The energy was "electric, beyond belief." Different affinity groups had organized different actions, and the police were all over the church, waiting for ACT UP to break the law. "They had dogs in there. It was nuts, but Cardinal O'Connor was determined to just continue with the service that day." Neil and Gerri stood up and others followed. Neil recalls that some people got up on pews. Some lay down on the floor. When demonstrators started speaking out and chanting, Neil recalls that the cardinal started singing and insisted that parishioners drown people out. "But the thing was, he couldn't." Neil observed churchgoers "punching" demonstrators who were in the church.

"Someone swung at me, but they didn't hit me. They were like baboons. They were animals. I was shocked—*these phony, hypocritical, self-righteous, uncaring shitheads who were there.* That's all I thought. And I thought, *What else is new?* . . . The noise level—people were still rising above the singing, and it was insane. There were so many police. It was frightening, adrenaline rushing, and a lot of people—parishioners— were in absolute shock. And with the police dogs there . . . it just felt like a police state."

MICHAEL PETRELIS

Michael Petrelis was born in 1961 in Newark, New Jersey, to a working-class Greek-Italian family. He was apolitical, but out in high school, after which he went to San Francisco, lived on food stamps, worked some restaurant jobs, and did a lot of partying. He moved to New York, and friends started dying even before the term *GRID* was coined. One friend's parents kept his boyfriend and gay friends from seeing him in St. Vincent's. Then in August of 1985, Michael was diagnosed with Kaposi sarcoma. "I thought I was going to be dead real soon." The doctor told him he had "about six months to a year." His roommate didn't want to live with someone with AIDS and said Michael had to get out. That person eventually died of AIDS. Very unusually, Michael went to the main gay rights group at the time, the Committee on Lesbian and Gay Rights (CLGR), and demanded that they find him a place to live. CLGR was not known as a social service organization and had very little power. He did the same at a community meeting at St. Vincent's. "I just let them have it. I didn't even wait for the Q&A part to start."

In this way, Michael blustered his way into the first group of residents at Bailey House, an AIDS hospice at the site of the former fifty-five-room luxury River Hotel on West Street, which had served wealthy gay men. At this point he joined his first activist organization, the Lavender Hill Mob. With Marty Robinson and Bill Bahlman, he decided to attend a February 1987 AIDS meeting in Atlanta with the CDC on mandatory testing of patients going into hospitals. They appeared in concentration camp outfits and started yelling, again before the Q&A. "How can you even talk to these people without screaming and yelling at them?" The demo was mentioned in *The New York Times*, and Michael got a phone call from Larry Kramer.

Larry came over to Bailey House, with a bag of food from the gourmet store Balducci's. He was very impressed with what the Mob had done. "And says that he's giving a speech at the [Gay Center]—I think within the next few days . . . *And you've got to be there, and you've got to get all your friends to come, and all the patients from Bailey House to come.* It's not any sort of invitation. It's an order to be there." The night of Larry's speech at the Center, "we were in that first-floor cafeteria room thing, our backs were to the men's room, and Kramer was by that door leading out to garden thing. And the room was packed. I remember, in terms of celebrities"—actor Martin Sheen, Christine Gorman from *TIME* magazine, folks from GMHC, Michael Callen, Michael Hirsch from the People with AIDS Coalition. "Kramer delivered a fiery speech and I remember he asked half the audience to stand up and he said, *You're all going to be dead in six months, now what are we going to do about it?* . . . Some of the people in the audience were silent or stunned or scared."

By the time of Stop the Church, in 1989, Petrelis had been deeply involved in ACT UP. But he had a social problem. "No one would let me in their affinity group . . . People felt I was too angry, too over the top and—you know, look, I guess I did set myself up as an isolated character for whatever reason." So when the morning of December 11 rolled around, Michael almost didn't go to the action, he was feeling so excluded, but he did pull it together and ended up inside the cathedral.

With his friend Carl Goodman, Michael walked into the ten-o'clock mass. He didn't see anyone else from ACT UP. Then he saw Bill Dobbs walking around, and he doesn't remember the police on the inside at this point. Carl and Michael were out in the middle of the church, right on the center aisle, and the mass began. Cardinal O'Connor made an announcement about there being *an expected demonstration* that day, and he wanted his parishioners to stay calm. O'Connor quickly led the congregation in a prayer, and it was at this point that ACT UP started the action. Different members of different affinity groups stood up, read statements about what was wrong with the church, its attitudes toward gays and lesbians, its attitudes toward AIDS and HIV prevention. Michael remembered that he wanted to be heard. And he didn't want to do a sit-down action. "I [stood] up on the pew where I was, and started screaming, *O'Connor, you are killing us. You are killing us!*

"And I couldn't hear myself, because there's this cacophony of competing voices from the parishioners saying the prayer . . . ACT UP demonstrators trying to read their statements, trying to be heard. I do remember hearing noises of the boots of the cops on the tiles, you know? Which I thought was kind of surprising because there was so much of this noise. And standing up and screaming, *O'Connor, you're killing us! Just stop it, stop it!* And then an usher for the church came over and asked me to sit down. I said, *No, I'm not going to sit down!* He goes away and then came back and said, *Please sit down.* I got down in a little bit. Stood up again, started screaming again. This time, there was a policeman who came over to me and said, *You're going to have to sit down.* I said, *Okay.* Sat down, and got up a minute or so later, doing it again. And I guess it was at that point, I went into this thing of *Well, it's a Fellini movie.*

"Listen, I'm half-Italian, so I felt like this was fine. This was more than fine for all of the surreal aspects of this. And I eventually was pulled down from standing up on the pews screaming, by two cops. They got me into the aisle. They put the handcuffs on me, and they're leading me out, and as they're leading me out, this fellow says, *Well, who are you?* and everything. And I said, *Why do you want to know?* It turned out to be a reporter from the *Times.* And [he] quotes me the next day and everything. Then I got all this hate mail. I was listed in the phone book."

When Michael got out of jail, he discovered that the action was big news. And a number of people in ACT UP were mad at him for having violated the group decision to have a silent die-in. But Michael's attitude was *Well, that's what I wanted to do.* "Someone had thrown a Communion wafer to the floor. And of course that action is what the church seized on, as this horrible act of blasphemy and outrageousness. It was like, *Oh please, you can get another wafer,* you can't bring your friends back from the dead."

TOM KEANE

Tom Keane grew up in a pro-Kennedy Catholic family in Mineola, Long Island, a home with "a kind of basic message of loving your neighbor and believing in sort of social justice and equality and that kind of thing." He went to confession after the first time he'd had sex with a guy, which was an unusual thing, because he never went to confession. "It was more like I didn't know what to think about this or what to make out of this." The priest told him that there are some people who will say it was probably just a phase and that he'd grow out of it, but that there are other people who don't think that at all, and no matter what anybody tells him, Tom should just understand that Christ never said anything about homosexuality.

Tom was a member of the Wave 3 affinity group and worked on the Fundraising Committee. By the time of Stop the Church, Tom had been representing the floor (the general membership) at the Coordinating Committee for a year. Mike Signorile organized an affinity group for the St. Patrick's action that was to be called Speaking in Tongues, "a reference to the old-fashioned way of taking Communion on your tongue, and the premise was we would go up to receive Communion, and instead of receiving Communion, say something, whatever we were inclined, whatever message we personally wanted to deliver. Again, mine was sort of still consistent with the [Target] City Hall demo. Mine was, *Opposing safe-sex education is murder.*"

The affinity group members came to the cathedral separately, dressed inconspicuously. Tom and his friend pretended they were Italian tourists and walked around speaking Italian. During the homily, he observed other ACT UPers, also dressed for church, rising from their various seats and lying in the aisles for the planned silent die-in. As those demonstrators were in the process of being arrested and carried away, the mass continued. When the call to Communion came, his affinity group approached.

"I hadn't premeditated like I was going to take the host or toss it or whatever, but eighteen years of going to church, I'm there, I put my hands out, and suddenly I have the Communion wafer in my hands, and the priest says, *This is the body of Christ,* and I say, *Opposing safe-sex education is murder.*" Then I sort of—I didn't really know what to do, and I think in some sense, some part of me was sort of saying, *Well, fine. You guys think you can tell us that you reject us, that we don't belong, so I'm going to reject you.* So I took it and I crushed it and dropped it. Didn't spit it out. That was all over the papers that—I think afterward, like six or seven people they said had, like, *spit the Communion wafer out* or whatever, which I remember being sort of amused by . . . they came scurrying, a bunch of them, to kind of sweep up the little bits, and I'm not sure what they're supposed to do with them after something like that, but they were definitely going to collect them and preserve them . . . I don't remember if there was a plan about what we would do after we said our thing, whether we were planning to get arrested or not, but I lay down and was arrested."

New York Newsday featured a cover that showed the priest stepping over Tom to continue to give Communion to the people in line. So clearly the media was paying attention and showed up at the church in time to get that shot. Tom recalled press clippings from all over the world. "I think if we had protested outside the church, it would have been local news and it would not have been a major story. I think once we chose to go into the church, it was going to be seen very differently."

AFTERMATH

The post-action meeting at ACT UP was high drama. The packed room was divided between people who were thrilled by the vast global media attention and people who were mortified by the fact that our plans had not only gone awry but ended up so far from the silent protest that we had all agreed on. Yet, interestingly, even though Michael, Neil, Tom, and others had acted against the organizational plan, no one was ever threatened with any kind of exclusion, shunning, or punishment. People were angry and debated their differences; they said how they felt, and the discussion was heated. But, with the exception of a political cult, the New Alliance Party, which had attempted a take-over of ACT UP and was asked to leave, no member or person in the ACT UP community was ever kicked out. And like most things, this was just the way it was, not the consequence of any kind of ideological or theoretical debate. Why? Because on some very deep level, ACT UP had mercy; we needed each other in order to survive and make change. And people in ACT UP were not in the kind of supremacy positions necessary to declare someone else a nonperson. We were suffering, and despite the hubris, the pain was accompanied by some kind of humility, a recognition of humanity, and a desire to get better.

TOM KEANE

Tom got up in the post-action meeting and told ACT UP that he wasn't going to apologize, and he recalls that this statement mostly got a cheer.

His perception was that, by and large, while there were people who had reservations, the bulk of ACT UP was supportive. "Well, I know Peter Staley was unhappy. He had been opposed to people going into the church at all, and the whole silent die-in during the homily was, I think, sort of guided into being as a plan by him . . . So I knew he was not happy about that. But I remember Richard Goldstein (of *The Village Voice*) wrote about it. He basically compared us to Cossacks, which I thought was a little bit over the top."

VICTOR MENDOLIA

About two weeks later, the Catholic Church was opening another hospice for people with AIDS. And Gabe Pressman, an older, familiar news reporter on NBC, asked Cardinal O'Connor, *Don't you think it odd that you continue to open up hospices for people to die, yet you oppose condoms and safe-sex education?*

"And that question would never have been asked [previously]—in New York, the press did not ask questions of the cardinal. They only took what he said, and reported it, and they never questioned him . . . He had always been completely unchallenged. And it was the first time, ever, that I had seen it done. And then I knew that we won. It was the time that made everything change, to this day. Now you talk about *the cardinal*, and they're like, *Well, who is the cardinal?* The church does not hold the power that they once had in this city. And I believe that it was our doing . . .

"I don't believe in untouchable and unquestioned authority. I believe in questioning authority. And in this city, at that time, there was no higher authority that was unquestioned than the church . . . And they are responsible for so much misery in this world. Certainly, as we continued on, people and corporations and institutions understood that we were serious, that if we were going to go after you, there were going to be serious problems for you. As we started targeting the drug companies more specifically, they really grew to fear us, for good reason."

Victor had not been tested for HIV until around the time of the Stop the Church action. Well, he had been tested, but didn't go back for results, three times. And finally he had the nerve to do it, and did it, he said, "because I had all these fierce people around me who were positive, who were living, who were going on, and were powerful, and getting all these powerful things done. And it gave me the courage to go and do it. And of course I tested positive, and I've been completely healthy, [or] relatively healthy since then."

LARRY KRAMER

"I think the most successful demonstration, in terms of what it accomplished for us, was the St. Patrick's thing. I remember going to the meeting after it—everybody was terrified, because it had been in the paper and every editorial page in town had dumped on us. People were scared, and I remember saying, *Are you crazy? Are you crazy? They're afraid of us now! That's the best thing that could ever have happened to us!* And it was true, it was true."

MIKE SIGNORILE

Mike felt that, ultimately, the public was very open to the message that ACT UP was putting forth about the church meddling in government, and using its power and affecting the epidemic in extraordinary ways.

"There was always a fine line in ACT UP, which was a great fine line. It always is what made the group electric . . . The anger always made ACT UP very powerful, and it was a balancing act. It was always a balancing act of, just show enough of it, that the rest of the message isn't obscured. You show too much of it, and then you're just an angry mob. But showing none of it would have just been a really dull group that would have gone nowhere. So to me it was always a balance. And I got off on the anger, almost all the time, that ACT UP was expressing . . . Then I think you get into a larger discussion of what is the purpose of the action—of any action? Is it to express our anger, or to get the message out? Or both? And it certainly was successful at expressing the anger. And sometimes, some actions just are about that."

MAXINE WOLFE

"There were seven thousand people outside—that was the biggest, ever, picket/demonstration we had . . . And the Catholic Church in New York had never had that many people to say publicly, *You are killing people. Your policies—not your religion—your policies and your money are killing people* . . . People [in ACT UP] started backtracking, [thinking] that we had offended people . . . I [didn't] have any of those feelings. If you do things that have public policy implications, I don't care where you are, I'm going to come and get you, and you can't hide behind the church."

TRANS WOMEN AT STOP THE CHURCH

Interestingly, in an episode that aired in 2019, the television series *Pose*, produced by Ryan Murphy and Janet Mock, depicted ACT UP's action at St. Patrick's Cathedral but added Black trans characters from the series going to the demonstration, performing civil disobedience, and being taken away by the police. In reality, one trans woman was arrested at St. Patrick's, but they were white: ACT UP facilitator Kathy Otter (later Ottersten). Writing on the ACT UP Alumni Facebook page, Robert Vázquez-Pacheco and Moisés Agosto-Rosario both expressed anger that corporate representations of ACT UP inserted nonexistent people of color while ignoring the people of color who actually were there and did the work. Once again, ACT UP still had no control over its own representation, but this was 2019, thirty-two years after its founding.

ANN NORTHROP

"It was the demonstration we did that got the most worldwide press coverage in tones that were horrified. And there are people who to this day think it was a very big mistake for us to do that because they think it was very negative publicity." Ann almost got fired from her job at Hetrick-Martin. "Damien Martin almost had a heart attack in the hall, screaming at me about this." Andy Humm, who is one of her closest friends to this day, whom Ann works with and plays golf with and lives next door to, screamed at her for doing it. Ann found that many gay people and straight people and all sorts of people hated the action and thought it was absolutely horrible.

"But I, in my heart of hearts, think it was a brilliant and wonderful and positive action, because it brought out the issues. And we said for years in ACT UP that our job was not to be liked—that we were not doing what we were doing to get the public to like us. We were doing what we were doing to accomplish something about particular issues, and I think we did that, enormously successfully. And we weren't liked, but we forced people to pay attention and forced change, I think, much quicker than it would have happened now. We didn't accomplish nearly what I would like to accomplish, but to the extent that we did things, I think it was tremendous and had nothing to do with being liked or admired. That action did end up on the front page of every newspaper in the world, I think, and mostly because Tom Keane crumbled the host, which I support him doing . . .

"But my favorite story, actually, is from Gabriel Rotello, who, several days after the action, talked to his mother in suburban Danbury, Connecticut, who said to him, *You know, my friends and I have been talking about this*—as was the whole world, at that point—*and we've decided that before this demonstration, we thought gay people were sort of weak and wimpy. But now, we think gay people are strong and angry.* That was it, for me. That did it. That was exactly what I wanted to accomplish, and I couldn't have been happier."

GREGG BORDOWITZ

Gregg was very frustrated by Stop the Church.

"People point to it as a success because we got an enormous amount of press. But no, it got us nothing. It might have broken the symbolic taboo. My Catholic brothers and sisters, I know, were exorcising an enormous amount of shame and guilt that they had been made to feel through the church. And I'm very sympathetic to that. I was sympathetic to that . . . being Jewish and having a different frame of reference for my shame and guilt. I could never imagine going to a synagogue. But the church is different—it's hierarchically organized—it's very different than going to like Temple Beth Israel of New Hyde Park, or something like that. So I understood and was sympathetic. But no, in the end we didn't get anything. And we exhausted an enormous amount of resources. And we were lost after that, because I don't think we knew what to do after that. We were trying to produce a spectacular achievement that didn't really work . . . It was becoming apparent to everyone then, after that, that this kind of politics of the spectacular were not necessarily going to carry us forward . . . I felt that ACT UP was a health-care movement and that ACT UP could achieve universal healthcare within New York State. That's where all of my organizing went."

But actually, ACT UP's greatest victories were still ahead.

Remembrance: Robert Garcia

KAREN RAMSPACHER

Karen met Robert Garcia when he was a facilitator for the Monday-night meeting. "He just had such a shining personality that I was immediately drawn to him." And they were close until his death in 1993. "He had a great mix in his personality, where he was very electric, but at the same time he was very focused and organized. In his day job, he was a secretary in an insurance company, which made total sense to me because he could be so together and step by step, which also made him a great facilitator at the meetings, and then the other side being so magnetic and really drawing people to him. He was a great party friend. I mean, we went to clubs and danced, and then he'd go off and go to the back rooms, and I'd say, *I got to go find some straight guys.*"

They had lived together at the loft on Warren Street, and then Karen moved to Avenue B, between Twelfth and Thirteenth, and Robert did, too. He lived with Victor Mendolia in the apartment upstairs. "So it was still a house, and he had keys, and he would come in and he would borrow my dresses to go cocktail waitress, and I'd come home, and my best dress would be trashed. But, you know, it went both ways. He'd lend me stuff to wear too. I'd wear his leather jacket." At the time, he didn't have a steady boyfriend. Later he met Bob

Scarpa. Then his brother Danny came from L.A. to live with him.

As Robert's best friend, Karen was in his primary care group. She felt like his sister. She went out with him to L.A. when he first decided to go tell his family. They knew he was gay. He had been out to them for a while, but they didn't know he had AIDS. She was back in New York when he had a heart attack, which could have been related to drug use. So Karen went back out and stayed for a week. Since she had been there when he told them he had AIDS, she could help bridge the gap with his family. So when he got ill, Karen was the person who organized his care group, because she knew that she couldn't provide all the support by herself. He had dementia, and he would be walking through the East Village in winter, in his underwear, thinking that he was Jesus. "That was a really hard time. People would call me and say, *Robert's in the East Village in his underwear again.* I'd say, *Well, did you get him inside?*" This was before cell phones. Usually, somebody would go out, tuck him in. Sometimes friends would get him to St. Vincent's Hospital and they would take rounds, because St. Vincent's was so overcrowded at the time that Robert often couldn't get a bed. So he would be in the hallway on a gurney, and friends would sit with him, because they didn't ever want him to be alone. They set up shifts so that no one person had to do it 24/7, because it could take days to get a bed. And once he got a bed, there wasn't much more to hope.

At that point Robert had seven T cells. He had some opportunistic infections. So friends were just trying to make him as happy and comfortable as possible. "He was very clear on what he wanted. He never really wanted [AIDS] to impinge on his life, and I can't say I blame him. He just wanted to keep being the Robert he was, and that meant going out as much as he could and participating as much as he could and not slowing down, and, as he used to say, *not eating right.*" Karen paid his insurance premium when he couldn't work anymore.

Robert finally went home to L.A. to die. "He was really tight with his family and he loved his parents and his sister and his two brothers, older and younger. He was tight with the nieces and nephews, so he was really right in with his family. I actually wasn't there when he died . . . By that point, he wasn't cogent anymore, and so I actually decided not to go, which was a really hard choice. But I wanted to remember him the way I knew him, and he knew I loved him."

PART III

Paths of Leadership

This analysis of how leadership functioned in a direct-action movement grapples with three critical stages of ACT UP's development. First, the role of three influential individuals: Larry Kramer, Maxine Wolfe, and Mark Harrington. We then follow Mark to the second iteration of Treatment and Data, where activists set the research agenda to win new treatments, rose to positions of real power, and came to identify as insiders, ultimately eclipsing the organization that fostered them. Finally, we follow Maxine Wolfe in a very different direction to the sprawling coalition that was ACT UP's four-year campaign to change the Centers for Disease Control's definition of AIDS so that women could qualify for benefits and become models for the development of new medications. In this way, dramatically different approaches to change also propelled the self-concepts of the activists who created them.

5

Inspiration and Influence: Larry Kramer, Maxine Wolfe, Mark Harrington

In 2018, I wrote a piece for *The New York Times* about the complex role of branding in political movements. The young, white, gay, male editor corrected my use of ACT UP to "Larry Kramer's ACT UP." I told him that if I went on record with the term *Larry Kramer's ACT UP*, I would have to move to China. Over a year later, Larry forwarded me an email from the same editor. He wanted to organize a photo shoot of surviving members of ACT UP, but "only" if Larry would be in the picture. Regardless of the reality, this editor wanted to brand Larry with ACT UP.

It is remarkable how many people in high places, of all ages, in multiple spaces, think that Larry was "the leader of ACT UP." Of course, that phrase alone shows how little others know about our movement because ACT UP had no singular *leader*, although we had many *leaders*, and needed and depended on them. People love and hate Larry. Most people credit him with being the catalyst for creating this movement through his inciting speech at the Gay Center on March 10, 1987. And in this way, some people credit him for being a force that contributed to saving their life. In the early days of ACT UP, Larry encouraged a treatment focus, and helped, with Vito Russo, to legitimize Iris Long's contribution, which set ACT UP on one of its most productive trajectories toward tangible change. But soon, inside ACT UP, Larry was often absent, regularly in conflict, and not very influential on applied policy or activist matters. What Larry did do, which makes him exceptional, is that, as a rich gay man with cultural and political connections, he screamed bloody murder, made demands on his high-end relationships, and used his currency to insist on change for people with AIDS. And very, very few people with his level of privilege did any of those things.

Larry went to Yale with someone from Bristol Myers, could get op-eds in the *Times*, could get famous people on the phone, could get on television. And he used all of that access for people with AIDS.

The many leaders in ACT UP had visions for concrete actions toward ending the AIDS crisis. They had imaginations that expanded our collective reach and impact. They encouraged and inspired action and commitment in others. They had ideas, they did the work to realize these ideas, and they coalesced small communities within ACT UP to achieve specific, concrete campaigns. Sometimes, as the interviews reveal, they became myopic about their small groups, confusing them with the greater movement. Within ACT UP, they created worlds that were productive, responsible, and in some sense comforting against the enormous weight of living and dying within a mass death experience. They could also be cliquey, mean, superior. There were probably a hundred people like this in ACT UP, in substantive positions of influence and responsibility, and the group's organization allowed and encouraged individual visions to coexist. In every interview, people name others who inspired them, collaborated with them, built the movement together. They helped other people become effective, sometimes one-on-one, sometimes in large numbers. They were bold. Many of them died.

Everyone else in ACT UP was just as necessary because they were, on some level, implementers. They did not have the big visions, the original ideas, the innovative approaches, but they cooperated. They enthusiastically supported with all their hearts and bodies. They did necessary tasks. They showed up. They followed through. They made posters, they went to demos, they worked on committees, they did essential labor like xeroxing, painting, marching, selling buttons, training, and engaging in civil disobedience. Even wearing T-shirts or buttons with ACT UP slogans and looking graceful on television ultimately performed an impactful service.

Scanning the interviews I conducted with a wide range of ACT UPers, the two names that emerge most often in reference to internal leadership are clearly Maxine Wolfe and Mark Harrington. Whether people loved them or hated them, these two were repeatedly named as profound influences. Mark and Maxine were two personalities of great ability who in some ways were equally polarizing and unifying. They ultimately represented two different points of view on political organizing, yet they shared a great deal in common. It would be a mistake to say that Mark was about treatment and Maxine was about access, because it could easily be argued that Mark's main work was access, and Maxine's was treatment. Mark's most impactful work was on access to effective treatments by forcing the government and pharmaceutical companies to create them. Maxine's most impactful work was winning treatment for women and poor people. Of course, even that assessment is too narrow. They were both hugely influential in every aspect of ACT UP's work and culture, rooted in group relationships and bonding systems. They cooperated with each other on many crucial events and projects. And they inspired both devotion and animosity in significant numbers of ACT UP members. Ultimately who they were, in the origin of their life experiences, produced what they each wanted the movement to become. As Marisa Cardinale, a TAG activist, told me, "For Mark AIDS was a puzzle, and for Maxine it was a political movement." Their interviews showed that they were like a number of other leaders in ACT UP, including sometimes Larry, in that they were hard-core, effective, and inspiring, and possessed endless energy and vision. They also were sometimes dismissive, manipulative, and brutal. Often unable to be self-critical, even in retrospect, they played hardball. These are the two people most often blamed for ACT UP's downfall and self-defeat, and the two most frequently named at the center of ACT UP's victories and strengths. As a sign of how much individuals were valued by the quality of their work for the movement, regardless of who they were in the outside world and what occupations they held, ACT UPers often worked intimately with others without knowing their last names. But everyone knew Larry Kramer, Mark Harrington, and Maxine Wolfe.

LARRY KRAMER

Larry Kramer was born in 1935, of Russian Jewish origin. His father was a government lawyer, and his mother ran a suburban chapter of the American Red Cross, in Mount Rainier, Maryland. "I grew up late. I was a late bloomer. I was a very unhappy child. I was a very unhappy teenager. I tried to kill myself at Yale. And it took a long time to pull myself out of those troughs." He got prestige positions as an assistant to studio presidents at United Artists and Columbia Pictures and was transferred to England to work on their films. "That's what probably saved my life in a way because I was able to be psychoanalyzed for very little money, and it was enormously helpful. I wanted to write and I was terrified to write. I was afraid to write, as so many young writers, wannabes, are. And through the analysis, I was able to work through all of that, and the first thing I really wrote was my screenplay for *Women in Love*, which turned out to give me a certain amount of confidence." Larry came back to New York and was frustrated by a gay community that he felt was too sex-oriented. He wrote the novel *Faggots* about his hurt at how an emphasis on sex interfered with him finding an intimate relationship. He had never been politically involved, but AIDS changed all that.

"We needed help and you had to scream for it, and I asked for it nicely, originally. We tried to be very nice to *The New York Times* and to Ed Koch and you learn very fast that you're a faggot, and it doesn't make any difference that you went to Yale and were assistant to presidents of a couple of film companies, and that you had money. You suddenly know what it's like to feel like a faggot or a nigger or a kike. I remember the day it happened. And I didn't like it."

In 1982, Larry, along with Dr. Lawrence Mass, writer Edmund White, Nathan Fain, Paul Popham, and Paul Rapoport, founded the Gay Men's Health Crisis. An answering machine in the home of GMHC's first director, Rodger McFarlane, became the world's first AIDS hotline, receiving over one hundred calls the first night.

With help from Larry's brother Arthur's law firm, GMHC was granted tax-exempt status, which meant that it had to have a board. Larry turned to "the guys I danced with" and put them on the board, and then learned that they didn't agree with his approach. Larry felt they thought he was too loud and too confrontational with city hall and Mayor Koch. Larry felt that GMHC was overly structured and controlled. Yale and work in the film industry had not prepared him for the job description.

"*What is a job description?* I didn't know what the fuck a job description was. Why did we have to have a job description? Why can't we go get the best person? And then it became all this business about—you know, you had to take people whether they were good or not, because they represented certain genders or certain colors. We didn't have many women in the beginning. The first paid employee of GMHC was a Black person—Phil Patrick. We couldn't get Black people there. So somehow to have to deal with all of that when I always say *get the best person*, somehow—and you get in a lot of trouble with stuff like that. No offense meant."

At ACT UP's first meeting, people knew they had to perform a public action because it was the only way to get attention. Somebody said, *Let's go against the FDA*, because they were so slow in approving things. So Larry was able to use his connections to place an op-ed piece for the *Times* called 'The FDA's Callous Response to AIDS.' It ran on the very day of the first demonstration on Wall Street, March 24, 1987. Through his connections he got Joe Papp, the founder of The Public Theater, whose son died of AIDS, to make an effigy in the theater's shop of Frank Young, the head of the FDA, who was then "hanged" on Wall Street.

Larry became "very attached" to the first iteration of Treatment and Data. "Iris Long was this incredible thing that happened to ACT UP. Just incredible . . . And she took two or three people initially, and then there were four or five and then they were bigger. And she taught them everything she knew." Using his connections with pharmaceutical companies, Larry once took Mark Harrington to a meeting and found the businessmen thinking that Mark was a doctor. "We were at this incredible meeting at [Bristol Myers], in some big office building, and we had a break in the john, and then the schmuck from [Bristol Myers] . . . we were pissing next to each other in the men's room and he looks over at me and says, *That Harrington, it is Doctor Harrington, isn't it?* I just kvelled—he was one of my children."

Although not involved directly in research, Larry felt he "was trotted out to scare people." He recalled a meeting at the pharmaceutical company Hoffmann-La Roche during which the man next to him at the conference table was shaking. Larry turned to the pharma guy on the other side and said, *What's wrong with him?* The man replied, *He's scared of you!* "And I thought *Hey, wow*."

Larry, like much of his milieu, believed in an Inside/Outside strategy, in which there would be insiders cooperating with government and pharmaceutical companies, and outsiders being threatening via street organizing. He did not seem to be aware that the ACT UPers who could be insiders looked and acted for the most part like the white Ivy League–educated men who ran government and pharma. "There was a lot of flak from people like Maxine [Wolfe] about going inside, when we were finally able to go inside. And I said, *Are you crazy? Of course, you go inside! They let you inside! What can you do from the outside? . . .* The destruction of ACT UP was the severing of this dual nature."

Larry felt that the "downfall" of ACT UP occurred when Mark Harrington and TAG left.

"They became drunk on hubris—drunk on their brains, drunk on the very things Maxine predicted, I might add. They were drunk on their power. They could sit down with the head of [Bristol Myers] or the chief scientists. They could call all these people up and they could do it on their own from then on, and they didn't need anyone fighting on the outside for them. And perhaps they became a little ashamed of us, I don't know. But I will never forgive them for it."

Despite how impressed Larry was with Maxine and Iris, he was often unable to see the diversity of ACT UP. When I asked him where he thought the Inside/Outside strategy came from, he gave a typical Larry Kramer answer:

"We were mostly white and privileged, and there was a lot of flak against us in the *community* because of that . . . It became a place to go where all the hot guys were. And they all wore their black jeans and their black boots. It became a look. And those were, unfortunately, the people who were sick. But enough of them came so that that gave us the image. And there was a lot of criticism of that by people who didn't look like that or didn't want to look like that . . . We had guys teaching us civil disobedience. I don't know if you remember that. We had some big Black guy who had done something for Martin Luther King or something come and give us civil disobedience lessons about how to lie down in the street and let your body go limp and all that. All of those things . . . I got Mark Harrington a book deal, after the Fast Track thing was fashioned because of us—when we were still talking. And he wrote the book and it was never published. I was never given the opportunity to read it because by then we'd stopped talking. So I don't know if it was any good, but it was indeed about the mechanism of all of this and how we had fought through all of this."

Larry famously was permitted a liver transplant later in life, despite being HIV-positive. When he came out of the fog he did a lot of thinking—*Why me? How did I live through all of this? Why didn't everybody fight?* He did not believe in God, but he theorized his advantages as luck. "When I needed a [hepatitis B] drug, it suddenly was there, in an experimental trial. When I needed a liver, it was suddenly there— timing . . . If I've been spared, it's been, I think it's because I'm here to tell this story. I'm the only gay writer who was on the front line—that's still alive—who was on the front line from the very beginning. And I know where all the bodies are buried—figuratively and metaphorically, no, actually and metaphorically. And that's what propels me, every day—seven days a week."

Just for the record, when he made these comments he was not "the only" gay writer on the front line who was still alive, but that was Larry.

I think Larry never really understood the wide range of people who were in ACT UP, where we were coming from, and what we were doing. He was able to recognize when women had something to offer that ACT UP needed, but he never integrated the AIDS politics of women and people of color into his worldview, despite repeated exposure. Perhaps in some way, this false image that he was "the leader" was very palatable to the media and the men with power, who saw the world in fundamental racial and gender lenses that made only white men important. And the world thinks of Larry as "the leader" of an organization that he didn't know and never claimed to lead because of the desire for a mirror of power, the power that was itself detrimental to both ACT UP and the communities of people we were fighting for.

MAXINE WOLFE

Maxine Wolfe was born in Brooklyn in 1942. When she would ask her immigrant mother who she was voting for, the answer was none of them were worth voting for because none were for the working class. In high school, Maxine had a friend whose father was in the Communist Party and had moved his family into Maxine's neighborhood to organize the workers. The girl took Maxine to a concert by the Weavers, when they were blacklisted. When they sang "This Land Is Your Land," Maxine believed them. *This land was made for you and me.* At Brooklyn College, she was the first person in her family to get a BA. Maxine got married at nineteen, "and then I spent ten years figuring out how to leave."

She started graduate school toward a PhD in philosophy at the CUNY Graduate Center in 1961, at night, while she was working. Her mentor was Hal Proshansky, who later was the president of the Graduate Center. Her first political involvements were with the Congress of Racial Equality, and she attended Martin Luther King Jr.'s 1963 March on Washington. She had two daughters and finally left her husband when her youngest was one. She joined a short-lived feminist consciousness-raising group in the late 1960s and there met a woman who belonged to the leftist party International Socialists.

Maxine Wolfe and her daughter Amy marching with ACT UP at New York City's Gay Pride parade in 1989 (Photograph by T.L. Litt)

Maxine took courses at the Marxist School, which was Trotskyist, and read Marx. She felt there was a lot of grandstanding and false claims coming from the Left at the time. "In the years that I was in the Left, a lot of what I learned was really important to my future organizing, but it wasn't politics. It was about doing politics . . . If you really want to organize, you have to have some authenticity in what you do." Her experiences in the Left, and in reproductive rights, formed the foundations of her influences on ACT UP.

ORGANIZE THE UNORGANIZED

Maxine observed that the Left would do their organizing around existing groups. They would ask for endorsements from other organizations that they were already in relationship with. "It was not about people," she said, it was about coalitions. She saw organizations claim to represent more people than they had actually activated. Coalitions would produce flyers with many organizational names listed as endorsers. But very few people would actually show up "because there was no membership, in the sense that eventually something like ACT UP would have . . . And there was no way to construct a membership, because unlike unions and stuff like that, people were not organizing unorganized people." Maxine also came to understand that the leftist convention of "principles of unity" was constricting. The groups would fight forever, over the wording of their agreements, and it closed down participation. "That top-down model didn't speak to most people . . . You're not reaching anybody, you're not changing anybody's mind, you're not changing the politics of what's going on."

In 1979, she moved into Left feminism by joining the Committee for Abortion Rights and Against Sterilization Abuse (CARASA). Like a number of women in ACT UP, including Marion Banzhaf, Maria Maggenti, Tracy Morgan, Dolly Meieran, Karen Ramspacher, Risa Denenberg, myself, and many others, Maxine came to ACT UP from the reproductive rights movement. And in ACT UP, these women, in turn, influenced large numbers of women and men to embrace a multi-issue perspective. At CARASA, Maxine learned more about "looking at the world as it really is and organizing unorganized people."

Although CARASA presented itself as part of the women's movement, since it was a women's organization, Maxine had no idea that it actually was composed of mostly socialist feminists. "It wasn't, like, *feminist* feminists. It wasn't radical feminists. It was socialist feminists. And some of those people were also connected to parties." Inside CARASA, Maxine got involved in the national committee, starting what eventually became the Reproductive Rights National Network, and also served on the steering committee. "But it was also driving me a little crazy in that organization, because people were also doing the same kind of thing, where they were organizing with other groups and not really with women—even though they said they wanted to do that."

Around 1982, well into Ronald Reagan's first term, Maxine, CARASA staff member Stephanie Roth, myself, and a few others joined what was eventually called the Lesbian Action Committee. From Maxine's perspective this move was highly controversial. Maxine experienced that many of the straight members of CARASA were very uncomfortable, anxious, and/or upset about specifically lesbian organizing in the organization. "As soon as we started mentioning lesbian stuff, it was like—everything else we had done in the organization disappeared. And, I can see in hindsight, I could understand why, because we had totally different politics! . . . The first thing we did was an educational—that immediately got interpreted that we were trying to make everybody a lesbian. It was classic stuff."

CONFRONTING THE CHURCH

In 1981, Maxine became a representative of CARASA at the first coalition of left-wing gay groups, the Committee Against Racism, Anti-Semitism, Sexism and Heterosexism (CRASH). Joan Gibbs, who later was a lawyer for ACT UP, was there as a representative of Dykes Against Racism Everywhere (DARE). Other groups included Radical Women, the New Alliance Party, the Committee of Lesbian and Gay Male Socialists, Black and White Men Together, Lavender Left, and others. "So we all started meeting, and it was like a revelation to everybody, because it was the first time that we—any of us in the room—had kind of brought together a gay politics with our leftist politics." They started working on the Family Protection Act, which was an omnibus bill that had been put out in 1980 by the Republican/Evangelical coalition that elected Ronald Reagan. The Family Protection Act established the anti-gay, anti-abortion social issues agenda that the right wing has followed to this day. The entry of right-wing Protestantism into the mainstream of the Republican Party was, at the time, a new political event. The Left had always had radical religious people involved, and there had historically been a fear of confronting religious organizations. In fact, abortion was an issue that was highly controversial in progressive coalitions because of the presence of Catholic leftists in peace and social justice circles, thus isolating feminists.

The Family Protection Act, using religious arguments, laid out step-by-step plans for restricting abortion rights, with the goal of outlawing abortion completely, while keeping homosexual sex illegal under sodomy laws that would remain intact until 2003. The Family Protection Act envisioned a furthering of the oppression of queer people and women. "It had stuff about not allowing women on welfare to use Legal Aid for divorce. It had to do with separating the sexes in sports." So CRASH organized a conference about the Family Protection Act and set up some demonstrations. Still, "it was a time where there was no mass movement." CRASH then organized a community meeting about the Neighborhood Church, which was a right-wing, fundamentalist Christian church, provocatively opened on Bleecker Street in the heart of gay Greenwich Village. The meeting led to a demonstration at the church, as a kind of early precursor to ACT UP's later, more significant action at St. Patrick's Cathedral. A tone was being set about directly addressing churches that were collaborating with the right-wing government. Some people in CARASA objected to targeting churches, which they felt alienated working-class Americans. They also objected to the fact that Maxine was spending so much time on lesbian and gay male politics.

DIRECT ACTION

In April of 1982, Stephanie Roth and I and some other women from CARASA and the D.C.-based feminist newspaper *Off Our Backs* organized a direct action called the Women's Liberation Zap Action Brigade, against an anti-abortion congressional hearing for a bill called the human life statute. We interrupted the hearing with signs reading A WOMAN'S LIFE IS A HUMAN LIFE. The hearing was on live television, and so the demonstration received broad national exposure. "Now, you have to imagine," Maxine said, "that [CARASA was made up of] lefty feminists who never did any direct action I have ever known of. The most they ever did was to picket somewhere. So they got freaked, because Sarah was creating this thing, where all of us were going to go to

Washington and break up these hearings . . . and we got huge amounts of publicity. And they were freaked that we got huge amounts of publicity, and it wasn't them that did it. So then they didn't want to support the people."

CARASA did not support direct action and accused us of "substitutionalism," which was an old left term, in which activists substituted themselves for the working class. Direct action was not common at the time, and, except for some feminist sit-ins at *Ladies' Home Journal* and *RAT* and some gay liberation zaps, direct action hadn't been used as part of a mass movement since the Vietnam War. CARASA believed that direct action was a vanguardist gesture, when the real goal was to motivate mass movements. What CARASA was missing here, and what ACT UP understood instinctively, was that, as young women at the time, we saw ourselves as the very constituency that we were organizing. We weren't reaching out to someone else. And so we were not substituting, but actually *being*, which was a reality that ACT UP would come to embody.

Maxine found herself continually at cross-purposes with CARASA.

"We had these ideas about organizing that I think came very directly out of—not just a set of lesbian feminist politics that was sort of out there at the time, but also out of the *lesbian* part of the lesbian feminist politics, because we knew that you wouldn't reach lesbians by asking for a lesbian group to join your demonstration. You know, if you were going to find lesbians to organize, you would have to go looking to where lesbians were. You'd have to go to bars—you know what I mean? You couldn't just pretend that they were going to be at some lefty conference. It wasn't going to happen. And . . . they basically pushed us out of that organization."

Maxine was accused of being "*an unconscious lesbian separatist. That's such a Marxist term, right? . . . That's literally what they thought.*" This experience convinced Maxine that she wasn't going to work in the feminist movement again. "I didn't want to work with straight women. That was it."

The lesbians kicked out of CARASA started a new group called Women for Women: fighting for women's liberation with warmth and a sense of humor, "which people on the left thought was ridiculous. They didn't even get that we said *sense of humor*. They thought, *What could you have a sense of humor about in the world?*" Women for Women joined the Reproductive Rights National Network (R2N2). We did a teach-in at the yearly conference on the pro-family left and the pro-family right. Just as mainstream Democrats were going to the right, so was the Left going to the right. Michael Lerner and Cornel West had started a "pro-family left" movement that overtly said they prioritized the family over gay rights. Maxine worked on the steering committee of R2N2, which was, "basically, all lesbians, and it was, at least, half lesbians of color. A majority of the lesbians on the steering committee were working class, and so we were trying to put all of those politics really in and not just verbally into what people were doing. And that's when all of this stuff just showed up—the subtle kinds of racism, all the subtle kinds of homophobia."

To combat the anti-abortion bill known as the human life statute, R2N2 made up stickers that said A WOMAN'S LIFE IS A HUMAN LIFE. "We couldn't make up enough of those to give out across the country. As an organization—the Reproductive Rights National Network—we must have produced, easily, a hundred thousand of those stickers, and we could have produced a million, if we had the money . . . sort of like the *Silence=Death* stickers eventually were."

CONVERGING POLITICS BEFORE ACT UP

In the early 1980s, Maxine became aware of AIDS, but none of the gay men in her life were infected. Then a gay woman wrote a letter to *Woman-news*, New York's feminist newspaper, arguing against lesbians being involved with AIDS. "*It's their problem.* And, *Why should we waste our energy taking care of men?*" And Maxine and Joan Nestle, cofounder of the Lesbian Herstory Archives, wrote a letter back rejecting this perspective, saying, *How many Nicaraguans do you know?* "Because everybody was doing work on Nicaragua [and it] didn't seem to matter that they didn't know any Nicaraguans."

Maxine attended a meeting of the newly formed Gay and Lesbian Alliance Against Defamation (GLAAD), which started off as an activist group focused on media, featuring people like Vito Russo, Jewelle Gomez, and journalist Peg Byron. They'd called a community meeting to organize a demonstration at the *New York Post*. "And there were [four hundred] men in this room and hardly any women. One of the guys who was sitting next to us said, *Wow, this is amazing this is happening, because nothing has happened in this community for the past fifteen years.* And I thought to myself, *Where have you been?* And then, Marty Robinson got up, and he started talking about . . . the commissioner of health threatening to close gay bars," because of AIDS.

In 1984, Maxine met Jamie Bauer, who would do substantive work training ACT UP in civil disobedience. Women for Women arranged to sit in at a New York City Council hearing that again failed to pass the gay rights bill; the documentary videotape *Just Because of Who We Are* shows the women being arrested. When the *Bowers v. Hardwick* decision came down from the Supreme Court, Maxine again participated in a civil disobedience action, organized by Nancy Langer and Allison Smith of the Committee of Lesbian and Gay Male Socialists, that attracted thousands of people. The marchers refused to get a permit or negotiate with the police and walked through police barriers in large numbers.

By 1986, Maxine was "looking for something to do . . . I wasn't a reader of the [*New York*] *Native*. I was not in the grouping of people who even knew who Larry Kramer was. He was irrelevant to my life. I would never have shown up at the community center—you know what I mean? I wouldn't have known that he was going to be there that night, or that it mattered, because he was not the person that I—or, that whole grouping were not the people that I looked to for information about political stuff." Meanwhile, she had started a group at CUNY, where she was a professor of environmental psychology, called CUNY Lesbian and Gay People, which allowed her to keep a hand in organizing when nothing else was happening. And so the CUNY group was marching in the 1987 Gay Pride parade that year, when Maxine's friend Rachel Pfeffer invited her to check out a new group that was meeting at the Center.

The contingent in front of Maxine and CUNY Lesbian and Gay People at the Pride parade was ACT UP, "with that incredible concentration camp float that they had that year." She went up to one of the men and asked, "*Are there women in your group?* Because, I saw mostly men. And he said, *Yeah, sure.* I said, *Oh great.* And so, Monday,

I showed up and that started [my involvement in] ACT UP, and there was something like four women in the room."

As someone who had been so politically active, Maxine was surprised to see that there was nobody in that room she knew. Marty Robinson looked familiar, as did former gay liberation activist Marc Rubin. But "there wasn't a lefty in the room. There weren't any of the lefty men that I knew. None of the lefty lesbians were there." Maxine didn't speak at meetings for the first month she went. She was just listening to what people did, because she had no idea of who these people were or how they operated. But she really liked the way the meetings unfolded.

"I liked the idea that people got up and they said what they thought, and that people got up, and they had an idea. And it seemed like if you had an idea, you could do it. I got the feeling then, which is a rare feeling, I think, that people felt that lives depended on them. That it wasn't like an abstract form of politics. There were people in that room who were infected. There were people in that room who had lovers who had died; people who had died. It was not an *interesting political point*. It was real. And that came through in that room. I mean, people were driven to do something."

It was obvious to Maxine that most of the people at ACT UP were independents and didn't have established or fixed ideologies. Instead, the group had a kind of an anarchistic framework. There were no principles of unity that anyone had to adhere to aside from being "committed to direct action to end the AIDS crisis." Maxine loved it when people brought leaflets to the floor. The floor didn't micromanage or hyperedit. The language was understandable, and "you didn't have to read Marx to know what the person was saying. It didn't sound rhetorical. People were really interested in putting out the facts and not embellishing them." And they were interested in doing actions, wherever they needed to get done. They didn't care if it was in Queens or in the Bronx. They were happy to go beyond the Village and the gay community. Maxine appreciated that people were not afraid of the media. "On the left, everybody was afraid of the media. If you got covered by the mainstream media, you must be doing something wrong. And here there were people who actually believed that it was good to be covered by the mainstream media. Not to play up to the mainstream media, but to get them there, so that they would get your message across. It wasn't so that you would perform for them."

For Maxine, it felt easy to fit in. She sat there. She didn't know anybody.

"One of the things that used to go on was that people used to be really *bitchy queens*. People would get after one another. They could not just say, *I don't agree with you*. They would have to do some kind of theatrical number about it. *People are dying! Why are you talking about that?!* . . . The idea that it would fall apart because people were fighting with each other just drove me crazy . . . So Michael Nesline, the facilitator, had ended the meeting, and I stood up on a chair, because I was so scared, and I said, *People, people, you have to listen for a minute, okay?* And Michael said, *The meeting is over*, and I said, *I don't care*. And I just said, *I can't believe that people are going to leave feeling this way, because this is so bad. This is so important that we do this work, and I would just say to people, go home and think about who the real enemy is, because we are not each other's enemies*. And then I got off my chair."

Somebody later told her that Larry Kramer had asked at that point, *Who is that woman?* At the beginning of the next meeting, Eric Sawyer, a housing advocate who always came to ACT UP meetings after work in his suit and tie, showed up wearing a hula skirt and a lei. He stood up at the beginning of the meeting and he said everybody had to go *m-m-m-m-m*, and he made everybody zone out and hum together. *Let's just cool out*, he said. *Let's remember what we're here for*. And then the meeting went forward.

The first time Maxine said anything in a meeting that was political was in June of 1987—when ACT UP was planning a twenty-four-hour picket of Memorial Sloan Kettering Cancer Center. "That's what I mean about people being committed. If you say to people, *Twenty-four-hour picket today*, and they go, *What? Well, I don't know if I can make it*. Nobody was like that . . . It was twenty-four hours a day for five days." ACT UP chose Sloan Kettering not because they were the worst regarding their AIDS services but because, nationally, there were supposed to be ten thousand people in clinical trials for potential HIV drugs, when in reality there were, Maxine said, "like eight hundred." So the idea was to use Sloan Kettering as an emblematic location to make a national point. Also, Sloan Kettering was still just testing AZT, which had been released that March, and excluding the other drugs that ACT UP wanted to be made available.

At one meeting a man came from an AIDS service organization and spoke out against the action. He claimed that *Sloan Kettering is the best place in New York City, and we're going to get them really angry with us, and they're going to close down their clinic, and it's the only place to go.* And he brought with him Dr. Bruce Lee, who was a doctor at the clinic and who stood up "like the savior" and said, *I'm not going to close my clinic, but I don't think it's the right thing to do.* This brought uncertainty to the floor. People were intimidated and started trying to adjust the action to accommodate Dr. Lee. Someone suggested that we should carry signs that praised Sloan Kettering, but made the point that the action was about the larger system. This really upset Maxine. "The idea of saying that some mainstream medical place was great was not my thing.

"So I stood up and I was very careful the way I said it—*You know, I would have a hard time carrying a sign like that and here was my reason.* And I said, *If people are concerned, why don't we write a leaflet that we give out to the workers who go into the building, saying that this is not about you, this is about the institution.* And so, people thought, that was a good idea, and so it was passed. And then, afterwards, a lot of people came up to me and said they were really glad that I said that . . . So that was the first time I said anything political, and then it just took off from there. Then, I just felt like I could speak."

MARK HARRINGTON

Mark Harrington was born in 1960. In the spring of 1982, he was taking a semester off from the visual and environmental studies department at Harvard to do a photo project in his hometown of San Francisco at the UCSF Medical Center. He was working in the nursing department. They were typing up protocols for how nurses should take care of people with AIDS, and they were very short and ended with *Give palliative care, assist with pain, to death.* There was no Bactrim and no prophylaxis. He was only twenty-one. "It was pretty scary. But it was also—it seemed like it was far away and happening to people that I didn't know." At that point in his life Mark thought he was going to be "somebody in the arts," like a writer or a DJ or a musician or a graphic artist or a collage artist. His thesis project was a translation of a 1930s work by Walter Benjamin.

Mark and his lover had some friends who were in New York's downtown art scene, and friends of theirs were getting AIDS in the early 1980s. And so he would hear rumors. A friend of theirs, David Armstrong, the photographer, had a lover who died of AIDS in 1983. So "it was semi-tangible." Mark and his lover would come down to New York and go to openings and see people "that were quite serious about using pretty hard drugs at that time. And we were pretty serious about sex ourselves. So there was a lot of risk going around." But when Mark was back in Cambridge and Boston, it seemed to him like the epidemic was happening somewhere else. In June of 1986, after meeting a man who lived in New York, in the East Village, Mark moved down to the city. He participated in East Village gay life. He went to clubs like the Pyramid and the World, and big dance clubs like the Roxy. He went to an amfAR event, "Art Against AIDS," with performance artist John Kelly in 1987, and remembered being "blown away" by that.

A friend had a show at the Robert Miller Gallery and came to his opening with what was obviously Kaposi sarcoma. He denied it. Mark sat with his lover, talking about it on the street. His boyfriend had had an affair with the sick friend, "so I was suddenly going, *Okay, I can draw the line where I could possibly have been exposed* via this lover—very important guy in my life. Then, when we broke up, subsequently over different stuff, I recall him violently not wanting me to test or us to test—in '87." But in 1988, another friend of Mark's began to develop symptoms. He was losing weight, coughing a lot, having fevers, and, most frightening of all, experiencing nervous psychological issues. "I could easily see myself in his shoes." ACT UP was already there. So Mark went across town and joined it. "I had drawing [class], usually, that night. And, instead of going to drawing, I went to ACT UP. And I actually never went back to drawing."

NO MORE BUSINESS AS USUAL

Mark had never been politically active before, had never belonged to a gay organization. When he walked into ACT UP in 1988 he saw two very attractive young people, Maria Maggenti and David Robinson, who was in a dress, facilitating the meeting. He saw many of his own generation in a large room of enthusiastic people planning the upcoming action, Wall Street II, to mark the anniversary of the first action on Wall Street in 1987. ACT UP had become much larger in a year, and the slogan this time around was "No more business as usual." Mark remembered many different affinity groups doing different actions at that demonstration. Gran Fury—the artist collective—made fake dollar bills that had PEOPLE ARE DYING WHILE YOU DO NOTHING stamped on their face. Mark was part of a new affinity group that just had been trained for that action called Wave 3, with Marvin Shulman, Jim Eigo, and Russell Pritchard. Later, Scott Wald, Pam Earing, Richard Deagle, and Ken Woodard joined. They sat on Trinity Place and Rector Street, right near the World Trade Center towers, and blocked traffic until they were all put onto a bus and taken to the police precinct. This was Mark's first time being arrested. "It was really exhilarating. It felt, in a way, safe, too, because we'd done this training. Gregg Bordowitz was one of my *CD trainers* . . . I felt very protected and part of a group. And then, when it was over, I felt like we'd crossed this barrier and it was very exciting." Wave 3 spent the rest of the spring trying to get arrested "as many times as we could." The group met every week, and became "close colleagues, I would say, as opposed to close friends." Mark made an installation for the Gay Pride parade that year called Hall of Shame. It was a list of AIDS criminals, each face on its own huge poster, accompanied by one of their horrible statements. So it had George H. W. Bush, and it had Ronald Reagan, and it had Cardinal O'Connor. It had presidential candidate Michael Dukakis; it had Jesse Helms. "It had people that we thought were particularly egregious."

The first committee Mark joined was Actions, in the summer of 1988. Then Wave 3 invited Iris Long's subcommittee, Treatment and Data, to give a teach-in to the affinity groups, so they could understand the treatment and research issues in preparation for the upcoming Seize Control of the FDA action. Mark then joined the Issues committee, and Iris's Treatment and Data became another base for his activity. He also joined Gran Fury and worked on some poster projects, ultimately participating on a lot of different levels of ACT UP.

Because he worked a part-time job and could set his own hours, Mark was attending Actions, Issues, Wave 3, Gran Fury, and the Monday-night meeting. "It was an entire way of life. It was totally engrossing. And then, everyone would go to Benny's Burritos afterwards, and have margaritas and burritos and talk about it. It was great. It was really, really exciting."

In 1988, AZT was the only treatment available. The first issue related to medications that Mark took on was accessibility: he found the language being used in the Treatment and Data subcommittee needed to be explained to the rest of ACT UP. He went to their teach-in, wrote down every word that he didn't understand, looked them up, made a glossary, and distributed it to ACT UP at large in July 1988. He felt it was very important for people to understand what the issues were so that the FDA demo could be a success.

The second issue Mark embraced was to get drugs to be studied faster. ACT UP had a list of drugs, like AL-721, dextran sulfate, and peptide T, that we thought the FDA should approve or test faster. In those days, a lot of people thought that the FDA actually tested the drugs. They didn't understand that they would actually just oversee the testing, which was done by the NIH or by the industry. There was a whole lot of explaining about institutional structure, regulations and laws, and some scientific concepts that had to be done within two months, so that everybody in ACT UP could understand and get across the message to the American people.

An example was pentamidine, used to treat pneumocystis pneumonia (PCP), the pneumonia most likely to kill people with AIDS. It was available by a special compassionate-use protocol from the Centers for Disease Control, on an intravenous basis. And at some point in the 1980s, the supply ran out because doctors were getting it sent to hospitals where people were dying of PCP. Pentamidine was very toxic, with a lot of bad side effects. Dr. Don Armstrong from Memorial Sloan Kettering was trying to figure out if the drug could just be given to the lungs, which is the area principally affected by PCP, thereby reducing the toxicity to the rest of the body. So the hospital developed a series of different devices to do that, and did studies in both New York and San Francisco, to show that it worked—and it did, although it later turned out that Bactrim, which is an oral pill, was more effective.

However, this basic information was impossible for a nonmedical person to obtain. The research into treatment was just getting off the ground. Once Iris's work to identify these studies and make them available was in place, they revealed that there were really restrictive entry criteria. Examples included women of childbearing age being excluded from a study. Period. Or, if a person had already experienced one opportunistic infection, they couldn't get into a study for another given opportunistic infection. But with AIDS, one person could have twenty-three different opportunistic infections. Or they couldn't be on two experimental meds at the same time. Well, the only approved drug was AZT, so everything else was experimental. So people were regularly excluded.

Because of and in addition to the restrictions, "all the trials were empty." They were accruing really, really slowly. And people in ACT UP who were in trials were not discussing the conditions.

"In that time in ACT UP, there was not that many people that were really talking a lot about their experiences with HIV and AIDS. I mean, I remember when Peter [Staley] got up at the Town Meeting in May of '88, and talked about having HIV, it was a memorable moment for me. And the same when Gregg Bordowitz announced it in April . . . There were some people, like Vito, that would talk about it. But a lot of people . . . maybe they would talk about it in their affinity group, or in a smaller setting, but they wouldn't necessarily get up on the floor and talk about their experience. And so, in Treatment and Data, we would do a lot of things like reading John James's newsletter [*AIDS Treatment News*] to try and find out gossip and rumors about potential treatments. And we had talked to people at CRI [Community Research Initiative]. Or researchers. It was hard to get information in those days."

Mark saw that very few of the people in the first group of treatment activists had AIDS, except Vito. Jim Eigo was negative, Garry Kleinman was negative, David Z. Kirschenbaum was negative, Iris was negative. Mark didn't know his status at that time. The late Herb Spiers was positive. A lot of the people weren't on treatment, even if they were positive, because there was so little that seemed to really help. So it was hard to get experiential evidence. Once the activists had a list of potential treatments that they thought were interesting or had potential, they would assign a member of Treatment and Data to become that drug's buddy, and this person would do the follow-up work. They would call the primary scientist serving as investigator of that treatment, if there was one, and try to find the literature about their drug, write a little report about it, and bring it to the group to see what could happen next. For example, dextran sulfate was being studied in San Francisco by Donald Abrams. So the drug buddy would have called Donald, who was a very community-friendly doctor, and try to find out what was going on in that study. A lot of the drugs weren't even in studies. Some of them that the community was using weren't being studied, or ACT UP was trying to get the government to do a study.

For example, the egg lipid AL-721.

"There were a lot of things for which there was no possible scientific basis for how it might actually work—that we wanted to be studied—because some group in the community was using it and trying it. I mean, AL-721 was this greasy, sort of buttery crap that you sort of spread—it was pretty disgusting, but . . . there was nothing else, you know. And then there were all these flaky substances like IMREG-1 and IMREG-2, where you met with a sponsor and [would] say, *Well, what's in your product?* and they'd say, *Well, we chop up the cells and it's something that comes out of that.* A lot of it wasn't based on very good science."

Mark didn't recommend anything to people. Instead, he focused on getting the information out. For example, AZT. It was toxic and it failed rapidly for most people—leading them to continued progression of HIV. And the toxicity, which included anemia, often made people sicker and more prone to other infections. One of ACT UP's early successful actions was an effort to force NIH and the FDA to lower the dose of AZT, which we did in, in December '88. There were five studies that showed a lower dose was better. And ACT UP wrote to Tony Fauci at the NIH, and to the FDA, and Gina Kolata covered it on the front page of *The New York Times*. They lowered the dose. While some people in ACT UP were taking AZT, "they weren't having debates on the floor" about their experiences of taking it.

In the spring of 1989, Mark was offered a two-month consultancy by David Corkery (an ACT UP member and a former employee of amfAR) to create a San Francisco conference for Community Research Initiative, Dr. Sonnabend's community-based research group, in conjunction with the National Institute of Allergy and Infectious Diseases and amfAR. It was typical that ACT UPers were often employed by AIDS agencies, some of which had political differences with ACT UP but offered paid jobs, which ACT UP did not. This conference was supposed to facilitate the community-based clinical research movement, which, at that point, not only was being funded by groups in New York and San Francisco but also had received several million dollars in federal funding, as a result of congressional hearings. Suddenly, there were going to be twenty different community-based research clinics around the country.

"And it was sort of ironic that they hired me to be the consultant, to help work on developing that conference, because at that point, I had not been to a scientific conference yet, at all. So I think Joe [Sonnabend of CRI] was suspicious about somebody from ACT UP, which he felt had a pro-AZT reputation . . . He was still not sure that HIV was the cause of AIDS. He exposed me to the arguments that it wasn't and, actually, the argument seemed to strengthen the case that it actually was. I mean, the more I thought about it, the stronger it seemed likely that HIV was the cause, but that didn't mean that everybody should be on AZT."

The controversy over HIV causing AIDS continued until the introduction of highly active antiretroviral therapy in 1996. These combination drugs were specifically designed to stop HIV, and would bring it down from a million copies in the blood to under fifty. Simultaneously, T-cell counts went back up to nine hundred, opportunistic infections went away, and people regained weight—strong evidence that HIV was the cause of AIDS.

But before the new drugs were made generally available, the conflict about HIV was dynamic. Some people who were HIV-positive (once the test was invented) never progressed to AIDS—later they were called *nonprogressors*. So it seemed that there was another element in the mix, a "cofactor" that needed to be present for a person to get AIDS, besides being exposed to it. And many people were concerned that this necessary cofactor was never identified. The fights over this question of HIV were vicious. ACT UP San Francisco split off from the national group because a faction strongly did not believe that HIV was the cause of AIDS. In order to perform treatment activism, ACT UP Golden Gate had to be formed, splintering off from what was ACT UP San Francisco. This fight got conflated with the confusion and pain surrounding AZT, which many people felt would save them, while others thought it was causing more death. It was an example of how brutal debates within the AIDS community could be, how high the emotional and literal stakes were, how desperate people were, how little anyone else was listening, and how truly destructive the pain and frustration could become.

"It was very violent and very unpleasant and actually, I think, very destructive. People on both sides of the debate . . . tended to try to de-monize the other side—there was a lot less goodwill than there should have been . . . Depending on your point of view, somebody would try to make you feel bad if you did or didn't try to use AZT. I think it was disempowering to the people with HIV that were actually having to make those really difficult decisions, because it turned it into a sort of ideological debate, instead of a discussion about medical uncertainty and personal choice . . . It wasn't as bad inside of ACT UP as it was in the broader com-munity. There was also, remember, the *New York Native*, which originally had some of the very best coverage of the epidemic in the early eighties . . . By the late eighties, it had become just a hotbed of flake, quake science—where every week, there was a different theory that HIV had come from a certain kind of monkey or dolphins, or you name it."

The cofactor debate focused a lot on what other things could be working with HIV to accelerate the decline of the immune system. And because of the way the immune system acts, any infection or activation of the immune system actually functions as a cofactor. So, if someone got tuberculosis, it would accelerate the progression of their HIV. If someone got pneumocystis, their HIV viral load might go up 80 per-cent, because of deviant activation. The virus is a parasite that preys on every instance in which the immune system gets activated. Therefore people who got exposed to many other infections might have been more likely to progress faster. In understanding AIDS, perhaps as a larger metaphor for life, oppositional ideologies and theories that caused ani-mus between people sometimes turned out to be informative in unpre-dictable ways.

Exposed uninfecteds and *long-term nonprogressors* were both issues that Treatment and Data thought were very interesting. The prospect of long-term survival was exciting. There were some people who didn't know why they hadn't gotten AIDS yet, and there were other people who had really low T-cell counts but were still doing pretty well. And treatment activists thought there might be secrets or scientific answers in looking at those people. It turned out there were.

MOVING BEYOND AZT

In 1991, Mark and the rest of Treatment and Data started getting very serious about basic science and pathogenesis, which is how the virus and the immune system interact to cause disease over the years from infection to AIDS. It was really clear to them that AZT-like drugs, ddI-type drugs, and opportunistic infection drugs were not going to stop people from getting AIDS and dying. They would only slow it down. And the evidence was all around them. There was a tidal wave of people in ACT UP who were dying in spite of being on AZT or even on AZT plus ddI, even if they had good prophylaxis or good doctors, like Joe Sonnabend. Vito Russo died and Ray Navarro died, and there was, Mark said, "just a huge, huge number of people that were dying and a lot of them had been doing aggressive medical interventions with the very best that we and the medical system had to offer."

They started a pathogenesis group at Treatment and Data. Gregg Gonsalves had recently moved down from ACT UP Boston to join the group, and they started looking into other theories, wanting the National Institutes of Health to put more money into basic science, because they knew that more studies of AZT-type drugs weren't going to lead to answers. They also asked the NIH to hold a workshop about long-term nonprogressors and exposed uninfecteds. And they did. And the exposed uninfected inquiry "proved very, very interesting"; it led to discoveries about cellular immune protection that can occur in exposed people like a famous, later cohort of sex workers in Nairobi who appeared to have some sort of a protection, in spite of repeated exposure to HIV. Researchers found out in 1996 that there was a genetic mutation that was silent and harmless. If someone had gotten that mutation from both parents, their chances of contracting HIV were almost zero in spite of repeated exposure. This discovery clarified why some gay men who had been very sexually active throughout the seventies and eighties hadn't gotten HIV. "But it took seven years from the time we started pushing for them to study it for that particular discovery."

Treatment and Data put out a weekly newsletter to the floor about new developments in science. Possibly as a result, people with HIV began coming to T&D.

"They weren't necessarily coming and telling us what their T cells were or what they had, but they were sure coming and listening to the information and using it in their everyday life. And I think that's one of the good things that we did . . . It was really scary and I felt like I was often asked questions that I didn't know the answer to, but I also felt like I could sometimes give people information that might help them make a treatment decision."

As more treatment choices became available, more people with AIDS came to Mark and to T&D for solutions to their own health issues. This was in marked contrast to the first iteration of T&D, when almost nothing was available. Mark and other treatment activists' field of knowledge and responsibility spread widely. Yet people were still dying. And once someone was immersed in ACT UP, the deaths were frequent and the debilitation was intimate. One of the early deaths in ACT UP that affected Mark, and a lot of other people, was that of the performance artist Brian Damage (né Allen).

Remembrance: Brian Damage

Brian joined Wave 3 in the summer of 1988, before the FDA action. He got sick and had mycobacterium avium-intracellulare (MAI), a severe respiratory illness, and had a long stay at Beth Israel. This was Mark's first time going to see a person with AIDS in the hospital. It was all happening at once in Mark's life: learning; studying; meeting reporters, scientists, and doctors; being part of the ACT UP community. And attending lots of meetings.

Wave 3 would go to the hospital every day, and different people, like the late Sally Cooper and Richard Elovich, would have shifts, to talk to Brian and to the doctors. There was no approved treatment for MAI, so doctors used a variety of tuberculosis drugs in combination. Brian had a very good intuition, and he would take out a drug that later turned out didn't do anything. And then, one day in May, Mark went to his room and Brian wasn't there, and Mark started to panic until the nurse offered, *Oh, he's in the park.* He was sitting outside in his wheelchair with some people from Wave 3.

"It was a nice moment. I think he probably lived longer than he would have because of the kind of collective love and support that people in Wave 3 had provided him over those months. And I think a lot of affinity groups were really busy with that kind of activity in those days. And some of it was medically specific, but a lot of it wasn't—a lot of it was just being there, being able to question the medical person or being able to help the social services or going out and getting the food and cleaning up. There was so much of that kind of collective activity. That was really, really powerful and great . . . A lot of gay men didn't have a family that supported them. The alternative family was what supported them . . . We had a discussion about whether or not we thought we should keep on working to keep Brian alive. It was very, very painful. We went and sat in—I can't remember which park we sat in—but there were some in Wave 3 who thought that it was hopeless and that there was not really more that we could do, and that we should just sort of [give] palliative care and try to help make his last, whatever, period of time as comfortable as possible.

"Then, there was another group that thought we should really try to go push back as far as we could with the doctors on the MAI treatments. That group prevailed, and he did live for six more months. And I'm not saying that the people who thought we should sort of move to palliative care were wrong or bad, it was—you know, it's just—the decisions are very hard to make. And of course, what we did is we went back and said, *Brian, what do you want to do?* And he said, *I want to try—everything.* So we did that with him."

In Wave 3 people talked openly about AIDS in a way that was not being discussed in ACT UP. It was felt deeply in Wave 3 when Russell Pritchard came out as HIV-positive. He did so at the group's retreat, at Tommy Tune's house in Fire

Island, which the ACT UP treasurer, Marvin Shulman, had arranged. It was really significant because nobody else in the group had done so. Brian had joined as an already totally out person with AIDS—and already quite sick. And Russell was healthy and looked healthy. Next, schoolteacher Mark Fisher, also in Wave 3, came out. "I guess we were very close. I mean, we did everything together and we loved each other in a certain way."

WHAT IS A LEADER?

It would be hard to find two people with so much difference in the same movement. Maxine came from the working class, went to school at night while raising children, had a full career as a professor, came up through the Left, and spent her time in ACT UP organizing the most marginalized HIV communities. Mark, more than a generation younger, graduated from Harvard, never realized his wish to be an artist, was supported by his father, was financed by a MacArthur grant, and landed a big book contract through mentorship by Larry Kramer. He spent his time in ACT UP bridging the gaps between the most sophisticated and highest-access communities of people with AIDS and their scientific and governmental counterparts for the larger field. Yet Maxine and Mark both succeeded as leaders because they coalesced community, attracted and inspired collaborators and followers, and were part of astounding and unprecedented victories for their divergent constituencies.

Both Maxine and Mark illustrated that leaders, in activist movements, are the people who do the most work. And that that work is partially research, partially conceptualization, and significantly repetitive on-the-ground pushing of power boundaries. They lead by example and they inspire by example. Neither Maxine nor Mark was particularly charismatic. They didn't have material reward to promise or grant followers. They did create groups that met in person with regularity, giving people support and group identities, relationships of ongoing experience, in both cases rooted in discussion and discovery. They both read extensively and shared books, articles, and written material as part of their group relationships. And they were both relentless and tenacious, and inspired fear in their opponents—both in the government and in the AIDS activist community.

When the stakes are high, and actual, real change is necessary, leadership delivers the goods, not the promise of aura or shine. And both Maxine and Mark delivered, until their differences and personalities overwhelmed. And then their division became as historically important as their coexistence had been.

6

Treatment and Data #2: Citizen Scientists

One of ACT UP's great realms of leadership and concrete gifts to the world was provided by the rigorous, disciplined, and creative reimagining of its second wave of treatment activists. Beginning with ACT UP's 1990 treatment agenda, and in full swing by 1991, Treatment and Data evolved from advocates to citizen scientists. The first group of treatment activists in the late 1980s was facing a wasteland. There were no medications effective against AIDS, and the government bureaucracy was a mystery. But by carving structure out of chaos, this first group started to win victories and lay foundations so that some treatments slowly became available. By the 1990s, there was still no functional sustaining treatment, but there were now prophylaxis drugs for preventing some lethal opportunistic infections, and new medications like ddI squeaking into availability. Doses were being adjusted, and concepts were evolving. As the virus spread, as more people found themselves infected or symptomatic or sick, and more possibilities for treatment emerged, more HIV-positive people were attracted to T&D. It became a kind of mutual aid headquarters for strategizing the creation of new, more effective medications. And the more success they had, the more people with AIDS came to rely on T&D for lifesaving information.

Mark Harrington, Peter Staley, Garance Franke-Ruta, and Gregg Gonsalves were just four of the central figures who transformed Treatment and Data into a force of citizen scientists who moved from influencing the *way* drugs were studied and made available to changing the direction of research in terms of *which* drugs were studied and what approaches embraced.

Protesting government inaction at New York City's Federal Plaza,
June 30, 1987 (Video still courtesy of Testing the Limits Collective)

MARK HARRINGTON

This acceleration corresponded to Mark Harrington's relationship to his own HIV. In July of 1990, he went in to see Dr. Joe Sonnabend (founder of Community Research Initiative), had his T cells finally looked at, and learned he only had five hundred. So obviously he was HIV-positive, but Mark decided not to take any of the inadequate available medications because he was still healthy. But his friends were not as lucky. His ex-boyfriend Jay was getting sicker. And with knowledge came increased pressure and responsibility.

"I tried to be very careful about giving information and then [made] it clear which was information and which was my opinion . . . For example, my friend Scott, who all this time is dying—we finally get ddI out on parallel track in October of '89, and I haven't seen Scott for several months, so I don't know that he's wasting away, looking really gaunt. I remember calling him up, saying, *ddI is out*. He said, *Mark, you know. It's way too late for me*. And I went out and saw him in December and I said, *Well, maybe it is*, but, you know, I was pretty naïve, too. I had sort of this funny kind of information without existential experience. I hadn't lived through the horrible eighties, the way a lot of people in ACT UP had—here in New York, with lots of their friends dying all around them. I hadn't lived through that."

Having so much information that other people needed may have been overwhelming for Mark for a while. So many people were desperate, and relationships in ACT UP were about staying alive, in all kinds of ways. "I think it probably went to my head in a way that, in some respects, I regret, in retrospect . . . It was very hard to deal with all that energy and passion, and I think there was a certain kind of power that came with it for a while that was both attractive and dangerous."

Unlike the first generation, who had to invent the structures, the second incarnation of Treatment and Data had to negotiate and revamp these partial, flawed, and inadequate relationships that made up the AIDS industrial complex. There were greedy pharmaceutical companies, like Burroughs Wellcome; there were community-based organizations like Community Research Initiative and the PWA Health Group buyers club; there was a corporate-dependent government bureaucracy; and there was *The New York Times*. And PWAs were desperately clamoring to try medications that simply were not going to work, constantly driven to take and try any new treatments, any way they could.

On October 19, 1989, ACT UP and key government officials met for three hours at the Gay Center to discuss AIDS policy.
     Front, left to right: Peter Staley, Jay Kevin Funk, Mark Harrington, Simon Watney, Margaret Hamburg (assistant director of NIAID), Anthony Fauci (director of NIAID), Richard Elovich, Charlie Franchino
     Rear, left to right: David Barr, Ken Fornataro, Spencer Cox, Larry Kramer, Dr. Suzanne Phillips, Keith Alcorn, Steve Rosenbush (Photograph by T.L. Litt)

TREATMENTS AND *THE NEW YORK TIMES*

ACT UP's relationship with Gina Kolata and other reporters at *The New York Times* was painful. For years the *Times* had neglected to cover the AIDS crisis at all, and we were dependent on community-based newspapers like the *New York Native* instead. The *Times* wouldn't use the word *gay*, would not allow obituaries to mention gay partners, and had a hollow understanding of both the scientific and social issues related to AIDS. "It was a tricky relationship," Mark Harrington said, "because we really felt like we needed to use [Kolata] to get into *The New York Times*, because *The New York Times* often set the agenda for the rest of the media."

For example, Marty Robinson was angry about DHPG, which was a drug that was the only available known treatment for CMV retinitis, an opportunistic infection that causes people to go blind and/or have terrible diarrhea. The FDA and NIH were causing the limited access to that drug to be shut off, so that everyone would have go into a placebo study. Marty brought it to T&D, and they were outraged. ACT UP could not allow people to be forced into a placebo study if being on the placebo meant that they were going to go blind. Marty "taught us about using the media, because he was from the seventies." T&D pressured Gina Kolata about DHPF. "Here's her phone number," Marty told them. "Call her up." She started running the information ACT UP provided in the *Times*.

"So then she would use us, because it was part of the story, and it was a good part of the story. But she didn't always get her facts right, which created a lot of problems. She would overexaggerate side effects that happened in a trial of an expanded access program for ddI . . . thereby endangering the whole expanded access. On the other hand, we weren't objective, either. We wanted her to run a certain message our way, and she didn't always do that. But she did it a lot. She covered stuff like a naïve science reporter who really thinks that science works and that it's not affected by business or politics or other social forces. She had trouble putting together the business, the science, and the political and, sort of, the personal. That wasn't her specialty. Her specialty was explaining, you know, *why randomization is a good idea* or *the basis for placebo studies*. So she had a sort of limited frame."

Lawrence Altman, the *Times'* chief medical reporter, who'd covered

AIDS since 1981, was "fundamentally a very lazy reporter. And you can see him at conferences watching [reporters] Laurie Garrett and Jon Cohen, and trying to figure out what they're doing, and what they're covering. He, at the International AIDS Conference, almost never leaves the media center to go to the real conference and talk to the real people that are there. He likes to do that kind of medical coverage where there's that one, lone, heroic researcher guy that discovers the cure . . . that kind of reporting—where you just make this one little hero—- it totally doesn't tell the story . . . I think *The New York Times* has always had trouble putting the story together . . . Good AIDS reporters at *The New York Times* have always had trouble getting support from management."

ANATOMY OF AN ACTION: BURROUGHS WELLCOME

In January of 1989, Peter Staley was planning his zap occupation of the Burroughs Wellcome headquarters in Research Triangle Park in Durham, North Carolina. He wanted to have a meeting with people in the company first—to set up the issues and let them know what our concerns were. He invited Mark to come as the "science guy." So the two of them went to the building—Peter said, *Oh, that's a really nice fountain, that would look really great dyed red, blood red, in a demonstration.* And the PR woman "sort of grabbed his arm and said, *Let's go in here, where the meeting's going to be.*"

One of the reasons people were so willing to take Burroughs Wellcome's product, AZT, when it really didn't work was that most people at the time were conceptualizing the treatment for AIDS as one pill that would fix everything, and AZT fit that fantasy. But even while Burroughs Wellcome was selling AZT, the highest-profit-making pharmaceutical in the world at the time, both it and the citizen scientists in T&D were starting to realize that *combination* therapies were the concept for the future. At the headquarters, Mark and Peter met with Dr. David Berry, who was the head researcher, and had been actually involved in the AZT teams since the very start. They had a "very stimulating, weird conversation" with him about science and business and price. And Berry said, *The only way to treat HIV, which mutates so rapidly, is going to be with powerful combinations of drugs. That's the direction this disease is moving in.* In that respect, he was very aware.

Mark and Peter were saying, *AIDS is a problem around the world, not just in the United States, and your price for AZT is way too high here, and it's totally out of reach for people in Africa.* And Berry retorted, *Even if it was free, they wouldn't be able to use it in Africa.* He floated the argument that drug companies still use about infrastructure, poverty, and illiteracy restricting medical treatments in developing countries. Mark was so affected by Berry's attitude that he came home and wrote an article for *OutWeek* called "Interview with a Vampire." It was Mark's first exposure to drug company people. He thought Berry was evil, at the time. In retrospect, with much more exposure, Mark now considers him to be a fairly typical drug company scientist. Later, Mark and Peter did the fountain action and got arrested.

PETER STALEY

Born in 1961, Peter Staley came from a high-achieving and wealthy family. He originally trained to be a classical pianist at Oberlin but attended the London School of Economics instead and came to New York in the summer of 1983 to work for J.P. Morgan.

"I went straight back into the closet [in New York], and then my relationship to the gay community was just kind of socially on the weekends. It was a bar relationship. And I was even very careful about not getting too emotionally hooked up with a guy because that would have been harder to hide. So it was just a lot of semi-dating and just sex . . . I didn't know about the *New York Native*. I didn't know that GMHC had been formed already and I didn't know who Larry Kramer was. I didn't have that sense of community. I definitely didn't sense or have any knowledge of the politics."

When Peter was twenty-four he seroconverted (in other words, tested positive; seroconversion is the transition from being infected with HIV to building up a detectable presence of the virus in the blood). He and a boyfriend, also named Peter, were watching the first television movie ever done about HIV/AIDS, *An Early Frost.* The lead character, played by Aidan Quinn, had PCP and was coughing a lot. Staley had had a prolonged cold and was coughing a lot, too, at the time. The cold just wouldn't go away. "We were sitting there on the couch watching this thing and Peter jokingly says—*He sounds like you!* And I said—*Oh, maybe I need to go to the doctor.*" So he went to see Dr. Dan William. Based on the cough and based on what was going on in his office at the time, where many patients were seroconverting and dying, if any of his gay patients came through the door with so much as a cough, Dr. William would run a complete blood count just to see if there was anything going on with their immune system. And sure enough, he could tell there was something wrong with Peter's white blood cells. He did a further T4 test, and Peter had 360 T4s. So he was already immune-suppressed. His lymph nodes were swollen, and he had mild lymphadenopathy, all of which was enough for a diagnosis, handed out early in the epidemic, of AIDS-related complex (ARC).

Peter's brother, James E. Staley, now CEO of Barclays, was high up at J.P. Morgan and eventually became its CEO. At the time, James knew that he had had a gay boss. "He would call him *that fucking faggot.*" Peter asked his brother to approach his boss, who was very high up in the bank, and ask him whether Peter should keep his HIV status a secret. So they met. And the boss's advice was to keep it a secret—"'cause he had gotten quite burned by the fact that many knew he was gay within the bank."

Peter then became a major donor of the PWA Coalition and became "the granddaddy donor" of the newly formed Lavender Hill Mob, which he'd read about in *The Wall Street Journal.* The Mob had zapped the head of HHS, the head of the NIH, and one of the Reagan officials. One morning, Peter was walking to work on Wall Street and someone from ACT UP handed him a flyer.

"They were going to do the sit-downs on Wall Street, and I usually got to work at seven. But I got handed the flyer and went up to the trading floor at J.P. Morgan—I traded U.S. government bonds—and a couple of other guys had gotten a flyer. Trading floors on Wall Street were like locker rooms, with just vile, homophobic, sexist, racist language, testosterone up the wazoo . . . The lead trader on the floor was my official mentor . . . a guy named Mark Warner. There was this argument going on about AIDS because of this flyer, and he was saying to one of the saleswomen, . . . *Well, if you ask me, they all deserve to die 'cause they took it up the butt*—and I just had to sit there and steam. I couldn't do anything, except just kind of agree with a smile, which just is so—ugh. But I got home that night and the lead story on Dan Rather was, not maybe the lead, but it was there—it was on national news. And I said—*Wow! That's power.* And there was the FDA who actually responded, saying *We're going to do this and this and this . . .* At that point it was still bullshit. But they were reacting. And I said, *This is Lavender Hill Mob to the nth degree.* So I went to the very next meeting and didn't miss a meeting after that."

Peter started writing checks and got to know Michael Nesline, who was the first head of ACT UP fundraising. Peter would come to meetings after work. He was one of the coat-and-tie guys "that made the room very diverse." He got to know Michael well and started hanging out with him, and they became boyfriends in the summer of 1987. "Those were just wild times, wild times, favorite time of my life, that year, that and '88 . . . They were everything, they were my church, they were my social life and they were where I became sexually active again, starting with Michael."

Peter accompanied Michael to a Coordinating Committee retreat in the Hamptons in August of 1987. "It was this ritzy little Hamptons house with a pool and we all just got smashed and swam around all weekend and got to know each other." Between 1987 and 1992, they sold over $1 million worth of ACT UP merchandise around the country. The fundraising committee ran a mail-order business, and in the Gay Pride parades ACT UP would sell "$20,000, $30,000 worth of merchandise at a pop." The biggest seller was always READ MY LIPS. Even more than SILENCE=DEATH.

AZT came out the same month ACT UP was born, and Peter tried the recommended dose at the time, which was very high. But it made him anemic, to the point where he actually nodded off at his trading desk, "which is very hard to do, given how loud those rooms are and busy those rooms are." He was pale and just looked terrible, so he had to stop the AZT. Then, in March of 1988, his T-cell count was on a downward curve, and it went below the danger level, hitting 107. He was seeing a shrink at the time, trying to help him deal. Peter was so into ACT UP that he was head of fundraising by that point. He even was starting to go to demonstrations holding a sign right in front of his face so that his identity wouldn't be revealed on TV. Peter tried to participate in the demos; every night was ACT UP, every day was Wall

Street, and the cycle was tearing him apart. Then there was Black Friday on Wall Street in the fall of 1987, and the market became very hard to trade. Peter was beginning to lose money. By March of 1988, his T4s crashed, "with the Dow, I like to say." Peter finally decided it was time to take care of himself. So he walked into his boss's office and told him he had AIDS and needed to go on disability, "and they knew in Tokyo, five minutes later. It's that kind of market, the news goes fast.

"We were all taking [AL-721] and [dextran sulfate] and grabbing everything we could possibly try, most of which didn't work. You know the AZT was largely unhelpful for most of us as well. I ended up going back to AZT on a whim, after I hit that hundred and seven T4s and went on disability. I told Dr. William, . . . *Why don't I just try taking as much AZT as I could tolerate, and no more, even if it's suboptimal.* And I went on three hundred milligrams of AZT, which even by today's dose is considered barely optimal. But—it actually worked—I had a huge rise in T4s that slowly started falling again, but even the baseline it fell to was higher than when I had started it. And the same thing happened a couple of years later when I added black-market ddI to the AZT. I did a very low dose, half the dose recommended, and I had a huge pop in T4s. And I stayed on a low-dose AZT and a low-dose ddI until the protease inhibitors came out. And that kept me above three hundred T4s for over ten years. The low-dose dual therapy nukes, which obviously was more luck than the meds. I just happen to be one of the few; I was on the outlier of the curve of how these nukes worked. They worked well for me, even at low doses. As long as I didn't have to deal with the toxicities. And AZT at three hundred milligrams was a completely different drug than AZT at twelve hundred milligrams."

Given his personal and professional background, it was natural for Peter to be staring down the pharmaceutical companies. Burroughs Wellcome and Bristol Myers were the only two in the AIDS game for a while, and they were viewed, right from the get-go, as gross profiteers. For example, Burroughs Wellcome set the price of AZT at ten thousand dollars a year—the highest price of any drug in history at that time. The profiteering shocked everyone, not just people with HIV but also most of the editorial boards of most newspapers in this country. "For very much the same reasons that we were dealing with a logjam at the FDA, very strong personalities were involved at Burroughs Wellcome that felt what they were doing was the right thing and justified. And very self-righteous, *we know what's best* kind of white-coat mentality."

AZT won faster approval than any drug in history. And all the subsequent AIDS drugs were approved very fast as well, largely because of the pressure of AIDS activism. Peter understands that pharma stood to benefit greatly. But it wasn't actually until years later when the Treatment Action Group took a position against an accelerated approval of an AIDS drug (saquinavir) that some AIDS activists had decided that the ball had swung too far in one direction.

"At the time we were saying, *Listen, you didn't actually have to do much. This didn't cost you nearly as much as a normal drug. The government did most of the research, [and] because of us it got approved in record time. You didn't actually have to spend much to bring this thing to market. So how dare you charge the most of any drug in history? . . .* There was this feeling that if you're going to benefit from what we're doing with the FDA and activism, then you've got to play fair with us. We want you to have a fair return and we want you in this business, but we don't want you stabbing us in the back like that."

INSIDE/OUTSIDE

In these early actions against Burroughs Wellcome, the roles of Insider and Outsider (i.e., face-to-face negotiator and in-the-streets demonstrator) were played by the same people. But some members of T&D were of the same demographic as the corporate suits, and as a result the relationships between them deepened. During those early contacts with pharma, Peter and Mark were often given the red-carpet treatment. They would be offered both a morning and an afternoon meeting with senior management of the company, including a very nice lunch in between. So there was an effort to kind of impress and respect, while at the same time there was "a real defensiveness about the radical nature of the organization that they were sitting down across from, and what we were capable of. There was a palpable fear of that. They had entire PR departments working overtime on us."

In these negotiations T&D used the executives' fear of the Outside, the ACT UP of women, radicals, and people of color, the street activists who could turn out in large numbers and to whom the corporate men could not relate. "The threat was demonstrations, being called vicious names in the media, being called *murderers*—which ACT UP did a great deal of. We would frequently personalize it. We were doing quite a job on certain senior people at the FDA at the time. So they saw that." ACT UP had never been violent, but there was the constant fear from pharma that we would be. In their early meetings with Peter and Mark and others like them, the executives were "definite walking-on-eggshells." ACT UP demanded a price decrease for AZT from Burroughs Wellcome, and threatened actions and demonstrations if they didn't lower the price. "They ignored us and I organized a small group of people to invade their headquarters in April of '89."

On April 25, 1989, Blaine Mosley, James McGrath, and about five others planned the action. They arranged for their own media spokesperson, who didn't go inside or risk arrest. They called their affinity group the Power Drill Team, for the sexual innuendo as well as because they used battery-operated power drills. They got into the Burroughs Wellcome headquarters in Raleigh-Durham, North Carolina, and, using screws, sealed themselves into an office after convincing the woman working there to evacuate. All over the local news they received very sympathetic coverage. It was one of the stories that got the whole country on ACT UP's side from the beginning. Everybody seemed to be offended by AZT's ten-thousand-dollar-a-year price tag. A few months later, the campaign to lower the cost really got going full steam when the government released new data on AZT showing that it not only helped people with full-blown AIDS but also looked helpful for people with what was still being called ARC. It was clear that the market was going to expand for AZT.

T&D started working in coalition with mainstream AIDS organizations and held a series of conference calls with GMHC, Lambda Legal, AIDS Action in Washington, and amfAR. They were all trying to work on multipronged ways to pressure Burroughs Wellcome. AIDS Action was looking at pushing for congressional hearings with Ted Kennedy and Henry Waxman. And in fact there were congressional hearings that brought in the executives of Burroughs Wellcome to explain the ten-thousand-dollar price. Media pressure, too, was being generated with *New York Times* editorials.

ZAP AT THE NEW YORK STOCK EXCHANGE

ACT UP's Stock Exchange action on September 14, 1989, was the last push to lower the AZT price. First, about two weeks beforehand, ACT UP met with Burroughs Wellcome in coalition with all the other AIDS groups. The meeting took place at a hotel outside the company's North Carolina headquarters, because Burroughs wouldn't let Peter near after his earlier action with the Power Drill Team. ACT UP told the Burroughs Wellcome public relations people that the Stock Exchange action was going to happen. Not the secret one planned for inside, but the public one announced for outside. If Burroughs Wellcome wanted ACT UP to cancel the action, it had to lower the price of AZT. Once again, that meeting was a corporate stonewall.

ACT UP had a member who worked as a trader on the New York Stock Exchange and was able to report on how lax the security actually was. There was an entry door right under the front columns facing Broad Street. Once inside, three steps to the left was a little landing, and another three steps up, someone could get on the floor. It was that close to the street.

The action was to take place on September 14, 1989. There was just one security guard at the NYSE, with no metal detectors. Peter started quietly putting together a crew. Many had done the action earlier down in North Carolina at Burroughs. Gregg Bordowitz was involved, and James McGrath again. There were, in total, seven men. Robert Hilferty was one of the photographers, assigned to record the action inside because the press could not be alerted in advance. To prepare, the activists needed to get trading badges. So a couple of weeks beforehand they acted like tourists and took video cameras during lunch when many of the traders were standing outside smoking. They zoomed in on one of the badges, and then drew up a copy based on that design and took it to a rubber stamp shop in Greenwich Village. They gave the proprietor a story that they were doing a skit for a holiday party. The thick plastic rectangular white tags had the traders' numbers on them with the name of the firm underneath and a black line through the middle. The traders all had photo IDs, but their contact on the floor told them that everybody kept those in their wallets. Nobody had to show them to get in. It was just kind of a visual look. If someone looked like a broker and had the white badge, that's all that was needed. The fabricated badges looked great and the crew decided to do a test run to make sure they worked.

Counting on the fact that this zap group looked like and were the same demographic as the actual brokers, Peter and two others from the group went down to the exchange on the Tuesday before the action, which was planned for that Thursday. Traders stood outside the door, smoking their last cigarette. At 9:25, they stood around with them in trader drag, with suits and ties and badges. The ACT UP people moved in with the rush before the opening bell at 9:30. The security guard didn't bat an eye, and all of a sudden they were on the floor of the New York Stock Exchange. Doing intel for the upcoming action, they walked around as the starting bell was ringing, trading was starting, and everybody was busy. The ACT UPers actually pulled out little pads of paper to look even more like traders, and discovered an old wooden VIP balcony that wasn't used anymore, with a steep little staircase. It was perfect because it had a big NYSE banner hanging over it, which would be a great backdrop for the photo. And there was no gate in front of it. Because it was unused, they didn't have to push anybody aside or have anybody wrestle with them once they got up there, and Peter said, *This is great*, and *You guys'll just stand on the floor, we'll have two cameras—in case one of the shots doesn't work—with high ASA film so that flashes don't go off, or anything like that.* And they decided they would chain themselves up there and do their routine when the day for the real action arrived.

But then, suddenly, Peter got stopped on the trading floor. An older man came up to him, and greeted him, *Hey—you're new!* And Peter said, *Ah, yeah!* and started to sweat. The man said, *Bear Stearns.* Peter replied, *Yeah, yeah*, because all of their fabricated badges said BEAR STEARNS. They'd just picked a firm out of a hat. And the man said, *That's weird—#3,865, the highest number on the floor is 1,600, there are only 1,600 traders here*, and laughed. Peter replied, *I don't know. This is the one they gave me*, and he also laughed. Peter started to sweat more and then the man said, *Well, I guess so, I guess they're trying a new system, well, welcome*, and he shook his hand and that was it, he walked away, and Peter was left thinking, *Holy shit!* Later, they went back to the shop and had a whole new set of badges made. It was forty-eight hours before the demo was planned to happen.

The morning of the demonstration, the men met beforehand at a McDonald's on Nassau Street, nervous as all hell. There were seven of them. Five would go up to the balcony, and two photographers would take their picture and get out right away to hand the cameras over to runners who would bring them up to the Associated Press. Each had materials under their T-shirts. One person had a huge banner that was all folded up. He looked a little fat. Peter had a gigantic chain wrapped in a fanny belt so they could chain themselves to the banister at the top and so that it would take the police a while to pull them off the balcony. They all had handcuffs in their pockets as well as ear-piercing marine foghorns that they'd use to announce their presence. They also included a special touch in honor of 1960s Yippie leader Abbie Hoffman, who was the first person to organize an action on the stock exchange. At what was then the visitors' gallery, now walled off with glass, Hoffman threw down dollar bills onto the trading floor of the stock exchange, real dollar bills, as an action against how capitalism was funding the war in Vietnam. This time, the ACT UP activists had fake hundred-dollar bills that on the back said FUCK YOUR PROFITEERING, WE DIE WHILE YOU MAKE MONEY.

"So we all piled in at 9:25, walking right past security, and the five of us walked up the stairs of the balcony, knelt down and pulled everything out from under our shirts and we waited for the bell, put the chain around the banister, all handcuffed ourselves to it, got the whole banner unrolled, which said *Sell Wellcome*. And at 9:29 and fifty seconds we jumped up and put the banner over and all let off the foghorns, you couldn't hear the opening bell, and it was extraordinary. The place just, for a second, just went dead quiet except for the foghorns as everybody tried to figure out what was happening. And they then started going into a rage as they realized . . . And the photographers took their pictures quietly and got out, handed the cameras off, but they saw that crowd . . . beginning to throw wads of paper at us and getting very angry and they were concerned, so they foolishly went back in and they quickly got nabbed.

"The traders were looking around for conspirators and they got real roughed up, shirt collars were ripped and stuff like that. And these guys were just raging at us, and I used to work with that testosterone and it was, ah, it was really one of the most gratifying moments of my life, 'cause I realized it was done. We had succeeded, we got through security, it was done. The picture was taken, this was a gigantic news story. And they could scream all they wanted, but we were going to be on the front page of *The New York Times* and *The Wall Street Journal* the next day . . . Three days later they lowered the price by twenty percent. Which was the first, and unfortunately the last, time an HIV drug has had its price lowered in the U.S. But fortunately we've seen very dramatic price declines in the developing world."

CITIZEN SCIENTISTS

MARK HARRINGTON

But progress was not fast enough. Even as the science evolved, and ddI started to become available, in 1990 and '91, AZT still dominated the marketplace. Mark Harrington knew that a lot of people were on AZT even if it didn't slow down the progression of their disease. But it didn't accelerate it, and so, later, these people would be called *slow progressors*. There was also a significant group of people using the drug who started too early or didn't really need it. As Moisés Agosto-Rosario had observed when he joined T&D, some of its members had and created access to cutting-edge treatments beyond AZT that were elusive to most PWAs, even those in ACT UP, if they didn't participate regularly at Treatment and Data. "There were probably some people in T&D that started on a combination therapy earlier than some other people," Mark said. "But, at the same time, we weren't pushing it. We were saying it was *being studied*, and that some people thought it was a good way to go, but we were also saying, *There is no evidence that it is any better, yet.*"

Between the FDA demo in October 1988 and the Montreal AIDS conference in June 1989, Treatment and Data had developed some experience. Not all the drugs that ACT UP had asked for in October at the FDA really panned out. The activists started to understand a little bit more about the science, and their standards got a little higher. So, by 1989, Treatment and Data decided that the federal government didn't have a research plan for the epidemic to comprehensively cover everything from opportunistic infections to HIV and to women and children. So they wrote their own treatment agenda and brought it to the conference. T&D's treatment agenda had concrete proposals for what the government and pharma should study and how they should study it. They gave examples of sixteen AIDS drug development disasters and had specific demands for different agencies and institutions in the government—from the National Cancer Institute to NIAID, the FDA, the CDC, Congress, and the president, as well as the community and the press. They held a press conference with Michael Callen, Vito Russo, Dr. Joe Sonnabend, Peter Staley, and nine other speakers. They said, *Look, the federal government doesn't have a plan, we do, here's what they should do.*

GARANCE FRANKE-RUTA

Garance Franke-Ruta came from a long line of mostly Jewish European writers, artists, and intellectuals; both of her grandmothers went to college. She dropped out of high school at sixteen in Santa Fe, New Mexico, and moved out over a conflict about her sexuality, but ended up living back with her parents in New York at Westbeth Artists Housing at seventeen, the year she joined ACT UP. Garance was attending a meeting for queer kids at the Gay Center, and Neil Broome came to recruit for the FDA action. It was her first protest experience.

"I was very naïve." She had no idea about the 1960s, or any other periods of radical protest. For the March 28, 1989, Target City Hall action, she joined an affinity group called CHER. They ironed images of Cher on white T-shirts and wore them to the FDA action, joking that *CHER* stood for "concerned homosexuals enduring reality." Still under the age of eighteen, Garance was arrested at that protest, with a group of other people.

Garance never felt treated differently within ACT UP because of her youth. "There was this real democratic spirit about it, little-D democratic. And everything was about, to a large extent, the work that you could bring to the table around whatever it was you were doing. There was a certain amount of it that was about personal charisma. And you could see that; the way certain people just were listened to more intently than others. But that happens in any group." But Garance also held her own with governmental agencies.

"It was fun and—there [were] a lot of moments where it was scary to do things. You didn't know how people would react. You'd go to these, National [Institutes] of Health hearings, or National Academy of Medicine hearings, and be dealing with all these people with PhDs and MDs and get up there, in your little East Village outfit, and ask questions. And it was one of these things where, I don't know why I had the guts to do what I did . . . It's one of those things where if you don't yet have any inkling of what's possible or impossible or proper or improper, then you're much more likely to do things that actually wind up moving the bounds of the possible. Rather than if you just accept there's those fixed categories. And I think that was the really cool thing about ACT UP, is a lot of people were just very fresh to social organizing. There was obviously huge connections with the older new social movements, like the feminist movement and the earlier gay rights movement and so on. It was a great tutorial."

In 1989, after experiencing the Montreal AIDS conference, and the death of her friend Costa Pappas, Garance decided to join Treatment and Data. She also started working in publications at the PWA Health Group. "It all sort of blurred together, as one continuum of stuff that I was doing." She was constantly researching new medications. Unlike the misrepresentations in the Oscar-winning but inaccurate 2013 film *Dallas Buyers Club*, AIDS buyers clubs were founded and run by queer people. The PWA Health Group was the first organization in the United States to import the antibiotics azithromycin and clarithromycin, which are now standard FDA-approved treatments for various conditions. It was importing the antifungal drug fluconazole before it was approved in the United States. It also organized a medication exchange for people who had excess stocks of ddI and wanted to leave it for others to use after their deaths. For a while, Garance wound up funneling some ddI to Peter Staley. People had to be "very, very aggressive" in pursuing new approaches and treatments in order to stay ahead of their condition.

A group started gathering at Mark Harrington's apartment, a walk-up on East Ninth Street. They called themselves Science Club.

They met once a week and read medical journal articles, as in a doctor's weekly rounds meeting, choosing a particular problem to discuss. They assigned themselves immunology and virology textbooks, and read them. They even made a goofy little logo for themselves, cohering their relationship and identity.

"It was this weird mix of sort of East Village DIY, and high-level science . . . It sort of dissolved into what we called Tequila Club, where we'd basically just go sit up on his roof and drink margaritas and talk about science . . . Honestly, I don't think that my personal friendships at the time were very personal. We were all so work-focused and so activity-oriented, and it was all guys. And gay or not, they were not hugely necessarily forthcoming about their lives. People [would] talk about sex endlessly, and they would talk about politics, and they would talk about science, and science politics, and they'd talk about the work people were doing in ACT UP. But they did not talk about themselves and what they were feeling, or their backgrounds, or even, really, their families that much."

While Garance did have female friends in ACT UP, like Anne-Christine d'Adesky, Anna Blume, and Joy Episalla, she felt alienated from the Women's Caucus.

"Maxine didn't like me . . . She was awful to me. She was very mean to me . . . I just felt like, *Well, okay, she's the queen of the Women's Committee, so I'm going to go do something else* . . . They always accused me of being *male-identified* . . . which is like a total seventies thing to say. It's like a seventies feminist thing to say. Who talks about these things anymore? *Male-identified.*—Anyway."

INSIDE/OUTSIDE

Garance went to some very early NIH meetings with Anthony Fauci and Mark Harrington and a couple of other people, when she was still only eighteen. "And I can't even imagine what he thought of us." She recalled that Fauci and Mark "got to be a bit, friends," in later years.

"And it's funny, a lot of those people who were working at NIH, who were sort of enemies at one point, or there was this real clash between the activists and the scientists; it turned out we couldn't have picked a better group of people to target, because they're data-driven, and they're empiricists, and they're hypothesis-based. And so if you bring them new information, they're probably the most likely group of people you could approach who would be willing to change what they're doing or how they're doing it."

The ACT UPers felt a constant sense of urgency and disaster. Garance recalled going to one of the meetings with NIAID. It was held at a bucolic, flower-surrounded, glass-walled, large-windowed building. The whole thing felt suburban and calm and serene. She interacted with the government people who would drive there from their homes in Maryland, whose behavior was very low-key. And then, at the same time, in the same meeting, there was a group of people who were coming down from a crisis center, in the East Village, where so many people they knew were dying and in crisis and in pain and grieving and not even allowing themselves to recognize the full extent of what was happening, and impoverished on top of this, because they're doing activist work. "There was obviously a lot of better-to-do people in ACT UP as well, but—the East Village at the time was still much more of the *East Village* as well." She remembered that Mark would smoke at these meetings. And that raised eyebrows. Because people could still smoke inside at the time, but even so, it was not common. He would be getting up and down, and smoking, and wandering around.

The meetings between T&D and government agencies exhibited a real clash of lifestyles and mentalities. For Garance, bringing ACT UP's sense of urgency and a belief in letting the affected communities direct the course of things was very important, as was letting people who had a direct stake in what they were doing have a voice in the process.

She remembers that Mark was always evaluating the level of the interaction. *Well, they didn't treat any of us with the same respect.* But that wasn't personal to Garance.

"We were obviously these outsiders. And usually we had some demand for something that they didn't want to do, because otherwise they would have done it already. And usually it was something that was going to make them less money, and lead to embarrassment for someone who made a lot of money and had a very high-status social position, and didn't like being embarrassed."

After a while, Garance came to believe, the pharmaceutical companies realized that loosening requirements for drug availability could actually work in their favor. T&D would go to meetings at Bristol Myers on Park Avenue, and "they'd put out these spreads of food for you, and sort of chat with you and—[it couldn't] hurt them to have a conversation. They would get more buy-in for their drug when it went to market."

COUNTDOWN EIGHTEEN MONTHS

By November 1990, Garance's main project was called Countdown Eighteen Months, a precise treatment agenda developed by T&D for pharma and the government. That was partly because she worked as a staff member at the PWA Health Group, and was involved in importing these medications and researching them. For her, it was about recognizing the situation: there was one antiviral, AZT; there was maybe another one in development, ddI; and people were dying from the consequences of immune suppression. And if there was nothing that could be done yet about fixing their immune systems, or suppressing viral load, which activists weren't even talking about at the time, then at least medicine could treat the five most common conditions that were killing people. If doctors could treat these opportunistic infections, then they could keep people alive. And if they could keep people alive, then there was hope. And if there was hope, then maybe people would be around long enough for something else to happen, and something else to get discovered. "And that in fact was very much how things worked."

Countdown Eighteen Months was released in November 1990 and was written by Jason Childers, Chris DeBlasio, Jerry Jontz, Derek Link, Rich Lynn, Kim Powers, Scott Slutsky, and Garance, all of ACT UP's Treatment and Data Committee.

"We picked Eighteen Months," Garance said, "because we thought it was ambitious but doable for scientists to get answers on medications for opportunistic infections within that period. And also because it was the average time from AIDS diagnosis to death for people with HIV who were white male, non-injecting. For other demographic groups, average time to death was shorter. The project goal was to help people make it through the gap years between the first generation nucleoside analogues and whatever was going to come next. We could see the gap, and the antiviral treatments weren't coming fast enough and weren't good enough yet to keep people from dying. It was the opposite of looking for a cure. It was people looking for a way to stay alive a few more months or even years so that if real treatments came along they would be there to try them. And barring that, to forestall blindness and suffocation and wasting for as long as possible."

But the gap years were far too long, even for activists on the cutting edge of treatments. Jerry Jontz died at thirty-five in 1991, Scott Slutsky died at thirty-seven in 1992, and Chris DeBlasio died at thirty-four in 1993.

The five infections targeted by Countdown Eighteen Months were pneumocystis pneumonia (PCP), cytomegalovirus (CMV) retinitis and colitis, toxoplasmosis, mycobacterium avium-intracellulare (MAI), and the fungal infections cryptococcosis, histoplasmosis, and candidiasis. Garance brought the proposal for Countdown Eighteen Months to the floor of ACT UP, which was quite large at that point, and it was approved.

"It was like Athenian democracy. And after I went to college, and started reading these books about the origins of democracy, I was like, *You know what? I experienced direct democracy in ACT UP in a way that is so rare in American life.* Because it was a thousand people who came together once a week, every week. And everyone had a vote. And everyone was equal, and everyone had a voice. And—it was a different thousand people every week. So you never really knew where things were going to go, because you didn't know who was going to show up and who wasn't going to show up. And it was just, you know, it worked by Robert's Rules of Order. Facilitators in miniskirts and big hoop earrings."

And that was just the men.

Garance felt that at that time in ACT UP, it didn't seem like anybody had to do a huge amount of politicking to get anything done. Anyone who had an idea that seemed like it could possibly help, and that had any kind of validity behind it, seemed to get their idea approved. The sponsor of a proposal would come up with a budget for what they wanted to do. And Countdown Eighteen Months did not require a large budget because it was not a demonstration-based project; it just required a lot of meetings with scientists talking to them about their research strategy. It was about trying to make the research process more intentional. Because if something's driven by principal investigators, and ideas come to a committee that then evaluates them through a peer review process, and then approves them, Garance said, "well, that doesn't necessarily get where exactly you want to be, from a research perspective, where you need to say, *Okay, these are the things we need to get answers to, fastest.*" Instead, Countdown Eighteen Months was about trying to make the whole process more intentional, directed, and results-oriented.

Many of the targeted medications eventually got approved thanks to activism and refocused scientific priorities:

- Foscarnet for CMV was approved by the FDA in September 1991.
- Itraconozole for fungal infections was approved by the FDA in September 1992.
- Trimetrexate as a salvage therapy for PCP was approved by the FDA in December 1993.
- Clarithromycin to prevent MAI was approved by the FDA in December 1993.
- Rifabutin to prevent MAI was approved by the FDA in August 1996.
- Azithromycin to treat MAI was approved by the FDA in June 1996.

Countdown Eighteen Months was never envisioned as a solution. It was always a stopgap. It was about just keeping people alive until something better came along.

RETROSPECT ON FDA

In retrospect, Garance and others came to realize that while some of the FDA reform, especially the speeding up the drug approval process, had a huge impact on saving lives, it also created an incentive for the pharmaceutical companies to do research. As a result, it lowered their research costs.

"I don't think that we realized at the time that this was part of the broader gutting of the FDA that we've seen since; that there was a lot of political agendas that we just happened to be in sync. I mean, the pharmaceutical companies wanted a weaker FDA, too. And so do a lot of political figures. Our FDA, right now . . . acts as a complete politicized joke. And it's sad . . . it seems like it's gone too far in the other direction—and not just for AIDS—where you really had a crisis situation, where it made sense. But there's a really strong pharmaceutical lobby against the FDA as well that I don't think we were aware of. I know I was not aware of it, at all. I just know that in later years, I realized that this probably had something to do with the fact that a lot of other people wanted it, too."

TRYING CUTTING-EDGE TREATMENTS

MARK HARRINGTON

Mark made the decision to start trying new cutting-edge experimental treatments himself in 1991. At the seventh annual International AIDS Conference, held that year in Florence, Italy, Tony Fauci gave a talk about how HIV hid in the body before progression to AIDS—when the person was still asymptomatic. And this information dovetailed with Mark's interest into the issue of long-term nonprogressors, and what was really happening with pathogenesis. He started having some talks about it with Dr. Don Kotler, at St. Luke's Roosevelt, in New York, who was taking care of Mark's ex-boyfriend Jay, who had developed horrible wasting syndrome. "And Don is probably one of the best AIDS G.I. doctors anywhere." Dr. Kotler did a biopsy and found out that Jay had a kind of *E. coli* that could be cured with the antibiotic Cipro in two weeks. So he extended Jay's life. In the middle of those conversations, Mark was talking to Donald about what Fauci had said and how it applied to lymph nodes, and whether it was true, and if so, did they need lymph nodes, because he'd be willing to give one. They did in fact need lymph nodes, and Dr. Kotler was willing to do the surgery. It was elective, so obviously, Mark's insurance wouldn't pay for it. It was science. Not *medically necessary*. Mark had a lymph node taken out in April of 1992. Then, when he gave a plenary talk at the eighth annual International AIDS Conference in Amsterdam that July about pathogenesis and activism, he was able to actually use pictures that were taken of that lymph node that showed the HIV inside it, and showed the immune response to it as well, which at that time was a healthy immune response. It gave him an opportunity to talk about the unanswered questions about AIDS and pathogenesis and how people with AIDS were giving their bodies for clinical science.

BASIC SCIENCE

GREGG GONSALVES

While a student at Tufts University, Gregg Gonsalves found out that his boyfriend was HIV-positive. He joined ACT UP Boston in 1988 and became part of Harvard Treatment and Data, a group of eight or so who learned science together. Gregg decided with his friend Derek Link to come down and work with the New York chapter in 1989. Derek became Garance's roommate, and they both joined T&D and attended the committee's meetings at the Center, in a small room on the third floor. These gatherings were very crowded—lots of fast talkers. Somewhere between twenty and forty people, or even more. Ken Jacobson was the Treatment and Data moderator. The meetings would feature full reports as well as little snippets of information on a wide range of updates. Then there'd be more substantive discussions about various different issues. "It felt like you had to know what you were talking about or you were going to get jumped on. So I think people felt a strong responsibility to being informed about treatment and research . . . it was very fact based, analytical, sometimes—but also, very passionate, at the same time."

Gregg attended a meeting in a hotel room, to which T&D invited the governmental leadership of the AIDS Clinical Trials Group. Once the officials arrived, the Countdown Eighteen Months group presented its manifesto on five or six opportunistic infections that could be prevented and treated.

"It was a pretty bad, bleak time. There's not drugs. People are still dying. There's no antiretroviral therapy . . . It was a fascinating moment for me, because all of a sudden we were in a hotel room, where all the ACT UP people were staying, and the researchers were all coming to us . . . this group of people like Judy Feinberg and other opportunistic infection researchers who are pleased to have people interested in opportunistic research . . . Countdown Eighteen Months work did make the federal government and the ACTG shift resources to more strongly work on opportunistic infection, prevention, and treatment. So I think it was one of the better things that ACT UP Treatment and Data did. It really put the spotlight on opportunistic infections and raised the profile of researchers who were working on it so it gave them more clout within the decision-making apparatus."

ACT UP had built credibility with scientists. Treatment and Data's early connections with researchers trained them in the language of science. There was the political credibility of ACT UP, and the accrual of skills through their work with T&D. And now, the second generation of AIDS researchers wanted to assert more of their power in the decision-making on AIDS research on a national scale. T&D got closer to pharma and to scientists; sometimes there was literal overlap. For example, Rich Lynn, from T&D, worked for Pfizer.

LONG-TERM NONPROGRESSORS

As the crisis developed, PWAs observed that while some people died quickly after diagnosis, others lived on for years without symptoms. Their disease simply did not progress. Gregg Gonsalves was working at a basic science laboratory, and Mark Harrington had sent a letter to Tony Fauci about long-term nonprogressors. Through T&D, Gregg got the NIH to do a conference on the question, which was the first time it had ever been looked at seriously.

Gregg, Mark, and Joe Sonnabend went to meet with the NIH. They shared their observed experience that there were people in our community who had not been on AZT or ddI who were doing fine. Despite being HIV-positive, their disease was not progressing. Gregg, Mark, and Joe insisted that the NIH had to study why this was happening. Later that year, Gregg was at Columbia one night, and suddenly an influx of pages came through the fax machine. He was in the administrative office, so he could see them spilling out. He picked them up, and the files showed that, in the Multicenter AIDS Cohort Study, there was a small group of people who'd been infected in the 1980s—ten years before—who were doing fine: they had really high T-cell counts, and a really slow rate of decline. So there was now evidence of the existence of nonprogressors. This revelation meant that AIDS was not one issue, but rather an umbrella condition with many different modes of expression based on as-yet-unidentified factors. And that if something was keeping these infected people from progressing in their HIV disease, then maybe that element could be isolated and understood and ultimately used to help others. This motivated Gregg to go back to basic science.

"[Dr. Joe Sonnabend] was an incredibly influential person in how I thought about things, and Joe was like, *The way they think that HIV causes disease is not true; there are all these other ways it could happen.* Remember, we didn't have *viral load*, and there was not a lot of basic information on how the disease worked. And there were also other alternative theories about immune activation. There's a lot of different thinking that came in the middle of the eighties, towards the end of the eighties. In the nineties, it started dying out—trying to figure out reasons how HIV makes the immune system collapse. And Joe was very influential in wanting people to sort of revise how we thought about things.

"But I think also, there was some feeling that *the drugs we have aren't working*—there have to be other ways to confront what's happening. *Is there a way we can intervene in the immune system? . . . Can we figure out what these [nonprogressors] are doing right? Or have right? And can we bottle it?* Are there other ways to approach treating HIV other than antiretrovirals or immune-based therapies? . . . And so, there were significant unanswered questions back in the early nineties that I think drew our curiosity, but also our hope that there are some unanswered questions that might lead to therapeutic advances."

These years were filled with intense emotional experiences. Eventually, after Gregg joined ACT UP, he and Mark started a relationship. After five or six years of work on AIDS, Gregg himself seroconverted. His gay cousin died of AIDS. A member of Countdown Eighteen Months, Jerry Jontz, got very sick. Sick people were increasingly asking T&D for advice. Gregg recalled how one guy at a Monday-night meeting came up to him in the hallway, extremely gaunt and wasted and wanting to talk about cryptosporidiosis (a disease caused by a parasite), and what was available. And Gregg remembered very clearly not being able to say that there was very much out there for him. "I said, *These are the alternatives. Nothing seems to work very well.* It was clear that he was going to die soon of this, and he did." Gregg, Derek, and Garance went to the bedside of Countdown Eighteen Months member Jerry Jontz. It was a desperate time. In the hospital room they sprayed [peptide T] up his nose, "while he's just raving like a madman. He obviously had AIDS-related dementia or some brain infection, and we're, like, going day after day to give him [peptide T]—which, you know, in our saner moments we knew that it had no hope of working for him, but he had fixated on it, at some point." Later, at a meeting with Bob Rafsky—during the transition period, when twelve members of T&D left ACT UP and went to TAG—Bob said, "These people are going to save my life."

MARK HARRINGTON

At this point, like many other people in all aspects of the organization, Mark found that his entire life was involved with AIDS. He was on conference calls every month, plus the Opportunistic Infection Committee (OI), the Community Constituency Group (CCG), T&D and its many subcommittees, and the Wave 3 affinity group, which would meet intermittently. He was working on treatment every day. "I had the part-time job, where I set my own hours, when I started. And then, I was able to get consulting gigs from '89 until TAG started, and then when that wasn't enough, I was able to get money from my dad." After DHPG was approved for CMV retinitis, people would come up to Mark and thank him for saving their eyesight. He saw concrete output from his work that would "help people that we knew and also people that we didn't know." There were huge changes that had happened in the FDA and the NIH, in the way that research was done, and he dreamed that ACT UP could get closer to "a democratization of science and research in our country and that ultimately that could benefit a lot of people, and right now, it could benefit people with HIV and people that I knew and people that we didn't know."

And yet, at the same, as with many people in ACT UP, Mark made huge personal sacrifices to save his own and other people's lives.

"Well, there was that whole, sort of other path of what I thought I was going to be doing with my life. And, I remember once, somebody from the Film Archive said . . . *Maybe you'll just be an activist, Mark*, and I was horrified. I said, *No, I'm going to become, like, a—I'm going to be in the arts. I'm going to be a writer or I'm going to be a filmmaker or something.* And there wasn't any such career as an AIDS activist at that point. And it took a while to realize that we should get to the point where there was available resources to pay people to do this kind of work, because it was worth it. And that was also part of what the formation of TAG was about, although, that wasn't so clear at the start."

GARANCE FRANKE-RUTA

"If AIDS had not hit a group of reasonably empowered, well-educated, extremely talented gay men, in the center of the media universe, in New York City, it would have been a very different national experience. Even if it had only hit San Francisco and not New York. But New York is a unique culture. And it's been much harder for heterosexual African Americans to get attention directed towards AIDS than I think it was for gay men. And also because homosexuality was so stigmatized, still . . . so people had a lot less to lose . . . They weren't embedded in families, either. So it was easier to create an organic alternative community . . . I think it's harder for anyone who has children to be involved in an activist organization . . . ACT UP was very effective, because it couldn't afford not to be. And that's the critical difference between it and probably any other organization I'll ever be involved with, is that— it's like having an antiwar group where everybody in the group is also the frontline soldier . . . Its failures were the failures of every movement and every activist group, which is the kind of turning inward and people being unkind to each other.

"I sometimes wonder if there had been less of that, if certain other things could have been accomplished more effectively, or if it could have gone on at a high level for longer, or something like that, but it provided an education for a whole generation of people in New York City, you know . . . I used to joke, when I thought I was going to get a biology major in college: I used to say I was going to go for a basic BS, since I'd already got my advanced BS degree, with ACT UP . . . And it created a whole set of institutions in New York City that still exist. And artistic and community services and research-oriented and advocacy and policy. And it was just—I don't know—it was like the last of the great new social movements of the twentieth century."

ACT UP at the New York City Pride March, 1989 (Photograph by T. L. Litt)

The ACT UP Latino Caucus, 1990. Back row, left to right: Pedro Galazar, Walt Wilder, Alfredo Gonzalez, Juan Mendez, Andy Vélez. Second row, left to right: Gilberto Martínez, Luis Salazar, Luis Lopez, Moisés Agosto. Third row, left to right: Patricia Navarro, César Carrasco. Front row: Guadalupe Sequeria-Malespin (Courtesy of César Carrasco)

Iris Long, 1990 (Photograph by T. L. Litt)

Ortez Alderson being arrested at the
New York Department of Health on
July 19, 1988. In the background:
Jean Carlomusto and Gregg Bordowitz
filming (Photograph by T. L. Litt)

Jim Eigo being arrested at the New York Department of Health
on July 19, 1988 (Photograph by T. L. Litt)

Seize Control of the FDA, October 11, 1988 (Photograph by T. L. Litt)

Lei Chou and Cathy Chou at the Stop
the Church action, December 10, 1989
(Courtesy of Lei Chou)

Jim Hubbard filming, with Richard
Elovich at the left and Mary Patierno
at the right, at the Stop the Church
action, December 10, 1989

Julie Clark and Neil Broome protesting *The New York Times* in front of publisher Arthur Ochs Sulzberger's home on July 25, 1989
(Photograph by T. L. Litt)

Macky Alston and John Shaw protesting for abortion rights at the Stop the Church action
(Photograph by T. L. Litt)

The House of Color video collective. From left to right: Pamela Sneed, Robert Garcia, Julie Tolentino, Jocelyn Taylor, Wellington Love, Idris Mingott, Jeff Nunokawa
(Photograph by T. L. Litt)

Larry Kramer protesting mayoral candidate Rudy Giuliani in 1989. David Dinkins ultimately won the election. (Photograph by T. L. Litt)

Mark Harrington, with Richard Deagle at the right, speaking from the floor at the Fifth International AIDS Conference in Montreal on June 4, 1989 (Photograph by T. L. Litt)

On September 14, 1989, ACT UPers—dressed as brokers—disrupted the New York Stock Exchange with the banner "Sell Wellcome," referring to the manufacturers of AZT. From left to right: Gregg Bordowitz, James McGrath, Lee Arsenault, Scott Robbe, Peter Staley (Photograph by Robert Hilferty)

Phyllis Sharpe at the Health and Human Services Protest in Washington, D.C., on October 2, 1990 (Photograph by Donna Binder)

Garance Franke-Ruta with Illith Rosenblum (at left), Robert Garcia (at right), and other members of ACT UP New York, on June 24, 1989, the twentieth anniversary of the Stonewall riots, participating in a renegade march up Sixth Avenue to Central Park. Themed "In the Tradition," this march followed the same route as the original march twenty years earlier and was designed as a rebuke to the corporatization of the gay pride parade. (Photograph by T. L. Litt)

Tracy Morgan being arrested at the Centers for Disease Control in Atlanta, Georgia, on January 9, 1990. Allan Clear, who took the photo, was arrested shortly after. (Photograph by Allan Clear)

Below: Heidi Dorow and Ray Navarro at the Abortion Rights March for Women's Life in Washington, D.C., on April 10, 1989 (Photograph by T. L. Litt)

Let the Record Show, 1987 display window at the New Museum

New York City Gay Pride, 1989. From left to right: Douglas Crimp,
Alan Robinson, Rand Snyder (Photograph by T. L. Litt)

7

Changing the Definition: Women Don't Get AIDS, We Just Die from It

Women were mistreated by the drug development system in two basic ways. First was by a fear of liability, rooted in the thalidomide scandal of the 1960s. That drug, given to pregnant women as a treatment for morning sickness, produced nearly ten thousand children who were born with missing limbs. Companies and governments had to pay hundreds of millions of dollars to the parents and children. This not only gave pharmaceutical companies strong motives to exclude all women from trials but also severely toughened approval processes for all drugs. Second, at the same time, science did not think about women. And so some of the exclusion was basic neglect. Winning the essentials for women with AIDS turned out to be almost the opposite endeavor of winning for men. Early on, AIDS activists, like government officials and scientists, had not conceptualized that women had separate epidemiologic patterns and health-care needs from men. Social and economic conditions were dramatically different for many women with AIDS as compared to middle-class gay men. Not only did the contexts and medical issues diverge, but the responses of the government and the media were opposed as well. The people in power did not know or identify with women with AIDS and therefore could not imagine integrating their needs because they refused to meet with or speak with them.

Unjust shunning always provokes resistance, and often that resistance, though necessary and appropriate, is pathologized. Those in power consider it to be an inherent right to ignore, exclude, and neglect people with whom they do not identify. For these reasons the campaign for women with AIDS—ACT UP's longest-lasting and farthest-reaching effort—required tactics and consciousness that were far from lunches with pharmaceutical companies, meetings with Ivy League alumni, and chats in corporate men's rooms; none of the activists happened to also be employed at the companies that held their fate in their hands. This exclusion from power created necessary differences in strategy and approach, which often resonated with the life experiences, and consequent ideologies, of the mostly white, mostly lesbian ACT UP women who fought for women with AIDS. This paralleled the way that the modes of approach fit the backgrounds and sensibilities of some of the men working on treatments. If you go to Harvard, you learn the insider playbook, even if you are gay, even if you are without civil rights or family support, and even if you have AIDS. For lesbians and women with AIDS fighting a government from which people like them were excluded, there was no playbook for accessing elite power systems. At its height, ACT UP had a place for every kind of person to act in a way that made sense to them organically, based on how they had lived and the powers they confronted. But conditions not being equal, the methodologies had to differ as well.

Most important, for those of us building activist moments today, we have to understand that ACT UP's CDC campaign was, by necessity, messy. There was the central action of a lawsuit, but it was filed by a young lawyer in an underdog organization, surrounded by a lot of chaos. There was no path, and so there was no genteel agreement among the players. The women had significant differences among themselves, not only in strategy, not only in how to evaluate outcome, but even in the literal narrative of what actually occurred. If they had been expected to be clean, to be orderly, to move together like a machine, to be calm, to be appropriate, to be principled at all times; if they had been expected to play fair, to always tell the truth, to be reasonable, to share credit; if they had been expected to behave, I think history confirms that there is no way in hell that they could have won. AIDS was a sentence of desperation, and the desperate need to win. Winning on an unfair playing field means not playing by the rules. And yet, when you make that call, there are consequences. A streamlined version of a complex story can be told by looking at the work of a poverty lawyer, Terry McGovern; members of ACT UP's Women's Committee, like Maxine Wolfe, Linda Meredith, Rebecca Cole, and Monica Pearl; a nurse practitioner, Risa Denenberg; an ACT UP member also representing an AIDS nonprofit,

Marion Banzhaf; HIV-positive women Keri Duran and Katrina Haslip; and two ACT UPers, Heidi Dorow and Tracy Morgan, who went so far as to employ handcuffs to get their message across.

RECOGNIZING A DISASTER

REBECCA COLE

Rebecca grew up in Wexford, Pennsylvania, a rural working-class town forty miles outside of Pittsburgh. Her father was a traveling salesman and her mother was a homemaker. She studied theater at Northwestern and in 1984 moved to New York to be an actress, bartending at the Raccoon Lounge. A friend told her about a request from the National AIDS Hotline, which required volunteers so that it could open. So Rebecca signed up. The office was at Park Avenue and Nineteenth Street, on the twelfth floor. The workplace aesthetics were "horrible" with a "horrible carpet." The conditions were spare. There was no computer system. Each worker had a phone that was a direct line to the central number. The phone would ring, and Rebecca would answer, "Hello, National AIDS Hotline." The volunteers were not trained. There was a booklet of the most likely questions and the most likely answers. The subject most likely to come up: *mosquitoes*. The callers ran the gamut from people who were clearly infected to those who really hated people who might have AIDS. But many were also people who thought they might have AIDS, and described their illness, asking where they should go.

"First, one call would be some redneck, basically, who wanted to shoot people. Next one was, *My kids go to the local swimming pool, and there's someone there that looks like a girl* and they're terrified, *what am I going to do?* And, *I've been sick for about six weeks now. And I used to weigh a hundred and eighty pounds, and I now weigh a hundred and ten. And I've got these big black marks all over me; and where should I go?* . . . We really were on, to say the front lines, and everyone calls something the front line: we were on the naïve front line. We heard what people really thought. Because this is all anonymous . . . And it was relentless, call after call after call, of the diversity of questions, and not one answer that we could give anyone. We didn't really even know if you could get it from a swimming pool! We wanted to say, *Well, you're crazy, you should send your kids to swim.* But we didn't know . . . how it was transmitted yet. HIV was just even becoming the term, but it wasn't even yet there."

Soon, through the hotline, Rebecca realized that many more women were sick than any public conversation recognized. And when women called, no one knew what to say. *I got diagnosed with some opportunistic infection . . . There's no treatment. What am I supposed to do? Should I breastfeed my children?* Rebecca would follow up by calling the CDC looking for answers, and they'd say, *Call the National AIDS Hotline.*

She went by herself to the second ACT UP meeting, and then ACT UP came and protested government inaction by sitting in at the hotline during Rebecca's shift. From then on she was part of both groups. Soon after, a woman called from Connecticut, and she had AIDS. She lived near a trial for a drug called Ampligen, and she qualified in every way. But they wouldn't let her in because she was a woman. And Rebecca found that hard to believe.

"*Eh, I'm sure you got the information wrong. That can't be—No no. They said because I'm a woman. Honey, you gotta be wrong.* And—what did I do? Hung up the phone; called the trial; asked them what the criteria was. I said, *Do you exclude women?* They said, *No. We exclude people of child-bearing potential,* that was the term . . . And I said, *You mean like, you have a period?* And they said, *Well, that's how you interpret it* . . . So I called someone from the ACLU . . . Because I thought, *Well, that seems like sex discrimination* . . . I called a number of other clinical trials, because we had the lists . . . and everyone had this *child-bearing-potential* rule . . . So I called up the ACLU, and I said, *Did you know?* And they said, *That can't be true.* And I said, *It is true!* . . . So they call the NIH. They find out that they have a rule that's been written since, like, 1957 or '63, or whenever the NIH was formed . . . And there has not been a woman in a clinical trial in thirty years . . . Anyway—I called up Anthony Fauci. And said, *We need a meeting.* And they're like, *You can't have a meeting.* I said, *I'm with ACT UP!* And somehow back in those days, that—it [was] like, *Ooh, we, maybe we'd better.* And I said . . . *We're going to start a movement here. You better meet with me.* And he did; he met with me."

Rebecca went to Washington, D.C., with an ACLU intern, and these two young women sat down and met with Anthony Fauci. He gave them really thorough arguments explaining why women couldn't be in clinical trials. But the women insisted that that was going to have to change. "And you can either change it yourself, or we're going to have to do a big lawsuit against the federal government." Later, a "big muckety-muck" from DuPont, the manufacturer of Ampligen, came up by helicopter to take Rebecca out for a meal to talk about how activists should allow Ampligen to go forward in the clinical trial, because "if we stopped it now, and either let women in or changed the trial, it could be years before it got to the market, and I could be killing people . . . So they actually pulled the trial. They did pull it, out of that . . . I thought, *Oh my God, what if that's the one drug?*" But it turned out to be worthless.

TERRY McGOVERN

A second-generation New Yorker whose grandparents came over from Ireland, Terry McGovern was born in the Bronx. Having come out as a lesbian in her first year at State University of New York (SUNY) Albany in a class on feminism, she got involved with the Seneca Falls Women's Peace Encampment, which was a radical antimilitaristic community, and then went straight to law school at Georgetown. Reagan was president, and the campus gay and lesbian group wasn't allowed to be recognized. The administration wouldn't let the reproductive rights group exist. It was very conservative, and it wasn't very pleasant, but it was a very good place to learn to be a lawyer. Basically, nobody agreed with Terry, so she had to learn how the other side thinks.

Her first legal position was with Federal Defenders of San Diego. Every morning she would walk into a holding cell and there'd be seventy-five people, and she'd have to represent them in front of the magistrate. Working in the jails of Tijuana changed her whole life path; there was no going back. Jimmy Carter was elected, and she returned to New York. Terry got a job with a civil legal services program created for people who were under the National Poverty Index and got placed in the Hell's Kitchen office as a housing lawyer.

"I started to see all these HIV cases . . . I couldn't believe what I was seeing . . . Extremely sick people. Women, gay men of color, who lived in the projects, who wouldn't say they had HIV/AIDS, but they were clearly dying of HIV . . . Very early on, in the Poverty Law offices, there was huge stigma. I mean, in one office they used to spray the seats with Lysol after my clients came in. There would be these intake meetings where people would say, *I can't take it, I have a family* . . . So I ended up taking the cases."

Terry started the HIV Law Project, opening their first office on pre-gentrification Avenue A and Fifth Street, in what was then still a poor neighborhood, near the projects on Avenue D. Terry's clients were being evicted. Some had lovers who had died, and they were losing their apartments while being extremely ill. The issue of lease succession rights had been dealt with in a rent-stabilization, rent-control context. There were a lot of cases taken on by the ACLU and Lambda. But nobody had thought about people in public housing. Terry was seeing through the poverty lens on HIV, and she felt that "the poverty law community certainly failed these folks." A lot of the legal groups that existed in poor communities where this was happening wouldn't touch it. And then there "wasn't the expertise" among gay male groups to deal with women with children. When it came to getting benefits for clients, like Medicaid and Social Security disability, Terry saw a strange pattern. These clients weren't able to qualify. And women couldn't get into clinical trials. "It almost was like everything you looked at, as a lawyer, you couldn't fix it. Like you couldn't just have the hearing and win, because the problems were at the top. And I had never seen anything like that."

What led Terry to ACT UP was one specific case.

"This man came in, extremely, extremely sick—convulsing, practically, in the interview—and after a long time, told me that—and it was very difficult to get the story out—that his lover had died of AIDS. They'd lived together years and years, actually in the Douglass Projects, up on One-Hundredth Street and Amsterdam . . . He was dying himself; they were evicting him. I said, *We're going to have to disclose that you were partners. And . . . have a hearing with the local project manager.* And we had to prepare a lot, because he was very nervous. We went to this hearing. And again, he was so ill. And they were horrible to us. I mean, vicious. *You're telling me he's gay* . . . And it was one of the most insulting, vicious kind of encounters I'd ever had. I waited a couple of days, started calling the client; and he wasn't answering, he wasn't answering, wasn't answering. And basically went there, and he was dead in the apartment. And I don't know whether he committed suicide; I don't know what happened. But it was just horrific."

Terry went to ACT UP, told the floor what was going on. But while she was sitting at the meeting, she heard the Women's Caucus speak, and they were talking about the CDC definition of AIDS excluding women from being able to get an AIDS diagnosis and qualify for benefits. "So that made me go back and really begin to get onto that trail."

MAXINE WOLFE

To build community for gay women in ACT UP, Maxine started to host "Dyke Dinners" at her home in Brooklyn. From that arose the ACT UP Women's Caucus. They began organizing a number of events and campaigns. Maria Maggenti and Jean Carlomusto created actions against *Cosmopolitan* magazine for claiming that heterosexual women could not get AIDS, and produced a film on the subject, *Doctors, Liars, and Women*. Debra Levine and others organized a bold action at Shea Stadium, where the New York Mets played baseball. A large contingent of ACT UPers converged on a night game and designed an action to support straight women asking men to use condoms. They displayed huge banners: NO GLOVE, NO LOVE and DON'T BALK AT SAFER SEX. Then the Women's Caucus started working on opportunistic infections that affected women with AIDS. Being a caucus meant they didn't have a representative on the ACT UP Coordinating Committee. But as a newly constituted *committee*, their position in the organization was solidified, and they started to have a set meeting time so women could freely come instead of having to be invited in through social networks.

RISA DENENBERG

Risa Denenberg was born into a Jewish family in Washington, D.C. She went to public school and was part of the first generation of her family to go to college. In 1968, at the man's insistence "with threat of violence," she had an illegal abortion performed by a woman who did them in her house. When Risa was nineteen, she gave birth to a son in a hotel room in Afghanistan. She and her boyfriend moved to Miami, where she enrolled in community college, and then Florida State. "I think I knew I was a lesbian, even when I got pregnant the first time." She finally came out and moved to Tallahassee.

There, Risa started working at the Feminist Women's Health Center, while getting a BA in nursing and her RN license, and ended up staying for fourteen years. With fellow collective member Marion Banzhaf, "we were the people that went around, showing our cervixes, and showing women how to use a speculum. And we did abortions . . . once a week . . . anywhere from eighteen or twenty to sometimes as many as thirty or thirty-five." The collective had Black leadership and began to serve the Black community. "We were basically—and not entirely, but basically—a group of lesbians, providing health care to straight women . . . and we were not taking care of ourselves."

In 1988, Risa came to New York to go to graduate school in the nurse practitioner program at Columbia and roomed with Marion, who had moved before her and who was already going to ACT UP meetings. Risa went along during her first week in New York. While she was at the Center, she visited the Community Health Project (CHP) and found out that, despite their name, they had no services for women. So she started a lesbian health program there and began seeing clients. She was also employed in the emergency room at Beth Israel Hospital. She then got a job as the nurse practitioner for Dr. Kathy Anastos at Bronx Lebanon Hospital Center, and was doing most of the gynecology exams for women with HIV coming through the clinic. Risa had already seen a few HIV-positive lesbians at CHP, so she had a heads-up about what she was going to see gynecologically. In the Bronx, she saw at least two hundred women. Day in and day out, she could see what was going on. The various conditions resisted treatment. Women came in with vaginal warts; Risa would freeze them and they'd come right back. The cervical problems would be treated, and they, too, would come right back. The patients had a lot of irregular, heavy periods. Many women came in with pelvic inflammatory disease that was hard to treat. But the most profound thing was the high rate of abnormal pap smears, which she immediately tried to document. This data collection became the basis for doing a full study of pap smear results from HIV-positive women. She quickly decided that these women needed pap smears every six months.

Terry McGovern asked Risa to look over her clients' charts in preparation for the lawsuit. There she saw the same patterns. Women returning over and over for urinary tract infections and pelvic infections that didn't respond to treatment. And no one was doing pap smears. Risa concluded that the women Terry was talking to "were getting horrible health care."

AIDS COUNSELING AND EDUCATION (ACE)

MARION BANZHAF

At college in Gainesville, Florida, before *Roe v. Wade*, Marion Banzhaf got pregnant. The editor of the school paper, the *Alligator*, broke the law by publishing information from the Clergy Consultation Referral Service on how to get an abortion in New York City, where they were legal. Unfortunately, Marion didn't have enough money to get to New York.

"Four of us went out to the college quad. And I'd approach people, and say, *I'm pregnant, and I don't want to be. I've got to get to New York to get an abortion. It should be legal. Will you sign this petition, and will you give me money too, so I can get up there?*" After she raised three hundred dollars, she flew up to New York with the address of the Center for Reproductive Health. "They told me how to get from the airport to the clinic. *Take this bus, then take a cab.* And when I got to the clinic, there were probably about four hundred women in this clinic. It's like, everybody east of the Mississippi."

She got her abortion.

By 1975, Marion had dropped out of college, moved to Tallahassee, and gotten a job at the Feminist Women's Health Center. They did abortions for half the price of local doctors. "We were definitely on the left of the women's health movement. We'd go to Planned Parenthood conferences and confront them for population-control policies, and we'd say, *Women should be able to have as many or as few kids as they want.*" She came out at the health center, and had a relationship with

Risa. Then Marion started to get involved in anti-imperialist politics, first being influenced by Marxist Iranian students standing against the shah, and then by revolutionary women from Zimbabwe. She moved to D.C. and, with her lover, the lawyer Judy Holmes, went to hear a talk by Silvia Baraldini of the May 19th Communist Organization, a descendant of the Weather Underground and the Movement for New Afrika, an offshoot of the Black Panther Party. Soon some key organizers from that movement, Laura Whitehorn, Mary Patten (who later joined ACT UP Chicago), Eve Rosahn, and Judy Clark, were all were staying at Marion and Judy's house. Marion joined a May 19th offshoot, the John Brown Anti-Klan Committee. Then, in 1981, a Brink's truck was robbed by former members of the Weather Underground and Black Liberation Army, and a guard was murdered. Some people associated with May 19th, including Silvia, Eve, and Judy Clark, were arrested. Silvia was deported to Italy, Eve served time for contempt, and Judy Clark served thirty-seven years at Bedford Hills.

"The first person I knew . . . to die from AIDS was Kuwasi Balagoon, who had been a member of the Black Panthers and had also been a member of the Black Liberation Army. And he died in prison; Judy Holmes was his lawyer. He had gone from being this strapping hulk of a guy to completely wasted from PCP, in a matter of four months. And that was, did I say '85? And he was a very interesting guy, because even though he was part of the Black Liberation Army, he was also an anarchist. And he was also in love with a Black drag queen. And I made a quilt panel for him [on the AIDS quilt] that had a big black panther on it, and was in red, black, and green."

While incarcerated at Bedford, Judy Clark and former Weatherman Kathy Boudin were involved in cofounding AIDS Counseling and Education (ACE) with other women. ACE was both an education project and a support project focusing on incarcerated HIV-positive women. It provided buddy services when women got sick; it provided safer-sex information for when they came back out on the street. It was connected to various groups, not only ACT UP but also Life Force and Health Force. "Because Judy and Kathy had both been organizers, they did outreach to various groups who would come in contact with women on the outside, and hooked people up, so that they would have someplace to go. And I think also those women had been influenced by Kathy and Judy's political education that they had imparted. And so also came out feeling like, *Oh, you can fight the system, actually.* As opposed to so many other people, who feel like, *I can't do anything about this situation.*"

Around 1987, Marion was protesting a new recruitment program by the New York Police Department at the Gay Center. She would see large groups of people gathering at ACT UP meetings, and decided she would join when there were at least ten women in the room. "And so I did." Marion joined the Women's Committee and became the Coordinating Committee representative with Monica Pearl, even though other committees only had one person, because the Coordinating Committee was all men. "We organized the floor to give the Women's Committee two seats, so that it wouldn't be just one woman in the Steering Committee, by herself."

WOMEN AND AIDS TEACH-IN

MAXINE WOLFE

"We had people in the Women's Committee, who had been working in different clinic situations, and knew what kinds of infections women were coming with . . . We found out that women would show up at hospitals with what seemed like pneumonia, and nobody would do a bronchoscopy. People would assume it was bacterial pneumonia, or they would assume that it was flu and they would give people aspirin and tell them to go home, and women would die." Maxine met Iris De La Cruz, Katrina Haslip, Lydia Awadala, and Phyllis Sharpe—"just a whole bunch of women that had been connected, most of them, to [ACE-OUT], which was the group that Katrina had started when she left Bedford Hills, for women coming out of prison who had HIV." Bringing the campaign to ACT UP started with the Women's Committee doing a Women and AIDS teach-in, Maxine said, "which I loved about ACT UP . . . the teach-ins . . . educating ourselves about issues, and then creating booklets." The handbook that they created "went all around the world . . . in its xeroxed form."

MARION BANZHAF

People in ACT UP were worried about threats of mandatory HIV testing. They knew that if anonymous testing was not permitted, people would not get tested and would die faster. Marion was discussing this with David Robinson and others, and she said, *We should just set up our own testing clinic. Why don't we? We could do that . . . Then, if they make it mandatory, we'll just have an underground clinic that people could go to, so you could still find out. But you wouldn't have to go through the state.* Marion wanted to share information about the women's health movement, and how other people had actually forced the FDA to do certain things before ACT UP. "And even that the women's health movement sort of paved the way for AIDS activism, in terms of challenging the control of doctors in the first place, and starting to democratize health care."

MAXINE WOLFE

The more research the women did, the more they found that infections specific to HIV-positive women were not on the CDC's radar. They realized that women with HIV were getting out-of-control yeast infections that did not respond to treatment. For example, there were various forms of tubercular bacilli that would form in women, in different places than in men. HIV-positive women's groups started forming in other parts of the country, and a National Women's Committee started having conference calls and thinking collectively.

WOMEN, AIDS & ACTIVISM

MONICA PEARL

Monica Pearl was born in 1964 and raised in suburban New Jersey. She started coming out in boarding school, then at Connecticut College and Smith College, and she first found out about AIDS by reading *The Village Voice*. Then she went to donate blood and was rejected because she was a lesbian. Monica knew ACT UP facilitator Maria Maggenti from Smith and started going to meetings.

What started as a handbook from a teach-in became a huge project of the Women's Committee when Monica and Cynthia Chris cochaired an extended effort to create the first full-length book about women and AIDS. With Marion Banzhaf, Polly Thistlethwaite, Zoe Leonard, Maxine Wolfe, Maria Maggenti, and others, the book, *Women, AIDS & Activism*, was eventually published by South End Press and distributed around the world.

"There were concerns women just didn't have information about what was risky for them, what kind of sex was risky for them, what kind of drug using, what kind of childcare, breastfeeding . . . What was great about the book is that besides having really great chapters on women having sex with men, women having sex with women, women using drugs, women and children . . . the chapter in the book that was about women with AIDS in prison was written by women with AIDS in prison . . . There was also a great list of resources in the back, and that was very important to us that we put that together."

GATHERING THE FACTS

LINDA MEREDITH

Linda was born in the 1950s in Southeast Georgia. Her parents were "avid and dedicated proselytizing members of the Southern Baptist Church. And so I grew up with the church being the center of my very small world . . . All things emanated from there." She started questioning religion at age nine or ten. Her hometown was legally segregated until Linda was in junior high school. They had separate water fountains at the department store labeled *White* and *Colored*. She went to one of two white high schools. After mandated integration, Linda was asked to be on a committee with faculty supervision to figure out how to change the school once integration was established. "So that was the first time I figured out that there were other people with whom I needed to share."

Linda got married to a soldier and had a son. After her divorce, she went back to school, earning a BA and an MA in immunology. She came out in 1979 in Augusta, Georgia, into a lesbian community organized around bars and softball fields, then moved to Atlanta, where a friend died of AIDS in 1985. Linda took a job in a CDC-financed lab, screening the blood supply with surrogate markers before there was an HIV antibody test. In 1988, she put her name on a list to house activists coming to the Democratic National Convention in Atlanta, and she got Maria Maggenti, Maxine Wolfe, and Maxine's youngest daughter, Amy Wolfe. "We're just staying up till three o'clock in the morning, talking about everything . . . Smoking our faces off . . . Maxine and I stayed in very close contact. Literally, we talked on the phone every day. And I helped start an ACT UP Atlanta."

Linda worked closely with ACT UP New York on a number of projects. With Risa Denenbeg, she went to the offices of physicians in New York and looked at blinded records to see what symptoms women were manifesting. They found extrapulmonary tuberculosis (TB) and invasive cervical cancer. They were documenting what women with AIDS were sick with and dying from at the time "in a very un-placebo-controlled way." They could tell very quickly that the list of opportunistic infections that were in the current CDC definition had no relation to the things that were making women so sick.

TERRY McGOVERN

By this point, particularly for women with AIDS and those battling state definitions, word began to spread that Terry would take their cases. There was a real problem with women qualifying for Social Security disability and Division of AIDS services, and the larger problem of the official definition of AIDS excluding women. Terry started to take referrals from the Women's Prison Association and began to see a lot of women who were coming out of the Bedford Hills women's prison.

"They all talked about that they had been helped on the inside by this woman, *the Muslim lady who worked in the law library*. And I was amazed, because . . . they had their medical records; they kind of knew what was going on; they understood the whole issue of the definition. And so I kept hearing about this person who had helped them. And that was Katrina [Haslip]. And not only did I see the evidence of how good her work was, but they all loved her so much. It kind of fascinated me, because their faces would light up about Katrina, and they'd talk about her . . . They all talked about how shocked they were to learn that she was positive, and that she was fearless."

Terry McGovern (center) and Katrina Haslip (right) protesting
at Health and Human Services in Washington, D.C., on the day
of Katrina's release from prison on October 2, 1990 (Photograph by
Donna Binder)

KATRINA HASLIP AND THE FOUNDING OF ACE AND ACE-OUT

Katrina Haslip was one of the most important and influential leaders
of the movement of HIV-positive women fighting for their rights. A
vibrant, charismatic, and energetic young Black woman, grounded in
her Muslim faith, Katrina was a fierce advocate for incarcerated HIV-
positive women. She was born in Niagara Falls, where she grew up with
twelve brothers and sisters. After two failed marriages she started using
intravenous drugs and was stabbed in 1983 and treated with a blood
transfusion at a time when the blood supply was not screened. She
never knew exactly the source of her HIV infection. Arrested at age
twenty-six in 1985 for pickpocketing, Katrina had been a sex worker
with a drug habit who survived by stealing. Sentenced to five and a
half years in a maximum-security prison, Bedford Hills, she found
out she was HIV-positive while incarcerated. With Judy Clark, Kathy
Boudin, and others, she cofounded ACE for HIV-positive women
inside Bedford Hills Correctional, and, after her release in 1990, she
cocreated its sister program, ACE-OUT, to help women with AIDS
once they were released. "They have to deal with, *How do I get my kids
back?*" she told *The New York Times*. "*Where do I move to? How do I stay
drug free? How do I earn money without stealing?*"

ACE was started because of the enormous stigma against HIV-
positive inmates, who were physically and verbally abused by other

inmates to the extent that their cells were set on fire. In a memorial tape, edited by Catherine Gund, Katrina testified that "we knew very little about AIDS, we knew we needed education from outside forces." They got volunteers to come in from Montefiore Medical Center, from ACT UP, from the Department of Health, to do trainings. "As a result we were doing counseling one-on-one informally, in the yard, in the shower, wherever people ask questions. We just tried to be supportive to one another."

In one of its most remarkable achievements, ACE started a buddy system inside the prison.

"We began to link PWAs up with buddies who would go up to the hospital to see them, who would do their shopping or clean up their cells or help them in the shower or take them out for recreation. And we noticed that it was really becoming something, changing the community, and we saw ourselves as a community . . . We were supposedly 'criminals' you know, the outcasts of society, that was responding to the epidemic in a way that some communities outside weren't even responding . . . As a result of all of that, the AIDS Institute noticed that we were responding and they awarded us a quarter of a million dollars to run a program, to be staffed, and set up office equipment and supplies that we really needed. And that's how we actually became ACE—AIDS Counseling and Education."

The more aware Katrina became, the broader her agenda grew. ACE members realized that HIV-positive incarcerated women were being denied access to treatments and were being studied, without positive outcomes for the patients.

"It is important to us that we educate ourselves that we learn what treatments are available and how effective they are and that we be given unlimited access to them . . . We should no longer be asking the question *What does reoccurring vaginitis mean?* . . . There was a blind study done in Bedford Hills Correctional Facility on women. What is the purpose except to accumulate numbers when there is no follow-up or options or availability to treatment?"

Katrina herself had long suffered repeated yeast infections before being tested for HIV. She knew it wasn't normal for her, but she could have been treated two years earlier if somebody had known that it was an early sign of HIV infection.

TERRY McGOVERN

Working with these women as clients, Terry tried to find a legal way to get at the problem of an inadequate official definition of AIDS from the CDC, which was the primary obstacle for women. She couldn't sue the CDC, because they didn't give away the money. She had to figure out a legal strategy to get at the benefits programs for imposing an unfair definition to qualify for an official AIDS diagnosis. So Terry surveyed all the poverty law offices and amassed a large group of plaintiffs who had been denied Social Security benefits for definitional reasons. On October 1, 1990, she filed a class-action suit against Social Security, while working closely with ACT UP. In fact, that day, she filed the suit in the morning, and then got on a bus to Washington, D.C., for an ACT UP action, which was a women's demonstration in front of Health and Human Services.

POSITIVE WOMEN'S ACTION AT HEALTH AND HUMAN SERVICES

MAXINE WOLFE

"The first demonstration that we did, which was at Health and Human Services—all those women came. And by that time, we had done more outreach. Tracy Morgan had joined ACT UP, and she was working, doing some counseling for homeless women. And there were women from her center that came. And then Terry McGovern had been doing some stuff, and women that she had been representing in Legal Aid came—so, it was a pretty broad range of women."

The action's slogan was "Women don't get AIDS; they just die from it." The action included tombstones and a speak-out of women with HIV talking about all their infections, followed by a large demonstration. If the CDC did not include HIV-associated infections in their definition, then there would not be relevant research. Without research, there would be no treatments. So the actions articulated issues beyond the crucial question of qualifying for disability benefits. They wanted female-centered research and treatments, with access for women to appropriate experimental drug trials.

LINDA MEREDITH

"These women just wanted a voice. They wanted to speak, and they knew the stuff, and they were dying to get their story out, because— talk about the invisible of the invisible. They could have a megaphone, a bullhorn in their hand, and say what was happening, [and] I think in certain ways without a definition and without drugs, it kept them alive . . . There were a few people from Boston, a few people from L.A., a few people from Atlanta, and then from D.C. . . . We all spoke to each other on the phone all the time. We had a phone tree with each other . . . We would fax each other fact sheets that we were working on. People would bring them to the floor of their own thing to try to get an endorsement. But really the hub, the mother ship, was in New York City."

TERRY McGOVERN

ACT UP had the resources to pay for thirty HIV-positive women to come to D.C. for the action. This included Iris De La Cruz, a highly engaged activist. Iris was also a member of Prostitutes of New York (PONY) and wrote a very popular column for *PWA Newsline*, "Iris with the Virus." In D.C., Terry saw Lydia Awadala and other members of Life Force, another self-empowerment organization for people with AIDS. Terry also saw Phyllis Sharpe, who was a leader of the Women with AIDS movement, one of the plaintiffs in the lawsuit, and a speaker at demonstrations. Black, sometimes homeless, with a recurring drug habit, Phyllis knew exactly what was at stake. She publicly testified to having uncontrollable yeast infections and pelvic inflammatory disease, which were emerging as key infections afflicting women with AIDS that were not on the CDC's list of recognized symptoms. Katrina Haslip had been released from Bedford two weeks before the demonstration and so was not allowed to attend because she was on probation. But she showed up anyway.

"This population was completely excluded from everything. And ACT UP had been consistently raising that [fact], and had been really effective . . . But I think the combination of having the litigation and the demonstration and all this ACT UP work that had gone on finally started to scare the government a bit. Because they had to respond in court. And they could see that . . . big allies were developing at this point."

The Center for Constitutional Rights had signed on. Jill Boskey from Mobilization for Youth Legal Services and Leslie Salzman from Cardozo Law joined in. Even the American Medical Association came in on the lawsuit, which for Terry was a "crazy, unbelievable" victory. Terry observed that the support of these very prominent groups made the government nervous. "Suddenly people were seeing positive women as leaders, also, who were saying *I've been denied disability*. So it wasn't just generalized complaints. There were specific things that needed to be changed. So I think it was an extremely powerful moment in this whole struggle."

The lawsuit and direct action worked together. The U.S. government moved to dismiss the case three times, but the federal court refused to do so. The government "littered" Terry's tiny office with papers and tried to basically outwork her. The judge in the case read about the protests in a *New York Times* article about the women's demonstration and campaign. And so all of the components worked in unison. Terry did legal research to figure out how the Social Security Administration was using the definition of AIDS to enforce discrimination, and ACT UP used the information in teach-in materials. And then together Terry's law office and ACT UP did widespread community education, which Terry observed not only affecting many positive women but also affecting providers. The collective coalitional effort was hugely important to moving things forward. From the beginning Terry was clear that a lawsuit, alone, was never going to be enough if there wasn't massive community organizing.

SOLIDARITY WITH CONVERGING EPIDEMICS

After the action in D.C. and the *Times* story, the word spread nationally. Terry got calls from providers and drug facilities, prisons, women's doctors, people in community health clinics. She got hundreds of calls from people who were dealing with HIV-positive people who couldn't meet the definition and were experiencing the same disability issues. And she was contacted by a lot of small HIV-positive women's groups around the country. Everybody wanted information; everybody wanted to start doing teach-ins. The original AIDS definition was used by Social Security as the gate into getting benefits automatically, but it was also used in all local programs for local benefits or for housing for people with AIDS; it was used everywhere. So nationally it was hugely important to get that definition expanded for women, and also for low-income people. The original AIDS definition was not looking at the concept of converging epidemics. As a result, tuberculosis wasn't in it; bacterial pneumonia wasn't in it. Terry saw that it wasn't just women; it was lots and lots of poor people, to pick a denominator.

CONFRONTING THE CDC

LINDA MEREDITH

The first direct-action strategy aimed at changing the definition of AIDS was to try to get the Social Security Administration (SSA) to buck the CDC on some kind of compassionate-care model because women were terribly sick and dying and had no way to live financially. The very first action was a picket at the SSA. But that didn't work; clearly the CDC was setting the pace. "We called them. We had fax zaps. We had letter-writing campaigns," Linda said, aimed at the CDC's HIV Surveillance Project, which was headed by James Curran.

"He was super obstreperous and he was a sexist pig. He tried to argue with us about the science, because he thought he could shut us down if he said more about *the pure nature of epidemiology* than he thought we knew. But we knew a ton. And actually, unlike a lot of the other campaigns that I worked on, the CDC was very much behind those walls in that brick building. There was no public face of the CDC. We would fax stuff to him, we would call him, we would bomb him with letters. We would see them at public health conferences and interrupt them and all of that—but there were not meetings."

Curran argued that since many of the HIV-positive women had been IV drug users, if they had—for example—extrapulmonary tuberculosis, it was a function of their lack of access to health care, their socioeconomic class, their injection drug use, or their homelessness. He was looking for anything to claim that their suffering was not as a function of the fact that they were immunosuppressed.

"He had characterized the disease in such a way that it was *only men*, and he had created a whole program around that . . . He just didn't want to change it. He couldn't see women. He didn't know that anybody had a vagina or cervix. And he just didn't want to see it, because it would have to make him rethink the way he constructed his entire department."

HEIDI DOROW

Heidi Dorow grew up with her German grandparents in Michigan. Wanting to be an actor, she got into a conservatory in St. Louis but was expelled for being in a relationship with a female dance professor. She hung out with theater people in Chicago for a few years and then got into Hampshire College. There, she quickly became an activist and ended up getting arrested at the Supreme Court in D.C. during her very first demonstration. At Hampshire, she met Maxine Wolfe's daughter Karen. Heidi had never met anyone with AIDS, but Maxine invited her to an ACT UP meeting, and that was it—she never went back to Hampshire.

"The CDC still had not changed the definition. And so, as I recall, Tracy [Morgan] and I—who were lovers at the time—said, *Let's come up with a year-long campaign to win, to get them to change the definition. How do we get from here to here?* and *We are going to make their lives miserable. They will have to change the definition, because we are going to be at them at every turn.* So this plan had several different layers. It was a campaign. And these are the components that I remember. I think the first one was a postcard campaign. And the front of the postcard was a picture of James Curran, who was the head of the HIV-AIDS division at the CDC. Had a big target on his face. And then the text on the back, it was addressed to him . . . It said something like, *Hey, Curran.* And basically said, *Change the definition; we're coming after you*, or something. And so we, I think, got ten thousand of those postcards printed up. We sent them all over the country; we got people in, obviously, ACT UP, but then we tried to get doctors, social workers, AIDS organizations; we tried to flood Curran with these postcards. That was one thing we did."

Heidi and Tracy got a hold of Curran's travel schedule. They found out that he was coming to New York and that he was going to be passing through the airport. So they met him at the gate, with these huge signs that were the cover of the postcard: his face, with a big target on it. They yelled at him, from the second he got off the plane, went to baggage claim, and got a cab. They followed him around, screaming at him.

Activists realized that there were local CDC offices. They worked with ACT UPs around the country and organized a day of simultaneous national actions at CDC offices. In New York they had made a huge, long banner that said CDC KILLS. And it was vertical. Heidi and others climbed up on the roof of the building, "risking life and limb." They crawled out on a ledge that had no guardrail and tossed the banner over the ledge, draping the front of the building. "I'm not sure that I would do that again, I was terrified, but also I didn't think twice about it. And there were other people who did the same thing. Anyway, so in the middle of this big action in front of Federal Plaza, the banner comes down! Whoo! *CDC Kills*! It's five stories high. It was beautiful!"

MAXINE WOLFE

The national team spoke anywhere in the United States they had invitations. They got lots of groups to sign on to the campaign. They got people to send postcards, sign petitions. The more they worked, the more sophisticated their understandings became about AIDS categorizations, and the ways the disease and infected people were misconceptualized. Drug use was a stigma that dominated the government's approach to people with AIDS. If someone had ever used drugs, that became their primary identity as a patient. Women who may have sexually contracted HIV were often categorized by their drug use, which was confusing because sexually transmitted AIDS could manifest as Kaposi sarcoma, whereas AIDS transmitted by needles did not. Eventually, three hundred different groups from across the United States signed onto the CDC definition campaign.

TRACY MORGAN

Tracy Morgan was born in 1962 in an upper-middle-class suburb of New Jersey. Her first action was in grade school, when she wrote a petition demanding that girls be allowed to wear pants. In high school she was homecoming queen. She majored in women's studies at SUNY Albany, where she had her first relationship with a woman, then went to London with a boyfriend and came back to New York, where she got involved with WHAM! Tracy met Risa Denenberg when she volunteered at CHP and started working a lot in ACT UP.

"We had the feeling that . . . we could do something really public, not just public at the CDC, but something more public. So we said, *Hey, well, we could run one of those last-minute ads at* The New York Times, which are a little more discounted, you don't know when it's going to run within—like buying a flight. Within three to five days, you can get the cheaper deal . . . Avram Finkelstein, and Gran Fury came up with 'Women don't get AIDS; they just die from it.' I don't know who put that phrase together, but once that phrase was enunciated, we knew we had to use it. So we began to do a postcard campaign, and getting people from all over the country, from community-based organizations that got their money from the CDC, and they received CDC funding to provide services to people with AIDS, and they began to take a stand, saying, *Change the definition.*"

The groups involved included the Caribbean Women's Health Association in Crown Heights, the Community Family Planning Council, and the National Black Women's Health Project. The process of signing on was politically complex. Tracy went "out in person" to talk to local groups about signing the ad, while national communication took place on the phone. For example, an organization receiving $250,000 from the CDC in Crown Heights, providing services to HIV-positive women, would have to be very committed to oppose the CDC. It would be a decision involving everybody on their staff, on their board, thinking this through. ACT UP had to provide them with the educational materials,

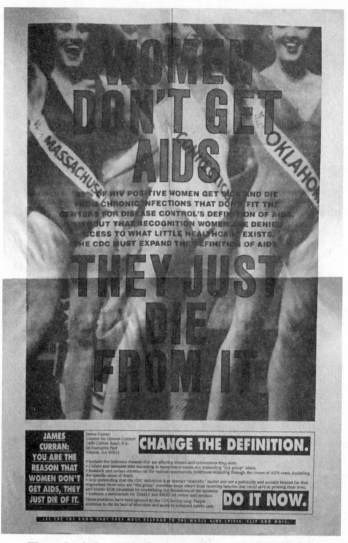

Women Don't Get AIDS, They Just Die from It, Gran Fury, 1991;
Offset lithograph on newsprint; Insert, "ACT UP REPORTS,
1991 / 2"; 22.50 inches high x 14.75 inches wide
(Image courtesy of Avram Finkelstein)

do the teach-ins, go meet with them, make sure that everybody understood what was involved and what the win would be, that there was going
to be a huge win, but in the short run they might get hurt. Organizers
in ACT UP San Francisco, ACT UP Chicago, and others were working,

building relationships with organizations and individuals who might sign on. When it got to five hundred signers, the ad finally ran in the *Times*.

FORCING THE GOVERNMENT TO DO A CONFERENCE ON WOMEN AND AIDS

MAXINE WOLFE

"Over that year we had been pressuring the National Institutes of Health to do a conference on women and AIDS. And they didn't want to." The campaign found many creative ways to let the government officials know that women and AIDS had to become an area of study.

LINDA MEREDITH

At the big ACT UP action Storm the NIH in Washington, D.C., on May 21, 1990, Linda Meredith and Marion Banzhaf dressed up "like businesspeople and went past security" and let the rest of their affinity group, the Costas, in through a fire escape door to the office of Dan Hoth, director of the NIH's AIDS division.

"We went up the stairs, and we were in his office for a couple hours. On his bulletin board was Tony Fauci's number, so we called him a whole bunch. We had fact sheets about what the ACTG (AIDS Clinical [Trials Group]) needed to study, from our point of view, specific to women with AIDS. We put those fact sheets in every Pendaflex folder in all of his filing cabinets. Then we all were arrested."

After the NIH action a few women were allowed to observe the ACTG quarterly meeting.

"Our direct action was both on target and hilarious. They would have these cocktail receptions, starting at five, after the regular meetings were over, and we had these custom fortune cookies made up. We got one of the servers at the hotel to let us have one of those silver trays, and we put the fortune cookies on there—right with the cheese platter, and whatever. The fortunes all said, *NIAID, Form a Women's Committee*. When you opened up the cookie, that's what it said. And the looks on the people's faces when they saw what the fortune was in those cookies, really, there was nothing better."

At the sixth annual International AIDS Conference, held in San Francisco in June 1990, there was a large ACT UP contingent that would meet and caucus. Dan Hoth was giving a major plenary talk the next morning, and the women brought to that local ACT UP group the suggestion of an action to disrupt his plenary talk because the ACTGs were not studying the role of medications for women with AIDS. A vote was taken about the action, and Linda recalled that the women were told that while they could hold a banner, they couldn't say anything.

"There was a [vote:] *Everybody raise their hand if you want to allow this affinity group, this onsite affinity group, to be able to go do this. Yes or no? Lots of no. Why? Because it's a scientific conference, and we want to dialogue with the researchers, not disrupt the information that is given there.*"

The opposition came from David Barr and Mark Harrington of Treatment and Data and ACT UP Golden Gate—a new chapter that had split from ACT UP San Francisco when it was taken over by HIV denialists.

"From our point of view, we were working on trying to get the government to study women with AIDS for a lot of reasons. There was a paucity of data, and they weren't doing anything. So what possibly, scientifically, could have been shared there if nothing existed?"

This moment was a huge conceptual rift. The women believed that science that excluded women was not valid science. The men knew instinctively, if not always consciously, that they *were* being studied, and so the information would be relevant to them. The women made a huge banner that night that said NIAID, FORM A WOMEN'S COMMITTEE. There were about eight or ten ACT UPers involved, including Marion, Risa, and Linda. They unfurled the banner so that it faced the speaker. And they had made some spray-painted T-shirts on the fly. Previously, Dan Hoth had said about a research and treatment agenda for women, "We've not actually paid much attention to how we actually do these trials." So they spray-painted that quote from him on the backs of their T-shirts and put his name on them. In this way he was looking at his own words as he delivered his speech.

MAXINE WOLFE

"But then, Linda Meredith handed him a note and the note said, basically, *We're coming back to your office.* And he was not wanting to talk to us on the phone, but when he got that note, he spoke to us on the phone, and we forced him to hold a Women and AIDS conference—the first one—which was held in December of '90. Originally, they wanted us to be part of the planning, and Linda was part of the planning, but we made it clear that we would not rubber-stamp what they did. And so, at the beginning, it was really interesting because there were all these women, who were from all over the country, who had been waiting for this day, because all of this stuff had been suppressed. There had been women researchers who had been pushing for this for years and nothing was happening. And, in fact, one woman said to another woman at this planning board meeting, *How did we ever get this conference? We've been pushing for this conference for years, and nobody did it.* And another woman said, *Because twenty people sat in at Dan Hoth's office, and he got scared to death.*"

The conference, officially titled National Women and HIV Conference, was held in Washington, D.C., on December 1, 1990. But even though they finally got in the door, women with AIDS were treated very differently from men. Maxine experienced that the women were all willing to do the best conference possible, but the government wasn't. She recalled that what the government had consistently done was run its own conferences, putting in researchers who would say whatever the government wanted them to say. "And at the point, what they wanted people to say was that there was no difference, whatever," Maxine said, between women with AIDS and men with AIDS. Maxine remembers that after the whole schedule had been set, the government people took it over and "totally decimated it and put only their people there." ACT UP wanted the government to pay for women with HIV to come to the conference, and the government wouldn't do it. So at that point the activists wrote up their first Women's Treatment and Research Agenda and handed it out at that conference. When a CDC representative spoke, they opened up a banner and "everybody started screaming at him about how wrong he was." They did a lot of actions at that conference, but Maxine felt that the main event was that a lot of women with HIV came from all over the country, and they formed a group.

"Tony Fauci was speaking, and he was basically saying that they didn't know anything about women and AIDS, but he was going to talk about men and AIDS, and he started doing AIDS 101—all hell broke loose . . . And everybody got up to the microphone and said, *Hey, you sit down, we have something to say.* And they had written up a whole statement about, you know, the three things that they needed; they needed the CDC to change the definition of AIDS. They needed women in clinical trials, and they needed to get their disability payments, and that sort of got a lot more women involved, and then they—a lot of those women—came to the CDC action, because then they got in touch with us."

MARION BANZHAF

The conference was attended by about a thousand people. Marion was there representing both the New Jersey Women and AIDS Network and ACT UP.

"We hounded Dan Hoth, I think, and Tony Fauci, during that conference. And they were definitely isolated. ACT UP's position was that we had to add cervical cancer, pelvic inflammatory disease, bacterial pneumonia, endocarditis, and two hundred T cells or less [to the definition]. And that it had to be *all* those things. And meanwhile . . . the state and territorial AIDS directors, from all the health departments, from all over the country, also wanted to get the AIDS case definition changed, because health departments were recognizing these other diseases, too. And they wanted access to the more money that they would have if they had more people with AIDS identified in their own states."

FORCING A MEETING WITH FAUCI

LINDA MEREDITH

Linda and her colleagues decided that they were going to get a meeting with Tony Fauci, no matter what. They called his office, "and called and called and called and called and called." Finally, he agreed to meet with a group. Nine or ten women, including a few HIV-positive women but "honestly, at that meeting, not many," arrived at the conference room. Fauci was to meet with the women for an hour or so. This was the only time Fauci had ever met with any activists around women and HIV, and they were offended that he was only going to give them an hour.

They sat at a big conference table and started going around explaining their issues. "Other than, *Hi, I'm Tony Fauci,* he hasn't really said a word," Linda thought, because the women were talking. Linda was thinking, *You haven't done the research, so what the hell are you going to tell us? We're here to tell you, and that's what we're going to do.*

About thirty minutes in, Fauci said, *Let me just stop you for a minute. We basically have—our time is almost half up, and if you don't allow me to speak, we're going to run out of time.* And Linda recalled the women saying, *Okay, fine, because we don't really care to hear what you have to say. We're here to tell you.* And she remembered him getting very ruffled. He said, *I have an agreement with the men in ACT UP that they don't speak to me in that way.* "Honestly, pretty much, the meeting went downhill from there. I think Maxine said, *Well, you don't have that agreement with us.* And then I said, *I've never even met you before. How could we possibly have that agreement?* So, instead of talking about the research and treatment agenda, the rest of the meeting really devolved into that."

MORE TENSIONS WITH T&D

According to Linda, no one from Treatment and Data was involved in getting the ACTGs to study women. The men in ACT UP who supported the women's campaign included "David Robinson, . . . Lee Schy, and Joey Ferrari just to name a few." Even in 2013 when I interviewed her, Linda was still processing the lack of support from T&D.

"I couldn't bear to think that many of the men in ACT UP—after having had politicized, radical, fierce lesbians side by side with them for years—couldn't change their minds . . . When I was in grad school in '87 when ACT UP first formed, I was the person who used to xerox the articles that were coming out in the peer-reviewed medical journals, and I would send them to Mark [Harrington,] and I would be on the phone with him for hours, essentially having a journal club to tell him how to read them."

THE SECOND CDC ACTION

MAXINE WOLFE

For the second CDC action, the activists went down to Atlanta, Georgia, on December 3, 1990, and did a large demonstration in front of the CDC headquarters. They managed to take over the office of the head of the CDC, Dr. William Roper, and a number of people got arrested.

"It was the most pouring-rain day I've ever seen in my life. It was not to be believed. And people stayed out there. Women with HIV stayed out there. It was just really powerful . . . So, after that, they thought that that was it and that we would give up. And I think this is what was really important—we just kept going. We didn't just do direct action after that. We did a lot of small things. We monitored what they were doing, and every time they tried to change the CDC definition and not put in women's stuff, we would do something because we had this mailing list now, from all over the country—so we would send out an alert. *James Curran is trying to change the CDC definition. He's not putting in any of the women's infection. Write to your senator, call your congressperson, tell them you're demanding a congressional investigation of the Centers for Disease Control.* Boom, he would stop."

TERRY McGOVERN

"Then the Washington groups got involved. Which led to its own problems."

Terry started hearing from gay, women's, and AIDS organizations based in Washington, D.C., that tended to have full-time staff who were cozy with government officials and, in some ways, resembled them. Most women with AIDS were such a different demographic than most white gay men with AIDS that these well-funded organizations had no direct relationships with HIV-positive women. The D.C.-based groups began getting invited to the meetings instead of the ACT UP activists or the positive women or the grassroots attorneys. A new chapter of struggle began as the newly established and funded AIDS industry moved in and start negotiating on behalf of women with HIV when they hadn't even been aware of the problem at its inception.

"There were some issues with some folks from GMHC [Gay Men's

Health Crisis], and there were issues with folks from the ACLU, and there were issues with folks in Washington . . . All of the rights issues that surround that in people's lives, nobody can speak to that as effectively as HIV-positive women . . . And I think, I have always really seen our role—lawyers' roles, or anybody's role—as kind of working together so that the women can do the best advocacy job possible. But also moving out of the way when you can so that [positive women] can take the seat. And that's just not the mentality of a lot of folks that are in these Washington groups, et cetera. They think they're the best representative, or maybe a more cynical read is it's about the power and the access. But I think who ends up suffering from that are the directly affected people."

TRACY MORGAN

"There was one action we did when things felt like they were going to fall apart."

The entrance of established organizations into the conversation was a threat to the more marginal groups of people who had been doing the real work beforehand. Finally, a meeting was set with CDC officials to discuss women and HIV, which felt to Tracy like a tipping point. She knew that the ACLU and GMHC would be there, and would dominate despite having no background in the issue. Tracy felt that these national organizations were completely willing to step on the grassroots communities that had created this moment. So Tracy and Heidi and their coterie went down to D.C. to confront them. Tracy and Heidi's group included 50 percent HIV-positive women, and some ACT UP members, including Rand Snyder, Walter Armstrong, and Bro Broberg. But this was not an official ACT UP action. They had not informed ACT UP and had not asked them for money or support.

"It was a closed-door meeting, and we kept saying, *We want to come* . . . and the answer was *no* and *no* and *no* . . . We drove down to D.C. We got a bus . . . I don't have the feeling ACT UP paid for this, because this was not approved by ACT UP . . . We went down and we had hotel rooms, and six in a room or whatever, for the night. Got up the next day . . . A busload . . . thirty-seven, forty-two, or something of us came in, and we said, *We need to have a seat at this table*."

Tracy felt that the response was: *"Well, we're not going to just do what you want because you want us to do it."* To which her group replied, *"Well, you're not going to have a meeting, then. It's pretty simple. Because we're not going to let you make this move, because we know who's at the table and we know their background, we know their politics on this issue of AIDS epidemiology, and we can't let you move forward with the imprimatur of GMHC and the ACLU, because their point of view is not the point of view that's going to save anybody's life . . .* We knew who was with us and who wasn't with us. That was that. Then we had handcuffs, and we handcuffed ourselves to people at the meeting."

As they handcuffed themselves to members of the ACLU and GMHC, Tracy emphasized that she and Heidi were "the ringleaders," but they were acting independently and not on behalf of ACT UP. Yet not everyone in the room understood that difference.

MARION BANZHAF

Marion and many ACT UP members looked on this action with dismay. "If you were going to handcuff yourself to anybody at that meeting, to demand that they listen to you and deal with you, it should be the CDC, right?" Not other progressive groups. However, Marion did concede that many ACT UPers "did see GMHC as this mega-cooptation instrument, sort of, that would just come and grab all the glory and all the money, and all the credit; and you'd wind up with an end result that didn't serve people with AIDS."

USING A LAWSUIT TO BUILD SKILLS

TERRY McGOVERN

When Terry filed her lawsuit against Social Security for discrimination based on an inadequate definition of AIDS, she joined an ongoing grassroots campaign run by ACT UP and women with AIDS.

"ACT UP had done all this work, way before even I got there, right?—on the AIDS definition, on women. And suddenly there was this lawsuit. And then ACT UP and us were completely excluded from all these meetings at the CDC, from all these meetings. All these folks were suddenly meeting, and not even telling us."

Terry moved her legal office to the city building Performance Space 122, on Ninth Street and First Avenue, with a young Black lawyer, Martha S. Jones. There were people from ACT UP in Terry's office typing papers at night. ACT UP also gave her their press capabilities; Laurie Cotter and Robin Hauser, press people from ACT UP, came and wrote press releases for the lawsuit. "We file the lawsuit; we're in Washington. And it's on the front page of *The New York Times*! That was ACT UP!

"It is a joke to think that a woman living with HIV (under 1980s conditions) is going to understand how the UN works or how the FDA works or how Social Security works." There had to be mutual exchange. There had to be technical assistance, advocacy, and capacity building. HIV-positive women got hours of press trainings so that they could speak to journalists on their own behalf, share their experiences and perspectives, and clearly describe in detail the ways in which they were being denied disability instead of making a generalized complaint. Terry saw that this ability to communicate with reporters on terms that the reporters could understand was very empowering. "The level of resources that ACT UP brought to this thing was incredible.

"A lot of the men had the education, had access, had a sense of entitlement, and also had the skills. I mean, not to say that they didn't have to be really activist and really push to get in the door. But it was a whole different level of access than certainly the people that we were dealing with." Terry felt that the CDC was very comfortable excluding HIV-positive women (most of whom were women of color), the mostly white lesbians from ACT UP, and poverty lawyers from negotiations. Unsurprisingly, the government was much more eager to meet with highly educated and professionalized white males from the national organizations.

Because she had the litigation in process and was being papered to death by the government, Terry became afraid the suit would be thrown out of court, "because it was a kind of a wild legal strategy." It was scary from a lawyer's perspective. She was very young—not even thirty— and launching a class action against the federal government claiming that the Social Security Administration was violating its responsibility to fairly define disability by using a definition that was based only on one portion of affected populations. It was risky and easily could have been thrown out. But at that point a number of the health-care providers who had been seeing these patients started publishing their articles. People like the late Helen Rodriguez-Trias, who was the co-founder of the Committee to End Sterilization Abuse, supported the suit.

"And then of course there were issues like the plaintiffs' dying without ever having gotten disability," Terry recalled. Signs at demonstrations said DEAD BUT NOT DISABLED, because that was the language appearing in the case reports of those who had been denied disability after they had already died.

MAXINE WOLFE

"They tried, at the CDC, three or four times in the next two years, to change the definition to what they wanted it to be, which was, basically, two hundred T cells, and no specificity of women's infections or the infections that drug users got, at all. And the main reason that people supported the two hundred T cells, is because there were a lot of health-care providers who were seeing people with those T cells [and] who are not considered to have AIDS, because they didn't have the infections that were on the list. And so they weren't getting reimbursed from the government. So they wanted the two hundred T cells, and they didn't care about the rest of it."

When the eighth annual International AIDS Conference took place in Amsterdam in the fall of 1992 and women from ACT UP showed up, women from all over the world joined with ACT UP and confronted James Curran. They told him directly to his face, *You have to change the CDC definition of AIDS.* But he still didn't want to do it. So ACT UP demanded that he hold a public hearing to show that his position denying different symptoms based in sex was correct. Maxine recalls that at first, Curran tried to manipulate the hearing, and to only present his kind of researchers. But ACT UP found a broad range of people to testify that he was wrong. And so he finally agreed to a hearing that took place in Atlanta. ACT UP fought for women with HIV to speak there, as well as doctors who had actually been doing the research. Again, ACT UP raised money to transport women with HIV down to the hearing. They got the media down there as well. This was after the campaign had been going for four years, and the women were finally being heard.

TERRY McGOVERN

Things began to shift in 1992. Bill Clinton was elected president, and Terry began to see some evidence that the government was going to expand the AIDS definition. By this point, there had been lots of infighting within ACT UP. In the summer of 1993, the CDC decided to hold a meeting to talk about what the new AIDS definition should look like, and Terry hadn't been invited. After a lot of protesting, she was added to the meeting at the last minute. It is very emotional to note how much sexism and antilesbian bias we faced every day in every aspect of life, but especially how our contributions were ignored and our voices were consistently excluded when it really mattered.

But clearly, what happened was that the CDC understood that it needed to expand its AIDS definition, and it was looking for some way out of the suit. Finally, it gave in partially and wanted to add bacterial pneumonia, tuberculosis, and anybody with fewer than two hundred T cells to the definition. And this would have helped a lot of people, but it explicitly excluded specific symptoms that only women had. The one female-only condition for which there was the most medical evidence was cervical cancer, which was excluded from this new definition. Terry was always looking at it from the perspective of what was legally provable. And ACT UP was "rightfully" looking at it from the perspective of what *should* be there.

"There was a huge difference of opinion about that, among everybody, including positive women, positive men. A lot of people felt the two hundred [T cells] should be there because a lot of people would come in under it, and that was more important than the listing of PID [pelvic inflammatory disease]. Other people felt differently. A lot of the physicians that we worked with were saying to us, *This is as good as it gets*, and *Don't be stupid; push to get cervical cancer on there so that there's at least a signal to the world that women and gynecological disease is part of this. And that's the only one you're going to get.*"

Some of the physicians who became close advisors were Machelle Allen from Bellevue and Helen Rodriguez-Trias. Terry was getting very strong advice from them: *You should push for one female condition, but there's not enough medical evidence on this other stuff.* Meanwhile, she was hearing from a lot of activists: *Forget it; we should bag it; we shouldn't compromise at all.* Some people didn't want to work with the CDC at all at that point. Others wanted to push to include cervical cancer. There were a number of blowout meetings at Performance Space 122, with some people storming off and others unclear about their positions. And ultimately, Terry took the stance that she was going to push for the CDC to include cervical cancer in its expanded definition of AIDS.

Terry got to the meeting with the CDC in September 1992. There were some ACT UP people there as well. Marion Banzhaf was representing the New Jersey Women and AIDS Network. And Mary Lucey, a lesbian from ACT UP LA who was HIV-positive, was there.

"At the meeting, I was given five minutes or something . . . The way I tried to handle it was I talked very closely to this group of positive women who were plaintiffs, and Katrina, and asked them very closely, *What should I do?* And often they gave me very different advice from what the activists were saying, because they felt like it was hugely important; the two hundred T cells was really important because so many people they knew had died with six T cells and didn't qualify, so they didn't really care. They were afraid."

When she began to get pulled into serious conversations about how to develop the new Social Security criteria, Terry brought positive women and physicians to help figure out, *How do we write these guidelines?* "And it was really a very difficult situation to be sitting there with these very conservative government people, pushing for as much as you could possibly get." It was hard for her to make a judgment about how far to push, when she knew she risked losing everything. And in some senses, Terry recalled, a lot of times, the positive women were really thinking about how many people would lose benefits and how many people would die if they pushed too far. It was very hard to navigate. As an attorney, Terry worked for the clients. So that, in some ways, was helpful to her. But things got very difficult with some of the activists, because often she felt like what they were saying, in regard to pushing as hard as possible, was ultimately right.

MARION BANZHAF

What wound up finally happening was that at the second National Women and AIDS Conference, held in 1993, Terry McGovern and Marion Banzhaf and a bunch of people from the CDC side hammered out a compromise. The women won cervical cancer. They lost pelvic in-flammatory disease, but they got both endocarditis and bacterial pneu-monia included in the official AIDS definition. And we got to keep the two hundred T cells marker.

"I wound up making the announcement of it, at this conference, and called it a *compromise*, and said that people should still be on the look-out for pelvic inflammatory disease, because it was still a real thing for women. But ACT UP, sort of, by that time, was not recruiting people in AIDS service organizations to be its allies anymore. Instead, AIDS service organizations had become sort of *the monster*, and just *the AIDS industrial complex* . . . I think it was about the changing landscape of AIDS."

After the compromise, Marion estimated that eligibility for women with AIDS went from "10 percent to 50 percent . . . overnight, people who had T-cell counts of under two hundred became eligible for ben-efits as a result of that. And that's thousands of people, hundreds of thousands of people."

LINDA MEREDITH

Most of the HIV-positive women activists died. The few survivors in-cluded Mary Lucey and Michelle Lopez, while Marina Alvarez lived for a few years. The women died far more rapidly than some of the men. The reasons were socioeconomic, and lack of access to health care. A lot of these women were way sicker than the men before seeking treatment, and they were not diagnosed until it was essentially too late. Many of them had an aversion to swallowing the early medications because they hadn't been tested on women, and they didn't know what the dose would be, and it made them sick. AZT made a lot of people sick. Those were just some of the reasons. "And isolation, I think."

According to Linda, the standard-of-care treatments available to people with HIV today were barely tested on women.

"It's very difficult for a woman—still—to participate in a clinical drug trial of any medication, despite what the FDA says. Especially for the drugs that are available even now—but certainly for the first cou-ple of waves of protease inhibitors. You can tell how many people were in those trials by looking at the package insert by demographic. Very small numbers of women were in those studies, because the way the

pharmaceutical industry takes care of a potential lawsuit for teratoge-
nicity [i.e., the capability of a drug for producing fetal malformation
when taken by a pregnant woman] is to keep the women out."

For example, a package insert for the AIDS drug Sustiva reveals that
only about 12 percent of the people in the pivotal studies that led to its
approval were female. According to Linda, drugs would never be approved
if it were men who were excluded. But regulators run down the side effects,
and then they look at the overall population and say, *Yep, no difference.*
"Now, if that was men, they would say, *Well, we can't make that judgment
because we don't have the statistical power to do that.* But for women, it's always been okay to just make a cursory look and check a box and say, *Done.*"

Remembrance: Katrina Haslip

MARION BANZHAF

"Katrina Haslip was an amazing woman. She was a Muslim.
She was one of these people who would just electrify a room
when she walked into it. And she could give the most amazing raps about women she had known in prison, who she had
lost in prison, women she was in touch with back out on the
street. And she was fearless. Some of her closest friends on
the outside wound up being lesbians, like Terry McGovern. I
wouldn't count myself as one of her closest friends, although
I loved her dearly."

Katrina's post-incarceration organization, ACE-OUT,
had its own support group. And its members were working
on setting up housing for women coming out of prison.
They were working on getting kids reconnected emotionally and physically with their mothers, on permanency
planning, so that HIV-positive women could be part of
figuring out what was going to happen to their kids when
they died. "Every time she did a new thing, she felt like she
could do ten new things." Marion felt that so much more
would have been accomplished had Katrina continued to
live because she was just at that point in her life where she
was encountering new places and people and things, and

she was just conquering them, one at a time. Except for HIV.

TERRY McGOVERN

Katrina was literally dying in the hospital just as the final CDC meeting took place in 1992. As one of Terry's clients, she didn't qualify for benefits. Because of the definitional gap, Katrina never officially had AIDS, even though she was dying. She had bacterial pneumonia. And she had no T cells, but the definition hadn't been changed. So she actually didn't qualify for Division of AIDS services and therefore couldn't get a home attendant. As she was leading the movement, she kept falling in her house. Terry would send HIV-positive women who were volunteers with the HIV Law Project to pick her up and take her to the hospital. But Katrina was ultimately another victim of the AIDS definition. She never got the care that she needed. She had to fight every step of the way to get anything.

"And it was incredibly tragic, actually. And so it was difficult for me to maneuver with these compromises because I didn't want to hold up people qualifying for benefits, because the results were so horrible. And they were right there in my face, even among the people that had been so activist . . . So Katrina herself, even though totally disgusted, was saying, *We've got to get this moved, we've got to open it up.* So she died, and never qualified, never met the AIDS definition, which is just quite incredible."

NEW YORK TIMES **INTERVIEW**

Three weeks before Katrina's death, *New York Times* reporter Mireya Navarro published a "conversation" with Katrina, which was really a bedside interview at Roosevelt Hospital in New York City.

> Ms. Haslip was so weak she spoke in a raspy whisper. Her room was cluttered with flowers, food, stuffed animals, newspapers and romance novels. Her eyes were often closed when she spoke . . . Ms. Haslip, who has been

confined to a hospital bed in New York City for a month with bacterial pneumonia, and has a CD4-cell count of six, would be added to the national AIDS caseload in January, when the new plan is expected to go through . . . "I am, and have been, a woman with AIDS despite the C.D.C. not wishing to count me," Ms. Haslip said after the Government's announcement last month. "We have compelled them to."

There is harrowing footage, shot by Catherine Gund and Debra Levine, of Katrina in a hospital bed, very thin, angrily retelling an experience she had of discrimination in Roosevelt Hospital. "A woman came to the room with mask, gown, and gloves on to take my temperature. I kicked her out and said, *Don't send anyone to my room with a mask on to take my fucking temperature. I told you I am an activist and I am not having it.*" In the final piece of footage, shot from her bed, Katrina told Catherine and Debra, "I feel very calm, very focused and very centered. It has a lot to do with the fact that spiritually I am in another space. I feel good about being more into my religious beliefs and it's giving me this balance."

TERRY McGOVERN

After the meeting with the CDC, Terry went to see Katrina in the hospital and told her that the CDC was only agreeing to one women-only symptom to add to the official definition of AIDS, even though other diseases were being added that would help poor people and drug users access benefits and be studied for drug trials. Although she was too sick to attend the press conference, Katrina wrote a statement that another HIV-positive woman read: *I'm not going to smile. This is only happening because of us, and you let us die.*

Katrina died on December 2, 1992. The *New York Times* obituary acknowledged that "because of her efforts, the Federal Centers for Disease Control and Prevention last month announced plans to expand its definition of the disease to include more illnesses that affect women with AIDS."

The CDC definition of AIDS was expanded one month later, on January 1, 1993. Terry eventually went to work for the Ford Foundation in AIDS, and for many years after she saw a lot of AIDS time lines. They would feature Rock Hudson's death, or some other popular cultural moment, but they never include December 2, 1992, when Katrina Haslip died of a disease that she wasn't permitted legally to have. Or January 1, 1993, the date when thousands of women and poor people became officially included in the community of people recognized as deserving help. By the time the Social Security Administration criteria were expanded in July 1993, theirs were even broader, and finally pelvic inflammatory disease was included in the definition. The official numbers of who was considered to have AIDS went up significantly, and more people got benefits.

By the time of the Social Security Administration's capitulation there weren't widespread celebrations by ACT UP members—a lot of the women who had been at the demonstration were now dead. The CDC was taking credit. Terry summed it up: "It went the way these things go. So it happened. And I think it was a victory that was very confusing."

Remembrance: Keri Duran

LINDA MEREDITH

One of the HIV-positive women Linda worked with closely in ACT UP was Keri Duran.

"Fierce, awesome dyke from Worcester, Massachusetts, who was mostly part of ACT UP Boston. She was one of the first women who was HIV-positive, who had AIDS, that I knew that publicly disclosed for the purpose of activism, like ACT UP kind of activism . . . She went on *Oprah*, because Ryan White bailed. This was a different kind of partner for me in the fight, and we became very close."

In 1995, Maxine and Linda took Keri on a trip to Key West, just to get her out of Boston. It was a brutal winter, and she was very sick. So the three of them went to stay in a little bed-and-breakfast just to warm up and hang out and, essentially, to say goodbye. But they got kicked out of the B&B because the staff saw Keri's medications on the dresser. *No people with AIDS in Key West.* At first, the owner tried to claim he was kicking her out because she had left the air conditioner on in her rooms when they had gone for a walk. So Linda got in the guy's face and started yelling at him. And then he said, *You people.* That was kind of it. It was a big scene; they got kicked out. Maxine took Keri and they sat on the curb and cried, and Linda went and told the owner she was going to call her credit card company and not pay for the rooms. Keri died about six months later.

WHAT VICTORY LOOKED LIKE FOR WOMEN WITH AIDS

One major lesson of the successful campaign to change the CDC definition was that women and people of color and activists—some of whom were poor; some of whom looked like dykes—could win changes from the white male power structure. But they had to fight longer. They were not welcomed in at any point, and they had to use direct action constantly. It was through grassroots, outsider tactics that this ACT UP coalition literally forced the government to change against its will. And while they did not win everything that was needed, they were able to gain benefits, access to research, and access to medication for thousands, if not millions, of people. Because every drug that was developed in America that included women of color in clinical trials became a drug that is still used internationally to treat women with HIV. This victory is felt every day by HIV-positive women around the world who are kept alive by medications.

MAXINE WOLFE

"They were so afraid of us by that time. We had done all these demonstrations. We had gotten groups that were so diverse to support this campaign, from all over the country. We showed that we could get congresspeople who would start to investigate the CDC. We used every single tactic that you could possibly use. It was really like community organizing and political organizing at its best. It went from the grassroots up, and we had this committed group of people . . . There were women who were dying because they were being denied food on their table, because people wouldn't admit that they had HIV, when they had HIV . . . [The CDC] didn't change the categories, but they did put in the infections, and they put in infections that both women and drug users get . . .

"But it was an incredible victory, because it was something that affected [hundreds], thousands, millions of women, probably, across the world, eventually. And yet it was incredibly political. It had a whole set of radical politics associated with it, and it was using every kind of organizing technique. And it also showed—you know, people came together to work on that, that everybody said would not work together. There were gay men, there were women of color, straight women of color, lesbians of color. There were straight women. It was every possible kind of person came together to work on that thing, that that's what was amazing about it."

From Maxine's point of view, there was no *This is about you, it's not about me.* Even in her own affinity group—which had twenty-four people in it—there were only seven women; several of the men had HIV, several of them died of AIDS. The whole group spent four years working on a campaign about changing the CDC definition for women and for poor people and for drug users. "And that is something that nobody ever says about ACT UP. They always talk about *gay white men, gay white men, selfish gay white men.* We got tremendous support in ACT UP for that work, and from other places, too. So I just want to say that."

PART IV

Radical Resistance and Acceptance

Acceptance is an essential part of effective political action. It doesn't mean defeat, withdrawal, or diminishment, but rather a necessary recognition of conditions as they actually are, so as to better address them. Here we see how ACT UP's reality-driven culture expressed itself in the most intimate realm. Through the eyes of Patricia Navarro, we see how she and her ACT UP community constantly adjusted to face the impending death of her beloved and gifted son, Ray Navarro. And we see politically how the same process of internalizing what is actually happening in people's lives brought ACT UP to take on the value of "harm reduction." Specifically, ACT UP took on the issues of IV drug users from the grassroots toward, eventually, significant legal transformation. This necessarily radical, nonpunitive, and lifesaving approach to the problem of HIV transmission through sharing needles relied on ACT UPers' lived experiences of narcotics and illegal drug use, developed in the context of realistically facing, without judgment or idealism, the mass death experience that was every day in the lives of AIDS activists.

8

Mother and Son: The Death of Ray Navarro, the Vision of Patricia Navarro

Hundreds of people who came to an ACT UP meeting, action, or party died of AIDS. Some of those deaths had profound effects on the organization, the movement, and the subsequent lives of the survivors. One of the most devastating and impactful losses was the death of artist Ray Navarro. At ACT UP's first public reunion at Harvard University in 2010, speaking from the podium, Gregg Bordowitz burst into tears and cried, "Why did I live when Ray died?"

I interviewed Ray's mother, Patricia, in her Simi Valley, California, home in 2008, eighteen years after Ray's death at age twenty-six. Patricia's story is important in ACT UP's history for a number of reasons. She was perhaps the only parent of a person with AIDS who stood completely and firmly as an active member of ACT UP. She was a heterosexual working-class Chicana who crossed many subgroups and committees within the organization. But most importantly, Patricia is an individual who embodied the spirit of being realistic yet proactive in dealing with the disease and its ravages.

Patricia Navarro was born in a San Diego housing project for people who worked in the aircraft industry. Her father, a carpenter, had come from an Arizona copper mining town looking for employment as a construction worker, while Patricia's mother worked in the garment industry. Growing up, Patricia's family never talked about her future. "There were limited interpersonal skills there." She was educated by nuns and priests. "I always questioned authority from the time I was little. Very little. And even though I knew that they didn't like it, I still, for some reason, continued to do it . . . I've always had that about me, that I wasn't concerned about what other people thought about me, if I thought I was right about something."

When she was twelve, she ran away from her father's alcoholism, and after two weeks on her own was found and placed in juvenile hall, a lockdown facility for youthful offenders. That was her first exposure to homosexuality, specifically to lesbians. "I really liked them! They were really cool! They had a good sense of humor. And they liked me, and they protected me." She already knew that she was heterosexual, and she had a cousin who was gay, but his homosexuality was never discussed. At sixteen, she had a daughter out of wedlock with a man who was later killed, and she then married a friend at eighteen. He desperately wanted a son, even though Patricia didn't want any more children, but she felt obligated. So when her son, Ray, was born in 1964, she felt relief knowing she would not be pressured into having more children. "He was the most loving little baby. And even though I did not know how to nurture my daughter, he taught me how to nurture. There was something very special about him, even as an infant."

Patricia went to community college and started to encounter feminism. During a brief separation from her husband, a friend took her to a women's reentry program for adult women to gain access to higher education, and a whole new world opened up. She read Germaine Greer and Simone de Beauvoir.

Her parents were assimilated. Living in Arizona, English was their second language, but by the time Patricia came along, it was their primary language. She was not taught Spanish. Yet, as a teenager growing up, she identified as a Chicana, hung around with Chicanas, and only dated Chicanos. In the reentry program, after she moved to L.A., she took Chicano history and all the Chicano classes that were available. "I discovered liberation. I discovered that we should not put people in boxes and categories."

Ray's personality and tastes emerged at an early age.

"There were two little girls next door—Raymond used to go and get into the trunk that they used to get into, and put on dresses and hats, and have plays in the driveway. I thought that was wonderful! I never thought that that meant that he might be gay. He was always artistic; he was always drawing . . . He was *the* most popular boy, with all the girls . . . He was a good dancer, so the girls even liked him more because of that . . . He was the snow prince of the junior high school. I couldn't have asked for a happier kid, and he was very good academically. He was in honors classes, and what do you call them? *Pre-college advanced placement.* And he was self-motivated, which of course made it very nice for a parent."

Patricia and her husband ran an auto parts store, and she continued her education at Moorpark College. More of an activist than a student, she became very involved in the activist group Mujeres Unidas and remained part of it for years. Mujeres Unidas joined in broad coalitions on a wide range of Chicano issues focusing on education, employment, health, and housing. They were part of a Dole boycott in support of the United Farm Workers. Patricia took Ray to demonstrations and brought home political handouts from various grassroots socialist and community-based groups.

Ray started as an art student at Otis College of Art and Design at Parsons when he was nineteen. He lived with his grandparents to save money. His foundation year involved handmade work in painting, drawing, and ceramics. He would put things in the kiln that he knew were going to explode. "And he just thought it was so cool. And I just thought, *Raymond, grow up! You can't do this! This is very expensive!* I mean, even though he was on scholarship. We didn't pay his tuition. We could never have afforded it." When her son went to Otis, Patricia had a real fear that she was going to lose him to ambition and materialism, because a lot of the students at that school were very well-to-do. His roommate came from a very rich family. And they rented an apartment together.

While at Otis, Ray got a job in the first crew at the Museum of Contemporary Art, which opened in a temporary building east of downtown Los Angeles before the museum opened in 1979. And he was hired to work at the ticket booth. For the first show the museum held a huge reception that he worked, and Ray invited his mother. "That night he said, *Oh, Mom, I'm so excited, I'm in a relationship* . . . I said, *Oh, Raymond, I'm so happy for you. Are you happy?* And he said, *Yes, Mom. I'm in love.* And I said, *Oh my God, who is it?* And he says, *It's a guy!*" They sat on some steps, and he told her a little about the guy. His name was Todd, a Latin American political science student at UCLA. And he just kept saying, *So what do you think?* And Patricia said, *Okay, Ra—Raymond; if we have a little, few minutes here, talk. I'm scared for you. Because I grew up in a racist, sexist world, Raymond. And you've got a lot of stuff out there to deal with. I'm afraid.* He grabbed her and hugged her. And he asked if she was afraid about AIDS. "And it went right over my head. It literally went right over my head."

After two years, Ray moved through Otis's video program, and then went to CalArts and worked at the New Museum of Contemporary Art. He kept in close touch with his mother, inviting her to openings, talking about his new projects. Ray then moved to New York with his lover, Anthony Ledesma, to attend the Whitney Independent Study Studio Program. He attributed his seroconversion to 1987 or '88, when he had a lot of sex in West Hollywood before moving to New York. Anthony, a dancer/choreographer, came from a different family situation. He was one of four boys with a single mother, and the youngest was twelve when Anthony got sick. Anthony was diagnosed with PCP in June 1989, while he and Ray were attending the Montreal AIDS conference, and was hospitalized in Canada.

"All I could think of was, well, if Anthony's infected, surely [Ray's] infected." Patricia went to the library, checked out all six books that they had about AIDS, read them the next day, and called the AIDS hotline. "I wanted to know everything about HIV. I anticipated that Ray might be HIV[-positive]. But I wasn't ready to anticipate that he could have full-blown AIDS . . . Finally, after a couple of calls from Canada, I asked him about getting tested. And he said, *Well, there's no way I'm getting tested up here. I won't get tested till I get back to New York and go to an anonymous test site.*" Ray was diagnosed in January 1990. Patricia had first heard about AIDS activism from her cousin Abie, who made and sold tamales and would donate proceeds to different groups. Abie told Patricia that he had made a donation to ACT UP, which was the first time she'd heard of the organization.

Ray and Anthony had been living with filmmaker Jennie Livingston in New York, but when they returned from Montreal she wanted them to move out because of fear of tuberculosis, and Patricia had trouble getting hold of them.

"I know he really liked Jennie. He was real happy with this woman that they were living with. And I guess she was a filmmaker, too, and he only had really good things to say about her. And then all of a sudden, they had, when he was in the hospital, they had to move, or whatever.

But he came down with the TB. And I tracked him down, and found out that he was in the hospital. He got really pissed off that I tracked him down, but I don't know how I did it, but I did."

Finally, Patricia asked him: *Raymond, did you ever get tested?* And he said, *Yeah, Mom. I'm positive. I found a doctor. And he's a very good doctor.* Anthony had been getting stronger, but then was really taken down, with PCP. They had a very dynamic relationship. Patricia would listen for hours as Raymond talked about all their problems. But, in the middle of it all, he talked about all the things he was doing with ACT UP.

"What I remember him being the most excited about was DIVA [TV] [Damned Interfering Video Activists Television]. He went on and on about DIVA . . . I remember him talking to me about—*If we can get all these artists—because artists, we all have these egos, Mom—to agree to work on this collectively, it's going to be fabulous, it's going to be absolutely fabulous.* And he just went on and on about DIVA; about stuff they had shot; and he'd just interviewed somebody, or whatever . . . That's all he would talk when he went to New York [to attend the Whitney program]. He didn't even talk about school. School was like, *Oh yeah, yeah, we're doing this stuff at school,* and—*I have to [write] a paper,* whatever. But it was like nothing; it was like work. Everything that excited him to talk about was ACT UP; and DIVA. And he went to this party. And he met this fabulous this, and this fabulous that. *And oh, Mom, it's so wonderful, I'm so glad I came.* The kid was just in seventh heaven. And it was nice."

Soon Ray started to exhibit symptoms. He had a seizure on the subway.

"He was all excited because he wanted, more than anything, to do work in the Chicano community. And he felt alienated, because he was this assimilated little suburb kid, who for all intents and purposes acted white, because that's where he grew up. Some people weren't very kind to him. And he wanted to establish credibility in the Latino community, the Chicano community. They were having a film festival in San Antonio. And Ray was presenting a program about video activism, how to use video to teach and to stimulate activism about AIDS. He put together a catalog, I think . . . about video and making catalogs . . . He had his fingers in ten different things to try to make money to survive.

Because he was very poor. Living as an art student in New York, and an activist."

Then Ray came down with tuberculosis. Increasingly, by 1989 and 1990, people with AIDS were frequently contracting TB, often in emergency rooms. The drugs Ray was on interfered with his writing, and he had articles that he needed to finish so that he could get paid. Everything was about trying to make money to survive and pay his rent. He truly was a model of the struggling artist/activist. People told Patricia that they used to feed him. She told him, *If somebody invites you to go to a meal, and you let them know you don't have any money, if they offer to pay, you can graciously accept that and pay them back in other ways. But if somebody's going to make a comment, you don't want to have anything to do with that person. I don't care how much money they have. They obviously have no manners. You don't have anything to do with them!*

Ray left the hospital and went to Jean Carlomusto's apartment. He told his mother that Jean was the finest person he had ever met. Within three days of getting to Jean's he developed a horrible headache that he couldn't get rid of and was back at St. Vincent's, this time with a diagnosis of cryptococcal meningitis.

ACT UPer Aldo Hernández told Patricia that Ray was back in the hospital. Patricia asked the neurologist over the phone, *Doctor, do you think I should come? Should I come now? I want to come, but he doesn't want me to.* And she said, *Well, Mrs. Navarro, if you don't come, it might be too late.* So she booked the first available flight for the next day. Robert Garcia and Anthony picked her up at the airport. They got to the hospital and walked in Ray's room. And there he was, sitting, like on a throne, with all these visitors, having a conversation. Zoe Leonard was there. "She had just come back from a show in Belgium or Berlin or someplace with a *B.* Hunter Reynolds was there. Ray introduced his mother to everyone. That's where she met Jean Carlomusto. And she gave Patricia her first ACT UP button, SILENCIO=MUERTE. Patricia called Mothers of AIDS Patients (MAP), and got the contact information for a mothers' support group. "I was going to need it."

She went to the hospital every day. And she was horrified to watch as Ray was in pain and drugged and hallucinating from the medication. The following week, Patricia attended her first meeting of the support group for mothers and her first ACT UP meeting.

At first she was overwhelmed. She walked into the Center and remembers really liking that it was an old building. And then she was
just kind of blown away by all the people. She especially loved all the
facilitators—David Robinson, Robert Garcia, and Ann Northrop. She
would later sit in the meetings with Roma Baran. "I think they were all
lesbians; I don't know . . . We never really talked about them being lesbians. I knew they were lesbians; they knew I was heterosexual. I didn't
talk about my heterosexual life, and they didn't talk about their gay life.
We talked about politics, and women's stuff." People had such a high
regard for Ray that she felt instantly accepted by everybody. "And that
felt really good." People would ask about him. And she would encourage them to go see him. And slowly but surely:

"ACT UP became a rock for me. Because when I was in there, it
was empowering. Outside of the ACT UP rooms, I was vulnerable. The
mothers' support group fed my heart; they gave me what I needed, support and love from other women. But it wasn't political. ACT UP made
me feel there was something that could be done. It gave me hope; it was
intellectual; it was emotional. I fell in and out of love in those rooms.
And that was—that felt good. That was my humanity coming out."

Patricia never missed an ACT UP meeting. Then she started attending WHAM!, and every Tuesday attended the mothers' support group.
At forty-seven, she was one of the youngest, and Ray was one of the
youngest children, until one mother came whose son was twenty. Patricia stayed at Ray's Seventh Street apartment unless he came out of
the hospital, in which case she would stay at Jean Carlomusto's. The
writer Florence Rush, from the mothers' support group, gave Patricia
her apartment on Jane and Hudson Streets, where she lived on and off
for eight months. She played poker with Susan Brownmiller, the writer,
who lived in the building's penthouse.

"I needed ACT UP. Okay? I didn't give very much to ACT UP;
ACT UP gave me the strength to keep going. I went to the meetings; I
went to some demos; I really couldn't do a lot. And some of the discussion, it was way over my head."

Finally, Ray lost his sight and much of his hearing. He fell out of
bed. One morning Patricia walked into the hospital and he was tied to
the bed. She was very upset and raised holy hell. She then saw that he
had hit his head. It turned out that he had gotten up during the night

to go to the bathroom, and he'd fallen. And to protect him, the hospital staff had tied him down. She realized she needed a private nurse to be on call, but she didn't have the money. So Patricia needed people from ACT UP to take shifts with Ray in the hospital.

"I think Kim Christensen—who's a beautiful, wonderful person, another dear friend of Ray's—I think she kind of let the word out, at the meetings. And pretty soon, people kind of knew." There were regulars, like Lola Flash and Julie Tolentino, who were a couple at the time. People were reading books into tapes, once Ray was blind. They recorded *The New York Times*. Deb Levine was a close friend. He loved the time with Catherine Gund; he made art with Zoe Leonard.

"He said, *Mom, I'm going to make art.* I said, *What are you talking about?* He described to me these photos that he was going to have Zoe take, because he was going to get them ready for this show, the Army of Lovers . . . he described to Zoe everything, and according to Zoe, she was doing it, exactly what he wanted. She was his prosthesis . . . The thing that Raymond told me, more than anything, is that he didn't want people to forget him. And I thought that was really incredible, that he was able to, to say that—that he knew how important that was to him. *Mom, I don't want people to forget me.* And I thought, *That's interesting, for a person who knows they're dying, to say.* I don't know. I've always thought about that."

9

Harm Reduction as a Value, an Ideal, a Way of Life and Death: ACT UP's Campaign for Needle Exchange

It has long been both known and assumed that ACT UP was primarily an organization of people with AIDS, queer people, and, secondarily, of women, people of color, and all intersections therein. But there was another constituency that was overlapping, influential, and effective: the community of former and current drug users and addicts. At first these ACT UPers were hidden in other identity groups, but as the impact of sharing needles as a major cause of HIV infection became better known, and then irrefutable, it was clear that ACT UP would have to lead in creating solutions. The New York City Department of Health, under Mayor David Dinkins, did institute a small and controlled program, but it wasn't challenging the larger problem of illegality obstructing large-scale needle exchange. The reason that clean syringes were prohibited was rooted in a deeply punitive and puritanical culture of response. The prevalent ideology of the day was that drug users were antisocial people, inherently criminal, and therefore not deserving of modes of assistance that fit the reality of their lives. The government offered abstinence or imprisonment.

Harm reduction was a new conceptual frame, one rooted in the recognition that people are complex and nuanced individuals, and that addiction renders their human vulnerability even more acute. If sharing needles spread AIDS, ACT UP recognized, then it was more effective, and also more humane, to give users clean needles than to insist that they stop using drugs or die. It was about meeting people on their own terms, instead of pathologizing them. In this way, harm reduction was a mature position, developed by young people already accustomed to the brutalities of AIDS, but also familiar with abandonment and disregard.

Here we look at a diverse group of ACT UPers, some with drug pasts, some who lost their lives to addiction while they were in ACT UP, or lost their accountability because of their addictions, and who worked together to defy antiquated prohibitions by deliberately breaking the law so that the law would have to change.

IDENTIFYING A SOLUTION

RICHARD ELOVICH

Born in Kew Gardens, Richard Elovich met the poet Allen Ginsberg in 1974 and ended up working as his secretary for a few years. He then moved to a loft building, 222 Bowery, which was an old YMCA gymnasium where abstract expressionist painter Mark Rothko had done his iconic Seagram's paintings. Richard was living with James Grauerholz in the locker room, which literally had urinals in the bathroom and authentic graffiti from the 1930s. Grauerholz was closely associated with the writer William S. Burroughs, situating Richard's life in the literal tradition of the Beats, with all the queer and drug content that relationship implied. After Ginsberg, Richard worked for Jasper Johns, then briefly worked for John Ashbery, by which time he was thirty.

Richard started getting "liquor'd up" as part of learning to talk to men in gay bars. But the heroin scene was completely separate. He had a boyfriend from Brussels who was using heroin, and Richard got hooked.

"It just knew my name. It was so great. It was one of the happiest moments of my life. I had my fist in his lap. And he was shooting me up. And it was so erotic. It was like this blanket just dropped over me, like I was shivering my whole life, and suddenly I just felt wrapped in this embrace . . . I would, every so often, try to stop using heroin . . . It wasn't until I went out to Minnesota for drug treatment—my family did a kind of intervention . . . I wrote a check, and the check bounced. And those guys weren't kidding around . . . I was looking to get out from underneath a lot of this. And so even when I was on methadone, I was still shooting speed . . . And then I took a deliberate overdose."

Sober by the time he got to ACT UP, Richard represented the organization at a meeting on 103rd Street about pushing teaching hospitals to provide AIDS services. Anthony Fauci was speaking, and Richard asked him why injection drug users (IDUs) were not being enrolled in AIDS clinical trials. Fauci responded that they were part of "a noncompliant population." In other words, Fauci and others in charge believed that people infected with HIV through narcotic needle use would not comply with the consistent regimens of medications, and that this would render the findings of the trials useless, as well as possibly building immunity in the patient. This noncooperation could produce future drug-resistant strains of HIV, which was constantly mutating. One block away on 102nd Street was Richard's former methadone clinic at New York Medical College, a place he had been every day for two years. "So it brought me home . . . I just became enraged, and hopefully in a more measured tone said, *There's no such thing as a noncompliant population. I'm part of that population.* Again, at that time, not knowing—did I know?—that was the first time I came out as an IDU."

One weekend, Richard had the transformational experience of going out on a needle exchange with Jon Parker, an activist from New Haven. Once he saw needle exchange happening, he was completely persuaded. Within a week, Richard and ACT UPer Dan Williams went to the floor of ACT UP, described their experiences, and brought needle exchange into the movement. While the Needle Exchange Committee ultimately orchestrated an action, during which they were arrested and went to trial, it was the previous two-year experience of actually exchanging needles, and the group-related activities surrounding that experience, that was the real "action," illustrating again how ACT UP's approach to direct action took untraditional and long-term form.

DAN KEITH WILLIAMS

Dan Keith Williams grew up in Beaufort, South Carolina, where his parents were stationed in the military. He had a difficult childhood, never really fitting in.

"I basically asked a lot of questions that people never wanted to answer. I was very inquisitive. I come from a family where men, basically, are passive. And that relationship has to do with slavery, and how Black men had to basically stay in the background . . . On a certain level, my family was trying to protect me by trying to keep me quiet. And, the more they tried to keep me quiet, the more questions I asked and not getting answers . . . *Why do white people have this, and Black people have that.* I was just very confrontational about inequality, and what I perceived to be wrong."

After college in Spartanburg, South Carolina, Dan moved to New Orleans, and three years later, when he and his boyfriend broke up, he joined the navy, hoping to get away from the gay life. But the navy was filled with gay men. Out of the two thousand people on his ship, he knew of three hundred who were gay, including the lieutenant commander. After an incident in which he got beaten up, Dan remained in the hospital for two and a half weeks. He was on a ship where he was ostracized and felt that if he went to sea, he would be killed. So he went AWOL to join his lover in Rome, where he stayed for five years.

When they broke up, Dan went to New York. His Italian lover developed AIDS and died quickly, and Dan joined ACT UP. He felt like, *These are my people.* It was empowering, and on the other hand, he found it scary, because Dan didn't really know anybody. The crowd was "relatively white, very white." And "even though those issues are not totally, totally important with me, they're there."

Remembrance: Ortez Alderson

One very influential Black gay man in ACT UP who inspired Dan was Ortez Alderson.

"I ran into Ortez, and . . . if I ever had an idea that I was getting away, it wasn't happening, because, he's, like, *We need more Black guys like you.* And that was it . . . His philosophy was just totally in tune with what I wanted to hear. And I considered myself to be in training at that point, because I felt a lot of things, but I couldn't really sort of vocalize them. And he just really helped a lot. He helped me put a lot of the anger, frustration and rage I had in words that I could do something about . . . I would never think to go and confront people and Ortez just sort of, like—*We're going here. We're going to confront this person and we're going right in their office. We're not even stopping at the secretary.* I'm, like, *Huh?* . . . And he helped me . . . But that is something that he inspired."

Dan and Ortez represented ACT UP at the National Black Leadership Commission on AIDS, under the directorship of Debra Frazer-Howze. The first time they went there, in 1987, their approach was very confrontational. They got accused of being *sent by the white boys.* And that was painful, because Dan felt that because he came from a mixed organization the Black groups were nonetheless suspicious, implying, *No, you can't do anything on your own, you have to be directed.* He felt set up between two flawed systems. On one hand, he clearly saw that there was "internalized racism" in ACT UP, "and they have no clue that they're doing it." On the other hand, he faced Black people, also active in the AIDS movement, whom he considered his allies, who were now calling him an Uncle Tom because he was involved politically and personally with the gay white activists. Ortez and Dan stayed in ACT UP but continued to work in Black cultural contexts; they even fought to get on Black Entertainment Television (BET) to talk about AIDS in the Black community. The segment was canceled three times, but they finally did get on.

THE ACTION OF NEEDLE EXCHANGE

Working with ACT UP's Majority Action Committee, Dan heard about needle exchange and got interested. Dan went out a few times with a group pulled together by Richard Elovich and was outraged that this essential service was illegal in New York.

"You're trying to help somebody, and somebody wants to arrest you for it—it just played totally with me. And so I just did it. It was ugly, it was nasty, but it was very eye-opening, because you've got all these guys—people who hadn't slept for days, people who've got big open sores on their arms. At first, I was taken aback by it, for a second, but I got over that real quick, because it was, like—if I say, *I want everybody to have access to whatever preventative measures that there are out there,* then I can't be sort of selective about who can. So once that sort of clicked in my mind, it was all over. And I was living on the Lower East Side, so it just made sense . . . If not using a condom can contribute to the spread of AIDS, then distribute condoms. If sharing needles can contribute to the spread of AIDS, then we need to distribute needles."

RICHARD ELOVICH

It started with a small crew: Richard, a young man named Dan Raymond, and Jennifer Lacy, a choreographer whose mother was a nurse and who got the team red infectious waste containers for discarded needles. Richard's therapist, Paul Pavel, was an animal rescuer, and he showed Richard how to get syringes out of veterinary catalogs. Then they learned that syringes were legal in Seattle and began buying them there. Then Rod Sorge became the manager.

Rod took on a lot of responsibility. Rod was living, at the time, with Heidi Dorow on the Lower East Side. And every Friday night, people would gather and put bleach kits together at their apartment. At some point, Rod and Richard went up to Montefiore to meet Ernie Drucker, a psychologist in charge of the methadone programs at the hospital. Needle exchange was ACT UP's longest civil disobedience, because it went on for two years, from 1988 to 1990. But ACT UP was doing it because none of the nongovernmental organizations could organize such a thing and keep their tax-exempt status. They went out to Brooklyn, at a single-room-occupancy (SRO) building, and then on the street in what was pre-gentrification Williamsburg. ACT UP Needle Exchange covered Bushwick, Harlem, Mott Haven in the Bronx, and Manhattan's Lower East Side, where Attorney Street met Delancey. There was a little schoolyard there, where they went out on Saturdays.

Richard knew a Black man from Narcotics Anonymous meetings who turned out to be running a soup kitchen in Mott Haven, right where ACT UP was doing needle exchange. Richard went into the soup kitchen, and they were having an Alcoholics Anonymous (AA) or a Narcotics Anonymous (NA) meeting there. At that time, needle exchange and harm reduction were controversial for some people in twelve-step programs, because of threats they posed to abstinence. But that was not the way Richard felt. He would talk, in AA meetings, about the fact that he was doing needle exchange, and the ways it was helping people. And that's how Allan Clear got started working with the group.

ALLAN CLEAR

Allan Clear was born in Portsmouth, England, and raised in Cornwall. His father worked as a mechanic, as a postal worker, on the buses, and in factories. Allan's mother answered telephones in a bicycle store and then at a gas station; they weren't connected in any way to any kind of counterculture. By June 1983, he'd moved to New York. "You'd be sleeping, there'd be cockroaches crawling over you, and I thought that was just how people lived in New York." He started working in restaurants and was a busboy in a bar on Fifty-Fifth Street between Eighth and Broadway. It was the eighties, and there was a drug market working out of the bar, with eight or nine dealers at a time selling little packets of coke. Somewhere around 1986, some of the regular coke customers "began to wig out . . . just disappeared in a cloud of smoke, basically. I remember a good friend of mine who was also a dealer . . . said, *These kids are selling something called base.* I guess that was the beginning of the crack epidemic . . . There'd always be these streets where the sidewalks were just littered with crack vials. It was like you were walking on broken glass just walking down the street."

By 1987, Allan had quit drugs and started going to AA and working in more high-end restaurants. "Very often I was the only straight waiter there." So Allan would be going to AA and NA meetings in the West Village and the East Village, and "literally, literally, literally every other person that spoke would say something like, *I've been sober for ninety days and just diagnosed with AIDS.*" He became overwhelmed by the pain of this suffering. He felt lucky that he didn't have HIV. He heard Richard Elovich speak at a twelve-step meeting, and he talked about being in ACT UP, and Allan quickly decided to join.

The Needle Exchange Caucus grew. Gay Wachman, a lesbian ACT UPer who was a doctor, would receive some needle shipments. People would make bleach kits on Friday nights, and Saturdays they would go down to Attorney Street and set up on the chess tables in the corner park. ACT UP would distribute bags that contained a plastic bottle of bleach, a plastic bottle of water, a cooker, cotton, condoms, and instructions on how to bleach a set of equipment. Users would come along, and if they exchanged ten syringes, they'd get twelve back, so they got a bonus of two. "In terms of actual public health or even HIV prevention that [amount] was pretty useless, but it was what we had."

On Saturdays there were so many people doing syringe exchange that Allan thought it was silly. He'd go down to Attorney and there seemed to be twenty people there "all in black leather jackets and black boots and tight black pants," and they would be gathered around as one person came up to get their syringes. And Allan said, *I can't do this.* So he started doing the exchange on Wednesdays, and decided the way to do it was to keep it really small. Thereafter, there were never more than about four ACT UP activists at a time, often Allan, Juan Mendez, Donna Binder, and Debbie Gavito. One of the drug users from the Lower East Side named AB took them around on Wednesdays during lunch to places where addicts gathered.

The tour included Tompkins Square Park, and the shantytowns under the Manhattan Bridge and on Eighth Street between Avenues C and D. Large numbers of homeless people were living in Tompkins Square Park, in hand-built shelters. They'd sleep on the benches and build structures over them. Within those encampments, the drug injectors would often be in one place, so the activists would know where to go. They built relationships with people and would walk around saying, *Free works. Syringes, syringes. Free works. Needles, needles.* And people would say, *Wait up,* and then ask for all kinds of referrals from housing to health care to food. The late ACT UPer Juan Mendez worked for the Lower East Side Family Union, a social service agency, and he brought in a woman from the health department, Raquel Algarin, who then worked at the Lower East Side Harm Reduction Center. They would meet in a restaurant called the Daffodil on Seventh Street, just off Avenue A, and have breakfast there. Raquel was told by the government she had to walk one block behind the activists to do referrals, "which, of course, she never did, because that's absurd." Allan talked to drug users about the Knicks, about the weather. He became that same bartender that he was when he worked in the bar. "It's not solely about providing help or social services. It's about treating people like people."

LEI CHOU

Lei Chou was born in Taiwan and came to America in the winter of 1984 to study sculpture at Cooper Union. He came out to his family once he got to New York. Douglas Crimp was teaching a theory class, but he incorporated a lot of activism into his pedagogy.

"So it was a very fascinating subject for me, personally. I certainly got very much involved with it . . . I was thinking a lot about being gay and coming out and, sort of, that unfairness of gay people having gone through all this persecution and finally found a way out, and all of a sudden we have this disaster on our hands. And it's such an injustice. It really pushed me to think about why that is going on, and if there is anything that I can do to change it." Crimp "did a specific presentation on the FDA action— some video work and posters and documentations that came from it. And then he would say, *Well, there's a meeting right across the town, if you want to go to one of the meetings. It would be interesting*, so I just went."

Lei's best friend was Rod Sorge, and Rod got involved with needle exchange through Lei. They would do bleach kits at Rod's house. They'd paint the needles to identify them as having come from the exchange program. They did some outreach into shantytowns, including one at the foot of the Bowery, by the Manhattan Bridge. There were some Chinese people who lived there. So Lei and his sister Cathy had a translated fact sheet in Chinese to hand out with their bleach kits and clean needles, often twenty or thirty packages at a time.

While in ACT UP, Lei was also involved with Gay Asian & Pacific Islander Men of New York. The group led a campaign against the use of yellowface in the casting of the Broadway musical *Miss Saigon*. Lei started the Asian Pacific Islander (API) Caucus inside ACT UP with Kathy Chou, Ming-Yuen S. Ma, Yukari Yanagino, and several others. Their focus was to bring AIDS issues to the API community. They did fundraisers and safe-sex awareness at Club 58, a gay Asian bar. One time they went down to a middle school in Chinatown, to an after-school program. The activists brought out bananas and condoms and did a show-and-tell in Cantonese, in English, and in Mandarin. "They'd never heard anything like this." They went to colleges and to an Asian student conference. Then they pulled together with Majority Action and Latino Caucus to organize a national People of Color AIDS Activist Conference. Lei wrote a piece in

OutWeek criticizing GMHC's lack of prevention material and got "hate mail" in response. The API Caucus looked at several prevention brochures and drafted its own version of one, and then went to gay Asian groups and asked for volunteers to translate them. In the end they produced one brochure that had six different Asian languages on it.

RICHARD ELOVICH

ACT UP Needle Exchange was joined by an urban anthropologist, Joyce Rivera-Beckman. She observed that Latinos would weave dolls into the city trees as a recognition of children born HIV-positive who were dying. Joyce's mother was addicted to crack, living in the soup kitchen, and because of her connections and the fact that she had grown up in the neighborhood, Joyce managed to get needle exchange in alongside the people who were standing in line to sell drugs. So this work involved many different scenes, communities, and approaches. ACT UP kept that circuit up for two years.

But being around needles and organizing with addicts did turn out to be dangerous for people in recovery. Richard knew that this work required being exactly in the place everyone told him to stay away from, the *people, places, and things* that NA and AA supported addicts in distancing themselves from. What Richard didn't know was that a couple of activists in ACT UP were actually active users who were hiding it.

ANN PHILBIN

In 1970 and '71, Ann was part of a small group of gay students at the University of New Hampshire. They tried to organize a dance and ended up in court because the university tried to expel them. The ACLU defended them and they won the case. By the early 1980s, Ann was working in New York City, as an art dealer and a curator for Livet Reichard (directed by Ann Livet and Steve Reichard, who died of AIDS), which was an organization that raised money for amfAR. She was involved on a daily basis with the positioning, packaging, and branding of the organization. Politically, amfAR and ACT UP had a lot of friction. "And both had their place in the world, I would say . . . but the necessity of the ACT UP component during that period of time was obvious."

Ann started attending ACT UP.

"They were just the most impressive people I ever saw. It was really an amazing group of people. And the leaders, the people who would surface, the leaders—of course, there aren't supposed to be any—were completely brilliant. You just—you wanted to sit in that room because first of all, you had no place else to go with your anger, but also it was incredibly entertaining. They were gorgeous, you know, they were sexy, they were angry. It was better than any TV or movie. It was really—it was high entertainment, but also just the place to go to relieve yourself. Because you actually felt like something was getting accomplished there . . . the beauty of—of these young, angry, brilliant people was so overwhelming in a way that it was glamorous."

Remembrance: Brian Weil

When she first started getting involved with ACT UP, even though she had been a lesbian most of her life, Ann fell in love with Brian Weil. He had started the first needle exchange in the Bronx, called Bronx/Harlem Needle Exchange. And together they hosted a lot of fundraisers and awareness groups specifically focused on needle exchange at the Drawing Center in SoHo, where Ann was the director. People came from the Bronx and Harlem to SoHo for these events, where her gallery functioned as a community center for AIDS activism.

"The goal was to give clean needles to as many people as possible, and to raise awareness about the fact that it was going to be the next spike of the epidemic. And I think that's very clear to everyone now, but then it was completely—the notion of giving clean needles to intravenous drug users was just—that was even more radical and more unsavory than homosexuality to most of the world."

Brian was a documentary photographer with various bodies of work that reflected marginalized, edgy, and dangerous worlds. He started a group that went to hospitals to help children with AIDS. For about two years, Brian had a group of six guys who went and held babies in hospitals. In this way he became very close to a particular family, a woman whose husband was ill and died along with two infected infants. Brian "had a huge ego in a way. He could be enormously helpful to people and actually pave the way through the medical system." He spent a lot of time helping people fill out their forms and get the right doctors, hanging out in SROs, and assisting people that he had met on the needle exchange.

"I think there were enough straight people that really affiliated themselves with ACT UP, so it wasn't a big issue . . . He had very good friends in ACT UP, too, so—but—but he definitely felt, I think, at some point that going into the Bronx and organizing people, you know, IV drug users in the Bronx, was a place that he actually could feel more empowered. He was not a—he was not the kind of person who would stand up in front of an ACT UP meeting and lead that way."

It was one of the needle exchange community's painful experiences when Brian died of an overdose himself in 1996 at age forty-one.

THE TEST CASE—WILMINGTON, DELAWARE

ZOE LEONARD

Zoe Leonard's mom was a refugee from the Second World War, descended from Polish aristocracy, and her father was American, but she doesn't know a whole lot about him. He disappeared and died when she was young. She lived in Harlem as a child. "We were not even working-class; we were just really poor." She dropped out of high school in her second year. The artist Jean-Michel Basquiat was a classmate, and they moved in together. They went to the Mudd Club every night, went dancing and out to see bands, sneaked into nightclubs, and attended art openings, and, Zoe said, "that just felt like my life." But she'd never been to a protest, never been to a march or a meeting until ACT UP politicized her.

Zoe was friends with the artist David Wojnarowicz. She called him one day just to say hi, and he was really upset, crying on the phone, and said that he'd just tested positive. He was on his way to an ACT UP meeting, so she went and met him at the Center. That first night, the facilitators were Robert Vázquez-Pacheco and Maria Maggenti. "This was so amazing, a place to bring your rage and a place to bring your anger and your fear and your sadness, and actually try to understand how the virus, how the disease had been made into a crisis."

ACT UP had been largely focused on gay men having AIDS and on transmission through sex. Needle exchange was the broadening of agenda. Zoe had shot drugs when she was younger, and it seemed really clear to her that drug users were another population that the government wasn't interested in protecting. She also understood the correlation between negotiating safe sex and getting high, particularly concerning issues of self-esteem and the trials of growing up. She knew that queer teens were more likely to use drugs, and in a lot of those situations were not as able to negotiate safe sex.

"Back then, which is really hard to remember in the post-Giuliani gentrified New York, but the Lower East Side was all about drugs. I mean, that's what it was. A lot of us lived in the East Village . . . And Lower Manhattan, it was a drug economy . . . You couldn't get around drugs. There was really no way to talk about anything without talking about people buying and selling drugs on the street and people getting sick because they didn't have clean needles and didn't have access to any kind of health education or health care."

While getting arrested and forcing a test case in New York City was part of ACT UP's plan, there was a simultaneous strategy of going state by state. Zoe, Gay Wachman, and two men chose to support local activists doing needle exchange in Wilmington, Delaware. The risk involved a big minimum sentence, "maybe twenty years." The activists were taking on something that was considered a serious crime, and needle exchange didn't completely have the same kind of support that some of ACT UP's other work did. But Zoe felt it was really important, and she'd been in ACT UP a few years already and really trusted the organization's legal support. So she thought, *All right. I really hope they don't make an example of me, but let's do it.*

The four of them, along with a small support team, drove down to Delaware. They met with a small local organization and wrote a press release. They set up a table with their needles, sharps containers, and harm reduction packets. After only fifteen minutes, they were arrested and in the police van.

"It was all just a blur for me. I was just like, *Oh, please, don't let me go to prison over this. I really, really, really don't want to go to prison.* They kept Gay and I together, which was great, so we were sharing a cell for at least a good part of it. I remember really having some doubts. It was really scary, actually . . . It was a different state. We'd prepared as deeply as we could, but there was the wild-card factor."

They got out on bail and came back a few weeks later for the trial. In the end, the lawyers were successful in getting the charges dismissed and a precedent set for needle exchange in Delaware.

Like many ACT UPers, Zoe felt that the organization played a central role in her life. She had a number of relationships there, including a long one with Gregg Bordowitz, and she was lovers with Suzanne Wright for a year and had an affair with Catherine Gund. For a few years, it became her social life as well as her political life. One day Zoe accidentally got stuck with a "really dirty, like a really filthy, crusty needle, and the wisdom at the time was if there was a potential that you'd been exposed, which I probably wouldn't have been because any virus on that needle probably would have been dead a long time ago and whatever, but just as a precaution, the thing to do was to mega dose on AZT for twenty-four hours or forty-eight hours or something. It's kind of like a morning-after pill or something. If there was any live virus, that would potentially prevent transmission." She got some AZT from Gregg, and, she said, "I did it for a few days, and I was like, *Fuck, this is really not fun.* Everyone talks, *Oh, this [AZT] is the solution,* and, *Oh, yeah, you've got your drugs.* And I was like, *I feel crazy. I feel nauseous and lightheaded and speedy and disgusting, and I can't believe people have to take these drugs every day, and that's the best thing we have to offer, and that's our solution.*" Zoe learned directly that even the solutions to the problem weren't acceptable solutions.

Remembrance: Rod Sorge

RICHARD ELOVICH

Richard Elovich recognized that Rod Sorge was capable of something that none of the others could do. Rod was twenty years old, and the women on the street adored him.

"They adored him for being there; for being as cute as he was; for being such a loving person. And so when we hit the street, we'd all be greeted; but Rod was really greeted by people. They loved the fact that he was out there. And that he learned people's names. They knew him. And that's what made it a maximalist thing going on . . . He was doing case management. Rod would start referring people into services out of it, without us conceptualizing it as that."

LEI CHOU

The first time Lei met Rod, it was at a Housing Caucus meeting, and Lei thought he was "one of those really smart people." For Lei, every word that came out of Rod's mouth had a concrete meaning and was well-thought-out and well planned. Lei found pleasure in just knowing people like Rod, who was doing this work, using everything he had. Lei went with Rod up to the Bronx, where he would know the location of crack houses and would go inside. Lei would say, *I'll wait outside for you. Just let me know when you come out.* "It was kind of scary, because it was obviously a very dangerous neighborhood, but Rod didn't give a hoot, and he met a lot of clients there." Rod went out to New Jersey and got arrested for needle exchange and went on trial for it. Governor Christine Todd Whitman wouldn't allow needle exchange at all. "It's just ridiculous how many people got infected in New Jersey because of that stupid policy—murderous policy."

First Rod came down with a really bad case of shingles. Lei thinks that Rod pretty much knew all along that he was infected, but a lot of people, at the time, didn't really feel the need to get tested, because there was simply no treatment. And Rod was one of those in that camp. *If there wasn't anything you could do about it, why find out?* But as it turned out, Lei later understood, Rod should have gotten tested. By the time he got an official diagnosis, it was too late for the drugs to do any good.

"I've wrestled with that thinking for so long now. I've

come to an understanding that Rod is one of those people that so firmly believes in justice, so firmly believing in living a life with a principle that he couldn't understand why drug use is illegal, and he couldn't understand why people were persecuted for that. He understands people use drugs for many different reasons, and the least of it is for the fun of it. Most of it has to do with people struggling with their daily realities and just trying to cope, with self-medication. That's very much his own take on drug use. I don't think that it was either drug use or AIDS treatment. It wasn't ever really a split on that level. He had tried to quit several times as well. When he found out, he was just so sick that he did try the medication. None of it ever worked out . . .

"Because he had track marks, he would get discriminated against on every level of service. Doctors wouldn't take him. Emergency rooms would confiscate his bag or search his bag. He was, basically, being treated as a criminal, rather than a person needing medical care. He got locked up in isolation wards a couple of times, because they had thought that he had TB. The level of discrimination that he faced was ridiculous, and still goes on. You never hear about that."

A couple of hundred people came to his memorial service, held at Housing Works in 1999. Some people wanted to do it at Judson Memorial Church because Rod used to prepare needle exchange bleach kits in the basement. But Rod was adamant in his will that he didn't want to have any association with religion, even if the church had been decommissioned. His friends thought Housing Works was an appropriate alternative site. When he passed away, there was a tremendous hurt being felt by so many people, just because of who he was. ACT UPers were surrounded by death, but some individuals' demise hit the collective especially hard. "I still don't know what memorial services are good for. I don't know if it helped me deal with it better, but it was nice to be in a roomful of so many people that knew Rod." Lei had actually not gone to a memorial service before. He tended toward focusing on proactive solutions rather than on the stark reality of death.

At the time of our interview, Lei had had the urn with Rod's ashes sitting out on a table in his small apartment for a number of years. But he had finally decided to let it go. "I'm just going to give it back to his mom. We've tried to figure out ways to—something to do with the ashes. We thought about taking them over to New Jersey and dumping them on Christine Whitman's lawn, or go to the White House, or go out to Fire Island. I just never really have the heart to do it. I want to let him rest. He's worked too hard. I don't think he wants to end up in New Jersey, anyway."

ALLAN CLEAR

Allan had breakfast with Rod the week he died. "The residual feelings you have around the impact of someone like Rod dying [are] as clear to me now as [they] ever were." They worked together at the Harm Reduction Coalition. When Rod did needle exchange in the Bronx/Harlem, Allan did it on the Lower East Side. They worked together in ACT UP's Needle Exchange Caucus and were very close. Rod didn't take care of his health. He had fifteen T cells before he even went to a doctor, yet Allan felt that the medical system screwed him over in the end.

Rod was seeing a doctor to get methadone through a clinic system. His doctor prescribed it officially for "neuropathy," but really it was to stabilize him so that he didn't have to go and score drugs. Allan had experienced working with Rod when he was using heroin. Rod would come to work at eight o'clock in the morning and would have his drugs delivered to the office. Allan and Rod wrote to the gay rights philanthropist Henry van Ameringen, who sent them a check for fifty thousand dollars. Henry took them to the Rainbow Room, but Allan and Rod showed up without the required jackets. Rod had blood all over his sleeves, and they had to borrow the jackets. Then he got misdiagnosed with spinal meningitis/TB. He was prescribed the antibiotic rifampin to deal with his spinal TB. Rifampin metabolizes methadone at a much quicker rate. The doctor then had to raise the amount of methadone that Rod

> was on, and the doctor finally said, *I cannot prescribe you any more methadone.* Allan recalled that the doctor just cut him off with no notice, no tapering, nothing. Rod was suddenly left to have to go and scramble and buy "a shitload of heroin that he didn't need to do before his methadone was being raised and raised and raised." He was left with a habit he had to deal with, and that crashed his health care. He died after injecting—no one knows if he died of a drug overdose or if he died just because he was sick with AIDS-related conditions. But decades later, Allan still felt the impact of losing him suddenly.

THE EVENT

RICHARD ELOVICH

Members of ACT UP's Needle Exchange Committee wanted to take the next step and actually change the policies that kept antiquated restrictions on the books. In 1990, they decided they had to get arrested exchanging needles to provoke a test case in the New York City courts. They met with ACT UP attorneys Jill Harris and Mike Spiegel, and activist Debra Levine. The Needle Exchange action was set up like any other ACT UP demonstration. The group tried to figure out a moment when the larger ACT UP would really be behind them.

The action took place on March 6, 1990, on the Lower East Side. The team met up at Katz's Deli—a number of ACT UP people and one woman no one recognized, named Cynthia Cochrane. She said that she had heard about the action and called somebody, and they said *Come to Katz's Deli,* and she just showed up. She was an older white woman, "very WASPy-looking, I guess." A picture appeared in the press of her being hauled away in her little scarf and her gray hair.

Ten people prepared to get arrested and go to trial as a test case.

DEBRA LEVINE

Debra Levine grew up in a Jewish family in Peabody, Massachusetts. The synagogue youth group became a refuge when her father died when she was nine. "I didn't know any other kids who were from single-parent households." After graduating from the University of Pennsylvania, she moved to New York and worked in theater for a while as an Equity stage manager, and then went back to Columbia and got her MFA in theater directing. She had never been to the Gay Center before, identifying as a straight woman, and crossing that threshold was really something major. Then she sat down in an ACT UP meeting and just listened. "I was blown away by that first meeting. I was blown away by the political analysis, by the level of information that was going on, by the incredible debate. It was hilarious. And then I was really chastened by the fact that I didn't know much."

Deb joined Outreach, working with Robert Garcia, and also attended the Women's Caucus, right before the Shea Stadium action.

"It was more than a little intimidating . . . I was really intimidated by some of the women because of their political experience and also their adamant insistence that because lesbians had been really kind of oppressed in other political organizations, that lesbian issues would be key and always a priority. And I felt as a straight woman, I had to figure out my own relationship to this and make sure that I was super careful . . . I was just very concerned that politically I would be incorrect, and I guess that was actually the real lesson that I learned in ACT UP, is that it was okay to be, and it was okay to be shouted down, and you could be argumentative about it, but there wasn't going to be the same kind of oppression that other people had experienced in other groups happening there."

Prior to the Needle Exchange action, Debra had gotten arrested with the affinity group the Box Tops at a demonstration for HIV housing, and ended up in a group of women ACT UPers who were strip-searched in jail. She joined the Needle Exchange Committee but only participated a few times before the purposeful arrest action. She recalled that the action itself became "just a real circus." She even had a hard time getting arrested that day. "It was hilarious." The team all had needles and sharps containers, having very carefully planned on how to handle the needles, because of concerns that there would be a lot of people around. The Guardian Angels, a controversial volunteer street safety organization, came, and as Deb was walking down to the site where they were going to give out the needles, she was mobbed by the press. There was news media, there were Guardian Angels surrounding the activists, there were the people who were supposed to receive the needles, and there were cops converging on all of it. One police officer took Deb's needles away from her, and he said, *You don't want to get arrested, honey. Here, I'll take them from you, and it'll be all okay.* And she was like, *No, I want to get arrested*, and she had to grab a needle from someone else and pull it back.

Deb was eventually arrested and charged with felony possession of a needle and felony possession of a syringe without a prescription. The trial dynamics were unconventional, of course.

"There was this great moment when Kathryn Otter [later known as Ottersten], who was sitting next to me the whole time, got up on the stand, and when they were talking about where we were doing the action, Kathy said, *Oh, it's right near these shops. I get my clothes there.* And [Judge] Laurie Drager was like, *Oh my God, I shop there, too.* So all of a sudden this judge and this great trans woman were just talking about discount shopping on Orchard Street, and it was one of those perfect New York moments where there was some sort of humanity in it."

KATHY OTTERSTEN

Kathy's father worked for General Electric, so the family moved around a lot. Kathy went to school at Fordham in New York and learned resistance tactics from the Catholic left. Bisexual since age twelve, Kathy came to ACT UP in 1989 in the middle of their gender transition. Homeless for two of their years in ACT UP, Kathy got involved with the developing Housing Works. In 1991, Kathy was elected facilitator, along with David Robinson.

"I never went into a trial expecting to win . . . I didn't know [about] my physical body and who I was, how I'd be treated. I figured that there was going to be a very tough time. But you roll with it . . . I talked about running the soup kitchen and seeing people who were needle users and exactly what happened to them with AIDS, and seeing what it meant for their families and just, you know, that it was really aimed towards why we needed to be doing what we were doing. I mean, in a lot of ways, that's what we were all trying to impress—*This has to happen.* It's not an option anymore. Any right-thinking person would know you don't condemn people to death just because they have a drug addiction. That's not what we do. It is not an executable offense, and that's what effectively it had become."

THE TRIAL

RICHARD ELOVICH

The six-day trial began on April 8, 1991. What the defendants first went for was a Clayton motion, a provision of the New York Criminal Procedure Law known formally as a "motion to dismiss in the interest of justice." The ACT UPers argued that they were breaking the law but not harming the community because their actions created a greater good. Attorneys Mike Spiegel and Jill Harris, and defendant Deb Levine and supporter Rod Sorge, did a lot of the work preparing for trial. They took affidavits several inches thick and prepared witnesses. Don Des Jarlais came on as a researcher, making the case that the President's Commission on AIDS had actually said that "the first line of defense is needle exchange."

But the Clayton motion was denied by Judge Laura Drager, who had presided over an earlier ACT UP case involving a campaign against New York City health commissioner Stephen Joseph. And so the defendants prepared for a medical necessity defense. In the meantime, Richard Elovich was serving on an advisory committee to the CDC and so was Joseph, who had long been a target of ACT UP's wrath. The campaign against Joseph, whose department was undercounting AIDS cases, included phone calls to his home and actions at his office, which he felt was abusive, while the activists working on him were driven by desperation.

"One of the times we went down to Atlanta, there was a really bad hurricane that was happening in New York. And we couldn't take off from Atlanta. So I ended up spending about three hours with Steve Joseph at the airport in Atlanta, with, also, Don Des Jarlais. And somehow, we kind of made peace. And just around strategy. And I never said, *You're right*. But he was able to vent his rage with me about the attacks on his home—the stalking, with the red hand—that went way beyond seeing him as someone who occupies an office to, again, just an uncontrolled rage. So he was able to kind of get that off. And I was able to get him to agree, by the end of it, to be a witness on our behalf. And that was really important. Because that was important for Laura Drager to see, that Steve Joseph was willing to testify now, on our behalf."

ACT UP attorneys Jill Harris and Mike Spiegel orchestrated a piece of legal theater, figuring out what everyone's role was going to be. Stephen Joseph's role was to tell the history of medical necessity defense. In a certain sense, each one of the defendants had a symbolic value. Richard was the former addict; and he went pro se, so that an addict was actually speaking for himself, though he had Jill's guidance.

JILL HARRIS

Jill Harris grew up in Oregon in the 1960s. When she was in high school, Gloria Steinem came to speak in Portland, and her mother took her out of class so that they could go up together to hear her. Jill came out after her freshman year at Harvard and came to New York in 1982 to go to NYU School of Law, and she went to work for Legal Aid as a criminal defense attorney.

Her first legal work for ACT UP was the Seize Control of the FDA action in 1988. Like the Media Committee, ACT UP lawyers didn't have that much of a role in determining the strategy. It was more a facilitating role and kind of an informational one. If Jill had questions about a strategy, she would really try hard to pose those questions not as a lawyer, but rather just as an individual, and she didn't discuss street action strategy often. At the FDA action, one of the things lawyers did was go to the affinity groups and find out what they were planning because different actions had different legal implications. For example, Peter Staley wanted to use a smoke bomb as part of his performance at the FDA. Jill felt strongly that he shouldn't do that. She looked up the statute on incendiary devices; theoretically, using a smoke bomb could have been interpreted through that lens and considered a pretty serious crime. She thought that the smoke bomb could endanger people, and that it could make the cops feel like they needed to escalate the thing, "just freak people out" in a way that would make it unsafe and take away from the message. And so she tried to talk Peter out of it, but he was not dissuaded, and it ended up being fine. After that, Jill did not try to talk activists out of their chosen path.

Lambda Legal usually refused ACT UP–related cases, so the organization built its own internal legal team. Over the years the list of lawyers in ACT UP grew: David Barr, Jill Harris, Joan Gibbs, Karen Moulding, Mike Spiegel, Mary Dorman, Lori Cohen, Terry McGovern,

Bill Dobbs, Michelle Adams, Steve Statsinger, Roma Baran. None of them ever got paid. Needle Exchange was Jill's first ACT UP case that went to trial.

Personally, she was philosophically opposed to the idea of going to trial. She knew that for the defendants it felt like a powerful thing. But for her, as someone who was in the criminal justice system all the time, she knew trials didn't slow down the system. They don't throw wrenches in the system at all. If they do, it's to the detriment of other people who are actually in jail, who really would like to be out of jail, and who need their trials faster. So anything that slows the system down hurts the people in jail rather than the system itself, which, Jill said, "is just not subject to that much influence."

Attorney Jill Harris in court with three Needle Exchange
defendants in April 1991. From left to right: Kathy Otter (Ottersten),
Dan Keith Williams, Debra Levine (Photograph by T.L. Litt)

But, for Jill, the Needle Exchange case was a different thing completely. The ACT UP defendants were mounting a necessity defense, which meant they weren't saying, *We did this. We sat down in the street to call attention to the fact that the government is not doing what they're supposed to do on AIDS*. Instead, the ACT UP defendants were acting to save lives, which should have been the work of the government, which was doing nothing. It was a different type of defense, conceptually.

ACT UP was doing the right thing, and should not only *not* be punished for it, but should be able to keep doing it. In fact, the government should do it. As a result, the trial had the potential to change government policy on needle exchange.

The defendants were Richard Elovich, Gregg Bordowitz, Jon Parker, Deb Levine, Kathy Otter (Ottersten), Monica Pearl, Cynthia Cochrane, and Dan Keith Williams, all of whom had been arrested at the action. One woman arrested on-site did not go to trial.

Mike Spiegel was the other attorney working with Jill, and the two of them worked closely together. "It was really a great collaboration and a great relationship." They'd call each other in the middle of the night— *Okay, I thought of this great thing*—and it was "really exciting and fun to work with him." They did have group meetings at which they talked about strategies, but mostly the defendants deferred to them on the legal issues. For the most part the lawyers set the trial strategy. They divided up the defendants and went over their testimony because they wanted to bring out specific points with each witness and make sure that they got to say what they needed to say about why the action took place and why needle exchange was important. Jill worked closely with Richard because he was representing himself, which she supported. She felt his voice, as an addict, was really important, and helping him get his voice out there was essential.

The necessity defense is used for an action that's ethically required to prevent imminent harm, when there's no other way you can achieve the same end. The defense claims that the action designed to prevent something worse from occurring. Stephen Joseph had tried to start a needle exchange program in the past, but he centered it at the Department of Health, about a block from the police headquarters, so no one would go and get needles there. That was under Mayor Ed Koch. Then Mayor David Dinkins came into office, and he was very ideologically opposed to needle exchange, so he got rid of it. And he had a new health commissioner, Woody Myers, who also opposed it. So when Richard Elovich persuaded Stephen Joseph to testify as one of our witnesses, it was exciting. Joseph discussed why the program had failed, and why

Dinkins had stopped it, Jill said—"that it was about politics, that it was a good idea and that it should've been kept."

ACT UP had Don Des Jarlais, who was a leading expert on HIV transmission and an advisor to needle exchanges all over the world. ACT UP also had Velmanette Montgomery, who was a Black state senator, come and testify that needle exchange was the right thing to do. She testified that she had tried to get it through the state legislature, and that that route was not going to be successful, and so there was no way to accomplish this legislatively. Marie St. Cyr, from the Haitian community, did a lot of work with women and HIV. She testified about the variety of groups that were affected by the illness. So different witnesses made different points to prove that without needle exchange, there was grave, imminent harm. And that there was also a way to ameliorate it. Needle exchange simply saved people's lives.

Both Jill and Mike did summations, and Jill concluded, *These defendants, they took action. They did what was necessary, and each one of them knows that they saved a life. They saved lives. They don't have to have studies to show that they saved lives. They know they saved lives. And, Your Honor Judge Drager, you know it, too.* And Jill recalled that Judge Drager's eyes got teary. She stood up rather quickly, and she left the bench. Jill remembered thinking, *Wow, that was good.*

STEALING MONEY

DAN KEITH WILLIAMS

When Dan was on the stand, he had been out the whole night before and was still high as a kite. "It was screwed up to say this, but," he said, it worked out perfectly, because when the DA asked questions, Dan had free-flying answers for him.

"Everybody was just rolling, laughing—the judge just had to make everybody shut up after a while. So it just worked to my advantage. No, I would never do that again, but it was funny . . . I was being sarcastic the whole time. And so it worked for me, anyway. But that was that. After that, I don't know—my whole world had started to become unraveled. A number of people had died."

Dan was profoundly affected by the death of his lover, and by the deaths of Ortez Alderson, Alan Robinson, and Ray Navarro. Alcohol had eventually got the best of Dan, and he was burned out. When he heard other people talking about the dying, he would start to laugh.

"I couldn't cry no more, couldn't feel sad no more, because I'd done it so long. I was just burnt on it . . . People were talking about going to a memorial service. It was, like, *Let me go to a bar and have a drink—let me have ten drinks, let me have twenty drinks. Let me just knock myself out* . . . Everybody sort of hung out in the East Village. We sort of took over the East Village and we said the 'regular' gay guys could have the West Village, the East Village belongs to us. And there was that whole dynamic, because ACT UP became a world of its own . . . But even in that safety, there is a lot of vulnerability because . . . death was still there."

RICHARD ELOVICH

At the time of the arrest, Richard and the committee had to go to the floor of ACT UP to announce that Dan Williams had stolen upward of ten thousand dollars from the organization. And it tore the Needle Exchange team apart. There were a lot of drug addicts working with them. Though he never knew exactly what had happened with Dan, Richard thought perhaps he was doing coke, or he could have been a compulsive debtor.

"But he was such a nice guy. And he was such a great partner for me in it. None of us saw it coming. And then Rod started raising the red flag when we couldn't do an accounting . . . And I remember realizing we had to take this proactive [stance], and actually go to the floor and announce it. And my thing with Dan was to get him to come to the floor with me. Because I thought if we didn't do that, it was going to tear ACT UP apart, along race lines. And it still did. Even with him coming out and acknowledging it . . . ACT UP was taking on more and more things that were no longer exclusive to the gay community. And there were lots of divisions that were emerging."

DAN KEITH WILLIAMS

"I would go on trips and buy needles—and I think it all started out very innocently enough. Unfortunately, what I discovered later is, I'm bipolar, and I just sort of just let my imagination take charge of me, and I just did what I wanted to do. I never spent any money on myself . . . People like to say, Dan took the money and bought drugs. I never bought any drugs. I don't do drugs. I can't do drugs. Part of my being bipolar, it doesn't work. I can't drink that much alcohol. I don't have—no one can ever say I had a big party . . . They said, *We need for you to give us back this money* . . . And I'm like, *I don't have it*. And I didn't . . . At that point, I was scared, I was embarrassed, I was upset with myself, on a number of levels—but that was just part of it. And it took me a long time to get a grip with what was going on with me . . . I think one of the things that bothered me about how someone might perceive it is that they might use it to diminish what Majority Action might have done and Needle Exchange might have done. This is something that Dan Williams did, and if you want to hate me, if you want to think I'm a crook, if you want to think I'm the worst person in the world, that's your prerogative. I put it in perspective. I did something wrong. I made a big mistake. I own up to it. I own up to it because I did it, but I understand why I did it myself."

WAITING FOR A VERDICT

RICHARD ELOVICH

It took more than a year for the verdict in the Needle Exchange case to be handed down. In the interim a lot of events took place. John C. Daniels, the African American mayor of New Haven, Connecticut, went ahead and had the city back a needle exchange program. Which in turn impressed Mayor Dinkins. In New York, city council member Ruth Messinger was about to come out in support of needle exchange, and Dinkins didn't want to be behind her. In addition, his political advisors were telling him, *Get out in front of this.* There was a budget crisis, and Dinkins had dissolved 1,100 drug treatment spots that had been set aside specifically for pregnant, drug-dependent women. As a result, the mayor had nothing to show in terms of what he was doing about the drug problem. And that was the argument, largely, of the National Black Leadership Commission on AIDS. Needle exchange, then, fit the mayor's political needs.

Dinkins communicated that he was going to go with needle exchange but that he needed support. Tim Sweeney and Richard Elovich had to go up to the National Black Leadership Commission on AIDS and make the argument. And Debra Frazer-Howze, the director, characterized them to the members of the commission as *two gay white men*, not realizing that Richard was also an addict. Eventually, everyone on the commission would come around.

Richard also went to Phase: Piggy Back, a group of Black Muslim men who had put together a drug treatment program. They had been against needle exchange.

"I'm meeting this guy for the first time," Richard said, "and we sort of recognized each other. And then I started the meeting . . . but this guy—I think his name was Assad—and he was wearing an Islamic cap. And I said, *I'm a former drug user, in recovery.* And he looked at me, and he said, *I'm a former drug user in recovery.* And a dialogue just started with us, and no one else was talking. It basically was about us. And at the end of it, he said, *I can't support needle exchange. But I will go to Dinkins's Blue Room, and I will say that we shouldn't stand in the way of this, because it's saving lives* . . . If you believe in the day-at-a-time, that relapse is likely—who are we to deny another drug user the means of survival? . . . Phase: Piggy Back got behind us. And we all stood behind Dinkins. And Dinkins reversed his position."

A number of other steps were taken at the same time:

- A researcher named Ed Kaplan concluded a study showing the efficacy of needle exchange.
- Don Des Jarlais and the President's Commission on AIDS issued a report in 1991 on the interlocking epidemics of substance use and HIV. *The New York Times* reported that "the commission said the Administration had failed to recognize the link between AIDS and drug use, a failure it called 'bewildering and tragic.'"
- The AIDS Link to Intravenous Experience (ALIVE) study from Johns Hopkins followed a huge cohort of IDUs in Baltimore. The researchers were able to pick out a group of IDUs who either themselves were diabetic or had a family

member who was diabetic and required insulin injections. Everything else remained constant; nothing else distinguished this cohort from the rest of the drug users, except that they had access to clean diabetic syringes. And they had a dramatically lower rate of HIV prevalence.

- City council member Ruth Messinger came out to the street. She observed the syringe exchange, but she also saw what was happening between people, the therapeutic relationship aspect of the communication.

Finally, before the verdict in the Needle Exchange case was even issued, Mathilde Krim (of amfAR) said she would pay for the program. There was a meeting at her apartment with a collection of people from different AIDS foundations, including nongovernmental organization representatives like Yolanda Serrano from ADAPT and Ronald Johnson from the Minority Task Force on AIDS. All agreed that they would support needle exchange. The AIDS Institute took on getting the regulations changed; even if the law was upheld, it would work to get a state of emergency declared in New York. Richard went to GMHC and said, *You guys are doing nothing on drug policy. And you need to.* That was when Tim Sweeney, David Hansell, and David Barr helped Richard write up a proposal to actually start a program for drug users at GMHC, and they ended up hiring Richard as a consultant using state and private funding.

THE VERDICT

On June 25, 1991, Judge Laura Drager found that medical necessity was proven.

RICHARD ELOVICH

After needle exchange became possible, Richard said, "I think it got as high as maybe nine or ten programs."

AFTER

DAN KEITH WILLIAMS

"It's kind of funny, when I think about it, because us being arrested and going to trial, and winning the case, and having the state law change, does, sort of, have an effect on me, yeah! And, sometimes, you know, when people piss me off really bad, and it's like—*You sit around and don't do nothing.* I'm like, *Yeah, have you been arrested and gotten state law changed?* And that usually shut them up, but that's me being a little egotistical, but still. When three hundred people do the same thing, change happens."

ALLAN CLEAR

"As far as I'm concerned, there's been two major successes in AIDS in the United States. One is mother-to-child transmission and the other is amongst drug injectors . . . Drug users actually did it for themselves. They came in. They collected the syringes. We created an environment where it was worthwhile for them to come to it, because people aren't going to go to a service or a place if they don't feel comfortable, especially if you're a criminalized population. And when we started doing this, New York City was the global epicenter of HIV injection drug use. People don't talk about New York City in that way anymore. You cannot find a bloodborne HIV transmission pretty much in New York City anymore because of what we've done . . . I'm sure people share needles, but not to the extent that it was. It's barely a blip on the radar screen in terms of HIV transmission among people who share syringes now. It's really, really rare . . . because of syringe exchange. It's like when you have a pot of spaghetti and you've only got one fork, you'll share that fork, but if you have two forks, you use your own. It's not cultural and it's not a death wish. It's not any of those things. It's just the fact there were not enough syringes in circulation, and that was a policy thing."

The fact that many of the needle exchange programs around the country came out of ACT UP is not something that's really at the top of the list when the movement's accomplishments are remembered. But needle exchange changed the trajectory of HIV in many parts of the country and, by extension, had an impact on the rest of world as well.

DAN KEITH WILLIAMS

Although no charges were filed against Dan and he never paid back the money, he did stay around ACT UP for a short time. A member of the Majority Action Committee, he also belonged to a short-lived Black Caucus. According to Cathy Cohen's 1999 book, *The Boundaries of Blackness: AIDS and the Breakdown of Black Politics*, a new group, Black AIDS Mobilization (BAM!), grew out of the Black Caucus of ACT UP. Black individuals frustrated with what they perceived to be racist actions of some members of ACT UP, and the narrow interests of many men in the organization who wanted to concentrate the group's resources almost exclusively on the process of drug approval, decided to build an alternative organization. Cohen defines BAM! as primarily focused on political battles centered around AIDS in communities of color and working within their limitations to draw attention to the spread of AIDS in communities of color.

Although BAM! did not last long, it did organize a campaign against Enoch Williams, a Black five-term city council member representing Bedford-Stuyvesant, Brownsville, East Flatbush, and Crown Heights from 1979 to 1997. Williams opposed a series of gay rights bills in the 1980s and told *The New York Times* that the city helped spread AIDS by "condoning homosexuality." BAM! and ACT UP held an action, at which the *Times* reported that activists interrupted a council meeting with demands for Williams's resignation and shouts of *Help me! I'm dying* and *You are killing us!* He also opposed needle exchange. Ron "Raan" Medley, an ACT UP member who was also in BAM!, repeatedly wrote articles in *Tell It to ACT UP (TITA)*, an in-house newsletter published by Bill Dobbs, trying to encourage ACT UP to attend BAM! events. Months after Dan left the organization in response to the group's anger about his theft of funds, Jane Auerbach, a Black Jewish lesbian in ACT UP, reported in *TITA*:

"Thanks to everyone who showed up at the City Council meeting. We really gave it to Enoch Williams. Tom Duane's speech was hard-hitting and the ACT UP presence was nothing short of disruptive. This is not a guilt trip but merely a commentary; in the recent past it has been difficult to get large numbers at our demos. Well, guess who showed up at the City Council demo this past week? Dan Williams! Just another thing that makes you go hmmmm."

BOOK TWO

ART IN THE SERVICE OF CHANGE

Do you resent people with AIDS?

Do you trust HIV-negatives?

Have you given up hope for a cure?

When was the last time you cried?

PART V

Art Making as Creation and Expression of Community

A movement gets misrepresented when images of it are skewed, but also when the images it produces are sorted and prioritized by historicizing institutions of power. That ACT UP attracted so many artists may be a reflection of its queer and marginalized origins, but it is also a reflection of its connected and aspirational impulses. There was a wide range of communities—both aesthetic and cultural—making art in ACT UP. From streets to museums to nightclubs to public space to Macy's, ACT UP was sometimes the honored guest, other times the confrontational and unwelcome truth-teller. The SILENCE=DEATH Project and the Gran Fury collective designed our public images. At the same time, the visual and performative exploits of Action Tours and Church Ladies for Choice, and the theatrical and visual strategies of the Asian Pacific Islander Caucus used artistic ideas to communicate with communities from Asian gay bars to abortion clinics. ACT UP lived the nightlife through Meat and the Clit Club as artistic expressions and coherence of community while also working with ART Positive. GANG engaged a variety of media, and the Anonymous Queers performed their theatrical emotions through their manifesto, "I Hate Straights." ACT UP confronted museums by taking on the responsibility for photographic images of people with AIDS. Some seized new technologies and formed video activist collectives like WAVE, Testing the Limits, and DIVA TV, while others used video to collaborate with formerly incarcerated HIV-positive women to document their realities. Jim Hubbard, Christine Vachon, and Jim Lyons described their work in film, both narrative and experimental, to respond to AIDS. Activists inside ACT UP had to adopt different playbooks based on their access and identifications. The same was true for artists. Only by juxtaposing the simultaneous diversity of expression can the cumulative power of ACT UP's use of visual art, design, performance, and venue be revealed, and its collective impact assessed.

10

The Artistic Life of Resistance

Movements have looks, and most come organically from the people in the streets. But there is also intentionality: Black civil rights workers in suits and ties carrying mass-produced signs written in clean lines proclaiming, I AM A MAN. These were assertions of seriousness, citizenship, faith, and also respectability in the face of dogs, water hoses, arrests, bombs, and assassinations. Black Panthers moved to leather jackets and open-carry weapons, telegraphing resistance, self-defense, and strength, despite the violence and rage of the state. White students resisting the war in Vietnam sported long hair, bell bottoms, and graffitied army jackets, reaching toward psychedelia; their message was rebellion, refusal, alternative values. Mattachine picketers for early gay rights insisted that the lesbians wear dresses to show they could. Occupy Wall Street brought back the hand-lettered sign on cardboard, each person appearing as an individual without an apparatus. #BlackLivesMatter and the more amorphous #MeToo seized the most contemporary means of communication and signified with the hashtag.

But ACT UP was probably the first movement of deeply oppressed people whose lives were at stake to have included such a large group of designers, advertising professionals, studio artists, marketers, and publicists well versed in the visual language of branding and experienced in the selling of ideas, fresh out of art school and with relationships to institutions of cultural influence. ACT UP not only adapted the aesthetics of advertising but also benefited from activists who were actually the people who *created* the aesthetics of advertising. Because of the way homophobia functioned at the time (no legal rights or protections, no accurate representation, and profound familial homophobia), coupled with the nightmare of AIDS (no treatments, plus stigma, isolation, and exclusion), people could have Ivy League pedigrees, corporate training, cultural currency, and positions of power in creating mass media—with decent salaries and significant discretionary income—and *still* have no rights and be abandoned to suffer and perish.

There was a clean edge to much of the ACT UP aesthetic. And like all things about ACT UP, images spoke simultaneously to the past and to the present. The first gay generation to be decimated by AIDS was the "clones," a gay take on the hypermasculine—plaid shirts, longish hair, mustaches, western wear—that was associated with the West Village and Chelsea in the 1970s. The heart of AIDS activism included younger people, and they rejected the clone look while creating a new aesthetic as a mode of identification, one that distanced us from the devastated previous gay generation. ACT UP was the queer East Village, the clean-shaven face, short hair, white T-shirt, tight black jeans, and stomper Doc Marten boots advertising the sexy, powerful, healthy-seeming PWA, in defiance of a media saturated with images of decline and death. But it also functioned as an antidotal model negating the past and the present. To quote the character David, a gay man with AIDS, from my 1995 novel (written in 1993), *Rat Bohemia*, published before protease inhibitors became available:

"Everyone looks clean. Short hair, white T-shirt, clean jeans, pierced ear, collegiate. We're trying out for the Varsity Squad because clean boys don't have *it*. Only the dirty ones have *it*. So I'll talk to some wide-eyed young queen who went to Vassar or Brown, or some Euro-Trash passing in East Village drag. We look into each other's eyes, feel the heat pass between our pumped-up gym chests. We both know for certain that the other one's underwear is clean. For that moment I don't have it and neither does he."

And T-shirts played an enormous role in the movement. They not only united a look, a membership, a commitment, but also provided the first source of fundraising for the new organization.

Michael Nesline spoke about the role of the T-shirts and the united look associated with ACT UP: "The finance committee financed the manufacture of, I believe, six hundred buttons. And . . . they flew out of our hands at a dollar apiece . . . So didn't we want to make more? And didn't we want to make T-shirts for the upcoming Gay Pride Day Parade? . . . So, in the middle of this painful conversation about whether or not it's appropriate to make T-shirts, Larry Kramer jumps up and screams, *You sissies—people are dying, and you're talking about T-shirts.* So we just tabled that conversation and we took it on ourselves to make T-shirts. The Coordinating Committee just decided that we should make T-shirts. I actually believe that that's the only independent decision that the Coordinating Committee ever took. But we took that decision and we made the T-shirts, and we had a table at Gay Pride, where Karl Soehnlein and Alan Klein tabled, while the rest of us marched. And then, afterward, people took turns selling T-shirts from the table, until, by the end of the day, Larry Kramer had elbowed everyone out of the way and was thrusting T-shirts in people's faces and demanding that they buy them and was just thrilled that he's making so much money.

"And, I was thinking, *Larry, you big sissy, you're selling T-shirts and people are dying* . . . We did the demonstration at Wall Street. We got amazing coverage for that in *The New York Times* and on the local press. Of course, what the media was impressed by was the uniformity of our presentation. I mean, all of the posters are black posters with big pink triangles. It looked really organized. That was not a completely conscious strategy at that point. It quickly became a conscious strategy, because we realized that it worked, for the media." —Michael Nesline, ACT UP NY

The range of artistic strategies, venues, aesthetics, working styles, and intentions was as broad as any political movement in memory, yet each strategy functioned to cohere relationships, to express collectively, and to telegraph ideas about queer people and people with AIDS that transformed public comprehension and group self-understanding. In this way, the simultaneous production of art in varying modes created a counterculture of both opposition and attachments, rooted in a belief that change was possible. It can be said that the art of ACT UP created a new kind of person, one who was living with HIV (infected or not) and who could change the world. It reached for and confirmed power, both as self-perception and ultimately reality.

WHEN AN IMAGE LEADS A MOVEMENT: THE SILENCE=DEATH PROJECT
AVRAM FINKELSTEIN

Avram Finkelstein grew up on Long Island, where his mother was a research scientist. Like many post-Holocaust Jews, he was interested all his life in the question of silence. In high school, he made a lithograph of a quote: "Sheep, who die silently, are no use as victims." Avram went to art school and then became art director for Vidal Sassoon, cutting hair for twenty years. His lover, Don Yowell, first showed AIDS symptoms in 1980 and died in 1984.

Don was a musician and didn't have health insurance, and the first time he was too sick for his friends to cope with, they called an ambulance that took him to Bellevue, which had a well-deserved reputation as a snake pit. And it was horrible. The orderlies and hospital staff wouldn't bring him food in the room. They left it in the hallway. They wouldn't even pick up his trays when his friends put them back in the hall. The workers wore masks and gloves. There was blood underneath Don's bed from a previous patient, because the orderlies were too afraid clean it. Avram and his friends brought in cleaning supplies and cleaned the room. Don was terrified.

At dinner with his friends Jorge Socarras and Oliver Johnston, Avram and his group started talking about AIDS, and it became very obvious that they needed a place to continue this conversation, so the men decided to form a group. "We didn't know at the time, but we formed a consciousness-raising group." They weren't sure how big it needed to be, but they decided to start by each bringing a person the other people didn't know, and then to see what happened. The goal was to talk about issues of being gay in the age of AIDS. Chris Lione, Brian Howard, and Charles Kreloff joined, and from then on they met every week. Four of the members were graphic designers.

At the time, in 1986, there was a lot of construction in Manhattan as the transition from some still-shuttered businesses to high-gear gentrification was in play. Eighth Street was literally papered with posters, manifestos, and diatribes. Avram remembered this as a very vital way that people communicated in the street. He told his group that he would pay to create some posters if the others would split the cost of putting them up. Everyone agreed. Then for the next six months they tossed around ideas that eventually became the SILENCE=DEATH poster. Because they weren't sure what kind of political responses they were going to be calling for, but they knew it would have a radical bent, they decided that it would be better to be anonymous. This method and process mirror Maxine Wolfe's observation that when focused on action instead of theory, the theory will "emerge" as collaborators make active decisions and, through action, their values become articulated.

"As is typical with collectivity, it really is about tossing out a lot of ideas," Avram came to understand. In March 1986, conservative pundit William F. Buckley Jr. called for people with AIDS to be tattooed. So for a couple of weeks the group talked about what a poster responding to that might be. It seemed startling; the idea harked back to the Nazi concentration and internment camps, and it was controversial enough. They thought at first that this would be a good issue for a poster, but as they began to really look at it, they realized, *Okay, well, so it's a photograph of a tattoo on somebody's butt*. Okay, well, whose butt is it? Is it a man's butt? What about the women? Is it a white butt? What about people of color? The issues surrounding representation made it impossible for them to pursue. They realized it wouldn't be inclusive enough and discarded the idea.

ACT UP demonstration at Foley Square, Federal Plaza, June 30, 1987.
From left to right: Steve Gendin, Mark Aurigemma, Douglas Montgomery,
Charles Stimson, Frank O'Dowd, Avram Finkelstein
(Photograph by Donna Binder)

The collective thought politically about how to build a campaign and how to develop consciousness; it was a conversation with an imagined constituency, not just a one-shot deal. It was more about connection than simply expression. At first they had some poster ideas about a call to riot, but then decided "there would be no point in having a call for a political response that was that severe when there hadn't been the first levels of conversation that might lead to even developing a communal response, much less a radical one."

Knowing that the poster would be wheat-pasted on the street implied a series of responsible considerations to create the maximum impact. They decided that it would not be hand-wrought or manifesto-ish, and would not involve a lot of text because they would be competing in the public sphere for people's attention, and text is not attractive. They decided it would have to be an image. Then they agreed that in order to compete in an urban context during the height of Reaganomics, it had to look slick, to appropriate the voice of authority. They set very clear goals that then determined the means. At the same moment that they were trying to stimulate political activity within the lesbian and gay community, they wanted to seem threatening outside of the community. They wanted people to think they were more organized than they actually were.

"We had to figure out a way to define our space discretely with one poster, and that's how we ended up with black, to neutralize the context . . . So then we began the debate over . . . what abstract image will signal to the lesbian and gay community we're talking to them? . . . We talked about the lambda. We thought it was kind of antiquarian. Younger lesbians and gays might not even know what it was. We loved the labrys, but [it] wasn't specific enough and the men wouldn't know what it was. We talked about the rainbow flag. We *hated* it. It was ugly. It was too friendly and, I'm not going to lie, just too ugly. Then there was the pink triangle, which we also hated. We hated all of them. The pink triangle we hated because it intoned victimhood, obviously, but it seemed like it might have the most chance of being clear enough to the lesbian and gay community, more clear than the other images we were discussing that were abstract, and graphic enough to be intriguing, interesting, compelling to people outside of the community who didn't know what it was."

They turned the Nazis' downward-pointing pink triangle, sewn onto the uniforms of gay men in concentration camps, so that it pointed upward, thereby permanently connecting the AIDS crisis visually to the legacy of the Holocaust but at the same time subverting it.

Avram had read something in *The New York Times* about the silence of a community being deafening. Later, while they were tossing around ideas for the poster, they were trying to talk about the fact that there was no communal response. Avram said, "What about *Gay Silence Is Deafening?*" To which Oliver responded, "What about *Silence is Death?*" And then someone else said, "Oh, no, it should be *Silence Equals Death.*" And then someone else said, "We should use an equal sign." Avram summed it up: "It was literally that fast. It was four comments."

They hired an underground, Mob-controlled "company" to illegally wheat-paste three thousand posters on walls and wooden boards propping up on construction sites, on semi-abandoned billboard spaces in SoHo, the East Village, the West Village, Chelsea, Hell's Kitchen, and the Lower Upper West Side. They were looking for areas that were art-related so there would be a non–lesbian and gay audience who might be sympathetic. "Or, as we say in advertising, *influencing influencers.*" They chose the spring because in New York during the winter, street life dies down. So they decided on March. Coincidentally, this was within a few days of Larry Kramer's speech at the Gay Center on March 10, 1987.

Avram knew about Larry Kramer from reading the *Native,* and he'd read in the *Voice* that Larry was going to replace film director Nora Ephron, who was scheduled to speak at the Center but had canceled. So he said to the rest of the guys in the group, *Why don't we, instead of meeting at someone's house this week, go hear Larry Kramer speak? I don't really know, but he may have something to say, or maybe we might get to meet him and maybe we can exchange ideas. Why don't we go there?*

At his talk, Kramer said to the crowd, "Okay, this half of the room, stand up." And they did. He said, "You're all going to be dead within a year." That's how he began the conversation, and Avram found it to be a very compelling piece of stagecraft. Larry was extremely hostile and was holding everyone's feet to the fire. In the Center, that main floor had a very low ceiling, it was a very tight space, and there was no escaping it. There was no escaping how urgent Larry had made the situation.

MICHAEL NESLINE

Born in a suburb of D.C., Michael Nesline was living in the East Village, driving a taxicab, and running a nightclub called Limbo Lounge. His ex-boyfriend Joe Hollis got sick and Joe's family in Georgia told him that he could not come home. Michael invited Joe to come stay with him, for as long as Joe needed to. There were no medications for HIV at that time. Joe died, and Michael enrolled in nursing school.

Chris Lione, who was a member of the support group that later came to be known as the SILENCE=DEATH Group, told Michael that he had attended the talk at the Center that Larry Kramer gave. Chris said that there was going to be a follow-up meeting to that, and invited Michael to go along. So he attended the second meeting. There were about sixty people there, and the meeting was being facilitated by GMHC executive director Tim Sweeney. It was clear to Michael from the very beginning that Tim didn't really want to be facilitating, but that he felt under some obligation to do so. The thrust of the conversation was, *What are we going to do?* It seemed to Michael that what was established was *We're all really upset that this is happening to us,* and *It feels like it's happening in a vacuum,* and *We're being ignored, and we're middle-class white guys and we're not used to being ignored* and *What can we do to get what we want? And what we want is for other people to know what's going on, and we want* The New York Times *to write about it, even inaccurately. So we needed to draw attention to ourselves and to our problem. So we probably should have some kind of demonstration.*

Michael started attending every Monday, after that first meeting. And, very quickly, majority rule decided that Wall Street would be a really good place to have a demonstration. So everyone began to make plans for that. Avram Finkelstein, Chris Lione, Mark Simpson—those were the people Michael knew best. Eric Sawyer was there with his new boyfriend, Frank Jump. Michael Petrelis was there, Marty Robinson was there, Larry Kramer came to the follow-up meeting. Barry Gingell, who was the medical information officer at GMHC, was there, Michael Savino was there. In preparation for the first demonstration, it was decided that everyone needed to organize into working groups, and Michael agreed to participate with a group of people who were going to put together a fact sheet. They met at Barry Gingell's apartment. Steven Webb was Barry Gingell's roommate. And Steven stood in the corner, sort of scowling and skulking as five people tried to write one document.

Finally, Steven ended up commandeering the process to make it more efficient. And then, after that, he began attending the meetings.

AVRAM FINKELSTEIN

Avram recalled people suggesting blocking bridges and tunnels, going to the National Institutes of Health, the Food and Drug Administration, the health commissioner—all suggestions that ACT UP would eventually take up. A group met a few days later and started planning the first action at Wall Street about the price of AZT. They realized they had to tell everyone who they were. It was then that Steven Bohrer stood and suggested *ACT UP*.

MICHAEL NESLINE

"What I remember is somebody who looked like a flasher—someone who was in, like, a trench coat—stood up and said, *I've been sitting in my room for the last three years thinking that something like this should happen, and I've been trying to think of names for an organization that would do something like what . . .*"

AVRAM FINKELSTEIN

"*. . . I've always had this idea. I thought it would be great to name a group ACT UP, the AIDS Coalition To.* Well, he hadn't actually fully realized the acronym. I think he proposed it as the *AIDS Coalition To*. It was that he wanted it to say ACT UP, and I think it was actually hashed out as to what the *U* and the *P* would be, but it was what it was . . . As in any collective environment, there is a hierarchy. In this particular case, it was a hierarchy of urgency, and I think almost everything was made in deference to the dying, the sick or the dying. So the arguments that were most compelling were the ones that seemed time-sensitive, and they were the ones related to drug therapies. Ancillary to that were questions of access, but they came later in ACT UP, when people who were accustomed to organizing realized that you couldn't have the one without the other. It was the myopia of ACT UP to buy into the idea that if we could just get them to release the drugs, everything would be okay."

MICHAEL NESLINE

Michael remembered that Michael Savino, who worked as conductor James Levine's personal assistant, had real organization skills. At one of the early meetings, he stuck his head across a row at the Center and looked at Michael Nesline and said, *Tim Sweeney's not going to be here tonight, can you facilitate the meeting?* And Michael was like, *Sure, I can do that.* So he got up and started facilitating the meeting, and then, for the next nine months, was one of the main facilitators for ACT UP.

"It's just a skill, a talent that I was born with . . . the ability to listen to what people are saying and what other people are saying and look for the common thread and have the main conversation and what are, sort of, the sub-conversations that come under that and how to connect all those things together, without becoming too distracted. And how to cut off a distraction without making people feel alienated."

Right around this same time, somebody stood up and asked about the SILENCE=DEATH posters that had been appearing around town. Of course, the people who had made those posters were in the room, but nobody said anything that night. The next week, Avram stood up and said, *I'm one of the people that made those posters. Most of us are in the room. We talked about it after last week's ACT UP meeting, and we decided that we want you all to know that we made those posters and we want ACT UP to be able to use that poster and that image for whatever purposes ACT UP deems appropriate. So it's yours.*

AVRAM FINKELSTEIN

At some point it was suggested that the collective copyright SILENCE=DEATH so that it couldn't be copyrighted by somebody else, preventing ACT UP from using it. The image was never intended to be owned, and no one was ever prevented from using it. So Avram had to go to the floor and explain that they were copyrighting it, that the copyright didn't mean anything and ACT UP still could use it. "Well, they almost ate us alive." So Bill Olander, who was the curator of the New Museum, contacted ACT UPer David Meieran and said he wanted to offer ACT UP the window of the museum. David Meieran called Avram and said, *Bill offered the window, and I don't really want any part of bringing this to the floor*, because of how intimidating it could be to navigate art questions on the floor of ACT UP. So Avram replied, *Well, I don't personally know if I'm interested in this, because it is too art-specific, but it is actually a window, so it's a public space, and I think ACT UP should be made this offer. I'm not in a position to make that decision. I'll bring it to the floor.* And he did. That was the beginning of the gathering of ACT UP artists and activists to create the New Museum window, a group that subsequently decided to continue working together as Gran Fury.

GRAN FURY: ART DIRECTING A MOVEMENT

The best-known, but certainly not the only, art collective inside ACT UP, Gran Fury functioned as an affinity group that designed posters and art projects (which often became T-shirts) in conjunction with ACT UP actions. Their intention was to enhance public awareness of issues related to ACT UP campaigns in ways that simultaneously spoke to the art world. More than any other sector of the movement, Gran Fury was art-world-conscious; it applied for independent funding, and the collective moved into institutional spaces that were individually advantageous for some of those with art careers. At the same time, they were enormously influential on ACT UP's public face in communicating through the media to both the general public and to other queer people nationally and around the world who emulated and embraced Gran Fury's images. Without its visual message of sleek, defiant power, ACT UP would not have been as coherent as it was to the outside world.

TOM KALIN

Tom Kalin was the youngest of eleven children, raised in a Chicago Lithuanian/Irish Catholic "leftie" family. He moved to New York in 1987 at the age of twenty-five to do the Whitney Museum Independent

Study Program, where Gregg Bordowitz, Ellen Spiro, Ray Navarro, Alexandra Juhasz, Catherine Gund, Sandra Elgear, Robyn Hutt, David Meieran, and many other ACT UP members studied.

"It was the Whitney Program that opened the door to class-jumping, and it was the connections provided there that led, one way or another, to ACT UP. And then, certainly, ACT UP was a social melting pot for a lot of these things . . . Those places become breeding grounds, definitely, and ambitious people in those situations end up making connections and going places."

Amy Heard, from the Whitney program, brought Tom to ACT UP in September of 1987.

"You come in, it's like, the complete [community center] smell and vibe. The narrow, skinny hallways papered with all those leaflets of every single kind, *seeking roommates, substance abuse*—you name it—*size 12 pumps for drag queens*, everything. You go into the room. It's kind of a crappy room with linoleum floors—green and black, if I remember correctly—with white iron poles all through the room—long in shape. The axis of the room, instead of being stacked the long way, facing this way, was used in the wide way, so there's kind of a wide open—maybe ten seats deep, facing the front of the room. Maybe there was a teeny little thing you stood on, like a podium, but probably not. I doubt it. Certainly, there was no lectern or microphone or anything.

"And my first impression when I came in was, like, first of all— *Who are all these people?* Because it was such an incredible mixture, an impressive mixture of people. But also, it was like every fantasy I ever had of thirties New York, socialist, communist meetings. It was like, it reeked of it. It was like the sixties again. I was in *SDS! Oh my God.* It had that romantic whiff to it, because it seemed utterly urgent, completely improvised, totally responsive and nimble in that early stage, because it was a fairly small group of people—highly intelligent— terrifying to raise one's hand . . . My God, I was in a room where people were talking about AIDS openly and were not just terrified and checking their glands—that there was this ferocious and angry energy that was going to do something, *goddamn it*. So that instantly reduces your fear. I just felt a sense of community and a sense of calm and purpose, being there. And it was just irresistible."

MARLENE McCARTY

Marlene McCarty was born in Kentucky and grew up in a religious Christian environment with no art, no artists—she did not see a real painting until she was eighteen. She was most influenced by magazines and record covers and hoped to be able to grow up to design those kinds of products. She studied design at the University of Cincinnati and then in Basel, Switzerland, for five years. "Ninety percent of design is about making corporate ventures look fantastic. And that can be music or it can be banking."

In Europe she saw the political posters of Klaus Staeck, which helped her understand that "design could be used in a non-passive way—in other words, it could be used in an assertive or even aggressive way to make a statement, as opposed to just making somebody else's statement look nice." In 1983, Marlene moved to the East Village, into a derelict building on East Fifth Street, where her neighbor was artist John Lindell. She then met artists Donald Moffett and Felix Gonzalez-Torres.

LET THE RECORD SHOW . . .

In fall 1987, Lindell and Moffett were involved with a group of ACT UP artists creating the window exhibit for the New Museum in Tribeca. Marlene went to a meeting at the offices of architects Terry Riley and John Keenan. She met young filmmakers Todd Haynes and Tom Kalin and the other people working on a piece called *Let the Record Show . . .* The installation was built against a background photographic reproduction of the Nuremberg trials, with front pieces of tombstones for politicians actively hurting people with AIDS, like North Carolina senator Jesse Helms, the Catholic Church's Cardinal Ratzinger, and conservative pundit William F. Buckley Jr. The image/title relation implied the threat: that these people would be eventually be called to task as some Nazis had been at Nuremberg and made accountable for their lethal crimes against people with AIDS. In that sense, it would prove to be a utopian work, since no one was ever made accountable for the suffering and deaths of people with AIDS. The mainstream press coverage of highly public deaths and funerals of Ronald Reagan, George H. W.

Bush, and Jesse Helms did not mention their roles in oppressing people with AIDS and escalating the global death rates.

LORING McALPIN

Loring McAlpin's father was a Presbyterian minister in East Detroit and Princeton, New Jersey. The family inherited wealth from banking and had the freedom to make choices about how to live. After boarding school, Loring studied photography with Reagan Louie at the San Francisco Art Institute before completing his degree at Princeton. He heard about the window project *Let the Record Show* . . . and got involved just in time to help de-install the work.

"It was probably one of the very first events in the art world to focus attention on AIDS, certainly in a[n] explicitly political way . . . I think there are two things going on. One is the wish that there will be some final justice served. But I have to say, I think the other thing that's being expressed there is rage, and theatricality. So in a sense, I would say that was just as operative. And that served us well. I think it was—we were making a media campaign. And who knows how many people recognize the Nuremberg [trials]? And I think probably many people didn't even get that. Maybe the art writers got it, for *Artforum* . . . But for us, I think it matched the rage that we felt, and so it kept us engaged in it . . . I think we were more interested in rallying a broader attention to the whole epidemic, and getting a response, getting our needs met."

TOM KALIN

Tom's thesis show in Chicago was large, blown-up photographs taken mainly from World War II—many of them from the Nuremberg trials. He went to the first meeting for the New Museum window and heard someone say, *We need to make a giant picture of the Nuremberg trials.* And he jumped in, offering that he'd made photo murals, and was headed to Chicago the next day where he had the negatives they needed. So the relationship was fortuitous as the images of AIDS criminals and Nazi leaders quickly segued together. This was already in the air in part due to Larry Kramer's overt parallels between AIDS and the Holocaust, and reflected in the choice of the inverted pink triangle in the

SILENCE=DEATH Project. The group decided that they wanted to put these U.S. leaders on trial.

"We had . . . concrete slabs that had quotes of various officials—whether from the Reagan administration or international figures—who said particularly heinous things around AIDS and HIV. The quotes had to be cast in concrete. And, in order to do that, individual letters had to be cut out of quarter-inch rubber, and then glued, reversed backwards onto a sheet, and then concrete poured onto it and cast and pulled off. So every period, every comma, every *S* with all the loops had to be hand cut. So there were meetings after meetings of these cutting out of these insane rubber letters. There were so many parts to putting the thing together."

MARLENE McCARTY

"I literally was cutting letters out of rubber, to make those tombstones."

Tombstones were central images in ACT UP's work from then on, even though very few of our dead were actually buried in grave sites with stones. Assotto Saint and his lover Jan had prepared a grave site with a stone that said NUCLEAR LOVERS, but this was rare. At the FDA action, one affinity group did a die-in, holding up cardboard tombstones over their own inert bodies, which became a standard gesture at ACT UP actions. Some of these people holding prop tombstones would eventually actually die of AIDS. Most ACT UPers who died were cremated, and their ashes became symbols of our losses and despair, and then moved beyond the symbolic.

"That was the one time when we tried to do something ornate, and it didn't work . . . We were not about being in the rarified, contemplative environment. Not to say we didn't wind up there, but that was a goal—not to be there, but to be outside, where people might read some of these texts or images who would not necessarily go into an art gallery. So, given that as sort of a fundamental basis of, *We're going to be in the public*—I think that had a large effect on a kind of shying away from the contemplative image."

For Marlene, that inaugural piece in the New Museum window was not one of ACT UP's most successful. She felt that there were no clear messages. "It was a mess." So many people were involved, and everybody wanted to say something, but there was nothing that rose to the top. "It was just a lot of minutiae." Mark Simpson had a potluck dinner, after it was over, to try to coalesce people into continuing to do those kinds of projects. The collective was formed and called Gran Fury.

FOUNDING GRAN FURY

MICHAEL NESLINE

"I aspired to an artistic career without making art anyway, so this was like a ready-made art career for me. And it was stimulating. Douglas Crimp edited an issue of *October* magazine—and I didn't know who Douglas Crimp was from a hole in a wall, but he wrote an artistic justification for ACT UP's Gran Fury's display in the window. And he gave it his imprimatur, and his imprimatur made the art world comfortable with Gran Fury as an art entity. The art world wanted to do something about AIDS. Artists were dropping dead left and right, and the art world—which is, basically, a conservative world—didn't know what to do. So now they knew what to do. Here's this little Cinderella group that makes art that can't be sold, because it doesn't exist, and they'll give us money so that we can produce our art projects, which are actions, and the art world can feel really good about themselves, because they've now contributed to the AIDS crisis—to ending the AIDS crisis—and we can feel really good that we've taken their money. So we've used them, and we're not going to give them anything in return, because there's not going to be any art product at the end of it that can be re-sold and could accumulate in value. So our status as Cinderella was preserved."

TOM KALIN

They came up with the name Gran Fury, after the Plymouth automobile that the police department used as the undercover car during the late eighties in New York. They thought they were "being very clever," Tom said, because, as an anonymous public art group, they were an undercover agent, but the name also gestured toward a big anger—Gran Fury—except it didn't have a *d*. And at that stage, Gran Fury was not closed. A lot of people came in and out of that group at that early stage, including Anthony Viti, Todd Haynes, and Mark Harrington.

MARLENE McCARTY

Gran Fury never came together and said, *We're going to make art.* They had an entirely different mission. Their goal was "in as raw and rambunctious a way as we could" to get out certain messages that they felt were not reaching the mainstream world, which is why they adopted the mainstream look of advertising. More than art making, the purpose really was about wanting to engage discussion and bring issues to a head, or to at least put them out into particular spheres where people could engage with them.

LORING McALPIN

Gran Fury meetings tended to be weekly. They would be either at somebody's house or at their workplace. And they rotated around. After about a year and a half of an open group, there was a core group of about ten, and they decided to close ranks. When they were more closely aligned with ACT UP in an official capacity, they'd have to present their idea to the floor, and then 350 people would be weighing in. Loring found that in terms of group dynamics, seven to ten is really an ideal number. Because when a collective gets bigger than that, it becomes much more difficult to process. People who were locked out of Gran Fury resented the closure. And Loring understood that there were some people who really wanted to do the work and were not allowed to. But he recalled that the decision wasn't made lightly. "We certainly didn't do it to exclude anybody. And there was, for the people that were there, they were the people that had showed up consistently, and we included everyone who had done that over that initial-year period."

TOM KALIN

"Being in an anonymous collective was incredibly liberating . . . along with catching your eye—the core value of it was a political message—trying to challenge or provoke or incite the viewer . . . I class-leapt utterly.

The art world has been the absolute entrée in so many ways to rooms I never thought I'd be in. And, even perversely and complicatedly—and even divisively . . . but, in the moment of ACT UP and then subsequently, Gran Fury, and my literally first major recognition as an artist, was absolutely all around AIDS . . . The central tragedy of my life has also been the central jettison—it's that thing that has propelled me. It started my career. It gave me visibility, and I don't have much complicated emotion about that. I have always felt like I've been as truthful as I can be in my work and in my life. But I'm also not deaf to the weird paradox of that."

MARLENE McCARTY

Then money started to come to the group. It was a little money. And no, the members did not make any money from Gran Fury. "In fact, it was a negative financial investment." They did start to get some small grants or offers from people who were in the art world, like the Whitney Museum. *Why don't you do a piece for Image World, and we'll pay for the production?* In response, Gran Fury created a piece titled *Welcome to America: The Only Industrialized Nation Besides South Africa Without National Healthcare.*

"It had a baby on it. So we did that piece, but at that point in time we were still saying, *Okay, we'll do a piece in conjunction with your show, but we won't do a piece to be shown in the museum.* So what we did was, we did billboards around town. That was always an issue. There was always a lot of argument as these offers would come in. *Should we do them? Should we not? Are we preaching to the converted? Is there the potential that people who could actually benefit from some of this information, or from this discussion . . . will someone besides art-world people be able to see this work?* So that was always an argument."

TAKE DIRECT ACTION

PATRICK MOORE

Patrick Moore was born in Iowa, went to Carnegie Mellon, and moved to New York in 1984 with his lover, Dino. He worked at amfAR and at the Estate Project for Artists with AIDS.

Patrick and Dino were in a relationship that was supposedly mono-gamous. Except that both of them were having sex with other people, albeit with constraints. If Patrick was having anonymous sex, he never had anal sex, and usually, at the beginning, he tried to use a con-dom when he had oral sex. What he didn't realize was that Dino was HIV-positive, and Patrick was having unsafe sex with him. "So it was a very convoluted way of not really thinking about what AIDS meant." They felt fear and shame. Shame that they had a sexual relationship that wasn't the kind of relationship they thought they should have. They thought they should have a monogamous relationship, and yet they didn't.

"It was the 'elephant in the living room' syndrome, where it became more and more terrifying as we didn't talk about it. And also, as [Dino] began to exhibit symptoms, then it became just crazy. It was crazy. He lost thirty pounds in a year. And both of us knew what was happening, but we just couldn't bring ourselves to talk about it."

They were in Fire Island, enjoying a very drunken weekend. And Patrick remembered getting drunk, and they were going to have sex, when Dino said, *I have this spot on my ass, and I don't want to have sex with you until I know what it is.* It looked like a mole, but immediately Patrick knew what it was. He knew that it was Kaposi sarcoma. Finally, reality pushed over the top and they felt like they had to confront it.

"And it was a very confusing process, because he was quite sick, and I didn't appear to be sick at all. But we both went in to be tested . . . But my test results were lost. Dino's came back positive right away, which was not a surprise. But mine were lost for—it was a significant amount of time, like two or three weeks, where I assumed that I was positive and I actually told my job that I thought I was positive and that I didn't know what was going to happen . . . I had, the week before, started at the Alliance for the Arts as the director of the Estate Project for Artists with AIDS, and they were incredible."

Maria Maggenti took Patrick to ACT UP for the first time. And he went to it with a kind of obscure feeling about AIDS and the ne-cessity of doing anything about it. But he was fascinated with Maria and was infatuated with her and her world. Once he went, there was an immediate connection with the energy of that room and the people. Also, many of the artists he was working with at the time as public relations director at the Kitchen (a dance and performance space) were around ACT UP, people he liked and admired. "It was so beautiful, and I was just completely enthralled with these people who seemed to be so committed and were so cool and were so—they were just everything I wanted to be . . . I had been completely apolitical up until that point."

Patrick persuaded the Kitchen to let him hire artists to design their public relations materials. He wanted to hire Gran Fury to do a poster, one that would be wheat-pasted all over the city and then mailed out to ten thousand people. So he talked to Don Moffett from Gran Fury and met with them, and they produced a poster that was just a black sheet with white type that said WITH 42,000 DEAD, ART IS NO LONGER ENOUGH. TAKE DIRECT COLLECTIVE ACTION TO END THE AIDS CRISIS.

"And it just sort of changed my life, because for the first time, all of these things had been drawn together in my life. Art was drawn together with gay men who I kind of got and respected and responded to, and also this incredible sophistication. Because that was the thing about ACT UP, there were these incredible graphic designers and— you know, people who were very professional in their lives, and who brought with them that whole world that they had learned outside of ACT UP. So I think that was kind of what cemented my relationship, and I remember feeling very, very proud."

Unfortunately, the people at the Kitchen were extremely upset and angry. The back of the poster advertised which artists were performing there at the time, and a number of these artists felt like they had been co-opted into the message. Not that they necessarily disagreed with it, but they felt that it had been grafted onto them. The board of directors was very unhappy because the poster was saying that to be an artist is not enough, that it's not an active way to participate in the AIDS crisis, to simply make work about it. In the end, the conflict caused Patrick to resign. "That's kind of what ACT UP did for me, it raised the importance of AIDS so high, its effect so broad-reaching in my life . . . So there was just a tremendous amount of anger about that that I had never really felt before. Everything that seemed important before didn't seem important anymore."

LORING McALPIN

Gran Fury created the poster *Read My Lips* for ACT UP's Nine Days of Action, then made it into a T-shirt and later into postcards. The collective was doing its own fundraising efforts at that point. Loring remembers ACT UP contributing five hundred dollars, and he estimates that the work for the poster was done for under three thousand dollars, which was basically the printing costs. Donald Moffett was working in a graphic design studio, and he did a lot of the mechanicals for these projects on his off time.

TOM KALIN

For the Nine Days of Action, Tom remembered Gran Fury producing the poster *Men Use Condoms or Beat It.*

"That poster always made me uncomfortable. Must we have a large erection on that poster? The sex-positive people were like, *Yes, we must* . . . I also liked the version of the piece that was just text . . . Donald Moffett did the paste-up of the poster—'Read My Lips' if I remember correctly, it was a slogan that stuck in my head and I brought it to the meeting, and it was almost exactly parallel to Bush using *read my lips*—and it just leapt out. I was looking for aphorisms. I was in Barbara Kruger/Jenny Holzer mode. So—looking for these kinds of things. Then Mark Harrington, specifically—no, for sure, he's the one—brought the picture of these two sailors kissing, and I remember setting the type—Futura Ultra bold. Things would come together in that way. One, two, three people would be the kernel . . . The group would have these organic connections between people, that would—two, three, four—sometimes all ten or eleven or twelve—would talk, and then there would be smaller sessions where they would get pasted up. We would agree what we were doing, then we'd print them and post them."

As the art world continued to ignore AIDS, in some ways it satisfied its conscience by offering space to Gran Fury, creating more and more conflict inside the collective and inside the larger ACT UP about the question of careerism. There were other professionals who brought their skills and enriched ACT UP, like lawyers. But ACT UP lawyers worked for thousands of hours for free and did not have their careers enhanced. Most people's professional lives were obstructed by the time they gave and the sacrifices they made to ACT UP, but Gran Fury met a need within arts institutions to show that they cared. And Gran Fury's work deeply benefited ACT UP and raised visibility for AIDS issues, sometimes beyond the parameters of the art world. The one instance that was the most controversial along these lines was when Gran Fury was invited to the Venice Biennale.

THE VENICE BIENNALE

MARLENE McCARTY

One of Marlene's early jobs when she came to New York was working in the graphic design department of the Museum of Modern Art, and one of the curators she worked with regularly was Linda Shearer, who later went to Williams College to run their art museum. But that year, Linda Shearer was selected to be the American curator on the Aperto panel at Venice. And she called Marlene up and asked, *Would Gran Fury do something?* And she said, *If they do do something, I know these three granting agencies that I can help you get funds from, to fund the project.* So of course, Marlene went back to Gran Fury to ask—and there was a lot of back-and-forth. A few people were so mad that they wouldn't even consider going to Venice. They tried the approach they'd formulated for the Whitney—*We'll do a project, but we won't do it in the space.* But the curators turned that option down. Finally, Gran Fury decided they would do it because it was a big international stage—people come from all over the world to the Venice Biennale. And secondly, the Catholic Church was such an obvious target that they just couldn't let go of it.

"To be catty, Avram [Finkelstein] was the one who was most anti the project, and probably did the least amount of work, and refused to go to Venice. But everybody else kind of, eventually, came around. We called it *The Pope Piece*. And we had a big quote from the New York cardinal O'Connor talking about how safe sex was a lie, and that that would not protect you from AIDS. So we just basically reprinted this quotation from him under an image of the Pope . . . Then we had a parallel image, which was *AIDS Rears Its Ugly Head. Men Use Condoms or Beat It. AIDS Kills Women, Too*—because in the Catholic Church, they're so down on homosexuality that they were like, *If you're not homosexual, then you won't get AIDS* . . . We had just finished working on a piece which was about the CDC definition of AIDS, and how their definition of AIDS was so male-centric. Basically, women were showing up in emergency rooms and being diagnosed with pelvic inflammatory disease and being sent away with antibiotics . . . So it was in our heads, and it just kind of synced up."

Marlene recalled that Gran Fury did a number of pieces that were about women or involved women. But, thinking about the faces in the room, with the exception of Marlene herself, it was all male. *Why would they care?* In retrospect Marlene believes that it was a kind of "forced political correctness of just like, *We know we need to deal with these issues*." She felt that sometimes Gran Fury may not have been coming from a truly heartfelt place. The way the dynamic worked was that, oftentimes, things would be in discussion in ACT UP, and then that would kind of trickle down and be brought up in discussion in Gran Fury.

After so much argument about *Oh, it's going to be in this rarified art thing and nobody's going to see it except art people*, Gran Fury at the Venice Biennale wound up being a huge scandal because the people who ran the Biennale ultimately feared the work. They thought it was blasphemous. They thought they could not allow it to be mounted, because they feared that the Catholic Church would shut them down. They kept the piece in customs and wouldn't release it to Gran Fury for the opening, so the group staged a sit-in in the director's office. Finally, the Venetians decided to let the work out, and magistrates from the church came to judge whether or not it was blasphemous. If it was blasphemous—because Italy doesn't have freedom-of-speech laws—all of the artists faced going to jail. They had to gather at the Arsenale early one morning, before the show opened to the public. And the authorities brought in their tubes, unrolled the posters, and these men from the church walked around, examining the work.

As the only woman, Marlene worried that if they were arrested, she would be going to jail by herself. Finally, the magistrates reached a conclusion. They told the Biennale people, *Well, we don't know if this is art. We don't know if this very good art, but it's not blasphemous, so they can hang it on the wall.* So the work was hung. Marlene recalled that Gran Fury's goal was always to generate discussion, particularly to generate discussion in the real world. In Venice, they started out that week in arguments with the Biennale people, who responded, *Why should we put this up? We don't have AIDS in Italy. This is a New York issue. This is not our issue. We don't have any of these problems. People won't understand it.* But after the show, "every newspaper in that part of Italy, [including] the *Express*, had huge articles on AIDS" and how it was an undiscussed problem in Italy that people had to become aware of. The collective was overjoyed, because the work had now leapt out of that art-world exclusivity that they feared.

"I probably have to be honest and say that my affiliation with Gran Fury probably helped some of the galleries take notice of my work or me or whatever they take notice of, but the work wasn't the same kind of work. But I'm sure it did help me get my foot in the door with some of those art people."

FOUR QUESTIONS

TOM KALIN

At that point, anybody who had fewer than 250 T cells, and whose viral load was skyrocketing, usually was quite visible because of the side effects of the current medications, particularly facial wasting. Other visible side effects included neuropathy, the inability to walk, and Kaposi sarcoma in an exposed place of the body. There were few places where these people felt fully comfortable and welcomed. There was one piece that Gran Fury created, before they disbanded, that addressed the feelings and the core emotional values of people with AIDS. Mark Simpson and others were involved with a project called *The Four Questions*. It was a giant sheet of paper, and, printed very small, were these four questions: *Do you resent people with AIDS? Do you trust HIV-negatives? Have you given up hope for a cure? When was the last time you cried?*

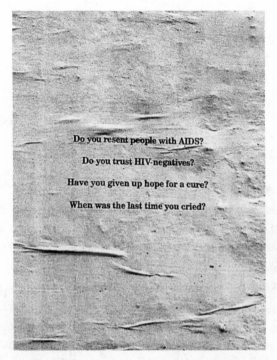

Gran Fury's *The Four Questions* poster (Courtesy of Gran Fury)

Robert Vázquez-Pacheco and Mark Harrington were involved with creating this poster, and they were both HIV-positive. It took a different direction than every other piece of work that Gran Fury had made. "It was plaintive and emotional and small-scaled and completely humbled and non-visual, almost to an extreme."

VINCENT GAGLIOSTRO

For Vincent Gagliostro, the point of the poster was to change the tactic of a message. The Gran Fury artists had decided that they didn't have any more statements to make, just a bunch of questions. The poster took a year. "Gran Fury got there through a lot of tears and a lot of sadness and a lot of fights and a lot of hurt feelings. It was a very, very emotional piece." They didn't know if viewers were going to write answers to these questions. They had no idea how it would be received. As usual, there was never a mechanism set up to gauge the results. There was no contact number.

"As any artist is always faced with, whether you're doing a political piece or painting, it's not yours when it's done. That has always been so easy for me. Because I am so not nostalgic about anything."

AVRAM FINKELSTEIN

"The forgotten part of the AIDS crisis, the thing that Gran Fury did not get to articulate, and, in fact, very few people were, was that there were actually people involved in this work and people who were traumatized, and while maybe the moment had passed to talk about, in wise rejoinders, in one-liners, the bigger issues, there was another big issue that was totally left off the table, and it was the trauma of it. That's what this poster was about . . . The poster was basically a big white sheet of paper with tiny, tiny text, so that you were forced to confront it. Scale is really essential to a message. The idea, the arrogance of the use of that space with its blankness, had the same arrogance of the blackness of the *Silence Equals Death*, but it had no rejoinder, nothing you could see from a car. You were forced into it, and it was incredibly hostile in that way, more hostile, and intentionally so."

Two of the four questions were in an HIV-positive voice or the voice of someone with AIDS, and two were in the voice of somebody who was HIV-negative. There was a tremendous amount of conversation at the time about the hierarchy of positive and negative. "It was in almost everything we did. I don't mean to intone that it was a secret undercurrent or a subtext." They were very candid. Gran Fury chose questions that were provocative. Avram remembered the meanings behind them:

- *Do you resent people with AIDS?* "We were giving voice to things that people weren't saying but we felt were clear. There were a lot of people, like younger people, who felt like they had been robbed of their own sexual history by the fact that people had behaved badly and now there was AIDS. That was part of what's in there, but there were other things as well."
- *Do you trust HIV-negatives?* "Because there were a lot of people with AIDS who didn't, who thought there was a subtext to their actions, who felt betrayed by them or insufficiently cared for on every possible level."

- *Have you given up hope for a cure?* "There were people who became so absorbed in the idea that you could treat it as *a chronic manageable condition*. The day I heard that phrase, I knew we were in for it . . . There's no money in curatives. There's money in medications for people who are sick. So the second that people agreed to the idea that it would be okay to continue to be sick, I realized that the entire dynamic had changed, the entire dialogue was changed, and that's what that phrase was about."
- *When was the last time you cried?*

Remembrance: Mark Simpson

TOM KALIN

Tom helped his friend Mark Simpson take his own life. Mark had tried to take protease inhibitors, but they didn't work for him. In 1996, he decided to take his life with an overdose of pills. He had had a devastating childhood in a very difficult family, with a schizophrenic mother "and very deeply bonded but damaged relationships with all the siblings." Tom spent the last week of Mark's life with him; he fed him caviar, because he'd never had it. They talked and just did everything someone could possibly do with their closest friend before they died. And then Tom stayed while Mark took the pills.

"Mark took his life, in part, because his body was conspiring against him, and he couldn't sit in his apartment in the afternoon and have sunlight in his face without him feeling like a vampire and feeling scorched. So the simplest things he enjoyed were no longer accessible to him. Mark took his life as much, though, for a profound sense of loneliness that no person could fill. I was never Mark's lover, but I was always really, really close friends with him, and no one can fill that space for another person. But God, maybe I could have tried more. And I feel like that's what was devastating—was that, Mark was always somebody who—you know, Mark never filed income taxes as an adult. Mark was an old-school, East Village type, who never had his career window open. By the late eighties and early nineties—Mark wasn't sexy in the way that he might have been in 1983. He was there and knew everyone to know, but he wasn't go-go eighties. He wasn't succeeding economically. And that's a drag to be around, maybe, while your careers and your lives are going in different places. And I'm not attacking anybody. I'm not criticizing really anybody.

"But I think people's lives went different places, and it wasn't missed on Mark, though, the kind of profound irony—that the place he felt most at home, the [places] he felt most embraced were in those meetings and were with ACT UP. The place that made him most able to fight against his own sense of being marked and being sick was what went on within Gran Fury meetings, and that those very people weren't able, as much as maybe they wanted to or as he wanted them to, be around—to visit him. Again, I have a very skewed perspective, because when a close friend is dying, you see every single minute, and every single day of it. And somebody else—two weeks go by, and it's a minute. *Oh shit, I need to see Mark. I need to call him.* And I know many people wanted to. I've had conversations with the people I'm close to who felt—who either thanked me because they were like, *You were such a good friend to him, and you carried such a burden for him.* And that's not how I saw it. There wasn't a choice. I loved him. He was somebody I wanted to be with as long as I could be with him. For me—and again, that's a very personal thing—that was painful to see."

After many emotionally difficult and exhausting days, Mark died in the middle of the night. Tom had to call the coroner's office and have Mark strapped to a gurney and brought down the stairs of his apartment building. Then Tom called Mark's family in Texas.

"So I'm tiptoeing around this whole, insane subject—the sister with whom I have the closest relationship, Linda, comes—and at the end of the time, she's like, *Do you think Mark took his life?* And I just collapsed into a bag of beans on the floor and said, *Yes, of course, Mark took his life, and God bless you for asking, and I was so afraid you'd never know.* She's a fundamentalist Christian, Baptist . . . Mark had described them and made them seem incapable of dealing with something that, sadly, they weren't incapable of dealing with. And that was something that really broke my heart the most about it. Linda was like, *Look, my husband died of cancer. If he hadn't died of cancer when he died, we were going to pursue euthanasia. He was going to take an overdose or take his own life, because he couldn't deal with the suffering.* She was just completely matter-of-fact about it. So I was devastated to think, *And he never knew this from his own sister.* What's the gap that would make you think that your own family couldn't, in this case—?"

Completely spent and depleted, Tom hauled himself home. It was a Sunday, and he showered and then sat down with the Sunday *New York Times.* There, on the front page of *The New York Times Magazine,* was a cover story by Andrew Sullivan. "I kid you not." It was Sullivan's infamous piece "When Plagues End," which Tom characterized as, *AIDS is over for white fags like me.*

"Andrew Sullivan embodies to me that kind of privilege. *Well, bully for you. You got the drugs. You're an upper-middle-class, white gay man, who has access and is connected in an urban environment and getting your hands on them and take them, and they work for you. Yippee, I'm so happy.* Now, what about all the other people who, for class, race, access—all those reasons—could not get their hands on the drugs? Why is the narrative of your life and your survival somehow more important or more interesting than all those other people? It's devastating. Then there's the personal kicker, which is, Mark Simpson got more or less slowly eroded away by a staph infection, which is one of those things that is just miserable and grisly and horrible. He tried to take the first wave of drugs and he could not tolerate them in any way, shape, or form. And watching your very best friend—it was like a horrible cartoon, where they're holding onto a rope, and then it's a series of ten strings, and then it's a piece of dental floss.

And then it's stretching, and then it snaps, and they fall and they're gone, while other people are climbing up and totally fine. It's just devastating. I was enraged, and it just seemed so brutally, brutally unfair."

MICHAEL NESLINE

Mark Simpson and Michael had an enormously disappointing separation. They had been very good friends before ACT UP ever even existed, and they had worked together in Gran Fury. When Mark learned that he was HIV-positive, all of the underlying tensions in their relationship, and the kind of caretaking that Michael had already resented in his relationship with Mark, came to a head, and Michael was unable to rise to the challenge. Mark felt rejected, and they had a very ugly falling-out. It marked a big change in Michael's personal life to no longer be part of Mark's world. Michael didn't miss him for a long time, and by the time he did miss Mark, too much time had passed to heal the breach. It had been assumed, initially, by both Mark and Michael, that Michael would be Mark's primary caretaker, and then because Michael "bobbled it so badly at the beginning," Mark refused him any access to his life at all, and Michael was relieved. And he is still relieved that he didn't actually serve that role in Mark's life.

"I don't know if it's indiscreet of me to say—Tom Kalin took my role up and Tom and Mark and I—by virtue of the fact that Mark had become Tom's roommate—the three of us had a sort of triangulated relationship anyway, and Tom, I think, understood that he was assuming a responsibility that would have been mine, except that I was unable to assume it for whatever reason. And so he did, and that I owed him, and that he was going to do what he could for Mark. And he did. And he knew that I was grateful to him for that. But all of this was in the realm of the personal. None of this was public."

ART BUSINESS

MARLENE McCARTY

Gran Fury did make a mark, but never once was the goal to have traditional art-world success. Marlene felt that they weren't about finding the form that's never been done. It was more, *Let's take what works, and make it happen and rip off everybody, and not make any bones about it.* Marlene actually met Barbara Kruger, one of Gran Fury's most fundamental influences, and Marlene told her, *You know, we owed you a lot.* And Kruger said, *I know, but I'm glad you did it.*

In a way, the reason Gran Fury got money to create a number of their projects was that people in the art world had guilty consciences about the whole AIDS situation. "So money was shuffled our way to sort of like, relieve their conscience, and let us do the dirty work." In a similar way, the critics shied away from trashing them head-on, because they knew that Gran Fury was never articulating that work as art. Marlene recalled that the collective was only concerned about making a dent in the AIDS crisis. "I think some of the people who might have been more critical of us as art makers were maybe just more dismissive of just like, *Oh, that's propaganda.* Which was fine. We claimed that. We were making propaganda."

Toward the end, Gran Fury's calling card was a very flat-footed approach to really blunt topics. After a number of years, the whole landscape of AIDS had changed so that it was more common to discuss AIDS and its complexities. "We kind of lost our ability to really refine that kind of activist punch. We spent so many meetings towards the end, trying to decide how we were going to transform . . . looking for these formats of being able to talk about more complicated issues, because you can't do that in two lines." Marlene realized that advertising is great for conveying basic concepts, but complex ideas could not be conveyed through advertising.

MICHAEL NESLINE

Eventually, Gran Fury reached a dead end, strategically. The issues became so complicated—the issue of treatment and the efficacy of one treatment over another—that they didn't lend themselves to snappy one-liners anymore. Michael recalls that the strategy became too difficult to constantly reach. The challenge "of coming up with another snappy one-liner to try to summarize every single issue, with all of its nuances and roll it all up into a tight little ball that was completely packed, but packed so well, that each word meant something that you could, like, understand what each single word meant," no longer felt feasible. And so the artists started to have conversations about how they could restrategize.

MARLENE McCARTY

One of the things they tried doing toward the end was actually collaborating with other groups. They tried do a Guerrilla Girls collaboration. "They came to the meetings in those fucking gorilla heads. We were like, *How do we work with people who are in gorilla heads?*" They had a number of meetings, but it went nowhere. Then they decided to work with Prostitutes of New York (PONY), with Annie Sprinkle and the late Diane Torr, but that also wasn't fruitful. They did all come to a crucial awareness that the way they were working or had been working was no longer effective, and they had no desire to peter out while becoming more and more ineffectual. And in 1995, they finally disbanded.

"We kind of had no desire to die that death—of just becoming more and more incoherent. So actually, the thing that kind of brought it to a head . . . was some art institution around town invited us, yet again, to participate in a show. And we were just like, *We can't, we can't.* Then what we decided to do was to write a statement. I think it was a pink slip . . . There were about four people involved, who wrote a very succinct little statement about like, *We did our thing, it's time to go, we don't exist anymore.* And I think at the end, there was a very sweet goodbye. From that point on, the majority of us were like, *Gran Fury does not exist anymore. We did it, it's over, it's done.* There were a couple of people who then did try and do a couple of other projects—like, sort of revive it—but I think there were a couple of attempts, and then it just died out. But, for the most part, we all just decided it was time. It was done, we did our thing, and now we had to go figure out what else to do with our lives."

I HATE STRAIGHTS

I HATE STRAIGHTS

by Anonymous Queers (David Robinson, Maxine Wolfe,
Heidi Dorow, Vincent Gagliostro, Tracy Morgan)—
Distributed at Gay Pride, June 1990

I have friends. Some of them are straight. Year after year, I
see my straight friends. I want to see them, to see how they
are doing, to add newness to our long and complicated histories, to experience some continuity. Year after year I continue
to realize that the facts of my life are irrelevant to them and
that I am only half listened to, that I am an appendage to
the doings of a greater world, a world of power and privilege,
of the laws of installation, a world of exclusion. "That's not
true," argue my straight friends. There is the one certainty
in the politics of power: those left out of it beg for inclusion,
while the insiders claim that they already are. Men do it to
women, whites do it to blacks, and everyone does it to queers.
The main dividing line, both conscious and unconscious, is
procreation . . . and that magic word—Family. Frequently,
the ones we are born into disown us when they find out who
we really are, and to make matters worse, we are prevented
from having our own. We are punished, insulted, cut off,
and treated like seditionaries in terms of child rearing, both
damned if we try and damned if we abstain. It's as if the prop-
agation of the species is such a fragile directive that without
enforcing it as if it were an agenda, humankind would melt
back into the primeval ooze. I hate having to convince straight
people that lesbians and gays live in a war zone, that we're surrounded by bomb blasts only we seem to hear, that our bodies and souls are heaped high, dead from fright or bashed or
raped, dying of grief or disease, stripped of our personhood.
I hate straight people who can't listen to queer anger without
saying "hey, all straight people aren't like that. I'm straight
too, you know," as if their egos don't get enough stroking or

protection in this arrogant, heterosexist world. Why must we take care of them, in the midst of our just anger brought on by their fucked up society?! Why add the reassurance of "Of course, I don't mean you. You don't act that way." Let them figure out for themselves whether they deserve to be included in our anger. But of course that would mean listening to our anger, which they almost never do. They deflect it, by saying "I'm not like that" or "Now look who's generalizing" or "You'll catch more flies with honey . . ." or "If you focus on the negative you just give out more power" or "you're not the only one in the world who's suffering." They say "Don't yell at me, I'm on your side" or "I think you're overreacting" or "BOY, YOU'RE BITTER." They've taught us that good queers don't get mad. They've taught us so well that we not only hide our anger from them, we hide it from each other. WE EVEN HIDE IT FROM OURSELVES. We hide it with substance abuse and suicide and over achieving in the hope of proving our worth. They bash us and stab us and shoot us and bomb us in ever increasing numbers and still we freak out when angry queers carry banners or signs that say BASH BACK. For the last decade they let us die in droves and still we thank President Bush for planting a fucking tree, applaud him for likening PWAs to car accident victims who refuse to wear seatbelts. LET YOURSELF BE ANGRY. Let yourself be angry that the price of our visibility is the constant threat of violence, anti-queer violence to which practically every segment of this society contributes. Let yourself feel angry that THERE IS NO PLACE IN THIS COUNTRY WHERE WE ARE SAFE, no place where we are not targeted for hatred and attack, the self-hatred, the suicide—of the closet. The next time some straight person comes down on you for being angry, tell them that until things change, you don't need any more evidence that the world turns at your expense. You don't need to see only hetero couples grocery shopping on your TV . . . You don't want any more baby pictures shoved in your face until you can have or keep your own. No more weddings, showers, anniversaries, please, unless they are our own brothers and sisters celebrating. And tell them not to dismiss you by saying "You have rights," "You have privileges," "You're overreacting," or "You have a victim's mentality." Tell them "GO AWAY FROM ME, until YOU can change." Go away and try on a world without the brave, strong queers that are its backbone, that are its guts and brains and souls. Go tell them go away until they have spent a month walking hand in hand in public with someone of the same sex. After they survive that, then you'll hear what they have to say about queer anger. Otherwise, tell them to shut up and listen.

MEAT/CLIT CLUB—ART POSITIVE

Nightlife, when run by ACT UP members, became an influence on and an extension of the activist/community group relationship. Queer people need one another for love and sex, and so we will always try to find one another. Facilitating this need with care was the creation of group experience, one that was participatory, visual, ritualistic sometimes, cathartic other times, aural, sensual, and designed.

MEAT

ALDO HERNÁNDEZ

Aldo Hernández was born in Cuba and grew up in Corona, California. While living in Long Beach, California, in 1982, he would nude model with a man he was seeing.

"He had some spots on his ass and his legs. And I just thought it was funny that he had this big, kind of purple lesion spot on his ass, and I used to joke about it to him. I said, *Well, you know, when you go modeling, you're going to have to put something on that* . . . I don't know how much he really knew, because he died later in 1988. But I just remember that. And then, years down the road, seeing the same thing when I started seeing KS lesions and realizing, *Oh, it's the same look.*"

Aldo worked on a cruise ship, and then came to New York and got a job in 1986 at the Museum of Modern Art (MoMA) as a development officer working on fundraising. A lot of his friends were positive or sick, and he wanted to do something, so he went to ACT UP. For the first three years he worked for the arts administrators Creative Time and was involved in financing Gran Fury's *Kissing Doesn't Kill* campaign. Then in 1990, he started deejaying.

AIDS contributed to dramatic changes in nightlife and the club scene. In New York, the bathhouses were closed by order of city hall. Gay dance clubs associated with the clone generation, like the Saint, shut down as clients and staff died of AIDS. Some people isolated and became afraid of sex, socializing, and partying. Others went full force in the other direction. Public or backroom sex was both contested and embraced. "There seemed to be a division between the people that thought it was fine to do what you wanted to do. And some people started to feel that it was kind of hedonistic to just go out."

The lesbian nightspot the Clit Club, on a desolate strip of far West Fourteenth Street, started to share time with Aldo's men's party, called Meat. It was the Clit Club on Fridays and then Meat on Saturday. The idea was a place where queers of all races could go that wasn't expensive. It was five dollars, and people could have a good time being themselves, being out. He wasn't trying to run a sex club, but Aldo would put condoms in the bathroom, on the bar. Customers weren't supposed to use them on-site. But at the same time, Aldo felt obligated to provide them since he was creating a quasi-sexual environment. "So it was really just kind of an odd combination. Because once you introduce a condom . . . we realized that there had to be somebody watching it or it could be out of bounds."

Because Meat and Clit Club were both run by ACT UP members, there was a lot of spillover from the ACT UP rank and file. One of the ways that sexual equality between positives and negatives was maintained was through condom use, or "safe sex," especially when there were no effective treatments and many people didn't get tested or know their status. For the first few years of ACT UP safe sex was de rigueur, but then it started to break down, in part from AIDS exhaustion. When unsafe sex happened at Meat, ACT UP felt implicated.

"This is in '90 then, when I started doing the party. And it became kind of an issue for some people, because the problem was *Well, are people having unprotected sex?* Unsafe sex . . . I was the first one to find myself at four in the morning, going, *What am I doing back here, doing this?* And I immediately realized that this is not going to work if I don't do something here . . . It actually evolved over months, where we were like, *If there's people making out here, then why don't we just kind of make sure we have somebody watching the situation, without stopping it. But we're not going to have sucking and fucking here.*"

Aldo hired a series of monitors. Oral sex and anal sex weren't allowed at Meat, but things did happen. Then one Monday night, at the ACT UP meeting, somebody got up and denounced Meat on the floor, accusing Aldo of tolerating unsafe sex. He heavily contested the charge, especially because he'd never seen the accuser in his club. *I know you wouldn't pay to come in. So what you're hearing is hearsay,* while conceding the possibility that something might have happened "for a minute and it was taken care of." The tension over unsafe sex was new at that time of condom fatigue, and frustration over the feeling of the inevitability of infection. But Aldo really had a harm reduction approach to sex.

"Instead of saying, *I can't be sexually active, or I can't have my life, or I can't go out, or I can't go to a club or a bar,* it was more like, *How do we do this better?* And, how do we do this right? And, like Ray [Navarro] and myself would go La Escuelita [an iconic Latino drag bar] and hand out condoms . . . You had to find a waiter or waitress . . . who was sympathetic with our cause, and then they would put them on the drink trays and give it to people . . . So in order to break through that custom, and create a whole new environment where it's okay to bring the condom or other safe sex protection into the equation, you have to introduce it, and make so it doesn't become suspect—like somebody's got something that's dirty or bad to hide."

ART POSITIVE

ALDO HERNÁNDEZ

Bill Olander curated a show at the New Museum in 1989, and the artist Mark Kostabi was not included. Responding in *Vanity Fair*, Kostabi said, "These museum curators, that are for the most part homosexual, have controlled the art world in the '80s. Now they're all dying of AIDS, and although I think it's sad, I know it's for the better. Because homosexual men are not actively participating in the perpetuation of human life." Then Kostabi told the *Post*'s *Page Six* that gay men dominate the art world and "that's why there's so much bad art in the world."

Aldo felt that there was a lot of resentment against gay men in the art world. And a number of others agreed. So a group of people from the AIDS community who worked with artists or were involved in that scene decided to create an organization, ART Positive, to advocate for people with AIDS in the art world and to push that world to be more open about HIV. Starting as a committee in ACT UP, ART Positive advocated for a demonstration about the censorship of the late photographer Robert Mapplethorpe that was going on at the Corcoran Gallery of Art in Washington, D.C., and to remove the censorship of artistic content "that was beginning—which now has come to fruition. Forget about getting any funding from the government if you have anything to say that has any sort of upward, up-front, sexual, political, AIDS-related agenda. And I saw it coming very clearly then, and the division lines remain."

Most art making, like activism in ACT UP, did not advance the maker professionally. In ACT UP, "people were warriors on the front lines, and it wasn't something that people went and got medals for." Aldo was moved by how many ACT UPers were such hard workers, and how they came from so many walks of life. As many people have recollected, in ACT UP it was unusual to know more about someone than what they did in the movement. Often we didn't know each other's last names or professions. "Your validity there in ACT UP was based on your work there, not on anything else . . . We just did the best we could. And really—people from all walks of life. And that's something that's just so amazing—that that can happen."

LOLA FLASH

Lola Flash was born in Montclair, New Jersey. There was a large Black middle-class community there, with a strong educational system in which both of her parents were teachers and her mom became a principal. Every Saturday, if she wasn't in some class, Lola would go to a crafts store. She was interested in making all kinds of thing: boats, model cars, velvet paintings. As soon as she wanted a camera, her parents bought her one. They built her a darkroom. After high school, Lola went to Maryland Institute College of Art in Baltimore. And again, her parents were really supportive. They paid for the whole thing.

When she came to ACT UP, Lola got involved with ART Positive. She was part of Ray Navarro's care team at the hospital, and she was in a relationship with Julie Tolentino, cofounder with Jocelyn Taylor of the Clit Club. Lola was making a lot of flyers for ACT UP–related nightlife, working for club promoter and ACT UP media person Chip Duckett. Lola and Julie would go from the clubs to Ray's hospital room for the 4:00 a.m. shift. Then Lola and Julie ended up in the Gran Fury shoot for *Kissing Doesn't Kill*, and their relationship was memorialized forever on a classic ACT UP T-shirt.

"Julie and I had kind of just started going out with each other, so, for that time period, it was nice to have that represent us, plus to be able to go national, and be serving a larger cause . . . At the time, I worked in the Bronx, [and] I used to be standing there, waiting for the bus to come, and there is my big old face on the side of the bus. And no one knew it was me. And . . . now, the younger generation have no idea that that's who, that I'm the girl on the poster. So it only has a certain amount of fame time. But I think that—those people who . . . have done a lot of art history . . . they know about it. So it's kind of cool. I've done a few things where I've talked to younger students, and they're like, *Oh yeah, you're that girl. That's kind of interesting.*"

Gran Fury was mostly "boys." It was mostly white. And while Lola appreciated their work, ART Positive was where she contributed more art ideas. She recalled that it had been started because of the need for people of color in the movement to have more input, and to do so in an artistic way. "For me, one of my favorite parts about ACT UP was that whatever your specialty was, that that's what you were able to do."

THE CLIT CLUB

LOLA FLASH

Lola was in a relationship with Julie Tolentino when Julie and Jocelyn Taylor started the club. Lola was head bartendress, "with my boobs hanging out, and some kind of S/M-gear-looking thing on." And Aldo started off being the DJ.

"There was just so many types of women: sizes, colors, races, ages . . . The music was great. And as the years went on, it just became this institution for women who were coming out . . . Julie helped create this really happy, I think, loving community."

The Clit Club was the first lesbian bar in New York that wasn't racially segregated and didn't have racial profiling at the door, and probably the first that wasn't involved with the mafia. And because Julie, Jocelyn, and Lola, three women of color, and Aldo, a Latino gay man, were also in ACT UP, it brought in a political crowd as well as just dykes looking to socialize in a women-of-color-positive environment without racist pressure.

"Girls went there knowing that it was going to be a more open environment. If you're going there feeling like you're going to be ripped off at the door, or interrogated, then you're going to go there feeling sort of defensive. But if you're going to go there feeling like this is a place that's going to invite you, you're going to go with a nicer feeling. And that's why, I think, once everyone was in there, it was a happy feeling. It started off being happy. You start off from home, when you're getting ready, knowing that you're going to a family affair, in a way . . . Julie has a very magical way of just making things flow together, from the way she made the club look, to moving things from here to there."

Lola and Julie used to bring their own TV and their VCR from home to the club. Their home and business merged into one entity; their home answering machine would often have thirty messages on it. They were young, with a lot of energy for the community they were building and the culture they were enriching. "I suppose when your friends are dying it's not very easy to get tired; it keeps your momentum going."

THE ASIAN PACIFIC ISLANDER CAUCUS: ACTIVISM, ART, AND PERFORMANCE

Although it didn't bill itself as an art collective, ACT UP's Asian Pacific Islander Caucus did a combination of traditional activism and imaginative, performative organizing, sometimes with theatrical or display elements. Two of the main organizers, Lei Chou and Ming-Yuen S. Ma, both had art backgrounds.

MING-YUEN S. MA

Ming went to a semiprivate religious school in Hong Kong followed by three years in a boarding school in Connecticut and then to Columbia. His first two years in college, he didn't go to classes very much. Instead, Ming mostly hung out in the East Village in the clubs with drag queens, "being fabulous—no time for sex." In an artist's residency at Skowhegan he met John Tucker, who used to be the manager at the Pyramid Club. They became friends. John told Ming that his lover had died of AIDS. And then, through him, Ming met a whole group of queers, gay men, gay women, and artists, some of whom were people with AIDS.

On December 1, 1990, the second annual World AIDS Day, Ming met the guys from ART Positive, and felt a direct connection. He decided that when he graduated, he wanted to work with them. That was his last semester, and he soon started going to their meetings. Ming's roommate, Ken Chu, was also in ART Positive. Through those relationships, he started going to the larger ACT UP meetings. ACT UP allowed him to transform his personal anger into something that was collective, "to actually get off your ass and do something about it."

Most of what Ming did with ACT UP New York was through the Asian Pacific Islander AIDS activists' caucus. There were very few Asian Pacific Islanders in ACT UP at the time. But some of them were very visible activists in leadership positions, like Lei Chou. At the same time, when the API Caucus became active, there also was a resurgence of activism among the larger lesbian and gay Asian Pacific Islander community in New York. Groups like Gay Asian & Pacific Islander Men of New York (GAPIMNY) were growing. There was a revitalization of Asian Lesbians of the East Coast (ALOEC). AIDS activism had sparked a new energy that was happening in the community. Those activities included the formation of the first AIDS agency that catered to APIs in the tristate area, Asian & Pacific Islander Coalition on HIV/AIDS (APICHA). And Ming was involved with setting it up.

"I think that queer APIs of my generation—we are probably more privileged. We have examples, like ACT UP and Queer Nation—even though these are predominantly white organizations, in terms of just how the energy and the tactics of these organizations was very markedly different from what was available, which was set up by older generations at the time—which are more subdued and more, sort of social . . . The energy, the stance, the tactics of ACT UP—the image of ACT UP was influential in that sense, but it's complicated, because I think also one of the things I remember about us being involved in ACT UP is race politics, which was a very—especially towards the end—was a very divisive issue. I mean, there's always a problem there, but I think as more people of color decided to join and as the pandemic itself transformed, that it really became a very big problem and so part of being in API Caucus was also negotiating those issues—sometimes on a personal level, and sometimes on an organizational level."

Some of the principal activists were Ming, Lei Chou, Yukari Yanagino, Lisa Stur, and Kathy Chou. It was a very small group. People would come and go, and the membership never got huge.

"I mean, it's kind of terrible because, like, whenever we see a new Asian at ACT UP meetings—and we spot them, too . . . we try to involve them . . . people coming in to check it out, and I think we kind of scared them . . . They were Asian gay men. And they probably came to ACT UP meetings because, hey, ACT UP had sexy gay white men in little cut-off denim shorts and combat boots, getting arrested. That's probably the main draw. That was probably part of the draw for me, too. I mean, you know. And to then—to go to the meeting, you're completely nervous. You're a person of color in this huge room full of angry white people, right? And then to be approached by these crazy Asian activists—I think that might be a little much."

At the time there was no culturally specific AIDS education targeting Asian Pacific Islanders in the tristate area. And so a lot of the work of the API Caucus was not focused on demonstrations. Instead, its members went to the GMHC and to the Board of Health, trying to get across that there was a great need for materials with cultural specificity, which is much larger than language. It was about approach, modes of address, and who was doing the educating. At the height of the AIDS crisis, the New York AIDS Hotline had a single Asian-language speaker. The API Caucus of ACT UP knew that among Asian Pacific Islander gay men, many were closeted and didn't feel comfortable talking about their status. What if their families found out?

"We worked with one of the bars—*rice bars*, that supposedly catered to gay Asian men . . . Club 52 . . . a transposed version of what happens in, say, Thailand or the Philippines. It's essentially sexual tourism. Non-Asian gay men—predominantly white—who are interested or who have a sexual fetish for Asian men—for sort of the typical orientalist reasons—go to these places to pick up guys . . . 52 was kind of unique . . . The owners were gay, it was Asian owned, and they were pretty open to us doing some work there. So we started out handing out information, but towards the end, we actually did these club-event-type things there. I remember, one time, we did this whole drag show kind of club thing, and we used it to hand out information. So it was kind of fun for us, too . . . Instead of giving them a brochure, we put the information in these red packets, which were sort of lucky money that you get during Chinese New Year or Lunar New Year. That's one example, right? It's kind of cute, it's kind of—it's disarming, right?"

In 1990, the API Caucus helped organize a national conference on people of color, AIDS, and HIV at Hunter College. People came from the Gay Asian Pacific (GAP) HIV Project: Steve Loo, Paul Shimasaki, Martin Hiraga from Washington, and Kyoshi Kuromiya, who was from ACT UP Philadelphia. The money came from ACT UP. Yet even with community building and working with other organizations, the API Caucus's work often came back to art making.

For World AIDS Day in 1990, they did a window installation for Art in General, a nonprofit alternative art space, located in what used to be the Chinatown/Tribeca border, at 79 Walker Street, where Ming had worked. At the street level they had a window for artists to build installations and displays. They actually created a project that addressed the Chinese gay community, living inside the Chinese immigrant neighborhood in Lower Manhattan. The piece was focused on AIDS and HIV. At the time, Art in General did not have much of a connection to the local community. The API Caucus imagined an audience of neighborhood and working people who might just pass by on the street and see their display. Because of this approach, the artists did not have a conduit to measure the reaction—beyond the knowledge that it was available to be seen by implicated passersby. It was three windows on two sides, containing a scroll-like painting with written information in Chinese, but in calligraphy. And then in the center, there was a light box. Half of it was an image of Guan Yin, a Buddhist goddess of mercy, very much invoked in relation to hardship and disease. Below her were paper cutout images illustrating how to put on a condom, how to clean works. All this in a public space. In the background were little shadow puppets showing the same kind of activity. The artists were playing with the public and private division—how these issues are desperately relevant to the community but are often hidden—and presented in a culturally specific, folk-art manner.

ACTION TOURS

Although extremely visual, Action Tours was both an art collective and a direct-action affinity group that was theatrical and zap-oriented. Its members were never involved with institutions, nor did they seek arts funding. Their images usually were accompanied by some kind of performative action using their personas as tourists. Less interested in building orderly, consequential campaigns, they most often chose the theme of sounding the alarm of emergency about the AIDS crisis. And they enacted this through almost two hundred actions.

JAMIE LEO

Born in West Union, Iowa, near Amish country, where his father was a dentist, Jamie Leo went to the Iowa Writers' Workshop and was exposed to Kurt Vonnegut and Tennessee Williams. Then he attended the Iowa Theater Lab with Richard Schechner and Polish director Jerzy Grotowski, whose idea that "art's capability is to effect profound change in people" felt "just as beautiful as it can be." In 1977, Jamie and his boyfriend moved to Christopher Street, where Jamie got a job running the follow spot for Ntozake Shange's *For Colored Girls Who Have Considered Suicide/When the Rainbow Is Enuf* at the Public Theater for ninety dollars a week.

JAMES WAGNER

James Wagner was born in Muncie, Indiana, to a Republican family with ninety-five first cousins, many of whom were priests or nuns. When he joined ACT UP, James had never been in a gay march or any kind of demonstration beyond an event for architectural preservation.

With Action Tours he helped organize a "blood-in" at the New York State Senate. Since it was going to be very difficult for activists or protesters to get into the government building, James and some others decided they could pretend to be somebody else. Eventually, this became the modus operandi of the group: to use disguise or to pretend to be part of the target in order to move freely into spaces that would be off-limits to activists. Their other gimmick was to pretend to be part of an organized tour. And so they had little plastic nameplates with name cards affixed to their clothing. They also prepared leaflets, flyers, and theater blood. The idea was "The state has blood on its hands."

The action started at the top of the grand staircases at the statehouse. There were about ten ACT UPers participating. They dressed pretty conventionally middle-class, drenched themselves in theatrical blood, and started running from the top of the stairs down, all the way through the bottom, and out the front door, where there was a rally already and everybody was chanting. They had thrown the police off guard quite quickly and kept moving fast. No one got arrested because of the blood. The police didn't know whether it was real or not. This began a pattern that they repeated in one form or another for the next few years.

"Jamie is pretty good at theatrics. So I think he did that even more than it was really necessary . . . The costume varied from something like suits—which is the most common—to tuxedos and gowns, which was very difficult for the women. Most of the women didn't have any access to gowns or even have any familiarity with wearing them, at that point. So the guys would help out. And that's what we did. We would basically get into banquets . . . I remember a Police Athletic League meeting."

JAMIE LEO

They also had a blood-in at the White House, which several people from the Catholic Left Plowshares movement helped them plan. The Berrigan brothers, radical Jesuit priests, were their teachers. About twelve members of Action Tours stood in line for hours to get inside the White House. They took a tour and then, while still inside the White House, they held a blood-in. They would always have the press in place, so that as they were leaving the White House, covered in blood, there was the photo! The news story became that AIDS activists emerged from the White House bleeding.

One of their standard props was "The Faceless Bureaucrats"— zombie-eyed masks that they would don for public hearings.

FACELESS BUREAUCRATS

JAMES WAGNER

"I remember we did that a few times. It worked very well."

Governor Mario Cuomo had an office in the World Trade Center. ACT UP had been constantly attacking Cuomo for not doing enough, even though sometimes he did say the right thing. But his office provided no leadership for AIDS funding, or simple AIDS awareness. On April 22, 1991, Action Tours decided to go to the World Trade Center plaza, because they couldn't actually get into the building itself or the governor's office. It was lunchtime and they dressed in suits and wore masks that said FACELESS BUREAUCRAT. These were plain masks, basically just ovals with holes for eyes. Jamie would print them and put them together with glue. They each carried signs like lunch boards against their chests, hanging around their necks on a string. Each sign presented an excuse: IT'S NOT MY FAULT, I DIDN'T KNOW ANYTHING ABOUT IT. NOBODY TOLD ME ABOUT THE OVENS, another ACT UP reference to the Holocaust. They used various forms of strong language, as though the bureaucrats had no blame, or couldn't imagine having any blame, either before or after something was done. And it attracted attention and got lots of media coverage.

THE *SATURDAY NIGHT LIVE* ACTION

JAMIE LEO

Then there was the night of April 11, 1992, when Action Tours zapped *Saturday Night Live* to protest the film *Basic Instinct*, which they felt relied on clichéd false images of gay people as predators that contributed to the hostile cultural conditions for people with HIV. By copying passes, they got backstage, hanging out at the commissary, snacking away, and acting like they belonged there. Just as the film's star, Sharon Stone, began her monologue, Action Tours burst through the doors shouting, "Fight AIDS, not gays," and set off marine whistles. They spent that Palm Sunday weekend in the Manhattan Detention Complex, aka the Tombs.

Once, Action Tours covered city hall with a banner that said HALL OF SHAME. "All it needs to do is be there for ten minutes, for you to get your photos of it and start to disseminate that image." Action Tours joined clinic defense for women seeking abortion and assisted the affinity group Church Ladies for Choice, a mostly drag a cappella choir.

CHURCH LADIES FOR CHOICE

ELIZABETH MEIXELL

Born at the end of the Second World War, Elizabeth Meixell came to New York to learn secretarial skills at the Katharine Gibbs School. She worked as a secretary at the World Trade Center, and then saw a flyer on Fourteenth Street about a demonstration about abortion rights. The *Webster* decision on July 3, 1989, brought her together with a lot of women downtown, and they walked up Broadway to Union Square.

"In the group were all these cute little guys in spandex, pink spandex, and they laid down in Fourteenth Street, which was shocking, and so did I. They had to help me up. I wore my pink polyester and patent leather shoes. Then these same young men came on bus trips with us to Washington [D.C.] for abortion rights, and they turned out to be young men from ACT UP."

Later Elizabeth worked at a law firm near Rockefeller Center, and ACT UPer Karin Timour happened to be one of the other secretaries down the hall. They ran into each other on the way to another demonstration, and were a little cool to each other at first, trying to figure out where the other one stood. Elizabeth was shy, but they were on the same side, and from that day on, she was a member of WHAM! and became totally involved with ACT UP and Action Tours. The Tourists met once a week, every Sunday evening; they would go through the newspapers to see what social events were happening and looking for ideas for actions.

Operation Rescue was escalating harassment of women entering abortion clinics. ACT UP and WHAM! had been doing clinic defense. Church Ladies for Choice often appeared at ACT UP events to help raise money, or just for fun. The members were mostly men, including Steve Quester, Brian Griffin, and Donald Grove. Then they started appearing at abortion clinics, in full drag, and singing their special repertoire to distract from the assaults of the anti-abortion demonstrators.

"They dress well. They are sometimes outrageous. But the goal of the New York Church Ladies is to break that tension, to interrupt an otherwise boring standoff. It's linked arms pressing up against another group who have linked arms. It's also to give the harassers a taste of their own medicine."

One of their best-loved songs was sung to the tune of "God Save the Queen":

God is a lesbian. She is a lesbian. God is a dyke. La la la la la. Send her a Victoria, Mary, and Gloria, she'll lick clit on the floor with ya, God is a dyke.

BILL CLINTON AND THE 1992 ELECTION

JAMES WAGNER

James went by himself to a fundraiser for Bill Clinton, while the then-candidate was in New York, just before he was nominated the first time. It was one thousand dollars per person, but he went into the entrance wearing his Italian suit and overcoat and fedora. They asked for his contribution, and he said, *Oh, my secretary must have forgotten to send it in—I'll have her do it tomorrow.* So they actually let him in, and James ended up talking to Clinton.

"I had props, so to speak. I had literature. I had copies of his record in Arkansas on homosexuals, which was not good at the time—to remind him of that. And I had a copy of . . . whatever it was that we were working on at the time. It was not a large group. There were probably only a few dozen people there raising money, in a town house. And I talked to him in turn—it seemed like five minutes, it was probably less. And of course, he was totally gracious. I'd never met him or seen him before, and he seemed very sympathetic about AIDS and that he was going to read what I'd given him . . . And then I walked away, and I shakily downed a glass of wine, I think, and walked outside. But when I did, there were other ACT UPers and Action Tourists, outside . . . He came out—apparently, he went across the street to a group of demonstrators and the media and said that he was going to talk to ACT UP. And he did. I think a day or two later . . . he actually did have a meeting in his hotel suite . . . This would be the '92 election—ACT UP and the various affinity groups—certainly ours, trailed all the candidates and tried to engage them with ACT UP's program to end the AIDS crisis . . . Even if one of them had come out totally subscribing to our program—as Jerry Brown did in the end when he was in New York—it wouldn't have been that ACT UP would support that candidate, it would just mean that the job was now to get the others to do the same thing."

FIGHTING CATHOLIC HYPOCRISY WITH COLLARS

In April 1989, the Catholic Church opened a very small, symbolic AIDS hospice. The inadequacy of service combined with the thought of people with AIDS being subjected to Catholic sanctimonious pity was painful, especially since the city was not fulfilling its responsibilities to provide appropriate housing to people with AIDS. Action Tours was there.

JAMIE LEO

Columbia University had just come forward with the numbers—there were twelve thousand homeless people with AIDS in the city. Action Tours was outraged to learn that the Cardinal Cooke Health Care Center—the former Flower Hospital on Fifth Avenue—was opening a room with ten new AIDS beds. Only ten! And that this was going to be a high-profile event! The church planned to start with a service and open up the auditorium, and the mayor and Cardinal O'Connor were going to be there. So Ira Manhoff and Charlie Franchino, a well-mannered chiropractor who did a lot of work with Treatment and Data, decided to act. They debated what we were going to do and decided to interrupt the event several different times. Jamie dressed up as a priest, a character named Father Achtung Toures. They all arrived at the opening of the chapel, and because they were in clerical collars they were escorted in and seated.

Charlie did his action first. Just as the president of the New York Medical Association was saying, *We are so proud today. We are proud to be here*, Charlie spoke out from the audience. *The homeless situation*—he was trying to get out a sound bite about the homeless situation—*how can we possibly be here, when the crisis is so much worse?* Then Mayor Ed Koch came up onstage and started his speech. But Ira then stood up and started talking. *It's a campaign ploy. You're a fraud. You're just here to campaign, this is a joke!* While the police were dragging Ira away, some of the medical professionals in the audience were saying, *Okay, ACT UP, we got it. Thank you.* Jamie had the misfortune of being number three. So, in his priest garb, he stood up, and later remembered this wall of white lights, as all these cameras turned to him, and all he could see was the face of Cardinal O'Connor glaring at him. And so, as a Catholic in recovery, Jamie started with a prayer. He said, *Heavenly Father, let us pray that we will use love and not cruelty to guide us here today, and that we will be true to family values and may we please find in our hearts to exclude, not include.* Silence came over the room, because no one would interrupt a prayer in a Catholic get-together. And Jamie said something about, *And may people who would take advantage of this epidemic for their own benefit—may they find compassion, and may they please—and, in a city of twelve thousand homeless people, may the people that open a hospital with ten beds realize that they are not doing something great to help people,* or something to that effect.

"Well, needless to say, it was the lead news story that night—that sound bite got it, it nailed it. I couldn't believe how long I went on. It went on too long. And, no one's hissing. And I'm like, *Oh my God, I'm going to get beaten to a pulp!* And this great big cop grabs me and I come away, and I realize that how he's holding me is not like the NBC guys. He's holding me and escorting me. The minute he gets me out—and I am wimping, I'm shaking like a leaf—and the second I get out, this cop says, *Oh, Father, now we've got to sit you down and calm you down.* And I was like, *What? No, no, Father, please, let me get you a glass of water, but we can't let you back in there.* It was like this sweet Irish policeman. I didn't know what to do. I was like, *I have my ID right here.* He said, *I'm not arresting you, you spoke your piece.* So he sits me down, and then he walks over and brings me a glass of water and goes, *Oh you know, Father, you think those two up on the stage—you think they know what's going on in this city? They don't know what's going on. They've never seen a hospital ward.* Whatever—the only weird part of the story was when the poor sweet man took me to the front door in the hospital and opened the door, and five hundred activists started cheering. That's a story of many. But it was an amazing experience to have lived. And to have seen that that number then got play, and then was quoted for some time, made us all feel that we had, that little tiny moment had been of some value."

THE STATUE OF LIBERTY ACTION WITH WHAM!

JAMES WAGNER

For James, the most dramatic action was July 29, 1991, when Action Tours literally veiled the Statue of Liberty with a banner while simultaneously unfolding a separate banner covering almost the entire base. It was a beautifully planned event. To prepare, James did intel by going in a few times to find the right wrench that would open these little bronze windows in the crown of the Statue of Liberty. The activists had to open at least two of the windows in order to hang a banner over Lady Liberty's face. So he went up once with some wax to make an impression against the hole to figure out what size wrench was needed.

Then he went back and tried it out. On the day of the action, there were a few dozen people carrying cinderblocks in handbags, or parts of cinderblocks, to anchor down the big banner, which was enormous and very heavy.

ELIZABETH MEIXELL

"None of us got arrested at the Statue of Liberty, because we were tourists, we looked like Italian tourists, or we dressed as family groups. Some people had to carry cinderblocks in their purses and look casual about it, and there were a bunch of moms of a certain age and there were kids who took their nose rings out just for the event and were willing to wear pastel sweatsuits. Can you imagine somebody from ACT UP in green sweatpants and a matching green sweatshirt saying *Chiefs* or something on it? But we did look really like tourists and took the boat over, and after much study and practice, dropped a banner from the crown without breaking the windows. Other groups have broken the windows. There's a key. You can buy the key at any hardware store. We figured out how to open the windows and drop the banner from the crown. *Abortion is healthcare. Healthcare is a right*, was a three-hundred-square-foot banner on the base of the Statue of Liberty. Then from the crown, the banner said *No Choice, No Liberty*."

SANTA CLAUS HAS HIV

JON WINKLEMAN

Jon Winkleman was born in Rhode Island in 1967. By the time he got to high school, he was feeling very alienated from everyone else. He was invited to the junior prom when he was a sophomore. And the night of the prom, all he could imagine was to put his head in a noose and hang himself. But instead he ended up calling a suicide-prevention hotline, talking for a long time, and they talked him out of it. Shortly after, he came out of the closet.

One week, there was a tiny article in the back of *The New York Times* about a lawsuit. A man named Mark Woodley was a Macy's Santa who had taken the job because he'd lost a lot of friends to AIDS and just wanted something to cheer himself up during the holidays. When he went back to reapply the next year, they asked him, *Are you taking any medications?*, and he knew they would do a drug test. So he said, *AZT*, and they decided not to rehire him.

Jon suggested, *Well, next holiday season, the day after Thanksgiving, we should go there, all dressed up as Santa, and do something.* So they all found these cheap Santa suits, for twenty-five bucks. There were twenty-five of them.

"And it was really cool, because we had Santas of color, we had [the ACT UPer] Harry Wieder, a dwarf Santa, which is great, because [at] Macy's, under a certain height, you're an elf. Everybody in Action Tours is Santa; we don't discriminate."

All twenty-five entered Macy's in their Santa outfits. They had Christmas cards that read *A Tragedy on 34th Street*. Inside was the fact sheet. They handed out the cards and started singing Christmas carols, on the busiest shopping day of the year. Then they got into the middle of the cosmetics aisle. Chains came out of their sleeves, and the ACT UP Santas chained themselves together in a circle. Then they started singing—*Santa Claus has HIV, fa-la-la-la-la, la-la-la-la. Macy's won't rehire he, fa-la-la-la-la, la-la-la-la. They think Mark Woodley's the best, fa-la-la, la-la-la, la-la-la. Till he took an HIV test, fa-la-la-la-la, la-la-la-la. Discrimination is illegal, fa-la-la.*

"Macy's kept coming up to us, saying, well—*We hear you, and we're glad you're here, but if you leave now, we promise, we're not going to call the police.* So on one hand, they needed to get rid of us, but at the same time, they were afraid to call the police, because they didn't want photos of Santa Claus being dragged out of Macy's in handcuffs. So they kept going to us, it's like, *No no no. Really! We promise! We won't call the police if you leave now!* And I'm chained to twenty-four other people, I really am not going anywhere. So then they started trying to put up those little screens that say, *Pardon our appearance while we're changing things.* So this amoeba of Santas is just snaking in and out of the cosmetics aisles. Until finally, they surrounded us, and they start cutting the chains. And this one little kid says: *What are they doing to the Santas?* It's like, *Macy's fired Santa. Macy's is bad.*"

GANG

ADAM ROLSTON

Adam Rolston grew up in L.A.; his mother was a yoga teacher and his father was an attorney. Both his older brothers were gay as well. When he went to college, he asked if he could go to art school. His father said, *No. I will pay for architecture school. I will not pay for art school.* So he went on to do both. In 1985, his brother Dean was diagnosed with AIDS and died. Adam went to ACT UP because of his brother. He couldn't do anything for him. Even emotionally there was no way to help, and he had to go somewhere.

Adam got together with some other artists in ACT UP—Wellington Love, Zoe Leonard, Jeff Nunokawa, Suzanne Wright, Martin McElheny, and Loring McAlpin—and started a collective called GANG, looking for a "subversive way to make people pay attention." The name was part of the "ironic, fake tough-guy image" of ACT UP, rolled-up T-shirts and jeans and big black boots.

Gran Fury was closed at that point. "It was a little bit like high school at its most base level." So smaller, independent groups started to form. Gran Fury had an emphasis on HIV, not homosexuality per se. The word *queer* was just starting to come back into usage, but there had always been a tension in ACT UP about gay issues that were not HIV-connected. GANG was founded before the direct-action organization Queer Nation started—in part by some ACT UP folks—precisely to focus on gay issues that were not necessarily AIDS-related, and their name and emergence made an empowered version of the word *queer* more common. GANG was frustrated by a lack of focus on gay subjects in ACT UP and wanted to not let that go. "We saw ACT UP as both a gay and AIDS activist organization."

GANG consisted of collective work. There was lots of fighting, lots of arguing and hurt feelings, but also a lot of closeness. Most of the art collectives in ACT UP were anonymous; the trajectory of the individual career was just starting for that queer, HIV-positive generation. Adam remembers David Wojnarowicz as "the first artist that moved into the gallery system." Adam made a sticker, I AM OUT THEREFORE I AM. He funded it himself, and with help from fellow GANG members, went out and stuck it up around town, and handed it out at ACT UP for other people to stick up. And there was a lot of that type of initiative, of people making things to give away and for other people to use and put up wherever they went. Then it was voted on the floor to use *I am out therefore I am* as an official ACT UP T-shirt for Gay Pride. "That was special for me."

GANG made a ten-second video meant to be inserted at the end of television programming, called *Color Bars or All People With AIDS Are Innocent*. It was created before the advent of twenty-four-hour television—at the end of the night, programming would come to an end, and the screen went to geometric patterns and color bars. The idea was that *All people with AIDS are innocent* would flash onto it.

ACT UP became Adam's entire life.

"Apart from my job and the gym, basically that was it . . . I walked into that room and I saw people like me, I think all of us—or a common trait was that HIV and the way that HIV was handled within our culture was an insult, and that none of us were going to let that stand. The common denominator was that we weren't going to just sit back . . . It was a culture, right? Not just an activist organization. It was a culture, and in many ways, I think that's what made the work so good. There was these just insane personalities, people that you otherwise probably couldn't stand, but because of their personality, just impossible, egomaniacal people."

ZOE LEONARD

Everything in GANG was done as a unit. They used to meet at Loring McAlpin's apartment and hammer out plans. Zoe joined because, in the beginning, Suzanne Wright was the only woman in GANG, and the two of them dated for a while. Suzanne really wanted GANG to take on more women's issues, and so she and Zoe started a project, *Read My Lips Before They're Sealed*, with a pussy photograph. There was a "gag order" at the time put out by the government, a threat that any health-care provider using the word *abortion* in any public conversation would no longer be eligible for federal funding, which would shut down not just abortions, but the ability to actually have family planning. So

Zoe and Suzanne were really interested in making the connection from that women's struggle to the struggle in ACT UP, which converged around the question of sovereignty over your own body.

"What AIDS revealed was not the problem of the virus; what AIDS revealed was the problems of our society. It was this fissure through which everything, all the ways in which our society isn't working, became really clear . . . People are complicated and societies are inherently fantastic and completely fucked at the same time. I feel lucky that I'm alive and that I survived, and for all of us in this room that we're making work, that we're making art, and you're making this document, and that we're able to talk about this as we're living it, is incredible."

11

Strategic Images: Photography, Video, and Film

TAKING ON THE MUSEUMS

RICHARD DEAGLE

Born in Germany while his father was in the military, Richard Deagle got a fine arts degree in Norfolk, Virginia, and moved to New York to study graphic design at Pratt. He came to his first meeting in winter 1988.

"ACT UP can be a really daunting thing, for a first timer . . . There were people that would show up and spend fifteen minutes and go, *Oh my God, I can't deal with this*, and never come back again. And then there were other people—this being, sort of the beginning of the Golden Age, if you will—who would show up and say, *Well, I don't know what they're talking about, but there are a lot of pretty boys there, maybe I can get some action.* So they would hang around until they snagged a boyfriend, or decided that they weren't going to. I never got any action out of ACT UP. I did get a boyfriend that I met at the AIDS conference in Montreal, but you'd hear these amazing stories like, certain people who I will not name, counting up how many people [they'd had sex with]. And there was this competition between certain people about—*Oh, I got this many guys* from ACT UP. Well, fine, I didn't."

In 1988, there was an exhibition of photos by Nicholas Nixon at the Museum of Modern Art. Nixon had photographed people with AIDS, many in late stages of wasting, lying in bed, covered with Kaposi sarcoma lesions, often with supportive family members. "Several people in ACT UP were really annoyed at it because it [only] showed all these limp, sad, *I'm-about-to-die* people with AIDS." ACT UP decided to confront the institutions who were maintaining the helpless PWA as the sole image in the culture. In this way, directly addressing institutions came from the needs and emotions of the members. The method of approach at ACT UP was that people could suggest an action, and all they needed to complete it was someone else who was willing to go along. There was no need to have to sit there and debate every fine point of theory and planning.

"We didn't sit there and say . . . *What would Kant say about this? What would be the Marxist theory of representation of people with AIDS?* You wouldn't necessarily do that kind of thing. It's, *Look, I'm really pissed off about this. I don't think they're showing what needs to be shown. Why don't we go up there and confront them about it?*"

ALEXIS DANZIG

Alexis Danzig went through the New York City public school system, from Music & Art to CUNY Graduate Center. Her parents broke up and her father came out as gay. In 1987, she found out that her father had AIDS. When her father died in February of that year, she joined ACT UP in March. Her father's partner died two years later.

Alexis found out about the Nicholas Nixon exhibit when someone made an announcement about it on the floor at a general Monday-night meeting. It was very clear to her that "utterly decontextualized" images of PWAs were being shown at MoMA, without any explanation about the AIDS crisis and/or the lives of the people in the photographs and beyond. She felt strongly that MoMA had to be challenged. She didn't know Nixon's photographs, but Alexis had graduated from the School of Visual Arts the year before and had a very clear idea of "how stupid and dangerous people in power could be, especially people in the corporate art world." Queer politics and the politics of AIDS were just beginning to be discussed in general.

"None of this was yet mainstream or mentionable . . . Fuck stupid straight people with power. It made me furious that PWAs were being exploited as *art photographs* at MoMA, on which Nixon was continuing to make his career while real people with AIDS suffered, and most people wallowed in their own ignorance and distaste about the syndrome."

The activists had at least one smaller meeting to determine what their response would be, and they settled on images of their loved ones with AIDS, signs with clear messages, and a fact sheet to hand out, which Alexis wrote. They planned a silent protest that would contrast Nixon's photos with real-life images and real information about the AIDS crisis, until they were asked to leave by guards/officials.

"I remember vaguely thinking of [ACT UPer] Catherine [Gund] Saalfield—as she was known at the time—and her mom, Agnes Gund, on MoMA's board. No one spoke of that connection."

Alexis took a color photograph of her father smiling and had it copied onto a piece of large poster board. She hand-wrote on her sign that the photo had been taken when her father was *LIVING with AIDS*. ACT UP photographer Ellen Neipris and Alexis sat on a bench in the museum, in the middle of the Nixon exhibit, with their signs and images, and handed out their information until it was all gone. She remembered thinking that she could have made three times the number of leaflets and stayed all day. Alexis felt obscured by the setting—the expensive curated show, the power of the institution, the self-righteousness of the artist, to whom no one had yet said, *Why?* She also felt defiant.

"Art has always been, will always be, an argument about power. I remember people studiously avoiding us while they looked at the exhibit. I remember a young man, my age, talking to the woman he was with about the formal concerns of the photograph they were looking at. His nonchalant conversation about *framing the image* filled me with rage and sorrow and underscored my commitment to showing up. He was refusing to see what he was seeing . . . I remember uniformed guards. I can't remember if we were asked to leave. I vaguely remember reporting back. I vaguely remember the roar of support from the floor: we'd done a necessary, useful job of making a non-issue into an issue, of *reframing* the conversation from formal to substantive, to change perception and bring all the affected to the table. The power of that interventionist/ educational moment helped inform much of the subsequent work I did in ACT UP, and afterwards."

CHANGING THE PHOTOGRAPHIC IMAGE OF PEOPLE WITH AIDS

Quickly ACT UP moved on from challenging institutions' narrow representations of people with AIDS and started creating their own images.

Not only did artists like Ellen Neipris, Tracy Litt, and Donna Binder transform how people with AIDS were depicted in still photography, but as activists, they fought directly with photo editors in the mass media to explain and demand that a new dimension of pictures be presented in corporate and movement newspapers and magazines.

DONNA BINDER

Donna Binder grew up in Oyster Bay, Long Island. Her mother was a social worker at Head Start, while her father taught and eventually became a high school principal. In 1986, she started photographing people with AIDS. She found it unavoidable. From her point of view, anyone working as a social documentary photographer, whether they were gay or not, would have, and should have, confronted the crisis. The *Native* sent her to shoot ACT UP's first meeting. Her portrait included Larry Kramer, Vito Russo, and actor Martin Sheen.

At the time, Donna saw that the prevalent journalistic image of people with AIDS was "the victim look." What people wanted in magazines all over the world was the tragic AIDS victim. Which was why, in 1987, when ACT UP first formed, she found it so amazing to have pictures of, and to be able to send out images of, a mixed group of people with AIDS who were strong, fighting, and completely turning around the victim concept. After ACT UP started, Donna would go out and photograph the demonstrations. And mostly, people in editorial positions in the mainstream media would say: *We don't want pictures of AIDS demonstrations; we want pictures of people with AIDS.* "And I'm like, *Well, some of these people have AIDS.*" But the editors rejected the images.

Persuading mass media took about four years.

"The Stop the Church demo—which I think a lot of people at the time viewed as kind of a failure—I think was probably, at least in terms of media coverage, a huge turning point. Because even though, whatever you want to say about that demo; it got the attention of the world. And after that, people wanted pictures of ACT UP demonstrating. They didn't just want people dying . . . there have always been gay people in media outlets, and . . . some of them were out, or whatever. But I don't think that was it. I think it's about a turning point in people's brains. The major magazines follow; they don't lead. So an idea has to be out there first, and then you'll see it across the pages of *Time*, or *U.S. News*, or *Newsweek*."

Donna was in a pivotal situation: shooting what was happening and then being the point person with photo editors, trying to convey to them why active photos were important, illustrating directly why standing up to her own immediate contacts in power positions was so crucial. In the very early years, she didn't have many editors that she could talk to or bring her work to consistently. That happened later, when she was closer with editors and frequently on the phone with them. She started working with the photography collective Impact Visuals, and loved being at a photo agency, deciding what images were being sent out. Of course, Impact Visuals had no control over what publications used, or how they used it. That, as a photographer, had always been incredibly frustrating. Yet, after Stop the Church, she saw that her activist photos were now going to other countries: England, France, Germany, Spain.

"My credentials always were challenged, no matter what I was at." Donna remembered being on a bus with Nelson Mandela in 1990 and Peter Magubane saying, *Why do they always pull you off?* She realized it was a combination of being a woman, being young, and maybe being a lesbian; to the authorities she looked like a demonstrator, and they couldn't imagine a woman who looked like her being a professional. She had all the same equipment as the men and the same credentials, but there were so many more men.

"They once took my credentials, in front of St. Patrick's. They just ripped them off of me. And I was on assignment for *Newsweek* that day, actually. And I told them I was. *I'm working.* And *You need to give me those back.* And [the officer] was like, *No, you're going to come and meet with me.* And I actually had to go down to police headquarters to get my credentials back."

It was obvious to many of us at the time that the media favored images of white males, and in this way gave the wrong impression of the dimensions of ACT UP's actual activities. Donna observed that it was bigger news to people with power that white men were getting arrested. As a result, a lot of her images that ran were of white men. After all, most of the people running the media were white men. But the reality was that ACT UP was diverse.

"There were also a lot of white men who were very outspoken. There were some tense meetings, and it was a mixed bag. There were certainly a lot of women that were involved, and there were lots of people of color. And certainly at a lot of the demos, too. But there was a core of white men—that I think spoke to the media a lot and were at the forefront of things . . . *Oh, look; these guys look just like us.*"

Later, there were people Donna considered to be great photojournalists who also photographed ACT UP, like Donna Ferrato. "Even though some of her early pictures of ACT UP are all victim things." There was Mark Peterson. "We won't go there with Alon Reininger, because he was like the champion of the victim pictures." But Reininger also started taking photos of the demonstrations. He was often at ACT UP actions. French photojournalists showed up, and people who were war photographers. When Donna flew to Atlanta to shoot the CDC action, Frank Fournier, a well-known French photographer, was on the same flight. "After Stop the Church—[everything] had just blown open, and everyone was interested in what ACT UP was doing. And things became really clear, I think, for the rest of the world and as ACT UP had successes, and really impacted policy and treatment."

CREATING AIDS ACTIVIST VIDEO

In the early days of documenting AIDS, the camcorder was not yet in general use. People still had film cameras: Super 8s and 16-millimeters. There was no technology for recording off a television set. People would have to aim their film cameras at the TV screen and hope to get something valuable. Video was a team sport. VHS started to be used in 1975. The equipment required two strong people: one to carry the huge "deck," which was larger than a piece of carry-on luggage. The other had to hold up a boom mic on a stick over their heads to capture sound. The three-quarter-inch camera weighed about forty pounds but was self-contained. Portable, low-cost video came into availability during ACT UP and stimulated the creation of video activism. Small cameras came into use in 1988, Video 8 in 1989, and the High 8 was used by ACT UP video activists like DIVA TV after it became available in 1989. In a time before the internet, sharing images in the precursor shadow of YouTube meant making copies of action footage and sending it in large envelopes through snail mail. It was laborious, but it worked. As activists were learning to use video, they also were learning to conceptualize it, and a number of the early influential individuals and collectives in ACT UP innovated foundational practices in activist video.

JEAN CARLOMUSTO

Brooklyn-born from an old-school Italian family, Jean Carlomusto was teaching a course in educational media at NYU in 1986 when she met Joey Licante, a person with AIDS who worked at GMHC. "Girl," he said. "We can use you." She volunteered in the Education Department in a building on Twenty-Sixth Street with halls that were "being urinated in regularly. It was a different kind of GMHC than later evolved." GMHC needed someone to coordinate audiovisual aspects of their expanding mission. So she took the job. It was a difficult decision that meant leaving a full-time job at NYU. Jean was in the middle of trying to get a master's degree, so she was giving up the free tuition. "But the best jobs aren't necessarily ones that you apply for; they are ones that you make." So she went for it because she thought that the movement needed to shape a new message. And being at GMHC would become a way to do interventions around representation. The first thing she said on the job was, *Hey look, we need to get a camcorder.* And that made it possible for her to do the cable show *Living With AIDS* and to produce her own material, so that she was not beholden to a local gay cable impresario whom GMHC would have to pay to use the same set that every other gay group was using. She wanted to fashion something different. And her show, which ran once a week from 1986 to 1994 on Paragon Cable channel 53 at 10:00 p.m., was different.

The message coming from the mainstream magazines and television at the time was, *First of all, AIDS is not your concern because you're straight.* The message was, *AIDS is very stigmatizing, so much so that we cannot show you this person. We are going to show them in silhouette, because if they show their face they are going to be subject to extreme discrimination. Plus, they are just so humiliated at their situation, why would they want to be on TV?* That was true for a lot of people, but it was not true for everybody. And being at GMHC, Jean was working with a lot of people with AIDS who were really out about who they were and who were also strong, charismatic advocates.

There wasn't a lot going on with treatment at that time in 1986. But an early show might have brought the viewer to the PWA Coalition living room for a makeup session, because Kaposi sarcoma was such an awful disfigurement. Having these lesions meant that it was going to be hard to get a cab or to go into a grocery store. So having a makeup specialist, who was just like any other makeup specialist or any good hairdresser, put HIV-positive viewers at ease. Jean's show ran once a week. Gregg Bordowitz was producing for *Living With AIDS*, and later Juanita Mohammed and Charles Brack stepped in.

"We always worked on an informed choice model, especially then, because information was very vague. So the idea was to get as much information out there to the potential person who was dealing with the treatments, enough for them to make the right choice based on their given circumstance. And testing was, at that time, a case in point. There were no treatments, so really, *Why are you going to test? Who is going to have access to this information?* It was more a matter of bringing up all of the subtext to the forefront so that people could analyze the situation for themselves. The dying was constant. I had a number of my supervisors who were telling me they had just tested positive, and then it seemed like a year later I was cleaning out their desk."

ALEXANDRA JUHASZ

Alex Juhasz grew up in Boulder and attended Amherst College. "I was a sheltered good girl, who wanted to be edgier and more radical." Alex came into the AIDS movement as a political act. She had been in New York for a year and couldn't find a place to be a political activist. She started going to meetings in the summer of 1987.

"A mix of sexiness, fashion, style, and an intelligence and a goal and community. And I haven't felt it since . . . I don't want to romanticize it, because it was born from grief, and it inspired grief . . . Even when everyone was flirting, and even when everybody looked so beautiful. It was clear, always in that room—what was at stake for people."

In the summer of 1987, Alex went and knocked on Jean Carlomusto's door at GMHC and said, *I know how to make video, can I work? Can I help you? Can I work in your department?* At that time Jean was working in a talk-show format, and wanted to make a show on women and AIDS. Alex was a feminist and saw issues through the lens of women's experience. So she thought, *Well, I'll research it and I'll make this documentary.* Alex just started talking to women around New York. There were lots of people who knew women who had AIDS; there was organizing that had been going on within social services. So she made what she believes was the first video on the subject, *Living with AIDS: Women and AIDS*, in 1987.

JEAN CARLOMUSTO

On the morning of the first ACT UP demonstration, Jean brought her camera to Wall Street. There were a lot of police around, and everybody was skittish, clearly nervous about what they were doing. When the activists were sitting in the street, she could sense an element of the unknown. Jean had seen so many different events depicted in a predictable modality: performer/audience. Yet here, all of the boundaries were erased. It was sidewalk/street. The people inhabiting either of these places were moving around. It was exciting and powerful.

She met Gregg Bordowitz and David Meieran that day, and they started sharing footage. Because there were all these actions that were now being generated, and all these footage opportunities, they needed to coordinate their efforts so that they could cover it all. They also served a purpose in terms of police surveillance, making sure that no one got roughed up, and making sure that the police were following procedures. For example, one instance that Jean documented was included in a tape about the demonstration at *Cosmopolitan*. In the shot, Maxine Wolfe is talking about how every time a certain officer came up to her, she would take his badge number down. And finally the officer just got so fed up with her and said, *You have taken my badge number five times.* The viewer can see that he started pushing her down the block. Jean's work here showed how Maxine was being handled. But it was also very important to see that footage as education about the rights of demonstrators: it taught activists to get the officer's badge number down. Later that information became part of basic ACT UP civil disobedience training. But at the time, ACT UP was just learning these techniques for taking to the street and dealing with police.

ALEXANDRA JUHASZ

One of the big ideas that Alex was trying to work through, as a scholar of documentary in addition to being a maker, was how to represent people truthfully; she was trying to work through divisions of difference and power and otherness more ethically than had been done previously with a camera. It was an intellectual, political, and practical concern of all of her work, and it came to a head when she made the *Women and AIDS* tape, which was a very traditional TV documentary. She recalled that she went to the homes of the subjects and interviewed them, just like a journalist would do. These were women who were dying, and she was talking to them about their dying. The women were living in very severe forms of poverty, and some were abused by their husbands, all of which came up during the interviews. And then Alex found herself leaving with her camera—"doing this thing which I find completely unethical and [which] also creates a system of representation which is about distance and judgment." This process of reflection and rejection of traditional approaches was an integral part of the evolution of AIDS activist video with its own ethics.

Alex made two more tapes for the GMHC *Living with AIDS* show, experimenting with different representational models. She eventually created the WAVE Project, with the Brooklyn AIDS Task Force, trying to move closer and closer to both a film practice and a political practice that was about mutual involvement, collaboration, and exchange between people who are different, but who have political allegiances. "And the camera—the power of the camera becomes a manifestation and a metaphor of a set of social relations." This collaboration was developed with Yannick Durand, who was working at Brooklyn AIDS Task Force and making videos, too. *Mildred Pearson: When You Love Somebody* (1987) was a portrait of a middle-aged Black mother who lost a son. At that time, admitting to being connected to HIV as a woman was a big deal. Alex found the film to be a beautiful, very poignant plea to Black Americans to love HIV-positive Black gay men, primarily those who were dying, and to not ostracize them. Brooklyn AIDS Task

Force was an underfunded social service organization staffed entirely by Black women "in some tawdry building" that served a large number of Haitian people in Brooklyn at the time. They held support groups, provided HIV education, and handled the nitty-gritty work of getting people housing and attaching them to entitlement programs. Alex wanted to collaborate with them, so she applied for a grant from the New York Council for the Humanities, where the artist Coco Fusco was a project administrator.

"She basically held my hand, and got me a large grant. Twenty-five thousand dollars. And, after I had that, then I went to the Brooklyn AIDS Task Force, and I said, *I have this money, I would like to do this project. The project is through a support group—could you run a support group? I'll finance it* . . . I had learned enough along the way to not ask to do that before I had the money . . . I had one VHS camcorder—it cost twelve hundred dollars."

Alex was able to pay the women twenty or twenty-five dollars a session and they got bus tokens and food. She had food at all the meetings. *We Care*—the video that that group made of the group sessions—continues to be shown in museums and film festivals, "and that has to do with the kind of capital connected to AIDS."

Alex found that "ACT UP–adjacent work" could access power very quickly. If someone did a project through ACT UP, it had infrastructure and support. If they did it anywhere else, she felt that power simply wasn't there. As a feminist, Alex knew that no women's organization she'd ever belong to would have the clout of ACT UP; specifically, no lesbian organization would ever have the clout of ACT UP.

"That was also alive for me, and it provided a kind of learning experience and attention . . . That men have access to money and power—especially white men, and lots of gay men . . . like a lot of the people who came to ACT UP—the politicos, who had come from other organizations and who had worked in struggles that stayed small and stayed poor and stayed invisible and stayed all the things they did. It's not like people were smarter in ACT UP . . . but, you know, people just tapped into money, the places where there's power."

At the same time, Alex felt that women were always in leadership in ACT UP, and that women ran the meetings. There was always a woman facilitator—she remembered there being few women in the room, but

they spoke a lot. "As much as it was vastly dominated by men, in numbers, women had a lot of power in that organization and were usually
treated with a great deal of respect, for the knowledge that they brought
about politics and organizing . . . If power and principle line up, things
can change in a way that matters."

DOCTORS, LIARS, AND WOMEN

MARIA MAGGENTI

Maria Maggenti first heard about AIDS when she was a twenty-year-old
Smith student, at that time a lesbian, and involved in anti-apartheid
politics. In 1986, she and her roommate, Laura Chapman, moved to
New York and volunteered for about six months at a battered women's
shelter in Harlem. They would hear about some of the clients losing
relatives to this new disease, AIDS, and they themselves had to have
an HIV test to even be volunteers. When they heard about the Buddy
Program at GMHC, Maria and Laura volunteered. GMHC assigned
volunteer "buddies" to work with people with AIDS who needed help
in all aspects of daily life. Most of these people died. It was a queer
community mutual aid program that was searingly formative on the
lives of the volunteers and the larger collective.

"The first man that I took care of as a buddy was an old flamer, who
worked for Fortunoff, and his lover in a highly decorated apartment in
Turtle Bay, and he was really bitchy and really funny. And that was my
first real introduction to a certain kind of gayness that I was not familiar with—which was a gay man who had his own sense of humor, and
his own sense of anger and was so not concerned with the things that I
was concerned with."

She went to an early ACT UP meeting at New York Law School and
found it very stimulating. "And, before you knew it, I was signing up
for everything." Maria signed up to be involved with the float for Gay
Pride. She signed up to be on the zap committee. There was something
about the energy of ACT UP that made her stay. It became her whole
life, every single week. In fact, it became so much of her life that she
had no real job or career. "Every job I got came from people in ACT
UP—temp jobs—it was always temp jobs." Within six months Maria

was one of two facilitators on the floor, and she was also on the Coordinating Committee, the Actions Committee, and the Outreach Committee. Along with Gregg Bordowitz, Maria is one of the ACT UPers most frequently mentioned by others as someone they were enamored with or inspired by.

One night in January 1988, Maria was at Maxine Wolfe's house for a Dyke Dinner, and someone brought in an issue of *Cosmopolitan* magazine with an article by Dr. Robert Gould, the husband of feminist novelist Lois Gould, author of the bestseller *Such Good Friends*. Dr. Gould dangerously claimed that women were not at risk for AIDS. ACT UP was just starting to take on the defense of women with AIDS and running campaigns to show that safe sex saves women's lives, so this article was the final straw in mass media's lies about women's lives and HIV. The women at Maxine's were so angry they just had to respond.

"The article claimed that if you had sex with an HIV-positive man and he came inside you, oh, your vagina was so resilient, there's no way you were going to get infected. This guy was insane. I can't even believe that they published this. And, P.S., he wasn't even a medical doctor. He was a psychiatrist, therapist psychiatrist—not even, like, doing research on anything. And so then we decided we were going to protest him, personally, first. And then protest *Cosmopolitan*."

REBECCA COLE

"His argument was . . . that the only way to really have the transmission happen was lacerations and, just the act of sex wouldn't give it to you. But if you had a cut, or something more, and that most of us don't have cuts when we're having sex with guys, and that unless you had sex in a—and I think he said *a cruel way*; and he said *like men in Africa*—He was being, wow. The fact that that got past the editorial board was—So, the guy was ridiculous. And *Cosmo* was ridiculous to do it. But it was almost like every other stupid article. Imagine if you protested every dumb article in a magazine today that's telling women—girls, young girls—the wrong things. There's a lot of them. But whenever it came to, this could kill you with this information, it was exacerbated . . . So, I think I called him first—Dr. Gould—and said that I'd read this article, and that I was confused by it, *and is it really true* . . . And he basically said everything he said in the article . . . So then we set up this, this, this sting operation. Like a video sting. Where we went to his office."

JEAN CARLOMUSTO

The subsequent action against *Cosmopolitan* magazine and the production of a video, *Doctors, Liars and Women: AIDS Activists Say No to Cosmo*, by Jean and Maria Maggenti, was the first time the women in ACT UP really got organized. It also was the first time in ACT UP that the video and the organizing were not separate. The organizing itself, from its very inception, had the component of video coverage integrated into it. But beyond it just being an action against a magazine, the ACT UP women wanted to do some different things. They wanted to try to interview Dr. Robert Gould, who actually was a fairly gay-friendly doctor. He had done a lot of work trying to take gay sexuality off the list of psychiatric impairments. But in this case, he had put information out there that was really harmful to women. And the activists wanted to know why he did this. So they just picked up the phone, and called him, and arranged an interview. Jean brought the camera along.

MARIA MAGGENTI

The women said, *We'd like to come to your house.* Gould lived on the Upper East Side.

"I'll never forget it because we were all in there and I kept saying to Jean, *Do you think he knows that we brought a camera?* And then—and he was a slight man, you know. He was slight. I mean, I probably would have more compassion for him now, but I hated him then. And he was a slight man, wearing a turtle neck, and he had gray hair and he was quite gracious, and then as soon as we—he sat down, we began to challenge him immediately, and how could he possibly—what was he talking about, that *the vagina is resilient*? Where did he get that research?"

Julie Tolentino, cofounder of the Clit Club, a queer and pro-sex lesbian nightclub that was operational between 1990 and 2012, working the door on March 19, 1993
(Photograph by T. L. Litt)

Alexis Danzig with a photo of her father, Allan Danzig, and Ellen Neipres with photos of David Summers and Mark Fotopoulos, inside MoMA protesting the Nicholas Nixon show in 1988 (Photograph by T. L. Litt)

Donald Moffett and Marlene McCarty with Gran Fury installation in Venice, 1990 (Photograph by Bruno Jakob)

David Wojnarowicz
(Photograph by T. L. Litt)

ACT UP

HAITIANS WITH HIV ARE BEING MURDERED
IN A US MILITARY CONCENTRATION CAMP

SILENCE=DEATH

Nearly 300 Haitian political refugees are locked behind barbed wire and armed guard at a US military base at Guantánamo Bay, Cuba. They fought for democracy in Haiti before the coup, and passed US immigration screenings for political asylum. Now the US government has held them prisoner for over a year only because they tested HIV-positive, the result of an inhumane Immigration and Naturalization Service travel and immigration ban for HIV-positive people.

HIV is not a crime!

The refugees protested peacefully for months, but the US military retaliated by beating them, detaining them in tiny boxlike rooms, and tying them outside in the hot sun. On January 29, they entered a hunger strike as a final act of protest against their imprisonment. They live surrounded by barbed wire and armed military guard. Their only housing is crude plywood shacks; they have no plumbing, only filthy outdoor toilets and communal cold-water spigots. Since the beginning of the hunger strike, many of them have refused to sleep in this "housing" which the US Centers for Disease Control calls a potential infectious disease disaster. They are sleeping instead in an open field. When they become unconscious from weakness and dehydration, they are carried into a tent and rehydrated. All have then walked back out to join the strike. Many of the refugees are very ill, and some are pregnant. The medical care on the base is negligently poor: there is no HIV specialist on the base, no Creole-speaking doctor, and no blood lab. Four of the prisoners have attempted suicide in the past week.

ACT UP's flyer
raising awareness of
the Haitian HIV crisis
at Guantánamo

US human rights abuses of HIV-positive refugees ARE a crime!

During his presidential campaign, Bill Clinton committed to lifting the INS's HIV ban. On February 9, he affirmed his commitment to that promise, but he set no time frame for change. His delay paved the way for an anti-immigrant and AIDSphobic conservative backlash. Though Donna Shalala, Secretary of Health, declared that there is no public health justification for the HIV ban, and said it should be dropped, on February 18, Senators Helms and Simpson passed an amendment in the Senate that would keep HIV on the INS exclusion list. Bill Clinton shut Shalala out of White House discussion on the ban, and did nothing to challenge the Senate.

We demand:

* *the immediate release of all Haitian refugees at Guantánamo to the US for medical treatment and political asylum*
* *an end to US immigration and travel restrictions for people with HIV*
* *the restoration of democracy in Haiti through President Aristide's return*
* *an end to the interdiction of Haitian refugees at sea and their forced return to Haiti*

Call your representative in the House (202) 224-3121: tell him or her to vote against any bill that comes to the House that would maintain HIV travel or immigration restrictions!

Pack the Court March 8: Come to Brooklyn Federal Court, 225 Cadman Plaza East, at 9 a.m. when the US Attorney General's office arrives to defend the Guantánamo prison camp! ▶

Sponsored by ACT UP (the AIDS Coalition To Unleash Power) (212) 564-AIDS and the Emergency Coalition for Haitian Refugees.

Charles King and Bob Rafsky being arrested at the New York City Housing
Authority while protesting discrimination against People with AIDS on
June 13, 1990 (Photograph by T. L. Litt)

Gerri Wells protesting against antigay police violence on October 25, 1990
(Photograph by T. L. Litt)

Michelangelo Signorile, the features editor of *OutWeek*, on his desk the day
the magazine shut down in June 1991 (Photograph by T. L. Litt)

Charles Hovland selling T-shirts at Gay Pride 1992 (Courtesy of the
Collection of Charles Hovland)

ACT UP seizes the stage at the Montreal Conference, June 4, 1989. From left to right: unknown, Neil Broome, Heidi Dorow (with arm obscuring face), Richard Deagle, Walter Armstrong, unknown, Garance Franke-Ruta, unknown (Photograph by T. L. Litt)

Dr. Joseph Sonnabend at the Montreal Conference, June 4, 1989 (Photograph by T. L. Litt)

Day of Desperation: ACT UP occupied Grand Central Terminal on January 23, 1991 (Photograph by Aline Allegro)

ACT UP demonstration at the Waldorf Astoria, 1990. Carrying the coffin is Assotto Saint. (Photograph by Dona Ann McAdams)

The Storm the NIH Action on May 21, 1990. Standing, left to right: Bill Monahan (obscured), Mark Bronnenberg, Maria Maggenti, Phil Montana, Heidi Dorow. Far right with arm raised: Rand Snyder. Seated in foreground, left to right: Tim Powers, Garry Kleinman; others unknown

(Photograph by Dona Ann McAdams)

Mourners at Tim Bailey's funeral on June 30, 1993. From left to right: Ioannis Mookas, unknown (obscured), unknown (in white shirt), unknown, David Feinberg, Michael Cunningham, Brian Fitzpatrick, Ken Bing (Photograph by Donna Binder)

Tim Bailey's political funeral, with Joy Episalla in the van, June 30, 1993 (Photograph by Donna Binder)

James Baggett at Jon Greenberg's funeral through the streets of the East Village to Tompkins Square Park on July 16, 1993 (Photograph by Donna Binder)

The Ashes Action, October 11, 1992, in Washington, D.C. Second from left: unidentified nurse with the ashes of her favorite patient; second from right, with handprint on shirt: David Robinson (Photograph by Donna Binder)

Latino Caucus thirty-year reunion, 2017. Clockwise from upper left (seated on couch): Alfredo González, Gilberto Martínez, Cándido Negrón, José Santini, Gonzalo Aburto, unknown, Jairo Pedraza, César Carrasco, Walt Wilder, Luis Santiago (in glasses) (Courtesy of César Carrasco)

JEAN CARLOMUSTO

Denise Ribble, Maxine Wolfe, Maria Maggenti, and Rebecca Cole were the people who were present at the Gould interview while Jean was behind the camera. Each woman took on a different mode of questioning. One person asked him why, in a work that supposedly was scientific, there were so few footnotes, and why the research was so dated. Part of the article's assertion was that women in Africa were getting AIDS at such a higher rate because *men in Africa take their women in such a brutal way*. Maxine brought up the point that many women in the United States are raped. *How can you say this? It's racist.* Denise Ribble talked anecdotally about her experience actually treating women—straight women—with AIDS, and how these women weren't lying. They did not get AIDS through anal sex, because this was what Dr. Gould was claiming—*that really healthy vaginal sex wasn't going to put you at risk, that basically the women who were getting sick were ass-fucking and not telling the truth.* The ACT UP women wanted him to write a retraction. They had a very specific goal. He refused to do it, and made a hasty goodbye out of the interview. The women were all hustled out very fast. When they discussed the experience, the women decided, *All right, fine, we went to him, we tried to have a normal conversation, we tried to treat him like an intelligent human being . . .* and immediately started organizing. They brought the issue back to ACT UP, and the men rallied around them. They wanted to be supportive of the sisters. They were ready for an action.

MARIA MAGGENTI

By the end of January 1988, ACT UP planned a confrontational action at the offices of *Cosmopolitan* magazine in New York.

"At the *Cosmopolitan* demonstration we did have some good graphics. And a lot of the men showed up. Of course they did, because it was an ACT UP action. But, I will say, it was seven and a half degrees that day. It was one of the coldest days that we had ever had—but it was a very successful demonstration, excellently successful . . . We got there early, and they had already set up barricades. They heard ACT UP was coming. And we had a very definite plan that we were going to try and get into the building, go upstairs, speak to the editors at *Cosmopolitan* magazine. They immediately shut down . . . and started asking people for IDs, would not let us inside."

Now, since the women had accumulated video footage from the interview and the action, and press coverage of the action, the mainstream media noticed! This was a new use for video in the movement: not only for documenting actions, and making arguments, but also using video to persuade and inform the mass media. This was video as a provocation.

JEAN CARLOMUSTO

"We brought this issue to the public eye, because then all of a sudden the mainstream media really picked up on it. Phil Donahue did a show on it, [as did] *People Are Talking*. They all wanted to do shows with, essentially, Dr. Robert Gould and some ill-equipped specialist to do some half-assed job refuting him. And the women who actually organized the action were not put on the panel."

REBECCA COLE

"*Nightline* had Helen Gurley Brown, and it should have been one of us. But we were too radical, and not sophisticated enough or something . . . Donahue did the same thing."

JEAN CARLOMUSTO

In response to being left out of the discussion, the ACT UP women took over the set of the TV talk show *People Are Talking*. They had brought the issue about the falsity of the article's claims to national attention, and all of a sudden they were not allowed to participate in its public debate. So a few women managed to sneak into the live television audience and then literally took over the show. Chris Norwood and Denise Ribble marched onstage and just sat down there and said, *Why don't you have any women on this panel? You're making us invisible. This is the message. You are killing women by making us invisible.*

"It was just so great to hear the host of the show say, *Can we get security in here?* to sort of shuffle these women out. That was the first time I really saw our activism subverting dominant media messages, taking over shows. And that would be something that ACT UP would do subsequently in a number of different interventions."

MARIA MAGGENTI

Some months later, *Cosmopolitan* published a retraction and an admission that Gould's piece was not the full story of HIV transmission for women. They now, for the first time, encouraged women to have their male partners use condoms. Jean and Maria's documentary of those events, called *Doctors, Liars, and Women: AIDS Activists Say No to Cosmo*, showed extensively. It was advocacy journalism. "And I was out of my mind with joy with that experience."

TESTING THE LIMITS COLLECTIVE

As the technology itself facilitated collaboration, and activists discovered ways to move video beyond documentation into a hybrid form interfacing with live actions, video collectives started to be created inside ACT UP. The best known was Testing the Limits, which included Gregg Bordowitz, David Meieran, Hilery Kipnis, Jean Carlomusto, and two Canadian art students, Sandra Elgear and Robyn Hutt.

SANDRA ELGEAR

Sandra Elgear grew up as an Anglophone in the context of a highly politicized Quebecois separatist movement. Her parents were conservative "farm folk." She made art from a young age and went to Ontario College of Art and Design in Toronto. She and her friend Robyn Hutt started collaborating on installations and were accepted into the Whitney program. "You come to New York and you get a studio. You get all these famous artists coming and talking to you. It sounded like a pretty good plan." There they started working with David Meieran and Gregg Bordowitz. Their first shoot together as a group was ACT UP's first demonstration.

ROBYN HUTT

Robyn Hutt grew up in the wealthiest small town in Canada, Oakville, just outside of Toronto. She came to New York to go to Cooper Union, then the Whitney program with Sandra, and then got a PhD in film studies from NYU.

The technology was evolving rapidly at that time. Cameras were changing very quickly. When Robyn and Sandra first started, they had big VHS tapes that went into cameras that were newly portable. By the time they finished school, much smaller tapes were available. It was a change that at first seemed to mirror the transformative moment in the early 1960s, cinema verité, when new advances in equipment gave film-makers a mobility they hadn't had before. And with video, the change in equipment also allowed affordability.

SANDRA ELGEAR

Because she was so short, Sandra was rarely behind the camera. She mostly did sound. When smaller cameras became available, she would sometimes do the camera work as well. On-the-scene documentary shooting was competitive.

"The big bruisers with their big cameras, with their passes and stuff, would always get the prime spots, or else they'd be right up there in front and you couldn't barge by them. And they're very aggressive. Of course, we would be so pissed off, because we'd be like, *We want all of this, and you're going to show ten seconds, max* . . . We eventually did get press passes; for a while we had bogus press passes that we used. But we eventually would get press passes for a lot of things, which was good."

At the time Sandra wasn't legally in New York, so she was never willing to get arrested. But because Testing the Limits was known and respected in ACT UP, people would talk to their cameras very readily. Before an action they would meet in a church or in a community center and get the logistics of how the day was going to progress, what groups were going to be where. ACT UP usually held a "pre-action meeting" to run through the upcoming day's events, and Testing the Limits would attend. Then they would shoot. Sometimes, when actions lasted more than a few days, they would look at what they had just shot that same night. *Oh, we didn't get this*, or *We need some of that*. All the tapes would be labeled as they were shooting, which could be a logistical nightmare sometimes. Batteries had to be replaced and recharged, and they had to make sure the batteries didn't run out, especially in cold actions. Tapes could be cumbersome and get placed in wrong cases, or misplaced. But, at the end of the day, everything would get logged, and the video makers would burn a copy.

The first tape the collective did together was a thirty-minute documentary called *Testing the Limits*. They had no workspace. Robyn and Sandra and Robyn's boyfriend were living in a loft in Greenpoint, and did their first edit of their first documentary all on paper. They had a long roll, laid out on the floor in ninety-degree heat, with no air-conditioning.

GREGG BORDOWITZ

The editors had marked time-code numbers down on index cards, and divided the huge roll of paper into three sections. Their documentary was set up according to three categories that activist Simon Watney had talked about in his 1987 book, *Policing Desire: Pornography, AIDS and the Media*, which were *civil rights*, *education*, and *treatment/activism*. That was the framing. So they threw each of the index cards within its category, and then ordered it from there. It was a painstaking process that went on for a week, and then they all went into the studio together and edited it.

Robert Vázquez-Pacheco gave them space at the PWA Health Group buyers club, and then the collective moved to Fourteenth Street. Using their fundraising skills from Canada, Robyn and Sandra had gotten money from the New York State Council on the Arts for Testing the Limits. There were other collectives inside ACT UP, like DIVA TV, and they would all share footage.

Testing the Limits was conceived of as an organizing project. The collective went around to all five boroughs to document various kinds of AIDS activism. The idea was to show how the various people involved in activism were all linked. Most of the city's activists hadn't yet met one another at this point yet. So, for example, there was Yolanda Serrano, who was doing needle exchange in the Bronx, and Suki Ports, who was working up in Harlem. The collective held *Testing the Limits* screenings where people made connections. The film had a life that was surprising to them. The American Film Institute showed it, and so did public television.

ROBYN HUTT

Then the group decided to make a feature, *Voices from the Front.* They again edited this collectively and fought about everything. *Voices from the Front* is quite different from *Testing the Limits* in a number of respects, including that it situates ACT UP in the history of AIDS activism. It acknowledges what came before, during the first five years of the AIDS crisis, when forty thousand people died.

SANDRA ELGEAR

"Our philosophy was all similar because we all were, in a way, products of a certain school of thought, which was to eschew traditional documentary style. As part of deconstructive theory, you don't have a truth. You don't have one side of the story. It's not just one presentation. So we didn't want to have the voiceover telling you, *This is what is happening. This is the truth. This is the story.* We wanted to say, *There it is. You tell us what it means to you.*"

At the end of *Voices from the Front,* there is an in-memoriam section, because it took so long to make the film that a lot of the people who appeared had died by the time it was finished. The collective discussed how to address this for a long time because, of course, the message of the film was, *We have to fight. It's not about people dying; it's about people fighting an illness, and making it so they're not going to die.* To end it with, *Okay, well, that guy's dead,* with a whole slew of people who were dead, seemed wrong. The collective debated this choice back and forth and ended up deciding that these deaths were a reality. These people did die. The audience had to know that. They had to acknowledge that as much as we fought, and did as much as we could, it was not enough. People were dying before our eyes.

DAMNED INTERFERING VIDEO ACTIVISTS TELEVISION (DIVA TV)

CATHERINE GUND

Catherine Gund attended Concord Academy and Brown University and then the Whitney program, which she called "a one-year Marxist-indoctrination studio-art program in downtown Manhattan." Whitney also offered critical studies, so students could be artists, or they could be theoreticians, or critics, or art writers. Catherine's parents were wealthy Democrats, involved with philanthropy, and her mother became president of the board of the Museum of Modern Art.

"Literally, the first thing I ever heard about ACT UP was that my mother told me about this organization she was giving money to . . . I remember when Robert Mapplethorpe got very sick, and then when he died, and he had been friends with my mother, and . . . he was someone I actually knew . . . He had photographed me as her daughter once, and I'd met him through that. And then I'd seen him a couple of times. But it just was a shocking moment."

In ACT UP Catherine brought her video skills to a number of different groups, including the collective DIVA TV, with ten to twelve people at its core and a periphery of close to forty people, including Ellen Spiro, Dean Lance, Ray Navarro, Costa Pappas, Jean Carlomusto, Gregg Bordowitz, and George Plagianos. DIVA TV's goal at the time it was founded was not festivals and certainly not TV broadcast. It was really for members of ACT UP to see a different perspective than they would have seen that night on television. It was to help us articulate and develop our perspectives by watching an extended interview, instead of just a sound bite. They would compile video tapes and sell them for ten dollars apiece. They mailed a lot of VHS copies to states and cities and towns around the country. "It was like ACT UP newsreel."

DEAN LANCE

Dean Lance grew up poor and Jewish in Canarsie, Brooklyn. He started making art in kindergarten and studied art at Brooklyn College but dropped out in his third year because CUNY started charging tuition. Later, he graduated from the School of Visual Arts.

Dean's boyfriend was on methadone maintenance and wanted to get off it, then he was diagnosed with TB. It turned out to be a false diagnosis, because actually he had AIDS. A woman from the Brooklyn AIDS Task Force was helping them, because there was a dentist who wouldn't treat Dean's boyfriend at one point because of his status. Dean joined ACT UP in March of 1989, and his lover was very proud of what Dean was doing, but he felt he had enough going on and couldn't get involved.

"Here's this horrible story. It's almost Dickensian. We were going to Thanksgiving, where they would let you have four God's Love We Deliver turkey dinners, which actually weren't bad, and we spent Thanksgiving together that year. Two days before he ended up going into the hospital. He was having a really bad stomach problem. It ended up he had a tumor in his stomach that they removed part of . . . It was on Christmas Eve he told me . . . *I have two weeks to live.* And he fooled them. He died after a week."

Dean was involved in producing three videos: *Like a Prayer*, *Pride 1969–1989*, and *Target City Hall*. He went to the first DIVA TV meeting because he wanted to get involved with video and also loved the idea of how DIVA was an affinity group but wasn't about archiving or documenting what was happening for posterity. "It wasn't that narcissistic." He loved the idea that one of the reasons it was set up was to do countersurveillance on the police.

"When you have ten or fifteen people shouting a cop's badge number into a rolling video camera they're less likely to deprive you of your civil rights or your brains, and it was a brilliant tactic . . . A couple years later, when the Rodney King thing happened, *Newsweek* did a cover story called 'Video Vigilantes,' and they gave two paragraphs to DIVA TV, Damned Interfering Video Activists. They explained . . . we were documenting people risking arrest by performing acts of civil disobedience, and they credited us for starting the whole concept of video activism."

GEORGE PLAGIANOS

George Plagianos was raised in Bay Ridge, Brooklyn, in a Greek family. His father was an electrician and a printer, and his mother was a seamstress. He came out to his mom in 1969 and started going to Gay Youth in 1974 and later to the Gay Activists Alliance Firehouse on Wooster Street, which was the first incarnation of a gay political and social center in New York City. In the early 1980s, his friend Michael got sick and there were no treatments.

"He kept saying, *If I ever get out of this disease alive, I'm going to go straight* . . . But he was getting weaker and weaker and couldn't go to the bathroom, and couldn't walk, and his mom would have to lift him up. He was probably maybe ninety pounds . . . He passed away, they had services, and they buried him right away, and I wasn't invited to the—well, maybe [his mother] was stressed out. She maybe couldn't find who I, where I was."

George worked part-time as a cleaner in gay sex clubs, for people like Walter "Wally" Wallace, who was the manager of the Mineshaft, and at the sex club in the Triangle Building, on Ninth Avenue and Fourteenth Street. He didn't get sick, but George saw other people getting sick, and he was looking to see how our community was responding, and how ethnic communities were responding, too. He didn't see any AIDS programs in the Greek, Eastern European, or Middle Eastern communities. He found that his own church, the Greek Orthodox community, was fairly silent on AIDS.

Within ACT UP, George worked on housing and joined DIVA TV. He got his first video camera and started recording how the police were treating people with AIDS and AIDS activists when arresting them. This was the precursor to the later trend of people filming police brutality on cell phones. George was not thinking at first in terms of "documentation" for the future, but rather he was working in the present to try to make the police accountable and to protect our people from fabricated charges and unjustified arrests. Due to rapid changes in technology, people in DIVA TV had different types of cameras. The standard was 8-millimeter tape, and Hi-8, but George could only afford a VHS-C, which just recorded and didn't play back. So he had to put the tapes in a little converter box. DIVA TV would have meetings every week or every two weeks. Member Ellen Spiro made phony press passes, which said COMMUNITY TELEVISION, that successfully "warded off the cops. It was almost like wearing an amulet."

ACT UP VIDEO AND HIV-POSITIVE WOMEN IN PRISON

DEBRA LEVINE

Through ACT UP lawyer Mike Spiegel, Deb was introduced to ACE. It was started by women at the Bedford Hills women's prison who had organized themselves into an advocacy and counseling group, and the women wanted to know what was going on on the outside and to have a liaison to activist groups. There were a number of activists from the 1960s who were prisoners at Bedford and who were working on what was going on around AIDS at the time. Kathy Boudin and Judy Clark joined, along with other inmates, including Ruthie Rodriguez, Ada Rivera, Awilda Gonzalez, Doris Moises, and Carmen Royster. They saw that a lot of women were getting sick with AIDS, and that incarcerated people didn't have access to experimental treatments, because historically experimental treatments had been tried on prisoners, and that was no longer allowed. The AIDS crisis presented many contradictory realities, including that experimental drugs were the only real kind of health care in existence, and yet no prisoners could enroll in an experimental drug trial. So that meant that they could only get AZT, which often did more harm than good. But even so, prison health care was really poor and people didn't get regular distribution of their drugs. Usually, AIDS drugs had to be taken exactly at the right time and regularly, or they could actually decrease a person's resistance.

There was also a tremendous amount of fear and stigma in the prisons, because women were afraid of transmission. There were real fears about transmission especially around tuberculosis, but there was also a lot of ignorance, including around using the same toilets and eating the same food as people with AIDS. Being sick in prison is dangerous because prison is a place where people get sicker faster. There is a lot of violence, and women were getting beat up if they were suspected of having AIDS or if they had a relative with AIDS. So people who had political organization skills in the prison recognized that it was a moment to say, *We can actually do something as prisoners for ourselves, because no one else is doing it.* A group of women had previously won a lawsuit against the state prison commissioner requiring more adequate health care, which empowered them to try to put together a more comprehensive health-care plan within the prison. Bedford Hills had what was considered a very sort of forward-thinking and liberal warden, Elaine Lord. This group of prisoner activists approached her saying, *We'd like to do something around HIV and AIDS where we can hold classes so that people understand really how AIDS gets transmitted, how to take care of themselves, and also how to treat others so that it would end the violence.* That kind of approach had already worked well with a mothering program to help prisoners whose kids were in foster care that also made sure mothers had relationships with their kids even while they were in prison. Because that earlier effort succeeded as a peer-run group, Lord saw the potential in the AIDS initiative, although she was very concerned about it as well, because it gave prisoners power, which was antithetical to the idea of prisons.

Debra met with Ada Gonzalez, an inmate in her early forties.

"She was a grandmother, a drug dealer, and completely intimidating, tough as nails. It took a long time for her to trust me. I was just like this white girl who was coming in from nowhere, and she was very wary. I talked to her. I don't remember who the other people talked to, because each of us had more of a one-on-one with someone. But she started explaining what ACE was to me, and I started explaining really the resources that we had that we could help them with. I was really intrigued by it. I was intrigued because it seemed to be prison issues were not the sexy issues in ACT UP, and a lot of people didn't want to deal with it, although they were supportive. Then we have women's prison issues where it seemed like more of the cases of HIV were in men's prisons, although there were a lot of women coming in there, and there were women being infected by their male partners and a lot of women who got it from drug use."

Ada Rivera was not HIV-positive, but she had a close relative who was. A number of the other women in ACE were HIV-positive, including Awilda Gonzalez, who worked in the beauty shop in the prison; Doris Moises; and Katrina Haslip. These women wanted information about all of the experimental drug trials because they wanted to know which drugs they should be advocating for. They were also interested in what was going on in other prisons. They wanted literature. They wanted to build a library for themselves. They told Debra and the other ACT UPers literally how to advocate for them. "It's a difficult dance because what you don't want to do is you don't want to offend the warden and you don't want to be banned from being able to go in [the prison]."

CATHERINE GUND

"Meanwhile, at the same time, Katrina [Haslip], who we'd met on the inside, got out. We'd already established this relationship with Katrina. And she was eager to immediately help the organization on the inside. And she also was trying to address some of the needs she was recognizing for herself and other women who are HIV-positive who were coming out, and then what was going to happen. And we did make a video with them. Debra Levine and I worked with Katrina and videotaped her and videotaped some of the other women as they were coming out."

DEBRA LEVINE

The resulting film, *I'm You, You're Me: Women Surviving Prisons, Living with AIDS*, was about the support group that was created with HIV-positive women out of prison. Katrina helped map out the film in a way that simply said, *Look. These are the issues that women have. This is the way women organize.* Catherine and Deb continued going to support group meetings and filming. They decided not to do voice-over narrative but instead to let women tell their stories and articulate their own experiences. They just showed portraits of women who were dealing with the real issues that set in when they got out. They had to cope in the world with getting their medication, making sure that they didn't get sick, taking care of their kids, finding health care, and finding housing. It was a short film, thirty minutes long, and it got distributed in prisons across the country. It was about visibility for women who were coming out of prison and understanding this was the way that they could organize themselves to support one another.

FILM AND FILMMAKERS IN ACT UP

There was a wide range of film and video made by ACT UPers. Maria Maggenti, Tom Kalin, Todd Haynes, Jason Simon, Moyra Davey,

Gregg Bordowitz, Ellen Spiro, Catherine Gund, Alexandra Juhasz, and others continued to make and produce features and shorts throughout the organization's existence and after. Video makers in ACT UP tended to focus on an active form of documentation, designed to enhance and encourage direct action and to educate about AIDS itself, but also to illuminate the specifics required for effective activism. And some of these makers went on to produce creative and artistic video features and shorts that were more expressive than the work they did in the movement.

But for filmmakers there were really two dominant trajectories. Some, like Maria Maggenti, Tom Kalin, Ira Sachs, Todd Haynes, and Christine Vachon, went on to make indie and mainstream narrative dramatic features, gathering larger budgets and receiving recognition at Sundance and Berlin, at Cannes and the Academy Awards.

JIM HUBBARD

The second trajectory, though, was less mainstream. There was also a large presence in ACT UP of experimental filmmakers. These were personal films, handmade, usually financed by the artist, that used visual and formal innovation to express emotions and ideas that were part of the counterculture of ACT UP. This was in part because of the "Downtown" influences on ACT UP resulting from the cultural location of queer life in the East Village, which was a center of experimental film. But this movement also happened because of the existence of MIX NYC Queer Experimental Film Festival, because the existence of venues helps create artists. If marginalized, unrepresented people know that they have a place to show their work, they are much more likely to make that work. Jim Hubbard and I founded MIX (originally the New York Lesbian and Gay Experimental Film Festival) in February 1987, a few weeks before the creation of ACT UP, and the festival still exists today, thirty-four-plus years later, with branches in Brazil, Mexico, and Denmark. Other festival codirectors included Shari Frilot, who went on to curate Sundance; Cannes-winning director Karim Aïnouz; Rajendra Roy, who became film curator at the Museum of Modern Art; and award-winning film and television director Thomas Allen Harris. MIX showed experimental film (and later video) by many ACT UP members, including David Wojnarowicz, Phil Zwickler, Karl Soehnlein, Gregg

Bordowitz, Todd Haynes, Christine Vachon, Testing the Limits collective, Maria Maggenti, Glenn Belverio, Emily Nahmanson, Catherine Gund, James Wentzy, Jean Carlomusto, Robert Hilferty, Carl Michael George, Jack Waters, Peter Cramer, Mary Patten, Jennie Livingston, Zoe Leonard, Alexandra Juhasz, Ming-Yuen S. Ma, Tom Kalin, Joe Ferrari, Jocelyn Taylor, Terry Roethlein, John Lindell, Ira Sachs, GANG, Stéphane Gérard, Lionel Soukaz, and many, many others who died of AIDS or who live with HIV.

Born in New York and educated at the San Francisco Art Institute, Jim Hubbard started filming gay demonstrations in 1979 and was usually the only person there with a camera. His early gay films include expressive artistic works in hand-processed Super 8, covering events like gay demonstrations against the filming of the movie *Cruising*, and community responses to the violent police raid at BLUES, a Black gay bar.

"I first started trying to make a film about AIDS soon after it became clear that it was becoming an epidemic, probably around 1982. I didn't want to replicate what the mainstream media was doing—barging into hospital rooms, stigmatizing people, showing people in their worst light possible. I guess I wanted to show what it was really like to have AIDS and its effect on the community. But it was difficult to find things to film. I started filming a friend of mine who was quite public about having AIDS, but very quickly it became clear that it wasn't working, that he didn't want a camera around all the time and I wasn't getting anything that would add up to a film."

Only one shot from that original attempt ended up in Jim's experimental feature, *Elegy in the Streets*. Then two things happened that changed that situation. First, Jim's former partner, Roger Jacoby, was diagnosed with AIDS in August 1984, and he wanted to be filmed. Jim filmed him on various occasions in various settings until he died in November 1985. When Roger died, Jim inherited his outtakes, in addition to footage Roger had filmed of himself over the previous twelve years. Second, ACT UP burst onto the scene, providing a highly visual, extremely energetic response to the crisis.

Jim first filmed ACT UP accidentally. He was standing on Fifth Avenue just below Central Park South, filming when the concentration camp float turned the corner at the 1987 Lesbian/Gay Pride March. Then he filmed the Sloan Kettering demonstration and filmed almost every big demonstration for the next two years, as well as numerous other demonstrations in the years following. Somewhere along the line, Jim realized that an elegy would be the perfect structure for this footage because an elegy starts from a private tragedy—the death of someone close—and moves to a public, political response to that death. So he started to capture filmic variations of some of the elements that are usually present in elegiac poetry—a catalog of flowers, a visit to the underworld, a black-and-white negative of two guys on the river's edge in the middle of the film, a procession of mourners, the ACT UP demonstrations. In the film, Roger becomes a very unlikely swain character—a rustic shepherd with poetic aspirations.

"With ACT UP demonstrations, there were usually at least a dozen people videotaping. Videotape was much more appropriate to the urgency of the epidemic. It was immediately available for viewing and could be quickly edited and distributed much more cheaply. Not only was I using sixteen-millimeter film at that point, but I was processing the film myself. Because I had to wait until I had a critical mass of film to process, there could be many months of delay before I could even see what I had filmed. Playing around with the colors of the image, changing the meaning of the image was very different from the directness of AIDS Activist Video."

He made some small personal AIDS-inflected films, *The Dance* and *Memento Mori*, the widely viewed *Two Marches*, and the experimental feature *Elegy in the Streets* before creating the full-length documentary *United in Anger: A History of ACT UP* (2012).

CHRISTINE VACHON

Christine Vachon's father was a photojournalist, and her mother was a French teacher. Her older sister, Gail, was in an influential early experimental women's band, Y Pants. Christine attended LaGuardia, the public arts high school, and then went to Brown. At that time, Brown was the center of semiotics.

"A poem wasn't just about emotion . . . a book couldn't just stand on its own as just a piece of literature that was part of a whole, like, cultural tableau, that was political, where race and sex and feminism . . . could be brought to bear, and that you could see a text in so many different ways.

And then it was much more like you saw the text in terms of what the author meant, and this notion that it doesn't matter what the author meant was a very radical idea." Now, "when we make a movie, I'm well aware that once you make it, it doesn't really matter what you meant to say. What matters is what people hear, and that works on a million different levels . . . That's how it exists in the world, and I'm totally fine with that."

At Brown she met Todd Haynes and Barry Ellsworth, an heir to the Kentucky Bingham fortune. After Todd and Cynthia Schneider made the feature *Superstar: The Karen Carpenter Story*, and Todd had the New York premiere of his first film, *Assassins*, at the MIX festival, Todd, Christine, and Barry formed a production company, Apparatus, that made a series of short films. At Brown she also made friends with Brian Greenbaum, who became the executive producer for her first two features. Brian later died of AIDS. Then her friend and mentor, the director of *Parting Glances*, Bill Sherwood, died of AIDS. Todd's boyfriend, the editor and ACT UPer Jim Lyons, was diagnosed. Jim, Todd, and Christine all came to ACT UP.

"I went to the meetings. I could tell that the committees were just like—like the process part. I still can't handle process, and everything has [it]—running a company has it. I could tell that was just not for me. I just was not going to be able to sit in a room with a bunch of people for hours and figure it—just couldn't do it. I was just like, *Put me where I can be the most effective and I'll do it. I'll get arrested. I'll march. I'll be a number. I'll be whatever those—I'll do all of that, but I cannot discuss [process]* . . . I got arrested four times."

Christine produced Todd's overtly AIDS-influenced features, *Poison* and *Safe*, as well as nurturing him his entire career. She recalled that some believe *Safe* is actually his AIDS movie, but that there were people who were angry when *Safe* came out because it was metaphoric. And Todd felt, *The whole point was to crack that all open and explore this whole notion of, you know, what makes you sick, and really do it in a way that makes you uncomfortable.* Through her company, Killer Films, Christine produced work by a number of ACT UP filmmakers, including two features by Tom Kalin—*Swoon* and *Savage Grace*—and work by David Wojnarowicz and Michael Cunningham.

Queer cinema had its explosion, Christine believes, because there was a sense of urgency and people believed that they would not live long. But from the producer's point of view, she was figuring out how to identify audiences and figuring out how to make a queer movie for the right price, so that if only gay people went to see it, it would still make its money back.

JIM LYONS

Jim Lyons grew up in a Catholic family on Long Island. He was strongly bisexual but was always drawn to "being gay," which he connected to reading Burroughs and Ginsberg at a young age. Soon he knew he wanted to be a film editor.

"I was very shy when I was younger—I don't know if I was perceived that way—but in my head I was very shy. And I had this very difficult-to-shake self-image that I think Irish families seem to propagate, but also being from a certain class seems to propagate. Because I got to college only through complete scholarship, and from that point on in my life I was always friends with people who came from a much wealthier background than mine. So even in college I knew that I was going to have to find some way to make money, and I picked film editing—which is what I do for a living—at that point, I had friends who were artists that were living on trust funds and making their art, and that was just not going to happen for me. I was estranged from my family. I didn't want anything from them. And although I was writing and making stuff . . . I was always writing and photographing, but I didn't allow myself to make that leap; instead I decided that I would cut films."

He experienced people in parts of his life who would talk about film *auteurs*, and he felt that NYU film school especially propagated that notion. He thought that approach "was really bullshit and that you really had to learn your craft." He learned by doing, and in the process of cutting other people's work he would come to understand that some mistakes were commonly made. So when he would go to make his own work, he felt he had already experienced fundamental problems with filmmaking. "I really came from no money at all, so when I started to hang out with Todd [Haynes] or those guys it was a very big thing for me, because I had no experience with people who could just go on vacation whenever they want." When Todd was making *Poison* in 1988, Jim acted in it and edited it. They were both already in ACT UP. *Poison* opened in 1990. The film's first showing was at a benefit for Treatment and Data.

Jim felt that he had gotten infected the third time he had gay sex, probably in 1981 or 1982. He experienced the severe "flu-like" symptoms that often appeared when a person was first infected. The doctor thought he had hepatitis. Then they thought he had CMV. The endocrinologist thought it was a virus that he had never heard of. And Jim left it that way. Of course, it took years for AIDS to develop. There was a little bookstore on St. Mark's Place, called East Village Books, where Jim found a tiny pamphlet talking about "the gay plague, GRID." He thought, *My God—maybe this is what I have.* At another point, he thought he had a venereal disease in his throat and went to Barbara Starrett, a well-known AIDS doctor.

"She basically scared the shit out of me. She talked about it—she said, *There is a terrible, terrible, terrible virus out there, and if you are telling me that you are not—you know that you are having unprotected sex, and doing this—you're gonna die.* And sadly, I think I was already infected at that point."

Jim went on a very high dose of AZT, and later he was on ddI and a new drug, dideoxycitadine (ddC), because he tried to jump on the new medications as soon as possible. He got saquinavir, the first protease inhibitor, and indinavir (sold under the brand name Crixivan), which was the second. Saquinavir was rushed onto the market without having enough supply for the amount of people who needed it. And the scientists knew that, so they dosed it at a much lower level than activists felt was needed. Jim's friends told him, *You gotta take twice the level of saquinavir that they are proposing because it won't work any other way.* He was very sick at that time, and very hopeful about it, but the efficacy of it only lasted about four months. "I've seen many, many people get sick and die over the time that I've been positive. It's been good, 'cause I'm still here, but it's bad in that I'm one of the people— like I just got out of the hospital a few days ago—I'm one of the people who has immunity to many of the medications." Jim died in 2007, after our interview.

Remembrance: Lee Schy

The street artist Lee Schy made public art about living with AIDS and the love of gay community. He orchestrated public events around the concept of "family" long before that word took on pronatalist implications.

I'd Rather Be Hit By a Bus—Lee Schy. Created to be wheat-pasted on the street and shared with the community and neighborhood.

JOE FERRARI

"ACT UP was a real period of growth for me. I always joked it was my formative years on a lot of levels, whether it was learning about who I am within a particular community, learning about that community and about our country and about politics and all of that, but also becoming comfortable with myself, and at first through expressing anger at what had been held back. I mean, I think that was a big part of it, or certainly an important part for me as an individual, was expressing anger. I don't think I did express anger as a child all that much. I was a nice kid. I was a good kid. I did what I was told, for the most part."

Joe met his life partner, Lee, in an Actions Committee

meeting in 1987. Lee had been creating a number of different artworks, many of them starting with photography, and then xeroxing images and putting them on the streets. ACT UP was a big part of both of their lives and their relationship. Lee was HIV-positive when he joined ACT UP. And he became educated and politicized, and that became part of who he was. His work never became dark or didactic. It was always tied to these kind and joyful moments with individuals and queer community. He tied feelings of connectedness into being gay and being part of a gay extended family. Not only did Lee do artwork about this experience, but he also started organizing some fun events tied around being gay, specifically July Fourth parties at Long Beach, "which were kind of genius." Some of them generated photographs that he would use in his work.

Once, Lee gathered a couple of hundred gays and lesbians on a typical straight New York beach, Long Beach, all of them being as queer as everyone could be, raising up a big pink triangle flag, doing a blanket toss, having people flying. There were women without their shirts on, which brought the police. Same-sex couples kissing was something rarely seen in public spaces at that time. While it was a blast and a fun presentation of gay culture and gay people, it also created an experience of safety and normalcy that affected straight people, as well as us. "If you had gone to the beach by yourself, two gay men, and made out, for example, you could get beat up. I mean, in those days, Lee and I walking down the street, people would give looks. People would say things. Every single thing we did felt political because of the world in which we were living.

"There was a real feeling in Lee's work that we were taking care of each other. We were there for each other. We had deep pain of watching people die, we had the extraordinary joy of being together, and we built a community, I think amongst ourselves, that really protected us and gave the community of people the strength to be ACT UP, to do the things that got done, to become the people that we were. That was really very much key because the rest of the culture really didn't provide a place to be yourself, to be gay, to be queer in that particular way, to be politicized in that particular way."

Lee died in 1995, just as protease inhibitors were starting to come into the market, so things at that time were really desperate. As his T-cell count went below two hundred, he began taking Bactrim in order to avoid PCP, but the drugs that he needed were still months away. "Lee had a lot of living to do, as he would say."

BOOK THREE

CREATING THE WORLD YOU NEED TO SURVIVE

Do you resent people with AIDS?

Do you trust HIV-negatives?

Have you given up hope for a cure?

When was the last time you cried?

PART VI
Activism Coheres Values and
Creates Counterculture

ACT UP emerged out of a broad, rich, wide, diverse queer counterculture. Having been excluded and ignored by straight power for generations,
deep undergounds of queer opposition were built in which our needs and
realities could be reflected and expressed and in which our authentic
concerns could be engaged. Familial homophobia was common, and
it allowed queer people to build primary bonds with those whom they
never would have known had they been straight. As AIDS revealed the
deprivation of many different communities who were, in a variety of
ways, excluded from mainstream recognition, it brought together people who were already used to identifying from the margins. From this,
ACT UP built a new countercultural social space, one in which people and their relationships were transformed, but its foundations were
already long in place. Communities inside ACT UP then saw values
emerging from their practice. The world did not give us what we needed,
so ACT UP was part of a nexus of people defiantly creating their own
realities.

Here we look at a number of milieus associated with ACT UP that
cohered to deal with AIDS in ways that queer people and people with
AIDS needed and wanted. ACT UP's Inside/Outside strategy continued
with a two-pronged media approach: ACT UP media activists worked

the mainstream press, while others created *OutWeek*, the grassroots journalistic voice of ACT UP's broader community. Dr. Joseph Sonnabend and his staff, including people like ACT UPer Susan Brown, worked at the Community Research Initiative to test new treatments outside of a corporate/government purview, taking on the profit motive behind AZT. ACT UPers worked in Haitian Solidarity and on the Haitian underground railroad between Guantánamo and New York, and there was a critical mass of lawyers with their eyes on justice who came to ACT UP to serve. ACT UP's foundational culture of nonviolent civil disobedience expanded skills and further cohered values as activists prepared for confrontations with the police, and one ex-officer used her own knowledge of NYPD culture to empower ACT UP to deal with police hostility.

12

Getting and Creating Media

CRACKING THE WALLS OF MEDIA EXCLUSION

Although there were closeted gay men in the corporate media, most of them did not jeopardize their privilege by confronting the institutions that employed and protected them. The press maintained a basic distaste for and separation from people with AIDS. As chair of the ACT UP Media Committee, Jay Blotcher—along with his predecessor, Michelangelo Signorile, and his associates, like Alan Klein—worked to break through years of exclusion of gay issues by the mainstream media. Jay employed a number of aggressive tactics to get AIDS activist news included as American news. Yet occasional inclusion or acknowledgment is still a container. And so a vibrant, radical, and independent gay press that was overtly political became essential. Only in this way could a queer point of view be presented and debated and actually cohered. This was just a few years before AIDS medical advertising transformed the queer and AIDS-centered press into a marketing machine. Corporate money was still shunning us, and so our content did not have to attract or appeal to advertisers. In this specific moment, a group of renegades led by Gabriel Rotello created their own weekly gay news magazine, *OutWeek*, expressly to make space for ACT UP's perspective. This dual strategy between ACT UP media and *OutWeek* broke through the walls of the public imagination without watering down the message.

JAY BLOTCHER

From the small town of Randolph, Massachusetts, Jay Blotcher came in on the ground floor with the Media Committee in an inaugural meeting at Vito Russo's apartment on West Twenty-Fourth Street. Somebody handed around a lined paper tablet and said, *Any of you who know fellow journalists, write down all their names, so that we have a group of people we need to contact, so that we can finally get somebody to write about this epidemic properly.* Up until then, as Larry Kramer's 1989 book, *Reports from the Holocaust: The Making of an AIDS Activist,* addresses, there was a virtual media blackout surrounding AIDS, except for gay publications and gay media. No one else was covering AIDS because they either just didn't care or found it distasteful. The people who had it had already been exiled to the outskirts of society and were considered to be expendable. So the group at Vito's apartment sat down and wrote the list of people they knew, which was formidable, considering that the ACT UP Media Committee was composed of journalists and publicists. David Corkery and Bob Rafsky helmed it at first. After them, it was Michelangelo Signorile, who passed it on to Jay.

It seems absurd now to think that people wouldn't be writing about AIDS with compassion and objectivity, but that was the brutal reality at the time.

"Either they ignored it, or when they wrote about it, they wrote in the most desultory of terms and described the AIDS activists as *troublemakers* and the people with AIDS as *outside the general population . . .* For me, it was a revelation. I don't think I was that naïve, but it was like, *Oh, journalism isn't objective, because if it were objective, then people would be covering this immense public health hazard with a greater interest.* So it became clear to me that the media pick and choose what they deem important—that it is political."

At a typical ACT UP demonstration, people in T-shirts or bomber jackets would be lying in the middle of the street yelling, pumping their fists up in the air. Jay would come on the scene, always wearing a suit and tie. "That was a really contrived, but focused way of trying to insert a little legitimacy in there." He wanted to show the press corps that ACT UP could play their game, too, and should not be easily dismissed. He would go up to the journalists and say, *Hi, you may want to know why these people are yelling and screaming. I'm the person to tell you, because I can speak in very calm, clear, collected, complete sentences.* "And, they would be soothed by the fact that a person with a seemingly sane face was disseminating the information." He felt that he had to play the role, because otherwise, we would be dismissed. It is important to understand that being openly gay, itself, often lost someone credibility. It was considered a sign of being inherently inappropriate and untrustworthy.

OUTWEEK: THE VOICE OF ACT UP CULTURE

In the 1980s and '90s, queer people were excluded from authentic representation in corporate television and film, both news and entertainment, and most lesbians as well as queer people of color could not get serious stage time for plays from their points of view. As a result, print was the most important venue for community communication. Queer and feminist bookstores were all over the country. In 1992, I was able to do a book tour that stopped in each gay bookstore in the U.S. South. Every big city had a least one gay and/or feminist newspaper, and some, like San Francisco, had more than three. Most heterosexuals, whether civilians, scientists, civic/political leaders, or cultural gatekeepers, did not read the queer or women's press because, frankly, they didn't know it existed. The walls between countercultural queer life and the official mainstream were thick and invisible. The queer press was made for queer people, and it both reflected and created the countercultural bonds that built community.

ANDREW MILLER

Andrew Miller grew up a "squirrelly, hypersmart, bookish, musical, isolated kid," who was also gay, and he was afraid early on because he lived through a time when lots of his friends died. But the cataclysm crept in through a kind of slow unraveling of the fabric of our community, "through lack of information, and fear, and not having answers, and being sick, and not knowing what to do, or having somebody else be sick, and not knowing how to fix it, and not knowing if you were gonna get it, and not having anybody that you could ask about it, or not wanting anybody to know . . . not being able to tell anybody else." Andrew remembered rushing out to get his passport, because there was a six- or nine-month period when President George H. W. Bush and Congress were considering making an HIV test a requirement for getting one.

Andrew joined the ACT UP Actions Committee and the Coordinating Committee while working as a stringer for out-of-town gay weeklies. He was writing for *The Bay Area Reporter* (San Francisco) and *Windy City Times* (Chicago) and, most of all, *Gay Community News* (Boston). At this time, around 1988, the situation in New York with the gay press was dismal.

"The only game in town was the *New York Native*, which had broken the story about AIDS and had some wonderful writing in it, originally, including by Larry Kramer, also some really solid reporting. But by this time . . . they refused to believe that HIV was the cause of AIDS and their reporting was getting very bizarre. They had become very hostile to ACT UP . . . My frustration was that often there were better stories about New York—often by me, but also by other people—in the papers in Chicago and Boston than there were in New York. And I hated this . . . there wasn't a way to circulate meaningful information."

Andrew met Michelangelo Signorile at ACT UP. Mike had been talking to Gabriel Rotello, who had access to someone who could provide funding. That person turned out to be a PWA businessman named Kendall Morrison, a phone sex entrepreneur who made his money from a service called 550-TOOL. Kendall was in ACT UP, and he signed on to fund the publication. A paper was also a way for him to have a vehicle in which to advertise his phone sex lines. "So he was a smart businessman."

MICHELANGELO SIGNORILE

OutWeek came about when a bunch of people who had been working on the Media Committee, along with others in ACT UP, were talking about how they needed a publication, something that would be the voice of the new bold, oppositional, and coalitional politics coming out of ACT UP. Sex was very much a part of the ACT UP culture, so having phone sex ads, as a result of Kendall's patronage, "just seemed appropriate and fine." There was never really a clear delineation between *OutWeek* and ACT UP—not only in the coverage but also on the business side. It was widely distributed on corner newsstands in the city, and "other people were reading it who hated ACT UP, and hated *OutWeek*, but they would read it." So it was broadening the debate to more people who needed to be engaged.

ANDREW MILLER

Gabriel was the editor. Mike was the features editor. Andrew was the news editor. Maria Perez became art director, and Sarah Pettit was arts editor. *OutWeek*'s cultural framework intersected with ACT UP's. It covered shows by ACT UP artists, reviewed books by ACT UP authors. Maria Perez's visual style was very downtown and contemporary, a combination of camp and sophistication. Handmade and sleek, it was interactive with ACT UP's countercultural aesthetic. When there were rifts in ACT UP, *OutWeek* covered them, and when ACT UP attacked politicians, *OutWeek* always asked them for a response. Its main political difference with ACT UP was that *OutWeek* endorsed candidates for public office, which ACT UP would never do. Even with a small regular circulation of ten thousand, the weight of being on New York's political and cultural cutting edge gave it a long reach. "Gay people weren't out in publishing, to the extent that they are today. *OutWeek* made it possible for there to be a National Lesbian and Gay Journalism Association." *Gay Community News* in Boston was the only other queer newspaper so closely aligned with activist movements. The national gay press, especially *The Advocate*, started out bold, but as the community expanded, it remained white male oriented and thereby became more driven toward assimilation. *The Advocate* also gave up its sex ads in order to attract the first mainstream brand, Absolut Vodka, that dared to advertise in a gay publication. One *Advocate* editor told me that when they put anyone but a white male on the cover, they lost sales. *OutWeek*, on the other hand, regularly had women, people of color, drag performers, or genderqueer people on the cover. The publication closed in 1991, a year before ACT UP's split, and no queer publication has been both that cool and that influential since.

GABRIEL ROTELLO

Gabriel Rotello was raised in "WASP Connecticut." His mother was a teacher, and his father invested in real estate. He moved to New York in 1974 and became a keyboard player. His partner, Hap Haddon, got sick in 1986 and died two years later. Gabriel went to a support group at GMHC and then saw ACT UP's concentration camp float at Gay Pride. What stood out for him in ACT UP was the structure. There was no hierarchy. There were no paid officials. There were no offices.

He joined the Fundraising Committee, and then, one day, "this light bulb went on in my head, and I thought, *Oh my God. What if somebody started a new publication that reflected what's going on in ACT UP?*" Gabriel went to Barnes & Noble and bought two bags full of books on how to start a magazine, read them all, and took notes. He made a list of, in his opinion, the smartest lesbians and gay men in New York who had been involved in politics in ways that he had not been involved. He called them all up and said, *Hi, my name's Gabriel Rotello. I'm going to start a new gay magazine in New York, and I would love to just meet with you, and you could just tell me everything that I need to know.* And every single one of them said *yes.* The way he understood it was that he created his own, independent affinity group, and *OutWeek* clearly could not have been an affinity group of ACT UP, because it was a commercial enterprise that cost about a million dollars overall. Yet it was far from traditional. Gabriel knew that they were not going to get corporate ads. "We were calling the cardinal *a fucking pig.*" Sometimes, when something particularly outrageous was on the cover, they could ramp up the print run to thirty or forty thousand and sell out. Even if it was just a typical week and it was the middle of summer, *OutWeek* could print fifteen thousand copies and sell out, running on a combination of circulation and queer-friendly and countercultural ad revenue. The pharmaceutical companies didn't even try to advertise.

OutWeek's biggest controversy had nothing to do with ACT UP directly, but everything to do with AIDS: outing. Initiated by Michelangelo, the goal of outing was to confront powerful people in positions to influence AIDS policy who hid their homosexuality—usually to maintain their currency—and in this way deprived the AIDS community of arenas of support and visibility that were necessary to shift the paradigm. "At the end of the day, I think you can put on the fingers of one hand the names of the famous people that we actually outed. We talked about it as breaking a barrier in journalism."

THE WOODY MYERS CONTROVERSY

The overwhelming majority of the lesbian and gay vote had turned against Mayor Koch because of his languid response to AIDS, and instead supported Mayor-Elect David Dinkins. As one of his first orders of business, Dinkins announced that he was appointing a man named Woodrow Myers to be his new health commissioner, who would be in charge of AIDS policy. Myers, who was Black, had previously been health commissioner of Indiana. Dinkins was the first African American mayor, and African Americans had a huge number of health issues in New York City. Gabriel began calling people in the Indiana state government to find out what Myers was like, and he discovered, to his horror, that Myers had advocated for mandatory contact tracing, mandatory name reporting, and the quarantining of people with AIDS in Indiana. And everybody Gabriel called said the same thing. "It was *common knowledge* in Indiana."

OutWeek came out every Monday, the same day as the ACT UP meetings. Gabriel wrote a story, five days before publication, during which time the mayor might actually appoint Myers. And Gabriel felt that the scoop couldn't wait. So he called *The New York Times* and said, *I have a story that I think that you're going to want to put on the front page of* The New York Times, *but it's going to be on the cover of* OutWeek *next Monday. But we sort of feel like we can't really wait, so I will give you the story, provided that you credit it to* OutWeek *magazine in your lede.* And they said, *Well, let's see what it is.*

So he faxed it over, and about five minutes later, they called and said, *It's going to be on the front page of* The New York Times *tomorrow, and it's going to say "*OutWeek *magazine" right in the lede.* And that started what has often been called the most bitter dispute of the Dinkins administration. In typical *OutWeek* fashion, they ramped it up: there had been a selection committee for Woody Myers, and there was a very prominent gay person on that committee named Tim Sweeney, who was the associate director of GMHC. Gabriel called him up before the *Times* ran the piece and asked, *Did you know about this? You were supposed to be vetting this guy or anybody for Dinkins.* And Tim said, *Yeah, I did know about it, but I didn't really think it was that big a deal. You have to understand, Indiana's a very conservative state. I actually felt that he was sort of taming even worse things that might have happened in Indiana. He was trying to keep it from being even worse than it was going to be. And he seems like a really nice guy, and I met him and he was really great.* Gabriel called everybody back up in Indiana and said, *What's up with this?* They were like, *Are you kidding? He was the guy. Nobody even talked about contact tracing or mandatory name reporting until he came along. It was his idea. What are you talking about?*

In *OutWeek*'s role of trying to keep gay leaders accountable to the grassroots, Gabriel wrote a strongly worded editorial, in which he excoriated Mayor Dinkins. He said, *He's broken the vow. We regret having endorsed him for mayor. He's proven himself to be an enemy of our community.* And then he called for Tim Sweeney to resign or, if he refused to resign, for the board of GMHC to fire him. That's the kind of thing that *OutWeek* did on a fairly regular basis.

"In ACT UP there was accountability. You got up to say something on the floor, and if you were an asshole, people screamed at you and told you. It was like Parliament in London, *Get off! Sit down!*, you know, whatever. But with our [greater queer] community, there was this self-perpetuating group of people, boards of directors that were dominated by very wealthy people. That's mostly how you got on a board; you were really rich and you had lots of money, then you would sit on the board and decide the policy and elevate various people, and there was just no accountability."

The next week the letter section exploded in *OutWeek*, with a number of leaders of gay and lesbian organizations calling for Gabriel's resignation. But Gabriel experienced a lot of people supporting him, indicating a more radical turn in the general stance of the community toward its own organizational boards. "And it just turned into this cacophonous thing." Sweeney did not resign, but Woody Myers did. And he was replaced by Margaret Hamburg, who had previously worked closely with ACT UP in Washington at the NIH. The threats of mandatory testing were averted, setting an entirely different tone for the future of AIDS in New York City.

"What we were trying to do—in *OutWeek*—was to take the vision, or at least my vision, of what the floor of ACT UP was, that energy, that anger, that whole worldview, and just send it out to the world. To people that could never make a Monday-night meeting because they lived in Des Moines, Iowa, or Tallahassee, Florida, to a high school kid that could never even get to New York. Just to send that out there to inspire people to believe that we could get through this nightmare, you know, with strength and positivity and power and humor and effectiveness."

Remembrance: Mark Fotopoulos

While media activists inside ACT UP were working toward accurate representation, and as the rank and file created collective protest with theatrical visual elements, some people with AIDS created their own one-person statements aimed at both the corporate media and the rest of the community. Mark Fotopoulos was an actor who had appeared in the Broadway revival of *West Side Story* as a Jet. His activist message for the media was to stand at every ACT UP demonstration with a handmade sign: LIVING WITH AIDS X YEARS, X MONTHS, NO THANKS TO YOU MR REAGAN. Every month he would change the numbers on his sign. Images of him are captured in most footage and many stills of ACT UP demonstrations and actions. Mark got sicker and sicker but still appeared when he could, over a period of years, in the background of many newspaper photos and five-o'clock news broadcasts. He was disintegrating in public, in defiance and denunciation. He did the most that one man standing alone could do to communicate his experience.

ALAN KLEIN

Alan Klein and his then-partner, the writer Karl Soehnlein, came to ACT UP right out of Ithaca College and quickly got deeply involved in the movement. Karl was elected facilitator, and Alan worked on logistics. Young and energetic, they were part of the sexual, loving subculture of ACT UP, bonding through eros, care, and friendship.

"Mark Fotopoulos, who was the first person with AIDS

that I really zeroed in on, first one that I knew who was also—who just happened to be absolutely exquisite. I mean, he was a really, really great-looking guy, and it was a mind-fuck at first, because AIDS and, you know, *hot* didn't go together in media at that time. That was, again, my first exposure to it . . . I wasn't supposed to be turned on by somebody with HIV, but yet there I was . . . we were not close friends. We were friends. We were *ACT UP* close."

Mark was a fixture of dignity and expression.

ACT UP demonstration at Foley Square, Federal Plaza, June 30, 1987. From left to right: David Z. Kirschenbaum (obscured), Anthony Viti, Mike Barr (obscured), Gregg Bordowitz, Steven Webb, David Robinson, Mark Fotopoulos, Michael Cowling, Deborah Alexander, Ortez Alderson, Michael Savino, David Strah (Photograph by Donna Binder)

"He was an actor, a good-looking guy. I think he was really concerned about his KS lesions, which were all over, including his face. I think that was a real issue for him. I think it was a problem. But, you know, I remember Mark being there with his—you know, *Living with AIDS. No thanks to you, Mr. Reagan. No thanks to you, Mr. Bush*, throughout ACT UP. And he was one of the people that I found an inspiration."

And then one day he was gone.

13

Community Research Initiative, Dr. Joseph Sonnabend, and the Battle over AZT

AZT loomed large in the public imagination. It played the reassuring role of hope, evidence that someone, somewhere, who was in charge was taking care of this thing. On Broadway, at the end of *Angels in America*, Roy Cohn has died of AIDS, and his nurse, Belize, steals the remaining doses of AZT for his friend Prior, hoping to save his life. It is a weird moment. First of all, if AZT worked so well, then why did Roy die? This is a leap of logic that the play doesn't address. But the bigger question is: Will AZT save Prior's life? The story is set between 1985 and 1986, but audiences watched it from 1991 on. Watching this play in 1993, the year it opened on Broadway, I, as an active ACT UPer, had already known since 1987 that AZT did not work. Yet the straight and mainstream audience in the Broadway theater did not have this information. Although not an intention of the play, a consequence was that as the audience left the theater each night, most left somewhat reassured that AZT meant hope. Those of us in ACT UP already knew that the greedy pharmaceutical company Burroughs Wellcome was not going to save lives. But for the general theatergoing, *New York Times*–reading public, well, they had no idea. As hard as we tried, the story just wasn't being accurately told or reported. The contradiction was representative of the battle between activists and pharmaceutical companies for the public imagination. Was a greedy pharmaceutical company going to save lives? As the curtain fell, only some people in the audience actually knew AZT was not the answer, because they already had this information before they took their seats.

Frustrated with inaction and greed by big pharma and the government, activists and renegade doctors created the Community Research

Initiative (CRI) as an independent organization to study treatments separate from the profit motive, looking only at what was best for the patients. CRI was actually testing treatments without the government or pharmaceutical companies. In this way they were a truly grassroots scientific and medical organization. The staff was comprised of people with very high personal stakes, bucking all the systems: both corporate profit and public myth.

SUSAN C. BROWN

Susan C. Brown was raised in Galveston, Texas, where her family were mostly accountants. She met her partner, Brad Taylor, in Houston, and together they came to New York to visit his brother Biff, who was gay and graduating from Juilliard for dance. They stayed.

Biff had pneumonia and had clearly lost a lot of weight. In a few months, he ended up in a hospital in Midland, Texas. The doctor had to get emergency permission, *compassionate use*, to prescribe pentamidine for pneumonia. And then Biff moved back to New York and stayed with Susan and Brad, who had become involved with ACT UP. Brad worked in the Spanish-Language Translation Committee while both he and Susan scanned the AIDS treatment horizons.

Larry Kramer made an infamous announcement on the floor of ACT UP. "They are dancing in the Streets in San Francisco," claiming that the drug trichosanthin (commonly called Compound Q), made from a Chinese cucumber, was a viable treatment. Susan tried to get Compound Q for Biff and ended up volunteering at CRI, where new treatments were being tested in a community-based environment. CRI never did take on Compound Q, which ultimately proved worthless and, in fact, toxic.

There was a man named Tom Hannon, whom Susan really trusted. She knew that Biff was on his way back to New York after his hospital stay in Midland, and she was trying to find a new doctor for him. She knew that he would be on Medicaid, and that certainly limited their options. She had access to a book of all the physicians in New York who would see people with AIDS. Susan would call and call and call, but nobody would take Medicaid. Finally, she appealed to Tom Hannon. And he said, *Call Joe Sonnabend. Here's his number. You'll wake him up, but it's okay.* And that's exactly how it happened. Joe told Susan, *As soon as he gets here, tell him to come see me.* And that was the beginning of a real relationship. Susan started working at CRI three days a week.

"There were no therapies out there. [Sonnabend] worked in a lab out at Kings County Hospital. And then he was at NYU, seeing people with STDs, because it was coming up more and more. So he started a little practice, where he just saw men with STDs. So—in the course of that, he began to see the trend of what was going on . . . Behavior was causing [the men] to be sick. As far as I understand, [gay men] went into their own community to try to articulate this. And it was not met with very much enthusiasm, because people felt like they were being indicted for their lifestyle . . . Originally Joe and Michael [Callen] and I guess Richard [Berkowitz] went into the bathhouses, and tried to do some teaching, instruction, education . . . I know they were not met with much appreciation . . . There were no treatments or therapies or drugs or anything."

CRI organized a community trial on AL-721, the substance made from egg lipids that men were spreading on their toast in the morning, believing it would increase immunity. It was a concoction that CRI literally made in a bathtub. CRI was also involved in aerosolized pentamidine studies. And when it was approved by the FDA, part of that progress was based on data CRI had gathered outside of corporate and governmental structures.

"Pentamidine was the most significant. At that time, I'm sure, as you know, everybody died from pneumonia, and they died real quickly . . . There was frustration because there wasn't anything to help Biff. So as he got sicker . . . he would go really up and down, with his two T cells . . . He had MAI, which really caused him the most sickness, because it causes terrible gastrointestinal problems. And he wasn't absorbing food, because his gut was just a mess. It was—*necrotizing* was the word they used. And [Dr.] Don [Kotler] put a tube in his stomach. I guess we were feeding that way . . . It worked very little, and he didn't get any satisfaction out of eating—and he had all of the visual symptoms of AIDS at that time. For this beautiful dancer, whose body was—not everything, but it was definitely nice. And it withered . . . He was certainly angry. He would go through sort of, an understanding of it, I guess—what are you going to do? You know what's happening to you."

Biff died in Susan and Brad's house in August of 1992.

CRI continued doing studies. They researched stavudine (d4T), which was very toxic. But it worked well in combination with lamivudine (3TC), "the first time they used a combination." CRI did the first ritonavir (an antiretroviral) study. And that was one of the times when CRI had a list of people clamoring to get a spot in that study, but they only had thirty places. Yet again, a much-sought-after drug did not pan out. People were not actually getting better, beyond gaining a few T cells, but they seemed to stop losing them. But all those early drugs, as many drugs today for serious illnesses do, had side effects. People ended up with facial wasting and buffalo humps—deforming lumps of fat on the top of people's backs—as their body fat depleted and redistributed. This was very depressing to a number of patients, many of whom felt that their looks were destroyed and that they now carried the telltale signs of being a person with AIDS, easily identifiable from the side effects of their medications. "But it certainly kept people going. And that's what it felt like at the time. It was like, *Oh, if you can just make it to this, then by then, we'll have more drugs.* Because they were coming then. It was ACT UP pressure that led to that."

DR. JOSEPH SONNABEND

Joseph Sonnabend was born into a Jewish family in Rhodesia (now Zimbabwe) and grew up in South Africa. Both his parents were Russian but based in Italy. His father was a sociologist, and his mother was a postrevolutionary physician. When anti-Jewish race laws were put into effect in Fascist Italy in 1929, the Sonnabends were ironically saved by transferring to jobs in colonial Africa. Joe went to medical school in Apartheid-era Johannesburg and moved to New York in 1967. When AIDS became visible, he started a practice for the first time, and did research, taught, and ran independent studies. He was deeply involved early with the process of producing interferon, which was later tried by others as a treatment for cancer and for AIDS, both of which he disputed based on his clinical experience. But Dr. Sonnabend's most controversial position, ultimately proven correct, was against giving people with AIDS long-term high doses of AZT.

"I have noticed, over the years, that clinical medicine in HIV is riddled with conflicts of interest. But so is all of medicine . . . the undue influence that marketing has on clinical practice . . . on the way that doctors are got to, and induced to prescribe for this and that disease . . . Their marketing people can make you an expert, calling you *an expert*, or *a decision-maker*, or *a thought leader* . . . They invent these things, and they confer on you, it's just some snit in the marketing department [that] makes you an expert, all of a sudden. And then you say something, and experts agree that this is whatever. And this is—as I say, this happens in everything."

AZT

Dr. Sonnabend recalled that the push behind AZT was not only the pharmaceutical company's profit motive but also the NIH's desire to make "a publicity killing," showing that it was on top of the epidemic. He found that this rush to victory created a "deadly sloppiness" in early studies that was, in part, a consequence of how devalued the lives of the patients were. "If this disease had been across the board, not been so localized in marginalized [populations]—would AZT have happened? And I suspect it may not."

The large trial of AZT conducted by Burroughs Wellcome enrolled three hundred people with an AIDS diagnosis simultaneously in a number of cities, including New York, at St. Luke's Hospital. The trial was advertised as "double-blind": half the patients would get AZT, and the other half would get a placebo. The foundation of a placebo trial is that neither the patients nor the doctors would know who was getting what, so as to not prejudice the doctors who might unconsciously treat patients differently knowing who was actually receiving medication. There were a hundred and fifty people, roughly, in each section. Then Burroughs Wellcome suddenly stopped the trial. When the reasons were presented to the public through a press release, the company announced that of the patients actually getting AZT over seventeen weeks—five months short of the expected completion of the study—only one person died. But, by sharp contrast, Burroughs Wellcome announced that in the placebo arm, nineteen people died. The findings between the two groups were so dramatically different that Burroughs Wellcome claimed this outcome as proof that AZT saved lives. And so it closed the trial and gave everyone AZT. The message to the public was clear: "Everyone has got to get AZT." From that point on, the floodgates were opened. AZT became widely prescribed as the standard of care, including for people who were positive but had no symptoms who were now being prescribed AZT as soon as they were diagnosed.

Celia Farber, writing in the popular music and culture magazine *SPIN* in 1989, covered the story: "Burroughs Wellcome stock went through the roof when the announcement was made. At a price of $8,000 per patient per year (not including blood-work and transfusions), AZT is the most expensive drug ever marketed. Burroughs Wellcome's gross profits for next year are estimated at $230 million. Stock market analysts predict that Burroughs Wellcome may be selling as much as $2 billion worth of AZT, under the brand name Retrovir, each year by the mid-1990s—matching Burroughs Wellcome's total sales for all its products last year."

But Dr. Sonnabend was suspicious. He felt that seventeen weeks was too fast for nineteen people to die. He knew from experience that even with PCP and no other treatments, he would not have expected that many people to die. And so he thought, *What's going on here? There's something wrong. Why did so many people die?* Martin Delaney, the director of San Francisco's Project Inform, filed a request under the Freedom of Information Act and received information from Burroughs Wellcome's records on this trial. When Joe Sonnabend saw the files, he found that they had been significantly redacted. So ACT UP New York got him another version, which was perfectly legible. It took him about three weeks to fully digest the findings. The first thing he did was try to find out why people died. What were the actual causes of death? After all, a person doesn't actually die of AIDS; AIDS destroys the immune system, which in turn causes people to die of an opportunistic infection. The word *AIDS* is a catchall, like the word *cancer*, for a wide variety of variations, strains, and manifestations that can be different in each person.

Dr. Sonnabend believed that, since people with AIDS die of an opportunistic infection, whether a person lived or died in the short term depended on how quickly the developing infection was diagnosed, and then how aggressively it was treated. When he examined the files, Dr. Sonnabend discovered that in many cases, the actual cause of death with not recorded. So while some patients were noted to have died of an opportunistic infection like pneumocystis pneumonia, others were simply marked as having died of AIDS. This was very sloppy for a major drug trial.

Another thing he discovered was that the deaths were not uniform. They tended to happen in certain places and not in others. For example, nobody in the AZT trial died in New York. People died in San Diego, people died in Florida. But in some places there were no deaths at all. Furthermore, there was no analysis of this discrepancy. He found that the FDA did not follow up on the deaths. For Dr. Sonnabend, whether a patient lived or a patient died of their opportunistic infection could be put down to kind of low-tech doctoring, what he called *patient management*. Quick diagnosis and skillful treatment—basic, old-fashioned doctoring—made all the difference with an opportunistic infection. How patients are initially examined determines whether they are at risk for a specific infection, which should prepare the doctor to monitor them. For Dr. Sonnabend, articulating patient management strategies of how best to look after patients would keep them alive and alleviate their suffering and certainly help them. Yet this was never articulated and emphasized in the discourse surrounding AIDS treatment. Instead, Dr. Sonnabend recalled, the emphasis was always about looking for *a drug*, a single gesture, one less labor-intensive than patient management. This led him to wonder if there was any reason to believe that the placebo group and the treatment group were managed in different ways.

"You'd think, *of course not*. Why do we [do] blind trials in clinical medicine? We all know it's important, but then you have to ask yourself, *why*. Well, we think it's important because we want to know whether an effect we see is a consequence of a drug, but not the consequence of something else. So bias can operate in many different kinds of ways. And so we don't want the patients to do anything; we don't want the medical people to do anything, in the knowledge that they are going to affect the outcome . . . because unblinding has led to bias."

But, as Dr. Sonnabend knew from his clinical experience, it actually was impossible to blind AZT. Doctors could go through the motions of blinding. But they could not succeed, because within a few days, AZT leads to changes in routine blood counts that the doctors can easily see. So they would know which patient was getting the medicine, and which the placebo. Since the doctors did know who was who, did they treat their patients differently, resulting in deaths in some cities? Because the trial had only lasted seventeen weeks instead of five months, Dr. Sonnabend felt that, with a halted trial, there was no evidence of the effects or effectiveness of AZT beyond seventeen weeks. And therefore, in Dr. Sonnabend's estimation, any further prescribing of AZT would be without knowledge, so "it would be inadvisable to continue AZT" for anyone beyond seventeen weeks.

The next issue to address was the question, revealed in the FOIA report but kept out of the Burroughs Wellcome press statement, of why deaths that caused the researchers to shutter the trial and declare victory were only in specific cities. In the New York trial at St. Luke's, Dr. Sonnabend noticed that every person who entered the trial had a doctor. The study doctor wasn't their doctor; they had their own doctor. And nobody in the placebo group died. But in Miami that wasn't the case. The study doctor was also the individual patient's doctor, so there was no uniform patient management.

This difference, also not addressed by Burroughs Wellcome, was significant, and it eliminated an entire layer of care and attention. Therefore, not only was the study not blind, but there was no second layer of support. The inherent bias of knowing that a person with AIDS was not getting any treatment may have impacted the care of that person, producing deaths in cities with no individual patient care, and survival in cities where even people receiving the placebo had two levels of doctors looking at their cases. Rather than proving that AZT worked, in fact, according to Dr. Sonnabend's assessment, the death rate only showed that when the study was not blind, and patients had only the trial doctor as their doctor, they died.

This trial was also giving AZT at the high dose of fifteen hundred milligrams, which Sonnabend called "ridiculous." People taking AZT soon began showing rising virus levels, but the virus was no longer the same, having mutated to resist the drug. This would become a key factor in ACT UP's split, later, when AZT was given to pregnant women. Today, AZT is sometimes prescribed in low doses, in combination with other treatments. But for years, in search of endless markets, AZT was given alone, as a monotherapy, in high doses that themselves caused deaths. In 1993, the Anglo-French Concorde trial, a three-year study of 1,740 HIV-positive people, confirmed that AZT does not ultimately improve survival or slow the disease in HIV-positive people, and that AZT was no better than a placebo in preventing the onset of AIDS and death. After three years, 92 percent of the AZT group was still alive as compared to 93 percent of the placebo group. So even though Sonnabend was proven correct by history, and his findings resonated with ACT UP's continued push for other treatments, and though studies eventually diversified away from AZT, thousands of people died either because AZT didn't work, or because taking it too early and at too-high doses made patients immune to future treatments. In this way, ACT UP, CRI, and others who pushed for more diverse development and study of new treatments were proven visionary. So, for example, the hero of *Angels in America*, Prior, might have actually died *because* he took AZT, instead of the implication that his life may have been saved by it.

"I'm very sad, for example, sad—I don't know, I can't find the right word—but if I think of the people in the earliest years, the patients who, or people with AIDS, who died horribly, and who did, I think, rather wonderful things on this earth, who completely just don't exist any longer. They've been—the things, some of the things they have done, the credit's been taken by others. They're just forgotten. Not that one needs to memorialize individuals, but—at the end of the day, maybe it's just sort of that the sadness of ineffable suffering is for nothing, in a way."

14

ACT UP and the Haitian Underground Railroad

Early on in the AIDS crisis Haitian people were targeted and incarcerated at the U.S. naval base in Guantánamo Bay, Cuba, as HIV was used as an excuse to exclude Black refugees from the United States. ACT UPers like Betty Williams and Esther Kaplan organized for two years to support legal battles, later winning them, and then finding themselves responsible for locating nonexistent "AIDS housing" so that freed refugees could finally settle in New York. Ultimately, the actions of a small group of people relocated and housed over one hundred HIV-positive Haitians in NYC. ACT UP held four demonstrations about the incarceration of HIV-positive Haitians in Guantánamo. Activists extended ACT UP's reach to this most punished and marginalized group of PWAs—incarcerated refugees of color—in what became ACT UP's first international relationship.

ANNE-CHRISTINE D'ADESKY

Anne-Christine d'Adesky grew up mostly in central Florida. Her family were white French colonials with strong roots in Haiti. Her father was born there, her grandparents lived there, and she grew up in a primarily French-speaking household, as English was her parents' second language. She went on to earn a journalism degree from Columbia. Haiti was under the dictatorship of Jean-Claude "Baby Doc" Duvalier, and Anne-Christine felt that she was in a position to document something from an insider perspective and to speak out. She got involved in human rights reporting, and would go back and forth to Haiti on journalistic projects. At first she wrote for progressive newspapers and magazines, like *In These Times* and then *The Village Voice* and *The Nation*. Eventually, she became a stringer for the *San Francisco Examiner* in the mid-eighties.

"I was white and working in a predominantly Black Haitian movement. And what impressed me was getting solidarity, feeling supported, in fact, by a community. When I was in Haiti, I was treated as a race traitor, always, by the elite and the middle class of [white] people who thought I should have solidarity with them. And, politically, I was very openly speaking out against them. And so I think that if anything, I was conscious of feeling embraced and there were probably times when I felt a desire to be able to have more contact with lesbians and gays in Haiti. I tried, but [queer] people were not that visible at that time. I did meet some of the people who later became AIDS activists in Haiti. But they found me, I didn't find them. It wasn't an easy place to be an open lesbian or gay man in the early eighties—at least, I didn't find it so."

In 1981 and '82, she was in Haiti, and there was an epidemic going on. Some of the first reporting that Anne-Christine did in those early years was for the *New York Native* on Haitian Americans in New York, and how they were being heavily stigmatized. Haitian Americans, like gay men and women, were not permitted to give blood. The groups excluded from donating were known as "the four *Hs*": hemophiliacs, heroin users, homosexuals, and Haitian Americans.

"For many years in Haiti, I don't think there was a death certificate that was signed that said it was HIV. But so many people were dying that, after a while, it became really obvious . . . A lot of the focus was really on the safety of the blood supply. It had a huge impact on people being able to get refugee status here . . . People were fleeing Haiti, trying to get status here, and being rejected because of HIV or concerns around communicable diseases. So, so much of the organizing here . . . wasn't really on the issue of the rights of PWAs or anything like that. It was just very specifically, *We're not gay, we're Haitians. We're being discriminated against, simply because we're Blacks.* So there was a racial discourse—the undertone of the official policy was racism. And, within Haiti, there was a real backlash. People were terrified to come out in any way or be seen as gay."

It's really difficult to know what the sources of HIV were for Haiti or for the Caribbean, but Anne-Christine believes that quite a number professional-class Haitians were posted to places in Africa where epidemics were developing, like in Kinshasa, Zaire. "Again, when your sexuality is so stigmatized, how can you possibly be really able to document whether someone was exposed through gay sex or through straight sex?" At the same time, the blood supply in Haiti was not very clean. Haiti is the poorest country in the Western Hemisphere. There have always been sales of commercial blood. A lot of Haitians engaged in sex work as a form of survival. And, for a long time, gay men and bisexual men from other countries saw Haiti as a place to have cheap and easy sex. Anne-Christine knew gay men, including some she met through ACT UP members, who had traveled to Haiti as sex tourists. Although the dominant narrative at the time was that AIDS in Haiti was heterosexual, Anne-Christine observed that, as in the United States, there were many Haitian gay and bisexual men who married women because of cultural demands.

Like many women in ACT UP, Anne-Christine came from the reproductive rights movement, which heavily influenced her perspective on AIDS activism.

"I actually think it was the closest to the reproductive rights work, because it was the angriest. People in reproductive rights were really angry. I didn't think the people in the peace movement were as angry at all. I thought that they were sort of morally high ground in the peace movement, but I don't feel like there was the same direct stake. And I think with AIDS, it was such a direct thing, because people were terrified . . . Coming out of Haiti, where a lot of people had died and were dying, it felt much more urgent to me. And so it was compelling in that way . . . One of the early experiences I had in Haiti was I was invited to an exorcism of a man who was dying of AIDS. And what I discovered was that he had dementia, and he was being prayed for and this was the kind of care that was available—palliative care. People were just trying to sort of usher this person from one realm into another. And it was very moving to me. And it was also frustrating to realize that he had a serious disease that was affecting his behavior and his brain. And I took that experience and went back to the States and tried to find out about HIV in the brain, and then shared what I knew with physicians in Haiti."

Anne-Christine consulted in the States with people who were experts on the brain, like Justin McArthur at Johns Hopkins, but the problem for Haiti was that they had no access to any pharmaceutical treatments, and those medications didn't work anyway for the most part. So Anne-Christine worked with members of ACT UP's Alternative Treatments Committee. She and Jon Greenberg spoke for hours about the brain, trying to find complementary treatments that could be applied to a deprived zone like Haiti. At one point they tried vitamin B_{12} shots. The situation was dire.

BETTY WILLIAMS

Betty Williams grew up in a rich family in Connecticut. "Well, basically, the people that formed our community were so privileged that not much bothered them except potential violations of the zoning laws or something, or, you know, a little bit of garlic getting in the salad dressing at the country club." In the mid-seventies, she became a Quaker, partly in response to the election of Reagan; she wanted to deal with the specifics of how people lived in more serious ways. Suddenly, a way opened. Betty had the opportunity to start a shelter for homeless people at the Fifteenth Street Friends Meeting in New York, with a friend, future ACT UP member John Maynard.

The church-run "so-called emergency shelter movement" began in 1980 or '81, during the Koch administration, after Reagan defunded housing, mental health care, and TB care, and large numbers of people who had been dependent on public institutions were literally out on the street. The Quakers started a shelter, and Betty was there every morning, every night, with a small band of volunteers, including some homeless people known around the neighborhood. The shelter served fifteen men and women with histories of mental illness and program resistance referred from drop-in centers. "It became quite clear that this was not a winter emergency just caused by cold weather, that it was a chronic state in people's lives."

Then her oldest and dearest friend, George Lahey, from Parsons, got sick the next year. He was one of the first 1,115 people to die in this country from AIDS, and his was the first memorial service for someone who died of AIDS held at the Fifteenth Street Friends Meeting. Then Betty was approached by some people at her Quaker meeting, who offered, *If you wanted to develop a residence for homeless people, you could do it here, because people think you're not a flake.* She had never considered herself to be a person that anyone thought would be capable of opening a residence, but she was moved and inspired to be trusted. She insisted that it had to be for people with AIDS.

"Of course, the horror stories came, mainly concerning women who were injection-drug users, who would get blown off by hospitals, who had PCP . . . and were told that they just had bronchitis. I actually believe that AIDS kind of existed among this group of people first, because if you look back, there was something called *junkie pneumonia*, there was something called *the dwindles* that addicts got, and I think this was another early AIDS population . . . The Quaker quarterly meeting, said, *Go ahead and try.*"

Betty had a friend who was chair of the Community Board 6 Housing and Social Services Committee, who invited her to a committee meeting at Bellevue Hospital. The friend told Betty, *I don't know quite what's going on, but they're accusing the HRA [Housing Resource Administration] of hiding people with HIV in the shelter there, and that's not legal, and everyone's making a huge fuss, and HRA is coming.* She walked in the room, and there was "the usual bloated alcoholic HRA public relations guys." Then there was this group of young men at the other end of the table, all wearing ACT UP T-shirts, shorts, and giant Doc Martens boots, and acting very wild. It was Eric Sawyer, Keith Cylar, Charles King, and Rich Jackman. The Housing Committee of ACT UP. "That was the whole *Housing, Not Shelter. AIDS Won't Wait. Let's go out and get arrested tonight.*" She immediately joined them and was at Eric's house for the committee meeting the very next week.

GUANTÁNAMO

A coup d'état ousted Haitian president Jean-Bertrand Aristide in 1991, and dictatorship resumed under General Raoul Cédras. Eleven thousand Haitians fled in boats, were picked up by the U.S. Coast Guard, and were then taken to Guantánamo, at the southeastern edge of Cuba. All of them, on their arrival there, without their knowledge or consent, were tested for HIV at the same time that they were given a high number of simultaneous immunizations. Many were people who had never been to a doctor in their lives. Anyone who protested was put in restraints to have their blood drawn. About three hundred were found to be HIV-positive.

The imminent ban on people with HIV from entering the United States had not yet been passed, but these refugee Haitians were herded onto little school buses one day and taken to a remote part of the base up against the Cuban fence line, which was mined, with the ocean on another side and arid wasteland on the other two sides, and no signs of human life. They were ushered into the camp, surrounded by big rolls of razor wire. The military had bulletproof plastic masks over their helmets, were carrying big batons, and had police dogs.

"Then a doctor in full military gear got up, and because it was believed that Haitians culturally did not have the same needs for privacy that the rest of us do, they were told over a loudspeaker, in the immortal words of Tuskegee, that they had *bad blood*, and that George Bush's doctor was going to fix them up, not to worry. They thought they were just lost, that no one would ever know where they were."

ESTHER KAPLAN

Esther Kaplan was born in Claremont, California, but her parents became back-to-the-landers and moved to rural Oregon to be subsistence farmers. She "entered Yale straight and left Yale queer or bisexual" and moved to New York in the summer of 1987. One of her housemates, Kevin Kennedy, was HIV-positive. That's when AIDS became part of her real routine of life, during the period when the treatments were toxic and brutal to endure. Kevin was having to do aerosolized pentamidine, which was very difficult. Esther joined ACT UP in the winter of 1987–88. Kevin then died.

"Gay lives were so suppressed, and part of what was so intense about ACT UP's presence in the streets was just all these gay people being gay in public and not apologetically so. And there was so much panic that that triggered, in police and media and everyone else, and so much emotional intensity for the people involved . . . The fact that there were so many people in ACT UP who managed to be really forthright about having HIV and [tried] so hard to be open and shameless about it, it's incredible."

In ACT UP, Esther worked in coalition with Black AIDS Mobilization, WHAM!, and then people from the Haitian pro-Aristide movement in New York, including Ray Laforest, and some affiliated with *Haiti Progrès*, a small progressive publication. Several lawyers and ultimately the Center for Constitutional Rights (CCR) got involved in fighting for HIV-positive Haitians stuck in Guantánamo. The CCR lawsuit was initiated by students at the Lowenstein Human Rights Project at Yale. At first Esther thought it was going to take a few months, but the legal issues dragged on. It was a year and a half, then two years, and the case was very complex. She was working with the Coalition for the Homeless and with CCR and the Yale Human Rights Project, driving the legal challenge through the federal courts. She was involved in constantly organizing or supporting little demos to keep the issues in the public eye. They never had huge protests, but every time Bill Clinton was in town, the Haiti group would hound him. And whenever there was any development in the court cases, activists would pack the court. At one point there was a Black judge on the case, and Esther remembered him being clearly impressed that there was a constituency for this cause, and she felt it made him pay a lot more attention. But it all kept dragging on and on. One person from the community died while still held in Guantánamo.

"It was just getting more and more dire. The numbers were rising up north of two hundred at one point. Then we won! And they all got released! . . . The State Department started compassionate-releasing the sickest people, and we started getting people out in dribbles that way. That was just due to the political pressure."

BETTY WILLIAMS

Betty, Bro Broberg, and some other activists went to Guantánamo after the legal victory. "[Bro] was not fearless, but he acted fearless." Betty was petrified the whole time.

"They were so scary down there. I had spent so much time standing in peace vigils, but I had devoted absolutely no thought to what it would be like to be on a military base in the clutches of really crazy military people. They were all these old Cold War colonels who'd come out of retirement to do this. They were all the Judge Advocate General, the

JAG colonels. They were like lunatics. We went at a loaded time. It was the week that Waco was going on. The judges' decision about closing down the whole place was way overdue. As we were getting in the cab to go to the airport, someone handed us a fax of a suicide threat signed by fifty people in the camp, so everything was very tense anyway. We got down there and the colonel took us into his office and they yelled—they don't ever speak in a normal tone of voice, they yell at you all the time . . . Later I said, *Colonel Kleff, why are you yelling at us like this? We're here to work with you and it's going to be really difficult to work with you if you keep yelling at us.* He said, *I don't want to work with you and I'm going to yell at you.*"

The activists had been able to meet with the camp president, a prisoner who was a selected leader, and had secretly made a plan with him that they would see the fifty suicide-threateners first. They couldn't let the military know, because Betty and the other activists did not have theater and area clearance to deal with people who were suicidal. They only had theater and area clearance to ask people where they would like to be resettled: Miami, Boston, or New York. The limitations imposed were absurd on an unjust situation. The activists had an interpreter, a law student whose father was a respected newspaper editor, and she came from a distinguished Haitian family. The military supervisors brought the people they called *the migrants* in their little school bus to meet with the activists on a former air base there.

It "was a beautiful, beautiful place, but they put us in this ugly, dark, dirty building, with one filthy semi-functioning toilet. We found old boxes of sheets . . . and we covered everything with white sheets and tried to make it look nicer. Plus, sadly, we had to use those sheets to pad the hard metal folding chairs for people that were really emaciated, to lie down when they came."

At Guantánamo, the detained Haitians received AZT and Bactrim.

"What was really amazing was that coming from a completely different information set and so forth, they made the same choices that I would have made. They didn't take the AZT. They had no shelter from the sun. It was treeless where they were. They were living in these horrible Quonset huts that became like ovens during the day. At that time, the theory was that AZT and full sunlight just crashes your immune system. They took the Bactrim, thank God, because they were familiar with it from Haiti. [The government] did horrible things, like they gave INH [isonicotinylhydrazine] to everyone who was in a Quonset hut with anyone who had had a positive PPD test [a tuberculosis skin test], which was just ridiculous. I had known about this because one of those pregnant ladies had said that she took INH. You never saw social workers run out of a hotel room so fast in your life. They started freaking out. I said, *Let's all calm down.* I asked her if she'd had *peau d'orange,* a reaction where she'd had a PPD test. She said, *No, they just gave it just on general principles."*

Betty questioned the people at the state Department of Health. They said, *That's a terrible thing to do,* first of all, because all TB drugs are harder on people of African descent, and especially on pregnant women, and giving INH for TB prophylaxis to people who don't need it creates drug resistance, especially since, of course, they don't take the full course of treatment. They just take a few and then stop.

"So when I pointed this out to the military, they all started yelling at me and said, *Well, that's what you do if a family were in a house. You'd give everyone in a house [the drug].* And I said, *Those huts are not houses, and the way you deal with that is give people medically appropriate housing,* which made them exactly as mad as the city's court council lawyers would get when we'd use that phrase *medically appropriate housing,* here in court cases. It'd make them so mad."

While this small group of ACT UPers focused on Haitians, the larger organization had four or five demonstrations about Guantánamo. They did an action at Rockefeller Center when there was the first hunger strike at Guantánamo. GMHC and Equity Fights AIDS were very helpful and bankrolled the action. The activists decided that going down and demonstrating in front of Federal Plaza was really a lost cause, because "it's cold and windy and no one sees you at all." Instead, they rented a huge Statue of Liberty and wrapped it up in orange netting. Since there was a passport office in Rockefeller Center, they chose that busy and central location on Fifth Avenue. There was a huge snowstorm, and all lay down in the snow. Jesse Jackson, Herbert Daughtry, Susan Sarandon, Jonathan Demme, Randall Robinson, and Al Sharpton joined in, as well as Olden Polynice, the Haitian basketball player. They all got carted off to jail. "Jesse Jackson goes to jail with his own security people around him."

ESTHER KAPLAN

"I ended up being the one that was trying to coordinate the pro bono attorneys for [the refugees], which was kind of a mess. We were training law students, and some people were getting really good representation and some really weren't. They basically got in, but they still had to each individually win their asylum case. And we were trying to find community housing. Betty ended up taking in a juvenile, young kid, and more or less parenting him . . . It was pretty awful. They hadn't generally known they were HIV-positive when they were in Haiti. They suddenly get a needle stuck in them by the U.S. government and then told they have HIV. So tons of them were convinced the U.S. government had given them AIDS—these were all left-wing people protesting the Duvalier regime. So it's like they didn't exactly trust the U.S. government. They'd been behind barbed wire for a year, year and a half, two years."

BETTY WILLIAMS

When the judge started freeing a few people under interim orders, suddenly the attorneys realized they didn't know what to do with them, and they came to ACT UP and asked for help from those who knew about housing. Betty thought, *Well, I know about housing. I can speak French. I should help with that.* ACT UPers Esther Kaplan, Keith Cylar, Bro Broberg, and Betty went to the first emergency meeting with people from the Haitian community.

"The next thing that happened was that the only child in the camp who was HIV-positive and her grandmother were released. I remember it was the very first cold day in December, it was December 11, and the plane was actually approaching Newark . . . They said, *Someone has to step up and take them or we're going to take them back to Guantánamo.* And Housing Works stepped up when they got off that plane in little cotton dresses and flip-flops . . . They also were releasing pregnant women who were exactly seven and a half months pregnant. They only had a medevac flight once every two weeks and they had this trap, like if they couldn't make that flight, they couldn't make it at all because in another two weeks they'd be eight months pregnant, and too pregnant to fly. So there was only one flight that was ever available to them, and it was that flight and they would call Bro Broberg and me at two o'clock on Friday afternoon and say, *The flight leaves on Sunday. Call us by the end of [the] business day today and let us know if you have secure supervised AIDS housing.* So the first few times we pulled it off. Then came a day we just couldn't. Housing Works would not take another person. They'd had it. Everyone else was full up. I walked over there twice and fell on my knees before Charles [King] and said, *Please.* They said, *No, no, no.* And Bro and I took a really deep breath and we lied. We lied to the Justice Department. We lied to the military and said, *yes,* we had housing.

"Bro was working for the Coalition for the Homeless, which had a hotel that was better than most and safer, where they put some homeless people in crisis, and we rented a room there. That was such a scary week. I remember just knowing that we were lying, first of all, and trying to assemble some warm clothes for people who were seven and a half months pregnant, who we'd never laid eyes on, et cetera. We got them in that hotel room, and some Haitian women that we had met in our various meetings would sleep over with them and babysit for them.

"We'd run around every day and ask people for enough money to pay the hotel bill that night. It was very nerve-wracking. Then we would walk them through DAS [Department of AIDS Services]. Our method was, we'd get that horrible little form filled out, and doctors never do it right, so then we'd have a friend who would get them on line in DAS the minute it opened. Bro and I would be crouching just down the block, outside the door of the HIV Law Project, waiting for it to open. When it opened, we'd rush in with a ballpoint pen and Wite-Out and doctor-up the forms and rush off and meet them at DAS. One day we were doing that, and of course, all the women had horrible colds because they'd just gotten here. They had to pee all the time because they were very pregnant, and there wasn't even a bathroom on the floor where people with AIDS were. Plus, there was such hostility toward people with AIDS, like where people went for emergency money, there'd been some attacking people and saying, *No faggot with AIDS is going to get their money before I do,* and stuff like that. So it was very dicey going there and sort of horrifying, showing people this kind of introduction to this country, with graffiti all over the walls, and sordid-looking bathrooms, two floors away, and menacing people lurking around, and having to stand back behind red lines on the floor, and all the cashiers giving out checks and money behind thick bulletproof glass.

"Halfway through the day, the supervisor called me into her office and asked what was going on, and I told her. She said, *You mean the city hasn't set up a special policy for Guantánamo people? We always had one for the Cubans, the Marielitos.* Well, that's all I needed to hear. I called [the city councilman] Tom Duane. I just ran to a phone and called Tom and said, *Guess what? Guess what?* Within a day, he had arranged with HRA a meeting. It was like the dream meeting . . . It was hard, in a way, seeing this meeting happen for Guantánamo people that we couldn't make happen for other people, the people we'd been working with for so long. But I feel the reason that worked was because we offered people a chance to be a good guy, a limited chance. So it was not going to open the floodgates to some huge new category of people all screaming for housing. For once, they could be the good guys that, in their secret hearts, I think all of them wanted to be when they took those jobs."

They resettled a hundred people and became what the Immigration and Naturalization Service calls a VOLAG, a voluntary agency.

15

Lawyers for the People

Of the different subcultures within ACT UP creating their own alternative structures to counter government indifference, there were a number of professionals who came to practice their skills without pay or professional advantage. Lawyers were the most impactful and among the hardest-working. There were basically three different areas of legal strategy in ACT UP: standard arrest, using the court as a strategy to overturn some kind of policy, and individual cases of police brutality/ strip search or if an ACT UPer was accused of harassment. Each of these fights had their own ideology and trajectory. This required an entire corps of lawyers, working for free, together, serving the larger movement.

THE STAKES OF ARREST FOR PEOPLE WITH AIDS

MARY DORMAN

Mary Dorman, whose parents were American diplomats, was born and raised in the Middle East, which always made her an outsider as a kid. She arrived in New York to go to law school at St. John's and came out as a lesbian in 1971. Then her closest male friend, Paul Paroski, a pediatrician, died of AIDS in 1989, and just after that she came to ACT UP, where she focused on defending people arrested in zaps and street actions.

"With ACT UP, we had supreme, supreme victories in court, from the individual to groups to the whole political movement . . . and it was a real, real team effort. It wasn't any one attorney who succeeded or any one client or member of ACT UP. It was really a group, and we came out of this very highly respected I believe . . . One thing that distinguished ACT UP from a lot of other activist organizations is not passion, but the depth of passion, because it was life and death. There was no doubt about it, a lot of the demonstrators and the activists were going to die, and did die, and knew they were going to die. So arrest was nothing to them, nothing. There was no fear. So they were going to participate in any act of disobedience until they were carried off. That's it. And once you're carried off, that's typically an arrest . . . Judges respected us because our clients often wanted to try the cases, go to trial. So we would go to trial, put the government to its proof. And a lot of arrests were bad. Most were good. But even if they took a plea, they had a wonderful constitutional right to make a statement prior to being sentenced. After they were found guilty, or even in ACD [adjournment in contemplation of dismissal], they could then make a statement. And those statements were some of the most eloquent things ever said. And they edified the courts and the personnel and the papers."

In one case, Mary represented a group of men who didn't mean to be arrested but were charged with obstructing vehicular traffic in a protest on the Upper East Side. They wanted to try the case. The arresting police officer took the stand, and the district attorney asked, *Were they obstructing vehicular traffic?* And the police officer said, *No, they weren't. They were demonstrating for their lives.* This abruptly ended the trial, and Mary was granted a motion to dismiss. Afterward, the officer came out in the hallway and told her that he had lost his brother to AIDS. "Where does that happen? He's a hero. So he was obviously directed by his supervisor to make these arrests and he didn't want to, and he was going to tell the truth."

Because ACT UP didn't have to pay attorneys, our activists were able to be arrested en masse and go through the system, and actually go to trial without legal expenses. Mary estimates that she represented ACT UP for a thousand arrests. One dramatic demonstration that stands out in her memory was when Bob Rafsky and others went out in the middle of winter, in full down bodysuits, and shackled themselves to the axles of pharmaceutical trucks. Mary recalls that these men were prepared to freeze to death. She found that her clients were willing to endure harm and risk of police abuse—which was happening—while many were in fragile and declining health. But she never saw them harm anybody. Her clients' intentions were about doing whatever they had to do to wake people up. They would go into a TV station and they would disrupt the evening news, or they would go into the office of an authority in the Department of Health or the Department of Education and not permit business as usual to continue, all while they were dying.

"A lot of our work was behind the scenes. You know, that the clients would just show up for court and think, *That is it.* And they would come in for five minutes and leave and not realize there were another fifty people behind them that we have to deal with—or the paperwork involved, or that kind of thing. I think my work was more—not in the public forum . . . Why was it that legal counsel and the legal support was mostly women? I think that a lot of lesbians are caretakers and that that was part of it. I felt very responsible for everybody."

LORI COHEN

A native New Yorker, Lori Cohen grew up in a housing project in Rockaway, Queens, and her family moved to Staten Island. She went to New York public schools through law school. She then came out as a lesbian and became a criminal defense lawyer, because that's where she thought she could help and affect the most people. At Legal Aid, around 1987, she met Jill Harris, who brought her into ACT UP. She had no previous experience with AIDS. Lori handled ten thousand cases for ACT UP, out of an estimated twenty thousand arrests. Like a number of ACT UP attorneys, Lori was a real criminal defense lawyer, so she knew how to defend people with rigor and discipline.

ROMA BARAN

Roma Baran was born in Poland in 1947, in the mountains, in a coal-mining district. Then her family moved to Montreal. After a long career in music, engineering and producing concerts, working with Laurie Anderson, she went to Rutgers Law School. She defended poor people. Roma felt a tremendous kinship with the approach to political process she saw at her very first ACT UP meeting. She recalled that somebody stood up and said, in response to an issue, *Why don't we write a letter?* And whoever was in front of the room said, *Why don't you write a letter? Are you willing to write a letter? And you mail it, okay? We don't need to look at it. Can you mail it by tomorrow?* Yeah. *Can you mail it to fifty places?* Yes. For Roma, this was a form of engagement around a political cause that was immediate and urgent and practical and iconoclastic and rule breaking. And it wasn't just that they broke rules incidental to what they were doing, but the point *was* to break the rules. "Their attitude towards the government and the church was not just a platitude, it was inherent in the functioning of the organization. And I just had a fabulous time."

LORI COHEN

Lori tried the St. Patrick's case—the Stop the Church action—which was on Court TV. "That was quite a show." ACT UPers decided that Cardinal O'Connor had made his pulpit a political stage instead of just a religious pulpit, and therefore they felt that he was open to be protested against like everybody else. Two hundred people were arrested at St. Patrick's, and eventually the total was whittled down to five people who went to trial, and Lori defended them.

"There was always this dichotomy. My belief was sort of you're not educating—all this talk about *We're going to educate the public by having public trials,* no one cared, in my view. I thought it was best to get people's cases taken care of, get them back out on the street to do what they wanted to do, and I think, for the most part, that's how people felt. They didn't want to have to come to court every day for two weeks. They had jobs or they had, you know, other things that they were doing. But I think these folks felt like it was time to stand up and take a stand: Ann Northrop, who represented herself; Charles King, who was a law graduate and represented himself; Kathy Ottersten . . . They were convicted, but the judge gave them community service afterward, so there was no real penalty . . . Because what kind of punishment are you going to give folks like that? Are you going to put them in jail? . . . Listen, what did they do? They went into a church service and they sat down, they spoke up. So what? What's the real harm in that?"

ROMA BARAN

"The [St. Patrick's] trial was fantastic. My favorite thing was in the first day, Ann Northrop stood up and—behind every judge in every court-room, it says, *In God We Trust* across the back. And she stood up and said, *Your honor, I'd like to move that, for the length of these proceedings, we shroud the sign behind you.* And the judge went around and everyone looked at the sign, and the obviousness of going to trial on this issue while the judge sat in front of *In God We Trust*—it just struck every-body in the courtroom. And she went on, "How could we possibly have a fair trial about the very issue that the court is conceding by sitting in front of a sign that says, *In God We Trust*? So there was an uproar. She brought it up several times."

LORI COHEN

Lori accidentally got arrested at one point. "Well, that was pretty scary." At some point during a nighttime march she saw a man who was not dressed like a police officer and wasn't wearing a badge pull out one of our people and start beating him. So Lori tried to intervene and the undercover cop turned around, threw her on the ground, and put her in handcuffs. But everyone in ACT UP knew she was a law-yer, and so now it became an unruly situation. Finally, the police gave her a ticket, and she had to go to court. "Initially there was more [police violence] because the police thought they could get away with it, and then they realized they couldn't, that we were smart, we had cameras, we were willing to call them out on stuff, and we were willing to sue them."

Lori sued the police in the notorious case of Chris Hennelly, who sustained a brain injury as the result of a beating by a police officer during a demonstration. At first the police tried to deny the violence, but when Lori and the other attorneys got the ACT UPers' long-delayed arrest photos, the photos became documentary proof of how truly bru-tal the beatings had been.

"It becomes so all-encompassing. You spend so much time with these folks, they're your friends, and, yeah, for those years, that's what it was. It was parties at people's houses and it was fun . . . It was easy to integrate into ACT UP . . . You know, for me as a young lawyer, it was amazing to be involved with people who really changed the world. You don't get that opportunity, and I really consider myself incredibly lucky that I was able to do that."

LEGAL TRAINING FOR DEMONSTRATORS AND TRAINING LEGAL OBSERVERS

KAREN MOULDING

Karen Moulding's father was a trust-fund baby, and her mother was a red-diaper baby. "That lasted about four years." She lived in Iowa, then L.A., went to college in Montana, and then came to New York to go to Columbia Law School and passed the bar in 1992. Karen started the Lesbian, Gay, Bisexual Rights Committee of the National Lawyers Guild.

In ACT UP, Karen organized legal observers. She held trainings in her apartment and took the new recruits for on-the-job training at demonstrations. Her main advice to observers: "Write things down. If you see any brutality, get badge numbers, and just as a backup, get the names of people as they're getting arrested . . . Once people are in the vans—the police vans—find out what precinct they're going to." And she strongly recommended that people wear an armband that said LEGAL. It warned the police to be on their best behavior, and it helped the demonstrators know that they were being watched and protected to some extent. Karen felt that her job was to provide demonstrators with services to protect their First Amendment rights. Her goal was to join demonstrators on the street and support them, and to run interference with the police.

Training people required many steps: knowing when the demonstrations were going to be, being there early, coordinating the legal observers and the other lawyers on-site, going to the precinct, and making sure that the processing was going well, that people got their medication, that nobody was held up for lack of ID. Then legal observers had to coordinate all the desk appearance tickets, or the summonses, and meet people in court on the various court dates. Karen often ended up doing all of that personally.

POLICE BEHAVIORS DETERIORATED WITH GIULIANI'S ELECTION

Working with the police under Dinkins, Karen would be on the front lines, running interference. For example, if ACT UPers wanted to block traffic on Fifth Avenue, they would send one attorney to be with the demonstrators and one to be with the police.

"And the police knew this—the more seasoned—like, Captain Fry, I remember him, a friendly guy, very Irish looking. He'd say, *Hey, Karen, how are you doing? Long time, no see* . . . If people were being arrested, they would tell me where people were going, and they seemed to understand the difference between nonviolent, going-limp resistance and active resistance . . . I never saw anyone get hurt or brutalized. And if that did happen, it was usually by an inexperienced cop, as opposed to the people that were higher up in the police force."

When David Dinkins was no longer mayor and Rudy Giuliani was in office, the first demonstration Karen remembers involved walking over the Brooklyn Bridge to demand homeless services for people with AIDS. There were a lot of elderly people in the protest, many poor people, people with foster kids. Often at AIDS demonstrations, participants were not healthy or in good shape. These demonstrators were met by a phalanx of motorcycle cops, and police with billy clubs holding plastic shields. "I mean, you're talking about old ladies in wheelchairs, and then these brutal-looking cops with these helmets, and they just bullied us out of doing what we wanted to do." From then on, Giuliani's police were much more aggressive with people with AIDS. At protests, they no longer respected the long-held and legal tradition of moving picket lines on sidewalks. Instead, they would set up barricades and force pro-testers into pens. When the twenty-one-year-old Matthew Shepard was murdered in Wyoming in 1998, there was a substantial demonstration where New York police herded queer demonstrators with horses, and people were picked off and held in jail overnight.

"It was just a different flavor, and, as is the way with most policies, I don't think they realize that the fact that they were mean made it worse for them. There was probably more disruption, a lot more tax-payers' dollars spent on people getting processed really slowly. When I didn't know what precinct people were sent to, that made it harder to even help out. Say, if someone didn't have the right ID or needed medication, it made processing slower for the police. It made it harder on the demonstrators. It made it harder on the pedestrians if there was more chaos."

GOING TO TRIAL AND WINNING IN COURT

In 1991, Karen defended ACT UPers James Baggett, James Learned, and Shraga Lev. In the annual *Sexual Orientation and the Law*, she wrote this entry:

> Defendants were arrested at a hotel, following a demonstration at a community advisory board meeting of a pharmaceutical company—Hoffmann-La Roche. Present at the meeting were numerous other members of the community, concerned about AIDS, and the failure of [Hoffmann]-La Roche to responsibly research, test, and distribute drugs potentially important for people with HIV or AIDS. The accusatory instruments and alleged facts indicating that defendants themselves took part in any demonstration—in any part of the demonstration—[show] that they didn't cause harm. The meeting itself was an event of grave, social concern, and the demonstration was conducted by responsible members of the community, deeply concerned about the AIDS crisis in this country and the world.
>
> This is evident from the fact, inter alia, that following the demonstration, 11 members of a 12-member community advisory board formally suspended relations with [Hoffmann]-La Roche until such a time as the company takes its role in ending the AIDS epidemic, as seriously as it must. Not only was there no real harm caused by this demonstration, but in fact a substantial amount of good may result from the attention drawn to the company's irresponsibility in the face of an extreme emergency. Thousands of lives a year in this country alone are lost to the AIDS crisis. And yet, for the sake of profit, [Hoffmann]-La Roche chooses to stall or withhold the release of crucial tools to combat the virus. That is the

real crime—not the important and successful attempts of the demonstrators to draw attention to the immoral practice of the company.

Her argument was successful and she won the case. This was a substantial victory. After making three or four court appearances and meeting with the defendants and drawing up motions, Karen won on the highly morally satisfying New York Criminal Procedure Law section 170.40, a "motion to dismiss information . . . in furtherance of justice."

BISEXUALITY IN ACT UP

Karen remembered "this thing from ACT UP—'A lesbian and a gay man sleeping together is still queer sex.' That was the thing about ACT UP, it was a little bit different. It was ahead of its time . . . What was it like? I was new and I was nervous, and I wasn't fully aware of my own bisexuality then. In a way it was like, I was very comfortable straight, and I'm very comfortable bisexual. But just as a pure lesbian I was a little bit awkward, I think, during that brief period when that's what I tried to be. I think I even tried to be butch for a while, which totally I'm not . . . First, it was Alexis [Danzig] and John [Kelly], and then they broke up, and then it was Alexis and [BC Craig], and then [BC] started dating somebody else, and Suzanne [Huber]—I remember first she had this little boyfriend with the shaved head. And then she was with women, and then she was with John. It was like that. There was a lot of shifting around and a lot of romance. I had parties. I remember a lot of parties."

GRATITUDE

One night Karen was at Cabaret Magique, "this nightclub—and this guy's like, *Is your name Karen? You were a lawyer for ACT UP, I know you, I know you.* And it was Vincent Gagliostro, and he said this—and I cried when I got home. He said, *You were my lawyer, you were my lawyer over and over again, and I watched you do that for years.* And he says, *And I knew you were doing that for love, and I never thanked you.*"

AIDS AND PRISON

JOAN GIBBS

Joan Gibbs grew up in Swan Quarter, North Carolina, population less than five hundred. There was a lot of Ku Klux Klan activity. When she was in the fourth grade, one of her female cousins was lynched, and the police quickly arrested and tried a Black man whom none of her family members believed was guilty. She came to New York in 1965 and in 1968 went to the Bronx High School of Science. She came out as a lesbian in the early 1970s, and with Sarah Bennett started Dykes Against Racism Everywhere in 1979. "By being lesbians and being active around issues of racism and the Left and particularly the Black movement, we could also challenge homophobia." Joan went to Rutgers Law School in 1982 and soon after started working at the Center for Constitutional Rights.

A friend of Joan's died of AIDS after his lover came out of prison and died. She recalled that when they came to get her friend's body, they put it in a plastic bag and threw it down the steps. She started volunteering at a Rikers Island prison in the men's AIDS unit. The facility was leaking so badly that rain was actually coming in. "It was just horrible, horrible. It was really horrible." Joan represented a Puerto Rican inmate who subsequently became her roommate, whom she got released on humanitarian grounds, because she found a doctor who'd sign an affidavit saying the man would die in six months. Once released with safe housing and Joan's care, he lived a couple of years. In that period, one of Joan's goals was to challenge prisons to treat people with AIDS fairly, appropriately, and equally. Then, of course, there was also an effort to try to get people out of jail on humanitarian grounds. She was moved to work on that cause because she was so offended and upset by the idea of a person with AIDS dying in jail. There was also the cause for condoms to be distributed in prisons.

Joan saw ACT UP as part of the Left. She knew ACT UP lawyer Mike Spiegel from work in the antiracism movement, and she started as a volunteer lawyer for ACT UP at the FDA action and the St. Patrick's trial. And she particularly stood up for men of color in the organization by representing Ortez Alderson when he went to trial for ACT UP after a sit-in in Stephen Joseph's office at the Department of Health. She represented ACT UPer Alan Robinson, who was her roommate until he died. "I had two of my roommates die, and I got sort of like, I didn't want to be involved in AIDS work, because you have two roommates die of AIDS, then you're like, *Oh, you know*. And I think that had impact on ACT UP. It's difficult, people constantly dying around you and going to funerals."

IMMIGRATION

PAUL O'DWYER

Paul O'Dwyer grew up in Kilkenny, Ireland, in a small town called Carrick-on-Suir. His grandfather, Michael Burke, holds the Guinness World Record for being a survivor of the world's longest hunger strike, ninety-one days. He came out as gay at university in Galway. After law school, Paul came to New York in 1987 and joined ACT UP.

Paul's primary focus in ACT UP concerned the ban on HIV-positive people coming into the United States. Another was access to health care and treatment for people who were non-nationals. Then there was the very practical question of what type of civil disobediences people who are non-citizens could get involved in, and what could they do without jeopardizing their status. Paul tended to be somewhat conservative on those fronts, and generally advised people to not get arrested. Yet at that time, immigration enforcement was not as severe it is now, so there were people who had no papers, who were completely undocumented, who went and got arrested and went to court, and nothing ever happened to them. In the 1980s in New York City, there was really no conversation between a local police department and the enforcement branch of the Immigration and Naturalization Service.

Paul represented the members of Action Tours who dressed up as Santa to protest Macy's firing a Santa Claus who was HIV-positive.

"I remember the judge saying, *They dressed up as what?* And I was saying, *Well, the allegation is that they were dressed up as a Santa Claus, and they were in Macy's and they chained themselves to the furniture, and I'm not sure what's illegal about that*. And the judge said, *Well, why were they dressed up as Santa Claus in Macy's?* And I was like, *Well, because that Macy's hires people to dress up as Santa Claus and go there and meet the people.* And the judge was like, *Well, were they working for Macy's?* And I'm like, *Well, I think you should ask the DA's Office if they worked for Macy's or if they didn't, because really that's for them to prove, not for me."*

Paul won the case.

KENDALL THOMAS

Of course, not all lawyers in ACT UP focused on legal work for the movement. A law professor and legal theorist at Columbia University, Kendall Thomas participated in ACT UP in a number of nonlegal capacities.

One of the cofounders of the Majority Action Committee, Kendall went with Robert Garcia, Ortez Alderson, and a few other ACT UPers to a meeting in the basement of the Abyssinian Baptist Church. It was for a group of cultural nationalist African American physicians, who were meeting to talk about what the African American community should do about HIV/AIDS. Jesse Jackson had agreed to write a very eloquent letter supporting predominantly Black and Latino churches in New York City for a day of solidarity and remembrance of people who were living with and/or who had died from HIV/AIDS. Kendall understood that there was no such thing as "the AIDS epidemic." There were several epidemics at a time when people from all communities were still dying in horrifyingly high numbers.

Kendall recalled that the gay white men who were getting sick, for the most part, had earlier and better health care and died under conditions that were materially superior to those of people of color, whose first point of access to the health-care system was through the emergency room. He knew there would be no effective political mobilization for a progressive AIDS policy that did not have an understanding of itself as an antiracist movement and as a movement committed to gender equality and to economic justice.

"The sex-positive, gay-affirmative, politically empowering force that was in that room and that [was] in the streets of New York or DC at ACT UP actions—I do feel it saved my life. And there was some great sex that came out of it, too. My roommate and I went to our first ACT UP meeting together, and the most beautiful boy I'd ever seen was standing across the room, on the third floor of the Center.

So there's that history at ACT UP, too . . . But there were any number of people—again, gay white men—who had been raised, before they knew they were gay, to this notion that they were where they were because of merit—that the world belonged to them. That the way things were was, basically, the way things ought to be. And then, they have the shock of being marked as queer and of being subjected to a politics of abjection, because people were dying.

"So, people who had been able to live their lives in the closet as gay men were being outed by the fact that their bodies were giving out on them. And that sense of not being willing to acknowledge their investment in the structures of social and economic and gender and racial power—even though that very same structure was killing them—was one of the most painful things in the world for me to watch, because these were smart people. But this willful refusal to recognize that their investment in this world was also killing them, because it was occluding a vision of the only kind of politics that would be adequate to the crisis we were facing. That willful refusal, to this day, is, for me, one of the most powerful examples of the strength of white supremacy as an ideology and as an institution—the way it can make white people, effectively, commit suicide, in its name, and not even see it as such."

16

The Culture and Subculture of Civil Disobedience

The most influential cohering experience in values inside ACT UP that almost everyone shared was civil disobedience training, and thousands of people experienced it together. Although based in an applied practice with tips and guidelines, all of the instructions were rooted in a very articulate and deep ethical belief system about community. The trainers became a moral center of this culture, profoundly influential on the movement as a whole, and specifically consequential on the individuals who shared this preparation and subsequent experience of nonviolent defiance.

JAMIE BAUER

Jamie Bauer grew up in Stuyvesant Town, in Manhattan. Their father was a salesman, and their mother was a homemaker. After Hunter High School they went to MIT to study civil engineering, architecture, and urban planning, and earned a master's in transportation, which had a one-in-eight women-to-men ratio. Jamie found the program to be not very intellectual. "Rigorous, but not very interesting." Although there was a small gay student union at the school, it was all men. On the other hand, MIT was in Boston, which had a huge lesbian community. And so Jamie came out pretty quickly and start making some connections into the mixed gay movement and into the lesbian movement, the two of which were still somewhat separate at that point. In 1981, they returned to New York to work for the MTA, eventually as director of subway schedules. About two decades after their time in ACT UP, Jamie started to live as nonbinary.

In the early 1980s, Jamie had heard a lot about the Women's Pentagon Action, a mobilization to create a large women's peace action directly confronting the Pentagon. They went to a couple of meetings and got hooked, "because these women were so interesting and so smart and creative, and knew so much. And I just thought—*Well I'm just going to sit here and hang out and absorb this.*" Jamie worked with Grace Paley, Vera Williams, Eva Kollisch, Donna Gould, Sharon Kleinbaum, Toni Fitzpatrick, Laura Flanders, Harriet Hirschorn, and other women peace activists. The group came together to make the connections between war, the patriarchy, women's oppression, the military–industrial complex. It was also an antinationalism group. They did not believe in borders, flags, or patriotism, and believed that women bonding together with other women could save the world. And at that time, 60 to 75 percent of the group were lesbians, but that fact was not acknowledged. "It wasn't part of the dogma of the group. We were *women*—which I found a little hard to stomach, because it was so clear that so many [of the] women were lesbians anyway, but they didn't want it to be a lesbian group." Jamie learned a lot about organizing, dealing with the police, insisting on the right to take space, and just everything about doing politics on the street.

BC CRAIG

BC Craig grew up in suburban Philadelphia. Her parents bred Great Danes. Her father worked for the Department of Agriculture, her mother was a tax accountant, and BC was raised in the Presbyterian Church. At seventeen, she got involved with the Movement for a New Society—eighteen communal houses, working together. She worked for the American Friends Service Committee and learned to do civil disobedience trainings and facilitate meetings. She lived at the Seneca Women's Encampment for a Future of Peace and Justice for a year.

FROM THE WOMEN'S PEACE MOVEMENT TO ACT UP

"The purpose of activism," BC said, "was really that old-school kind of speaking truth to power; and that you had the responsibility to be willing to do what was necessary to let government know that people were not simply going to go along with oppression and injustice when they saw it . . . When I came to ACT UP, it was a revelation to me, of a different way of thinking about what we were doing . . . Having spent years and years in activism where it was like—*Let's put on a demo! Okay. If everybody brings their own poster board, then all we have to do is pay for the markers,* or something like that—was about the kind of budget we were talking about. And early in the first fall that I was with ACT UP, they were working on a CDC action—in Atlanta. And it was, *Let's fly a hundred people to the CDC so we can have an action there.* And I was like, *Are you serious? You're seriously going to fly people? And then put them up in hotels? And then pay per diems for them?* Having come from years and years of, *You get there how you can get there; you sleep on church benches; there's often a place where they're handing out sandwiches,* it was just a completely different thing, in terms of the resources."

JAMIE BAUER

Jamie recalled that a lot of men initially came to ACT UP because it was the first time in their life that their white male privilege wasn't working for them, and they were outraged that the government wasn't taking it seriously, and that they couldn't get the drugs. They couldn't believe it. They couldn't believe that other people didn't think their lives were worth taking extraordinary steps to save. Jamie observed that some of these people had a hard time making the connections to others who didn't have that same privilege. But everyone in ACT UP knew people who were sick and dying, and, particularly in the beginning, when a lot of people didn't know their HIV status, no one knew who could be next. "So there was a certain emotionalism about it that was very different from [the] Women's Pentagon Action."

Influenced by the writings of Barbara Deming, Jamie picked up the concept that people have a right to free speech and freedom of assembly and should not have to ask permission for it. And if the state wanted to arrest us for it, that was their business, but the people were not going to ask the state's permission. So it was nonviolent civil disobedience rooted in an insistence on people protecting their rights by using them, and not letting the government take those rights.

When they first came to ACT UP, Jamie found it all very exciting. People were so charged up and just wanted to demonstrate, demonstrate, demonstrate. ACT UP would schedule five demonstrations in a week, and then the members would go to all of them. But Jamie found that they didn't know anything about demonstrating. For example, at the first Wall Street demo, ACT UP gave the police a list of the seventeen people who were going to be arrested, and each person who was going to be arrested wore an armband so that the police wouldn't accidentally take the wrong person. Jamie felt that this was overly orchestrated and made it impossible for anybody else to try to jump in. Jamie called this "Celebrity CD [civil disobedience]. They didn't want three hundred people, at that point, necessarily doing CD. They wanted a couple of name people, with recognition so that would be what would be in the press."

Jamie understood that ACT UP was trying to figure out how to use its anger, because it was a group with a tremendous amount of rage and anger at the system. Although New York City was the epicenter of the AIDS epidemic, the federal decision-makers were in Washington. It was very frustrating to go out into the streets of New York and demonstrate, because they were demonstrating against buildings that people in power weren't necessarily in. For Jamie, civil disobedience is an American tactic that people understand, in some ways. But Jamie had a particular commitment to a concept of safety. There were people who didn't understand issues of public safety, personal safety, the safety of the community, or taking responsibility for one's actions. Jamie and the other trainers really began to talk about civil disobedience as a safe tactic for making a stronger, direct, personal statement, and as a way of getting media attention. They tried to get everybody in the group trained for civil disobedience, because no one always knows when it's going to happen, or when they're going to want to do it. When dealing with the police, no organizers can guarantee people's safety; there are a lot of things that can make it physically safer than just haphazardly running out into the street.

COMMUNITY'S RESPONSIBILITY TO INDIVIDUAL AWARENESS

There were some situations in ACT UP when Jamie saw people lose it. But the group had enough mechanisms to pull them back in before it got out of hand. In a less disciplined group, Jamie felt, there would have been some violent actions. But in ACT UP, even with people kicking over police barricades, or jumping through a line of police officers to join a demonstration, there was no violence against the police. In one case, Jamie saw someone actually shoving a cop at a level that could get him a felony arrest. The ACT UP marshals were able to surround the person and get him back in. They physically engaged him and calmed him down.

"I turned to the police officer and I said, *He's with us. I saw what he did, we'll talk to him.* And I turned around and was like, *What's going on?* And you just talk to the person and try to get them to engage with you . . . Even in situations where you might have hecklers, what we would try to do is get some marshals to talk to the hecklers, so that the people protesting wouldn't stop protesting to focus on the hecklers, and that would defuse some tension. We tried to get people to not be provoked into doing things that they would regret . . . If someone in a group stands up and says, *Let's charge the barricade!* that you don't get up and charge the barricade. You say, *Well, why should we? What's the pros and what's the cons? I don't really feel like charging the barricade,* to defuse the situation, because you don't want a police provocateur or anybody else [to] be able to lead a whole group into doing something like that."

When the police would bring horses into a demonstration, running away creates panic, so people had to be trained. Although it is counter-intuitive, sitting down is safe if done in a group. "If you run away—well, who gets left behind? Well, the people who can't run fast—the people who are older or sicker or are just too dazed to figure out what they should do. And so you leave your most vulnerable people behind, to the police."

AFFINITY GROUPS AND CIVIL DISOBEDIENCE

Jamie believes that it is absolutely critical to establish an affinity group structure from a safety perspective. It also helps the staging of the civil disobedience, because groups can move in waves—so that it is not one large mass of people all doing the same thing at the same time.

"The most important thing about affinity groups is the support structure so that someone knows who you are, what you're wearing, where you were arrested, who to contact if anything happens. They know that you went into police custody, and they know when you came out of police custody, so you don't lose anybody, and everyone is tracked. And that is really important—so, if anyone gets injured, or if there's any brutality. Affinity group actions is that I think they are much stronger in terms of the solidarity of the people doing the action together, because you have much more connection to the people there. So I think you're less likely to do things that are stupid. And if you do have a question about what's going on, or something feels like it's getting out of control, you have people, who you're in it with, to talk to about it."

CIVIL DISOBEDIENCE TRAINING

Jamie and fifteen to twenty others trained over a thousand ACT UPers in nonviolent civil disobedience over the six or seven years that ACT UP was most active. And, with Alexis and BC, they resumed the trainings as part of Rise and Resist during the Trump years.

A typical training would involve twenty people, fifteen of whom would decide to get arrested, a couple of whom would decide to do support, and they would become an affinity group. There were some long-term affinity groups in ACT UP that stayed together for a few years, but there were also pickup affinity groups, formed by new people who came to a training. Jaime didn't want to be part of anything where people were hand-selected and it was closed. And they had a lot of arguments with people who wanted Jamie to train them, but Jamie would insist, *That's not how I work.* "There were some really obnoxious, difficult people in ACT UP, and I didn't want them in my affinity group, either, but I couldn't do it."

ALEXIS DANZIG

"None of us were there to do the work on the cops. We were there to make sure that people were safe—not only physically safe, but also legally safe. And it took a lot of time. It was like ACT UP meetings themselves; it was like participatory democracy, in general. It's messy; it takes a lot of time; you got to explain things three or four times; people don't get it. So instead of going up and saying to somebody: *Stop stickering that cop car*; you had to explain: *These are the implications of what your actions are*, and—it was boring, and people didn't listen, anyway, and—there were times when people were doing more egregious things—property-damage kind of stuff; and I'm talking about, like, spray-painting—where more people could have been implicated, and we would act, I think, more firmly to shut that down.

"Because here is an action that one or two people were taking, that other people had not agreed to, and that other people could become implicated by. If a cop is going to grab the person with a spray can, the cop may grab the person who's got the spray paint on their clothing, as well . . . We wanted to keep people as safe as possible, and not have to deal with jail time. Risa Denenberg went to jail for a week, for spray-painting on federal property during a demonstration in Albany. So we saw that this had real complications . . . So you have to reiterate the understandings that the organizers have created for that particular demonstration. And then you, at a certain point, you have to let go, and you have to say, *If you people want to go and do a CD in front of the—whatever, City Hall—by all means. But the demonstration is now officially over. See you at the next meeting.* And so it was sort of, it was sort of businesslike—friendly and businesslike. We tried very hard not to tell people what to do."

GERRI WELLS

Gerri Wells is from an Irish family in the Inwood section of Manhattan. Her father was a sergeant in the New York Police Department; her mother was a medical secretary. Gerri went to the police academy and became an officer. She worked in a child abuse unit in Harlem for a number of years. Then she started a contracting business. Her brother Easton, an actor, was also gay and they would go to gay clubs together.

Around 1987, Easton was in Cabrini Hospital with AIDS, and Gerri went to visit him only to find that his tray was being left outside his room. She was outraged, but she wasn't getting anywhere in the hospital. The nurses were too petrified to bring the tray in to him. A friend who was active in leftist politics, Michelle, said, *There's a guy named Larry Kramer who wants to start this group*, and gave Gerri his number. She called him and said, *Larry, what do you do with this anger? I'm really pissed off. What do I have to do, because they're leaving his tray outside his room?* It was just so unfair. And Larry said, *Well, we're meeting at the Center tomorrow night.* Gerri went to the meeting, and there was only a handful of people there. It was just the beginning.

"ACT UP was like, right on time . . . I was kind of shy; and totally not into the whole thing, the whole group thing, myself. So when I got there, something happened, something changed in me . . . I think when you're fighting for a member of your family or for a loved one, it changes who you are, in a way . . . I went every Monday night . . . I would teach people about how to bring police up on charges, how to get shield numbers. I'm the one that brought that into the group: *Get their shield number; document everything; write it down* . . . How to work the process. How not to get arrested, and how to get arrested and keep yourself safe when you see someone else getting arrested . . . Basically, you don't want to get into a physical thing with the officer, because then the charge changes. You're not doing civil disobedience, you're doing something else."

Gerri was arrested nineteen times. Sometimes she was a little manhandled, bounced into the wagon. There would be a little hostility, a little tight on the wrists. And she knew how that all worked. But when she was getting arrested, Gerri felt that she wasn't disrespecting the cops. Because she wasn't there against the police. She was there to bring solutions to the problems of the AIDS crisis. *Yes, officer. Okay. I'm moving.* It was never, *I'm angry, and fuck you, you're a cop.* That's not where she was coming from.

At trainings, she would talk about the penal codes and the law, do some role-playing. *Suppose I'm a cop and I arrest you. What do you do, how do you act?* She answered a lot of questions. People were nervous about getting arrested. Some cops were, and are, homophobic, and they couldn't control their bias. They would take it to work with them. "And that's where it's a problem, because you're arresting people, you're dealing with all kinds of people. And a lot of people were . . . they hit them with the baton; they'd kick, accidentally trip them. It's just like rough."

CHRIS HENNELLY'S BEATING

JAMIE BAUER

In 1991, a bunch of people went up to the police precinct at night after a meeting to do a demonstration there, and there were a couple of guys in ACT UP who resembled each other. One of them was in the cops' faces about police brutality. Jamie believes that the police mistook Chris Hennelly for Jon Nalley, who had a way of getting in the police's faces. Chris was a pacifist. He was wearing a white T-shirt, blue jeans, and a black leather jacket. He had blond hair. The cops took Chris hostage to end the demonstration by arresting him, but then beat him up in the privacy of the station as payback for the antibrutality chants. "Not that what he was doing was illegal or bad, but I think the police made an error, and thought that Chris was John." When the police got Chris inside, he was either thrown against a wall or hit with a police radio on the head and suffered nerve and brain damage—epileptic seizures, trouble talking—very, very serious impairments.

"I felt very badly about it, but I don't think it was the wrong thing to go demonstrate against the police, and I don't think that it's your responsibility if you demonstrate against police brutality and the police beat you up, that it's your fault. So, should it have happened? Absolutely not. Were we responsible for it? No."

RELATIONSHIPS WITH POLICE

JAMIE BAUER

When Jamie was marshaling a demonstration, their goal was to let the police know why ACT UP was there, and what the parameters of the demonstration were. *We're going to be setting up a legal picket over here. No, we do not want barricades. No, we are not going to take barricades.* If the barricades were set up when ACT UP got there, marshals would just set up in another spot, "and everyone knew that." Jamie treated the police with respect for their personhood, but not for their authority. Jamie tried to be friendly with them, to assure them that ACT UP was perfectly capable of maintaining our own demonstration without their help, but also tried to not give them a lot of information about whether there was going to be civil disobedience, where it was going to be, whether there would be a march, and where we were going to march.

"We don't need the police to do our demonstrations. We don't want them there. It's better off if they don't come. You know, it's 100 percent legal to do a picket without telling the police you're going to do it. You do not have to be behind barricades; you just have to leave enough space on the street for people to walk by. And we were pretty careful when we were doing demonstrations—that if we took up more than a block to go to a second block or across the street and set up other pickets, and to try to keep everything moving."

GERRI WELLS

Gerri was on the mayor's police council and fought for more sensitivity trainings. Once a month she would meet with Mayor Dinkins's liaison to the LGBT community, Marjorie Hill, the director of the Anti-Violence Project; Matt Foreman; and a number of others. The police chief would sit on one end of the table and Gerri would sit on the other. "And we would lock horns constantly." She brought examples to him. *This was a case where the officer used excessive force, and it's all documented, we have pictures of it, there's witnesses.* And he would say, *Not my officers.* And Gerri would say, *Are you kidding?* "And he would get really red." Gerri would insist, *Why can't you just admit that there's some bad apples in the force, and just get people sensitivity training?*

She did sensitivity training at some of the local precincts. Officers used to put on rubber gloves when they were arresting people from ACT UP, assuming we all were people with AIDS and HIV, and that we could infect them simply by being arrested. Gerri would tell the police, *Say whatever you want, this is all off the record. You could say whatever you want.*

"And they would go off. They would say, *Well, you guys went into our church.* That always came up; that was always one of the first things that come up. And I said, *Well, it's my church, too. It's not just your church* . . . But they would say awful things. *I never knew any dykes before*, and blah blah blah. And usually, by the end . . . there would always be three or four cops that would come over to me and say, *Thank you* . . . There would always be one or two cops that you knew were gay. And they would come over and say, *I'm so glad you came*. Because that's when the cops, they were peeing in your locker. If they thought you were gay, they would do all kinds of stuff. So they had it going on right with their fellow officers."

PERMITS

JAMIE BAUER

ACT UP tried to organize demos where permits were not necessary, which meant no rallies with sound systems. Often, the police would allow a bullhorn without a sound permit. But at a certain point, they stopped allowing this, so ACT UP stopped using bullhorns. Demonstrators can call for a march and not ask for a permit. But there needs to be negotiation with the police on-site either to march on the sidewalk or to get a lane, or to do a whole street closure. Jamie found that marshals could negotiate from a position of more strength when they had a thousand people than when two people go down to the police precinct to ask for the permit. So they tried to do a lot of negotiating on the spot. After time, Jamie observed that there were some people on the police force who understood that ACT UP was basically nonviolent.

"They understood the parameters of exactly what we were going to do, and they didn't feel a need to assert their authority in our doing what we were doing, and those were the ones we worked the best with. And there were other ones who were just like—they just couldn't stand the fact that we wouldn't tell them ahead of time, we wouldn't ask for permission, and we didn't want to talk to them when we got there, and it drove them crazy."

Although Jamie felt respected by a lot of people in ACT UP, they also recognized that a lot of people didn't want to be told what to do, nor did Jamie really want to tell them what to do. In the beginning, it was hard to get people to listen and really think about personal safety, that there was a method to setting up a picket, that there was a method to setting up a CD and that ACT UP would do a lot better as an organization to find a way to fit those methods to actions and demonstrations.

"I'm not a very passionate person in that way, and I think that the people who were listened to most were the people who have that fire and have that passion. And if they're cute and sexy, it sure helps, but I think—I mean, I don't know if Maxine [Wolfe] felt that people really listened to her, but I always felt that people really listened to Maxine, and Maxine, no offense, is not that young, vibrant, sexy—she's not Maria Maggenti. So looks and charm have something to do with it, but I think Maxine is very passionate, and I think passion has a lot to do with it."

CHANGING PEOPLE

"I really believe that anybody can change," Jamie said. "They can change because they want to change, or they can change because they have to change. And first you try to persuade people to change because they want to change, [but] that's not really why you do civil disobedience. When you want to get people to come over to your side, you talk to them, you write to them, you confront them. But there's a certain point where they don't want to change, but you can force them to change, and that's where civil disobedience, I think, really comes in—to either make it impossible for them to do what they're doing and not change, or to make them really have to face you face to face, if you can't get into them through some other direct methods. Civil disobedience also makes people understand the seriousness of what you're doing. And I think CD that is the most direct is like taking over someone's office, is a very powerful CD, as opposed to blocking traffic in front of their office building. So the more direct the action is and the closer it gets you to the person you're trying to change, or the institution you're trying to change, the better off you are. And the hardest thing in organizing any demonstration, whether it be a picket or a CD is, how do you get across to the people who are outside your demonstration, what it is that you are doing . . . the clarity of why you're there and what you're demanding, and that that has to be really simple and crystal clear, both to you and to [the public]—using props or signs or banners or whatever, to make that crystal clear, to the people you're confronting and the people walking by you. If that's what you want."

PART VII

Money, Poverty, and the Material Reality of AIDS

As the years passed and more people suffered and died from AIDS, poor people suffered the most. The neglect of the government was a constant impediment that ACT UP had to confront. Personal devastations from AIDS motivated some wealthy men to reach out, in different ways, to the poorest people with AIDS, in ways that they probably never would have before the crisis. At the same time, ACT UPers from poor and working-class backgrounds also worked across the class divide with even poorer people as well as richer ones. The emergency forced those who took responsibility to try to create solutions, at great levels of commitment and effort. Because we wanted to win, which meant to live, ACT UP had to rise to reality and create solutions to problems created by government indifference and incompetence, while continuing to insist that this work was the responsibility of the government and private industry. It was a simultaneous approach of literally designing change while escalating pressure on the society at large to step up and be accountable. ACT UPer Karin Timour masterminded a campaign to win insurance rights for people with AIDS that she ran in all fifty states before the existence of the internet. ACT UP's Housing Committee members Eric Sawyer, Gedalia Braverman, Charles King, and others developed policy that ultimately resulted in a new organization,

Housing Works, creating housing for homeless people with AIDS in New York City. Gay Youth organizing by Kate Barnhart and others transformed into the creation of YELL. And a porn photographer, Charles Hovland, and two arts administrators, Patrick Moore and Ann Philbin, raised $650,000 in an art auction for ACT UP, while an entrepreneur, Sean Strub, used direct mail to invent niche marketing for the AIDS consumer.

17

Insurance Equals Access, and Without Access There Is No Treatment

KARIN TIMOUR

The story of Karin Timour's years-long campaign to win insurance eligibility for people with AIDS is also an example of the very different paths and motives that brought people to their work in ACT UP. Timour was a hard-core strategist and her work is a textbook lesson in research, rallying the troops, coalition building, interacting with legislators, and the point-by-point demands of running a successful uphill campaign that benefited hundreds of thousands and ultimately millions of people.

Karin Timour, with Joe Keenan on her left, being arrested at the Woody Myers protest in Times Square in 1990. Ben Thornberry, in the lower left corner behind the police, was photographing the arrests. (Photograph by T.L. Litt)

Karin's landlords in Brooklyn were a Black gay couple who had been together about ten years. One of them got sick in 1985, deteriorated, went to the hospital, and died without a will. His family tried to take his property, including the building. Karin and her roommates accompanied their landlord to his lover's funeral against the will of the family, only to discover that the dead man's body was encased in glass because he had died of AIDS. The family banned her friend from the graveside, threatening to call the police if he showed up. While they were at the funeral, the family had the water and electricity turned off, so when they returned, the man could not even have a cup of tea in his own home. He also died, five months later, without a will.

Karin read about ACT UP in an article by the novelist David Leavitt in *The New York Times Magazine*. She thought, *Wow, a group that's not only politically active but actually gets things done*. Karin had moved to New York from central Indiana and was working as an HIV coordinator within the inpatient drug rehabilitation program at Phoenix House, a well-known transitional program for addicts. The federal government required that funding for drug treatment was dependent on having HIV services on-site, and she was one of the first waves of HIV coordinators hired to provide HIV care within outpatient drug treatment.

In 1989, Karin walked into the Gay Center for the first time to attend an ACT UP meeting. Almost no one spoke to her for the first three or four months, but she learned a lot. When her brother got a rare illness, she'd gone to the College of Insurance and started reading up on health benefits but had trouble getting anywhere. After going to ACT UP for about six weeks, the floor called for volunteers to start a Health Insurance Committee. Karen thought that it might help her with her brother, so she joined.

ACT UP decided pretty quickly that there was a lot of information that needed to be mastered. Some insurance professionals among that first group organized a series of internal teach-ins about how health insurance was structured. The committee included Bob Padgug, who was working for Empire Blue Cross and Blue Shield, and David Petersen, a private financial planner. They were joined by Wayne Kawadler and Barry Lapidus.

At the time, Empire Blue Cross and Blue Shield had something called *the million-dollar policy* for people with chronic illnesses. There was an open enrollment period every year, for only a month, but nobody else was insuring people with chronic illnesses. If a person with a chronic illness missed that month, then they didn't have health insurance. The Insurance Committee's first goal was to get a stop loss in Empire Blue Cross and Blue Shield. Most people, when they start using their health insurance, have a deductible, so for a certain period, starting in January, they have to pay 100 percent of the bill, and then, after a certain point, the deductible is met and the company starts paying 80 percent of what it has determined the bill should be—not 80 percent of what the bill is, but 80 percent of what it deems *usual, customary, and reasonable.* And then, in most cases, when the client hits a cutoff number in insurance claims in one year, that's when they reach their stop loss and the company has to pay 100 percent from that point on. But Empire had forgotten to put a stop loss on its new policy. So that meant that clients would pay 80 percent, until they ran out of money and went on Medicaid.

It's a fairly technical thing to get across in a demonstration and sound bites, but insurance is a stuffy industry and "they were really not ready at all for ACT UP to come and do demonstrations." Karin and only five other ACT UPers did an action with signs in front of the Empire Blue Cross and Blue Shield building on the corner of Third Avenue and Fortieth Street. They marched in a little circle in front of the company logo. Empire was extremely upset, and immediately invited ACT UP into the building. The picketers said that they could only negotiate if Empire would put a stop loss in, and the next week the company complied and changed the policy.

The next, and most significant, demand was that Empire put in writing that HIV was not a preexisting condition—that it would only consider AIDS a preexisting condition. Empire agreed to that as well. "It's very heady when you start out and there's six of you with foam core signs, and you win." In this small way, hundreds of thousands of people with HIV became eligible for insurance.

TEACHING ACT UP HOW TO FIGHT FOR INSURANCE

"I know it's not a wildly, sexy, fascinating topic," Karin said, but she and
the tiny Insurance Committee set out to start educating ACT UP. They
would keep getting up in meetings and saying, *Okay, it's coming—our
demonstration is six weeks from now, five weeks from now, four weeks from
now*, and they'd get the approval from the floor for fact sheets. *We need
the troops; you guys gotta come.* There were never more than ten people at
a meeting of the Insurance Committee. But they functioned like an action corps; they would do the research and then go to the floor, explain
it to ACT UP, and then people from the floor would show up in large
numbers at the actions. When the committee surveyed the floor one
night to find out if people had insurance, they found out that a third of
those present had no insurance, which is a very strong indication of the
class range of ACT UP.

This tactical mode of organization is highly efficient and can be
applied to any movement. A small group of people commit to becoming the experts. They do the work to design a solution. They present the
solution to the powers that be. When the powers refuse the change, this
vanguard/committee/affinity group holds teach-ins at which the facts are
presented in a clear, succinct manner to the larger community, preparing
them to act. They then organize a specific action for the larger group to
do, an action designed to force the solution they have already created.

In 1990, the National Air Traffic Controllers Association (NATCA)
wrote into their disability coverage that if members got AIDS because
of drugs or sex, the disability insurance wouldn't pay anything, but if
they got it through birth or blood transfusions, they would have full
disability coverage. ACT UP decided that was discrimination and that
it was outrageous. They started learning about disability insurance.
What do we need to know to turn this around? Insurance is regulated on
a state-by-state basis; there really isn't a national insurance standard.
ACT UP filed formal complaints charging NATCA with discrimination on the basis of disability in all fifty states and all the U.S. ter-
ritories with the help of all the ACT UPs in the country. A number
of state insurance commissioners responded positively. Kentucky, West
Virginia, and Arizona all said, *Yes, this has merit.* And what rapidly
became clear was that NATCA was going to have write two different

disability policies—one for the states that did find it a problem, and one for the states that didn't—so it changed the whole policy to cover all HIV-positive workers. "Every air traffic controller in the country who got HIV and who eventually got AIDS got the full disability coverage no matter how they got it, because of something that we did. And that was just, like, *wow*."

FINDING YOUR COALITION

The biggest win that the Insurance Committee achieved in ACT UP was realized in January of 1990.

Everybody who needed health insurance and could afford it bought a policy. But the cost of maintaining that coverage got to be higher and higher and higher. And so Empire had to raise the premium. Healthy people started going to other insurers, where they would get a 20 percent discount for switching. But sick people couldn't switch without getting a 50 percent increase. The insurance industry trade term for it was *cherry-picking*. ACT UP was just outraged. So the chairman of Empire Blue Cross and Blue Shield filed for a rate increase, and in those days, if an insurance company wanted a rate increase on health insurance, it had to have a public hearing.

Karin started calling all the organizations that represented people with chronic illnesses that she could find or figure out. The Heart Association and the Cancer Society—*Do you know what's happening? Do you know what they're talking about? Have you heard this?* David Petersen was independently doing the same thing.

"David had the brainwave of *Let's pack the hearing room. Let's get everybody and tell them to come down and testify* . . . I called the Hemophilia Association and—see, the secret story is that so many people with hemophilia are infected with HIV. And they were on it like white on rice. They were absolutely [in]—*We will be there* . . . There were a number of transplant organizations that got it, and they showed up . . . The Multiple Sclerosis Society—they were on board . . . The Epilepsy Society, they were there very early."

By the time the hearing came around, the Insurance Committee had thirty-four organizations signed up to give testimony. "We pointed out that, in fact, the hearing room was not a wheelchair-accessible space. And so they moved it . . . down the street, and they rented Town Hall Theater."

The Insurance Committee started meeting with these groups to share ideas about how to give testimony, because some of them had never spoken at an insurance department hearing before. They also planned a demonstration out in front. ACT UP had gotten the Brooklyn-wide Interagency Council on Aging involved. The idea of senior demonstrators "terrifies legislators, because seniors vote and they remember, and they care a lot about how much money it cost for health care." The Faceless Bureaucrats from Action Tours came on board. They had paper plates for faces and signs hung around their necks that had the name, in very formal script, of each person testifying for Empire Blue Cross and Blue Shield, and the words EMPIRE—WE DON'T CARE, WE DON'T HAVE TO with the annual salary of each person across the top. When the hearing started, the Faceless Bureaucrats stood up, walked down in front of the stage, and faced the audience and all the media, wearing the signs right in the middle of Empire's testimony. The print media rushed the stage, because they wanted to get a picture.

"*Good Morning America* came down and filmed us. We had a moving picket out in front. We had a banner that said, *Insurance Discrimination Kills People With AIDS—KILLS* in giant red letters—wide as a city block. And we had the general ACT UP picket, people who were in business drag, on their way to work. And we had people in leather jackets, coming home from the bars. And they're all, like, in this little circle. And then the school bus drives up that's been chartered by the [Brooklyn-wide Interagency Council on Aging]. It's all the seniors, with their box lunches. They're coming for the hearings! . . . A number of the senior groups in Brooklyn were made up of people who'd been very active communists and socialists in their youth . . . They all bop off the bus, canes and walkers and the whole nine—fists in the air, you know—and they just charged right in and got in the picket line. So now we had the leather guy, the guy in the suit, the little lady with a cane, and the guy with the leather. It was, like—it was just wonderful, you know. And they were trying to learn the chants, you know. So they were chanting. And then, when it came time to go into the theater, the media all wanted to know, *Are you guys going to do civil disobedience in there?* And we were like, *You'll have to find out.*"

Inside the hearing, just as someone from Empire was testifying that the company needed more money, two demonstrators got onstage and held up the banner right behind him so that he had to give his testimony to television cameras and the print media in front of the statement INSURANCE DISCRIMINATION KILLS PEOPLE WITH AIDS, with the Faceless Bureaucrats standing in front of him. At the end of the day, at five, there still were almost sixty groups waiting to testify. By the second hearing, they had named their coalition New Yorkers for Accessible Health Coverage. The actions led to direct negotiations with Empire Blue Cross and Blue Shield as well as other companies.

The coalition had a meeting to sit down and concretize its concept of a dream insurance. The members decided that individual people should be able to buy health insurance, regardless of their health status, and that using health insurance should not push its price upward. They were concerned about small business owners, because one of the things made clear from the hearings was that small business owners often wanted to have health insurance for their employees, but the costs were too extreme. The insurance company would give a break if there were 300 or 350 employees, but they wouldn't give that break if a business had two.

DEALING WITH THE LEGISLATURE

The New York State Senate was controlled by the Republicans, and the Assembly was controlled by the Democrats. So there had to be a Democratic Assembly sponsor to introduce a piece of legislation, or it was sunk. And there had to be a Republican Senate sponsor to introduce it, or it was sunk. So the Insurance Committee had to find a Republican senator who could get on board to introduce the legislation that we wanted. Committee members started going around and meeting with Republican senators, which primarily meant senators from Long Island and Queens. They met with the Health Committee and with the Senate Insurance Committee.

"That means, if the person that you need to get to, to sponsor your legislation, is sitting there, talking to you, with a giant dessert plate button that says, *I'm with the Pope, and I Vote*—then that's what you do. You sit and you talk with that person, you know . . . People had big pictures of dead fetuses on their walls and things like that . . . We were always very clear to have somebody from an AIDS group, somebody from a multiple sclerosis group—so we would pick which diseases. And if we knew that somebody in their family had a particular disease, we would move heaven and earth to get that person from that disease association in the room, with the legislator."

Openly HIV-positive state senator Tom Duane's office lent ACT UP a folding machine. It would jam folding more than four pieces at a time. But the Insurance Committee literally turned cases and cases of paper into little trifold folders that said, *Empire's rates are going up. Are you going to lose your health insurance?* And on the inside they put action steps. *Call your legislator.* They looked up the actual legislators for specific districts, did a different trifold for each district, and went out weekend after weekend after weekend to the malls on Long Island, to get those Long Island Republican senators.

"We had to, like, build a fire and get them to understand why it was important to pay attention to this. I would go to the floor of ACT UP. *I need like two or three people to come out this weekend on a Saturday . . . We'll provide the car, we'll get you out there.* And, *We're just going to leaflet the mall . . .* Sooner or later, mall security would figure out we were there and then, throw us out of the building, okay. So then we would leaflet all the cars, okay. So we're running around the parking lot, but when you would go up to people and explain it to them, people were galvanized . . . I knew that we were going to win the day that we walked into a very, very ritzy North Shore Long Island mall—they didn't have any plastic anything. They had teak everything . . . I, like, got myself totally geared—because I don't come from money. That's not my background . . . And I walked into this incredibly wealthy men's store. I'm certain that I never earned enough money to buy a belt in there. And I walk up to the manager and I explain the situation to him, and he got it, immediately. Not only that, he was [like], *Give me all you have.* So I gave him, like, fifty flyers. He got all the staff to come around and he said, *We're going to lose our health insurance on this job if these rates go up. We can't afford it. Here, I want you all to take a flyer, and I want you to all take one home to your family, and I want you to all call.*"

The organizing effort here was thorough, but it was also very efficient, because the direct contact with constituencies in target districts was not just informational: it gave them an action, something specific to do— call the legislator—and it told them what to say. Clearly, contacted people did take action, because in the last month before the vote, the insurance industry brought in a million dollars of lobbying talent to try to defeat them. But the ACT UP Insurance Committee was successful. They got through their legislation, the Open Enrollment Community Rating Law of 1992. *Open enrollment* meant that anytime a person wanted to go out and buy health insurance, if they had the money, they could buy it, and could not be refused because they were sick. *Community rating* meant that the price of health insurance—the premium— would not go up because the person went to the doctor. Those were the two major pieces of legislation. They also won *credit for preexisting conditions*. At that time most private insurance was employment-based. A lot of people were concerned because when they would switch jobs, they would face a preexisting initial waiting period, a certain number of months where they had to pay premiums but didn't have coverage for anything related to their particular illness. This new bill allowed people to transfer coverage for their preexisting conditions. This was landmark legislation when it was passed.

At the time of Karin's work, there were 633,000 people with AIDS in the United States. These changes in private insurance on national, state, and union scales became potentially available to huge numbers of people. But what about those who could not afford insurance? ACT UP simultaneously fought for inclusion in private insurance and made an even larger, longer-lasting, and continuing campaign to support people with AIDS who had no resources at all: the homeless.

18

How the ACT UP Housing Committee Became Housing Works, Housing for Homeless People with AIDS

ERIC SAWYER

Eric Sawyer grew up in a little hamlet called Quinneville, New York, and went to community college on an athletic scholarship and then to SUNY Oneonta, in upstate New York. His father was a long-distance truck driver, and his mother was a housewife who took in laundry and foster children to make ends meet. After reading in *TIME* magazine about the growing gay liberation movement, Eric decided to go to graduate school in Boulder, Colorado, and immediately sought out the Gay Liberation Office, went to his first gay bar, and within six months had broken up with his girlfriend and had a boyfriend. He then went to New York.

"I think I was infected on New Year's Eve—'79 turning into '80—after going home with two guys from Flamingo and having a three-way after doing acid. And I returned to Denver—to Boulder— and immediately had a horrible flu and flu-like symptoms—swollen lymph nodes. I was sick for weeks, and they thought I had mononucleosis. They thought I might have Hodgkin's [lymphoma], because I had so many swollen lymph nodes. They did a biopsy, it wasn't Hodgkin's [lymphoma]. Eventually, it kind of passed. And then, I moved to New York, in the summer of '80, and in '81 developed shingles. So, in retrospect, my doctors think that that was probably my conversion."

Eric had renovated a two-family house—a Victorian—with his ex-lover in Denver while he was in graduate school. He sold it and made some money. He was reading a lot of books on how to make money in real estate and was living in Harlem, renovating his second town house, while having rental income coming in from the first in Colorado. Early in 1984, a boyfriend came down with KS. "So by then I was pretty sure that I was also infected. As soon as there was a test, my doctor tested me, and I was positive."

Eric met Larry Kramer at the West Side YMCA when he very first moved to New York. They used to run around Central Park together. Larry had a little group called "The Network." He and Dr. Lawrence Mass and other people were writing articles about the *gay pneumonias, the gay cancers, the gay plague*, and sounding the alarm about it. Meetings were Tuesday and Thursday mornings at seven-thirty, in different people's apartments. But Eric was renovating a brownstone at the time and didn't stay involved in that group. Eric and Larry almost bought some buildings together, but Larry's brother, Arthur, objected to Eric buying single-room-occupancy buildings, as this was early gentrification: destroying low-income housing and replacing it with luxury real estate. Eric said, "When there was a desire to return to the cities like New York—from the suburbs . . . the creation of new housing opportunities for rich people—luxury housing—has to come from existing housing stock, or existing real estate. There's not a whole bunch of empty lots in New York City. And the most affordable places were welfare hotels, or apartment buildings, where a lot of poor people lived."

He was a gentrifier.

Soon thereafter, Eric got involved in caring for his boyfriend, Scott, who had pneumonia a few times and eventually died in 1986. And after he died, Eric became aware of a lot of homeless people with AIDS, partially because a homeless drug user in the area where he was renovating came down with AIDS and had nowhere to stay. Some neighbors were collecting money to rent him a room in a rooming house, a housing option quickly being eliminated by gentrification. Eric called Larry to let him know that Scott had died and told him about his new awareness of homelessness and AIDS. Eric told Larry that he wanted to use his housing development skills to develop some housing for people with AIDS, and asked to be put in touch with people, "because by then the Network had evolved into GMHC and Larry was one of the prophets of the epidemic."

Larry told him, *Sure, but I'm going to do this speech at the Center next week, and the NIH has got a hundred million dollars to test drugs, and there's a hiring freeze, and they're not hiring new researchers, so only one drug—AZT—is being tested. I want to start a protest group, like the antiwar movement, to try to sound the alarm and get the hiring freeze lifted, so that some of these drugs that are promising can get into trials. Do you want to come to the meeting? Why don't you be in the audience? But ask for volunteers. Stand up, be a rabble-rouser! Try and get other people to help organize the demonstration, and help me do the first demonstration.* "At that time my lover Scott had been dead about nine months, and I already had a new boyfriend, and his name was Frank Jump, and Frank and I went to the meeting."

Knowing a couple of people in the neighborhood who were homeless, who didn't have housing, was what sensitized Eric to the issue, and he started reading a lot about it. Eric started to realize that there was an entirely different AIDS plague, tied to drug use, that was very prevalent in homeless communities, and that there was an entire area where there were no services. There wasn't a group like the Gay Men's Health Crisis that was advocating for HIV-positive homeless people, other than the AIDS Resources Center, and Bailey House only had sixteen or twenty rooms. There were thousands of people already with AIDS and hundreds of sick homeless people in New York City. Eric heard lots of stories about people with AIDS being beaten in the shelters or driven out of squats or out from some of the areas, like under the bridges or in the subway tunnels, where many homeless people were living.

In the eighties, New York real estate had become prohibitively expensive, marking the beginning of a real estate boom. The Upper West Side, which had a lot of rooming houses, SRO hotels, and inexpensive housing was being snapped up by gentrifiers, who were throwing out poor people, the mentally ill, and underemployed people and making them homeless. There had been a big defunding of mental health services and drug treatment services, so there were a lot of marginalized people living on the street who were not given any job training or education or drug rehab. It was the Reagan years—the economy was booming, Wall Street was booming, banking was booming, and a lot of buildings were being converted into high-priced co-ops.

Eric brought a proposal to the floor that ACT UP should try to develop housing for people with AIDS. Response was mixed.

"Larry wasn't particularly happy that we were introducing things like a Housing Committee to ACT UP. Or that we were bringing up issues like needle exchange, or that we were doing a lot of work advocating for Medicaid cards and for income maintenance and expedited social services. A lot of Treatment and Data folks—and Larry—felt that we were diluting the energy and the resources of ACT UP, taking up too much time on social justice issues, and deviating from the intended purpose of getting drugs into bodies . . . Sometimes there would be outbursts by people complaining about the fact that we were spending too much time on those issues, and there were lifesaving therapy issues that we needed to be discussed. There was an amendment passed, a vote taken to block the first ten or fifteen minutes of the agenda of ACT UP meetings for lifesaving information—to share information about the latest clinical trials, or latest drugs coming onto market, or what have you. And so some of us kind of die-hards, like myself and Charles King, decided that we could play that game, too. And we asked for a vote for lifesaving information about housing and access to social services and Medicaid cards as well, because if poor people didn't have a place to live, or didn't have a Medicaid card, and didn't have health insurance, they couldn't afford the drugs."

What evolved was what Eric called the Social Justice Squad of ACT UP. "It was the Women's Committee, dealing with issues of women and children." (The Women's Committee actually did no work with children.) It included the Needle Exchange group and the Majority Action Committee. "We kind of had our little cabal, and alliances, that we would work." Eric learned a huge amount about how to work with networks and groups. From his perspective, ACT UP was a microcosm of society.

"There were power brokers, amongst varying populations or subgroups within ACT UP, or varying committees. And we were working the phones during the week, or having meetings or dinners or coffee with varying groups to get them to support our agenda, so we could get a demonstration or get money to go to Washington about a housing issue or whatever—horse-trading."

The ACT UP Housing Committee never actually got a meeting with Mayor Koch. But it did meet with several officials in the mayor's office and in the city's Housing Preservation and Development (HPD) Committee. Initially it was a polite meet and greet. *Oh yeah—we'll take your recommendations and your requests under consideration*, or, *You've got to understand, it's very political, we can't just be turning buildings over to groups. If every group who wanted a building turned over to develop low-income housing came to us and we handed them a building, imagine the mess we'd be in*—blah, blah, blah.

"And it wasn't until we started blocking the street and getting coverage on the five and six o'clock news on a regular basis, and really embarrassing the mayor at fundraisers for Richie Rich members of the gay community that we started, actually, making some headway in getting housing allowances. Actually, after the big demonstration we had in front of HPD, where we blocked the streets, Koch actually announced a twenty-five-million-dollar capital fund, to create housing for homeless people with AIDS, that was soon matched by New York State."

SHARON TRAMUTOLA

Sharon Tramutola was born in the Ironbound section of Newark, New Jersey. Her father, a union man, loaded trucks, and her mother worked in a school cafeteria. She went to one year of college and worked in day care for many years. "I always read books and stuff about other places. And from when I was thirteen, I was sneaking to New York."

In 1986, a friend of hers got sick. There were no services because he was a drug user, and once someone is labeled a drug user in the system, it is even harder to get any services at all. It was difficult to get him into rehab, because the programs were not dealing with AIDS and didn't know what to do. This friend was staying with Sharon for a long time. Sharon was bisexual and identified with the gay community. She was watching the news one day, and she saw ACT UP.

"And I was really pissed by that time. I mean . . . everything was really rough. And when I'd seen them on TV, they were talking about what they were going to do, and they interviewed them at the Center, I think, the first time. Then I'd seen them again—it might have been the Gay Pride march. And I said, *I'm going to go check this out.* So I came over and checked it out. And the first meeting I went to, I brought my girlfriend with me. And there must have been five hundred people, at least, at the Center. And it was really confusing. When you first came in at the beginning . . . it seemed like everybody knew so much. And they were talking about things that I never heard of before. And my girlfriend said, *I'm not coming back here. I don't know what's going on, I'm not coming back.* And I said, *No, you are, you are.* So it was right before the FDA, we joined. After the FDA, she said, *I can't*—she got hysterical. She got too upset when we went to the FDA. And after that, it was like, she didn't come to an ACT UP meeting again . . . You know what really made me stay? I was just telling my friend Lei [Chou] a little earlier. Maybe like the third meeting I came to—you know, I didn't understand everything going on, and I wanted to; but somebody came in the door and said, *There's a gay-basher on the corner with a bat.* And everybody in the meeting stood up and ran out the door after the guy. And I said, *Hey, these people really want to do something. At least they're not a bunch of punks saying they're going to [do] something, you know?* And I started coming back."

Sharon joined the Majority Action and Housing Committees. The issue at that time was that people with AIDS in shelters were endangered. They were getting tuberculosis and other illnesses from using the same facilities as other people, when they really needed their own rooms, their own bathrooms. A shelter was opening at Bellevue, and the Housing Committee was saying, *This is not a good situation for people with AIDS. They need something else.* ACT UP wanted more SROs explicitly for people with AIDS. Sharon worked on Housing with people from Majority Action, some women, and people of color, including Dan Williams, Alan Robinson, Robert Garcia, Robert Vázquez-Pacheco, Lei Chou, Emily Gordon, and a little later on, Wahn Yoon, Michael Wiggins, and Marvin Palmer.

"We did actions that went against just the system." Sharon did an action at Kings County Hospital, where people with AIDS were coming into the emergency room with symptoms, and they weren't being tested for HIV. Instead, doctors were giving them drugs for diarrhea and sending them home. And by the time they finally got an appropriate diagnosis they had two T cells. There were a lot of people with AIDS with Medicaid. And people with Medicaid, clearly, in all the hospitals, were not getting treated the same way as people with insurance. They marched to Kings County and did a die-in in front. They leafleted not only the hospital but the whole surrounding community. There was a lot of media at the action. The resistance was so public that hospital administrators were forced to come out and meet with ACT UP. Eventually, that emergency room got a little better for people with AIDS.

"There were two groups of people in ACT UP. There were the groups of people who thought that until they had AIDS, they thought that the government was out there, and working for them. And I went to an affinity group meeting with this guy, I don't remember his name; and he said it, quite clear. And he was really serious. He said, *I can't believe that my government let me down. I had a good job, I had plenty of money. But when I got sick, the government let me down. I wasn't getting the services, I got treated like a pariah.* Then there was the other group—and it wasn't only people of color; but there's another group, I think it's more of a class thing—who knew that the system stunk, and the system had been letting them down, for years . . . People with insurance were definitely feeling something different than people going in with Medicaid . . . There were people that socialized in ACT UP who would never, ever, in a million years, if it wasn't that situation, even talk to each other on the street.

"But I think that's the thing that held the group together so long, and made it work. Even people you didn't like in ACT UP, right—you would support them in some way, because you had the same issues . . . People were dying, it was urgent; a lot of people in the group were dying; and this was it. There was nowhere else to go but ACT UP. And I think some people came to ACT UP or they would have jumped out windows if they didn't come to ACT UP, because it was also, in a way, some kind of therapy for people coming there. Whether you were rich or poor, that was one of the only places you could talk about your condition, your friend's condition, whoever you were taking care of. That was the only place to talk about it. And I think that made an alliance that would have never happened anywhere else . . . And the anger was there. Everybody was pissed. They weren't getting the services; most people were still treated like pariahs, in the beginning."

RICHARD JACKMAN

Richard Jackman grew up in southwestern Pennsylvania. His father was a steelworker; his mother was a nurse. With a degree from Carnegie

Mellon in architecture, Rich moved to New York in 1987 and joined ACT UP in August of that year.

ACT UP's Housing Committee's main goal was to create housing for homeless people with AIDS in New York City. This meant dealing with housing discrimination and not-in-my-backyard (NIMBY) issues, wealthier communities reacting to AIDS housing as an extension of the reaction to affordable housing in general. There was a proposal to develop the Northern Dispensary in Greenwich Village into AIDS housing at one point.

"There was a lot of NIMBY about that. I remember specifically the owners of the Monster, the [gay] bar, were opposed to it. We plastered the neighborhood with posters that I think the headline was, *What kind of Monster would oppose AIDS housing?* Something like that. We supported squatters. We did some marches with squatters."

The Glass House was a big, old, industrial building in the East Village on Avenue C. Gay Latino councilman Antonio Pagán was trying to pit AIDS activists against squatters in order to facilitate gentrification, claiming that squatters were in the way of the development of affordable housing for people with HIV.

"You've got sick people who are homeless, and over here they are just doing what they can to help themselves, so they break into a building and they're living in the building, and over there, now you set up this nonprofit agency and you've got all these people working there and you get government funding and you do all this policy work, and that's how you do it, right? And one is not necessarily more efficient than the other, you know. I mean, that has a lot of overhead . . . I think we pretty successfully turned that around mentally. I don't know how successful we were in the end, but we forged some alliances, if nothing else."

GEDALIA (GEDALI) BRAVERMAN

In 1981, at age twenty-one, Gedali Braverman moved to Manhattan after Georgetown, expecting to be a businessman. His family was from Israel and had a diamond business. But Gedali found himself tabling on street corners for a pre-GMHC group. "The fact sheets were very basic—that there was some sort of an epidemic that was in progress, and that there were a few hundred people who had died already. I remember the day that we changed our little poster that said *999 Dead* to *1,000.*"

In 1983, he became involved in his first serious relationship with a man, "a boy—we were both boys." His boyfriend was twenty-two, and Gedali was twenty-three. A bit more than a year later, his lover became ill, was diagnosed with Kaposi sarcoma, and died seven months to the day from the time of his diagnosis, in 1985. Gedali's life became, essentially, taking care of him. "I lived in the hospital and that took over my life." People died so rapidly at that time, and all of his friends disappeared. Only one consistently came to the hospital to visit. Gedali didn't tell his family what was happening to his lover. His brother knew, but not his parents, because he knew that he was probably HIV-positive, and didn't want them to freak out. He wanted to focus on taking care of his partner, as opposed to having to deal with taking care of his parents around his health.

He would leave work at five and walk from Rockefeller Center to the hospital, where he had a bed in his boyfriend's private room. Gedali slept there, and he would wake up in the morning at seven, walk to his apartment on Thirty-Sixth and Park, take a shower, and go back to work.

"The nights there were very interesting and very sad—very difficult nights. It was 1985, a period where, in a lot of hospitals, there were reports of the staff leaving food outside of the doors and the nurses not wanting to attend to the people who were diagnosed. A lot of young gay men, appearing at the hospital, lying in the emergency rooms until they could get a room—with no family and no friends. I developed a very close relationship with the nursing staff—all of the nursing staffs for all three shifts. And I developed this strategy of bringing them a lot of gifts—chocolates, foods, whatever—and endearing them to us, so that Roy would get good care during the daytime hours when I wasn't there. And they developed a relationship with me, where they would wake me, in the middle of the night, when new cases came in, because they were generally boys my age—in their early twenties, leading very, sort of, last days of abandoned existences. And I would sit with these other boys, while Roy was sleeping and talk to them about life, whatever.

"So I was, over the course of those last three months, making a lot of friendships with boys who lived for a few days. And it was a surreal time. They were mostly in shock and overwhelmed. They came in such what we would later call *late-stage* conditions that they would generally only have a few days of consciousness before they would end up in respiratory failure, whatever. The more angry and dire cases were the ones who arrived with massive, rapidly progressive KS, and you would see boys who you could barely ascertain where their eyes were on their face. Their features became just mottled."

Gedali recalled that in 1987, with AZT, there was a glimmer of hope that there might be a cure that galvanized people, because they wanted to reach for that brass ring. He also remembered that feeling of randomness—those who survived felt the randomness of the loss and realized that they might live for another year or longer. After his lover died in December of 1985, he hid from life for a little bit. For a couple of years, he said, "I just wanted to be an audience." He went to the theater. He wanted to escape what he'd experienced in his lover's loss and the losses of these other people he'd met, who had died quickly. He pursued his love for the arts in what he believed might be the last days of his life. After a couple of years, when he wasn't dead yet, he remembered seeing ACT UP at Gay Pride and seeing the force of it, and thinking, *That's where I need to be* . . . "I knew, of course, I was HIV-positive . . . In the early days of ACT UP, I think, there were not a lot of us who were out about being HIV-positive, and I was one of those people."

His boyfriend, Roy, had been doing graduate work in public housing when he died. Roy was always interested in housing and disenfranchised populations, and Gedali took that on in his memory. "But I also— somehow, I think, I identified more with issues that dealt with minority populations and populations that were just what we later called *disenfranchised* or *harder to reach* people who really had the least opportunities to survive."

The first meeting of Housing Works was called by Bill Bloom. I also attended this gathering, held at the West Village brownstone of gay historian Jonathan Ned Katz. There were probably about twenty of us there, and the meeting was called in order to decide what was going to happen with a demonstration at Trump Tower, which was for Thanksgiving of 1988; we wanted to begin creating affinity groups, to look at how to orchestrate the action. At the time, Donald Trump had developed several properties and received tax abatements from the city, and the overall feeling from the activist community was that instead of wealthy landlords getting tax abatements and incentives to develop housing for rich people, the city should be providing funds and services to people who were homeless or on the verge of becoming homeless, which would help the conglomeration of problems that occurred as people became ill and lost jobs. So the idea was to target the Trump Tower, which was, at the time, the symbol of real estate gigantic-ness in Manhattan, and to essentially shut down the tower at Fifty-Sixth and Fifth, in order to call attention to the fact that people were already homeless and living with AIDS.

RICHARD JACKMAN

The Housing Committee–organized Trump Tower action was dubbed Trumpsgiving. Rich saw the protest as a way of "countering this whole glorification of gentrification and this just disgusting kind of Trump-ism." Trump was getting tax breaks, basically corporate welfare, while there were homeless people with HIV on the streets. But, Rick realized, ultimately it wasn't about money, because it always costs more to have people in shelters and on the street than to house them.

"And it's not even about not wanting to spend money on *those people* . . . It's about hate and fear. Ultimately it's very important that people are afraid of being homeless, that you are afraid of losing your job, that you could see how far down you could slide, and our society has to maintain the possibility of personal disaster to keep people in line, and that costs money."

There were different affinity groups doing different actions, mostly in the courtyard mall within Trump Tower. ACT UP handed out empty paper plates saying HAPPY TRUMPSGIVING. Somebody blockaded the front doors. "There were a bunch of things happening simultaneously. It was semi-organized chaos."

GEDALIA (GEDALI) BRAVERMAN

The Housing Committee's demand was for the city to provide fund-ing for scattered-site housing and independent housing for people with HIV, as well as group homes. In 1988, *The New York Times* esti-mated that 1,500 to 2,000 infected people were in the shelters alone. That didn't take into account the numbers of unsheltered and inad-equately housed homeless people. Activists believed there were already five thousand homeless people with AIDS living in the city's streets and in the shelters. There was almost no housing available at the time. So ACT UP began targeting the Dinkins administration and its Housing Preservation and Development (HPD) Committee. The com-missioner of the city's Housing Authority then was a Hasidic Jewish man, Abraham Biderman, who was very unapproachable. ACT UP stormed his offices, demanded meetings, and came up with a series of proposals for scattered-site housing. Within the first six months, ACT UP was able to get the Housing Authority to earmark six hundred units through persistent, creative demonstrations. The Housing Committee set up house outside the HPD office building, with beds, sofas, and desks. They brought furniture onto the sidewalk and chained themselves to it. They embarrassed Biderman so greatly that they were able to get meetings. "And, interestingly, there were some gays and lesbians on his staff who were sort of our inside moles, who would feed us information as to what his level of flexibility was, and how we should next approach his weak spots."

Once ACT UP was able to get the city to start moving on housing issues, it then targeted the Catholic Archdiocese of New York, which, at the time, was the single largest property holder in the city and had also received tax incentives and abatements for development of skilled nursing facilities. There was an abandoned building that the archdiocese opened in the East Village. The city gave the archdiocese a ninety-nine-year lease.

"It was to be a skilled nursing facility, specifically for people with AIDS, which we thought was rather heinous, given the fact that at the time—not that it's that different now—but, the Vatican and the arch-diocese obstructed anything that was done in terms of safe-sex educa-tion, condom distribution, educational programs in high schools. And we thought it was just a great slap in the face to gay people who might be homeless, to have to spend their last days in a nursing facility that was run by the archdiocese, where they'd be dying and judged simul-taneously, and where the state and the city were providing funds to the

Catholic archdiocese for these people's care. So, from that point, we started targeting Cardinal O'Connor."

ERIC SAWYER

There was over one hundred million dollars' worth of city, state, and federal funds allocated to create housing and nursing homes for homeless people with AIDS. Eric recalled that the Catholic Church was trying to get all of the money set aside to fund AIDS nursing homes. And they were refusing to allow condom distribution. They didn't want to provide gynecological services or abortion services. They didn't want to provide drug treatment. They wanted only clean and sober establishments. They also wanted ten-year limitations of those facilities being used specifically for AIDS patients. "Okay, we'll take all of your money. We'll create these nursing homes. We'll treat the nice, polite faggots who don't use drugs, but they can't be pregnant women, they can't be drug users, and we won't talk about sex. Or let them have sex, or whatever. They can come here and die, and then after ten years we want to turn them into nursing homes for elderly Catholics." And so the Housing Committee organized an aggressive campaign, which succeeded in stopping Cardinal O'Connor and the Catholic Church from receiving the money. But stopping the church was not enough. Someone else had to actually create the kind of housing needed by people with AIDS in New York City.

RICHARD JACKMAN

The members of the Housing Committee realized that they would have to leave ACT UP if they were to be the ones to create this housing.

"To actually produce housing, you have to go in a somewhat different direction. You have to become a service agency of some sort. That's what it is. ACT UP was never a service agency. It's not meant to be. It's an activist organization, and that's something very different. I mean, Housing Works still has a very activist character to it. I'm very happy about that, that it ends up being the largest AIDS service organization in the city and it's very—it was Charles King. He's very charismatic, and he just bulldozed it through and did what I think everybody thought you couldn't do, which is have a service organization that was actually going to get government money at the same time that you're doing civil disobedience against the very departments that you're getting money from. But it worked."

CHARLES KING

Born in Delaware, Charles King grew up with a father who was a fundamentalist evangelical minister and missionary. "He thought Jerry Falwell was a liberal." Charles's mother was a housewife. Charles grew up on a five-acre farm with nine siblings. Being queer propelled him out of the community he grew up in. The first ten years after he left home, Charles recalled, was all about doing his own personal healing by working with marginalized people—with homeless people and abused children—doing street ministry at the First Baptist Church of San Antonio. He started a support group for male street prostitutes. And it was in the context of working with them, saying to them, *God made you who you are, God accepts you, God loves you,* that he was able to come to terms with his own sexual orientation.

Charles went to Yale Divinity School and became assistant minister of the Immanuel Baptist Church of New Haven, Connecticut, a white minister for a predominantly Black congregation.

"AIDS was what actually brought me out . . . So it actually wasn't until our minister of music was terminally ill that I really was forced to grapple with it, and he'd been ill for a while. I had visited him . . . at Yale New Haven Hospital. This is early eighties, '84, I guess, and I went into his room. Clearly wasting syndrome, thrush lining his mouth, he was gaunt, blisters, the whole classic image of somebody dying of AIDS. He was laying in his bed, eyes half open, and I went over to him and I said, *Richard, it's Reverend King. Would you like me to pray for you?* He mumbled something, and I wasn't sure I heard him, and I repeated my question, and then he very clearly said, *It won't do any good . . . God's punishing me because I'm a homosexual,* and that broke the dam for me. I said, *That couldn't possibly be true. If that were true, I'd be in the next bed."*

The summer of 1988, Charles started going to ACT UP and quickly joined the Committee to Demand Housing Now for Homeless People with AIDS and HIV. Their first action was a sit-in at the Housing Resource Administration, demanding a placement for a homeless man with AIDS named Wayne Phillips. They won.

In ACT UP, Charles met Keith Cylar, really the "first true relationship" that he'd had. They met at a government-sponsored Minorities and AIDS Conference in Washington, D.C.—the first ever—and Charles was determined to get some homeless people to the the next conference and get them a speaking venue. So he went to go to the floor of ACT UP to ask for support.

"The Housing Committee endorsed it, but the politics of ACT UP, the Housing Committee was not—we weren't like Treatment and Data. ACT UP had its own fascinating politics. You had the Peter Staleys of the world, who came from places of tremendous privilege, and AIDS had outed them and taken away their privilege, and for them it was all about *drugs into bodies* . . . There was no real appreciation by a powerful minority within ACT UP of the socioeconomic factors that were really drivers of the epidemic. It wasn't so much sexual. It never was about sexual orientation. It was all about social and economic factors, sexual orientation just being another one of those factors, discrimination, marginalization, and what that does to people."

But, as Charles recalled, Majority Action, the committee of people of color within ACT UP, had much more clout than Housing. "They were probably disdained as much as Housing, but they always had the white guilt factor." So Charles decided that Housing needed to go to Majority Action and get their support for this trip. He brought two homeless people who were his clients with him to that meeting, and they presented why they needed to go to the conference and why they needed Majority Action's support.

"And this big Black guy gets up and starts challenging my cred, like, *Who's this white guy coming to us, and what's he doing here?* The committee was split, and, ultimately, they made a very Solomon-like decision. They decided that they would support going to the floor of ACT UP asking for the money, on the condition that Keith and I work on organizing this trip together."

Charles didn't realize that Keith was a coke addict at the time. The floor gave them a little bit of money. Lei Chou, who was then a student at Cooper Union, gave his whole meal allowance for school, and that's what paid for the trip. They planned to take the train to Washington on Sunday, Charles remembered, but Keith had stayed up all night doing coke while xeroxing their materials. He had stuffed the papers into a huge box that fell apart on the platform. As the train was pulling out of the station, Keith jumped in with Charles's clients and left Charles behind, saying, *Catch the next train. Bring all of our stuff!* Charles had to go dig through the garbage to find boxes, rebox everything, and get it down to D.C.

"I think Keith gained respect for me. I gained respect for him . . . At an ACT UP meeting, they needed somebody to write a fact sheet, and you know how ACT UP would call. ACT UP was like going to church, and they were constantly calling for people to come forward to do something. So they called for volunteers to work on the fact sheet. I remember I was the only person to raise my hand. I'm forgetting which moderator it was, but one of them said, *Okay, we have Charles King. Do we have someone else to work on the fact sheet?* Keith's hand went up . . . *Okay, Keith Cylar is going to work on the fact sheet. Do we have anybody else to work on the fact sheet?* And Keith says, *I think two is quite enough to do this fact sheet.* So he comes over to me about five minutes later and says, *I think we should go ahead and knock this out right away. You want to come over to my place and do it?* So I said, *Sure.* We walked over to his place, and I sit down on the couch and pull out my note pad out of my book bag, and the next thing you know he's kissing me and seduced me, and that was it. We were partners for life . . ."

It was in the context of his relationship with Keith that Charles was able to fully imagine creating a new organization for homeless people with AIDS.

"I think the conceptualization of Housing Works would have happened. I don't know if its actualization would have happened if we hadn't been in a relationship. I actually seroconverted just a few years before he died, and it's interesting, being HIV-positive wasn't something that I—it was stupidity on my part not to be more careful than I was, but I have to say I never could have taken on the role that I was left to take on if I hadn't been HIV-positive."

FOUNDING HOUSING WORKS

At the time, Charles remembers, "AIDS organizations wanted absolutely nothing to do with homeless people. The whole reason Bailey House was founded was because GMHC didn't want to touch homeless people. And Bailey House wouldn't take homeless people who were using drugs." Homeless people with HIV had to prove sobriety to get admitted into Bailey House. At the same time that AIDS groups excluded homeless people, homeless organizations did not want people with AIDS. Charles went to his first board meeting at the National Coalition for the Homeless, and there was a Catholic nun on the board. She made some remarks about how, *Well, I'm fine if we have to take this project on, but I think we should be very careful to make clear that we recognize that these people did something wrong to get infected. Otherwise, we'll lose all of our support.* Charles got up, not being recognized, very much in ACT UP mode and said, *Well, actually, I think the majority of people get AIDS by having sex, which is a very natural human thing that at least most of us in this room engage in.*

"I never thought that ACT UP itself really was about poor people and poverty. ACT UP, at its core, was gay men and their allies fighting for their lives. I think there were more conscious and politicized people within ACT UP who saw the relationship to poverty and classism and racism, where I think the core of ACT UP saw homophobia, and that was all they saw, and they never saw the other connection. At best, it was the sort of thing that Larry Kramer might give lip service to, but really not even that. The number of times Larry went to the floor and made some, if not racist, at least racially insensitive statement, often referring to Majority Action or to the Housing Committee—I think ACT UP was clueless about that. So, yeah, in terms of socioeconomic issues . . . I really truly believe that the LGBT community officially abandoned AIDS with [Andrew] Sullivan's article in *The New York Times*, and the reason they abandoned it was, for them, it was over. It was now a Black disease, not their disease. You can almost see the mark of that article and sort of the handoff: *This is no longer our problem. We're going to move on to gay marriage and other things that pull us in towards the center,* with the presumption that everybody wants to be in the center instead of at the margins." Yet, true to the ACT UP tradition of alienation, Charles was defining "ACT UP" by the people he disagreed with, not by himself and his allies.

GEDALIA (GEDALI) BRAVERMAN

As the ACT UP Housing Committee started the transition process into creating a new organization, the activists articulated and designed their visions for AIDS housing. They were specific about what the actual, physical layout of a unit or a site should be—what the needs were of a person living with HIV, in terms of making sure that there were kitchenettes and refrigeration for food and that these places allowed for independent living. They wanted to ensure that residents wouldn't be monitored in terms of coming and going and that there'd be certain sanitary standards and minimum square footage in the units, and that they not be congregated in one location. The Housing Committee was clear that they didn't need a building for people to go and die; instead, the units should be developed from around the city, the same way low-income units weren't grouped in one neighborhood.

Public perception of the need for AIDS housing was changing as AIDS became better understood and gentrification affected more and more people's daily lives. What would have, otherwise, seemed to be peripheral issues were finally growing media-worthy. This gave the activists a lot of confidence. Gedali recalled that some people were beginning to do cost analyses around HIV and AIDS, and it was clear that the cost of hospitalization was so high—especially with rising tuberculosis cases among homeless people—that creating interventions like housing would help keep people healthier longer. Housing would keep people out of hospitals and out of more expensive places like skilled nursing facilities, for a longer period. ACT UP stepped in and was able to provide a sort of cost-benefit analysis to the city at the same time.

Gedali remembered several people in the Dinkins administration who were supportive. "You know, the Koch administration was the worst. There was no one to talk to. Anybody who was gay was homophobic in that administration." But there was a change with Dinkins. First his staff said, *We won't meet with you at all. We have no need to talk to you, and you have no authority to engage us.* But a couple of months later, after some ACT UP actions and phone and fax zaps—during which activists would disable an institution's fax machine by sending it, for example, a mile of black paper, or repeated leaflets arguing against its policies—the Dinkins team became more responsive.

"Oh yeah, it was very widely criticized. I think that, for the most part, the gay male community felt that these tactics were harmful. That the general population would see us as more of a fringe community, that we would alienate straight people, that any progress that we had made in terms of gay liberation would be set back. I think there was a phenomenal amount of negative feeling about the activist movement—certainly in the first years . . . Why were we able to succeed with the first proposals? Because we were right, and that ultimately, the bureaucrats saw that there was just so much lying that they could do, and the facts spoke [for] themselves."

CHARLES KING

Virginia Schubert and the Coalition for the Homeless sued the city in 1988, in a case called *Mixon v. Grinker*. Charles recalled that this suit is responsible for all of the AIDS housing that exists in New York City, because as it wound its way through the courts, the city and state kept putting more resources on the table to make it go away. Although it wasn't won until 1995, *Mixon v. Grinker* served as a model and an agenda. Mayor Koch had come out with a plan to segregate the public shelter system. The city's idea was to run a curtain down the middle of the huge Fort Washington Armory and have people with AIDS on one side and everybody else on the other. "Like, oh, boy, that's going to really help folks," Charles said. The activists' position was *an apartment with a private bathroom for everybody who is HIV-positive.* An HIV-positive gay man was deputy commissioner at HRA, and he testified that *homeless people with AIDS were all better off in the mass-congregated shelter system because they were all either mentally ill or chronically chemically dependent, and in the shelter system they would be less of a menace to themselves and others.*

In 1990, Charles had had a client actually beaten to death by the guards at a shelter and left in the snow in January of that year because they had seen his Kaposi sarcoma lesions when he showered. Charles was listening to the gay HRA commissioner's testimony and reported on it to the ACT UP Housing Committee meeting that night. Activists were totally disheartened. Charles said to the group, *Look, if we're going to get the people we care about housed, we've got to come up with a way to do it ourselves.* And that was it. By the end of the meeting, they'd even come up with the name Housing Works. It took them another five months to write their mission statement and bylaws, because, "of course, typical ACT UP, we had to process everything." The basic team included Charles King, Keith Cylar, Richard Jackman, Sharon Tramutola, Lei Chou, Conyers Thompson, Natasha Grey, Betty Williams, and Gedali Braverman.

BUILDING HOUSING WORKS

CHARLES KING

The first step was to throw down the gauntlet and issue the city a challenge. *If housing active drug users is so difficult,* Housing Works said, *give us a contract, we'll do it.* Housing Works wanted a city contract that included a requirement for at least 50 percent of the people they housed to be active drug users or people who were mentally ill. The Housing Works team went to court and the judge ordered the city to invite them to participate in the bidding process. They put in a proposal and won! The award was for forty units, twenty scattered-site apartments in Lower Manhattan, and twenty in Brooklyn. Charles liked to say, "It was the first housing contract in the nation that required us to keep fifty percent of our residents using drugs at all times."

There was always an assumption, broadly in the field of supportive housing, that drug users were unhousable, and they had to hit bottom, get cleaned up, and only then could be helped. Housing Works disagreed and shared a slogan with the Needle Exchange Committee: "Dead addicts don't recover." The name Housing Works represented the idea that before somebody can deal with addiction, with mental illness, with medical problems, they needed a safe, secure place to live, and that this was the threshold to anything else that a person might need.

"I think that's actually where Keith added in so many ways his greatest contribution to Housing Works, because not only was he out, by the time we started Housing Works, he had been tested and actually had an AIDS diagnosis, but he was very open about the fact that he was a drug addict. I remember wanting to get somebody into detox, and Keith's going and buying the guy some heroin so that . . . he could calm his nerves to stick around for this long enough to get into treatment. Supporting people's drug use when they were dying and saying, *You know what? Not only should we not be trying to take their drugs away from them, we should be helping them get them. What's the point if somebody's dying? If they want to smoke crack, let them smoke crack. Help them die as well as they can. Help them die happy. Help them die with whatever they need.*

"[Keith appreciated] the whole business of drugs and the players and the problems getting caught up with loan sharks, because Keith himself had been caught up with loan sharks. So he just had a real understanding for the depths of that. And also helping us to recognize the fact that [because] somebody was addicted didn't mean they couldn't contribute. There were days when Keith was totally dysfunctional and couldn't come into work, but when he was on, he was on, and he made an amazing contribution to the organization. That always stood as this powerful thing for us, that we weren't ashamed of who we served, we weren't ashamed of who we were. It was a part of creating what we then called and still call a healing community that recognizes that every single one of us comes to this experience in need of healing."

ERIC SAWYER

The first building that Housing Works got on was East Ninth Street and Avenue D. ACT UPers didn't want to do AIDS housing; they didn't want paid staff; they wanted to do activism. They didn't want to create housing or provide services. The Housing Committee would come to the floor and tell people about their search for buildings, and there was a huge outcry of, *You can't have paid staff, you can't get governmental contracts. That's going to limit what we say. It's going to compromise our voice.* Housing Works could actually provide the services. It got a thirty-unit scattered-site contract, which gave it a base and a government contract to recruit paid staff who could supervise construction, obtain Medicaid licenses, and open clinics.

CHARLES KING

"I think the deepest core issue that has continued to be a part of Housing Works was realizing that we had gone from being these pure activists who could do no wrong. We were always on the side of right and justice, to even back then realizing that we were becoming part of an industry. So the biggest challenge for us at that moment was *How do you keep yourself honest?*"

Housing Works decided that a third of its board had to be consumers elected by consumers, which led to a commitment in its mission statement to job creation. At one point, Housing Works was the largest nongovernmental provider of housing in New York City. It had an inventory of over 350 apartments and was adding 100 more. "That's when we got into our little pissing match with Giuliani." Housing Works sued the administration over the mayor's plans to eliminate the Division of AIDS Services. It won that lawsuit, but Giuliani yanked six and a half million dollars in contracts, so the organization lost all of its housing.

"However, we have continued to grow in many other ways, in large measure thanks to a decision we fell into accidentally, but very early on [we] became committed to being entrepreneurial and as independent as we could from government contracts as a way of being able to maintain our advocacy voice. So by 2010 we ended up . . . with revenues of fifty-eight million dollars. We have over five hundred people employed at any given time. We're serving about twenty-five hundred clients on a very, very deep level. We're providing them with primary care, intensive case management, psychosocial services, job training, legal services, so just a comprehensive integrated care system. [As of 2010] we've built our inventory of housing now back up to maybe 170 units. What's different about this is, we own the lion's share of our housing units, instead of pissing away rent money to private landlords, and so that's a positive thing. But we've always regretted that we haven't been able to build housing that keeps apace with our consumer base.

"I'm very proud of the fact that for many years graduates of our job training programs, all formerly homeless people with AIDS, represented over a third of our staff. As we've moved more and more into health care and had to hire a lot more doctors and medical professionals, they still remain twenty-five percent of our staff. We have a three-chair dental clinic. We have [a] comprehensive primary-care center as well as AIDS adult health care. We have four centers, two of which are co-located with housing, two of which are freestanding. We'll probably open a fifth center in the Bronx. We're still very true to our mission. Our clientele is people with AIDS, people at risk of AIDS, who other organizations either cannot or won't serve."

Remembrance: Phyllis Sharpe

When Charles King got to D.C. for the conference on people of color and AIDS, he met up with Phyllis Sharpe, who had worked on the campaign to change the CDC definition. She was a leader in the movement of women with HIV, fighting for benefits and access to experimental drug trials. She signed on to the class-action suit against the government. Phyllis spoke openly about her experiences as a woman with AIDS; she spoke at rallies and to the media. She'd lost her three children to Child Protective Services, which was an unending debacle. First it was that she couldn't get her children back until the HRA gave her an allowance for an apartment big enough to house them, and then the HRA wouldn't give her the apartment until she had custody of her children. Finally, she got the apartment, but Child Protective Services would not give her youngest daughter, Siouxchie, back, because Phyllis didn't have a crib for her, and the HRA wouldn't give her a crib until she had the baby. She wrote a powerful fifteen-minute speech about her experience.

Then Phyllis and Keith Cylar got asked to go on *Nightline* and were very effective. She was then hired to work at Housing Works with Keith and Charles. They were able to help her get a really beautiful three-bedroom apartment in the Bronx. Charles and Keith used to go over there every year for Thanksgiving dinner. "She was in an abusive relationship with this Trinidadian guy, but I give him points because he could do the best pickled pig feet in the world."

Phyllis went through the Housing Works job-training program, and became part of the staff, and worked at their bookstore for a while. Eventually, she started using drugs again and her life became chaotic, and she passed away.

19

YELL: The Evolution of Queer Youth Politics

When my parents first started punishing me for my homosexuality, there was no place I could go. In 1975, my high school guidance counselor told me not to come out to the other students because they would "shun" me. There was no concept of protecting or advocating for gay kids.

By the time ACT UP was founded, twelve years later, the situation had transformed. Ann Northrop had come to ACT UP from Hetrick-Martin, later called Harvey Milk High School, which was an alternative high school for kids who had been driven out of their classrooms by homophobia or transphobia. But the queer youth situation did not leap from zero to complete service. In the interim, there was a radical and ragtag process of gay kids demanding their rights.

ANER CANDELARIO

Born in Puerto Rico, Aner Candelario graduated from Bronx High School of Science. In 1976, at age sixteen, he had a revelation on the 6 train that he was not bisexual, he was gay. And so, being a practical person, he looked in the Yellow Pages and found under *gay* the Gay Switchboard, and called and asked, *Do you have a group for kids, teenagers?* And they said, *Yeah, it's at the Church of the Beloved Disciple on Fourteenth near Ninth Avenue*, which was a condo building that had converted into a church, and, after gentrification, went back to being a condo. Aner showed up to his first meeting, and there was an older man outside smoking a cigarette, the archbishop. Aner was really nervous to go in. The clergyman said, *Are you looking for the youth group?* Aner nodded. *Well, we're going to start in a second.* So Aner went up with him, and there were three or four other kids, and they were kind of shy. The meeting lasted about two hours, and Aner thought, *Well, it wasn't my erotic fantasy, but this is important. This is important.* He kept coming week after week after week, and eventually the kids got rid of the archbishop, because he was a bit of a misogynist and chain-smoked and the gay kids didn't need him. It was a *youth* group. And so at age sixteen, Aner started running Gay Youth, which he did for five years, and it eventually went from a core of about 10 to 160 kids at a meeting; they had to split up in two groups of 80. They were at the Triangle Building in the far West Village under the Metropolitan Community Church on the third floor for years. Mostly it was a support, social, and community-building organization, but it also provided public education. Members would go before the gay synagogue and speak. They met with gay teachers, and they even spoke with the North American Man/Boy Love Association (NAMBLA).

"We were a very above-average group of intelligent young people, I must say, and we heard about NAMBLA and we heard a lot of rumors and things . . . So one week NAMBLA was the topic, and then we found out that several of the people in the group were in NAMBLA. So they said they're having a party, we're invited. So we went en masse to a NAMBLA meeting, and we found out that it was a bunch of nice gentlemen, varying ages from, like, thirty on up, who were very kind of suburban. And we saw our fellow friends, who had lovers, and we talked about why, the benefits of having an older lover. They have an apartment. They have money. They can feed you. And we realized that the power was with the youth. We heard a lot about youth being exploited, but in all the situations, we found out it was the youth that had the power, because the youth, if anything happened, they could say, *Oh, he molested me.* So there was always the threat of being turned in and the illegality of it. Not that any of my friends ever had any problems. They always spoke highly of their partners who were twice their age. And we had the gay teachers talk. We spoke with everyone, and we held our own with all these groups, and we never felt exploited, and we stood up."

Aner was the youth representative to the first Gay and Lesbian March on Washington in 1979. His speech got a standing ovation. For years, he tried to go to every significant community meeting to represent Gay Youth.

"I had no idea what I was doing. I had no roadmap. I made many mistakes, and I just was kind of fearless . . . When I realized that I was gay, it was such a self-empowering act to own my sexuality . . . I'd go to a Gay Youth meeting on Saturday and a demonstration on Sunday, and we would go to Queens and we would protest against representatives in the city council who wouldn't let the gay rights bill [get] out into the General Assembly. And we protested in the winter, in the snow, in front of their houses in Queens, and we were fearless. We protested in the West Village to a gasoline station who wouldn't take gay money. We were fearless . . . Years later I ended up living on Fifty-Third and Third, and I saw a street hustler for years living on the street and slowly saw him decline. And I would give him socks and underwear and clothing. Everything I grew out of, he could still wear because he was just frail. And I remember seeing him on the coldest night, going out for something, and see him like in a box, like skeletal, and then the next days after, he was gone. So it was brutal [for young queer people]. It was brutal."

While Aner was one of the few ACT UPers who came from a background of political organizing with Gay Youth, the ways queer kids organized in ACT UP had changed dramatically from my generation. The open nature of AIDS organizing welcomed a new generation of queer kids who came out into existing institutions, even though some continued to face familial homophobia and were grossly overrepresented in youth homeless populations in New York. As the Catholic Church deliberately interfered with AIDS education in the public schools, minors were put at risk, and it made sense that ACT UP would produce a sector of kids fighting for their own lives in radical ways.

KATE BARNHART

Kate Barnhart grew up in Carroll Gardens; her parents were gay-friendly and involved in the Park Slope Food Coop. The first person she knew who died from AIDS was the choir director in a Catholic chorus she sang with at public school. She visited him at Cooperative Care in NYU when he was dying. Kate and her best friend, John Won, were the two out gay students at Stuyvesant High School. They organized an HIV peer education team and used to get notes, in John's locker, that would say, *I'm gay, but I can't tell anybody.* When Nora Gibbons from ACT UP was gay bashed on the street, John and Kate and a gay friend skipped school, went to the trial of the basher for a week, and as a result failed some classes. Kate also joined a group of high school kids from private and public schools called Students Against War, and they did an action with a new committee from ACT UP called Youth Education Life Line (YELL). When YELL first started in ACT UP, it was mostly adult teachers who were concerned about the lack of AIDS education in the New York City public schools. In fall of 1989, adults from YELL and youth from Students Against War took over Brooklyn borough president Howard Golden's office (the Golden Is Silent action), because Golden was the only borough president who was not taking a position on AIDS education in the school. They stuffed his files with condoms and dropped a banner out the window at Brooklyn Borough Hall, disrupting everything, and they all got arrested. That was Kate's first arrest.

"We're all sitting there, and for some reason, instead of separating us into cells, they had us all chained together in the waiting room of the precinct—men, women, adults, youth, everybody together. So that gave us a lot of time to talk and get to know each other. So we all went to the ACT UP meeting, and it was at Cooper Union, and it was full—hundreds of people. And we stood up in front, and we passed the microphone along the line, and just talked a little bit about the action. And there was just such an overwhelming sense of support from that room that I was just, like, home. You know? And I never left ACT UP after that."

As YELL started doing more organizing and mobilizing youth, more people joined, including Lazar Heyman Block, Sarah Kunstler, William Barnes, Jonathan Berger, and Alice Eisenberg.

There was no AIDS education in the schools, and YELL was fighting for the creation of an AIDS curriculum. They were also fighting over the content of that program—they were fighting to get condoms in the schools, and over how condoms would then be *available* in the schools. In 1990, the New York City Board of Education had seven members, and two were David Dinkins appointees, with the other five each appointed by a borough president. This produced a split on the board because some of the borough presidents were so conservative. Every month, the board of education would have a hearing on a Wednesday night starting at five, which could last until ten-thirty or eleven. YELL mobilized doctors who worked with adolescents, teachers, young people, and parents to come to the hearings, packing the meeting. It was an open agenda, and people could testify for two or three minutes. Wayne Fischer, who was in ACT UP, would get up there and say, *I'm a teacher and I have HIV,* which was very effective, because very few teachers were openly gay, and it was very rare to find teachers who were openly people with AIDS. This kind of heartfelt testimony was effective, and the board decided that, *yes,* an AIDS curriculum was a good idea. Board members then put together a curriculum development committee that actually included a few young people from YELL.

As the issue progressed, the Christian Right started mobilizing massive opposition. And its supporters would be out in force. Once, at a hearing, Wayne Fischer said, *I just want everyone to realize, people with AIDS are people, too.* And one of the Christians shouted out, *No you're not!*—"and it became a melee." School safety people were trying to separate the activists from the Christians, trying to put one group in the cafeteria and one group in the meeting room. And for some reason they were not able to successfully identify who was who.

"It seemed pretty obvious to me—the ones with the rosaries are the Christians and the ones with the pink triangles are the activists. So they wound up with two mini-riots—one in the cafeteria and one in the main hearing room. But then what happened was, there began to be fighting about what was allowed to be included at different grade levels . . . There was a big fight over whether anal sex could be mentioned—even in, like, the reference notes for the teachers, which were not to be used in the classroom. At one point, the Christian Right went completely bananas—this one lady got up there and she started going on and on about how gerbils in the classroom were problematic because gerbils were living in homosexual relationships in classrooms, because people keep the same gender gerbils together in the tank." Kate stopped here to laugh. "They were wild nights. Another point—some lady got up there and started testifying about the morally damaging influence of dental floss, and how dental floss should not be taught in the schools. And of course, she meant dental *dams.* So there were some really humorous moments, and there were just some intensely painful moments."

A number of churches were well organized, and the pastors said, *Get out there and fight the infidels and get rid of those condoms.* They passed their collection plates. Staten Island and Queens always had the most conservative people representing them to the board of education.

"Some of them had just flat-out delusions. I remember a lot of them firmly believed that condoms had holes in them. A lot of them didn't believe that young people should be having sex. And they thought that if you got AIDS education, that would cause you to have sex, which is ridiculous, because if anything, if you say to somebody, *Having sex could have potentially fatal consequences*, does that make you more likely to want it? That doesn't make sense. They just didn't respect the ability of young people to make decisions and to think for ourselves. They kind of felt like information would be dangerous. They just wanted to control us. They thought of young people as property—they really did. *My children—I have the right to control what they think. I own this kid,* you know?"

John Won came out as gay, on impulse. He was so outraged by what he was hearing at these meetings that, when it was his time to speak, he just blurted it out in front of the media and it was reported on the news. His Korean parents, living in Queens, saw the report, and John had to stay with Kate after that. "He ended up living with an older man, which was something that I was not so comfortable with. It seemed exploitative to me, but it's something that a lot of LGBT young people wind up doing when they can't stay at home anymore."

The Christians wanted what was called an *opt-in*, which would mean that in order to get a condom, a student's parent would have to sign them up for the condom availability program, actively. ACT UP knew that it wouldn't have worked. YELL advocated for condom dispensers in the bathrooms or somewhere private. Failing that, they supported special training largely for gym teachers, "who didn't necessarily have a great deal of sensitivity." In the end, students were supposed to go to the designated teachers to get the condoms, which was an awkward thing to ask a young person to do.

"At Stuyvesant, John and I were on the scene, and we were known to have condoms and dental dams and everything else you can imagine.

One day, we were looking for our subway passes. They didn't usually ask for them at this station, so we didn't have them handy. But this cop was there, and he said, *We need your passes.* So John Won and I both kneeled down, open up our bags and start rummaging, and what's coming out is strips and strips of condoms and dental dams and ACT UP flyers and pink-triangle buttons and all kind of things. Finally, the cop just said, *Look, just go ahead.* He didn't want to know what we had in there."

YELL met weekly at the ACT UP workspace, and then the following Monday, its members would go to the ACT UP meeting. And at that time, it was very competitive to get a slot on the agenda and to attract people's attention, but YELL's proposals often got unanimous support. "I really never got a hard time from the floor of ACT UP. Many other people did. So ACT UP would approve it, hopefully pay for it—at that time, they could—and we would be off."

20

Funding ACT UP's Campaigns

As a political movement, and not a social service agency, ACT UP did not file for not-for-profit status during the period covered in this book, 1987–93. Even though Testing the Limits, Gran Fury, and Housing Works applied for outside funds, ACT UP itself never did. Therefore, as we were winning access to health insurance for people with HIV, fighting for housing for the homeless, organizing to serve teenagers in public schools, and helping other impoverished communities, ACT UP had to raise the money somehow.

Most of ACT UP's funding came from selling buttons and T-shirts. I remember tabling once at Wigstock, the annual free drag celebration that was held in the East Village's Tompkins Square Park every Labor Day. I had never seen more opened wallets in my life. People would buy a one-dollar button and give a twenty. ACT UP also held many fundraisers at nightclubs. In its first years, ACT UP raised about one hundred thousand dollars annually. All of the money came to ACT UP from its communities, but the largest sum of money raised by ACT UP was through a high-profile, high-concept art auction that allowed many contemporary artists to donate their work to bankroll radical activism.

FUNDRAISING FROM THE COMMUNITIES

CHARLES HOVLAND

Charles Hovland was born in a small town, Northfield, Minnesota. He grew up on a farm. He met his first boyfriend at a gay bar and started going to his lover's art school classes. When he first came to New York, he got a job in the bookshop of the Guggenheim Museum.

He had a friend who wanted to answer some personal ads. In those days, people had to send a photograph along with their response letter and mail it to a post-office box. So Charles took pictures of him, and then that friend told a friend of his, and so Charles started taking photos for personal ads. Then it turned out that he'd photographed one of the editors of a magazine who really liked the pictures, and he said to Charles, *Why don't you get a portfolio together and bring it down to the magazines, and I can use the photos. I can print them.* That's what started Charles's entry into the porn business. He shot for *Mandate, Honcho, Playguy, Torso, Inches, Black Inches, Latin Inches, Heat,* and *Stallion.* Finding models was the hardest part of the porn business; it's the most guarded aspect. He'd go up to people on the street, take out ads, and go over material from agents.

"Once a model knows they have found somebody who's reliable, who will pay them and will not put them in any kind of precarious situation or demand to have sex with them, then they tell their friends and it gets to be a word of mouth . . . There were times, a couple of times, people came to me and needed money and had lesions, and we used makeup."

Around 1981, Charles had a friend who died very quickly. They barely knew what was going on, and all of a sudden he was gone. This was the performer and artist Hibiscus, who was in the Cockettes and Angels of Light. Gradually, Charles had other friends who were dying, and he wanted to do something but didn't know what. Then in 1985 he read an article about God's Love We Deliver, which was just starting. The founder, Ganga Stone, was cooking meals in her apartment for her friends who had AIDS and was looking for people to deliver the food to her friends. Charles responded, and there were no questions besides *What's your name? Could you deliver this food?* Charles said yes.

"Everybody was so grateful, and it was a wonderful program, but, man, I'd be delivering food to some of these people, and they'd be living in terrible, terrible squalor, terrible, because they'd be so sick that they couldn't take care of themselves. Most of the people had no place to turn, and I'd come back and I'd be so upset, and I'd tell them God's Love has to do something. They have to get involved, and it can't be just food. It also has to be medical and housing. They'd say, *It's just not our mission. We just can't do all of this, but we've heard [about] this new organization called Gay Men's Health Crisis. Why don't you go to them and see if they can help* . . . And I did, I went to them, and, of course, they were so overburdened with taking care of all these people, and I'd say, *I went to this place, and this place was terrible. You have to go and help this person.* And they'd say, *We just can't take on all of this. We just don't have the resources. We don't have the people. We can't do it.* This would happen over and over again, and I was getting so angry and so frustrated. And then I started seeing these notices about ACT UP demonstrations . . . and it was great right off, because I could see now, here's a group of people that feel the same type of anger."

Charles joined ACT UP's Fundraising Committee. They sold so many Keith Haring–designed T-shirts at the Gay Pride rally that Charles had to go home early because he had thirty thousand dollars in cash on him. Keith was coming to some ACT UP meetings. Charles remembers that there would be buses going to demonstrations, and Keith would raise his hand—*I'll pay for it.* ACT UP rarely got large sums of money from individual donors because it refused to be a 501(c)(3), meaning that donations were not tax deductible. Charles remembers a few two- or three-thousand-dollar gifts, and once somebody gave ten thousand, but never more than that. So ACT UP was always looking for new sources.

Then the idea for an art auction arrived on ACT UP's doorstep. Charles recalled that art dealers Matthew Marks and Paul Morris had been doing an internship with a gallery in London, and they had both come back to New York. They were starting to be involved in the art world, but they wanted to do something to get some excitement and to really get their names out there. So they came up with the idea of doing an art auction for ACT UP. Ann Philbin and Patrick Moore had been working with amfAR on another art auction and had been traveling around the country for quite a while, so they had experience, and these two different groups came together at the same time. *We have contacts in the art world. We can make it happen.*

PATRICK MOORE

Patrick was in ACT UP but had been running Art Against AIDS for amfAR with Ann Philbin.

"I really knew that whole world, and I thought, *Why am I raising all of this money—through selling these incredibly important art works for amfAR, when I don't believe in amfAR?* . . . [amfAR director] Mathilde Krim did a benefit dinner in Chicago with Elizabeth Taylor—it was shortly after the governor came out for mandatory testing. So ACT UP Chicago decided that they would infiltrate the dinner, and I was in this weird situation of being in ACT UP but also working for amfAR. So they flew me to Chicago to meet with ACT UP, and, you know, there was no resolution to it, basically. ACT UP Chicago wanted the governor to withdraw his statement and he wouldn't. So, as I recall, there was, like, a protest out front. And that's when I kind of couldn't work [at amfAR] anymore . . . I went there, like, two weeks before the dinner, and they didn't let me go back for the dinner."

Plans got under way for a major art auction to benefit ACT UP. The textile designer Jeffrey Aronoff was in charge, and he and Patrick would meet regularly at Jeffrey's scarf company on Twenty-Third Street, surrounded by "all these incredible queeny-like" chenille scarves, throws, and shawls. The team included Ken Silver, who was an art history professor at NYU; Charles Hovland; Tony Feher; and Ann Philbin, mostly people who had been Patrick's friends already. The artist Robert Gober had come to sit in Patrick's apartment with Patrick's ailing partner, Dino, when Patrick went to work. "And he was kind of my hero during that." Ann and her lover, Brian Weil, who also was in ACT UP, on Needle Exchange, came and stayed with Patrick the day Dino died. It was a close group.

"The whole reason the auction worked was that Robert Gober—who was probably the hottest artist in the world at that moment—basically made everyone in the art world participate. Every gallery contributed, every artist gave something significant. And Mira Rubell was a great collector of his, or aspired to be a great collector of his. And they, at the moment, controlled what was Guggenheim/SoHo . . . That floor above the Prada store on Broadway was sitting there empty. And he convinced her to give that floor free to hold the auction. And his dealer, Paula Cooper, gave everything, in terms of showing the work."

The event planning started in spring 1989 and took six months.

CHARLES HOVLAND

Charles was in charge of the framing, so he would get phone calls, *So-and-so is donating a piece. Will you go pick it up? And then you have to find out who will donate the framing, and then go pick it up and then store it until the auction.* Often, he would call the gallery that represented that artist and say, *What is the framer that you use?* Then Charles would call that framer and say, *Okay, you do a lot of work for this gallery. Now, this gallery has donated the artist's work, so would you be willing to donate the framing?*

PATRICK MOORE

"Probably the most important piece was Robert Gober's, which was a sculpture of a man's leg coming out of a wall made out of wax, and it sold for—I think, a hundred thousand dollars . . . There was a man who was a very important collector and dealer in Switzerland named Thomas Mann, who had a representative come. And we had already discussed how much he was willing to pay. So I sat in the audience, actually, and bid for the house to bid it up to the reserve. And then he paid a bit more."

ANN PHILBIN

"Eric Fischl gave something big, I remember. April [Gornik] and Brice Marden and obviously [Robert] Rauschenberg, and people that you would assume. But a lot of people that were very surprising that helped us. It was kind of amazing. [Julian] Schnabel I remember gave a big piece . . . Because we were losing people in droves. And it was so clearly [at] epidemic proportions for the art world. It was just—it was such a time of huge grief, whether you were a dealer or a curator, no matter who you were, it was very clear that this was—that the world was changing right in front of us because of this. The whole art world, the trajectory of the art world, the marketplace—everything."

PATRICK MOORE

"There was, as I recall, an important Warhol, an important Lichten-stein . . . And, we didn't do a catalog for it, because it was too expensive. But, basically, every major artist working or represented in New York at that time participated, and not with some stupid print."

CHARLES HOVLAND

The art auction organizers hoped to include a piece by the famous graffiti-inspired pop artist and activist Keith Haring, who was at the time dying from AIDS, but the recently established Haring Foundation wouldn't donate, which upset Charles.

"I put a notice—I called *Page Six* [of the *New York Post*], and *Page Six* did something, and the next day we got an explanation from the Haring Foundation. They said that they had been getting advice from the Warhol Foundation, saying that when an artist first dies, they really have to be careful about what money and what art they donate, and so because of the Warhol Foundation telling them that, they were pulling back all donations to any causes for a while. So that's why they wouldn't."

Patrick noted, however, that someone else donated a piece by Haring so that he would be represented. Somebody told Charles, *I know somebody that has a stack of Basquiat drawings, and she'll probably donate one.* So he went over to this woman's apartment, and, yes, she had a stack of these drawings. She said, *Pick out the one that you want.* She didn't say, *You can't have that one,* or, *This one's too good.* It was just a stack of them on the floor. It went for a fair amount at the auction. There was a Mapplethorpe, a Ross Bleckner. Then there were pieces that didn't sell. Somebody donated a space and took everything left over, and Charles sat there for about three days afterward calling people and calling galleries and saying, *This work is left over. Could you come over and look at it and either give us a bid or give us an offer or something?* Because they had to get rid of it. They weren't going to give the stuff back.

Charles remembered that the auctioneer was a big problem. Bob Gober said, *I will make sure that we'll get this big auctioneer from*

Sotheby's. Bob talked to the auctioneer, who said, *Fine, sure, great, I'll do it*, until he found out that it was with ACT UP, and then he wouldn't do it. That was after the Stop the Church action, and Charles believes that there was so much negative publicity toward ACT UP at the time that it may have been a factor. Charles didn't know if Sotheby's put pressure on the man or if he worried about having the same clout with his rich clients, but he backed out.

PATRICK MOORE

The auction took place on December 2, 1989. At least one hundred artists ultimately participated, including Meg Webster, Jeff Koons, Lorna Simpson, Barbara Kruger, Jenny Holzer, David Salle, and Cindy Sherman.

"Basically, every hot artist . . . There were a number of ACT UP artists in it as well. And people who weren't so well known—the way we dealt with that, is that I think we allowed everybody to participate—that some people were in the silent auction, and then there was a live auction. I remember my friend, Robert Farber, gave a painting and was very pissed off, because it wasn't—he thought—placed in the right place, and—so there were things like that. And, you know, Donald Moffett was a part of it and Zoe Leonard. But I don't think it was as crass as that. It was just, sort of, I think, for all of the artists saying, *We're a part of this too, so we want to be represented* . . . I have no idea how many people attended, but I know that that huge floor of that huge building was completely full, so there must have been well over a thousand people."

THE CONSEQUENCES OF BIG MONEY

CHARLES HOVLAND

Bringing all this money suddenly to a small grassroots organization had some unforeseen consequences. The amount was announced at the next Monday-night meeting. All of a sudden, everybody's hands went up. *Well, I know how we can spend it. We need* . . . Everybody wanted money, and that's why the Finance Committee said, *We have to sit down and think how to use this money wisely, because it could be gone in two minutes.* Up to that moment, most funding came from selling T-shirts, posters, and buttons. There was a direct relationship between ACT UP members' efforts and the funding we had for events. Not only did this new infusion of funds pay for actions, but ACT UP New York was able to give money to other ACT UP chapters. We were flush with cash and spent heavily. Charles continued to fundraise for ACT UP for fourteen years.

PATRICK MOORE

In Patrick's experience, the big sum of money that came from the art auction was the worst possible thing that could have happened to ACT UP. He remembered that somebody would say, *Let's buy a full page in* The New York Times, which, at that time, was fifteen thousand dollars. And his problem was that one day ACT UP was marching around the *New York Times* offices and complaining about the paper's AIDS coverage, and the next day it was spending fifteen thousand dollars, supporting the paper's advertising revenue.

"And those things didn't reconcile to me. But they were done in such a way during those meetings that had become increasingly hideous and long, that people just got frustrated. And, you know, I think spending of money became one way to have power."

There was a lot of money spent on needle exchange, which Patrick thought was a very valid cause. But the Needle Exchange Committee and Housing Works, both "had this kind of strange relationship to ACT UP—it was almost as if they were their own organizations, but they were born out of ACT UP." At that point, ACT UP bought all of the needles and other supplies. There was a lot of money spent on sending people to conferences, too, Patrick said, "which, I suppose, was a valid expense, as well." There weren't any salaries, which Patrick remembers as "one great thing about ACT UP." There also was rent on the hall when the meeting moved from the Gay Center to Cooper Union, due to size. Patrick recalled when Dan Keith Williams stole money and made a promise to gradually pay the money back, but never did. This incident had a negative impact on ACT UP's ability to raise money. Patrick had people coming to the Fundraising Committee, saying, *We're not going to raise money for ACT UP, because of this.* "So that's when my relationship with ACT UP kind of got strained, and it really was—money was very poisonous for ACT UP, I think."

DIRECT MAIL AND THE COMMODIFICATION OF PEOPLE WITH AIDS

SEAN STRUB

Sean Strub grew up in a Catholic family in Iowa City. At age thirteen, he "jumped at the opportunity" to go away to a Jesuit boarding school. Among the teachers was the first Marxist he met, and the first time he ever saw gay male pornography was from the algebra teacher, Father Kidd. Sean came out in Washington, D.C., in 1976 and met "ultra-closeted guys" in politics, from members of Congress to senior staffers to lobbyists to important journalists and pundits. He found that there was no ideological distinction in the socializing. As it was the nation's bicentennial year, Washington was all cleaned up, and the bicentennial logo was everywhere. There were many new organizations, and direct mail as a fundraising mechanism had exploded. Advances in managing databases and postage rates suddenly made direct mail the funding mechanism of choice for broad-based mass marketing.

Sean was friends with Steve Endean, founder of the Human Rights Campaign Fund, and they would hang out at Alan Baron's town house. Steve was starting a gay political action committee (PAC), and Alan was constantly poring over data, a lot of direct mail for social-change groups and PACs. Alan said, *We need to frame this issue, of gay rights, in terms that anyone could respond to.* And he wanted to call it the Privacy Project. *You want to frame it on privacy, because privacy can be marketed as a conservative ideal as well.* Sean remembers them going back and forth on this before deciding.

The first mass fundraising letter for a gay organization, which Sean got Tennessee Williams to sign, was raising money for the Human Rights Campaign Fund, one of the more conservative national gay organizations, which did not use direct action or grassroots organizing. Using the word *privacy* was attractive to more reluctant and monied gay donors.

Sean started summer school at Columbia in 1979 and began a sexual relationship with Vito Russo in 1981. Vito worked at the snack counter at the St. Marks Baths. Sean would sometimes go down there and do his homework, and Vito would give him free carrot cake. They met in different cities when their paths crossed and happened to be together in Denver when the *New York Times* story on gay cancer broke.

The article "identified the three symptoms that a number of people shared; I remember really kind of—feeling, you know, getting a queasy feeling, because they all hit close to home. The symptoms were persistent swelling of the lymph glands, the weight loss, and the night sweats. And in the fall of 1980, I was at Sloan Kettering, because they thought I might have some sort of weird lymphoma. Columbia University health service, student health service, had sent me there, because they didn't know what was wrong with me . . . Early in 1982—I was walking along Seventh Avenue, at Christopher Street. And there were guys there, at a table, for GHMC. And I was, like, sort of standing there, reading the literature, but afraid to pick it up and take it with me, but standing there, reading it. And of course, a couple of the guys were very cute. And one of them said he had to go somewhere, and said, *Here, would you do this for a while?* And he gave me the can, just like that. Okay, quaking and shaking. And I remember somebody I knew walked by, and he sort of looked at me, and was like, *What are YOU doing shaking that can?*"

Over the next few years an increasing number of friends, lovers, and acquaintances got sick, and many died. Sean got officially diagnosed in 1985 after the test came out. The doctor took his hands and said, "Sean, these days, you can have two good years left."

Richard Viguerie was a right-wing organizer who used direct mail to successfully bring evangelical Christians into the Ronald Reagan campaign. As a result, direct mail was deciding the political destiny of America. Understanding the potential, Sean started writing fundraising copy to use in direct mail campaigns, and then turned it into a business.

He identified three niches to specialize in: One was in homelessness and urban problems. Another was environmental work. And the third was gay and lesbian issues. His company would develop a client that would pay a monthly retainer, two to four thousand dollars. And for that, Sean would produce a certain number of appeals per year, and he would produce a certain number of pieces of prospecting mail.

As he created his own database, he'd rent the names back to his clients, which was a key part of the service. Sean's company would make money on rentals of the database it created in-house. Senior Action in a Gay Environment (SAGE) was his first paid client, because he'd been doing their mail on a volunteer basis for several years. It was an enormously successful campaign. SAGE executive director Ken Dawson kept wanting Sean to do more and more. SAGE paid Sean one thousand dollars a month, which was a discount. He would do a test mailing that typically would be fifty thousand pieces of mail, asking for donations. And it would typically be ten to fifteen different lists; each list would be three to five thousand names. So, for example, to raise money for SAGE, Sean would mail five thousand requests to the ACLU list and the Gray Panthers list to see if these constituencies of people responded. It was an early example of data mining.

Whenever a gay publication was going out of business, or gay catalogs or travel agencies faded out, Sean would be at the bankruptcy sale buying their mailing database, creating as big of a list as he could internally. But it was a small universe. There were sixty to seventy thousand names available at that time, with many overlaps onto other lists. So, for example, the general ACLU list was too broad and generic for queer issues. But if Sean took just men on the ACLU list in zip code 10014 in the West Village, that might work. He would sort these things in many different ways. For example, addresses where the house number ended in a zero or a one were corner houses. They're more affluent, on average, than other houses, and affluence would bring a response up.

"Peter Staley called me. I had, you know, followed ACT UP in the papers . . . [He] introduces himself, and very businesslike he says, *I understand you're the direct mail guy. I'd like to come talk to you.* And he came with his briefcase. I think he had a jacket and tie on. And I think there's only five years' difference in age, but at that time, it seemed like he was a lot younger . . . And I came to a meeting, was sort of captivated by it. And then he wanted a proposal. And he said, you know, he would deal with the Fundraising Committee. And so we did the proposal for an initial mailing . . . and the letter was going to be signed by Harvey Fierstein . . . Keith [Haring] put up the postage, and we guaranteed everything else . . . I was using a lot of newspaper clippings as an insert . . . sort of cut around this wire, which gave it a little bit of a rougher edge, rather than a sharp cut. It looked a little bit more like somebody might have torn it out of the paper . . . that was the first piece we did, and I think it was fifty thousand pieces. I don't remember how much it raised, but it raised a fortune. It was immensely profitable."

In 1988, Sean brought in about thirty thousand dollars for ACT UP, the equivalent of over sixty-five thousand dollars in 2020. Minus his commission, and he got to add about two thousand names to his list.

PETER STALEY

"The big battle was direct mail. And I thought that was a way to really bring in much bigger cash for the organization and a fairly stable way of fundraising as well. 'Cause benefits were just hard, a lot of work, and were unstable . . . But direct mail has a smarmy nature to it. It meant that we had to hook up with a direct mail house who was going to profit from the relationship. And that's where I met Sean Strub, who was the lead direct mail guy at the time for gay and AIDS organizations. And, it took quite a lot of speeches on the floor and discussions before the final vote was approved to proceed with the direct mail campaign. And then it almost all fell apart, because Larry Kramer was supposed to be the guy writing the first letter—the signature. And that was during his first spat with ACT UP, his first break-up of many. He doesn't recall that he left the group many times. But he wrote this angry letter to the floor, which I read, saying he wasn't going to sign the letter and he wasn't going to be back, and all this stuff. So all of a sudden we were without a signer. So I called around, tried to get the phone number of Harvey Fierstein—who was really big at the time. And I got his phone number and I left a voicemail at his home in Connecticut and he called back within a day, saying [in his gravelly voice], *Peter, I'd love to do this. Yes you can put my name on it.*"

Peter felt that it was a huge success. The problem with direct mail is that mass mailings, at the start, typically lose money. It cost twenty to thirty cents per package. ACT UP was sending packages out to a hundred thousand people, requiring $150,000 to $200,000, and it didn't all come back. What the group did get was its own database, because the first lists it used were rented from Sean. ACT UP only got back the people who sent checks, which was usually 1 percent, which barely covered the expense of that first big mailing. This was something that had to be explained on the floor. It was complex.

"It sounds like a scam, even as I describe it now. But that's how direct mail works. And then, when you have that list, when you keep hitting them up in the year, it's almost pure profit and that's where you actually make a lot of money direct-mail-wise."

Sean's cut was 10 percent or 15 percent, and that was a problem for ACT UP, too. For the first time, the group was being asked to work with someone who was going to make money off working with us. But Peter recalled that the first mailing was a massive success. The letter got close to a 10 percent return rate, with Harvey's signature on it, which was just extraordinary for a mass mailing, and the group made way more than the amount that was spent on it. So ACT UP made money right away. And it did direct mail for the next few years, using a number of signers. "It definitely raised a great deal of money—probably for Sean as well."

In this way, Sean Strub became the only person in ACT UP's history, among everyone from artists to lawyers to scientists to journalists, from media specialists to video artists to insurance brokers to art auction experts to street activists, to actually get paid.

SEAN STRUB

By then, Sean was doing a fair amount of direct mail for many AIDS organizations. So he knew not only the people who specifically were giving to AIDS, but in some cases, people who were giving to more than one AIDS organization. He got the Federal Election Commission reports for not just openly gay candidates, because there weren't that many then, but also for officeholders and candidates he knew were gay but were not publicly so. He would get the lists of supporters of closeted politicians like Gerry Studds, Barney Frank, Pete Kostmayer, Stewart McKinney (who died of AIDS), and others. And then he would even find some repeating names of donors. In this way he identified a whole social circle that was very closeted, of people who were giving to these politicians—who were also very closeted. And so he'd overlay that data onto his lists, which ranged from politics to smaller communities. The Gay Male S&M Activists (GMSMA) had a list of thirteen hundred names. Not a very big list, but an incredibly responsive list. And a very high average gift.

In the fall of 1989, Keith Haring's career was exploding. And initially, he was going to come out about being HIV-positive in his direct mail letter for ACT UP. Sean talked to him in June, briefly, but he didn't have enough time to really discuss the letter. Then Sean saw him a month later in Paris. They were both staying at the same hotel at the same time. Sean recorded an interview with Keith, and sort of explained the direct mail process. Keith told him about some art magazines that he thought he could get names from; they were expensive lists, but they were available, subscribers to *Art in America* or something. "Pretty affluent profile."

When they composed the letter, Sean said, *We really need something we can print and send out.* So then Keith did a big poster titled *See No Evil, Hear No Evil, Speak No Evil.* It was included as a premium for people who gave ACT UP fifty dollars. And then, while they were in the process of finalizing the production on it, Keith gave an interview to *Rolling Stone* and came out about being HIV-positive.

"It was a huge, huge news story. It was just a couple weeks before our piece was going to mail. So I knew, when you can coordinate something with media like that, it's like unbelievable . . . So that's when I said, you know, *Let's just go for it, and mail two hundred thousand pieces.* But of course, ACT UP didn't have either the capital to put into something like that or, as a group, probably, the ability to sort of understand the economics of it, without people going crazy. And I was dealing with Peter on it. And so I said, *If you can come up with the postage*—because that had to be laid out upfront—that I would guarantee the printing and letter shop and list bills. And these were a lot of expensive lists. We used a lot of art lists and a lot of other lists beyond the ones we could exchange for or that we had ourselves. And so we did. And it was incredibly successful. I don't even remember how much money it made."

In December 1988, Sean's partner, Michael, had died, and from 1989 to 1991, Sean was, he said, "on some adrenal autopilot that I— it's amazing, what I don't remember." By that point, ACT UP's list was around six or seven thousand effective donor names. If there were four thousand responses, and the average gift was $45, that would be $180,000 that came in. And the mailing of two hundred thousand would have cost less than fifty cents a piece. It was less than $100,000 to send it out. So ACT UP took in about $80,000; Sean donated his percentage, but he came away with the names of donors. "We got the data . . . we [got the] advantage of the data, which was very useful, good data for us."

Sean now owned this gay database, and increasingly, he was getting inquiries from commercial companies that wanted to rent it. They were gay businesses as well as non-gay businesses, looking to come into the gay market, which was starting to be identifiable. They weren't ready to go on television aiming at gay consumers, because these companies didn't want the rest of their customers to see them with gay content. But direct mail enabled them to appeal to LGBT consumers without letting anybody else know. So Sean started little card packs with ads for different businesses and services, all sent to gay consumers from his database.

And here we see the beginning of niche marketing to gay consumers. But having databases with names of people who gave specifically to AIDS activism was a very special consumer base: the beginning of the PWA niche market.

DIRECT SALES AND MARKETING OF AIDS DRUGS

Various mail-order pharmacies began advertising in the card pack, because people with AIDS were afraid to go to their local pharmacy for medications. And, importantly, most of these mail-order pharmacies were waiving copayments routinely, just as a matter of course, which was a marketing advantage for them. They were getting paid enough by the insurance company, and it was wildly profitable. There was one advertiser, from Ohio, Mike Erlenbach, who had a mail-order pharmacy, whom Sean recalled proposing, *You guys should be the ones doing the marketing.* At first Sean was not interested, but he recalls that Mike was insistent. "And I was polite to him, because he was a good advertiser."

Stephen Gendin was running the card pack business, even though Sean was involved. And Stephen said, *This guy, he'll put up some money. He'll finance, it won't be any risk to us.* And so finally, Sean and Stephen said that if Mike would finance a newsletter, "we would use a newsletter as our marketing device."

Stephen had been an editor of *The Treatment and Data Digest* at the beginning of ACT UP, which was the first kind of newsletter for people taking AIDS drugs. Mike agreed to finance seventy-five thousand dollars for Sean and Stephen's marketing activities, which paid "most of Stephen's salary for a year." Stephen owned part of the company, and administered the day-to-day almost entirely himself. And it became profitable; they called it Community Prescription Service. The advisory committee was Peter Staley, Phil Wilson, Connie Norman, and Michael Callen. They each got paid a one-time fee of five hundred dollars.

"What was attractive and made it competitive was, it was owned by people with HIV; we routinely waived copays; and very importantly, we would go to bat with the insurance companies—because there were all these treatments coming out that insurance companies wouldn't cover, wouldn't recognize, or it was trouble. And Stephen was brilliant at that. And so it wasn't somebody going to their local pharmacy in Iowa City who only has so much time to deal with insurance company; we'd have ten or fifteen customers looking for this drug—and Stephen would know where to find the papers that were being published that suggested this would be useful. The customer service office was right in our office. And people called all day long, and then it'd be sent out from Ohio."

Sean would regularly go to ACT UP meetings, pick up T&D reports, and the next day, in his office, fax them to various friends around the country who needed treatment information. Very quickly, it was hundreds of people. That packet of information became a marketing newsletter for the prescription service. Then it became cheaper to actually produce their own newsletter, rather than xerox all these other things, so Sean started thinking about something that would create a larger sort of conversation.

"Something that not just the science club members, or people who went to ACT UP meetings or whatever, would relate to. And thinking like—like a *People* magazine, but just of people with HIV. Because in the media, every time the epidemic was referenced, it was inevitably fatal, dread disease, no survivors; a hundred percent terminal, yada yada yada. And yet, in my life, which was surrounded with people who had HIV, and all these incredibly vibrant people leading really interesting lives, despite this life-threatening challenge . . . Literally, *POZ* [magazine] was started just to talk about the people that were populating our lives, in our activism every day."

Before AIDS, pharmaceutical companies sold drugs directly to doctors. But AIDS became the first illness in which afflicted people were marketed to directly by pharma, with the intention that they would then ask their doctors to prescribe the treatment. Today, this is a common part of consumer life. We see ads for Viagra every day on television. But this started with the creation of the AIDS consumer, who often knew more about medications than doctors did. And advertising in Sean's new magazine, *POZ*, founded in 1994, was the perfect way for pharma to reach people with AIDS.

Pharmaceutical companies started to realize that there was a direct consumer market and they would start to create ads specifically for the PWA consumer audience.

"The first ads were very kind of dark and sad—they'd have somebody walking along the beach, looking up at the moon, you know. And then, the first ones where they were, like, showing somebody who was represented as a person with HIV; and then they'd have their little disclaimer, that they were, *This is not an actual person, it's a professional model,* or whatever and that, I just could not stand that. And so we wrote something about it in *POZ*, one of the very first issues of *POZ*; we said, *You know, if you're someone with HIV who's willing to be a model in one of these ads, let us know.* Right? . . . So we got fifty, sixty, seventy people who were delighted to, eager to do this. And we gave them to a modeling agency in California that created a positive models division, or whatever. And then they started supplying them to the companies. And so then they were using real people with HIV for a while. And then, the next kind of breakthrough was really the Crixivan ad, which was the rock climber. And the irony was that about a year after my health came back, I did go rock climbing for the first time."

The problem with direct consumer marketing in pharmaceutical advertising is that it creates, sometimes, inappropriate demand for specific medications that have good advertising copy. But the plus side is that these ads alerted huge numbers of people to the fact that there was treatment available. In addition to pharmaceutical advertising, *POZ* also carried viatical advertising, looking for dying and sick people who needed money to cash out their life insurance policies at percentages of the value so they could have cash at the end of their lives. Sean sold three different policies to viatical firms. His New York Life policy gave him 93 percent of the value, because the company thought he was going to be dead in a short period of time. New York Life didn't want to lose money on it, but it wasn't seeing Sean as a profit center. His Chubb policy was sold to a private viatical company, an investor group, who wanted to get it as cheaply as they could, and then they sold it to a group of investors. "So it is now owned by—I don't know, I think it's like eight or nine people, different entities . . . I still get, every six months, I get a little form I have to sign or whatever. *Yeah, I'm still here, sorry, you know.*"

The first issue of *POZ* came out in April of 1994. An ACT UP member gave Sean a copy of a memo that Ogilvy Adams & Rinehart had written for its client Burroughs Wellcome about *this magazine Sean Strub is starting*, and its history with Sean Strub, and his card packs.

"I just remember reading it, and being astonished they had any idea who I was, let alone how much they knew about the magazine and the plans. It was just—that was a very sobering . . . This is before the magazine even started."

Making people with AIDS a niche market, to be directly addressed by advertising, was perhaps the most normalizing action stemming from the activities of ACT UP and its peripheries. Openly and clearly asserting PWAs as a source of profit, ultimately, under capitalism, was the only way to guarantee that someone would be interested in them. And if PWAs needed images of vigorous men scaling mountains to make purchases, then this would ultimately seal the brand. In this way, the empowered image we fought so hard to achieve, combined with the whitening, male eye of a homogenous media corps further obstructing the representation of people of color, women, children, and poor people with AIDS, were ultimately co-opted to mutual service of pharma and patients living under a brutal market that, without profound structural change provided by the dream of a broad effective health-care system, ultimately offered no other path.

BOOK FOUR

DESPERA-
TION

Do you resent people with AIDS?

Do you trust HIV-negatives?

Have you given up hope for a cure?

When was the last time you cried?

PART VIII

Division

'91, '92, '93, for me they were dreadful in terms of people dying. People who had survived for a while were dying. AZT wasn't working. It was a very tough, tough time.

—RON GOLDBERG

21

Storm the NIH Action at the National Institutes of Health, Washington, D.C.: May 21, 1990

By 1990, the situation inside ACT UP was dire. Despite enormous sacrifice as an entire community of activists donated their lives to struggle, no effective new drugs had been discovered. And despite huge efforts that built radical infrastructure and a complex subculture, people inside and outside of ACT UP were still suffering and rapidly dying. Treatment and Data wanted more power on governmental committees. The lawsuit to change the CDC definition of AIDS so that women could get benefits and be in experimental drug trials was a few months from being filed, and women were still unable to get meetings with government officials. The gap between what levels of access different activist constituencies had was growing and, in many ways, determining group consciousness.

MARK HARRINGTON

"Within the AIDS Clinical [Trials] Group (ACTG) we wanted more resources to go to opportunistic infections research, and not just to AZT-type drugs. And after the big demo at the NIH campus, that actually started to happen . . . The consequence was a civil war within ACT UP. And, eventually, it led to the fissuring of the organization."

BRIAN ZABCIK

A Texas farm boy, Brian Zabcik came from Zabcikville, named for his Czech grandfather. There was one general store and no indoor plumbing at school until third grade. He first had sex at twelve. During college,

Brian didn't go to gay bars, he went to adult bookstores. That was the sex that he had, for most of the first four years. Brian's mother was a Republican activist, on the Moral Majority mailing list, and a Reagan supporter. One day she took out a clipping. *I want to read you something.* So she started reading this description of what happens to people with AIDS. This was about 1982 or '83, and for Brian, it was an awful experience. The first time Brian had sex with a guy whose name he knew was at age twenty. Brian graduated from the University of Texas, Austin, where he worked on the paper, *The Daily Texan.* Then, in 1987, he bought a one-way ticket to New York City.

A coworker at *Manhattan Lawyer* magazine, Mark Carson, brought Brian to ACT UP at the start of 1988.

"I would be wired after I left one of those meetings. I could not go to sleep for hours. I'd be walking. I'd be wandering around. My mind would be racing, just with everything that I had taken in. It was information overload, it was cultural overload, it was social overload. It was like grabbing onto the third rail."

At his first demonstration, at Metropolitan Life Insurance, Brian found himself silent while everyone else was chanting. He wrote in his diary, *Let's face it, I hate confrontation. I hate doing anything that I think might make people not like me. As I've said to myself many times before, one of my key characteristics is an intense desire for acceptance.* Brian put so much time into ACT UP that he lost his job.

"I did end up over time working most closely with T&D because of my personal friendship with Mark [Harrington]. I worshipped everything that he did . . . Mark was the only one who I had a real strong cultural fit with on T&D . . . A lot of it had to do with class."

Although Mark had gone to Harvard and was supported in part by his father, Brian identified with him and felt that they were both "poor."

"I'm not talking about class background. I'm talking about whether or not you could go to eat at Woody's with the rest of the people after the meeting or not depended on how much money you had in your pocket . . . I was basically making a half salary for the time that I was in ACT UP. Mark, I don't really know how he subsisted. I don't know where his income came from. There could be a trust fund behind there that I'm not aware of. Is there? . . . I'm pretty sure that there isn't, because I was pretty close to him during that time, and I was over at his apartment a lot and I saw what his apartment looked like. He had a cramped East Village walkup with not a lot of furniture, and books and papers all over the place. I also, too, know from his wardrobe . . . I just remember at one point everyone lit up at once, and pulled a brass lighter out of their pocket at the same moment. And the reason that that detail is telling is, is that the poor faggots I was hanging out with at the bars, we all had the cheap Zippo lighters that we bought at the corner Bodega. I'm not saying that these were that much more expensive, but when you had a little bit more money, that is what you would do. You'd buy a nice polished metal butane lighter instead of the cheap little plastic Zippos. Mark had a cheap plastic Zippo, if I remember right. So that's how when I talk about class, that's what I mean. I mean economic status."

Brian recalled that Mark and Maxine Wolfe represented two of the strongest poles within the group and he felt that they actually worked against each other in some ways. To Brian, Mark represented treatment issues. Maxine represented not just women's issues, but the whole history of radical activism.

"She had seen things fail before and was unhappy to see ACT UP making the same mistakes all over again. Mark, on the other hand, I place him with myself, Mike Signorile, and a few others. We hadn't done anything before, and so we were like tabulae rasae, starting out from scratch. Rather than taking our previous influences into ACT UP, we were shaped by ACT UP. ACT UP was what formed us . . . [Maxine] invited me over to dinner at her house several times, and so we'd have these long conversations about politics, like progressive politics and activism, and she'd give me reading lists and books to read . . . Mark and I talked a lot. We saw each other a lot at meetings . . . I was like a hanger-on at T&D . . . Mark and I would see each other socially and at the bars, weekend bar calls, like parties . . . I was the one who never had to figure out which black leather jacket was mine at the end of an ACT UP party, because I didn't have one."

When it came to the big action at the National Institutes of Health in May of 1990, "Mark asked me to plan it . . . I just said, *Sure.*"

Much like David Barr asking Gregg Bordowitz to be the ACT UP front person for the FDA action two years before, Mark picked a younger man with relationships across various milieus that, since the

FDA action, had cohered into factions. And like Gregg, Brian did an excellent job.

Brian set about to create a large, national action focusing on the dysfunctions and indifference of a major governmental agency. He started with a simple list.

> Three biggest lies in AIDS treatment research:
> 1. "The U.S. is making progress against AIDS."
> 2. "AZT has made AIDS a chronic, manageable disease."
> 3. "Government scientists have added years to the lives of people with AIDS."

Brian was motivated by his political goals but strengthened by his personal connection to Mark Harrington.

"Basically, my kind of relationship with Mark was simplifying and translating and popularizing his stuff. He would come up with very, very long, detailed technical proposals, reports, and I felt like my job was to translate it to the floor . . . And I don't want to denigrate him. He did a brilliant job of explaining himself to the floor himself, but Mark loves density. Again, as an editor, I knew that you have to simplify the story for people who aren't familiar with it, so that people who aren't familiar with the story can understand what you're talking about. So I was constantly trying to simplify or pare down what he was saying."

In building the NIH action, Brian and his team were trying to keep a tighter focus on issues than ACT UP had previously done with a series of sprawling demonstrations in the state capital, Albany, and they were trying not to run all day, like ACT UP did at the FDA. Brian recalled that the NIH action was planned "top-down." Whereas the FDA action organizing committee had about thirty members, the NIH planning group only had about ten. Brian had concerns that there might never be real ownership of the NIH action by the larger organization. He remembered that during Monday-night meetings, when he would bring updates to the floor leading up to the action, there were few comments and little discussion, as late as the last Monday before the event. He had ten minutes on the floor to do an NIH Committee report each week leading up to the action, "but there really wasn't a lot of back-and-forth between us and the floor. We weren't getting a lot of questions."

To prepare, T&D took responsibility to come up with the issues and demands sheet, and Brian was doing the mammoth list of logistics, which included getting buses, motel rooms, speakers for a closing rally, the public address system. Then there was a series of rentals: cellular phones, walkie-talkies, megaphones, everything else. It was also his job to line up medical support, transportation to and from the courthouse and jail, the media table, a safe zone for the disabled. He coordinated sending out letters to NIH employees, provisions for storing luggage during the demo, and outreach with ACT UP DC for an AIDS vigil. Every component had its own issues. *Where do we do ticket sales?* At bookstores. *What to do about affinity groups who go down on Saturday?* Then there were demo props. The production of flames, banners, and posters. Finally, there was a meeting with the police.

The NIH action was one of the few times when ACT UP had a pre-action meeting with the police, in this case because they reached out to us. Jill Harris was head of legal for that action; John Kelly was head of marshaling. Both joined Brian on the shuttle down to D.C. During the meeting, Brian said, the police "were basically trying to pump us for information on what we were going to be doing. They told us arrest risk and stuff like that."

After getting to Washington, ACT UP held a pre-action meeting for the demonstrators. Then, at 7:00 a.m. on May 21, ACT UP assembled at the Metro station to march en masse to the National Institutes of Health. General protests were held against the gates and in front of the building. Affinity groups did a wide range of actions, including setting off sirens followed by multicolored smoking torches, breaking into an office, running banners up the flagpole, and other simultaneous theatrics. There also was a legal picket to march around the buildings, and civil disobedience elsewhere on the NIH campus. Archival footage in the film *United in Anger* shows a crowd of about fifteen hundred people, with each person and group a moving, and often individuated, part of a larger whole.

My own personal recollection is that there was a surprisingly vague understanding from the group at large as to why we were going to the NIH. I did go, and not with a feeling of unease, but rather with a complacent sense of trust that someone knew why we were doing this and therefore it needed to be done. But when interviewing for the ACT UP

Oral History Project, I started to realize that almost no one could tell me, in retrospect, what the demands were for this action. Then Jim Hubbard showed me some archival footage of a post-action meeting in which both Maria Maggenti and Bob Rafsky questioned the purpose of the demonstration we had all just attended. So, before interviewing Brian, I alerted him that I was going to ask him what was won at the NIH. What did the NIH action accomplish?

"Quite honestly, I don't know. That was not my department. My job was to run the action . . . I didn't really do the follow-up for the actions. I planned them. I was a freelancer. I was basically a caterer or whatever . . . After you told me that you were going to ask this question, I emailed Mark and I said, *Hey, what can you tell me?*"

The information he provided gives us the opportunity to contrast the demands of the action with its results.

According to flyers quoted by Brian, the demands for the NIH action were:

- Test all potential treatments immediately.
- Study the whole disease (not just retrovirals but treatments for opportunistic infections and cancers).
- Open closed committees and meetings.
- Announce results immediately.
- End medical apartheid (make treatments open to everyone, not just white gay men).

According to Mark Harrington's letter to Brian, this is what we actually won:

The short version is that the NIH demo got NIAID [National Institute of Allergy and Infectious Diseases] to establish the CCG [Community Constituency Group], put activists on all ACTG [AIDS Clinical Trials Group] and CPCRA [Community Programs for Clinical Research on AIDS] research committees, (with votes), increase the amount of support given for OI [opportunistic infection] prevention and treatment research, and led to the best practice model of community involvement with AIDS research, which has become almost universal since

1990. The NIH demo was on May 21st and [Anthony] Fauci relented to ACT UP's demands one month later at the International AIDS Conference in San Francisco. The longer version from my unpublished manuscript is attached.

"And," Brian added, "he has sent me the particular chapter of his ACT UP book that he's working on, which I was just—it's the first I'd seen of it. I was just staggered at the amount of detail. It's like a daily diary of everything that he did."

As a result of the action, some people from our community on the T&D side became part of the structure inside the NIH. Which Brian called "a big bone of contention later."

"My personal take is that I think some people got in and others didn't, and the people who didn't get in were the ones who were upset . . . I think the ones who got in had been working at it longer . . . Was it because they were the white men and they got in first? You could say that. I wouldn't say that . . . This is really key; they spoke the language of the people that they were trying to meet with. They kept up with these guys research paper for research paper, and so I think that the NIH people were eventually willing to take them on as equals of a sort, because they had figured out what it took to win their acceptance, and I don't think that it was just because they were white men. I'm not going to say that that might not have played a factor . . . It very well could have been . . . A lot of people were even at the end fuzzy about what we were doing and why. It is a new target, and maybe the reasons for why we were protesting at the NIH still haven't sunk in . . . I do remember that there were complaints from people from the floor, that they didn't feel invested in the action."

Just as David Barr reported that before Seize Control of the FDA he could not get his phone calls answered, but after the FDA action, "they returned the call the next day," Storm the NIH was primarily orchestrated—involving fifteen hundred people at a cost of sixty thousand dollars—to get access for Treatment and Data into government committees. But this was not made explicit to the membership, which is why so many people I interviewed did not know what was won at that action.

I wonder if the organizational consequence would have been different if everything was simply put on the table. Obviously, it was necessary to have people with AIDS on government committees. I don't think that was the problem. But the manipulating, the false fronts and puppet mastering, even just the difficulties with emotional communication—that is, the *method used by some of these men*—represented values and created a feeling of unease among some of the membership. It telegraphed a feeling of superiority and disrespect. Certainly, as we saw from the catered lunch at Burroughs Wellcome, there was a kind of identification and recognition between white, male, well-educated government officials and the mostly white and male T&D members. Perhaps the membership of ACT UP, those who normally occupied the Outside role, would have supported the same goals, had the goals for the NIH action been honestly stated, but they certainly would have demanded a more varied group of individuals represented "at the table." But would the government have listened to dykes, street queens, and women of color in 1990, when none of the above were represented in government, media, or pharma? The four-year campaign of women with HIV, who had to go two years without getting a meeting, definitively proves that the answer is a resounding *no*.

The men of T&D were people with AIDS, desperate for new treatments, and yet so were other people. As the women's campaign and the experiences of needle exchange reveal, demographics determined access, and access determined the playbook. So building and using mass demonstrations, peopled by the Outside for one sector to get Inside, without making that explicit, I believe was one cause of resentment, anger, and rancor within the group, even though penetrating government committees was important. Ultimately, six years later, the new drugs were researched appropriately and released, but only for people who had insurance or lived in a city or state where the medications were covered. And in this way, today, large numbers of people with AIDS living in the United States are still denied the standard of care for both AIDS drugs and preventive medications like pre-exposure prophylaxis (PrEP). As T&D got on the ACTG after the action at the NIH, women with AIDS were fighting their four-year campaign to get basics. Why did one event not help the other?

Brian's journal entry, March 8, 1991:

> People have been walking out of ACT UP from day one. That
> doesn't bother me, though it has been exacerbated by our
> larger size in Cooper Union. Used to [be], you were at least

in physical contact with your, quote, unquote, "enemies." The T&D section and the Maxine section used to be separated by, say, 50 feet, not 500 feet as it is now, and this physical proximity forced you to deal with your enemies more than we do now. Again, "enemies."

Remembrance: Brian Zabcik Remembers His Dead Friends
"So, okay. Dave Liebhart, *L-i-e-b-h-a-r-t*. Someone else who fought with me to flirt with me. We actually went on one date that I wasn't realizing was a date, and basically at the end of it, he said, *Look, I've got to know whether or not I have a chance with you or not, because my time is limited.* My God, what do you say to that? I was honest. I said, *Look, I really like you as a person.* He was about fifteen years older than me, and I just did like him as a person, even though he was very prickly. God, it was just the situations that we were placed in.

"No stories about these people. I just want to name them, some of whom have been named before, and I'm leaving names off, but these are just people who made an impression on me and that I wish were around. Lee Schy, *S-c-h-y*, his photographs, that's the ACT UP history that I want to see. I'm sorry. No one captured ACT UP better for me, that whole environment, than his photographs. Jon Greenberg, oh my God, such a sweet person. Luis Salazar, *L-u-i-s S-a-l-a-z-a-r*, he did not die of AIDS; he died of leukemia at twenty-seven. He and I also, too, went on a date once. He was in my affinity group the Awning Leapers. Ray Navarro, I do have to say this. This is my story about Ray. This symbolized what the time was like for me. He was sick in St. Vincent's, and I went up to visit him, and he was not fully lucid at that point. He was already starting to have a little bit—his mind was already starting to be affected at one point, and he had wasting syndrome. He was in his bed. He was moving around. He was only wearing a hospital gown. At one point, because he just really was not with it or totally there, he was moving around, and his gown rode up and you could see his naked body. It had withered except for his dick and balls, and that just—I mean, that was really a disturbing thing to see. And it made perfect sense, because the dick and balls, it's not muscle mass, there's not anything to wither. It's just blood, and you still have your full sixteen pints or whatever at the end. But that was just really hard. Still, I remember him for other things.

"Bob Rafsky, *R-a-f-s-k-y*, Kevin Smith, Robert Garcia . . . But, God, Steve Zabel, *Z-a-b-e-l*, he was the first person that I knew to die in ACT UP, and, in fact, he died in New York, and it wasn't AIDS. He was murdered, as far as I understand, as I remember, by a trick gone bad. Tony Malliaras, he was the guiding spirit of Awning Leapers. He was the one that drove that affinity group, and his line was, *We shocked the world for you*, which was a line for Maurice Villency and their advertisements in the *Times* Sunday magazine, and he would always say that. He was always saying campy things like that that I just didn't know where in the fuck he was coming from. Roger Pettyjohn, *P-e-t-t-y-j-o-h-n*, he was more at CHP. I worked with him while I was in ACT UP. I was also, too, volunteering at CHP with the PCP prophylaxis clinic, and he was the nurse administering the aerosol pentamidine, and I was the one who was cleaning the aerosol equipment for him. Mark Carson, who, as I said, was the one who introduced me into the group. Bill Baletka, who's the one non–New York person on here. He's a cousin of mine, *B-a-l-e-t-k-a*, in Texas. We grew up together in church camp, and he was my age, and he came out, I think, about a couple years before I did and started becoming sexually active about a couple years before I did and did not get the information in time and died in '88 or '89. Then, finally, there are the people who died since then that [were] not necessarily of AIDS, but that I still wish were around. Rod Sorge, *S-o-r-g-e*. John Gilbert, I did not find out that he died until about a month ago. Sarah Pettit, she wasn't really in ACT UP. I don't know why, but, goddamn, I cried like crazy when she died."

22

The Dinner: December 1, 1990

As more people moved Inside, women's issues were on a distinctively different pathway. The increased access of T&D simply did not ever seem to help women get the access and changes that *they* needed. And this growing divergence exploded one night in Washington, D.C., in a hotel bar.

TRACY MORGAN

Tracy was in D.C. for the NIH-sponsored conference on women and AIDS that ACT UP had fought so long to realize, seven months after the action. She was there with Linda Meredith, Risa Denenberg, and Maxine Wolfe. They had brought their treatment agenda for the NIH and done a lot of organizing, both with the NIH and with the floor of ACT UP. It was a daylong event with a lot of activity and flyering and asking hard questions. That night, Tracy returned to New York, and when she got back to her apartment, she got a phone call from Risa Denenberg, who was still in D.C. Risa said, *You won't believe this.* Tracy answered, *Won't believe what?*

Risa was with Linda Meredith in the bar at the hotel where the conference had been held. Risa said, *I just ran into Mark Harrington.* And Tracy responded, *What's he doing there?* Because he had not attended the conference.

"It would have been a dream to have Mark at the conference. To have Mark with us at the conference would have been a shape shifter in many ways, if not on the political front, at the level of micro politics in the organization. It would have been really terrific . . . I couldn't seem, even though it's NIH, to get the Treatment and Data interest around this Women and AIDS [Conference]. I remember. I felt heartbroken. It was just heartbreaking. I was like, *What's he doing there? He wasn't with us.* And Risa said, *Well, he was going to a dinner party with Tony Fauci.*

"And I cried. I remember, because it was so disturbing to me, that I was like, *How could he be in D.C. and not have been with us and then go to dinner with Fauci? Fine. But come throw your weight with us . . .* Because Mark was really extremely, clearly very intelligent, but also accruing a certain cachet and power that it would have been really great . . . And I was like, *Wow. That blew my mind . . .* I was like, *How—? . . .* We were very, very far apart and that the cleavage was already there . . . I was like, *This is not going to be good, this sort of thing.*"

ACT UPer Bill Dobbs used to publish a weekly newsletter called *Tell It to ACT UP* (TITA), and it was like a slam book. It was Twitter before the internet. People would submit anonymous statements: sometimes gossip, sometimes blowing off steam, sometimes substantial critiques that didn't have a place on the floor. Tracy's comment was "Pick of the Week":

I would like to know why, after Evil Anthony Fauci treated all the women at the Women and HIV Conference like dirt, Mark Harrington got to have dinner with "The Big Guy" that same evening? I find this revolting. In ACT UP are we merely acting as individuals or are we working together? What did the two of them meet to talk about—women and HIV? Certainly not. We must stop these private meetings and commit ourselves to acting publicly, where we reach more people with our message. What really floors me is this: As ACT UP at this conference we sent the government (Fauci being a cog in that wheel) a clear message of our disdain and fury. How does Mark's "private" and in fact "secret" (he lied to Linda Meredith and Risa upon seeing them post-conference, stating he was on his way to [an] "X-mas party") meeting with Fauci get with what went on earlier that day? I think we've got to get our shit together and not perpetuate the syndrome of good boys versus bad girls. I resent the lack of thought behind the planning of this secret tete a tete.

"And it really was one of those things. I remember somebody—I think it was Jim Eigo. He was really angry."

Jim Eigo responded in *TITA*:

> Tracy Morgan's criticism of Mark Harrington is wide of the mark—a distortion of facts and (more disheartening) inexplicably sour. David Byar is the chief biostatistician at the National Cancer Institute. He also has AIDS. Upon reading ACT UP's 1989 Treatment Agenda, he translated our demands into a proposal that dozens of this country's chief biostatisticians have signed—in an article published in [*The*] *New England Journal of Medicine* which credits ACT UP for being the catalyst for a new way of conducting clinical trials. One more ACT UP empowered PWA, Dave's become a good friend of several of us, and has been the catalyst/convener of several social occasions over the last year-and-a-half that several ACT UP members have attended. He was responsible for the dinner Tracy complains about. ACT UP member Rebecca [Pringle] Smith attended as well. Fauci's deputy Jim Hill hosted. (Mark was in DC primarily for another social occasion.) Before the dinner (no secret) Mark asked Treatment and Data members if we had any questions of Fauci. The guest list wasn't his. After 3 ½ years I can say it's not easy to work with ACT UP. We have no support system. Those of us of a certain age, have witnessed intimately an unending stream of sickness and death for over a decade now. Some of us have our own heath to worry about. All of us are overworked; a few of us have given our lives full time to ACT UP. We have a right, even a duty to criticize each other's work. But no ACT UP member deserves to be personally attacked from within ACT UP. Especially not Mark, who nearly three years ago virtually put his life "on hold" to work with ACT UP, and has with uncommon brilliance and commitment—to work so hard,

that some of his colleagues (like me) worry about his physical health and peace of mind. In fall of '89 I had occasion to say that Mark Harrington's joining T+D was one of the two or three most important events of its history; that was probably an understatement. Attacks like Tracy Morgan's make some of us wonder sometimes if working for ACT UP is worth it.

The next week, Tracy addressed this on the floor of ACT UP in person. She said:

What we're talking about here are tactics and strategies. If we are going to appreciate the work each other does, let's not undercut it. Mark's having had dinner with Fauci was a prime example of what I'm talking about here. I can't help but to feel that breaking bread with Fauci, in fact, being with him as he recovers from being called on the carpet by us for his negligence of women in the AIDS crisis did anything but let Fauci off the hook.

I used to think that it was a sign of our power that after we did a huge demonstration or beforehand, we got to meet with the people in charge, the people we were protesting against, but I've changed my mind. I think that as activists screaming in front of the NIH, for example, Tony Fauci knew that he'd meet with our rational factor later on so he could dismiss the rest of us and our anger. He could dismiss us as a political force. Any threat we could have posed to his power was turned into useless theater. All meetings with government officials, in particular federal ones, must be approved by the floor. We must not let ourselves be swayed as mostly lesbians and gay men by people in power, those people largely being straight men. And we do not have to understand precise details of the ACTG and NIAID in order to criticize them with fervor. Let's stop being pitted against each other, expert versus novice. Let's remember our impulses for justice that bind us together . . . My fear is that we've become acceptable, that if we let that become our fate, who will deal with the direct action we need to save our lives?

MARK HARRINGTON

Mark was in Washington for a dinner meeting that he, Rebecca Pringle Smith, and David Byar from the National Cancer Institute had with Fauci to talk about doing a different kind of clinical study that would be larger and simpler and would get answers that were more reliable. And the dinner was scheduled for the same time as the big Women and AIDS Conference at NIH, where there was a demonstration.

"There was a lot of legitimate anger at NIH at that time about not dealing well with women with AIDS. And so I think the fact that I, from T&D, had a meeting with Fauci at the same time as there was a demonstration and also a [Women and AIDS Conference], revealed that there was a lack of coordination if not outright distrust between these groups. And I'm sure that contributed to some of the mistrust and antagonism that was taking place."

REBECCA PRINGLE SMITH

Rebecca Pringle Smith grew up in Ann Arbor, Michigan. Her mother was a feminist who contributed to *Ms.* magazine. Her father was a basketball player in Brazil, secretary to the writer Stefan Zweig, part of the Group Theatre with the playwright Clifford Odets, and eventually a neuropsychologist. Rebecca came to New York to do Columbia's postgraduate premedical program and worked as a research assistant at St. Luke's Roosevelt Hospital. In 1988, she went to Community Research Initiative to work with Dr. Sonnabend, and also worked in ACT UP, primarily with David Kirschenbaum, Jim Eigo, and others on the Treatment and Data Committee #1.

When the conference on women with HIV at the NIH was being planned, Rebecca was asked to speak about whatever she wanted, and her talk was titled: "Mechanisms for Incorporating Community Input into Clinical Trials."

"And I couldn't get any feedback on my talk. And people were like, *We don't care about that,* and there was clashes going on. And I think I was too sensitive, in retrospect. So stuff was under way. So David Byar and Mark had wanted to meet Fauci to talk to him about large simple trials, and my view was, *This guy doesn't know—he can't spell clinical trial, you know. But if they want to do it, fine* . . . So whenever the conference was planned, we planned to get together with them if David was still alive, and we had no coordination with the women and I'm indifferent to Tony Fauci. But you know, he was talking to the guys. He wasn't talking to me, but I was involved in there.

"I had thought we should have a meeting together about what the tactics were going to be. And this is going to sound really bad, but I really feel that we should have coordinated, and that this view got put out that the [ACT UP] men were nice and the [ACT UP] women weren't, and Fauci liked the men better because they were nice, and the women weren't, and I think that's such crap. But the men and me bear responsibility for not fighting it out with the women beforehand about, *Look, if you want to talk to a fucking bureaucrat, don't waste it by just screaming at him. He doesn't have any decision-making power anyway. Figure out what you want out of him and get it.* And we should have fought that out, but we didn't . . . And so this got cast as me and Mark and Tony Fauci undermining the women, you know, and I can see it being cast that way and I'm willing to be accountable and talk to anybody about it . . . I think they *were* being marginalized. I think it's legitimate. I don't think this is bullshit. I think it's a process problem."

At that meeting Rebecca learned that, from Fauci's standpoint, his office had no power, and he and his colleagues just had to do whatever the pharmaceutical industry did, that "the ACTG was the pharmaceutical industry's bitch." She felt that ACT UP got nowhere with Fauci at that dinner regarding the large simple trials agenda.

"What use is it, having us on all those committees? . . . Well, you know, there was a power to ACT UP . . . that before there was an Inside, we spoke to each other . . . *Bureaucrats,* as my mom says, *they resist change.* They like their jobs. Their digestion is splendid . . . And I think for Tony Fauci, we became a mechanism through which he related to his work and it became more dramatic and more colorful and more interesting . . . maybe the Community Constituency Group was the right thing to have done. I saw it as co-optation in action, but I don't have a better alternative. I don't know how these things should be done. But I think that was the moment at which the old ideology started to die."

23

Day of Desperation: January 23, 1991

The first Gulf War started on January 16, 1991. Unlike most previous wars, it did not suddenly explode, but rather, President George H. W. Bush announced that the war would start on a specific date and then the world waited until he began it. Ten years before 9/11, the Gulf War was accompanied by manufactured anti-Arab sentiment and generalized fear, even though the exact reasons for the war were unclear to most Americans. For ACT UP, this was a monumental distraction from the real problems of the AIDS crisis, a huge waste of money, and an exploitative use of racism to justify a war.

VICTOR MENDOLIA

Victor proposed and then coordinated the Day of Desperation during the first Gulf War. He felt that the organization was at a roadblock. The lack of progress in finding medications that worked cast a pall over the group. ACT UP needed something cohering that would reflect our emotional state. He asked Larry Kramer for a meeting, went over to his apartment, and shared his idea to blockade all the bridges and tunnels. *We'll get press for that. If we have to up the ante and we have to do that, that's what we have to do.* And Victor felt that Larry was really happy that somebody had come up with something that maybe could break through the wall of indifference. The following Monday, Larry and Victor proposed the action to the organization. And over the course of several discussions and reality checks, they focused on Grand Central Terminal instead, with the idea of affinity actions happening elsewhere. Victor was saying, *We got to ramp it up. We have to do stuff we haven't done before, like break onto the sets of television shows, et cetera.* So then at one point, somebody came up to him and said, *Look: we're working on it, so stop talking about it.* And he did, Victor said, "and then the rest is sort of history, as far as that goes."

AIDS IS NEWS: FIGHT AIDS, NOT ARABS

JOHN WEIR

John Weir grew up in New Jersey. His father worked at NBC TV for forty-five years. And his mother had an animal talent agency. He went to Kenyon College and then moved to New York. His first boyfriend worked at GMHC.

"So immediately, it was about people dying, and having to take care of them . . . From '84 to '86, maybe, that was kind of all it was about, was going to people's hospital rooms, and dealing with them. There was no notion of what ACT UP later did, of intervening against any government agency. It was all about getting care for people who were sick and people who were dying."

CBS

ACT UP started planning for the Day of Desperation. The activists felt strongly that part of the stagnancy of government and pharma was because the media did not report on or reflect the rage and desperation of people with AIDS. Instead of showing ACT UP's perspective, news organizations were still objectifying and stigmatizing people with AIDS, without accurately reflecting our feelings of absurdity and almost hallucinatory pain. The purpose of this action was to break through the confinement of the media.

Ann Northrop had worked for CBS for a while and had an ID that she could get copied. The affinity group the Marys made plans to interrupt a network news broadcast the night before the Day of Desperation action in Grand Central Terminal. Others were doing CBS and ABC and NBC, and the Marys were doing the *MacNeil/Lehrer Report*. And when this idea was being surfaced, John thought, *Ha! If there's one thing*

I know how to do, it's how to get into a newsroom, because he'd grown up around them. His father had covered all the moon shots. John thought, *This action has my name written all over it.*

ANN NORTHROP

Ann donated her ID card, which she still had, because CBS had neglected to take it back from her, and ACT UP members copied it and put their own faces on, making their own ID cards. She diagrammed the floor plan of the CBS broadcast center building on West Fifty-Seventh Street, where the evening news was done. It was very simple, because they had just built a new *Evening News* studio, close to the front door. So she told everyone, *All you have to do is go in the front door, go by the security desk, flash your ID card—they won't look at it closely . . . make a gesture, and they'll let you go through. And then you go straight down this corridor, take a left, go through these doors, and you're in the* Evening News *studio.* She told them that if they dressed in business suits, and just stood off to the side, they probably wouldn't be challenged. If anyone did ask who they were, men were told to say that they were salesmen from Black Rock, the CBS headquarters building, and they were there showing clients the *Evening News* studio. And so they did a dry run of this, a couple of weeks before, and it worked. They stood there, about twenty feet from Dan Rather, live on the air, and no one said a word to them.

JOHN WEIR

John, Dale Peck, and Daryl Bowman practiced a couple of times. They made a little banner that said FIGHT AIDS, NOT ARABS—which they carried, folded up, wearing suits and ties. And they'd figured out what they were going to say ahead of time.

DALE PECK

Dale Peck grew up in Hutchinson, Kansas. He went to college as a Young Republican but within three weeks was completely radicalized. He became a vegetarian and was a member of the anti-apartheid group, the antiwar group, "and everything else." Dale also was president of the Gay and Lesbian Student Alliance before he even came out. In New York in 1985, he observed that "when you got off at Christopher Street . . . you saw AIDS the minute you got off the train. Those were the days when men with wasting syndrome were walking up and down the street, all over the place; when you saw people with large KS lesions, and everything; when you saw places draped in mourning, and everything else. It was really inescapable."

He joined ACT UP in December 1989, right after Stop the Church. "The AIDS crisis had been going on for a decade at that point. And the news coverage hadn't been getting any better. And it was like, we need to do this, we need to effect that."

JOHN WEIR

They got into the studio and stood to the side.

"We couldn't see a monitor, but we could hear the announcer saying, *This is the evening news, with Dan Rather.* And then we just ran on, the three of us, chanting, *Fight AIDS, Not Arabs!*"

DALE PECK

It was seven seconds into the broadcast, and as soon as the activists took the stage, the show went off the air for four seconds.

"Just hundreds of people seemed to jump on us. Nobody actually hit us. There was no violence, and all that. And in the adrenaline rush, everything gets very blurry. But there's a very funny shot. Only John's face got on the actual CBS News. And you can see him being shuffled off the side of the stage. And then they kind of took us back out into the lobby. And people were really excited, because they thought that we were Islamic terrorists or something like that. And they're like, *Who do you work for, who put you up*, all this kind of stuff. And we kind of let it be clear that we were with ACT UP, and all that. And after about fifteen or twenty minutes, everyone settled down. The police came, and all that . . . on the fourth day of the Gulf War."

ANN NORTHROP

"*Evening News* went to black and came back, and Rather was upset, apologizing to the viewers for this dastardly interruption. And this became such a big deal, that other newscasts took the clip of this and played it all over the world. I talked to someone who saw it broadcast on CNN, when they were in Jerusalem, doing war coverage. So it became a very big deal. And, meanwhile, another group went into PBS and managed to handcuff themselves to Robert MacNeil's chair, and, they may have gotten arrested ultimately, but he let them sit there for a while, and talked to them on the air, for a little bit. Before, then, I think, handing the broadcast over to Lehrer and dragging them out."

JOHN WEIR

The activists were held in the lobby for a while and handcuffed over a semicircular desk. The CBS people were circling around them, John said, "with *You Pigs* written on their faces." Then the police van showed up, and on the way out to the van they were still chanting, *Fight AIDS, Not Arabs.* The activists were taken to the Midtown North precinct.

"But for me, it was also breaking through this pasteboard mask of network—those network news shows are, they're scripted and they're full of lies, and there's just a glossiness to them, and a smoothness, and—an inability to deal with anything except the three issues that they're told to deal with over and over."

NBC

ELIZABETH MEIXELL

Action Tours organized into three groups, and one went to NBC dressed as employees. They had fake ID passes. To look like they belonged at NBC, they'd shed their outdoor clothing. That was the important thing about Action Tours; they looked like they belonged. In clean white shirts, a couple of ACT UP people got in front of the camera and said, *Money for AIDS, not for war! Money for AIDS, not for war!*

And they had a sign. The other news stations kept playing the tape on all the networks, so it was there that night, live on the six-o'clock news on CBS and on the eleven-o'clock news on all stations. "We were up late, jumping on James's bed and screaming."

SEIZING TELEVISION TIME: DISRUPTING *MacNEIL/LEHRER*

KEN BING

Ken Bing grew up on the Lower East Side of New York and went to Stuyvesant High School, dropped out of NYU, and came out at age twenty. He gravitated to Black and White Men Together.

"Living in New York at that time was crazy, because people are getting sick every day; three, four, five, six people that you hear about, being sick. And also, I'd seen people in the street that you knew were sick, because they were very emaciated, and they had lesions on their faces; they could barely walk. That was scary for me, because I would think, *Well, this could be me in another few months, in another couple of years.*"

In ACT UP he joined the affinity group the Marys with Tim Bailey, Joy Episalla, James Baggett, Jon Greenberg, Michael Cunningham, and others. Tim, who was one of the spark plugs of the Marys, was definitely getting sicker at the time.

For the Day of Desperation, the Marys picked the PBS *MacNeil/ Lehrer Report* to infiltrate, with the goal of getting on camera. Five of the Marys actually got into the studio and chained themselves to some equipment in the studio. Unfortunately, the action wasn't actually on camera. But viewers could see Jim Lehrer watching the whole thing. And he said, on camera, *There's a group of people from ACT UP in there, chained themselves. And, back to you.*

MARCHING THROUGH WALL STREET

KARIN TIMOUR

The morning of the Day of Desperation, there was a march early through downtown Manhattan. The Insurance Committee pulled out the banner that said INSURANCE DISCRIMINATION KILLS PEOPLE WITH

AIDS. "Lower Manhattan is insurance company heartland," Karin said. So they decided that wanted to take back an entire street, and chose John Street. They had bumper stickers printed up the size and shape of street signs, went out at four in the morning, got up on ladders, and replaced all the street signs that said JOHN STREET with bumper stickers that said INSURANCE FOR PEOPLE WITH AIDS STREET, the entire length of John Street.

THE CUMULATION: TAKING OVER GRAND CENTRAL TERMINAL

VICTOR MENDOLIA

Around three thousand people showed up inside Grand Central Terminal. ACT UP was on every stair, on top of the information booth, draping banners across the big Arrivals/Departures board announcing the numbers of AIDS deaths. Commuters could not get through. It was literally "no business as usual." The numbers were too large to police, especially with the normal rush-hour crowd interspersed. About seventy people were arrested outside, including me—one of my two ACT UP arrests.

"They put them through the system, it was a big deal," Victor said. "That was, I remember specifically that it was a much more severe treatment than we'd received before."

One affinity group snaked through the station looking like they were delivering balloons. But when they got into the main hall, they let go of the balloons, which had a banner attached—MONEY FOR AIDS, NOT FOR WAR—that sailed up and hung from the high domed roof of Grand Central, out of the reach of the police.

"We clearly made the front page the next day, of everything. So we accomplished what we wanted to do, which was at least just get AIDS in the news for a while . . . It was like a scream in the middle of the desert, really."

DALE PECK

"Shutting down Forty-Second Street on a bitterly cold day, and lying down on that street, and then all getting arrested and stuff, the classics of spending eight hours in a holding tank, when you have to pee and they won't let you out, and all that kind of stuff. And trying to do your homework, because I was still in school at the time . . . That was the beauty and the effectiveness of those early ACT UP messages. There were people who sat down with Tony Fauci, and sat down at the NIH, and had long, reasoned conversations about why double-blind studies were essentially condemning thousands if not hundreds of thousands of people to death, and why things had to be sped up, and all that. But when you're dealing with the media, you have to deal in sound bites; you have to deal in very concrete, discrete messages, because anything larger just gets garbled. And we were good at staying on point that way. So that was essentially the message, and I think that that's what was communicated."

GARANCE FRANKE-RUTA

Not everyone thought it was a success.

"Day of Desperation? We in T&D were [like], *Okay, what is the goal of the protest? What are you trying to accomplish?* . . . And they couldn't come up with anything, as I recollect, other than sort of—again, this was the moment where everyone was going crazy—other than just saying, *Hello, we exist, this is an issue, deal with this.* And in T&D, everything had become so goal-oriented and so focused and very specific. We would have, we wouldn't just do protests. To do a protest, on its own, seemed like an extremely inefficient strategy of creating change. First thing you do is, you figure out exactly what you want; what the changes are that you think need to happen. You write a letter to whoever is the highest-ranking person who you think can effect those changes. You send them all your demands. You ask for a meeting. You have a meeting. You don't get what you're looking for. Then you hold a protest. After that, again try and meet with the person. So there's this ongoing process, where everything was very targeted and goal-oriented. And T&D was also, so sort of scientific at that point, and sort of—specialized. It was divorced from, I think, the mainstream of ACT UP a bit at that point."

Remembrance: David Feinberg

Emotionally, people in ACT UP were devastated, as we were constantly watching our friends enduring psychic and physical suffering in the face of the indifference of their families and their government. In some cases, no one cared about the person's life aside from those of us in ACT UP, and some of the dying became brutal in the reality of their own destruction, as people tend to take out their pain on the people who care. One of the most punishing deaths was that of the writer David Feinberg, who made sure that as many ACT UPers as possible would suffer along with him. These kinds of high-profile deteriorations and consequent desperation made being in ACT UP even more difficult, painful, and high pressure. Something that only occupying Grand Central could address. Even if its only accomplishment was to show the world how we felt.

JOHN WEIR

It wasn't until he met David Feinberg, author of the novel *Eighty-Sixed* and the essay collection *Queer and Loathing: Rants and Raves of a Raging AIDS Clone*, that John started going to ACT UP. David had reviewed John's first novel, *The Irreversible Decline of Eddie Socket*, in *OutWeek*.

"It was a competitive review. It said—*I thought I wrote the best book about AIDS, but I guess someone else has! But I'm cuter!* It was a very funny review, and it felt like he was flirting with me, in his caustic, hectoring way. And I read. And then he came up, at the end of that reading, at A Different Light, in November, I guess it must have been, of '89 and said, *Hi, I'm Dave Feinberg*, and he was this little guy with a gigantic chest and these little legs."

John really liked David because of his honesty. John remembered thinking, *I'm going to keep this guy alive.* As that first meeting came to an end, John walked across the street and waved goodbye. Then David waved goodbye. And that went on for five minutes of waving goodbye. David turned around and waved, and then finally, he vanished. And John thought, *Well, this time, I have to, like, make sure someone doesn't die.*

"It was like a little deal we made somehow. And I think he understood that, also. Which of course didn't really work out that way, but . . . in particular, my starting to go to ACT UP meetings was kind of to keep track of David."

In 1992, David started getting sick. He'd call John on the phone, and say, *What have you done today to end the AIDS crisis, John Weir?* And John felt that he had done nothing. Every day David called him and woke him up with *What have you done today to end the AIDS crisis?* That was his hello, which became more and more, *What have you done today to keep me alive?* But shortly after that, in September of 1992, David really did start getting sick. After he got out of the hospital, he weighed 90 pounds, down from 150. David held a coming-home-from-the-hospital party called I'm Still Standing. I was at that party; it was in his Chelsea co-op; his health-care attendant was there. David was emaciated, surrounded by all his friends, wearing Calvin Klein thigh-length underpants, and then he got diarrhea and ran screaming to the bathroom. It was horrible, especially for the other sick people in the room staring down their futures. I was there with Stan Leventhal, and once David got diarrhea, Stan just left.

John recalled that by that point, there was practically a tradition of desperate, sick people screaming at ACT UP. Like at Vito Russo's funeral, when Larry Kramer yelled at the mourners, "We killed Vito, can't you see that?" David Barr, Bob Rafsky—a number of people let us have it.

"You get up and say, *What the fuck are you motherfuckers doing about my health!* And screaming and screaming and screaming. And, *Oh, I'm angry! Why aren't you angry! Where is your anger?!* And David was going to have that moment. It was like his farewell tour."

David came from St. Vincent's in his hospital gown,

dragging his IV to the Gay Center on a Monday night, and started yelling, *You failed because I'm dying!*

"There was a certain level at which I was like: maybe David was acting out my rage, also. And if he wants to walk down the street, dribbling diarrhea, and screaming at people at high noon, on Lower Broadway: then fuck it. I'm going to walk behind with a pooper scooper, basically, and be a part of this display. But that was my anger, also. But it was—it was really upsetting, certainly. And it certainly alienated me from my friendship with him, ultimately. Because he was just, at the very end of his life, just so angry, twenty-four hours a day. And he never slept, and he was—and everyone was the enemy. So that was hard to deal with . . . It didn't feel like David was the only guy who was losing something . . . I ended up angry with him, that he'd sealed himself off, and said, *This is only happening to me; you don't have anything to say about this, except to pay the cabbie, and help me out of the car when we get back to my apartment.* And there was a certain amount of that in ACT UP, I think, in general, of the people with HIV are sacred, and that people without HIV are somehow—aren't entitled to say anything about how they're feeling about it. Maybe it was just David; I don't know."

24

Are Women "Vectors of Infection" or People with AIDS? Clinical Trial 076, April 1991

While the four-year campaign to change the definition of AIDS to include women did get a lot of support from many people in ACT UP, the fight over Clinical Trial 076, which sought to test AZT on pregnant women, was so divisive that it became a breaking point for the organization.

The question at stake was: Should all people with AIDS be considered equally important, including mothers? Political conflicts came to a head in ACT UP as new parameters of AIDS not-for-profits and testing centers became institutionalized in a manner that challenged long-standing feminist ideas about what constitutes consent for poor women of color. Are pregnant HIV-positive women "vectors of infection" to be viewed primarily in relation to the future sero status of their potential children? Or are they people with AIDS needing treatment, deserving of the same standards ACT UP established for gay men? As the future of AIDS medications started to come into focus, was it ethical to give poor women drugs that could cause resistance later, or did the futures of millions of children who might be born HIV-positive take precedence?

MARION BANZHAF

Clinical Trial 076, conducted by the AIDS Clinical Trials Group (ACTG), was designed to determine whether or not AZT, given in the second and third trimesters of a woman's pregnancy, and to the newborn for seven days to two weeks, would stop HIV transmission from mother to infant. It was just being proposed and designed at a time when the ACTG had come under a lot of fire from ACT UP, and all over the country, for doing its work outside of community input. The ACTG had started its own Community Advisory Board, and there were representatives on the board from AIDS service organizations and different community-based organizations from around the country. These were straight people and people of color, not just white gay men. There were a few ACT UP people on the Community Constituency Group, which was also under the ACTG.

Marion Banzhaf had gotten a job as coordinator of the New Jersey Women and AIDS Network, which had been formed in 1988, and was the first statewide women-and-AIDS organization in the country. It was not a service organization, but an education-and-advocacy organization. The designers of the experimental drug trial 076 came out of University of Medicine and Dentistry of New Jersey (UMDNJ) and were based in Newark. New Jersey had the distinction of being the only state in the country where people who got infected from unsafe sex and people who got infected from drug use were about parallel; it was fifty-fifty from the beginning, and it stayed fifty-fifty. New Jersey also had the highest proportion of women with AIDS in the country. Because of this phenomenon, pediatric AIDS was identified first in New Jersey. So the principal investigators were out of Newark.

At the same time, Marion was having meetings with ACT UP, with people in Newark, and with community groups like African-American Women United Against AIDS, around this trial. Because in 1991, AZT was still the only available drug. There was a lot of discussion in the Black community about how AZT was poison. And there were also HIV denialists, some of whom were the same people. The history of medical experimentation on Black people was being reflected in the lack of treatments for African American women.

As the principal investigators were trying to woo the community to support the trial, Marion was trying to get the design of the trial changed. She believed it should not have a placebo arm, because that would deny those women access to the drug, and that's the only reason they'd be joining the trial in the first place. Marion felt that would be unethical. At that point, Marion felt that there could easily be a control group from women who were in another hospital, where the trial wasn't being done. And she also wanted the newborn requirement to be optional. As the trial was designed, women had to take the drug and give it to their newborns. But Marion wanted the women to be able to decide whether or not they wanted to give the newborn that powerful dose of the drug, because nothing was known about what impact that drug would have on a newborn later in life. There were other pressing issues as well. If the women took this drug during pregnancy, would they be able to continue getting it when they were no longer pregnant, if it helped them? Or would the women just be dropped when the trial ended?

For women in ACT UP with strong reproductive rights backgrounds, influenced by the earlier movement against sterilization abuse, this trial had many red flags.

First, women with AIDS/HIV were for the most part poor, and women of color were overrepresented. Issues of testing on women and children of color arose. The question Marion raised of placebo use—whether the test would be double-blind, with half the women getting sugar pills, as opposed to everyone who volunteered getting the AZT—resonated deeply with debates in the early 1980s about whether or not newborns with HIV, who were also mostly poor and of color, would be offered placebo or be tested against the current standard of care. No person with AIDS ever wanted to be in the placebo group of a clinical trial. But women desperate for their future children's health might feel that they have to risk it, while at the same time the fetuses could not consent to a potentially detrimental dose of AZT.

Second, a major issue was that women who took AZT while pregnant, to see if it would keep their fetus from seroconverting, could then be rendered resistant to the next stage of treatment development. In this way women were valued first as "vectors of infection," with the fetus's future deemed more important than the life of the mother. In this regard, the question of consent also resonated from the early questions around sterilization abuse. Many of the mothers felt guilt about how they got infected, or that they got infected and then got pregnant, and may have felt that they *had* to sacrifice their future care for the opportunity to prevent their fetus or future child from being HIV-positive. The question of sacrifice weighed heavily, and it was unclear if this kind of emotional pressure compromised consent.

Third, as ACT UPer David Kirschenbaum raised on the floor, his research showed that women being enrolled for 076 were not told that cesarean sections cut down the risk of transmission. Without cesarean sections, there was a 20 percent transmission rate, and with cesarean sections, there was an 8 percent transmission rate, because, evidentially, doctors were able to control the amount of the mother's blood with cesarean. This naturally brought up questions of patients not being fully informed.

Fourth, scientists' main concern was to stop new HIV-positive children from being born; they were less concerned with treating HIV-positive women. ACT UP's campaign to get the CDC definition of AIDS changed to include women was in full swing with no government cooperation or support. But when it came to *women as mothers*, science was willing to jeopardize these women's own future care. So it was about women's only value being as bearers of children, not as individual people with AIDS who deserved care. There were no plans to continue care for the women after the trial. Once the children were born, the women were forgotten.

Finally, it was unclear what side effects would be felt later in life in people who were given AZT in the womb. This harked back to a famous case in which pregnant women, from 1938 to 1971, were given the synthetic estrogen diethylstilbestrol (DES), and their daughters developed cervical cancer in their twenties.

On the other hand, not everyone in the communities serving women with AIDS shared these historically resonant concerns.

MARION BANZHAF

Janet Mitchell, who was an African American doctor based at Harlem Hospital, was strongly pushing for the 076 trial to happen. She thought it was a really good thing for pregnant women who had little access to treatment. And she had other differences with ACT UP. For example, she thought that AIDS testing shouldn't be done in separate AIDS counseling and testing centers; it should just be mainstreamed into regular health care from the very beginning. Some AIDS activists favored the separation because of confidentiality issues and a historic hostility to testing that had leftover repercussions.

Marion went to an ACT UP meeting and was really surprised at the position that ACT UP was taking. She recalled that some people in ACT UP were saying that the trial should not go forward at all. Some

ACT UPers were arguing that, since nobody knew what the impact was going to be on the fetus and the baby, women deserved to have access to all clinical trials, instead of being restricted to trials built around pregnancy. Some ACT UPers felt, *You can't use pregnant women for this trial, when your sole intention is for the baby, for the fetus,* and then exclude non-pregnant women from clinical trials for other drugs. "I wanted to reform the trial. [ACT UP] wanted to stop it," Marion said.

But not everyone in ACT UP agreed that the trial needed to be stopped.

DAVID Z. KIRSCHENBAUM

David got a copy of the trial protocol through the AIDS Treatment Registry, and he and Margaret McCarthy analyzed it.

He recalled that the protocol didn't tell women about defects in the trial. It was a big trial, widespread all across America, with seven hundred people.

"Well, a group of women [in ACT UP] thought it was their issue. I specifically was told at one meeting that maybe I should find another organization to work in . . . It was really ugly at moments. [Their position was:] *We need to stop the trial, period*—which wasn't my position. Women should have informed consent. Women should be knowing what they're getting into . . . People should have information on what they're doing in this disease."

MARGARET McCARTHY

Margaret filed a Freedom of Information Act request, and again huge amounts of paper flooded her house. Her big concern then was surrounding *women as vectors*—women being seen only in relation to men or to fetuses.

"Nobody cared about these pregnant women getting treated. Like, it's all about giving this treatment that *Maybe the baby will be born without HIV,* without really looking at, like, *Does this woman need HIV treatment?* At that point women were not getting treated. They were dying more quickly. Not every woman with HIV, but a lot of women with HIV already were poor, had little access to health care. They were really stigmatized. They didn't have the same social networks that some gay men had been able to form . . . A lot of the way that society was looking at women with HIV was just like, *We've got to nip this thing in the bud, like, make sure they don't pass it on to anybody else*, without saying, like, *Oh, this is a person who deserves to get medical treatment on their own.* You know, like, if this woman weren't pregnant, would she be able to get medication? Probably not."

MARION BANZHAF

Marion thought that the trial was going to go forward, in some way or another, regardless of what ACT UP did. And she felt that it was important to get rid of the placebo arm, and to make newborn inclusion optional. She knew that the principal investigators at UMDNJ had powerful connections and that their funding was all lined up. It was going to go forward. Furthermore, in talking to pregnant HIV-positive women, they were very invested in not infecting their kids, even at great detrimental outcome to their own health. Marion felt that women were really hoping that the trial would work. At that time, many women discovered that they were HIV-positive only when they were pregnant, since they didn't have basic health care. It was like, *Oh God, now not only do I have this dreaded disease, but now I might pass it on to my baby, and I might wind up killing my baby.* So they were clamoring for the trial, which, in Marion's view, was all the more reason why it shouldn't have had a placebo requirement.

DAVID Z. KIRSCHENBAUM

David brought 076 out of the realm of committees and directly to the floor of ACT UP.

"A group of women got very interested . . . The ones that mostly come to mind are Tracy [Morgan] and Heidi [Dorow] . . . There's probably eight to ten women . . . I'd set up a meeting with Fauci and a whole bunch of people from NIAID to meet in Newark Airport, I believe, at a hotel room. And we were going to talk about the protocol, talk about our issues—that was the first step in all of this. And we got to the meeting. Basically, [the ACT UPers] closed down the meeting, just started yelling and ranting and walked out. And I was like, *What's going here?* I mean, it was just screaming. No points were discussed, nothing. No actual input was put into whatever they were doing, and it just became like a yelling match."

MARION BANZHAF

"Some people decided that they were going to do an action at the Community Constituency Group meeting. And it was the first time that the clinical trial 076 was going to be talked about at the CCG. And people from ACT UP went in and started yelling at the principal investigators . . . the meeting got shut down, the principal investigators walked out. And the Community Constituency Group got really pissed off at ACT UP, that they hadn't been able to evaluate the information for themselves and been able to engage with the principal investigators. And so the conversation then switched from the design of the trial to that ACT UP's action wound up being racist. Because here was this group of largely people of color [who were participants]; and [ACT UP] didn't let them hear the information and make up their minds for themselves. So then this emboldened the principal investigators, one of whom was an African American woman, and the other was a white guy, they went on to work for a pharmaceutical company. And any discussion about the design of the trial stopped; and the trial went on as originally designed."

HEIDI DOROW

"There were some of us in the Women's Caucus who went to a meeting, a public discussion about the 076 trial. We disrupted it . . . There were people of color running the meeting, and some of the doctors involved . . . Most of the women who were leading this protest were white. So there was backlash: *What were these white women doing—disrupting this discussion, or talk about this trial, or trying to disrupt this trial, when it was giving access to women of color?* It was being led by women of color. That it was racist. Anyway, and we were denounced, that action was denounced by some members of Treatment and Data."

TRACY MORGAN

"The controversy about 076 was dual. So here [was] Janet Mitchell, a Black female doctor up in Harlem Hospital . . . It was perceived through this prism: white women saying, *This trial is a problem because it's giving women the garbage drug (AZT), it's privileging the fetus over the woman* . . . And these Black women MDs who were also increasingly a part of the establishment, the AIDS establishment, were saying that we were denying women health care . . . I think what was controversial *in* ACT UP perhaps was that it was a lot of people stepping into territory at a certain kind of level, right, stepping into a terrain that was not ours. In part it was about turf. We were at the AIDS Clinical Trials Group, if I recall. That was where the whole 076 thing took place. We, meaning Women's Caucus, not Treatment and Data, . . . were talking about drug trials. I think that we may have been perceived as going someplace where we weren't supposed to go . . . We were lay professionals stepping in and commenting about the politics of this without as much medical knowledge. We just didn't have that . . . I don't know what we should have done differently, but we definitely should have done something differently . . . because within ACT UP it created more tension and we're being delegitimized by these doctors, and it just felt terrible. It felt like we should be working together, and somehow I think—maybe we were just really naïve. Maybe we just thought that people would agree with us. I think I remember being shocked that Janet Mitchell considered a drug trial a form of health care. I was like, 'I understand it can give people some health care, but let's not stoop to that level.'"

DAVID Z. KIRSCHENBAUM

David found the whole debate really disturbing, and he felt attacked by Tracy and Heidi. He tried to bring the issue back to the floor, but he didn't feel that the floor responded appropriately. He didn't feel he was being supported. He wasn't being supported by the T&D, which was about to split off from ACT UP. Alienated, hurt, and frustrated, David quit ACT UP. He felt he had given the organization a lot, and he had enjoyed the work immensely, but he didn't like the way he was being treated.

MARION BANZHAF

"I think also what was part of it was that the AIDS landscape was also changing, in that just as in any kind of movement that happens, once you start winning some of your demands and actually forcing the government to do what you want, then, lo and behold, cooptation starts happening. So . . . I wasn't the only person who went to go work for an AIDS organization. There were lots of people who were going to work for AIDS organizations. And so I think ACT UP was trying to figure out how it was going to continue to position itself in this new AIDS landscape. And was it going to be a coalition-builder, or was it going to be the shamer? And I think in that action, it shows the shaming mode . . . I just wish that at that action, that people had figured out a way to meet with the CCG first; say, *Here's the deal with this trial, here's what we think.* So when the principal investigators come in, ask them these questions, and see what you think about it, too. And then let's strategize about how this can go forward in the best way possible. Or not. But since they thought that it shouldn't go forward at all, of course they wouldn't take that position."

So, in short, the rancorous differences between four points of view were:

1. No trial should sacrifice the future of HIV-positive women's lives by making them resistant to next-stage treatments in the name of potentially keeping their future child from seroconverting. The 076 trial must be stopped.
2. The trial should be reformed so that women are better informed and can fully consent. Information about the cesarean options should be added.
3. The trial should be reformed so that there is no placebo component, and women are not forced to subject their newborns to AZT.
4. The trial should proceed as is, because getting AZT in order to see if it stopped the fetus from seroconverting is a form of health care, and may be the only health care these patients receive.

In this way, pregnant HIV-positive women of color were now in the same position that white gay men had been years before—dependent on being in a trial in order to have contact with medical institutions and professionals, to get a medication that could be toxic or useless, and to subject their children to the same.

WHAT IF A CLINICAL TRIAL IS A SUCCESS . . . BUT ONLY FOR THE CHILD?

The 076 trial turned out to show success in limiting the seroconversion of fetuses, and subsequently science progressed to the point where it is extremely rare for HIV-positive babies to be born in the United States today. The standard-of-care treatment is no longer AZT but often Truvada. So the crisis of children being born HIV-positive in America came to a conclusion. But what of the women and children who were given AZT in the trial? As far as I know, no follow-up has been done to see if those children, or *their* children, ever developed side effects. And yes, at least some of the seven hundred or so women given AZT—although no one knows how many—were rendered resistant to some subsequent classes of new medications. No one has calculated how many of them died for this reason. And we do not know how many women and children who received the placebo died of AIDS— probably in the hundreds.

MARGARET McCARTHY

"They have actually been really successful in reducing the rate of maternal-fetal transmission, which is huge. And so, like, in that sense, like, maybe I was on the wrong side of the issue, because if it were my kid I would do anything not to have them, you know, be sick."

MARION BANZHAF

"I still wish it had not been a placebo-controlled trial. It did wind up showing the maternal-infant transmission rate had been about thirty-five percent, thirty-three percent. With AZT, it reduced it to eight percent. Now . . . it's down to practically zero. So it ultimately did wind up being a success. But not for all those women who were on it who got the placebo, not for those kids. The women who were in the trial did wind up getting directed into care."

MARK HARRINGTON

"There was a demonstration by one group of people from ACT UP at the ACTG to stop the ACTG-076 trial of AZT, to prevent transmission of HIV from mother to child, and later, that study broke out positive and became really influential, in terms of getting HIV treatment starting to be used in developing countries . . . It's dramatically effective in reducing . . . the transmission of HIV from mother to child . . . Well, they said that they were against it because it was using the mother as a vessel and not treating the mother [as a person]—and there was a lot of reasons on their fact sheet—why they didn't want the study to go forward, but that was one of them."

GREGG GONSALVES

"Now it is the only thing we can do years later for people all over the world to prevent mother-to-child infection . . . Maxine and Heidi— There's a bunch of people who were not in T&D who were mainly women who didn't support the trial, and then, there were all these men in T&D, who probably felt more strongly—that they needed to go ahead . . . Now thousands and thousands of women in poor countries are getting it during childbirth, and all of these infants are born HIV-negative."

MAXINE WOLFE

"I regret that we couldn't stop 076. To this day, I think it was a big mistake. I will always think it was a big mistake. The transmission from women to kids was minuscule. In order to save the next one percent of children, we've probably killed many, many women. I think that's a bad trade-off. So, I feel badly that we couldn't stop that. But you know what? It's all about *saving babies*. Linda [Meredith] and I tried to write an article about that in the *Times*, as an op-ed piece. We tried to get it published all over the country, and we could not. And we called it

'Saving Babies.' *Who makes drug policies, the government or Burroughs [Wellcome]?* . . . You say something's going to affect kids—and it doesn't matter if it affects a zillion adults. I regret that, and I regret the people who died."

WHAT WAS REVEALED?

REBECCA PRINGLE SMITH

In discussing the events around 076, Rebecca pointed out to me the dichotomy of what she called "good science versus good medicine." Scientists want studies with placebos, because it gives them sharper results. Both science and industry, in this case Burroughs Wellcome, wanted 076, because science wants data and Burroughs Wellcome wanted larger markets. Science and industry were willing to sacrifice women with HIV, and perhaps the future health of their children, in order to advance treatments and markets. But medicine is another matter. In medicine there is the doctor's point of view, and then there is also the patient.

In 076, "good medicine" from the point of view of Black women doctors meant getting women with HIV, often poor and women of color, into a clinical setting. Getting them a treatment that *might* work, when we knew what would happen if they remained untreated, was their strategy. But in the case of 076, there were three patient constituencies: the women who would get placebo and die, the women who would get AZT and be rendered resistant for future treatments, and the other HIV-positive patients in the future, who would benefit from their sacrifice. Which group of patients should have priority? The living and actual, or the imagined future? As in all matters relating to women and especially women with AIDS, the question is ultimately, *Who will decide?*

Regarding the question of placebo, Rebecca, as a practitioner who often sat on the activist side, also had some interesting contributions.

"At ACT UP, I was trying to talk about the placebo issue and saying, *You know, this monolithic opposition to answers is a mistake. We need access to answers, and in some cases placebo controlled is the way to go, but it depends on the question. And placebo control doesn't mean you take people who think they should be on the drug and you keep them on the placebo till they die. But in some instances, this is a good way to go.* And I remember we were all sitting around talking. I think David [Kirschenbaum] was there, and he was not buying it. He was like, *No. Trials are treatment.* Jim [Eigo] was there, too, and someone was there who was in the Lentinan study at CRI. And I defended it, and I said, *Listen, you know, this is a valid thing.* And this person said, *Well, I think anyone who would do a placebo-controlled trial is a murderer, and anyone who would be in one is a martyr.* And then I went off, and I was like, *Well, you know, I'm not into calling each other murderers here, but suppose there's a drug, a promising new therapy, that's toxic, that kills people. The drug companies are going to say they died of AIDS. They're not going to go with the idea that it was the drug . . .*

"There was a view that some of the nurses at CRI had that if people with AIDS wanted it, we should give them access to it, and I was like, *No. If people with AIDS want it, they can get it, but we need to give them an informed dissent. You don't just go along with it . . .* Jim Eigo's point of view, when we were arguing this, [was] that every arm of every trial should represent a legitimate treatment option for people with AIDS, this is not just good medicine; this is good science . . . Nobody's begging for access to placebos . . . If someone's sure they want the drug, and their doctor and they feel it's best, then it's unethical not to give it to them. If someone's sure that they don't want the drug, then it's not ethical for them to be in the trial. But for people where there is substantial uncertainty who want to participate, they should be allowed to participate. They should be allowed access. And that's called the uncertainty principle."

25

AIDS Hysteria: The Case of Derek Link

Fully understanding how much pressure people in ACT UP were living with is essential to a mature historical view of the divisions in the movement. In some ways, we went insane with grief. One example of how this pain played out was the case of Derek Link.

Being a very young person surrounded by constant death was implicating and terrifying. Watching other people suffer and die was threatening. Why them and not you? Especially as ACT UP became more sexual internally, including across genders, the fear level rose and expressed itself in emotionally reasonable but factually illogical ways. AIDS felt inevitable, and being left behind was unbearable. This combination of difficult factors created a kind of AIDS hysteria inside the ACT UP milieu. For example, unlikely targets imagined themselves followed by the FBI, out of proportion to their effectiveness in the movement. In another case, even though there was no proof of female transmission to anyone except children through childbirth, some lesbians started to practice unnecessary "safe sex," using finger dams for fucking, or dental dams and, in some cases, Saran Wrap for oral sex. When an ACT UP–attended, lesbian public sex back room emerged at Wonder Bar on East Sixth Street in the East Village, it was raised on the floor of the Monday-night meeting as a possible source of HIV infections. I had long been clear that there was no evidence for female-to-female transmission, but at a general meeting at Cooper Union, Maxine Wolfe said to me on the floor, "Women will die because of you."

As the deaths accumulated, ACT UP got crazier, in a sense more apocalyptic, as a reaction to the reality of suffering. Yet perhaps the longest-lasting expression of AIDS hysteria in ACT UP—and later

TAG—happened inside the Treatment and Data Committee, when core member Derek Link was revealed to have falsely claimed to be HIV-positive for almost twenty years.

GREGG GONSALVES

"I think Derek was young and wanted to feel part of a historical moment . . . a lot of us were obsessed and into the work, but I think Derek's identification just . . . his identification with the work and the virus became really superimposed. He's a little pathological because of the other details of his life that have nothing to do with AIDS. Maybe it was just anxiety about being negative and being afraid of seroconverting, or seeing everybody else around him getting sick and dying. But I think in a weird sense, it's an over-identification with the people around him. It's hard to explain."

DAVID BARR

David decided that he needed a support group of gay men who were HIV-positive and who were working full-time in the fight against AIDS. He felt that there were issues that he had around his personal life and his professional life, and surrounding how these two things interact. The lack of any boundaries between work and personal life was increasingly difficult. And so he asked his closest friends, who were also his closest workmates at the time, who were already living in a communal situation, to form a group. "It was all about the meeting and the dinner after the meeting. Mark Harrington, Derek Link, Spencer Cox, Gregg Bordowitz, and Peter Staley, and me."

They met every other week for dinner; they would rotate houses, for seven years. They had a structure to the conversation, where everybody went around and took a turn and said how they were doing and what was going on with them. It wasn't a conversation about work and it wasn't a gossip conversation; it was much more personal, and they all would go into it thinking, *We'll all be with each other as we get sick and die.* Part of the purpose of the group was to create that structure in the present.

"Derek arrived in New York in 1990 from Boston. He was adorable.

A little nerdy boy; cute, as cute as can be. And clearly smart. Immediately attached himself to Treatment and Data. Started coming to the meetings. After a couple of months, he changed his look entirely and became a punk, and had a green Mohawk. And he was like whip-smart. He started learning the stuff; he did really good AIDS work. Whatever the end of this story is, Derek did really important, good AIDS work. Derek and Garance [Franke-Ruta]; I mean, they were kids, they were little kids. Garance wasn't 20 years old . . . They transformed OI [opportunistic infection] research. They created this project where they selected the seven OI drugs . . . They went to Congress, they went to the NIH and said, *You've got to put more effort into OI research. Because we don't know what's going on with this antiviral stuff. And look at all the progress that we could be making treating OIs* . . . oh, fuck . . . It was very important work. Derek also uncovered over fifty million dollars' worth of AIDS research money that was being not spent on AIDS in the National Cancer Institute. That was one of the reasons Sam Broder lost his job. And Derek's work was very important.

"That said, he was very crazy . . . Derek came in; he's a person with AIDS. Joins the support group. He, Derek, once wrote a thing that he handed out on the ACT UP floor: *HIV-negatives get out of our way.* This is during all of this, all the disputes about who we should or should not be meeting with, at T&D, and Derek went on a rant. Derek not only was in a support group with me for seven years, we shared a house together, we traveled the world together. I supervised him for three years at GMHC, and he sat in the cubicle next to me. We eventually learned that every single thing that Derek had said about himself was not true. He was not HIV-positive. His grandparents did not die in the Holocaust. He was not Jewish. His mother is not a paleo botanist who lives in New Orleans. Just on, on, on, and on and on.

"I don't know what's true . . . I know the last version of the truth that I heard. I think he grew up in Kansas. I think. His father, I think, was involved in the aviation industry. Other than that . . . he didn't go to boarding school in England and have a nervous breakdown there. None of that was true. I don't know. The astounding thing about the lying isn't just the extent of the lying; it's how long he lived with it. It was [that] everything about him, about his identity, was a lie. And he lived with us, and—it must have been so exhausting, to have to continually remember all of the components that he had made up. And detailed discussions in the support group about his trip to New Orleans to visit his mother. He wasn't, hadn't even been to New Orleans. His mother didn't live there. It's kind of a great story. But it was terribly upsetting."

Gregg Bordowitz and David had been suspecting that there were things that were just not right about Derek's story. For one, his illness wasn't progressing. He clearly wasn't a long-term nonprogressor, because he said he had three hundred T cells, and it was always three hundred. This was one of many chinks in the story that David kept uncovering. And so one day, David said, *Derek, we got to talk*. They went out to dinner. David said, *Okay, let's start from the beginning. What's your name?*

"And he said his name was really Derek Link, and he just sort of spilled . . . Was there a sense of remorse? Uh—I guess. There was, clearly, there was some guilt. And more, I guess more than guilt, there was, not so much guilt; it was embarrassment. It was embarrassment. There wasn't really an understanding—I tried to continue to be friends with him, and to work it through. But that didn't last very long, because there was never really any remorse, there was never an understanding as to how deeply he betrayed me, all of us, by lying to us all that time. It was like I had this friend that didn't exist."

Derek said that he went to Hunter to study computerized mapping. But David never saw him at Hunter, so he doesn't know if it was true. He also said he was doing computerized mapping on electrical grids in northern Vermont. More than a decade after Derek left ACT UP, Mark Harrington got an email from a woman saying that she had been going out with this guy named Derek Link. And she'd Googled his name, and all this AIDS stuff came up. She asked him about it, and he told her that he'd fabricated this story about his brother dying of AIDS, and that's how he had gotten involved. Mark wrote back and said, *None of that is true; he has a history of lying, and you should know that.* Gregg Gonsalves talked about Derek in his ACT UP Oral History Project interview, and Derek let Gregg know that he had seen it. But that was the last anyone heard. When these interviews went up on our website, ActUpOralHistory.org, Jim Hubbard and I also heard from Derek. He said he wanted to be interviewed and wanted an opportunity to clarify.

So we set up an interview date. He confirmed it a few days before, and then he never showed up.

GARANCE FRANKE-RUTA

I shared this story with Garance during our interview and she knew nothing about it, having not been involved with ACT UP people in years.

"Oh my God, that explains so much! . . . There was one time I was in San Francisco. And they were selling, like, ddC through the [buyers club] in San Francisco. And I think I brought some back for him, because he couldn't get it in New York. And then there was some issue where he got this dog from the pound, and the dog ate his ddC, and then the dog died. And so then there was no dog. But I don't know if I even met the dog. It was just suddenly, like, there was none of this medication . . . We were roommates. I didn't live with him very long. I remember that he had a lot of issues."

26

The Split: January 1992

In interviews, many people characterize the split as theoretical: between people who wanted to work inside and people who wanted to work outside. But the split could also be seen as experiential, between people who were allowed inside, and people who were kept outside. How deeply does experience impact ideology? As for me, I really did not participate in the split. I went to all the meetings and watched the confrontations between the most polarized personalities. But I never took a side. I stayed in ACT UP after the split in 1992 but soon moved on later that year, when I co-founded the Lesbian Avengers, a direct-action group for women.

GREGG GONSALVES (TAG)

At the time of the split, Gregg felt there was a huge tension building between T&D, and Maxine, Heidi, and some of the women in ACT UP. There was a group who felt like T&D was making too many compromises by talking to the government and meeting with the drug companies, a belief that was only underscored when Risa and Linda ran into Mark in D.C. Gregg recalled that Derek Link started going after Maxine and a faction on the floor that was aligned with her with "a screed" demanding, *HIV-negatives get out of our way.* "In retrospect, it was just insane," because Derek was lying about his status.

MARK HARRINGTON (TAG)

During this period, Mark told himself that there was an ideological conflict in the group, and that those who stayed in ACT UP didn't like the style of activism that had evolved within T&D, which was centered on "trying to understand and change scientific culture and institutions, with political means, using citizen power." Mark believes that T&D's ideas were influenced by Michel Foucault, whom he and others had read when they were younger. These were ideas about how to engage with institutions that are your *opponent*, ideas that were based on "a different kind of antagonism." In other words, Mark believes that despite becoming insiders, T&D was still antagonistic to the NIH or to drug companies when they met with them. But sometimes, they would work with them on one thing and then fight with them about another thing. Back in New York, this led to a lot more unpleasant and very painful debates "about who we were and what we should be and how we should do things." This was in March of 1991. By August, there were serious discussions going on inside Treatment and Data about whether they could, in fact, stay in ACT UP, or whether they should leave.

"At one point, it was proposed that there be a six-month moratorium on meetings with people in the NIH system. And then other people wrote manifestos that HIV-negative people should get out of our way and people accused each other of slowing down research."

Like Mark, most of the people I interviewed about the split mistakenly remembered "The Moratorium" as a halt on all meetings between ACT UP and the government. But, actually, by the time it came to the floor for a vote, it was a halt on all meetings *about women* without group approval. Technically, this would not have affected T&D because they were not meeting with the government about women, and in a sense, the proposal was a recognition of defeat by the people working on women-with-AIDS issues, trying to systematize some kind of control of their own territory. As often happens, reality is too complex, and a false but easier to remember version of a moratorium proposal as punitive and sprawling has substituted for the historical reality.

THE MORATORIUM

TRACY MORGAN

"Maxine, I remember, asked me, and I remember being so surprised to be asked . . . *We're going to have a strategy brunch*, Max says. *Larry*

[Kramer] and I, we're putting this together. We want to get some people to put together strategy papers or something, and talk, so we can begin to think about strategy. And I was pretty surprised that she chose me. It was at the Center in a big room. It wasn't attended by that many people, as I recall . . . Larry, Maxine, myself, [Bill] Dobbs. I remember David Barr was there for sure. Heidi [Dorow] was there. I was very nervous . . . I remember being palpably nervous, and I remember writing and rewriting. It was handwritten, right? It was weird, but I didn't have a computer yet. Maxine had sensed I had an idea that was really not fully formed, she's pretty perceptive, so she sensed I had some nascent something."

Tracy looked back at her experiences in the reproductive rights movement, and said, *You know, the reproductive rights movement suffers from this kind of sort of insider politics . . . Who's in charge of the reproductive rights movement now? They're all people who have salaries.* She wondered if ACT UP wasn't at risk of heading in the same sort of direction, that would lose the best thing that we had, which was this incredible group of people who were "very obsessive and meticulous and thorough-going and very bright and very tenacious." These qualities created social change. She was noticing a drift in the organization to an Insider-Outsider fissure, which just struck her as very sad and tragic, because, Tracy thought, *The reproductive rights movement doesn't have a movement. They have a demonstration every two years that a million people come to, but what's happening on the local level? Nothing.* She felt that ACT UP needed to stay alive and lively on the local level, or everything was ruined.

"I said something like, *We're all vulnerable to the temptations of approval by those in power and those in authority. Nobody's beyond that. But let's hold hands with each other rather than let those that are in power divide and conquer us* . . . Well, [David] Barr [responded], as I recall—it was terrifying for me. I thought, *Oh my God, what have I done?* Barr said to me, *You know, what you're saying would kill me.*"

Tracy's idea was for a six-month moratorium on meetings with government officials; instead, ACT UP would pour our energy back into direct action and to working together. Tracy didn't think David was right, even though she understood his feelings. "And perhaps if I had been HIV-positive and I had Anthony Fauci's ear, I would have the fantasy that I, too, was going to be saved by that. But to my mind, that was just a fantasy."

There were distinctly different logics colliding in this moment. Tracy Morgan was coming from the perspective of her experience. The women-with-AIDS agenda was not advancing. She saw the mostly male T&D advancing their treatment agenda through their relationships with government, won by mass actions put on by the entire organization at the FDA and NIH. And she saw those men not using their new connections to help the women-with-AIDS movement in ACT UP. She saw the train leaving the station and leaving many people behind. As a survival strategy, she wanted T&D to look inward, and reconnect to a holistic AIDS politic in order to fix the relationship with the rest of ACT UP.

David Barr had an entirely different perspective. His experience showed him that the closer he and his friends in T&D were to power, the more they could help themselves stay alive. And so he was gazing up and not back. In some deep way he believed in an ethical trickle-down system, that whatever was won through these relationships between (mostly) men in ACT UP and in the government—men who identified with one another—would ultimately not only save his own life but also benefit all people with AIDS. He had faith in the power of the T&D/government relationship.

Tracy justified her long-range thinking based on the history of the co-optation and defanging of previous radical movements by bureaucracy.

David based his immediate thinking on his own feeling of himself in danger and the progress that his own strategy had already yielded.

It is impossible to evaluate who was right, or if they were both wrong.

One clear question is, What was David Barr's, and the splinter group TAG's, actual subsequent contribution after ACT UP? And could they have achieved these same concrete things if they had stayed and repaired the relationship? That is for another historian to address.

We do know that in 1996, four years after the split, protease inhibitors came into general use, and they remain the basis for the standard of care today that keeps people with HIV living a full life span, if they have health insurance. These drugs were not developed or released because of ACT UP directly. Only the culture around the drugs was transformed by our activism.

And we do know that many people living in America who are HIV-positive do not have full access to that range of care, because the health-care movement necessary to make the drugs available never manifested. We don't know, if ACT UP had healed, if it could have become, created, or contributed to that health-care movement.

We also know that twenty-seven years after ACT UP split, *The New York Times*, on May 28, 2019, published a piece by Apoorva Mandavilli in which she wrote:

> Women make up just over half of the 35 million people living with H.I.V. worldwide, and the virus is the leading cause of death among women of reproductive age . . . Even in the southern United States, new infections in young women are helping to sustain the epidemic.

The reporter echoes the concerns of Linda Meredith and others that women and men have different reactions to H.I.V. infection, but gay men make up the bulk of participants in clinical trials:

> A 2016 analysis by the charity AMFAR found that women represented a median of 11 percent in cure trials. Trials of antiretroviral drugs fared little better; 19 percent of the participants were women.

This matters because it is broadly understood that men's and women's immune systems respond differently to HIV:

> The immune system in women initially responds forcefully, maintaining tight control over the virus for five to seven years . . . the female hormone estrogen seems to lull H.I.V. into a dormant state. That may sound like a good thing, but the dormant virus is harder for the immune system, or drugs, to kill . . . Gay men have formed strong support networks that alert potential participants to clinical trials, and they often live in cities where the research is conducted.
>
> By contrast, women with H.I.V. tend to be isolated, and may not advocate for themselves. They may need help with

child care or transportation, or be more comfortable with female doctors—accommodations few trials offer.

For women of color, there is an additional hurdle: mistrust resulting from a long history of exploitation by medical
researchers.

It is clear, decades later, that women are still not getting the attention and services that they need.

Tracy never brought the moratorium proposal to the floor. "Maxine
did that."

MAXINE WOLFE

"Okay—the moratorium. Actually, it was Tracy Morgan's idea that
there should be a moratorium. And the reason she decided to do that
was, because . . . the Treatment and Data Committee were meeting with
the very people who we were fighting against . . . And this is where, I
think, that you know, what I brought to ACT UP was a little different
than what other people did, which is—I had been a political person for
a really long time. I don't get crazed about individual people, because
if it wasn't for this person, it would be somebody else—that's my attitude. There's a category, you know what I mean? So [Tracy] came on
a national women's conference call and had this proposal that we had
this moratorium on anybody meeting with any government officials,
because it was undermining the work that we were doing, blah, blah,
blah. I always thought that the good thing about ACT UP was that
people did both, and that that had been an ethos in ACT UP for a really long time. And I thought that the one-two whammy was the best
way to go. So it was a good cop/bad cop kind of thing. So I was not in
favor of that, at all.

"I said that I thought what worked equally as well was *everybody*
should talk about it. The government couldn't claim that one person
spoke to them. If you let women all over the country demand to meet
with the CDC, and let them say what they want to, then it would be
the same thing as not anybody talking to them, because they would get
so many different points of view, that who would they claim spoke for
anybody.

"In that discussion, Tracy backtracked and she got it to be that people should stop meeting with the government about women's stuff. And people voted and they wanted to do it. I personally couldn't have cared more or less. I didn't think it was a great idea. I thought it wouldn't be bad to try it, *about women's stuff*. . . Then, we all said that we would bring it to ACT UP. I have never felt that bringing something to ACT UP was a big deal. People vote it up. They vote it down. That's what it's about. That's what a democratic organization is. I always felt that that was a good thing to do. But somehow, word got back to Mark, and the people that were on—a certain group of people on Treatment and Data—that we were going to call for this moratorium. It was going to prevent people from doing anything. And they had already decided, in a way—that whole grouping of men—that their interest lay in pushing the drug stuff. And, unfortunately, their view of things, which was that politics was separate from medicine, prevailed, eventually. But, at that point, that was not what ACT UP was. The beauty of ACT UP was that it was about the fact that medicine is political.

"Weeks were going by. There was all of this tension. So I figured, *Fuck, I'll present it. I don't care.* So I got up on the floor of ACT UP, and I put it on the back table, and I basically said, *This was something that was on the women's phone call and we should discuss it and talk about it* and whatever. So that's why it gets attributed to me, because I was the public face of it—but I wasn't the public face of it because I thought it was the best thing to do. I was the public face of it because I brought it to the floor of ACT UP, because I was trying to get rid of that tension . . . and it was voted down . . . and I was fine about people voting it down."

Maxine recalled that TAG was going to split off anyway because they had become convinced that the way to proceed was to separate politics from medicine. They would sit on government committees, and wanted to take money from drug companies. "It was whatever they wanted to get out of it for themselves." Maxine remembered that TAG tried to reorganize the NIH in a manner that "would literally give them control of it." But this plan did not work. TAG claimed "that there were social issues and there were medical issues, and that they were about the medical issues." In the end, Maxine accepted the philosophical and historical view that groups have their time frame and they don't last forever, and that the level of mass movement involvement that ACT UP had was hard to sustain.

TREATMENT ACTION GROUP (TAG)

MARK HARRINGTON

Peter Staley "with his love of affinity group and guerrilla-like actions" had established a group called the Treatment Action Guerillas in August of 1991, and their mission was to go Jesse Helms's house and unroll a giant condom on his roof that said SENATOR HELMS, DEADLIER THAN THE VIRUS. The name TAG was already available when, as Mark recalled, there were agonizing talks in Treatment and Data about what to do about all the tension that was happening in ACT UP, and whether it was better to stay and fight or whether it would be better to leave and form a dedicated organization focused on research and treatment. There had been other groups that had been spinning off around that time, like Housing Works, but in much less hostile circumstances. Mark remembered that they didn't want to leave, or at least, that *he* didn't want to leave. The great majority of people in ACT UP didn't want them to leave. There was really a polarization between two groups, neither of which, Mark believes, spoke for the majority. "I think the majority wished that we would just work it out."

But he doesn't recall that majority having much of a voice at the time.

"We were on the edges and we were shouting at each other. It was very unpleasant. It was definitely getting in the way of us being effective and doing our work. So eventually we decided that it was not effective to keep on fighting . . . Personal attacks were being made also including Peter, who had, by then, had been appointed to the board of directors of amfAR, [and] had requested some money from Burroughs Wellcome for amfAR's community-based clinical trials network. And then, some people said that was a conflict of interest . . . In January, we had a meeting at Charlie Franchino's house—this is '92—and we decided we would go to T&D on, I think, January 22, and we would say that we were forming a separate organization that . . . [was] open by invitation to people that you feel like asking to join it."

TAG became a 501(c)(3) nonprofit organization with a board and a staff and consultants. It also eventually became Mark's day job, and he assumed the salaried position of executive director of TAG, solving his employment problem. The organization reached an annual budget of six hundred thousand dollars, with four full-time staff and the ability to pay consultants, and a newsletter. "So we became a small, professional organization, out of being a larger, volunteer activist organization, and the transition was very painful, from one to the other."

DAVID BARR (TAG)

"I think there were a lot of crazy people in the room, that were just attracted to us, you know. And they became problematic. They took up a lot of time. They created disputes on the floor that would take all this time and energy . . . I think the agenda that we were working on in Treatment and Data, we were seeing a lot of success with. It was moving faster and in a different way than other equally important agendas were moving. How the CDC was addressing the needs of women with AIDS was an agenda that was moving at a very different pace than drug development activism was moving. And that meant that the tactics that needed to be used were different . . . The CDC is a very different place. There's a different institutional culture. I think, most important, though, is that the agenda around addressing the needs, just identifying the needs of women with AIDS—then and, even more so, now—is an agenda that has to do with sexism; it's an agenda that has to do with poverty; and those are bigger, more complicated, longer-term issues than how you get a drug approved. Right? . . . And the pharmaceutical industry, as difficult as they were for us to work with them, had no problem with getting their drugs approved faster. Right? There was a lot of common ground on different ends of the table in the stuff that we were doing."

I asked David what he could have done differently.

"Been a little less arrogant . . . It's not like we all didn't, on all ends of this discussion, spend time trying to come to some terms, and find mutual ground. But I think we could have done it more."

ANN NORTHROP

Ann believes that the split occurred between "people who were interested in immediately saving their own lives versus those who had a bigger vision, bigger issues, or were interested in saving other people's lives." Ann saw that TAG wanted to get funding from pharmaceutical companies to do their work, and that was certainly unacceptable within ACT UP. If that was their focus, then they were, inevitably, going to have to break off, because that was not going to work within the group. She also recalls a sense of territorial control on the part of TAG.

"Their feeling that women wanting to work on issues pertaining to women was hurtful to them was wrong, and to bring issues of race into it—and they saw that as distracting or whatever, I think that was wrong. So I think they were short-sighted . . . They've done a lot of work with pharmaceutical companies in doing drug research and I'm sure some of that has been productive. The suspicion among the women of that group, I think, was also a little over the top."

PART IX

Living and Dying the Mass Death Experience

After the split, hundreds of people remained in ACT UP—people with AIDS and HIV needing treatment, and people working in a vast array of arenas for a diverse range of people with AIDS. As the deaths increased, ACT UP continued with a newly constituted third chapter of Treatment and Data, while in the face of unending suffering, the street activists intensified their strategies, doubled down on their commitments, and pushed their imaginations even further.

27

Treatment and Data #3

Most of ACT UP remained after the split and carried on doing work. A new core of treatment activists emerged, some of whom also attended TAG meetings while carrying on research and advocacy for ACT UP. Though the departure of twelve or so people into TAG was emotionally devastating, in reality there were still hundreds of people in ACT UP. And, looking back, we can now see that some of the most visceral public actions by ACT UP took place after the split. Yet the feeling of the split was, at the time, almost unbearable. After all, to be in ACT UP was to constantly lose the dead, and now there was the loss of the living. And worse, it was willful.

But in reality, ACT UP continued its hard work and continued to work on treatments. It wasn't only TAG that cared about finding drugs that worked. A new team rose to fill the seats of ACT UP T&D. And what typified T&D #3's strategic approach was its intense focus on individual drugs. Each member adopted one drug or illness or protocol and became an expert, engaging science and pharma on behalf of that specific project. Central to this new wave of treatment activists were Dudley Saunders, Kevin Robert Frost, George Carter, and Rick Loftus.

DUDLEY SAUNDERS

Dudley Saunders grew up in Louisville, Kentucky. He came to New York, after attending Northwestern, as a writer, musician, and performance artist, and worked the midnight shift word processing in a law firm. He came to ACT UP in 1987 and couldn't connect. "Like a lot of people in ACT UP, I had some kind of social dysfunction." Still, he stayed. Later that year, he and his lover, Chris Stewart, tested positive together and did not qualify for any experimental treatments. Dudley started off doing simple tasks in ACT UP, like photocopying.

"The only thing I knew how to do was to kind of clean up. And so I operated that way. And that was that true for a long time." Then he joined Treatment and Data after the TAG group left in 1992, and "I was allowing myself to be stupid. Because at the time, you know, these people just seemed so incredibly smart. And a lot of people in ACT UP were very, you know, intimidated by them. *These people can save my life; they're the [geniuses]; they can do the talking.* And the shock to me—I mean . . . I started the process of teaching myself the science."

In this third incarnation of T&D, the group put together a study group to study clinical trial design, having long discussions about what a certain clinical trial could reveal. Pilot studies can reveal that there is something interesting about a treatment, which then requires a full clinical trial to determine whether that's really true or not. Clinical trials would ultimately come out and say, *This is crap, it doesn't do anything.* But the pilot study made it sound promising enough to independently investigate further. So there was a group of people who were fighting to really, really believe in a treatment that science determined didn't have any value. "Talk about wish fulfillment problems. People wanted to believe that there was some kind of magic bullet, and that the scientists just weren't right."

Dudley worked on immune modulators. Interleukin-2 was a cytokine, a type of protein used as a way of clearing infected cells. He would learn about the modulators. And then he would go to conferences and talk to the scientists and try to find out where the science was. Dudley remembered going a conference on immune reconstitution—he would sit in the meetings, and then get up and try to redirect the discussion toward the treatment possibilities. *How can we think about this in terms of the patient?* The scientists were receptive but esoteric. And the repetition was maddening, as was the continual waste of resources. "We were constantly finding research grants given to people to do studies that didn't need to be done, which were designed to answer a question that had been answered by three other studies before."

Dudley also focused on mucosal immunity—gut health—because there were a lot of HIV-positive people who had constant diarrhea for no reason at all. This was a mysterious opportunistic infection. People were dying because they couldn't absorb any food, which just ran through them undigested. He would approach scientists with these issues directly, and try to get them to talk about it. In the end, it was a triple combo therapy, in which three different medications given together lowered the viral load and made a lot of stomach issues go away. When the patient did get the virus suppressed, immune constitution would come back and the gut would heal.

Dudley dealt mostly with scientists who were all over the country. He'd usually run into them at the conferences. Whether they were working directly for a pharmaceutical company was neither here nor there, because they were usually funded by a pharmaceutical company somehow. "A lot of the scientists knew about ACT UP and they agreed with what ACT UP was doing. So you could walk into a room and say, *Hi, I'm from ACT UP.*" He also joined TAG as well.

"I had had pneumonia that winter. It wasn't PCP, but my T cells were coming down. I was, like, 320 or something. And, you have to understand that at that time what that meant—what I knew I had to look forward to—what I was not fearing was death. I was fearing the moment when my life became about staying alive, managing illness. And I knew that the minute I would take my first AZT or what have you, it would be the beginning of the end. What this meant to me was the possibility— well, maybe there could be an extended future . . . At the time I started in Treatment and Data, there was a belief that we've got to do something different. We've got to look in a different way. So we were pulling back and approaching it from looking at the immune system directly; looking at other things that we could do. *Maybe we're looking at it in the wrong way. Maybe looking at the virus is not the right thing to do.* So we were kind of casting a wider net . . . It was a big push to do a lot of basic science, because a lot of the basic science had fallen apart."

KEVIN ROBERT FROST

Kevin Robert Frost was born in Tripoli, the capital of Libya. His father was a career air force man. Kevin grew up in Texas, went to college in Austin, and was a music major in school. Then he moved to Dallas and worked for the Moving Target Theater Company. There was a production in Dallas of *The Normal Heart*, which Kevin got to see. He moved to New York in 1990 to be a musician and got a job in the classical music section of Tower Records. One late night, Larry Kramer walked in.

"He was looking for an opera, some obscure opera recording, and I told him I'd help him see if we had it. After a few minutes, I finally said to him, *Listen, I just want to tell you that I saw your play,* The Normal Heart, *and it really, really moved me.* And Larry being Larry, looked at me and said, *Oh, that's great. So what the fuck are you doin' about it?"*

Kevin joined ACT UP's Treatment and Data Committee. He was one of a handful who, like Dudley, remained in T&D and also became members of TAG.

The specialization Kevin took on was AIDS-related blindness, CMV retinitis. Ganciclovir was the first drug treatment, but there was a new drug coming through the pipeline called foscarnet, owned by Astra, which was starting a trial that would compare the two drugs. Kevin immediately became the CMV guy in T&D, and started writing articles about it for treatment issues at GMHC and other places. It was difficult, because most people weren't diagnosed with CMV until they had fewer than fifty T cells. So the person had to be very sick by the time they were diagnosed. In the very first trial, the average life expectancy for someone in the study was nine and a half months. Young men (no women, of course) went into this study to go on terrible, toxic drugs, which they would tolerate for about nine and a half months, and then die. It was very difficult and very emotional for the staff and for everybody who was involved in the trials at that time. Both foscarnet and ganciclovir had to be infused through a Hickman catheter, which meant the person was hooked up to a drip, but the patient had to get it so frequently that these men lived with Hickman catheters, which were put into their chest, because it was an easy administration for an IV and went immediately into the bloodstream that way.

The foscarnet/ganciclovir trial was designed to be a progression study, which meant that it was designed to look at how fast the CMV retinitis disease progressed in one group versus the other, with the hope of finding out that one of these drugs was better at controlling the retinitis than the other. But CMV is endemic, an infection of the entire body beyond just the eye, and so most people who would get CMV retinitis were suffering CMV disease in other places, like in their intestines and other locations that weren't so easily identifiable. In the end, people on foscarnet were living three to four months longer than the people who were on ganciclovir. It was a very controversial finding at the time, and a lot of people argued, *Well, it isn't designed to be a mortality outcome*, but there it was. It was published in *The New England Journal of Medicine*, and it was considered an important study.

"Of course, the Astra people jumped all over that to declare foscarnet the second coming. But foscarnet was a horrible drug. I mean, it was a terrible drug. It had to be administered more often than ganciclovir, and it was incredibly toxic to the people who took it, and the side effects were just devastating. So there was an argument that even though people on foscarnet might have lived two or three months longer, the quality of their life was lower, and that led to a series of quality-of-life studies, which sort of followed to try and articulate even more clearly what the differences were. But they were both horrible drugs. They were both horrible for the people who were on them."

AZT caused anemia, especially in those days when people were getting really high doses. Ganciclovir, also a nucleoside analogue, caused anemia. People were having to choose between taking AZT and taking ganciclovir, because the anemia was such that a person couldn't do both. Basically, the choice was to die of AIDS (not take AZT) or go blind (not take ganciclovir). Foscarnet, when it was approved, was very expensive. It cost fifteen thousand dollars a year or more, and there were many protests in Massachusetts at Astra's headquarters, but the company didn't budge. "They were absolutely intractable about it."

CMV, like a lot of opportunistic infections, diminished rapidly when the drug cocktail was introduced. As soon as the viral load was driven down, CD4 counts would recover, and people would be at lower and lower risk for opportunistic infections. Pneumocystis, Kaposi sarcoma, CMV retinitis, and cryptococcal meningitis all started to diminish at a very rapid pace in the aftermath of 1997 and the introduction of protease inhibitors. Today, thankfully, CMV retinitis is very rare.

RICK LOFTUS

Rick Loftus was born in Detroit in 1969. After graduating from Yale, he moved to New York in 1991, when his partner got a job at *The New*

York Times Magazine. In fall of 1992, the first year after the ACT UP/ TAG split, Rick joined ACT UP's T&D #3, and he found the meeting packed and robust. There were about fifty people in the post-split T&D, and about fifteen people who were actively working on research and had projects to present and report on. There was always a second and third and fourth row of people who were there to listen and learn about their own treatment.

"It was the most amazing experience in self-education I've ever had. It certainly completely conditioned how I've approached my education on medical issues ever since, because I learned all kinds of stuff, on my own—immunology, virology, pharmacokinetics . . . I was reading huge amounts . . . going to conferences and presenting at ACT UP floor meetings, and people would come up to me and ask me, *Hey, are you a doctor? Because, I just got this test result* . . . I remember—after finally entering UCSF, as a medical student and then as a resident—looking back and thinking—*My God, we were operating at beyond PhD level, in our routine discussions.* That even applies—ACT UP Golden Gate, here in San Francisco—same deal. The kinds of things that people would bring up—the insights, the ideas. And then I would go back to my lab and say, *Well you know, blah, blah, blah, blah,* and I would present something that some bartender had observed at a T&D meeting or treatment committee meeting, and you'd have this bigwig fronts-of-the-newspapers, doctor-scientist say, *Really? Oh my God, what an interesting idea—I'd never thought of that, but that's true, isn't it?*"

After about ten months, Rick also joined TAG, so like with Dudley and Kevin, the separation between treatment committees for a while was really thin, while their social functions were quite different. Treatment and Data #3 was more approachable. TAG was meeting behind closed doors.

"[TAG was] probably meeting with a lot of big lobbyists and people in suits. And, for a lot of common folks who were trying to just get educated about their treatment options, that didn't seem very approachable. And TAG . . . had this image of being the ivory tower . . . People sort of perceived them as being these sort of über professionals. They were lawyers and doctors and well-to-do, and probably maybe would have never been activists, except that they got an HIV diagnosis, or somebody they loved was sick and all of a sudden they realized that they needed to be involved and do something . . . As cool as it was to be able to sit in TAG meetings and hear people talk about meetings with the FDA and the NIH—I mean, certainly we had people in Treatment and Data Committee who did that kind of stuff, too—it was important to continue my involvement with ACT UP New York because of those floor meetings, because that was where you'd have a hundred people filling the room, who were not going to be sitting at an FDA committee meeting, and probably couldn't spend a lot of time, listening to a lot of jargonese about what had happened at that meeting. They just wanted to know—they would come and tell you, *My partner just got really sick, and he's on his sixth treatment for MAC and his doctor doesn't know what to do—what do we do?* That's where those people would come to you. They weren't coming to the TAG meetings. The TAG meetings were closed. And for me, as an activist, *Why the hell am I doing all of this?* It's to help people like that. I guess that's in a way, a presaging of my work as a physician—it's just like, built larger, but that's the same thing I do as a doctor now. They come in and I have to treat them."

GEORGE CARTER

George Carter grew up in a small town, Greensburg, Pennsylvania. He dropped out of Carnegie Mellon when he lost his financial aid and joined a punk band, and spent about eight years as a needle junkie in San Francisco. In 1984, he moved to the Lower East Side and OD'd, and then relocated to Montreal and then back to New York in 1989, and finally quit heroin. A friend brought him to an ACT UP meeting, where Garance Franke-Ruta was speaking, and he was so blown away by her that he stayed. Eventually, he got involved in Alternative Treatments.

ALTERNATIVE TREATMENTS

In 1991, George started publishing the *AIDS Chart*, a comprehensive list of opportunistic infections and their treatments, and continued this service for over a decade. It included material about cells, immune modulators, cytokines, new antibiotics that were in clinical trials, what was known, and what was unknown, and followed all the latest medical literature. He was reviewing data, discussing people's experiences with side effects, and the differences with drugs that might be off-label or generic. He included botanical interventions, too: plants, roots, bark, leaves; botanicals and nutrition, and of course eating well, stress reduction, and anything else that could have a significant impact on outcome.

While working on the *AIDS Chart*, George started to attend some meetings of ACT UP's Alternative Treatments Committee. One of the conveners, Jon Greenberg, became his hero because he was saying exactly what George had been thinking. *Some of this stuff looks damned interesting. It seems to be keeping some people alive a lot longer. Why don't we do clinical trials and figure out if this stuff works?* There was a series of conferences called the Keystone Symposia, in Albuquerque in 1993, where Tony Fauci had given a presentation on superantigens, a deadly toxin. George went up to the microphone and said, *Dr. Fauci. There are people out there who are using a number of different interventions with a significant dearth of data. And I'm wondering, when is the NIH going to begin to do clinical studies of things like bitter melon and curcumin and glycyrrhiza?* And he could feel the temperature in the room plummeting as the scientists heard this litany of plants and vitamins.

"There's this cultural identification with those types of interventions as being flaky. And ineffectual. And certainly not as good as a drug. Then of course there's simply the monetary issue. You can't patent herbs and vitamins and things like that, so you can't make billions of dollars on it, so who the fuck cares?"

George became involved with Maxine, Avram, and a group inside ACT UP called the McClintock Project, named after geneticist Barbara McClintock. It was intended to be a kind of Manhattan Project on pathogenesis and the way HIV causes AIDS; specifically, how does it disregulate immune systems? The project received some very stiff opposition from some people within ACT UP who felt that this was not a good way to utilize resources. George found those arguments "somewhat despicable." He thought it would provide a lot more information about how the disease operates.

"They bought the notion that the only way we were going to find treatments for HIV was to follow the capitalist model, because that's what existed. And anything more radical than that, that was a threat to that, would stymie further research and development of drugs . . . The McClintock Project was not about drug development. It was about understanding how HIV causes AIDS . . . by collecting a group of scientists from disparate fields into a center or a site where their entire focus and effort would be—and well funded—would be to determine how HIV causes AIDS; and with that deeper understanding, understand better ways to treat the drug, from not only [an] antiretroviral perspective, but from a vaccine perspective . . . To the extent that pathogenesis work was being done, I think it was mostly being done at NIH. Drug companies don't do that; they don't care. What drug companies do—if they do anything at all, and not just wait until some small company comes up with an idea that they then purchase, or the NIH comes up with a drug—to the extent they do anything, what they do is drug development. And what they'll do is, they'll look at the protease enzyme, and then get a 3D crystal structure, maybe, and then try to figure out how to fit a drug into the pocket of the protease. But that's what they're interested in; they're interested only in the antiviral approach."

George believed the reason clinical studies of complementary alternative medicine were needed was "to bring science back into healthcare research. And science has been destroyed by the pharmaceutical industry." He felt that the industry dominated universities and hospital research, had taken over government research, and had turned it all into marketing tools to sell more drugs to people. "The real benefit of drugs gets lost in the haze of bullshit."

LIFE INSIDE ACT UP

KEVIN ROBERT FROST

Kevin's social life was ACT UP. His friends in ACT UP were the people he socialized with, went to actions with, went to meetings on Monday nights with, and went to T&D with on Wednesdays. For those years when he was involved, it was all-consuming and incredibly empowering. "ACT UP taught me that . . . you also sometimes had to challenge authority. It's that Margaret Mead saying. *Never doubt that a small group of individuals can change the world; they're the only ones who ever have.*"

DUDLEY SAUNDERS

Dudley go-go danced for ACT UP at Mars one time. He remembered that at ACT UP, he always wanted to flirt, because there were some very sexy guys there.

"And there were guys that were sexy because they were so driven and uninterested in you, which made them seem wonderfully unattainable. But I actually never really saw it really connect—in fact, there were usually people who would kind of avoid you—avoid me, sexually, because I was in ACT UP with them . . . Too close, you know . . . Later, I would run into a lot of people in sex clubs. There came a point in my life where it dawned on me that if I was going out to a bar and trying to talk someone up and pick them up—when I was just horny, I didn't really want to get to know them at all. It was a huge waste—it was like a misdirect, you know. So, it was much cleaner—like, to do sexual fast food in some kind of sex club; get it over with quick and get home, and then if you want to date, you date . . . I remember going to Club Bijou 82 on Fourth Street and Second Avenue . . . At that time, safe sex was the easiest thing in the world—it was just what you did. We were all in this together. I never had to think about it. It was so simple. In fact, safe sex was a problem before I got into ACT UP, which we've now seen in studies, the more disconnected you are from the gay community, the more likely you are, you know, to have unsafe sex. And, uh, once I got connected, it was fine. It was just kind of understood. There was no embarrassment about condoms. It was just matter of fact. But, then, AIDS was a part of our lives, where AIDS isn't really a part of people's lives now. Because *AIDS is a problem that people with AIDS have. People with HIV have this problem.* And, you know, I got to say, in a horrible way, at the time, it was really politically incorrect or, it was shameful to avoid people who had HIV sexually. It was just an outrage."

Dudley recalled that for a lot of gay men, there was significant shame around being gay.

"And then, to have gotten yourself infected—even if you'd done it before you knew anything. You'd done this dirty thing, and gotten this dirty disease, just as, you know, you deserved to get. You had nothing to be angry about. And, somehow, we did these things that tapped into this rage that people didn't know they had—didn't know they could have. I think people were surprised by it. Now, living in a state of rage, also makes you crazy. And so, maybe it touched into a wellspring of anger, and drew people to it who really couldn't handle the anger, once they had it out."

28

Ashes Action: October 5, 1992

DAVID ROBINSON

David Robinson grew up in Livingston, New Jersey, went to Princeton, and got an MFA in dance at NYU. Many people remember coming to ACT UP and seeing him facilitating meetings in a dress or skirt and earrings. "I was in dance school at the time and exploring the relationship between movement and gender, gesture and the way you hold your body."

WARREN KRAUSE'S LOVE AND DEATH

David met his partner, Warren Krause, in 1989. Warren was living in Atlanta and came up to Gay Pride, in New York. David saw him marching and thought he was really cute. Warren invited David down to Atlanta. David took him up on it and fell for him pretty quickly.

Warren knew he was HIV-positive. "He didn't tell me that first time, though it was totally safe sex. But when I went down there, to see him for a few days, yeah. He took me for a walk in the park and told me."

Warren and David were very different from each other. Warren had grown up on a dairy farm in Connecticut. His parents were Jehovah's Witnesses, and his mother was especially devout. He was dyslexic, which David didn't know until after he died; David just knew that he had had a lot of trouble getting through school, and that he didn't read very well. Warren ended up in Atlanta bartending, doing drugs, and having lots of sex, so by the time David met him, almost everyone Warren knew had died. He had about three surviving gay male friends. Warren was ten years older than David was, "but he looked fantastic."

"He was convinced that he was going to fight; that he was going to beat this. And here I am, with this logical mind. I said, *Well, yeah, there is, even though most people with the disease seem to just die, there are some people who are these long-term survivors. He could be one of them.* So I just committed to that."

Warren didn't fit in with David's friends, and New York was not where he wanted to be. David wasn't going to move down to Atlanta. Then David got into grad school in San Francisco, but the spring before they were going to move, Warren ended up in the hospital down at Grady Memorial. He had lost his health insurance, so he had to be in a public hospital, and it was awful; they initially left him for fourteen hours, writhing in pain. David flew down to Atlanta to be with him, and Warren recovered, but not fully. Soon after, the first KS lesion appeared on his foot. But they still thought, *Okay, we'll handle it.* That summer, they moved to San Francisco. Warren was still vibrant, and things were going fine. Gedalia Braverman had moved, too, and David and Gedali joined San Francisco's ACT UP Golden Gate.

Then Warren got very sick. Amphotericin B was the prescribed drug for meningitis in his spine. David called up Michael Nesline, who was now a nurse. Michael told him that people who had failed on amphotericin B could use fluconazole, which had a lot fewer side effects. Some people used that as first-line treatment, and they were having success with it.

David became a full-time caregiver. Warren did rebound with the help of fluconazole, and he was looking for other options beyond what was offered medically. My friend the writer Bo Houston had had a seemingly miraculous turnaround from an oxygen treatment from a Swiss doctor. Bo met with Warren and gave him the bare facts of how it had been before. Bo hadn't been able to even get out of bed. And then he went to see this doctor, because he had heard about it, and he came back healthy, out and about in the world again. David and Warren decided it was worth the risk. David wrote to everyone he knew, every acquaintance, and asked if they could contribute financially. Because Warren had to fly to Switzerland, it cost several thousand dollars. In the end, it didn't work at all for Warren, not a bit. In retrospect, David realized that Bo had been on AZT. And the Swiss doctor actually made patients stop AZT and all major meds they were on. Stopping AZT was probably really good for Bo, and good for a lot of people, because it was so toxic. Warren, on the other hand, didn't have anything dangerous in his system. The doctor injected Warren with an herbal mixture.

"I feel we were taken in. I think this guy was a total crook. But it was quite reasonable, based on what someone had seen, to give this a try. So I don't regret that. But then it was soon after that that Warren went really downhill . . . By the end, Warren had dementia. It was Gedali, a couple of my friends from graduate school who were sweet, wonderful straight women who knew no one who was in this situation, who came for caregiving. Warren's family were evil; his mother—wouldn't even—they had no contact. They were offered the choice, and they had no contact. My parents hadn't been good on this one. They hadn't been good on the relationship. The stuff about him being really poor, and this person is so different, they sort of freaked . . . They were very wonderful before and afterwards. At this moment, they got into their, *The spouses of your children are never good enough for their children*. And so it wasn't helpful. So I couldn't have them around."

THE ASHES ACTION

The idea of a political funeral had really struck a chord with Warren. If Warren hadn't gotten dementia, David knew he would have changed his will and arranged for his body to be brought to an action, but things progressed too quickly. Warren died in April of 1992, and he wanted to be cremated. This inspired what would become ACT UP's Ashes action in October of 1992. David was going to send Warren's ashes to the White House, privately, but it bothered him that no one would know. He talked with friends in New York, and they immediately said, *We'll organize an action*. And they did.

At the Ashes action, Alexis Danzig scattered her father's ashes on the White House lawn. Mark Schoofs brought his lover Mike Hippler's ashes; Eric Sawyer brought the ashes of Larry Kert, the actor who played Tony in the original *West Side Story*. People came from other cities. That was also the weekend the AIDS Memorial Quilt—the world's largest community art project, conceived in 1985 by San Francisco activist Cleve Jones and consisting of thousands of panels showing the names of people who died from AIDS—was being shown. And David had gotten to the point where he felt the quilt was being used mostly in a really dangerous way as a means to actually give the right wing cover for their inaction on AIDS, because the quilt was so beautiful, and everyone could come see it.

"But a lot of us agreed that we wanted to show the truth, the unvarnished truth: *Don't pretty this up in any way.* What has come out of this epidemic? It's ashes, it's bone chips—and so with ACT UP New York doing, really, almost all the logistics—and my providing just feedback and input from San Francisco—we arranged this action. I flew out there. And although it didn't get a lot of press, it was this extremely important moment for a lot of people who had been in ACT UP for quite a while. It was the way we dealt with our grief that time, in a way that we hadn't in a lot of other demonstrations."

ACT UP started marching from the quilt. About fifteen people actually had ashes; some had little urns, some just had a plastic bag. David had what he had been given from the funeral home, a cardboard box with gold lamé paper, almost like wrapping paper, with a plastic bag of Warren's ashes inside. There were lots of ACT UP supporters present, people who had come down to march. The ground rule was that this was not going to be a fake-blood action. "The idea was, you don't need anything fake. We want to show what have really been the consequences of this administration's, and the previous ones', action."

So many people joined the march from the quilt that, although the march started out with a few hundred, mostly ACT UP people, by the end, there were thousands. They marched up to the White House lawn, where the police, mounted on horses, tried to stop them.

"Shane Butler was [from] a new generation of ACT UPers who'd just suddenly come into their own. So he was this young kid. And I was already a veteran. I guess I was twenty-seven. And Shane was probably maybe twenty-two, or something like that. And he had been the lead organizer. They organized so well that our marshals, our people, being all linked, they kept these horses at bay long enough for us to get up to this fence, this black, wrought-iron fence. And we half scaled it, and stood there. And we threw the ashes, dumped the ashes, threw the urns, whatever . . . People were screaming and crying, and some people were screaming because the horses were there, they were frightened by that. Then we turned around, and we were hemmed in. I had no idea there had been that many people who had gathered. Because while we were marching, I would look periodically—and I remember I grew so hoarse from the chanting, but—by the end, when I turned around, it was just unbelievable how many people were there. And the police decided to really move in and try to, try to just get us out . . . They did charge us with the horses. And we had been prepped. The marshals had—to this day, I've repeated this when I do marshal training—if the horses are coming at you, *sit down*. The horses, they will charge into people who are standing. There's no guarantee of anything in life, but ninety-nine percent of the time, they actually won't trample on you if you're sitting down. And so we sat down, and sure enough, the horses stopped.

"ACT UP was my first gay community, and I can't believe how lucky I was . . . I didn't have to go to bars to meet people. Most of my first gay sex was in ACT UP, my first dating. All of [my] transferable job skills were almost entirely from ACT UP. I grew up there . . . But looking back, maybe the third year—I feel like I only had two emotions anymore. I had grief or rage . . . it was like I had skated further and further out on thinner and thinner ice, and I had no idea. And it just crashed . . . Now, in retrospect, I understand partly why I left [ACT UP]—I think I didn't know how to be there and remain healthy. But I still thought it was going to be there when I got back. And instead, these bitter, bitter divides had erupted, and TAG had broken off, and it was, not even just broken off, but they were actively campaigning against ACT UP, telling people, *The days of demonstrating are over, and ACT UP is dead*. And then people in ACT UP, some of them were [like], *They are the devil incarnate*, and—and I still wanted to be involved, so I got involved in the AIDS Cure Project [the McClintock Project].

"And I have to say—I had not been in on all those fights. And I'd had some good experiences with some of the guys in TAG . . . One on one I had gotten along with a lot of them. Not all, but a lot. But—the fact they actually went out and campaigned against the AIDS Cure Project—met with all these other AIDS groups and told them not to support it—broke my heart."

KAREN MOULDING

Karen went down to D.C. in a van for the Ashes action. She traveled with Andrea Dailey, Bob Rafsky, Shane Butler, James Thacker, and David Falcone, "who was really wild." Karen had just taken the bar exam and was doing a lot of ACT UP activity, trying to make friends, "and I was on the over-sensitive side." And there was Bob Rafsky, who was very well respected and beloved in ACT UP and getting sicker. They were going down there to do the very serious act of throwing people's ashes on the White House lawn. On the road, they started playing a game in the van, called "I Have."

"You hold up ten fingers and you say something that you did in bed, and if someone hasn't done it, they have to put a finger down. I was really sexually active with men, and then I was going to the Clit Club every Friday, and really sexually active with women. And there was like, all these experienced—very sexually active, HIV-positive, really older people than me in this van, and I won! Bob Rafsky and I were going head-to-head. And I was like—I don't know if I should say it on the tape—*threesomes and in the train and on the beach*. And this bisexuality—multigendered threesomes and this and that. I still remember—I was almost a martyr in ACT UP, because I gave so much and I was running around, trying to prove myself. I was a little hyperactive and young and new on the gay scene. And I remember at the end of this game, Bob Rafsky—there's a silence, and he goes, *Karen, you've just found yourself some newfound respect. We'll never look at you the same way again.*

"It was really fun. And, he's so serious, and he's got that deep voice all the time. And even when he talked on the floor of ACT UP, it was this baritone, and he was lecturing at us, and he was on *60 Minutes*, and he had his little girl and his Harvard degree—and that was fun . . . And I remember . . . at his memorial, with his little girl running in the hall and stuff—I just became hysterical. And I remember just losing it. And, I don't know, for some reason it really hit me."

ALEXIS DANZIG

"The idea was—for me, and that's the point that I have to speak from—to have a moment of clarified anger about anger and mourning.

And these had always been together, as ideas, and they can't be separated, in the AIDS crisis, or in ACT UP. But it was personal. And it wasn't just about, the people who this is affecting, or will affect, or the people who we've already buried. This is about my dad, and about bringing him, through my experience, into a sense of—into confrontation with the authorities. And it was something that I felt conflicted about, because my father was not particularly confrontational. My father was fairly respectful of authority, despite the fact that he was actively gay and had a very active sex life while he was alive. But for me—it was one of the last actions that I participated in. And it sort of bookends my own participation in ACT UP."

Alexis's father's ashes had been buried, without her consent. She was overridden by her family. And so there was a real sense of, *I can't participate legitimately in this action*, because she literally couldn't do the action of throwing her own loved one's ashes on the White House lawn. Then another person in ACT UP came to her rescue and shared ashes with her so that she could participate. "And—it [was] just incredibly meaningful to me. I could have used anything, right? But there was this sense of comradeship in this activity."

"Participating in such a central way was almost like an out-of-body experience. I can't turn off my marshal brain. But I was there to do a particular job. And I remember walking down the Mall, and how dusty it was, and that I was there with a bunch of other men who I typically didn't do actions with, whose names I can't remember at this point, even though I have some wonderful photographs. And the sense of purposefulness was very large that day. And having other people to do other jobs—getting to trust other people to do the work of marshaling—made it very powerful. To be able to participate in something which is very emotional and not also have to guard yourself was—yeah, a big gift from ACT UP."

29

Political Funerals

JOY EPISALLA

Joy Episalla's father was Sicilian; her mother, Italian. Her father started in the business of family camping on the East Coast with Coleman stoves and sleeping bags, and he graduated from those to trailers to motor homes. Joy had always been in situations where she had to act on the fly and had to adapt readily. ACT UP seemed like a good fit. James Baggett, a coworker from *Elle Decor*, brought Joy to ACT UP, and there she found "this wild bunch of crazy people. The energy was amazing . . . My first thought was, *This is interesting*. And I could see the desperation, I think. And I felt like I could give something."

Joy sat down with James and met his friends of his, including Tim Bailey, Jon Greenberg, Dennis Kane, John Stumpf, Mark Lowe Fisher, Steve Machon, and Barbara Hughes. She joined the affinity group the Marys. They had just done the FDA action, lying on the street with cardboard headstones. Soon the paper headstones and the die-ins would be replaced by real bodies, in real coffins. Tim, Jon, and Mark started having overt conversations about wanting political funerals after they died.

DAVID WOJNAROWICZ'S POLITICAL FUNERAL, JULY 29, 1992

The Marys were in Steven Machon's apartment, talking about what they wanted to have happen after they died. Burning of bodies on pyres was very high on the list. Tim and John and Mark started to discuss their deaths seriously. They were videotaped saying what their wishes were, and the others promised to carry out their mission.

In his memoir, *Close to the Knives*, published in 1991, David Wojnarowicz had written: "I imagine what it would be like if friends had a demonstration each time a lover or a friend or a stranger died of AIDS. I imagine what it would be like if, each time a lover, friend or stranger died of this disease, their friends, lovers or neighbors would take the dead body and drive with it in a car a hundred miles an hour to Washington D.C. and blast though the gates of the White House and come to a screeching halt before the entrance and dump their lifeless form on the front steps."

Joy knew somebody who knew David—Gene Foos—and she went to see Gene. She knew that David was sick, and the Marys wanted him to know that they were using his writings and would be there if some kind of public event was something that he personally was interested in. And Gene came back saying that David was too ill to make that kind of a decision. Then very quickly after, Joy was out in Fire Island with Tim, and they got the phone call that David had died. She called all the Marys, knowing that the community would want to do something because David was really important to a lot of people. They approached David's lover, Tom Rauffenbart, as well as David's friends, and went to David's apartment to talk with them. Carrie Yamaoka, Joy's partner, came with her.

"That was probably the hardest thing I've ever done. It was terrible. Most of those people didn't know who I was. I was an intruder. I had to basically convince them—suggest—that there were many, many people in the AIDS community that wanted to honor David and what they were thinking was this procession, but that we really would like their participation. Some of his friends were very against the idea. It was really hard to enter this room where these people were mourning this person."

Tom said that he wanted to think about it, but that it sounded very good to him. This was a couple of days right after David died, on July 22, 1992. Soon after, they were all in agreement and started to plan. ACT UP decided to do a procession from David's house down Second Avenue, past Tompkins Square Park, through the Village, ending up at the parking lot at the corner, near Astor Place. When they got to the parking lot they wanted to project this slide with text from *Close to the Knives*:

I worry that friends will slowly become professional pall bearers, waiting for each death of their lovers, friends and neighbors, and polishing their funeral speeches. Perfecting their rituals of death, rather than a relatively simple ritual of life— such as screaming in the streets.

But they needed a place for the slide projector to plug into. They looked down at the bottom of the streetlight and the plate was knocked off, revealing an outlet. As the procession came down the street, up went the slide, and there was a reading of *Close to the Knives* by one of David's friends. Tom was there, and he and David's friends were carrying posters of David and David's work—the piece with the shot of the buffaloes going down the mountain, and another of his big sunflowers.

Barbara Hughes and Joy carried a big black banner with white lettering that said DAVID WOJNAROWICZ DIED OF AIDS and gave the dates. People off the streets came to join the procession, and it got huge. Joy recalled Bob Rafsky being there, walking alongside her. She searched all over to get fabric that was not fire repellant, because she wanted something to burn. Joy had a can of lighter fluid, and was dousing the material, trying to light it, getting lighter fluid all over her. Finally, the thing took, and they pushed it out into the area between Cooper Union and the parking lot. It was burning, and they started throwing the posters they were carrying, and the sunflowers, onto the pyre. "It was unbelievable. So in a way, that was the first political funeral. From there it was really wild. That was July."

MARK LOWE FISHER'S POLITICAL FUNERAL, NOVEMBER 2, 1992
RUSSELL PRITCHARD

Russell Pritchard was born in Tisdale, Saskatchewan, in Canada, and moved to New York in 1979. He was a journalism major, focusing on advertising and public relations, and started doing photo assistant work, then art direction, fashion casting, prop styling, and food styling. He hung out in the Pines on Fire Island, which was one of the first identified gay communities with widespread AIDS. "You think you're all going to die in the next five years. So it was really just a matter of being supportive and trying to figure out what sort of treatment or course of action they should take." He had been HIV-positive since 1985 and came to ACT UP in 1987. Russell met Mark Fisher in the affinity group Wave 3, and they became very close friends. They traveled together.

"Mark and I decided to take a trip to Italy together, and he actually got sick on our trip. He got an infection in a Hickman catheter that had been installed, prior to our leaving. And that sort of aggravated his situation, and he went into toxic shock, and actually died on our flight home. So I was reeling from about a week of dealing with all of that—being in a foreign country—these hospitals in Southern Italy that were just deplorable. You'd walk in, there would be dogs walking around inside the emergency rooms, and just so having to decompress from all of that and he actually died beside me on the flight home."

RICHARD DEAGLE

"Mark knew he was in bad shape—a really nice guy. He worked for an architectural firm. He had worked on the team with Arata Isozaki, who is doing the redesign of the Brooklyn Museum . . . So, he and Russell are on the airplane, flying back from Rome. Mark's refused medication in Rome. They couldn't get a doctor. *Let's just go home. Let's not go early. Let's not do whatever.* Mark starts doing weird things on the way back, and dies in the seat next to Russell, on the airplane. And the stewardess and the crew come and they go, *Yes, in fact, he's dead.* They got met by an ambulance at the tarmac at Kennedy. I cannot think of a more horrendous thing to have happened than someone you've just spent a week on vacation with, dying, next to you on an airplane."

JOY EPISALLA

When Mark died, Tim Bailey was in the hospital with a collapsed lung. He came out of surgery and they put him on a machine that recirculates air; he had a chest tube and big staples in the back of his shoulder. As he was lying in bed, Joy, who was with him, got a phone call from Barbara Hughes. *Mark's very sick, he's on his way back from Rome . . . He'll come in at the airport, and they'll rush him to St. Luke's Roosevelt emergency.* Joy said she'd go downstairs and look for him. But she was talking slightly in code because Tim was in bed, and she didn't want to get him worried.

Mark Lowe Fisher's funeral. From left to right: Tim Lunceford, Joy Episalla, BC Craig, Vincent Gagliostro, Scott Morgan, Eric Sawyer (partial) (Photographer unknown)

Joy got off the phone and Tim said, *What was that?* And she said, *Oh, it's Barbara, I told her I'd call her back.* Joy left the room to go down the hall and called her back. By that time, Mark had died. He was going to be taken to Redden's Funeral Home, on Fourteenth Street, and the Marys were going to meet that night at Mark's apartment. So Joy went back to Tim's room, and he said, *I just took a Valium. Now you can tell me what's the matter.* She started to tell him and got very upset, and he let her cry. When she left Tim in the hospital that night, she went to Mark's. It turned out that Mark had left everything in order. His Rolodex was completely color-coded in the order the group was supposed to call people. It was all to do with what was now going to happen, which was what the Marys had all decided. They had been meeting with someone who was an undertaker, who knew the ins and outs. A person has to be embalmed for their body to be moved, and then it has to be brought back to the place of origin, from where it would go to cremation or burial.

"Steven and Barbara had talked to Redden's and the decision was made that we'd have him lie in state, basically, at Judson Memorial, and that we would then process his body out of Judson up Sixth Avenue, to Bush headquarters. And it was the night before the [presidential] election. Well, Mark died on—I believe it was a Friday, if I'm not mistaken—and I think this was on a Monday night? So we all went into gear, and we got a slip-lid casket, which in the Jewish religion is what they use, because the top slips off. So it wasn't like opening a casket, you could just slip the lid off. It was a complete frenzy, and I was going back and forth to the hospital to see Tim and we talked about what was going on. He wrote a note to Mark, that I was to read. It was very hard. It was very hard to watch Tim and [to have] Mark be dead and you were supposed to keep your brains about you, to move forward and not get upset. You didn't really have time . . . I don't think we at all forgot that it was about our friend—our comrade, our friend, and we were going to do what he wanted us to do. So that was the bottom line.

"We got Mark from Redden's, and we went to Judson Memorial and practiced walking around the room with him, with the casket up on our shoulders—because he wasn't light, even though he looked really skinny. And so it happened. There was the memorial, and James [Wentzy] has footage of all that. People got up and spoke, and then people left the building. Then one more time, we picked him up and we had taken the lid off, and we then processed out of Judson, onto the street there and then down to Sixth Avenue, where we passed Tim's apartment, where we had a big banner hanging off of his building. And that morning we woke up and it was raining out, and Carrie and I said, *Oh my God, Mark's going to get wet. We have to get umbrellas.* We went to the wholesale district and bought forty huge black umbrellas. Then we were back at Barbara Hughes's house, before we went to Judson. We had the black umbrellas, and we made those pyres that we'd used a number of times before—it's basically a broomstick with an empty paint can that you can buy to mix paint in, with toilet paper saturated in kerosene, and you light it. So we had these torches. I think we were all shaking and we were all in complete shock. We'd spent a little time with Mark at Judson before everybody got there. So we saw him . . . We did this procession down Sixth Avenue, all the way to Bush's headquarters on Forty-Fifth Street."

RUSSELL PRITCHARD

"We didn't try to get into the office. It was just sort of presenting to these people who were not doing anything. *Here is a loved member of our family who has died; we want to show you. This is his body—and you killed him.*"

RICHARD DEAGLE

They ended up marching from a memorial down at Washington Square, against traffic, up to the Bush campaign headquarters, which was up near the Algonquin Hotel, with Mark's body in an open casket, in the rain.

"It was just hellacious, but it was something we had to do. I don't think—because all the umbrellas were over the body—people actually knew that there was a dead body there on the street. It was just amazing. If that had been me, I would have wanted the same thing to have happened."

JOY EPISALLA

The police had started to come along as the procession passed, and Mark was covered with the umbrellas. The cops started to take their hats off, and they turned off their radios. Once ACT UP got to Bush's campaign headquarters they put the casket down. They had thought about the banner from the ACT UP action at George Bush's house in Kennebunkport, Maine, and thought it would be perfect for Mark's funeral, because Mark had worked so hard on it. The banner was strewn across his coffin, covering him up to his shoulders. Another Mary, Michael Cunningham, made a speech. And Eric Sawyer made a speech, as did Bob Rafsky. Then, when they finished, they had a station wagon, and they put Mark in and brought him back to Redden's. "And you know, it was a big blow."

"Things happened so quickly, and because of what Mark wanted or Tim wanted or Jon wanted, we followed through with their wishes. And I'd also say, about one's family—the crazy part of all of it, too, was that in fact, in one way, you felt like you knew each other incredibly well, and on the other hand you probably didn't know who their parents were or about their family. There wasn't enough time, somehow, either . . . I say that, in terms of Mark. I don't think I thought about it after a certain point. That wasn't important anymore."

EULOGY BY MICHAEL CUNNINGHAM AT MARK LOWE FISHER'S POLITICAL FUNERAL

"We who brought him here, all loved and respected him. We won't recover from his loss and we won't forgive it. A year ago, September, Mark helped organize a demonstration at George Bush's summer house in Kennebunkport, Maine. Mark and others carried a banner that listed the specific steps that George Bush could take, as president, to fight AIDS. It was a last desperate attempt to reach a president who had done nothing about AIDS. Who had never voluntarily mentioned the disease in any public address. Who had ignored every urgent recommendation of the National Commission on AIDS, a commission that included several of his own appointees. The list of demands was left within sight of his home and a police car ran it over. Mark and several others pulled it out of a ditch by the side of the road and carried it back to New York. Later, in response to a reporter's question, Bush said he cared far more about unemployment than he did about AIDS, because 'unemployment affects families.' We're here to tell George Bush and the other hatemongers that *we* are Mark Fisher's family. We have suffered an irreparable loss.

"Several months before his death, Mark said *I want my funeral to be fierce and defiant.* In obedience to his wishes we've brought his body to the doorstep of the man whose callous disregard, whose inhumanity, killed him as surely as did the disease. We've covered his body with the list of demands that Mark himself helped make. The demands for simple, inexpensive measures that have gone unheeded. Mark Fisher was a hero. We will never quit the battle Mark fought until the moment of his death. Some of us, like Mark, may not live to see the battle won, but we will win. We will fight the hatred so powerful and pervasive, it is no different from murder. There will always be more of us and we will never be silent. Mark, we love you. In your name we say to the world *ACT UP, FIGHT BACK, FIGHT AIDS. ACT UP, FIGHT BACK, FIGHT AIDS.*"

TIM BAILEY'S POLITICAL FUNERAL, 1993

JOY EPISALLA

After Mark died in 1992, Tim became seriously ill. Joy had met Tim's mother on a couple of occasions, and his sister and brother. It was summer 1993, in the midst of Gay Pride, and Tim had been in the hospital for about two weeks, and had lost his short-term memory. He had CMV retinitis, and it had traveled to his brain. Joy promised him that he would only be in the hospital for about a week, but now it was two. There wasn't really anything they could do anymore. So Tim wanted to go home. Then it was a process of making him comfortable. Joy had gotten a nurse to help out. "She wasn't quite a real registered nurse, but she was HIV-positive herself, actually. She was a sweetheart.

"Because he'd lost his short-term memory, he really wanted to smoke in the hospital . . . and we couldn't smoke cigarettes in the room. And I'd be pointing out the sign to him, and he said, *What kind of hotel is this?* I'd keep a dirty ashtray in the drawer and say, *Look, you did have a cigarette.* I felt terrible about lying like that, you know? But there was no real way to totally make sense of anything anymore. He always knew who I was and there was total communication, it's just that he didn't know where he was, exactly. And he was starting to lose his sight, as well. Well anyway, Tim was the menswear designer for Pat Field. So he was very into clothes and his appearance and everything. Anyway, one time I got a phone call—I was working at another magazine by then, actually it was *GQ*—freelance—and I got a phone call from the hospital saying they had tied him to the bed. Well, basically what happened was, he'd gotten out of bed and he was trying to put the sheet on, and he was asking the nurse, *Would you help me gather it here?* They obviously didn't want to help him out with his dress. So they tied him to the bed.

". . . I knew where things were going—we're definitely on the downswing, not the up. He had made certain requests for after he died, and I think there was a part of me that wanted final confirmation, if you know what I mean. Anyway, we had the curtain drawn and it was later in the evening. All of a sudden, he was wide awake. He was there—very present. And it was my moment. We had this great conversation, and he was totally present. And I said, *Wow—I've been waiting for you.* We talked about his political funeral, and that's what he still wanted . . . By the time—his doctor told me, there was nothing they could do . . . I basically was saying to them—*Listen, all the stuff that you're running here, I can do at home. I don't see any reason in keeping him here* . . . So that's what we did. And James came and had my car and got Tim in a wheelchair, because you've got to go out in a wheelchair and he couldn't really walk anyway. He was wearing his light blue denim shirt, and he put on his leopard-skin printed silk scarf, and his sunglasses, and he looked his fabulous self, and we put him in a car and drove down the West Side Highway, and it was a beautiful day. It was me, Tim and James and Tim Hamilton—Tim's friend from Ohio. And James said—*What's-her-name has come out with a Barry White song.* Taylor Dayne came out with that song, and James is talking about it and he turns the radio on and what is it on but that song? He turned it up really loud, and Tim's really getting into it in the front seat, and we're driving downtown—here we were, together again. This was great.

"Then, over the course of the next week and a half, two weeks, he really went downhill. He made me go to Gay Pride . . . That was a Sunday. Tim died on Monday. He died on the night of ACT UP. It was me and Tim Hamilton—we were with him. He couldn't breathe, and I called the doctor's office saying, *He can't breathe.* And they said there was this machine I could get to vacuum him out. So I drove like a maniac all the way up to Eighty-Eighth Street on the East Side, and bought this machine . . . I was driving up and that's when I thought, *It's over. You're going through the motions.* I knew. I picked up the machine, and I got all the way back downtown—and we did try to use it. We were out of our heads, really. He was already on a morphine drip. We put on Ella Fitzgerald. And then we stopped doing everything. And he was, like, *Are you all right?* We just kept saying that we were right there with him. You know, it's a real honor when somebody lets you be with them like that . . . It's very special. I think you kind of cross over, in a way. So I made a phone call to Barbara Hughes at ACT UP, and then everybody came to the house, to Tim's, and we all had martinis with him."

RON GOLDBERG

Ron Goldberg grew up in Great Neck, came out in college, and started auditioning for acting jobs. It wasn't until he got involved with ACT

UP that he actually knew people with AIDS. Ron was Chant Queen— which was about getting everybody enthused. *"Health care is a right—* it's not poetry, though it does have a rhythm if done correctly."

Ron got a phone call saying, *Tim just died. If you want to come in and say goodbye to him before they send somebody to pick up his body, then you should come down.* So all of the Marys who were available went to Tim's apartment, where he was laid out on his bed. Everybody had their turn, saying what they needed to say, while being next to him. Then they started talking about Tim, "reminiscing about how crazy he was.

"And probably three hours into our unofficial wake for him, we started talking about, *well,* what Tim wanted us to do with his body, as part of his funeral. And personally, I couldn't think about that too much at that time. I was still processing Tim's body being in the next room. But we knew that Tim wanted his funeral to be a political funeral. And he wanted it to be taken to D.C. And wanted to be placed in front of the White House. And there were three or four people who were working very hard to kind of do logistics for how this was going to go off. And we also announced it to the general membership, because we wanted a lot of people there. And a couple of members of his family reluctantly got involved."

JOY EPISALLA

"Then they came from Redden's, and we went into gear."

KEN BING

Tim's brother Randy was very helpful. The body had to be released to a family member so that they could take it from the funeral home.

"We knew we were going to run into resistance when we got there, anyway. But we, we were expecting to at least be able to go a few blocks, chanting, and then maybe stop. I don't think a whole lot of us thought it would actually get to the White House. But at least we wanted to be public, and let people know we had a person who was living with AIDS die because of government neglect. So we wanted that kind of picture to be out there."

JOY EPISALLA

"[Tim's brother] Randy came down with us for the funeral, and we had Tim in the van with us. It was the same deal—the slip-lid casket."

RON GOLDBERG

"It was very much about, literally, bringing the bodies of our dead to where we thought the blame [lay] and making that quantifiable . . . *Here's a dead body—this was someone who we loved, who we valued.*"

There were some delays in the car getting down there, and by the time they arrived in Washington, D.C., the police were on to them. When they arrived, the police started pushing back.

JOY EPISALLA

Barbara Hughes drove the van with Michael Marco, James Baggett, and Carrie and Joy and Tim's corpse. They had white roses and the banner. Tim had already set aside money to pay for buses for people to go down to Washington to meet at the pool in front of the Capitol. They drove right by the White House and did have a moment of thinking they should get out right there, right now. But then they thought, *No, we have to meet up with everyone, with our friends.* They stopped at a hotel to meet up with Vincent Gagliostro and get the sound system from him and Michael Cunningham. Then they passed the White House with the sound system. As they drove up, Joy remembers seeing people with signs already there, waiting. Soon they were surrounded by undercover and uniformed police. Barbara and Joy got out of the van and started to open its back doors. Joy had the keys and roses in her hands.

"The next thing I know is, this big guy has come in from the passenger side and he's fighting me for the keys, and he's got me by the arm and I can't remember what he was saying to me. I knew I wasn't going to give him the keys. I was fighting him off. And Barbara comes in and she's saying, *Get off of her!* And it was just like this completely bizarre experience. He finally got the keys—he was undercover FBI. They didn't want us to leave, obviously. And I think they thought they

were going to stop this, but they weren't. All these people were there—
Eric Sawyer was there and—I'm sure we put out a press release . . . All
those people with signs were pretty much a giveaway. There was FBI,
undercover, park police, and people in riot gear—cops in riot gear. It was
unbelievable. Jamie Bauer was there. I mean, there were tons of people
there. And Jamie was like, *Surround the van!* And everybody knew their
cue, and everybody surrounded the van. So there was a blockade between
the van: Tim, the van, these people, and the cops. Well, this siege went on
from something like one o'clock in the afternoon to six o'clock at night.
It rained. Everybody's emotions went from this to this to this within five
seconds flat. It was completely insane. We were trying—our whole thing
was that we were driving Tim's body down to the White House. We were
going to have this procession to show people what a person with AIDS,
who's died not only looks like, but looks like in its total. This person had a
life that's been lost. This is a terrible crime that you are letting go on, day
in and day out, and you're not paying any attention."

The night of Mark's funeral, Joy went back to the hospital because
Tim had done an absentee ballot and "voted for fucking Clinton." And
now here they were, full circle: Clinton was president and ACT UP
was out in front of the Capitol building, right down the street from the
White House, and they were being stopped by Clinton's police. This
went back and forth, with the Marys calling all people—*Who knew
who in the White House?* The police tried to make deals with the protesters, because the last thing they wanted was ACT UP on the six-o'clock
news. Finally, a deal was struck where the police would let ACT UP
drive Tim's body down toward Pennsylvania Avenue. The Marys were
all set to do it, but then the police did a reversal and they tried to stop
them again.

"Then we just said *fuck it*, so we opened the back doors, and we start
to take Tim out. That's the picture that was in the papers. You've seen
it—you see the casket—and Tim's brother was there, who is not an activist. He'd come down for Tim. Randy was on the side of me—on this
side, and I was on the outside of the casket, trying to hold—it was so
scary. And we'd had this whole run-in with the cops earlier, before this.
They wanted a coroner to make sure that he was dead the proper way.
So they actually wanted to look at him. I tried to negotiate for the set of
keys back. I got the keys back. I said, *I have the papers right here*, which

I did. I had them down the front of my shirt, so that nobody could get them. And they did—they examined him, with plastic gloves on. It was disgusting."

RON GOLDBERG

Tim's brother got very upset, screaming and yelling until he got arrested. ACT UPer Jim Aquino then took a bust because they didn't want Tim's brother to be in jail alone. "That was a really tough day."

JOY EPISALLA

The police tried to take Tim's casket out of the van, but ACT UP struggled and ended up getting Tim back in the van, basically deciding to leave and take him home, with the banner out. They started driving around the Capitol parking lot with activists following, but the next thing they knew, the van was cut off from everybody else by police and an ambulance and cops on motorcycles who started to escort them out of there. And there were a couple of squad cars in front of and behind the van that started taking them through a Black neighborhood of Washington. They had a sticker on the van that said FUNERAL. They waved the poster for Tim and were throwing leaflets out the windows, and started to get support from people on the street.

"They drove us through traffic—traffic was parted. We went through tolls—cars and ditches through tolls—all the way to Baltimore, with sirens. We get into Baltimore, and we're on the highway, and we're running out of gas. And Barbara's driving. She pulls up alongside one of the cop cars and says, *We're running out of gas.* So they take us off the highway, and they take us to a gas station, and we pull in and start to get gas, and the cop car's over there. So I walk over the cop car and I said, *So are you going to take us all the way back to New Jersey?* And he said, *No, I think we've all had enough for the day.* That's where they left us. It was unbelievable.

"We took Tim back to the funeral home in New Jersey. He was then taken from there to be cremated. His ashes—most of them, went to his family. I had some of his ashes. We were thinking about making a trip to Paris—so some of Tim's ashes are in Paris. It was pretty unbelievable, the whole thing. And I think we never totally got over it—any of us. About two weeks later, Jon Greenberg died. We had another political funeral for him in New York City, which went to Tompkins Square Park. It was unbelievable."

JON GREENBERG'S PUBLIC FUNERAL—JULY 16, 1993
GARANCE FRANKE-RUTA

The first political funeral Garance went to was Jon Greenberg's.

"It was the point, I think, where everyone was starting to go crazy without realizing it. It was this idea that, again, this idea of invisibility; that the world couldn't see what was happening. And so people wanted the world to see what was happening. And it was this idea of moving from the mock funeral, with the cardboard caskets and the little fake tombstones and all that stuff, into actually, when someone actually did die, to giving them a public funeral procession. And I know Jon Greenberg wanted that. And he and Risa [Denenberg] were really good friends, and they were on the Alternative Treatments Committee, along with Anna Blume. And they held a sort of memorial service for him in Tompkins Square Park. And it was just—this public memorial service in this public park in New York City. With his actual body; and with us going and saying our goodbyes in the park."

ANNA BLUME

Anna Blume was born in Los Angeles and educated at Williams College. After getting a PhD in art history at Yale, she came to New York in the winter of 1989. She joined ACT UP, became a Mary, and among many different commitments in ACT UP worked with Jon Greenberg on alternative therapies for HIV. Anna recalled Jon believing in a holistic approach to life. And that didn't just have to do with AIDS or treatment; it had to do with, *We're part of something so much bigger than us.* And whatever role we can play in those waves that dip and flurry, that's all we can do.

"And I think he felt he rode those waves pretty well. He was a beautiful being that could be angry and passionate and sad and in the moment. And I think his ability to stay in the moment, till the moment he died, is all he really wanted. And to be able to do that under the kind of physical and emotional stress of HIV disease is just a beautiful testament. So I really don't think he had any regrets."

RISA DENENBERG

"Jon was a beautiful man who was really a difficult guy, and that I, for whatever reasons—we just meshed, we just got along, we were like, I felt he was my best friend, for the years that he lived, that whole time I was in New York. Some of the things that he talked about were so out there, so revolutionary, that people wouldn't even talk to him. He was feeling like, *Well, I have these organisms in my body; and this war concept is really offensive to me, and I'm going to learn to live with them, I'm going to make peace.* And he wrote something called 'The Metaphysics of AIDS,' which is this lovely treatise. He wrote a number of things that I have that I don't know that they've ever gotten published. I'm simplifying it. But he was very smart. And he wrote about these things in a very compelling way. And a lot of people congregated around him."

Jon became interested in alternative treatments after receiving acupuncture from the Lincoln Hospital Acupuncture Clinic, a place where Susan Rosenberg and other members of the May 19th Communist Organization, and the Black Liberation Army, worked. He learned the philosophy by being a patient and a consumer. And he was just naturally skeptical, in a very similar way that Risa and other women were naturally skeptical of the medical industry. There were lots of different reasons why people didn't go on AZT. But to Jon, it was poison. And he believed, as he was in and out of the different alternative communities, that he could manage his illness without toxic pharmaceuticals. He could figure it out. "He was wrong, but he really believed that. And he really worked on it. And he had a lot of people listening to him. And he had a lot of really good ideas."

Risa and Jon lived in the same apartment building, both on the fifth floor. He would talk, like a lot of men talked, about how *AIDS was this lesson.* He was very smart, and Risa remembered that she had to listen.

"He could take a metalevel of what was going on in ACT UP, or what was going on in the treatment community and branch it out into a philosophy of how we could achieve world peace, or how people could learn to live together. Learning to live with the virus was about people learning to live together . . . He did things wrong, as I said. But he did everything thoughtfully . . . And he gave me a real sense, too, that I've carried with me, of what it means to die. He just said, *You can't save lives*. That was Jon's line. *You can't save lives; everybody dies.* It's so obvious. But he would say it in ways that startled you, it made you think. *What are we talking about here?* . . . He didn't want to die. But he was very aware that he was going to. And he didn't have any illusions about that until he was dying, at which time, he threw everything out the window, and didn't want to die . . . I think I fell in love with him. He was just so charismatic, for me. And so the relationship itself meant a lot, in terms of what my life was about. It was shocking. It was shocking to feel so drawn to a man. But it was also delightful. And it allowed me to think about things that were being thought about amongst the larger community of gay men and lesbians, trying to work together."

Risa felt that the Alternative Treatments Committee gave a lot of meaning to a lot of people. She felt that they were essentially right, not wrong, about the way that drugs were being developed. And she believed they were right that these drugs were no panacea, even though they became life-preserving.

"So they were right philosophically; they were just wrong factually. And so I don't know where people scattered over time. I know that Jon didn't change his position soon enough."

Jon developed cryptococcal meningitis and became convinced that the drug fluconazole would help him, even though the correct drug was amphotericin B.

"And he did tell us, one day, that he had fucked God . . . At other times, he seemed perfectly lucid. And he would have these horrible outbursts. But he had always had horrible outbursts . . . So I don't know how much was the disease; I never knew. Which itself was a great lesson, because I deal with a lot of people with disease, and I understand that you can't tell how much of anything is disease, and whether disease is something separate or integrated . . . it was the middle of July, he died on the twelfth."

Once, Risa was in the elevator with him, going to get either an induced sputum or a chest X-ray. They were in a medical building, and there were other people in the elevator, including a child. And he said, *Well, when I die, I want you to burn me in the street, and eat my flesh.* His idea of a political funeral was very different from the other political funerals. He did not want a traditional political funeral. But he was very active with the group of people who were planning political funerals, and he was very close with Mark Fisher and Tim Bailey and the other men who planned their own political funerals. Jon's body had been at a funeral home called Fisher's. Risa went to the home of Barbara Hughes, who had been in the affinity group the Marys with Jon. The two of them sat down and tried to decide, *Well, what did he mean? What would he want?* There was the in-the-street element. They were near Tompkins Square Park. And that influenced their decision.

Risa got the funeral home to agree to bring the body to Houston Street in a hearse. I was there with the other activist mourners. The pallbearers, including Jon's brother, the choreographer Neil Greenberg, carried the casket up First Avenue to a prearranged spot in the park, where they opened the coffin. Jon was dressed in drag, which Risa had selected. The smell of preservative wafted through the summer air, as we all looked at Jon's corpse. John Kelly, the performance artist, sang, and Jon Nalley of ACT UP said the kaddish. Then he was cremated, the ashes going to his family and to Risa. A year later, she scattered them on Fire Island with some friends and threw some flowers along with some of his belongings into the ocean. Then she asked everyone to make Jon's wishes come true and eat some of his ashes. Not everyone would, so she put them in the cole slaw.

KARIN TIMOUR

"There was a six-week stretch where somebody that I knew from ACT UP died every ten days—every ten days to two weeks . . . I think, like, four or five people died . . . I talked to Jon Greenberg about a week before he died, and I called—we were talking on the phone . . . He was living his life. He knew that he was very close to the end . . . When we took his body and went up to the park and then had a funeral in the park—and kids are playing on the swing sets over here and somebody's lighting memorial candles over here. And there's this open casket, lying in Tompkins Square Park. It was—for so many of those years, it was—I felt sometimes surreal, in terms of—*There's this war going on and I'm losing friends and people are dying here, and nobody is noticing.* And, I felt that a funeral in the park was very much a—*Somebody died here today. Pay attention, people. This is real. This is what's happening. This is a concrete reality of what's happening in that house, in that house, in that house—this is happening right here.*"

BARBARA HUGHES

When Mark Fisher died, Jon Greenberg wrote a eulogy for his friend that he was unable to deliver. So when Jon died, his close friend Barbara Hughes read that eulogy in front of Jon's open casket in Tompkins Square Park.

Jon Greenberg's eulogy for Mark Fisher, read by Barbara Hughes at Jon's funeral:

On January 22, 1991, Mark, Barbara, Anna, Steven, Lori, Neil and I sat in the cafeteria of Channel 13, waiting for a beep which would tell us to take those final steps, walk those final one hundred yards which would propel us down the passage and into the studio where Robin [MacNeil] was reporting on the [Iraq War] once again. We were nervous, frightened and fidgety. We were about to push through a social barrier; do what many had only imagined and fly in the face of convention and what was once considered acceptable social behavior, to declare our presence and force for the world to take notice. Our country, this world, had lost all perspective. And we were determined to reaffirm some truth, some reality into a media event where truth and reality had ceased to have meaning. We were prepared for everything we could possibly be prepared for. Mark had made sure of that. As many variables as we could control, we did control and that was largely because of Mark's extraordinary anal organizational abilities. But for all that, as we approached that studio door with the red light flashing outside, none of us knew what to expect on the other side. The red light was meant to scare us into staying on our proper side, control our actions with fear. But Mark and the rest of us, in spite of our fear, knew that it was only fear. And rather than let that stop us, we used it to propel us into further action, to confront and push through the barrier of our fear and be liberated even as our bodies were being arrested and jailed.

There was an otherness about those moments—we all felt it. We all knew that we had—if only for a moment, an hour a day—[become] larger than we had been the day before. We each became part of the other. And as a unit our collective spirit crossed an illusory boundary, which we only knew was an illusion after we had crossed it. We were each a part of Mark on that day and he was a part of us. And through our collective empowerment we declared who we were and how we felt and made a place for ourselves in the universe.

Mark has once again crossed a boundary that each of us will sooner or later have to cross, whether we have AIDS or not, whether we are angry or not, whether we are afraid or not, and whether we have a Republican president or not. The truth is that each of us will one day follow Mark to that ultimate otherness and the final liberation. Let us hope that we can do it as consciously, actively, and as well prepared as Mark has. To the end, Mark was unafraid of the consequences of his actions, or *if* afraid, he used that fear to propel him onward rather than to paralyze him and stop him from fully living. Mark knew he was going to die. We, each of us, will also die. Mark's life and death—if it is to mean anything—cannot be trivialized by wishing it away or pretending that there could be any other end.

Yes, we are in pain. We have lost a precious powerful friend and colleague, but to avoid that pain by blaming it on someone else robs us of our opportunity to experience and learn from a greater consciousness, a larger self, a fearlessness. Acceptance of our mortality as Mark accepted his, makes it possible to live life fully in spite of our fear, makes it possible to live life in real freedom because we are not afraid of the consequences of our actions. It is only after we see how trivial and illusory the political, social, religious and physical barriers of this world are, [that we can] begin to liberate ourselves from our fears and find our true power, consciousness, action and fearlessness.

Mark was honest with himself and with his life. He knew his death was unavoidable, he knew that to believe other-wise was to believe a lie and to give more power to the fear of the unknown than to the courage, strength and love that we can choose to face the unknown with. And Mark chose this action today as his memorial, making even his death an act of empowerment for his community, and giving each of us an opportunity to publicly declare our presence, our pain, our right to life and our right to be proud of our deaths. We can learn from Mark's death, learn about consciousness, em-powerment, fearlessness and action, and follow his lead, as I followed him almost two years ago through the barrier of our fears. Goodbye, Mark, and thank you for this final act of empowerment and generosity. Mark's final entry into his medical journal was *mind is clear, feel like a connected whole.* We honor that connected wholeness in our actions today.

Conclusion: The Myth of Resilience and the Enduring Relationship of AIDS

CÉSAR CARRASCO

César Carrasco was born in Chile. The Fascists came to power through a military coup when he was eighteen, in 1973. That was also the year he came out to his family. Augusto Pinochet's dictatorship was bloody. César saw people being arrested and taken to detention camps. Friends whom he'd played with in the neighborhood became college-educated leftists, and then one day, all of a sudden, they would be missing.

There was a little gay joint a couple of blocks away from Pinochet's military headquarters. Men could not demonstrate any sort of affection—kissing or holding hands or anything. But it was still a gay club. There were no places for gay people to dance, but they could just go there and have drinks and cruise. César recalled that there was no political gay community at that time in Chile. There were no queer movies or books. "It was like a culturally dead country."

He knew, though, that there was a lot of gay life in New York. César had friends who had gone to Europe, and they spoke of the wonders of Berlin and Hamburg and Amsterdam. But they talked mostly about how fun it was; the bathhouses and the clubs, and all the freedom that could be had. César had some sense that there was more to the gay future than just social life or endless parties, that there was a lot more gay power to be won. He understood that this freedom was not only about dancing and doing drugs, or going shopping, that there was a political movement. He had the idea that San Francisco and New York were the places where gay people lived very openly.

César was in a relationship with a man who was a naturalized U.S. citizen, an Argentinian immigrant who was much older. His lover was a chemist. César was finishing college, and he was very politically active. His partner would make donations to or help some groups that were fighting Pinochet or other "governments that basically are just so corrupt that the people are suffering." Finally, after many tries, César got a student visa to St. Louis University. He was appalled at the dramatic difference between Black and white people in St. Louis. "That was very, very, very evident . . . It was kind of like, *What the hell happened here?*"

He didn't have a car. It was twenty below zero—a winter that he was not used to. There was a gay church in St. Louis, and he was so absolutely amazed by the idea that in America, he could just go to a church being gay, and hold hands with a partner. Even though he was not religious, he thought it was wonderful. For spring break in March, he grabbed whatever money he had, took a Trailways bus to New York, and spent a week there. "It was kind of like, *Oh my God; I arrived in heaven.* It was a wonderful trip. And it was kind of like, *I have to live in this city. I don't know how, but I have to really make it to this city.*" He came to New York in 1982 at age twenty-seven, nine years into the Chilean dictatorship.

"I met this guy from Chile . . . There were a lot of men from Chile living in New York. And one of them was this hair stylist. He had his own shop on Greenwich Avenue. That's the first time that I met someone that is officially diagnosed with HIV, or AIDS, or whatever they called it then . . . In 1984, when we were all freaking out about AIDS, I became one of those buddies at GMHC. I did the training. And that's how I started doing work that was directly connected with HIV . . . I would visit—I don't know if they called them *clients*, but you had a number of people that you would visit regularly, once a week. They were like in East New York, or somewhere. And they were drug addicts, mostly injectors, who had contracted AIDS."

César was working in commercial art—advertising and illustrations. From 1988 to 1990, he used to go to ACT UP alone. He participated in the Media Committee, with Jay Blotcher and other people.

"But it was kind of like, I didn't have anyone. I would go to the demonstrations, the marches alone. I'm not necessarily a very sociable person in the sense of striking conversations and getting to know people and becoming friends—it's not necessarily my forte. And it was not until 1990, when all these Latinos in ACT UP decided to form the

Latino Caucus, that I really get deeply involved in ACT UP. But I was involved before . . . But I would be kind of like an invisible figure in the background. And so when I started—and that happens to many, many other members of the Latino Caucus—we all shift professions, you know, from filming and media at New School, or *whatever* . . . we started doing AIDS-related work in the community. And I started working at the Lower East Side Family Union, which is a foster-care prevention, you know, services for families where children are at risk. And I started working with women, Hispanic women, where the children were at risk of being placed in foster care, or having the system involved, not because the mother was neglecting them or abusing drugs or doing crazy things, but because the mother was dying."

That's when César began to get the sense of how terrible the epidemic was; the silence, not telling anyone, not wanting to go to the doctor if it was in your neighborhood, being terribly afraid that people would find out. And he met wonderful women, who were already getting some form of medications, "or at least kind of like getting the type of primary care that you would get in 1990." He had no idea that there were specific services for Hispanic people until he got involved with ACT UP's Latino Caucus. Then he learned about the Hispanic AIDS Forum, and the Upper Manhattan Task Force on AIDS on 125th Street. He became very disenchanted with his GMHC work. He felt the epidemic getting more serious, more and more sinister and horrible and dramatic, and that the whole purpose of GMHC was to go help people to die gracefully.

"And that didn't cut it for me anymore. I really felt that now, I needed to get involved at a more activist level; that this trying to be the pleasant, nice, Christian, generous, giving homosexual, was, like, *no*. My personal process with my own—now, *I* was infected . . . So ACT UP became a wonderful way of channeling all this frustration, all this anger, and also all this energy, in a way that I felt that it was productive and effective. Working now officially with women and people with AIDS at the Lower East Side Family Union, I was a direct observer of what taking AZT at those massive dosages was doing to people . . . When they were taking it like every four hours . . . Personally, I was not at the stage where I had to take [it]—my T cells were pretty high back then—so I could say *no*. I was afraid. I knew that it was kind of like a form of oral chemo; really altering the metabolism of the cells . . . I got into the ACT UP agenda; that we need different compounds, better compounds, approved fast. So even though I ended up doing a lot of community work with the Latino Caucus, at the same time, I'd remain a firm ACT UPer in the sense that I was there to make sure that the approval of new compounds would be expedited. Because otherwise, there was going to be no salvation."

All of a sudden, there was a critical mass of Latino gay men in the group, and to César it felt like a discovery. There was Robert Garcia and Joe Franco and twenty others in an apartment in Brooklyn for meetings. And that is when the Latinos in ACT UP voted to become a caucus, instead of being a committee, and they really started doing the work.

"There was Cándido Negrón, Mario Quiñones, Héctor Seda, Nelson Galarza, Pedro Galarza, Luis Salazar, there was, from San Francisco, a Chicano from San Francisco, wonderful, wonderful soul. Elías Guerrero, I think, I'm talking about the Chicanos. Elías Guerrero, Vic Hernández. And then we have, from Puerto Rico, we have Moisés Agosto[-Rosario], we had Gilberto Martínez, we have—wow—Juan Méndez; we have José Santini. Lots of Puerto Ricans, obviously. From Argentina, we had Sam Larson and Alfredo González. From Peru, we have Hernando Mariscal; myself from Chile. And we have Jairito Pedraza from Colombia; Luis Vera from Venezuela, Jesús Aguais from AID FOR AIDS, from Venezuela, Gonzalo Aburto, Cathy Chang, Carlos Cordero, Steven Córdova, Mario de la Torriente, Héctor González, Danette Lebron, Carlos Maldonado, Patricia Navarro, Víctor Parra, Luis Santiago, Amador Vega, Andrew Vélez, Walt Wilder . . . So it was like a really wonderful, wonderful group of people, from different countries . . . We had Lydia Awadala, with her own group of women. We have Rita Córdova that had El Centro in Harlem, Marina Alvarez, Carmen Royster . . . We were ACT UP; we were not a sidekick, like an adjunct group; we were ACT UP . . . We were heavily involved in basically every single action. And we were always kind of like going from one committee to another."

THE CONSEQUENCES

In 2014, when I interviewed César, he had moved far from commercial design. He was now working in mental health as a hospital clinician. And he had done a lot of thinking about postplague life, and how the events of the AIDS crisis dug a hole in people's psyches. He thought of the aftermath as *endurance trauma.*

"Not necessarily the classical PTSD. But the sense of danger in seeing in your life at risk of being annihilated; the in and the out, and feeling that there is little you can do to change that level of threat, or that level of danger. You know, month after month after month . . . 1992 was a hard year, when people started really getting very sick, or dying. So many of them were not coming to the meetings; they were in no condition to really get out of their homes. I mean, you remember. I mean, you know, people with AIDS at twenty-seven or thirty-five don't die in two days . . . They just linger and linger and linger."

César worked at Housing Works from 2002 to 2005, and then he went to work at St. Vincent's Hospital from 2005 to 2009. There, he would see people who were "survivors" of the epicenter of the plague, dying once a month of a drug OD or something like that. It was the post-epidemic condition; an epidemic doesn't just end. *And then we go back to the commercial, toothpaste and European cars.* That doesn't happen. Instead, the community was hit with a long-standing crystal meth epidemic. Even one of César's doctors got involved in drugs, and his career and life were ruined.

"There was no way to transition from total crisis and abnormal way of living into something that can be integrated with a daunting loss . . . People basically stay in crisis, but in a different form of crisis. In this case, it was the emotional crisis . . . I don't know if, when the Black Plague ended in the Middle Ages, people really learned that they needed to do something about the aftermath. I'm sure that they started going to church, and [trying] to rebuild their lives, and going back to normal. And it was not after a while that they realized that some of them are not making it, that they are all messed up in their heads.

"My theory, or my sense, is that the people that got involved in activism, like me, are much more aware of what happened. The ones that were not involved in activism, they don't know why their lives just do not make any sense. And their relationships don't make sense, and they are becoming more and more kind of like—alienated. I see some of that in the patients, the HIV, middle-aged patients that we treat in the clinic where I work. It seems that they remain alive, not to be able to connect the dots forever. Like there is something there that remains disconnected.

"[We need] some kind of acknowledgment that a post-epidemic generation doesn't remain intact simply because they have survived. At least that would be the lens. Once you put on a specific type of filter or lens, then you begin to see the kind of things that you need to take care of. But if you don't have a lens that allows you to see certain things, like those things that you see—you know, soldiers put to sea in the night, in the dark—then you don't see anything. It's been there in front of us."

And so César articulates for us that ACT UP and its relationships are, as Matt Brim notes, not just a model of activism but a model of making sense of the problem that activism is trying to address, and the problem that lingers in the lives of individuals, long after the activism creates some kind of positive permanent change. Activism is, consequentially, the process of making sense of one's experience of the problem that collectively we have transformed. It creates order, demystifies, and allows an understanding of systems that otherwise feel overwhelming and unaddressable.

"Spencer Cox gave a presentation at the Harm Reduction Coalition. I remember, I attended that. And they were asking about crystal meth . . . [They were] mostly heterosexual care providers. And there was kind of like a little bit of, *What the heck? I mean, you people, you know, waged this incredible war. You survived it. Some of you were heavily involved in making these incredible changes that we never thought that they were going to happen at the level of kind of like approval of new drugs, and treatments, and stuff like that . . . And now you are killing yourselves! You know, you're doing these drugs! Society is much more open; we are on the way*—this was several years ago—*we are on the way of maybe having kind of like marriage. What's up with you people?* It was like that, you know? And I remember Spencer talk about, and he said, *It's loneliness. It's just sheer loneliness.*

"When you are left with a whole bunch of people, but neither you or your friend has a narrative, then you don't want to talk, neither to you, to yourself, or to your friend. You just stay isolated. So developing a narrative for what happened afterwards, I think that would be very, very useful . . . To tell you the truth, if I were a sociologist, I would be running behind that. I would try to get grants to do this. Because when are we going to have another epidemic to document how this behaves? From the purely kind of like sociological, anthropological perspective, it's kind of like, it's a fantastic experience.

". . . That particular split—I think that should have been dealt [with] better by all of us. If we all lowered the volume a little bit on the rhetoric; if we all tried to get more practical, more pragmatic, about what is it that we want to do, and whether we can continue doing it, having very dramatically different, or diametrically different ideologies or perspectives, or angles, whatever you want to call it. But nevertheless, we see the practical. It's like, I'm sure that a lot of people in Treatment and Data never really understood the agenda of the Latino Caucus. To what extent they supported us, or not; some of them did, some of them don't, whatever. But you know, when they were negotiating inside the CDC, with someone there, and we were screaming outside; or when they entered the Wall Street chamber, and we were making kind of like a scary mess outside; we could see, you know, like in a few days, I don't remember how much, kind of like Burroughs Wellcome lowered their price of AZT. That's all what I care. I don't need to marry you, I don't need to really know that actually, what you are doing doesn't cover the whole spectrum of what I believe the political activism should cover. But if what you're doing is somewhat effective, and you're doing good work—if you are doing good work, I'll do my part. Is there a place for us?"

A Personal Conclusion

AIDS prepared us for everything.

—JACK WATERS

It's March 2018. I have been struggling with a serious genetic disease, caused by a Janus kinase 2 (JAK2) gene mutation, for a decade, and my veins have become scarred after two years of phlebotomies, given every five weeks. The nurse who has been patiently sitting with me and helping me, Trish Sullivan, used to be an AIDS nurse at NYU in the early days of AIDS. She's told me about the endless diarrhea that nurses had to deal with, and how they would try to clean up and pull patients together when their friends or parents came to visit. How the men couldn't keep any food down except milkshakes from McDonald's. So the nurses would pick up shakes on the way to work. It is very intimate to sit with Trish during the twenty-minute blood drain, and we talk about Trump, her son's football team, and AIDS memories. Then one day, at the end of the session, she says, "I won't be here next time because I took a job in another building. I'm going from five days to four days. But I didn't want you to come in and have me just be gone. It wouldn't be nice."

I am so moved by her kindness. This is the standard of how human beings should behave: acknowledging, communicating, informatively kind.

In the interim, a doctor at Sloan Kettering thinks I may have a second gene mutation and suggests a bone marrow specimen. He tells me it is an easy procedure and that I will be able to walk home. I show up at seven-thirty in the morning with evening tickets to see a play with Alan, a friend from San Francisco. They make a hole in my rear hip bone and take the specimen. I do walk home, but two blocks from my house the anesthesia wears off, and suddenly I cannot put any weight on my leg. I cannot move my leg. I cannot walk or stand. I am in the middle of Ninth Street, a block from my house, and I cannot move. I am filled with dread.

By holding on to the sides of buildings and moving an inch at a time I get to my place, and literally drag myself up the six flights—it takes about thirty minutes. Once I lie down on the couch, I realize that I can't get up. I can't stand at all at this point. In order to get aspirin from the next room, I have to lie down on the floor and slither like a snake. Two hours later I have to call Alan and cancel. The next morning, I have to cancel my participation in a meeting with the provost of the City University of New York about the new HIV/AIDS studies program I want to start there with my colleagues Matt Brim and Linda Villarosa. Perhaps because I missed the meeting, the program is never supported. In fact, I—a person who almost never cancels anything, who considers it a sign of honor to keep her word—has to cancel five days' worth of commitments because I simply cannot move.

The full genetic and molecular high-tech testing of this bone marrow specimen takes two months. And in the end, it shows that I don't have a second gene mutation, which is "good," except I still don't have an explanation for what is happening to me. But the Sloan doctor, a personable but nerdy young Jewish guy with a highly trimmed, graying beard, tells me that the hematocrit number of forty-five that I have been aiming for for two years is actually the standard for men, and that, as a woman, I should be at forty-two. Of course, I am familiar with this problem of male standards from AIDS. And I understand that I have been misanalyzed, part of a historically consistent erasure.

The next time I come into NYU, it is with the knowledge that I have to get to forty-two, not forty-five. It's a goal that is a bit daunting. Normally, I come in between forty-six and forty-eight, so getting down to forty-five with one blood draw has been relatively easy. But forty-two is a whole other matter. There is a new nurse and she seems to be in a rush. Because my blood is too thick, phlebotomy requires a large needle, and she goes into my vein but no blood comes out. She is impatient and starts digging around in my arm, trying to score the vein. For the first time in this entire horrible process of my mysterious decline and untreatable series of symptoms, I feel overwhelmed. She pulls out the needle and reapproaches using another vein, and that one doesn't work, either. She is digging around again, and I am feeling panicked.

The sensation of a carelessly operated needle digging into my arm, in futile search for a functional spot in a scarred vein, is a kind of invasion I have not experienced before. She takes the needle out, and my arm starts bleeding. She wraps it up and goes to my left arm. There, again, she makes two punctures and gets nowhere. My veins are scarred from so many punctures, and she can't access the blood. She goes to get two nurses from chemotherapy, who start rubbing and turning my arms. Then another nurse, sixty-something, Irish, like Trish, comes in. She tries my right arm again, and it still doesn't work. I want it to end.

We decide that I will go home and let my veins heal. Then I will come back in ten days and try it again.

The older nurse waits until the team has left.

"I'm Kathy," she says. "Ask for me."

So I make an appointment to see Kathy.

My friend Dudley Saunders, a long-term HIV survivor, suggests that I get a port so that they can stop poking me. It's a dramatic step, but I know I may need it. The fact that he suggests it so normally, and the fact I have seen a number of them in my friends, mostly years ago, makes it more imaginable and reasonable. I write to the doctor and ask him about a port. He calls me and says that if the phlebotomies become impossible, we will move to a daily low-dose chemo pill. The problem is that the pill can create GI problems, and I already have GI problems that are so severe and mysterious that my standard of living has dropped considerably.

In looking for management solutions for my genetically based GI problem, I have been to four hospitals. My out-of-pocket expenses for health costs last year were twenty-two thousand dollars. Thanks to my time in ACT UP, I know how to read trials, understand medical journal articles, and ask questions. For example, I know that if a doctor is prescribing a drug with bad side effects that probably won't work, he will raise the dosage before moving on. So I know—from history—to ask, "Have you had any experience of a patient with my exact condition benefiting from this drug?" But no matter how compliant I am, this is a question that my doctors, at least, don't want to answer. I also know—from history—that when looking at the results of a trial, it's not the percentage of patients who improved that should be influencing me; it's whether or not any of them had my exact condition. If even one person like me was helped, it is worth trying the drug.

Around the same time, my eighty-eight-year-old mother contemplates a move to assisted living and needs me to go through her photographs and divide them into parcels for my siblings and cousins. I spend three days sorting pictures of family events that I was excluded from: baby showers, weddings. I have spent forty years mourning the cruelty of my family, and performing this task makes me stoic about the whole thing. "This is the way it is," I tell myself. "This is the way it is," Dudley says when his stepmother dies. "This is how it goes," another queer friend says when his mother dies. But I am surrounded by straight people who find the decline of their parents to be tragic, and unbearable. My friend Jack Waters, another long-term HIV survivor, tells me, "AIDS prepared us for everything."

In the interim, as my veins are healing, I decide to go to Jeffrey VanDyke the day before the retry. Jeff has been my acupuncturist for a number of years, and I have sent many people to him. A painter in his late sixties, he had a huge AIDS practice in the 1980s, when there were no treatments. When I am on the table, we have long conversations about AIDS. Sometimes it surfaces that we both knew the same person, long dead and forgotten. And that is always a special moment. It feels great to say someone's name and to conjure up something about them, no matter how mere. This time, Jeff is trying to help me get ready for the return phlebotomy. The session is two hours, and we start talking about some of the dead people we have in common, only this time we are joking around, actually camping. "That one was such a bitch," Jeff says. "Yeah, he thought he was so glam," I respond. We are laughing, and devolve into full-on bitching, telling jokes about all the jerky things our dead people said and did. We are probably the only people in the world talking about them that day. Some have been dead for thirty years or more. It helps relieve the pressure, this intimate acknowledgment. Jeff does some Japanese and Chinese moves to help my circulation and blood flow.

The next morning, I come into the cancer waiting room. Everyone there is nice. The woman who works reception is kind and patient. The chairs are comfortable. There is a quiet room. There is light through the windows. They have coffee. My colleague from work who also has cancer is there that day; we hug. I am feeling optimistic that this time the phlebotomy will work.

Kathy comes in. She is very kind and very experienced. She talks me through the process, uses lidocaine to make the needle entry less difficult, and that lets her move the needle around without hurting me. A necessary innovation. As the twenty-minute slow drip starts, we start talking, and I tell her that I am an AIDS historian. Kathy tells me that she started working in nursing at NYU in 1980. And then she describes the suffering. The young men, with good bodies, in their twenties, riddled with KS. She told her boyfriend, *I saw someone with KS*, and he said, *No, that's impossible. You have to be old and Mediterranean.*

She saw someone with pneumocystis pneumonia (PCP), and her boyfriend said, *That can't be.*

A woman came in to give birth and she couldn't breathe. It turned out she had PCP; her husband was a sailor. Kathy says, "It was awful for them, for their families. I mean their friends. Most of them didn't have families."

She had a patient who would yell at the nurses and throw his urine. His friends came in and said, *This is not him. He would never act this way.*

Later they realized that the patient had dementia.

"There were no beds," she said.

Time is up; the blood bag is filled. She takes it and throws my blood in the garbage, as it is bad and cannot be donated. She wipes a tear.

We have not mentioned any names, but she is crying for all of them, and we two, end-of-middle-aged women, sitting in a hospital room, are part of the ashes.

"Thank you," I say.

"Thank you," she says. "Thanks for talking."

This, I know, is the enduring relationship of AIDS.

Appendix 1: ACT UP and the FBI

MARY DORMAN

"They definitely, definitely had detectives in ACT UP . . . There definitely were snitches. Absolutely . . . because they were informed about a lot of things. And I know, writing from the Freedom of Information Act for myself, that the FBI has files on me, NYPD has files on me, CIA has files on me. They're all organizationally affiliated and I know it's ACT UP . . . I have a good faith belief that there were undercover police there or informants, whether they were police officers or not. And I do have an idea who it was, but I cannot say."

GERRI WELLS

"I've seen cops sitting in ACT UP . . . They were so obvious, you know. You know, the white socks, the black bulky shoes. I mean—[LAUGHS]—dark glasses [and] a trench coat. I mean, they were so obvious. They just would stick out . . . They wanted to know when our next demonstrations were, where we were going. It made them feel like they had the inside scoop on things . . . I believe that there were cops that I can identify, and there were cops that we couldn't identify. I really believe there was an FBI involvement. Especially when we were going after the big drug companies. They had a lot of pull in this town. A lot of money, a lot of power. And I think, I really believe that they were getting all the information they wanted to get. It was okay; we weren't doing anything, we weren't making bombs. We were committed to nonviolence."

The FBI released 196 heavily redacted pages on ACT UP, but even with the thick black bars on most pages, it is immediately obvious that there was an informant or informants giving information about timing and content of actions. For example, a document originally marked SECRET on July 13, 1988, reports the following:

> On June 14, 1988 (REDACTED) provided the following information:
> (Entire paragraph REDACTED.)
> (REDACTED) advised the group was planning a variety of activities to increase their visibility, however, does not have any information regarding outward plans to disrupt the convention.
> (REDACTED) advised a demonstration and rally, plus a "kiss in" to be staged at the Omni Hotel, are planned for July 18, 1988. On July 17, 1988, [ACT UP] members will have a "visibility day" where they will distribute leaflets at busy areas like shopping malls, et cetera.
> (Entire paragraph REDACTED except for the word *advised* indicating that an informant was identified.)

In 1995, gay Massachusetts congressman Barney Frank wrote to the FBI asking about the nature of the informants. He wanted to know if they were undercover agents sent into the organization, or if they were actual ACT UP members who gave inside information. In other words, were the informants actually police officers who simply attended public meetings in plain clothes? Or were they, for example, ACT UP members who may have been arrested for drugs, let's say, who worked off charges by giving information?

The FBI general counsel, Howard Shapiro, responded:

> Typically a Bureau informant, who was operated as an informant for reasons wholly unrelated to [ACT UP], would report to his/her handling agent regarding planned protest activity by ACT UP. In many instances the informant information expressly referred to planned unlawful activity. The agent would record the information provided by the informant, and prepare an outgoing communication advising, through FBI channels, the relevant Federal, State or local police agency, or if the circumstances warranted, the United States Secret Service, of the impending [ACT UP] action. Quite often after the demonstration or other action occurred, the responding police agency would send a communication back to the originating FBI office describing the protest event and its police response, and frequently enclosing press clippings. On other occasions, press clippings were apparently provided by the informant . . . In each of these cases, the Bureau acted merely as a conduit, receiving the information from a confidential source and forwarding it to the relevant police agency. In none of these cases did the FBI undertake any investigation of its own.

The phrase *who was operated as an informant for reasons wholly unrelated to [ACT UP]* actually fits theory number two, that this was a person in ACT UP who owed the FBI something, possibly in exchange for dropping other charges. The statement *In none of these cases did the FBI undertake any investigation of its own*, I think, implies that the informants were not undercover agents, again reinforcing the idea that they were ACT UP members.

> To be sure, none of the reported [ACT UP] plans called for any violence. In almost all cases, however, the intended actions included interference with the Secret Service's protective responsibilities or violations of state and local law: trespass onto government property, crossing police barricades, taking possession of government offices, obstructing entrances to various public or private buildings, destruction of property, plans to harass and disrupt various speakers, including presidential candidates, and to sabotage various computer systems.
>
> . . . The unlawful aspects of the actions planned by ACT UP and reported to the FBI were not protected First Amendment activity.

The FBI then addressed the issue of the heavy redaction on most pages of the Freedom of Information Act–garnered material, obtained primarily by ACT UPers Duncan Osborne, Andrew Miller, and the late Robert Rygor:

> Exemption 7(D) of the FOIA permits the withholding of all information provided by a confidential source in a criminal or national security investigation. As virtually all of the documents in the New York file fall within this exception, being comprised of confidential source-derived information, they were properly withheld.

Whoever these informants were, and regardless of their motives, their information constitutes the substance of the FBI records.

Some other citations from FBI reports include the following:

- May 27, 1987. FBI Counter-Terrorism was alerted via an informant to potential for violence by ACT UP at the upcoming International AIDS Conference in Montreal.

- July 11, 1988. The FBI Domestic Terrorism Unit reported that "[ACT UP] and Skinheads" were protesting the newly imposed midnight closing of Tompkins Square Park by scheduling a demonstration at 12:01 am. (Sixteen lines REDACTED.)

- September 30, 1988, Counter-Terrorism Section, Domestic Security Unit. (REDACTED) "[ACT UP]" (REDACTED) Organization was planning to hold a demonstration on Tuesday October 11, 1988, in Washington DC at the Food and Drug Administration (FDA) Building. (Fifteen lines REDACTED.)

- January 1989. The FBI notes that ACT UP was a member of "The Ad Hoc Committee Against the Klan" in Atlanta.

- May 22, 1990. A report on the NIH action found that eight hundred to one thousand people attended, six to eight smoke bombs were detonated by ACT UP, eighty-two people were arrested for trespassing, and one person was arrested for resisting and battery of a police office. The report notes: "No infected blood or used condoms were exhibited or thrown."

- October 1990. In a lengthy memo, the FBI noted: "It is also recommended that all law enforcement officers who will be working at an [ACT UP] demonstration wear thick rubber gloves."

- November 16, 1990. Right-wing congressman William Dannemeyer complained to the FBI that ACT UPer Michael Petrelis was quoted in *Mother Jones* magazine saying "If someone took out Jesse Helms or William Dannemeyer of California, I would be the first to stand up and applaud." In seventeen lines of redaction, the only visible text reads: "[ACT UP], a pro-homosexual organization."

- An obscured date in 1991. An informant provided information to the FBI of a "possible threat to the safety of President George Bush" by ACT UP. The rest is redacted.

- September 30, 1991. The police report concluded that "[ACT UP] has protested at every public appearance of President George Bush during the month of September."

- October 1991. The FBI noted that eighty-five members of a group called The AIDS Coalition to Unleash Power were arrested throwing theatrical blood over the White House gate.

- Undated document. "Civil Rights Matter" (REDACTED) (Protect Identity) (REDACTED) "ACT UP, a radical Gay/Lesbian Organization" (REDACTED).

Although a few ACT UP members, notably Tracy Morgan and Heidi Dorow, told the floor that they believed they were being followed and harassed by the FBI, there is no mention of that in the released material.

Appendix 2: *Tell It to ACT UP*

In the days before the internet, ACT UPer Bill Dobbs operated a low-tech precursor to Twitter, in which every week people could write down anonymous comments on a slip of paper and deposit them into a box. The following week, Bill would distribute these messages, unedited, in a typed handout called *Tell It to ACT UP* (*TITA*). I have some editions of *TITA* from February 5, 1990, to June 1, 1992, covering the period of the split and after. Here are a few selected and edited highlights (and lowlights).

April 16, 1990 #10
PICK OF THE WEEK
I'm not your average TITA writer. In fact, I've often thought it's been a bit petty. However for Sean Strub to say that women aren't asked to sign said [fundraising] letters because there's no women in ACT UP "with a profile"—unlike Larry Kramer and Mark Harrington—points out how much sexism and chauvinism still exist in ACT UP. We should not approve direct M-A-L-E fundraising utilizing s-t-a-r-s. J.E.G.

ᘒ

I'm sick and tired of the way we [ACT UP] have our set-up. I'm talking about Media set-up. ACT UP should pick one permanent spot in the room where people who don't want to be on camera can sit. It's not fair to decide on a spot right before the meeting. I rush here right after work just to get a damn seat. If I [we] have to move, we have to stand until 11 pm. Just expressing myself to ACT UP!

ᘒ

I object strongly to the practice of using xeroxed information sheets as "place cards" on unoccupied seats. To find over half the available seats "reserved" at 6:30 is obnoxious and inconsiderate. If you want a seat get your butt to the meeting early! The meetings are not public performances—no reservations (except the first row of course) First come, first served. Be fair! Thanks. Woody Enoicaras.

ᘒ

Lets stop Peter Staley bashing! He is one of our most effective activists. He deserves to be valued.

ᘒ

Nobody ever gives his/her name before they speak. At the risk of feeding hungry egos, could we try to encourage this more?

ᘒ

If anyone has photos of the Albany action, specifically of a Black woman with reddish-brown dreads (that's me) being dragged away by a cop, please get in touch with me. Iris Mathew

℘

How about an action at the heinous Taj Mahal—Trump's newest hellhole. I realize it's not directly AIDS related but—how much more symbolic can this billion dollar wasteful monstrosity be during this crisis?

℘

Please thank Mary Dorman for her competent and gracious help during the Albany trials, She wasn't mentioned during follow-up. Gabriel

April 30, 1990
PICK OF THE WEEK
The only purpose that TITA serves is to allow ACT UPers to shit on each other and most of the time do it anonymously. TITA is partially responsible for the venom and divisiveness currently sweeping ACT UP. Lets get rid of TITA. Lee Arsenault

℘

We need a new space now! Tom Crimmins

℘

Querido Tom Shultz! Nos Preguntamos: Si fueras activista en un pais donde no se hablara Ingles, y donde un porciento elevado de los afectados por el SIDA fueran abnglo-parlantes: Te preocuparias por hacer llegar le informacion a ese gente en su lengua? PIENSA EN ESTO. Gilbert [Martínez], [Moisés Agosto-Rosario], Juan Mendez, Gonzalo Aburto.

℘

You: Fearless activist at the Stop the Church action. Me: Handed your Walkman and told "take care of this." I have been since December 10! Do you remember who you are? Call 533-4913 and I'll be glad to return your Walkman.

June 18, 1990
Every time you take a drag on a cigarette, you're sucking [Jesse Helms's] penis.

℘

Although our decision to go to San Francisco [International AIDS Conference] is a controversial one, it does not authorize people to behave like maniacs: In recent weeks people on the floor were completely out of order with boos, hissing, name calling, insinuations, cat-calling and screaming in general. When one person standing near me yelled to Ann Northrop, "you're trash!" I had to restrain myself and another person from belting him. R.J.G.

℘

Lets target the new bishop in Brooklyn. He is outspokenly anti-choice (praying around the clock etc) he says this is the church's #1 issue. He is also anti-gay. He replaced a much less militant one.

℘

I am still seeing fellow ACT [UPers] smoking Marlboro cigarettes. ACT UP/DC has been putting up "Ban Marlboro" stickers throughout their city. Why haven't we? It bothers me that such a small thing can't be observed. James Murphy

℘

I am writing this letter on the back of Marvin [Shulman's] ACT UP Treasurer's report. I am astounded that we have spent over $186,000 for the last three actions. I can't believe we are spending $83,000 to do San Francisco—too much of this money is going to subsidize people's travel. Some need the financial help and deserve it but not all. We are not a travel agency. Michael Marco.

August 13, 1990
If the members of ACT UP are serious about replenishing the treasury, they should put themselves on the auction block. Since they already prance around the room dressed as revealingly as possible, let them auction off their services as hustlers. The call boys who advertise in The Advocate at $150 or even $225 an hour so a night with one of the more virile adherents of ACT UP should be worth $1,000 at the very least.

℃

My bicycle was stolen out front last week.

℃

We all need to learn Spanish chants!

℃

Asian Outreach: Tell your Asian friends to join in.

℃

Whoever gave me a receipt from the Bush action—I have your money. Please see me tonight. Sukey.

September 17, 1990
PICK OF THE WEEK
The next time a gay person of color complains about being ostracized, try to listen and understand as best you can. Try to encourage your friends who are Asian, Latino/a or Black etc to come. Try to get as enthused about their issues as "mainstream" issues. Try to listen, and not ignore us when we talk. Only then will ACT UP truly be a coalition of all people. C Chin, A Realvyo, Lei Chou, Ming Ma, Kathy Chen

℃

Couldn't we earn money with anti-Helms stickers?

℃

We love Larry Kramer and think that, considering his venerable status as an AIDS-activist god, and his generally massive coolness factor, he should be allowed to say anything he damn well pleases during Monday night meetings. After all, isn't that what being Larry Kramer is all about? It's why we love him anyway. And we do love you Larry. And we love your new hair. Will and Michael.

℃

Why are people in ACT UP so rude to each other? Is it frustration and anger or just poor breeding?

℃

Garance's brain child "Count Down 18 months" in which treatment activists from all over the world work together toward the common goal of making all the major opportunistic infections treatable (and hopefully preventable) within the next 18 months is the news we all needed to hear. The concept is clear, powerful and obtainable. Garance, we love you. Lee Arsenault, Bob LaChance, Casper Schmidt

℃

Does ACT UP/Gran Fury know that bootleg versions of Silence=Death shirts are being sold at various boutiques and flea markets. (The one I saw was on Saint Mark's.) They're making money off a patented design. Should we do something about this? Glenn Belverio

℃

I'm scared to death that we are losing our focus—fighting AIDS. If it has to do with the room we have to try to focus even harder but I think it's bigger than just the room. Let's fight our complacency and revitalize ourselves this fall. Barbara Hughes.

January 28, 1991
I thoroughly enjoyed the demo at Grand Central Station. Everything seemed to go well, with the "banner in the sky" and the banner across the schedule boards. The coverage was wonderful and there were so many of us. But why did we have to leave Grand Central, what was the purpose, sit on a cold street to be arrested? The symbolism was lost and the wait in the holding cell was agonizing.

૨૭

Dear unsigned: Answer to question in TITA, January 7, 1991, concerning from Tracy Morgan fundraising letter: Received to January 22, 1991 $23,811. Cost of letter mailing $5,122.30. Profit to ACT UP to date $18,688.70. Marvin Shulman, Treasurer.

૨૭

Peter Staley, your anal retentive/obsessive compulsive behavior is making us crazy. It's a workspace, not the Staley residence. Honey take a pill and relax.

૨૭

To whom it may concern: Mary Grace Farley cannot receive any more telephone calls at work.

February 4, 1991
I was very proud of us on the Day of Desperation. Whoever thought of the balloons and banner for Grand Central was brilliant—it made for a beautiful and moving statement. But the day really made me think about our arrest-O-mania. Civil disobedience in its classic mode ([Gandhi], King) is about breaking a law in such a way that any onlooker would be forced to question the morality of the law. I don't really know what point is being made, what symbolic drama is being acted out by being arrested for blocking traffic on 42nd Street. Don Shewey.

૨૭

The Marys are way cool.

૨૭

To the people who wear fur coats to demonstrations.: please stop it. Your right to wear whatever you want ends where the cruel and unnecessary abuse of animals begins. Kevin O'Conner

૨૭

Cheers and hugs and kisses and champagne for our fabulous support people: Emily Gordon, Rafael Pimental, Patrick Carr, and Marlene Merson. They are the best. Love, Outreach/Disseminators—Tony Ortiz, David Levine, Mary Grace Farley, Betty Loos, Steve Dierna, Scott Wilson, Mike Nolan, Harbery Lerner, Charlie Welch, Michael Allen, Michael Long-acre, Steven Keith and Rick Mount.

૨૭

Although I thought the Day of Desperation was an experiment which worked brilliantly, I was disturbed by some of its aftermath. By late Wednesday night there was no one at Pitt Street (the police station) coordinating support. There was no master list of arrestees. There was only an incomplete pile of desk appearances tickets. No one really knew who was still in jail. When it got too late and too cold a lot of people just went home. Support implies commitment. It's a breach of faith with people who have been arrested not to carry through. Robert Marshall

☙

This may be denial but as an HIV+ person, I find a huge wave of negativity sweeps over me everytime some over-enthusiastic activist gets up and says "people are getting infected with HIV and dying" as some sort of political slogan. The statement is true of course but many of us are infected with HIV and are living, and trying to stay as well as possible. So, think about what you say and why you are saying it.

☙

Peter Staley—some of us think anal and retentive are quite becoming

☙

I'd like to thank the Latino/a Caucus for sharing a coffin with us (Asian and Pacific Islanders Caucus) on the Day of Desperation March. It was important that the coffin for David Dinkins was delivered by people of color. Ming Ma.

February 11, 1991
PICK OF THE WEEK
Raan Medley's "How to be A Person of Color in [ACT UP]" on the back cover of ACT UP Reports says the solution to straights' hesitation to come to ACT UP, due to being afraid of a proposition from a gay/lesbian, is, that it probably won't happen. We just talk about sex, we don't do it. BULLSHIT. The solution is work on your homophobia! An unwanted offer, straight/gay/male/female can be disposed of with a few polite words. To pretend otherwise is to condone homophobia.

☙

It is the greatest honor of my life to be able to represent ACT UP as the signer of the fund-raising letter. I hope that with each day my work, in and out of the classroom, continues to inspire and educate people about HIV and AIDS. In this way I can express to ACT UP, and the world, the gratitude I feel for the effect it has had on my life. It is ACT UP that serves as my greatest strength. With gratitude and Love, Wayne Fischer, A Gay Teacher Living With AIDS.

☙

Derek Link: I think the work you are doing is great and ever since you got your blue hair you've become a SEX BOMB! Love, Tony.

☙

Our government continues to oppress foreign nationals. But there are practical things we can do to help. Committed women who are willing to help a deserving activist, please call "matchmaker" Marvin Shulman.

☙

HOUSING AUTHORITY—please contact me if you have any information about the following: 1) You work at NYCHA (New York Housing Authority) 2) You're a NYCHA tenant or applicant 3) You know anyone with information about anti-PWA or other discrimination. Confidentiality respected. ASAP, please call Jim Davis. Thanks

☙

ACT UP/OKLAHOMA CITY would like to thank all of you for your incredible efforts in spreading the news to the hinterlands. We immensely enjoy the information. We have a long way to go in Oklahoma but because of ACT UP we will win the war with AIDS—Matthew Sharpe, Communication Committee

April 8, 1991

If the discussion over the moratorium teaches us nothing else, it should tell us that many people on the floor do not feel that they are being kept informed about the contents of meetings with government officials. Trust is not an abstract entity. It is based upon concrete information given to the floor on a regular basis. Yes it is a drag to write a report to the floor about every single meeting with every single government official. But it is absolutely essential to do so, to maintain a democratic flow of information in this organization, and to maintain cohesiveness in this organization.

℘

Why are we still arguing about AZT trials? Especially involving pregnant women of color? Must we continually—for years now—be held hostage by the 5% (mostly gay white men) of people who seem to benefit from AZT? It is a disaster of a drug, a chemotherapy foisted upon us by Dr. Fauci and Burroughs Wellcome. All of this talk about the right dose and stuff, we've been duped. Anthony dEllia

℘

It was very refreshing tonight to hear the guy from Treatment + Data mention that he has AIDS. As a HIV+ with ARC, I often wonder if anyone in ACT UP is even HIV +.

℘

Tracy Morgan thank you for your courage and work. Marisol Ruiz

℘

Has anyone ever noticed the uncanny resemblance between Peter Staley and the James Mason character in "Odd Man Out"? Raan.

℘

[Dr. James Curran] told ACT UP/Shreveport and ACT UP/New Orleans that he would change the definition of AIDS as it occurs in women if Anthony Fauci (his boss) told him to do that.

April 15, 1991

I am disturbed at how out of control these meetings have gotten. Our strength lies largely in the number of members who come and participate. Surely we can only function in these numbers if there is some order! Facilitators need to take some control. If they are not going to enforce things like "no cross talk" and three minute limits, then they shouldn't bother including it in the introduction. On that note, the guidelines even include bigwigs like Larry Kramer. I am appalled that he can get up and scream and yell at people and speak out of order and laugh at himself thinking it is very cute. Lets please begin to have some respect for ourselves and each other.

℘

In love of a friend Louis Fiero. Co-founder of ACT UP/Long Island, survived by his lover Greg Moore, sisters Cookie and Theresa and his mother Charlotte. His friends and family will live with his love. Ted Oneto.

℘

[Jamie] Bauer always says the greatest things.

℘

It is 9:30. There are 40 people ahead of me yet to make statements.

℘

During the April 8 meeting, a truncated discussion took place on the proposed six month moratorium on talks with the CDC and [NIAID]. The discussion was focused on HIV/AIDS issues in general which, I do not believe was the point of the proposal. The Women's Action

Committee was not saying that all talks with all government organizations should cease. The idea was that only women's issues be off-limits to discussion and instead be addressed in the streets publicly. Many people seem from their statements not to understand that women's issues are separate from HIV/AIDS issues in general. This isn't the ideal but it is the reality. Women are excluded in all health issues, from clinical trials. Women are taking drugs which have never been adequately tested on women. The CDC definition of AIDS is exclusionary of women. That was the impetus of the proposal and not some childish AIDSphobia desire to yell and scream, in direct action because it's fun. Chris San Miguel.

ᘓᕽ

Caution: The black and pink "The AIDS Crisis Is Not Over" sticker lose the words "Is Not" under long-term exposure to the elements. Stick them indoors only—subway, elevators, stores etc. Use your imagination but keep them inside.

May 13, 1991
Is ACT UP really distributing $9,640.00 worth of needles a month? Or does this include legal expenses for the charges pending in Criminal Court? This should be made clear because no one I know realizes this is an apparently open-ended commitment. Also, tonight I heard for the first time that Peter plans on leaving ACT UP. I will actually miss this Tory in radical clothing. As narrow as his focus was I probably agreed with him 50% of the time. The other 50% I hope will be subject to much reconsideration over the course of a long and diverse life. Raan.

ᘓᕽ

The [Gay Center] is too small and frankly that means healthy people ski in gaily from work and sit down by 7pm. [PWAs] on the other hand are lying down at home in the East Village on disability—7 comes around and we get on the bus for 55 cents and arrive at the Center at 7:30 to find every chair taken—that means no access to the meeting. So this PWA picks up the papers and tries again next week.

ᘓᕽ

Does OUTWEEK's arrogance really serve any purpose in our community? Not if you are an addict, PWA, person of color, or live outside the pretty boy activist community. Let them know we're all queers! Write!

ᘓᕽ

Must Scott Morgan, every week, sit up on the stage in such a provocative and oh-so tantalizing fashion? A girl can't hardly concentrate . . . An achingly frustrated admirer.

ᘓᕽ

Aldyn [McKean] darling, stay away from the sun (whilst recognizing your right to sun as much as you want).

July 1, 1991
The Immigration and Naturalization Service demonstration on June 26 had lots of eye catching posters but a somewhat fuzzy fact sheet. Most marshalls could be seen socializing with each other. ACT UP's biggies picketed, too deep in conversation to join in the un-catchy chants. Baylor.

ᘓᕽ

It is unconscionable that we let an ACT UPer steal $20,000 from us and spend $16,000 for an ad in the New York Times. It is ridiculous and paternalistic that we spend close to $50,000 to send 20 of our members to Florence when our European brothers and sisters can do the job as well as we can. Lets spend the little money that we have fighting AIDS. Roy Martin Hyman

ℰ℧

I thought I lost a roll of film from the Holocaust Museum. I found it and ironically found out the same day the friend I went to Israel with died due to AIDS complications. I'll miss you Richard Dana. David Falcone.

ℰ℧

Again, lets time the presentations with a clock.

ℰ℧

If Dan Williams stole $16,000.00 from us he must pay it back. He must sign an agreement saying how and when he will pay it back. It doesn't matter if all he is able to pay is $5.00 a week, he must pay it back. For him to do anything less is an insult to all the people who work at ending the AIDS crisis and the memory of all the people who died in the struggle, Mitchell.

July 29, 1991
More disturbing news on the Dan Williams scandal: On the same Monday night Dan "apologized" for stealing $20,000, he orchestrated another $2,200 disbursement of ACT UP funds to himself. Here's how he did it: Dan was originally representing Needle Exchange in Florence. He possessed his airline ticket when that sponsorship was pulled. Furthermore, his friend Carlos Garcia had a ticket paid for by ACT UP. Dan said he would be covering Carlos's travel expenses. I asked Dan to cancel their plans in order to save ACT UP $2,200. I also told him I found it ludicrous that we were lending $$ to someone who stole money from us to go on a two week trip to Italy. He replied that he would be working for Revlon for one week and would earn $12,000 most of which would be used to repay ACT UP. Besides, he said, he had already given ACT UP two checks to cover his travel expenses. The checks bounced because Dan issued a stop payment order against them. He willfully defrauded ACT UP soon after promising to repay us. No one should expect repayment anytime soon. Charlie [Franchino].

ℰ℧

For the start of every meeting, please: Strip Donald, Strip!

ℰ℧

AS a GBM I'm appalled at the racism and sexism in today's TITA . . . I have been an ACT UP member for three months and the people in this group need to get their shit together . . . Although [Mr. Williams's] actions are reprehensible and he should be legally bound to repay the money he stole, we should handle this problem ourselves. We've got the cops and the federal government against us and we shouldn't involve the law in certain [matters] unless we absolutely have to. L.J. Lambert.

ℰ℧

While I very much appreciated Rich Lynn's medical overview of the Florence conference, I was confused by some of the terminology and I know I am not the only one. Could Treatment and [Data] please do short teach-ins during the meetings on the following: Tat gene inhibitors (and relation of TAT to interleukins), protease inhibitors, TIBOs, cytokine levels (relation to disease progression). Hand outs would be helpful too. Thank you very much.

ℰ℧

I like sexy mature men and three of the hottest ones are in this room—Gene Fedorko, Charlie [Franchino] and Vince Gagliostro. I am blushing too much to sign my name. But don't worry they'll know who I am soon. You guys are gorgeous.

ℰ℧

Hey New York Times Obituary Department—My lover is not called "companion"! I don't even refer to my dog that way. A gay man.

&

Michael Cunningham is fierce!

&

Kudos to Ron Goldberg for clear funny, focused facilitating. Jamie Meyer.

&

To Mr. Andrew [Vélez]—my hat is off to you and I toast your eloquence. Your facilitating has a control that commands respect! Keep it up!

&

Candido, you are the hottest, fiercest man in ACT UP. I wish I had the guts to say this to you. An Ardent Admirer.

September 10, 1991
PICK OF THE WEEK
Kennebunkport brought ACT UP together!! It was overwhelming to see faces of those ACT UPers I often disagree with politically marching to Bush's estate. Fuck dissension within ACT UP—it was time for all of us to be together. Now, lets all come together for our action in Washington D.C. Michael Marco for the Girlfriend Militants

&

Just for the record, we were interviewing the citizens of Kennebunkport during the Target Bush action—two out of ten people were hostile. Most people felt that the damage that was going to be done to their town by us was media hype. We were surprised by the support we got. In that sense the action was successful. Duncan Elliot, Glenn Belverio.

&

Has anybody else noted the heroic evolution of Bob Rafsky (from the center aisle?) He's stunned us more than once with his brilliant locutions. To transform our anger and rage, our pain and grief and our aggravation and frustration into action is a rare and great gift.

&

Karin Timour, you are the best. You are the activist with the mostest I really love and respect you. You are everything I want to be. Donald Grove.

June 1, 1992 (apparently the final edition)
Stop the fighting, start the uniting. ACT UP is still worthwhile. ACT UP is still a valid form of social, medical and economic change. ACT UP is still needed . . . ACT UP, FIGHT BACK, FIGHT AIDS! Erik Krumm

&

The Democratic Convention. Since Bush and Perot answer to none—bring a friend to ACT UP next week! We can have powerful and passionate actions that can have an impact on National Democratic agendas, plus lots-o-media visibility. It's up to you. [Jamie] Leo.

&

Many thanks to folks on the Media Committee as well as Paul O'Dwyer and others who volunteered for the Judge Roth "Citizens' Arrest." Appreciations are also due to the Saturday Night Live defendants (sorry I can't remember all your names) who helped double our numbers! You all turned a mediocre turnout into a first rate zap. Raan

&

Thanks to everyone who showed up at the City Council meeting. We really gave it to Enoch Williams. Tom Duane's speech was hard-hitting and the ACT UP presence was nothing short of disruptive. This is not a guilt trip but merely a commentary; in the recent past it

has been difficult to get large numbers at our demos. Well, guess who showed up at the City Council demo this past week? Dan Williams! Just another thing that makes you go hmmmm!
Jane Auerbach

ﮋ

Pam's presentation about the Dan Quayle zap was great—everything open and a real activist statement. All of us can listen and learn—this is the real ACT UP, thanks to Campaign '92.
Emily

ﮋ

AS a lesbian of color I've felt totally unwelcome by the white lesbians of ACT UP. After approximately 18 months of regularly attending meetings, maybe two lesbians have consistently spoken to me. Furthermore I can immediately identify the straight white women, they are the white females who speak (read safe). I've seen lesbians of ACT UP on the streets and said "hi" and received no response. I'm not searching for dates here, just a simple hello . . .
Kim Edwards

ﮋ

Over and out. Bill Dobbs

ACT UP New York Time Line

(Sources: ACT UP, ACT UP Oral History Project, Ron Goldberg)

The story of ACT UP's accomplishments is not a chronological one because so many campaigns occurred at the same time, overlapped, and intertwined. This is a map of simultaneity, focusing on the prime years from the organization's founding in 1987 to its split into ACT UP and TAG in 1992. While ACT UP held meetings, zaps, and actions sometimes daily, here are the dates of a short list of key contextualizing events.

Stonewall riots: June 1969
Roe v. Wade legalizes abortion: 1973
Lambda Legal founded: 1973
New York's sterilization regulations: 1978
Hyde Amendment upheld by Supreme Court: 1979
New York Times article "Rare Cancer Seen in 41 Homosexuals": July 3, 1981
Gay Men's Health Crisis (GMHC) founded: 1982
Reproductive rights movement splits over lesbian liberation: 1982
Community Health Project at the LGBT Center founded: 1983
Denver Principles by People with AIDS: 1983
Minority Task Force on AIDS founded: 1985
AIDS Clinical Trials Group founded: 1986
Supreme Court *Bowers v. Hardwick* decision: 1986

1987

January/February—The SILENCE=DEATH collective (Charles Kreloff, Avram Finkelstein, Jorge Socarrás, Brian Howard, Chris Lione, and Oliver Johnston) design a poster with an upward-pointing pink triangle over the words SILENCE=DEATH. They wheat-paste it around gay areas of New York City.

February—The Lavender Hill Mob (Bill Bahlman, Marty Robinson, Michael Petrelis, and others) disrupts a meeting at the U.S. Centers for Disease Control (CDC) on mandatory testing, wearing concentration camp uniforms.

March 10—Larry Kramer gives a speech at the Gay Center on West Thirteenth Street calling for a political response to AIDS.

March 12—Three hundred people form the AIDS Coalition To Unleash Power (ACT UP), name proposed by the late Steven Bohrer.

March 19—The U.S. Food and Drug Administration (FDA) approves AZT, patent held by Burroughs Wellcome.

March 24— At ACT UP's first action on Wall Street, 250 people protest pharmaceutical greed and high prices, demand new drug approval. Seventeen are arrested.

June 1—ACT UP joins other activist groups in civil disobedience in Washington, D.C.

June 28—The ACT UP contingent participates in the Gay Pride march with a concentration camp float responding to threatened quarantine for people with AIDS.

July 21–24—ACT UP holds a silent vigil at Memorial Sloan Kettering Cancer Center for four days and nights, demanding that scientists run more clinical trials for drugs other than AZT, and that more people be enrolled in these trials.

October 11—ACT UP joins the National Lesbian and Gay March on Washington and civil disobedience at the Supreme Court to protest the *Bowers v. Hardwick* decision. Twenty ACT UPers are arrested.

October 23—*Testing the Limits*, from the AIDS activist video collective, is shown at the American Film Institute.

November 19—The ACT UP window display *Let the Record Show . . .* is installed at the New Museum by a group later to become the art collective Gran Fury.

December 10—The Metropolitan Health Association (MHA) affinity group occupies the office of NYC health commissioner Stephen Joseph. Eight are arrested.

1988

January 4—The AIDS Coalition to Network, Organize, and Win (ACT NOW), a national coalition of new ACT UP chapters, is formed.

January 15—ACT UP's Women's Caucus's first action. Five hundred people protest at the offices of *Cosmopolitan* magazine responding to the magazine's claim that heterosexual women can't get AIDS.

January—The film *Doctors, Liars and Women: AIDS Activists Say No to Cosmo* is produced by Maria Maggenti and Jean Carlomusto.

February—The Community Health Project women's program is founded.

February 1—Work begins on the AIDS Treatment Registry, the first collected data on AIDS drug trials across the United States.

February 14—Iris Long attends a roundtable meeting with Dan Hoth of the National Institute of Allergy and Infectious Diseases.

March 24—ACT UP anniversary action Wall Street II. Five hundred activists disrupt traffic for hours using a "wave" system, in which affinity groups take turns sitting in the street. More than 111 are arrested.

March 27—ACT UP holds its first anniversary party and talent show at Siberia.

April—Parallel track proposed by Jim Eigo and ACT UP's first Treatment and Data Committee to Anthony Fauci, head of the National Institute of Allergy and Infectious Diseases (NIAID).

April 29–May 7—"Nine Days of Rage." More than fifty national chapters coordinate local actions on IV drug use, homophobia, people of color, women, testing programs, prison programs, and children with AIDS.

May 9—Vito Russo presents his speech "Why We Fight" at an ACT UP demonstration in Albany.

May 11—The Majority Action Committee, people of color in ACT UP, holds its first meeting.

May 17—Bob Rafsky and Vito Russo meet with *The Village Voice*'s editor, Robert Massa, to discuss the *Voice*'s inadequate AIDS coverage.

June 23—ACT UP meets homeless people at a "Talk-IN" at Tent City in City Hall Park to protest the city's lack of policy on the homeless. ACT UP gives out fact sheets and distributes condoms.

October 10—"Why We Fight," Vito Russo's speech, is repeated at a rally in front of the Health and Human Services building, Washington, D.C.

October 11—Seize Control of the FDA. In its first major action, ACT UP shuts down the Food and Drug Administration.

October—The poster *Kissing Doesn't Kill: Greed and Indifference Do* appears on buses in New York City.

November 25—Trump Tower Trumpsgiving action. ACT UP protests lack of housing for people with AIDS (PWAs) in the face of tax breaks to wealthy developers. Activists are arrested.

1989

1989—The Community Research Initiative is founded to do independent treatment research.

1989—Operation Rescue escalates harassment at abortion clinics.

February 2—ACT UP protests the FDA's new protocols for DHPG, which would cut many users off from the drug. The FDA concedes and makes DHPG available under "compassionate use."

March 2—The FDA approves the use of DHPG, the only drug available to treat AIDS-related blindness.

March 28—ACT UP's second anniversary action, Target City Hall. Three thousand demonstrators focus on Koch's inaction. Two hundred are arrested.

May 2—The FDA approves aerosolized pentamadine.

June 4–9—ACT UP disrupts the opening of the fifth annual International AIDS Conference in Montreal.

June 11—Anthony Fauci announces federal implementation of ACT UP's "parallel track" design for clinical trials.

September 14—ACT UP members chain themselves inside the New York Stock Exchange, protesting the price of AZT.

September 18—Burroughs Wellcome lowers the price of AZT by 20 percent to $6,400 per year.

October 18—The ACT UP Housing Committee protests lack of desks and phones for caseworkers at the new Department of AIDS Services. ACT UPers bring furniture, and then handcuff themselves to it.

December 2—ACT UP's art auction raises $650,000.

December 10—Stop the Church. Seven thousand protesters join ACT UP and WHAM! outside St Patrick's Cathedral. Inside, demonstrators disrupt mass, objecting to the church's interference with condoms in public schools, abortion, and needle exchange. Two hundred arrests.

1990

January 8–9—Two Days, Two Ways to Fight for Your Life. ACT UP holds a double demonstration at CDC headquarters against the AIDS definition and sodomy laws, which were still on the books.

Febuary 13—ACT UP returns to Albany demanding AIDS funding. Thirteen ACT UP members seize the Division of the Budget offices, chaining themselves to desks. All are arrested.

March 6—ACT UP holds a deliberate illegal needle exchange action on the Lower East Side. Ten arrests.

March 28—Twenty-five hundred people go to Albany to protest Governor Mario Cuomo's lack of AIDS funding.

May 21—ACT UP's Storm the NIH action. Fifteen hundred people demonstrate at the National Institutes of Health in Washington, D.C.

June—The Latino Caucus goes to Puerto Rico to start ACT UP Puerto Rico.

June 13—ACT UP organizes a zap at the New York Housing Authority to protest discrimination against PWAs, protecting survivors of PWAs who are not lease holders from being evicted when their partner/roommate/family member dies.

June—The Latino Commission on AIDS is founded.

June 16–23—ACT UP holds a national action at the sixth annual International AIDS Conference in San Francisco. The Treatment and Data Committee issues its 1990 treatment agenda.

July—The drug ddI starts to become available.

July—The book *Women, AIDS & Activism*, originated by the Women's Caucus, is published by South End Press.

July—NIAID meets with women from ACT UP New York and ACT UP DC, who demand a conference on women with HIV, a women's committee for the ACTG, and a natural history study of women and HIV, which finally happens three years later, in 1993.

July–August—In a monthlong series of actions, ACT UP New York's Latino Caucus and others and ACT UP Puerto Rico demand programs for PWA in Puerto Rico.

July 25—ACT UP protests *The New York Times*'s lack of adequate AIDS coverage by picketing outside the publisher Arthur Sulzberger Jr.'s home.

October 1—HIV Law Project files a class-action suit against the Social Security Administration for denying benefits to women with AIDS.

October 2—ACT UP New York and ACT UP DC protest the Department of Health and Human Services (HHS) disability regulations, which discriminate against women with HIV, using the CDC's inadequate definition of AIDS to determine eligibility.

November—Countdown Eighteen Months is launched by Garance Franke-Ruta and the Treatment and Data Committee.

November—The sixth annual International AIDS Conference is held in San Francisco.

December 1—National Women and HIV Conference is held in Washington, D.C.

December 3—ACT UP New York and other AIDS activists return to the CDC in Atlanta to demand changes in the official definition of AIDS.

December 2—Katrina Haslip dies.

December 2—Larry Kramer gives eulogy at Vito Russo's memorial at Cooper Union. "We killed Vito. Can't you see that?"

1991

January 16—First Gulf War begins. Youth Education Life Line (YELL) demonstrates at the board of education to demand approval for condom distribution plan, and the removal of parental consent requirements.

January 23—The Day of Desperation:

- On January 22, the night before the Day of Desperation, ACT UPers sneak into CBS and PBS studios and successfully disrupt the live evening news broadcasts by Dan Rather and Robert MacNeil and Jim Lehrer, chanting, "AIDS is news. Fight AIDS, not Arabs."

- On January 23, the day of the action itself, ACT UPers march with coffins from Wall Street to the World Trade Center to city hall.

- The Housing Committee, working with Stand Up Harlem and Emmaus House, stops traffic in Harlem while the Latino Caucus sits in the office of the Bronx Borough president, and the affinity group the Marys does an action at the TKTS booth in Times Square.

- A large demonstration fills the hall of Grand Central Terminal, stopping rush-hour traffic. The banner MONEY FOR AIDS, NOT FOR WAR rises to the ceiling of the central hall on balloons. Two hundred sixty-three protesters are arrested on Forty-Second Street.

February 11—Protest against police violence at Midtown North precinct results in three arrests and an unprovoked police attack on ACT UPer Chris Hennelly, causing permanent neurological damage.

February 26—The Latino Caucus protests the Hispanic AIDS Forum's lack of response.

February 27—The board of education approves condom distribution in NYC public schools.

March 17—The Irish Lesbian and Gay Organization (ILGO) is banned from the St. Patrick's Day Parade.

March 25—Maxine Wolfe and Tracy Morgan propose a six-month moratorium on meetings with the CDC and NIAID on issues relating to women's health.

April 2—ACT UP marches through Lower Manhattan to protest cuts in the New York State AIDS budget. Action Tours demonstrates at the World Trade Center.

April 18—ACT UP votes down the women's issues group's moratorium bill.

May 21—ACT UP pickets at Federal Plaza to demand that the CDC change its definition of AIDS so that women can qualify for benefits and experimental drug trials.

May 30—The FDA approves ddC for people who have failed on AZT.

June—ACT UPer Dan Williams acknowledges that he took thousands of dollars earmarked for needle exchange.

June 16–22—The seventh annual International AIDS Conference is held in Florence, Italy.

June 25—Verdict in the needle exchange case: Judge Laura Drager accepts the necessity defense, and needle exchange becomes legal in New York.

July 29—Action Tours and WHAM! seize the crown of the Statue of Liberty.

August—The CDC accepts changes to its AIDS definition.

August 27—PBS cancels its broadcast of the late Robert Hilferty's documentary *Stop the Church* due to right-wing protests.

September 1—Target Bush! ACT UP converges on Kennebunkport, Maine.

September 5—Treatment Action Guerrillas (TAG), a Treatment and Data affinity group, puts a giant condom over Senator Jesse Helms's Arlington home.

September 11—NYC board of education removes parental consent from condom distribution.

October 14—Magic Johnson announces that he is HIV-positive.

November 3—Jimmy Somerville headlines an ACT UP benefit dance at the Palladium.

November 5—Mayor Dinkins reverses his opposition to needle exchange.

November 12—ACT UP zaps George Bush's New York visit.

November 23—Affinity group Action Tours disrupts a performance of *The Will Rogers Follies* on Broadway, attended by Ronald Reagan.

November 29—Twenty-five Action Tours members dressed as Santa Claus enter Macy's protesting the firing of an HIV-positive Santa. Nineteen are arrested.

December 2–5—Internal battle within ACT UP over ACTG trials 076 and 175 concerning consent and testing of pregnant women.

December 2 & 6—The ACT UP Women's Issues Committee meets with NIAID on HIV transmission and progression in women.

December 10—ACT UPer Michael Petrelis's New Hampshire Project disrupts Patrick Buchanan's candidacy announcement in Concord, NH.

1992

January 22—TAG officially splits from ACT UP. New ACT UP Treatment and Data Committee continues with over fifty members, some of whom belong to both groups.

February 15—AIDS campaign '92 kicks off around the New Hampshire presidential primary with demonstrations.

February 19—Members of ACT UP's CDC working group handcuff themselves, without ACT UP approval, to representatives of community-based organizations during meeting convened by American Federation for AIDS Research (amfAR) and American Public

Health Association (APHA). Protesters demand involvement of the full range of people with HIV.

March 18—ACT UP zaps Marilyn Quayle, wife of the vice president, at her book signing at Bloomingdale's.

March 19—Marty Robinson dies.

March 26—ACT UPer the late Bob Rafsky confronts candidate Bill Clinton.

April 4—The Clinton campaign organizes a 10:00 p.m. Sunday meeting with AIDS activists, volunteers that there will be a PWA speaking at the convention.

April 11—Action Tours disrupts Sharon Stone on *Saturday Night Live*.

June—Lesbian Avengers is founded.

July 19–24—The eighth annual International AIDS Conference is held in Amsterdam.

July 29—ACT UP organizes David Wojnarowicz's political funeral.

August 17—Two thousand ACT UP, Queer Nation, and Women's Action Coalition protesters march to the Houston Astrodome to protest the opening of the Republican National Convention. Mounted police charge the crowd, followed by more police violence.

October 5—Ashes Action. Protesters throw the ashes of their loved ones on the White House lawn.

October 29—Bill Clinton makes his AIDS policy speech.

November 2—Political funeral for Mark Lowe Fisher. At his request, three hundred mourners carry Mark's body in his casket uptown, through the streets, to Bush headquarters.

November 18—YELL organizes an action against the four board of education members who voted to block AIDS education in the public schools.

December—ACT UP, Housing Works, and Haitian activists organize an "underground railroad" to provide services for Haitian refugees from the Guantánamo detention camps.

1993

January 1—The CDC expands the definition of AIDS to include women.

February 20—Bob Rafsky dies.

May 16—Robert Garcia dies.

July 1—Tim Bailey's political funeral in Washington, D.C. At his request, ACT UP attempts to carry his body to the White House. The police prevent the march, creating a three-hour standoff involving a physical fight over the casket.

July—The Social Security Administration includes pelvic inflammatory disease in its AIDS definition.

July 16—Political funeral for Jon Greenberg. Activists and family carry Jon's coffin through the East Village and hold an open casket funeral in Tompkins Square Park. Jon Nalley says the kaddish.

December 27—Michael Callen dies.

1994

March 4—Aldyn McKean memorial march

March 14—ACT UP protests Mayor Rudolph Giuliani's move to defund the Department of AIDS Services.

March 21—Action Tours hangs AIDS HALL OF SHAME banner on city hall.

March 22—Over 1,500 demonstrators march across the Brooklyn Bridge protesting Giuliani's proposed AIDS cuts. Forty-seven are arrested.

April 10—Civil disobedience action is held on the steps of city hall to protest AIDS cuts.

April 11—Activists confront Giuliani at a town hall meeting.

April 12—ACT UP holds a sit-in at city hall following a New York City Council hearing on proposed AIDS cuts.

May 10—Giuliani leaves AIDS services funding intact.

May—Congressman Jerrold Nadler introduces HR 4370, the AIDS Cure ACT of the McClintock Project.

June 26—ACT UP organizes an "Outlaw" Stonewall 25 march, disregarding the city's imposed route, and invites all groups excluded from the increasingly controlled Pride parade.

October 17—ACT UP author David Feinberg leaves his bed at St. Vincent's Hospital to berate ACT UP for not being effective.

November 2—David Feinberg dies.

ACT UP Oral History Interviews

Available on www.actuporalhistory.org

Gonzalo Aburto, Interview #100, August 26, 2008
Moisés Agosto-Rosario, Interview #003, December 15, 2002
Tony Arena, Interview #148, September 22, 2012
Mark Aurigemma, Interview #169, September 11, 2014
Sam Avrett, Interview #168, March 12, 2014
Bill Bahlman, Interview #112, March 10, 2010
Marion Banzhaf, Interview #070, April 18, 2007
Roma Baran, Interview #034, November 5, 2003
Kate Barnhart, Interview #052, March 21, 2004
David Barr, Interview #073, May 15, 2007
Jamie Bauer, Interview #048, March 7, 2004
Andrea Benzacar, Interview #153, January 5, 2013
Donna Binder, Interview #121, June 25, 2010
Ken Bing, Interview #078, May 30, 2007
Jay Blotcher, Interview #054, April 24, 2004
Anna Blume, Interview #109, January 25, 2010
Gregg Bordowitz, Interview #004, December 17, 2002
Gedalia Braverman, Interview #019, April 20, 2003
Neil Broome, Interview #055, April 25, 2004
Susan C. Brown, Interview #114, March 24, 2010
Richard Burns, Interview #147, September 11, 2012
Aner Candelario, Interview #179, March 31, 2015
Jean Carlomusto, Interview #005, December 19, 2002
César Carrasco, Interview #166, March 9, 2014
George Carter, Interview #068, April 16, 2007
Blane Charles, Interview #161, January 7, 2014
Lei Chou, Interview #025, May 5, 2003
Cynthia Chris, Interview #159, January 3, 2014
Kim Christenson, Interview #122, June 26, 2010
Allan Clear, Interview #178, March 1, 2015
Chris Cochrane, Interview #110, January 27, 2010
Lori Cohen, Interview #163, January 23, 2014
Rebecca Cole, Interview #088, June 30, 2008
Steven Cordova, Interview #125, October 22, 2010

David Corkery, Interview #145, September 4, 2012
Mary Cotter, Interview #119, June 23, 2010
BC Craig, Interview #085, June 23, 2008
Peter Cramer, Interview #050, October 26, 2002
Douglas Crimp, Interview #047, May 16, 2007
Anne-Christine d'Adesky, Interview #016, April 15, 2003
Alexis Danzig, Interview #117, May 1, 2010
Richard Deagle, Interview #028, September 13, 2003
Risa Denenberg, Interview #093, July 11, 2008
Bill Dobbs, Interview #065, November 21, 2006
Mary Dorman, Interview #030, October 17, 2003
Heidi Dorow, Interview #069, April 17, 2007
Chip Duckett, Interview #182, April 26, 2015
Brent Nicholson Earle, Interview #150, December 11, 2012
Matt Ebert, Interview #081, July 13, 2007
Jim Eigo, Interview #047, March 5, 2004
Sandra Elgear, Interview #095, July 22, 2008
Richard Elovich, Interview #072, May 14, 2007
Joy Episalla, Interview #036, December 6, 2003
Eugene Fedorko, Interview #144, August 25, 2012
Blair Fell, Interview #134, June 3, 2012
Jeffrey Fennelly, Interview #104, January 4, 2010
Joe Ferrari, Interview #126, October 23, 2010
Jose Fidelino, Interview #057, October 13, 2004
Avram Finkelstein, Interview #108, January 23, 2010
Lola Flash, Interview #091, July 8, 2008
Jim Fouratt, Interview #066, November 28, 2006
Charlie Franchino, Interview #105, January 11, 2010
Garance Franke-Ruta, Interview #080, June 6, 2007
Kevin Robert Frost, Interview #142, August 23, 2012
Vincent Gagliostro, Interview #064, July 8, 2005
Debbie Gavito, Interview #096, July 24, 2008
David Gerstner, Interview #158, December 19, 2013
Joan Gibbs, Interview #138, June 21, 2012
Ron Goldberg, Interview #032, October 25, 2003
Gregg Gonsalves, Interview #041, January 19, 2004
Emily Gordon, Interview #127, November 5, 2010
Jeffrey Griglak, Interview #140, July 19, 2012
Donald Grove, Interview #089, July 1, 2008
Ron Grunewald, Interview #148, September 22, 2012
Elias Guerrero, Interview #051, March 17, 2004
Catherine Gund, Interview #071, April 20, 2007
Mark Harrington, Interview #012, March 8, 2003
Jill Harris, Interview #087, June 27, 2008
Jason Heffner, Interview #103, October 21, 2008
Aldo Hernández, Interview #013, March 17, 2003
Drew Hopkins, Interview #167, March 11, 2014
Charles Hovland, Interview #135, June 5, 2012
Bob Huff, Interview #079, May 31, 2007
Robyn Hutt, Interview #086, June 25, 2008

Richard Jackman, Interview #172, October 15, 2014
Alexandra Juhasz, Interview #008, January 16, 2003
Frank Jump, Interview #033, November 1, 2003
Tom Kalin, Interview #042, February 4, 2004
Esther Kaplan, Interview #146, September 7, 2012
Sandy Katz, Interview #058, October 15, 2004
Nanette Kazaoka, Interview #162, January 15, 2014
Tom Keane, Interview #176, February 24, 2015
Steven Keith, Interview #118, June 22, 2010
Charles King, Interview #107, January 20, 2010
David Z. Kirschenbaum, Interview #031, October 19, 2003
Alan Klein, Interview #186, May 7, 2015
Garry Kleinman, Interview #165, March 3, 2014
Larry Kramer, Interview #035, November 15, 2003
Dean Lance, Interview #136, June 7, 2012
Jamie Leo, Interview #037, December 21, 2003
Zoe Leonard, Interview #106, January 13, 2010
Debra Levine, Interview #128, December 21, 2010
Rick Loftus, Interview #022, April 26, 2003
Iris Long, Interview #026, May 16, 2003
Timothy Lunceford, Interview #115, April 28, 2010
Samuel Lurie, Interview #184, May 3, 2015
Jim Lyons, Interview #063, February 16, 2005
Ming-Yuen S. Ma, Interview #007, January 15, 2003
Maria Maggenti, Interview #010, January 20, 2003
Ira Manhoff, Interview #152, January 4, 2013
Loring McAlpin, Interview #098, August 18, 2008
Margaret McCarthy, Interview #175, February 9, 2015
Marlene McCarty, Interview #044, February 21, 2004
Terry McGovern, Interview #076, May 25, 2007
Raan "Ron" Medley, Interview #038, December 28, 2003
Dolly Meieran, Interview #181, April 21, 2015
Elizabeth Meixell, Interview #123, September 30, 2010
Victor Mendolia, Interview #097, August 15, 2008
Linda Meredith, Interview #155, March 10, 2013
Mark Milano, Interview #077, May 26, 2007
Andrew Miller, Interview #056, October 6, 2004
Patrick Moore, Interview #006, January 14, 2003
Tracy Morgan, Interview #149, October 12, 2012
Karen Moulding, Interview #039, January 16, 2004
Emily Nahmanson, Interview #023, April 27, 2003
Patricia Navarro, Interview #084, July 20, 2007
Michael Nesline, Interview #014, March 24, 2003
Nettles (Yaron Schweizer), Interview #061, October 17, 2004
Ann Northrop, Interview #027, May 28, 2003
Paul O'Dwyer, Interview #174, February 9, 2015
Duncan Osborne, Interview #185, May 5, 2015
Kathy Ottersten, Interview #188, December 28, 2017
Monica Pearl, Interview #129, April 11, 2011
Dale Peck, Interview #113, March 17, 2010

Michael Perelman, Interview #083, July 18, 2007
Michael Petrelis, Interview #020, April 21, 2003
Ann Philbin, Interview #011, January 21, 2003
George Plagianos, Interview #124, October 7, 2010
Russell Pritchard, Interview #021, April 24, 2003
Steve Quester, Interview #040, January 17, 2004
Lee Raines, Interview #137, June 8, 2012
Karen Ramspacher, Interview #094, July 12, 2008
Hunter Reynolds, Interview #133, June 2, 2012
Eric Rhein, Interview #164, January 25, 2014
John Riley, Interview #151, January 2, 2013
Scott Robbe, Interview #156, December 5, 2013
David Robinson, Interview #082, July 16, 2007
Rollerena, Interview #173, February 2, 2015
Adam Rolston, Interview #101, August 27, 2008
Illith Rosenblum, Interview #141, July 20, 2012
Gabriel Rotello, Interview #180, April 6, 2015
Ira Sachs, Interview #143, August 24, 2012
Dudley Saunders, Interview #009, January 18, 2003
Eric Sawyer, Interview #049, March 10, 2004
Stephen Shapiro, Interview #062, October 23, 2004
Benjamin Heim Shepard, Interview #183, April 23, 2015
Nathaniel Siegel, Interview #150, December 11, 2012
Michelangelo Signorile, Interview #029, September 20, 2003
Jason Simon, Interview #157, December 8, 2013
Rebecca Pringle Smith, Interview #170, September 18, 2014
Bill Snow, Interview #017, April 16, 2003
Karl Soehnlein, Interview #018, April 18, 2003
Joseph Sonnabend, Interview #187, November 12, 2015
Herb Spiers, Interview #090, July 2, 2008
Stephen Spinella, Interview #139, July 18, 2012
SPREE, Interview #060, October 16, 2004
Peter Staley, Interview #067, December 09, 2006
Charles Stimson, Interview #160, January 5, 2014
Sean Strub, Interview #171, September 30, 2014
Brad Taylor, Interview #116, April 29, 2010
Polly Thistlethwaite, Interview #154, January 6, 2013
Kendall Thomas, Interview #024, May 3, 2003
Karin Timour, Interview #015, April 5, 2003
Sharon Tramutola, Interview #092, July 9, 2008
Christine Vachon, Interview #177, February 26, 2015
Robert Vázquez-Pacheco, Interview #002, December 14, 2002
Andy Vélez, Interview #045, February 26, 2004
John Voelcker, Interview #130, May 30, 2012
James Wagner, Interview #046, February 28, 2004
Scott Wald, Interview #132, June 6, 2012
MaxZine Weinstein, Interview #059, October 16, 2004
John Weir, Interview #120, June 24, 2010
Gerri Wells, Interview #075, May 24, 2007
Betty Williams, Interview #099, August 23, 2008

Dan Keith Williams, Interview #053, March 26, 2004
John Winkleman, Interview #131, May 31, 2012
Daniel Wolfe, Interview #111, February 27, 2010
Maxine Wolfe, Interview #043, February 19, 2004
Brian Zabcik, Interview #102, September 9, 2008

Acknowledgments

Thanks to Jim Hubbard for our thirty-five-plus years of collaboration to represent our communities, and for our beautiful friendship through it all. And thanks to everyone who supported us in creating the ACT UP Oral History Project, especially Daniello Cacace, the remarkable historian James Wentzy, and Urvashi Vaid, without whom none of this would have happened. Big thank-you to Michael Bourret and the folks at Dystel, Gooderich & Bourret. Gratitude to Laird Gallagher for acquiring this book and to Jackson Howard for becoming my editor and working with sensitivity, respect, and understanding, as well as everyone at FSG. Eric Banks and Melonie Rehak at the New York Institute for the Humanities gave me invaluable workspace. Thank you to the City University of New York College of Staten Island, the Fine Arts Work Center, and Captain Jack's. Gratitude to the many friends who read and commented on this as a work in its long process. And thank you to those who read and commented on the entire manuscript: Matt Brim, Jim Hubbard, Dudley Saunders, Lydia Polgreen, and Candace Feit. Thanks to Leslie Harris for listening to the enormous first draft, read out loud, with ongoing guidance and feedback.

Thank you to the MacDowell colony, which has supported and sustained me since 1986, for a long and perfect residency that allowed me to complete the first draft of this book. You serve as a counterpoint to the market in supporting artists and thinkers who don't have approval or reward, at crucial stages of development. Your contribution to American letters is unparalleled.

During the writing of this book I had my own health emergency. My Dream Team of remarkable friends were there in the direst circumstances. Special thanks to Matt Brim, Jim Hubbard, Leslie Gevirtz, Nuar Alsadir, Claudia Rankine, Jack Waters, Peter Cramer, and Heidi Schmid (who literally cleaned blood off the floor of my apartment); Dr. Tu for saving the night; and Steven Thrasher, who went so far as to wash my bloody clothes downstairs at the laundromat. Lisa Balthazar, Jackie Brown, Jimmy Shack, Anna Betbeze, Kelly Roberts, Kathy Danger, Cynthia and Patty and Max Schneider-White, Rochelle Feinstein, Gaines Blasdel, Gordon Beeferman, Shelley Marlow, Jorge Cortinas, Will Burton, Chris Cochrane, Marcia Gallo, my cousin Marcia Cohen-Zakai, Lana Povitz, Barbara Spandorf, Keli Dunham, Gina Gionfriddo, Chris Freeman, Elena Comey de Junco, Tracie Morris, and Aruna Krishnakumar—thank you for cooking, garbage pickup, doctor drop-offs, dishwashing, canceling plane tickets, shopping, laundry, hair washings, shower help, plant watering, sheet changing, and helping me up and down the stairs, and for your snack baskets, time, visits, and care. Special thanks to Flying Squirrel Pilates and to all the doctors, nurses, and occupational therapists who actually listened, discussed, and brought their skill and compassion, and in that way actually helped me.

Index

Page numbers in *italics* refer to illustrations.

Clark, Judy, xvi, 236–37, 241, 396
Clark, Julie, 6, 140, 144
class issues, 16, 18, 40, 47, 471, 498
Clear, Allan, 47, 287–88, 310; Sorge and, 297–98
Clinical Trial 076 (of AZT on pregnant women), 430, 562–74; Banzhaf and, 562–72; Dorow and, 567–69, 572; Gonsalves and, 572; Harrington and, 571–72; Kirschenbaum and, 564, 566–69, 573; McCarthy and, 566–67, 571; Morgan and, 567–69; outcome of, 573–74; Smith and, 573–74; Treatment and Data and, 568, 572; Wolfe and, 572
clinical trials: abuse of people in, 81, 563, 585; placebos in, 573; women excluded from, 227, 230–31, 263–64
clinical trials of AIDS medications, 33, 39, 42, 43, 44, 53, 54, 56, 67–69, 74–86, 108, 184, 189, 221, 266, 396, 397, 504, 547, 549, 584, 587; AIDS Clinical Trials Group (ACTG), 43, 53, 74, 82, 83, 222, 251, 252, 255, 535, 540, 542, 548, 550, 563, 569; AZT, see clinical trials of AZT; children in, 74–75; consent issues in, 15, 75–78; death as endpoint in, 78; design of, 594; double-blind, 76, 101, 427, 558; drug users and, 283; foscarnet/ganciclovir, 596–97; parallel, 85–86; people of color and, 42, 81–83, 268, 562, 564; placebos in, 15, 75–78, 201, 427–31, 564, 567, 571; women in, 42, 56, 81–83, 189, 227, 230–32, 243, 254, 263–64, 504, 584
clinical trials of AZT, 75; blinded, impossibility of, 429–30; Burroughs Wellcome, 64, 427–30; Concorde, 430–31; on pregnant women, see Clinical Trial 076
Clinton, Bill, 91, 261, 364–65, 438, 623
Clinton, Hillary, 91
Clit Club, 143, 315, 352, 355, 356, 609
clone look, 100, 145, 318, 352
Close to the Knives (Wojnarowicz), 612–13
Club 52, 359
CMV (cytomegalovirus) retinitis, 71, 72, 201, 218, 219, 224, 596–97, 619
Coalition for the Homeless, 438, 442, 498, 500
Cochrane, Cynthia, 298, 304
Cockettes, 513

Cohen, Cathy, 311
Cohen, Jon, 202
Cohen, Lori, 302, 446–49
Cohn, Roy, 423
Cole, Rebecca, 13–14, 228–31, 385–88
Color Bars or All People with AIDS Are Innocent, 371
Columbia University, xviii
Committee Against Racism, Anti-Semitism, Sexism and Heterosexism (CRASH), 178–79
Committee for Abortion Rights and Against Sterilization Abuse (CARASA), 76–78, 177–80
Committee of Lesbian and Gay Male Socialists, 178, 182
Committee on Lesbian and Gay Rights (CLGR), 154
Committee to End Sterilization Abuse (CESA), 77, 260
Community Advisory Board, 563
Community Constituency Group (CCG), 43–44, 540, 550, 563, 568, 570
Community Health Project (CHP), 46, 82, 100, 234, 249, 544
Community Prescription Service, 527
Community Programs for Clinical Research on AIDS (CPCRA), 540
Community Research Initiative (CRI), 61–62, 64, 189–91, 199, 200, 412, 423–26, 431, 549, 573, 574
Compound Q, 68, 424
Concorde trial, 430–31
condoms, xxiii, 233, 352–53, 453, 508, 510–11; Catholic Church and, 9, 26, 138, 140, 146, 159, 493, 494; Men Use Condoms or Beat It, 337; "No Glove, No Love," xiv, 233
consent, 15, 75–78, 562–70
Cooper, Ellen, 69, 72–73, 75
Cooper, Paula, 516
Cooper, Sally, xvi, 194
Cooper Union, ACT UP meetings at, 52, 508, 519, 542
Copelon, Rhonda, 107
Corcoran Gallery of Art, 354
Cordero, Carlos, 49, 636
Córdova, Rita, 636
Córdova, Steven, 636
Corkery, David, 126, 190, 414
Cosmopolitan, 233, 381, 385–89